THE
Robert Carrier
COOKBOOK

Also in Arrow by Robert Carrier
TASTE OF MOROCCO

THE
Robert Carrier
COOKBOOK

DRAWINGS BY JANE CRADOCK-WATSON
Additional drawings by Leslie Dean

ARROW

Arrow Books Limited
20 Vauxhall Bridge Road, London SW1V 2SA

An imprint of Random Century Group

London Melbourne Sydney Auckland Johannesburg
and agencies throughout the world

First published by Thomas Nelson and Sons 1965
Revised edition 1970
Sphere edition 1967
First published in this edition by Arrow 1990

Photoset by Rowland Phototypesetting Ltd
Bury St Edmunds, Suffolk
Printed and bound in Great Britain by
Courier International Ltd, Tiptree, Essex

ISBN 0 09 072990 3

ACKNOWLEDGEMENTS

I am extremely grateful for my many years' experience as Food Editor of *Harper's Bazaar, The Sunday Times* and *Vogue*. Many of the writings and recipes included in this book first appeared on their pages.

Like most cooks, I am deeply indebted to the countless cookery writers of the past, both in this country and abroad. In this book I have drawn on several French, Italian and early American cookbooks for regional specialities of those countries. And I am especially grateful to those great English cookery writers – Hannah Glasse, Eliza Acton, Margaret Romford, Isabella Beeton, and Florence Jack. The very form of this book, its serious intent, a few of its recipes and some of its basic preparations come straight from their pages. For other recipes I am indebted to the many chefs and restaurateurs who have given so generously of their talents and their time to teach me their craft. Of those restaurants, I should like to cite by name the following, whose recipes appear in this book.

Restaurant Lapérouse, Paris; La Petite Auberge, Noves; Maxim's, Paris; L'Oustau de la Baumanière, Baux-de-Provence; Le Grand Vefour, Paris; Auberge du Père Bise, Talloires; La Mère Brazier, Col de la Luère, Lyons; Auberge Paul Bocuse, Collonges-au-Mont-d'Or, Lyons; Hôtel de la Côte d'Or, Saulieu; Grand Veneur, Paris; Relais Fleuri, Avallon; Fouquet's, Paris; Paul Chêne, Paris; Chez Victor, Aux Deux Marches, Paris; L'Auberge d'Armaille, Paris; Chez Michel, Paris; Le Petit St Bênoit, Paris; Bois Joli, Bagnoles-de-l'Orne; La Paillote, Bandol; La Voile d'Or, St Raphael; Chez Fifine, St Tropez; Caprice Restaurant, London; Mirabelle, London; Trader Vic's, London; Etoile, London; White Tower, London; Quaglino's, London; Festa del Mare, London; Mrs Beeton's Tent, London; Pickwick Club, London; The East Arms, Hurley, Berks; The Hare and Hounds, Marlow, Bucks; Four Seasons, New York; Forum of the Twelve Caesars, New York; Rainbow Room, New York; George's, Rome.

Finally, I wish to take this opportunity of thanking Jane Cradock-Watson for her drawings, which have made this book so visually attractive.

Contents

INTRODUCTION
The Art of Eating

Odysseus made his voyages first and then Homer wrote about them. To discover and to reveal: that is the basis of all art. Until we have learned to explore, our tastes are so limited, our experience is so narrow, that we can make no valid comparisons, can found no true judgements.

So it is with food. We must learn to eat first. Children like jam and peanut butter and coconut-covered cakes, it seems, by nature. Olives and caviare and such adult preferences, they abhor. We have to admit it: the more sophisticated tastes have to be consciously acquired. Acquire them we must. For one can pass through life not caring about music without much harm to oneself. One can proudly know nothing about art. But then, Nature does not compel us to attend two concerts of chamber music or spend two hours in an art gallery every single day of our lives, as she forces us to have lunch and dinner.

So we would do well to learn the subtleties of food, the delights it can fully hold – and learn them fast! For though we have so many meals – tens of thousands during our lifetime – these meals are numbered. Each slapdash one, each one that goes unappreciated, is lost for ever. Try as we may, it is difficult to have more than one lunch, to eat more than one dinner a day. And to succeed in multiplying meals may cut out a goodly number at the end, for did not Lord Houghton – friend of Thackeray and a great Victorian gourmet – sigh on his deathbed: 'My exit is the result of too many entrées'?

This is where the French have the advantage of us. Believing that human beings are like kittens, and that it is right and natural that their eyes should be opened as they grow older, they ply their children with good food and drink as soon as they can take it, with the result that it soon becomes, and remains, one of their great pleasures in life. To realize this, just think what the phrase 'to know how to eat' means on either side of the Channel. To the French it means to be a gastronome, a gourmet, to have a fine palate; to the British it means only to know how to behave at table. But how French children behave in restaurants! I remember one ploughing through a meal at a three-star restaurant with all the concentration of a fifty-year-old gourmet, though she cannot have been more than six. No fidgeting there. None of that horror for the parents that I remember we caused so skilfully in any public place in America when I was young. No. Serious business was afoot, and the food held her with all the power of her favourite game.

The British, when they travel today, are getting more adventurous as it dawns on them that one of the main delights of foreign travel is to get out of one's hotel and eat in a national and not an international atmosphere. In fact, so marked has this trend towards trying the true cooking of the country become, that the head of one of the great international hotel chains told me that it was their policy to cut down on the number of restaurants in their hotels and to open quite separate and anonymous restaurants across the street; the smiling management could then watch from their office windows as those guests who wanted to 'get away from the hotel' poured out to sample native fare.

Abroad is one thing, but people still do not experiment much at home. More garlic or more wine goes into our meals nowadays, but the food still has rigid class lines. Servants in England before the war would have been as outraged at being given rabbit as guests would have been if they had been served tripe – two high gourmet dishes in France. Different dishes now bear the stigma, though tripe would still make a good many people jump. For the lines can be broken. 'It's a wery remarkable circumstance, sir,' said Sam Weller in *Pickwick Papers*, 'that poverty and oysters always seem to go together.' Remarkable indeed, but cockles and winkles are still below the line.

There is a double delight about food. Once you have adventured your palate long enough to have acquired real taste, real discrimination, the time has come when you yourself can cook. And cooking is a truly creative art, though an ephemeral one. It is also the most selfless of the arts because it is the least enduring. A bite or two, a quick swallow, and a beautiful work of thought and love and experience is no more. And yet the chef will cook again, with as much care, as much skill, for the very next meal.

It was in Provence, I think, that I first realized that cooking was an art. I once stayed the whole year round in St Tropez. It was then, as the last yacht left the harbour in October and St Tropez turned back into a village for the winter months, that Fifine, one of the best natural cooks in Provence, had time to take me through the calendar of Provençal cookery step by step, and teach me the secrets and skills of that age-old cuisine. It was here that alchemy stepped in. Using the same ingredients, the same equipment exactly, no one, not her son, Robert, also a *restaurateur*, nor any of the other cooks, could approach what she did with simple basic ingredients. It was not just skill or long experience: she was operating on quite another plane. Each dish was an act of creation. It was the first time I had seen this and I have come across the same gift only a dozen or so times since. The people who have it are visited with awe, like the oracles of ancient times. I once saw Alexandre Dumaine at Saulieu refuse a Prime Minister of France lunch when he arrived because he was late. He was told that if he wanted to eat he would have to wait until dinner that night. And as I left, replete after a sumptuous meal, this famous politician was sitting, melancholy, in the bar, sipping a glass of milk, waiting to be admitted hours later to the mysteries from which he had been so cruelly barred.

You do not have to be a genius to cook. Take it slowly as you would any other branch of learning and you can reach the heights: not the summit itself, perhaps, but high enough to astound your friends and delight yourself. For there is something vastly satisfying about cooking. The blending of flavours (you must taste, taste, taste, when cooking) can be magical, as one augments them without destroying any of those already present. It is this lack of tasting by the cook that spoils most food. A great chef is always sipping, then adding a touch of this, a hint of that, which will transform the dish when it is served. But most of the truly great chefs measure the basic ingredients. No guesswork with them for the foundations of the dish.

'The art', according to Alexandre Dumaine, 'is the setting in value of the ingredient to be cooked. If one just cooks, it is not worth the trouble.' Take a note from the book of this great chef: learn to experiment with flavours, with textures, and above all, with heat. For heat is the most important friend or foe of the aspiring cook. How a fish or piece of meat is 'seized' in butter at its first contact with heat is as important to its final flavour and texture as its freshness and the quality of the sauce that accompanies it.

In oven roasts, casseroles and braised meats especially, the temperature at which the meats are cooked is of prime importance. For meat tends to dry out if cooked at too high a temperature and fibres 'toughen'. Do not follow the instructions too slavishly; experiment to bring out the best in the food to be cooked. Watch your oven heats and make sure your cooker really does simmer at its lowest possible heat. Many a sauce has been ruined, many an otherwise delicious casserole spoiled, because the meat was boiled when it should only have simmered.

And cooking is no mean intellectual pastime either. Even Dr Johnson said: 'I could write a better book about cookery than has ever yet been written; it should be a book upon philosophical principles. Pharmacy is now made much more simple. Cookery may be so too. A prescription which is now compounded of five ingredients had formerly fifty in it. So in cookery. If the nature of the ingredients is well known, much fewer will do. Then, as you cannot make bad meat good, I would tell what is the best beef, the best pieces; how to choose young fowls; the proper seasons of different vegetables; and how to roast, and boil, and compound.'

The Art of Cookery, which has been refined as Samuel Johnson prophesied, still embraces four of the five senses, giving taste, texture, and delight to the nose and the eye. No other art does that. And cookery seems to embrace half of human knowledge and all of human civilization, or so John Ruskin said:

'What does cookery mean? It means the knowledge of Medea and of Circe, and of Calypso, and Sheba. It means knowledge of all herbs, and fruits, and balms, and spices, and of all that is healing and sweet in grapes and savoury in meat. It means carefulness, and inventiveness, watchfulness, willingness, and readiness of appliances. It means the economy of your great-grandmother and the science of modern chemistry, and French art, and Arabian hospitality. It means, in fine, that you are to see imperatively that everyone has something nice to eat.'

Bon appétit!

The Dinner Party

'In this competitive age', wrote William Makepeace Thackeray in the nineteenth century, 'hospitality is being pressed into service and becoming an excuse for ostentation. Dinners are given mostly by way of revenge.'

The climax to this unhappy state of affairs was reached in America in the Gay Nineties, when a once-famous socialite decided to make her first big splash in Washington society. Abashed by rival political hostesses' habits of enfolding a costly jewelled or gold trinket in each guest's napkin, she decided that there was only one way to beat them at their own game. When her turn came to give a large dinner party, she wrapped a crisp new one hundred dollar bill in the napkin at each plate!

But the new trend in entertaining is away from big parties. The famous American publisher who had three guest lists for his equally famous parties – the 'A' list for Society; the 'B' list made up of actors, writers and other celebrities; and the 'C' list, a sort of catch-all for wits, favourite beauties and close friends – is a glamorous figure from a dead, dead past.

Small gatherings where everyone gets a chance to talk to everyone else are the new rule; intimate suppers for four, party dinners for six to eight, country luncheons for eight to ten, buffet parties and after-theatre parties for eight to twenty. The result: a more friendly feeling, and conversation of a more thoughtful and informed calibre – except, of course, at cocktail parties, where the talk is as impossible and improbable as it ever used to be. But one thing is true of today's parties: food is uppermost – everyone eats!

While some well-known hostesses explode like Roman candles with gimmicky party ideas to dazzle their guests, I much prefer the warm candlelight technique of the hostess who sees to every need but wastes no time on glittering pyrotechnics. Good seating, good food, good conversation: what more can anyone ask?

Well, I can tell you that asking your guests to 'come as you are' or 'as the person you hate' can backfire, and you may find that you are the one they hate most for such scandalous trickery. Entertaining, when properly done, needs no gimmicks. Try and mix people of all kinds and varieties at your parties . . . whether you are the guiding light behind a charity ball, tossing an after-theatre buffet at home, a highly perfected picnic in the country, or a dazzling dinner in town.

And give them something different . . . if you are entertaining visiting Americans, for instance, do not fall into the trap of giving them baked Virginia ham and candied sweet potatoes with marshmallows. Far better to lead them down the English byways of star gazey pie, Lancashire hotpot and old-fashioned treacle tart. The last thing in the world you want is to make visitors feel as though they were back at home. Far better that they should stagger about talking about the wonders of British cookery than merely observe that the English can turn out a damned fine hamburger!

To entertain with ease means planning as much do-it-ahead preparation as possible either in the morning or preferably the day before, so that you can then forget you are the host or hostess and just have fun.

Develop a repertoire of dishes that you do especially well and feel at ease in preparing. And then add a few new specialities to this list each year.

Do keep a record of the parties you give and the guests who attend each one. There is nothing worse for a guest than being served *paella* (no matter how delicious) every time he comes. In this way you can be sure you will not repeat your menus and serve the same people the same dishes each and every time.

If you are planning a new dish which sounds fabulous, try it out on the family or one or two close friends first. This gives you a chance to check on ingredients and on cooking times . . . and what is more important, allows you to add your own special touch to make the recipe more personally yours.

And remember, the true art of entertaining comes from knowing and being yourself. Do not struggle with a six-course dinner when informal casseroles are your *forte*. Being yourself means living by your own standards, not those of others. You can find fascinating ways, well within the scope of your own limitations, to entertain anyone, from a visiting diplomat to a visiting member of the family, without trying to do what is 'expected'.

A dinner party in Cannes, given one summer by the famous French *antiquaires* Grognot and Joinel in their luxury summer apartment overlooking the Old Port of Cannes, taught me what true simplicity can be. Four courses, if you count the gloriously simple green salad, made up this meal . . . and the only wine served with it was Sancerre, a *vin nouveau*, the perfect accompaniment. The first course was *rougets à la niçoise*, a dish of lightly grilled red mullet, followed by *poulet au blanc*, a tender chicken cooked in cream in the manner of Mère Blanc, well-known restaurant owner of Vonnas. A green salad with herbs and a *salade des fruits* completed this delicious meal. When one thinks of entertaining in terms as simple as these, it becomes more of a pleasure.

Entertaining in our day is so much easier than it was in Edwardian times. Of course, you may not have the scores of domestic servants that some families enjoyed in those days, but neither do you have twenty people sitting down for Sunday lunch, and your dinners do not have to go on for course after heavy course of complicated foods to keep up with the Joneses. Nor do you have to go twice a year to Baden-Baden to recover from these excesses. Today we have our electrical equipment, the know-how of modern refrigeration, science and merchandising . . . and we have our four-course dinner with the continentally inspired casserole as star performer.

Although I entertain frequently, I like my parties to be simple and intimate, in keeping with the kind of life I live. Never any fussy cocktail bits with the drinks, but, for special occasions, bacon-wrapped prawns, prunes or chicken livers served hot, tiny *brioches* filled with *foie gras*, or iced celery stuffed with caviare and cream cheese – or no cocktail food at all but quantities of good food after: practically never more than four courses at any dinner party, but each course substantial and interesting in itself.

Two words of warning for the unwary: be realistic about your budget and stay within bounds. And stick to a dish you know you can do successfully with no last-minute grilling or warming up while your guests sit fidgeting at the table. A casserole answers that problem, for you can prepare it in advance, even the day before, and as such, it can be something spectacular – so much better than a roast (it needs carving) or grilled cutlets, even when stuffed with curried chicken livers (they need last-minute attention).

Choosing Your Menu

The conventional opening for a formal dinner used to be clear soup, followed by fish, an entrée and a pudding. But why be conventional? There are no rules for this sort of thing . . . I much prefer the hostess who began a memorable meal with *crêpes aux sardines*, a recipe brought back from a holiday on the Basque coast – served with imagination and pride – to all the clear soups in the world. I shall always remember those *crêpes*, crisply golden, with their delicately blended filling of fresh sardines, pounded over ice and mixed (like *quenelles*) with whipped cream and egg white, and indeed, I have since served them (the sincerest form of flattery) at my own dinners. The *crêpes* were followed by *poulet à la basquaise*, chicken in a white wine sauce, served with baked green peppers stuffed with saffron rice.

So be adventurous and try new ways with old favourites – serve cold lamb with *mayonnaise comme au Pays des Landes*, creamy mayonnaise lightly flavoured with garlic; try the humble mussel, skewered *en brochette* with alternate slices of bacon, the whole rolled in flour, egg yolk and breadcrumbs, deep-fried in golden oil and served with *sauce béarnaise*; or slit 'pockets' in thick lamb chops and stuff them with savoury garlic and herb butter. Delicious!

Serve a fillet of beef *en croûte*, but first cut your fillet into thick serving pieces; spread each slice with a paste of finely chopped mushrooms and onion which you have sautéed in butter until soft; and insert a slice of cooked ham or boiled bacon between each slice. This is skewered together and roasted in the usual way before being wrapped in its envelope of puff pastry and baked to golden perfection. It is as delicious cold as it is hot and makes an excellent buffet party dish as well. And for a gala party with no holds barred, precede this dish with salmon soufflé mousse with a prawn and lobster sauce. The mousse – a *quenelle*-like mixture – can be prepared in individual soufflé dishes or in one large ovenproof dish. Sometimes I turn it out just before serving and cover it with its sauce; at other times I serve it in the dish it was baked in, with the sauce passed separately. Either way it is a most attractive first course.

Your menu depends to some extent, of course, on the amount of time you have for preparation and on the time it takes to gather your guests to the table. I like to plan all dinner parties so that nothing, absolutely *nothing*, will spoil if kept waiting.

If guests *are* apt to be a little late, it is a good idea to copy the Russian *zakouski* table, set up in a room adjoining the drawing-room and wheeled in. I find this an easy and rather stimulating way to soften the cares of service, and often produce *hors-d'œuvres*, both hot and cold in the Russian manner, in the drawing-room before going to dinner, where a hot casserole – or a hot fish dish followed by cold meats and salad – awaits the guests.

The meal can start in this way with something which requires absolutely no preparation: the thinnest slices of smoked salmon served with fresh wedges of lemon on an oiled platter, or rolled (budget notwithstanding) around sombre cargoes of Russian caviare; smoked eels or sturgeon, served on beds of chopped ice; and firm pink slices of tongue and ham with olives. Perhaps greenhouse cucumbers, marinated in a sour cream and chives dressing, could bring a touch of early spring to your menu.

The Enjoyable Kitchen

The kitchens most of us love and remember best are tied in our subconscious by an appeal to all our senses. The first kitchen I recall was my grandmother's, the busy centre of a pre-revolutionary farmhouse in upper-state New York. Its wide-planked wood floor, its rough-textured brick walls, and the big wood-burning range my grandmother used to cook on, made this kitchen the warmest, friendliest room in the house.

On cold winter mornings, Old Ted, the family dog, used to curl up under the range, Grandma would take up her position in the Boston rocker by the window, and I would sit at the huge scrubbed table, creaming butter or peeling 'taters'. Grandma did not believe in new-fangled notions; there was no central heating or electric light in the little farmhouse; but the air was heady with the fresh-baked smell of new loaves, and the fragrance of burning wood not only contributed to the delicious aromas of the room, but imparted its smoky flavour to the country dishes simmering on the stove.

Those were the days when I used to come down to breakfasts of fried steak, hash-browned potatoes and hot corn bread. It was Grandma who taught me how to make baking powder biscuits and how to butter-fry the first sunfish caught by myself in the neighbouring creek. I was only eight when she died, but I felt a real loss, for in her spare, Yankee way, she had made me love the good, the simple things of her farmhouse kitchen.

The second kitchen to leave its outline on my memory was the super-modern 'clinical' kitchen attached to the new twenty-four-room house that my mother built with such perfect timing in 1929, the year of the Crash. I shall never forget the spacious kitchen with its imposing battery of white cabinets and mammoth, if unpredictable, electrical appliances.

The floor was of particular interest. Made of one of the new American plastics, it was a symphony of rectangular tiles in soft shades of green, and it stained irrevocably when even water was spilled on it. This floor was a constant problem to my mother, as were the big house and kitchen, when servants became an impossibility instead of a necessity. My two brothers and I used to help out in the kitchen after school hours, taking turns washing up, drying the dishes, preparing vegetables, and as our skills grew and we became more and more interested in good food, we began to cook special dishes for the family. I still remember with pride my first Thanksgiving dinner at the age of twelve, and I still make the Mexican *chile con carne* with red beans and rice that I cooked in those early days.

When I first left home at the age of seventeen for a job in a New York bank – one of my main duties seemed to be mixing martinis for resplendent visitors when they came to call on the president – I was reduced to cooking in what was little more than a cupboard in my one-room Greenwich Village apartment. And though this taught me the pleasures of improvisation – I can remember a host of 'one-dish dinners' served with aplomb and a bottle of cheap Italian red wine – it was not until I reached Paris during the war, and decided to stay on there, that a kitchen proper once more played an important part in my life.

Classic French cuisine was the lesson here: mayonnaise whisked with a fork slowly, drop by drop; sauces stirred patiently in a *bain-marie* to the proper consistency; country casseroles simmered for eight to ten hours in the lowest of ovens; *crudités*; *charcuterie*; and the whole gamut of French wines and cheeses. Naomi, my *cordon bleu* cook-housekeeper, was the undisputed Queen of my Paris kitchen for five long years; great is my gratitude for knowing her.

My first kitchen in England was located in an old house at the top of Berkeley Square; it was a large country kitchen with an antiquated gas range placed in the old fireplace, a huge refrigerator represented modernity, and a large, solid, wooden-topped table in the middle of the room spelled comfort. Here I used to make pigeons in wine, chicken with bananas in cream, and the host of English pies and puddings that I came to love so well when I was first here: beefsteak and kidney pie, old English chicken pie with forcemeat balls, an oyster pie from an eighteenth-century recipe, apple pies made with great fluffy Bramleys, suet pudding, summer pudding, Yorkshire pudding, and even pease pudding.

When I began to plan my new London house, I decided to fulfil an ambition of many years: to have two kitchens – one for work and the other for play. A professional 'cook' like me often spends days on end testing new recipes for an article or book, creating dishes for colour photography, or just trying out some new piece of equipment. For one's own peace of mind it is almost imperative to have a small, uncluttered kitchen – free from fuss and bother – where one can retire to whip up something casual for one or two guests, or something more elaborate for a full-scale dinner party.

Kitchen for Play

This play kitchen – with two ovens, an American 'charco' grill, a refrigerator-freezer and a custom-built cooking top for maximum ease and efficiency – would always be stocked with certain prerequisites of good cooking: well-flavoured basic stocks, eggs, cream, Parmesan and Gruyère cheese, and vegetables for soups and casseroles . . . Spanish onions, turnips, carrots, etc. Each casserole and saucepan would be a personal favourite; each knife or gadget kept in its appointed place, and only those utensils necessary for good cooking allowed 'a place in the sun'.

This was only a dream until I moved into my new London house. Here at last was the perfect room for a second kitchen, right behind the dining-room, with only two steps down to the garden, and the outside summer dining-room, covered over for inclement weather, but still warm and pleasant enough to eat in for six months of the year.

The kitchen itself is a narrow galley passage, fourteen by nine feet, designed by David Vicary, with a wall of major equipment on one side encasing a new high-fired open grill from America, which forms the central pivot of the room's décor. The cooking top with four drop-in gas burners is set into an Italian mosaic counter below.

On the other long wall is a continuous working surface cut only by a built-in electric blender and a sink for washing salads and vegetables.

Dish-washing is not play, so there is no clean-up centre in this kitchen. All dishes are washed downstairs in the main work kitchen. Instead, a porcelain salad and vegetable sink, with its own waste disposal unit, is set into the long chopping block unit. The electric food waste disposal unit is a cook's aid I would never be without.

Above this long counter top are three slender, pine, open-fronted cupboards to house jars of flour, sugar, salt and spices, and a collection of casseroles and cruets.

The décor is simple – white-tiled walls, white vinyl floor, and stainless steel units, warmed by the honey tones of the pale woods and decorative tiles.

Finished like fine furniture and handsomely styled, the cabinets are topped with a hard beech chopping block in the play kitchen, and polished teak in the work kitchen. There is no tell-tale hardware to distinguish cabinets and drawers: pulls are mercifully part of the design. All are horizontal black battens – designed to match recessed coving – and grooved underneath for fingertips. Specialized storage includes flat drawers for flatware; individual sliding deep-file drawers specially partitioned for baking tins, for wine, for trays and for casseroles.

The two narrow walls of the kitchen are glass-fronted: wide double french windows lead out to the garden at one end, opening flush with the walls, and a large glass-fronted cupboard finishes the other. Lighting is accomplished by an ingenious system of separately controlled spotlights which light up every work surface, giving a sense of gaiety and immediacy to the entire room.

FOR COOKING

Nowadays most people cook on gas or electric stoves. But commercial design is still far from perfect, with the exception of one or two firms which are continually experimenting to bring ever-new improvements to their ranges. As a result, the cooker – the most important piece of equipment in the kitchen – is often the least integrated with the design of the kitchen. Most combined oven-cookers are too narrow, too confined. I like to be able to chop on the cooking top if I want to; to be able to pull a saucepan off the heat to cool for a moment before returning it to the flame. And I do not like the saucepans crowded too closely together: this creates an uncomfortable closeness when cooking, and a danger of scorched handles or fingers.

Today, with split-level cooking – separate ovens (one for roasting, the other for baking), and a custom-built cooking top at just the right height for stirring a subtle sauce – this can be remedied. For split-level is more than just an attractive way of decorating a kitchen. It actually works; lets you put ovens where you want them, and gas or electric burners or ceramic hobs where you want them – at exactly the right height.

We took the split-level one step further with the following set-up:

A custom-built cooking top in cool white mosaic, fronting an imported American grill for open-air grilling and indoor barbecuing.

In operation, this cooking top is really the star of the show. The four drop-in gas burners are generously spaced out in the white mosaic surface. The cooking surface is lower than usual in commercial models to bring the tops of deep saucepans to normal working height, making it easy for the cook to see and stir.

An American 'Charco' grill – a new acquisition for the play kitchen – is rapidly becoming my favourite cooking unit. This combined grill and salamander features a bed of 'coals' made out of one of the super-plastics created for missiles, that are capable of absorbing great heat. Fired by high gas flames from below, they rapidly heat to a fiery glow which sears steaks, chops and joints in a minute. Fats and juices dropping from the grilled meats create a flame that chars the meat, adding superb 'charcoal' flavour and sealing in juices and savour. This method of grilling gives a new dimension to the cooking of chops and steaks and patties of minced beef with no loss of natural juices, and a dark, crusty exterior is quickly formed.

A large salamander rack just below the grill is perfect for toasting, braising, top-grilling and glazing, just like those used in professional kitchens.

Two twin balanced-heat, built-in electric ovens by Westinghouse take care of all roasting and baking. No stooping and bending for this pair; you can watch your roasts or soufflés through the extra large heatproof windows. An extra addition is an electrically operated rotisserie grill, so good for self-basting roasts, poultry and fish.

The easy-to-set automatic controls are big convenience features of the two built-in ovens. They bake and roast and turn themselves on and off at pre-set times and temperatures. Both ovens are lit from within to allow perfect visibility.

FOR STORING
The Westinghouse refrigerator and freezer takes care of all my cold storage problems. The refrigerator – with special compartments for fruit, vegetables, butter, milk and eggs – is roomy enough for all needs of this auxiliary kitchen. The freezer holds more ice trays than even I can use.

Kitchen for Work

The first requisite for a hard-working kitchen is an efficient working plan. When I set about the task of creating a workable, livable 'work' kitchen out of a nondescript extra room in my present London house, I wanted the charm of the kitchens of my past combined with the myriad conveniences of the most modern equipment: a refrigerator that never forms frost; surfaces that require minimum upkeep; storage space for everything from a turkey platter to proper freezing equipment.

A long counter wall was a must, with surface cooking units – mobile if possible – and a built-in chopping block with special slots pre-cut to hold all my chopping knives. No more searching in crowded drawers, no more cut fingers; every tool in its right place. Whisks and wooden spoons, too, must be slotted away, within easy reach, yet hidden from view.

All equipment was to be built-in, with cabinets plentiful enough so that everything could be put away at its point of use but out of sight: each storage unit located as logically as possible.

David Vicary solved these seemingly insurmountable problems with his usual good sense. And to them he added the interest of glazed tile walls; continuous working surfaces topped in glowing teak; spacious storage cabinets faced with Pirana pine; adequate shelf space for my ever-growing collection of French and Italian casseroles; and enough space for kitchen appliances that easily transform my kitchen from the calm and friendly country classic of my dreams to the hectic food factory that it becomes on days when there are photographs to take, recipes to test, visitors on the day's agenda, and a dinner party for twelve scheduled for that evening.

A warm colour-scheme of wood-tones and browns, spiked with orange, sun yellow and off-white, sets the scene for this country kitchen, sparkled by the warmth of copper and flame accessories.

The working arrangements of the room are planned so it can function as a one-cook kitchen, yet easily accommodate additional help when necessary.

Each of the main activities such as cooking, washing dishes, serving food, storage, etc., is not only given a work-top and appliance area, but also accompanied by storage fitments in which all the tools and requisites are housed close at hand. The kitchen is, in fact, planned in five basic working areas or centres joined by continuous working surfaces:

The clean-up centre – the most frequently used work area in the kitchen – is made up of two sinks: a single-basin sink unit, with teak counters on each side and adequate storage cabinets for all supplies and utensils used in this area, and a stainless steel sink with fitted stainless steel top. An electric food waste disposal unit pulverises waste food and washes it down the drain.

The food preparation centre is close to the sink and clean-up centre, as more trips are made between these two in the average kitchen set-up than anywhere else. Here we have located the built-in gas cooker top with its copper ventilation hood. The cooking surface, as in the Play Kitchen, is lower than usual in commercial models to bring the tops of deep pots to normal working height, making it easy for the cook to see and stir. Two deep pull-out drawers, one lined with baize to protect precious silver serving dishes and delicate casseroles from scratches, are planned to house necessary cooking implements.

The mixing centre Modern kitchens are filled with mechanical hands to make light work of heavy jobs, freeing the cook for the thoughtful preparation of food. When I make bread, cakes or pastry, I need a multitude of ingredients and tools close at hand, and a good clear surface to work on. Once the job is done, I like all these things cleared away without fuss. How much easier to think this work area out in terms of a mixing centre equipped with a slide drawer filled with lidless bins of sugar, brown sugar, flour, cornflour, baking powder, raisins, rice, pasta, dried beans, etc. Just a touch of the hand and the proper quantities of these ingredients can be scooped up from their appropriate bins, and with a touch of hip or elbow the drawer can be pushed shut again with no fussing with jars, bags, boxes and the usual paraphernalia of messy baking. I keep a pastry board and mixing bowls in position on this work-top at all times.

The mixing centre houses my three electric mixers too; the Kenwood has six lightweight attachments that blend, mix, juice, grind, shred and sharpen. The Braun, with its extra powerful motor, I use for mincing meat for *pâtés*, *terrines* and mousses. And for complete flexibility I have had a Cannon blender built permanently into the counter top. The blender is measure-marked for accurate filling and makes frozen daiquiris in a flash for cooks in thirst.

Baking, roasting and grilling is done in a built-in electric Westinghouse oven with eye-level grill, complete with electrically operated rotisserie spit.

The fully automatic controls and drop-leaf door are big convenience features of this built-in wall oven. A miniature hood over the door catches overflow heat and protects the wall from fume stains. The oven is lit from within to allow perfect visibility.

The large Westinghouse refrigerator and freezer has special compartments for fruit, vegetables, butter, milk and eggs, and the freezer works like magic for quick-chilled dishes of all kinds. I use the freezer to keep stocks and sauces in small-quantity jars so that they may be taken out and used in a jiffy for emergencies. Small quantities of beef stock, chicken stock and fish stock can be stored in the freezer indefinitely until ready for use, and most cooked sauces – especially meat sauces and gravies – are excellent freezer standbys for pasta, rice, and a variety of dried bean dishes.

Freezer-to-cooker-to-table utensils make it possible to take the same casserole from the oven directly to the freezer without bothersome cooling-off time. The same casserole, stew, or meat or game pie can then be transferred from freezer to oven and on to the table.

A quick trip through the kitchen and china departments of the main London stores – Liberty's, John Lewis, Harrods, Heal's,

Fortnum & Mason, and Selfridge's – will give some idea of the general range and variety of cooking utensils and appliances now available in this country. Most good cookbooks will serve as a competent guide to the basic equipment necessary for the new kitchen. No list, of course, can be definitive; your own needs will be dictated by the type of cooking you want to do. If pastry-making is not your idea of a favourite pastime, it would be senseless to stock your kitchen with a complete battery of baking tins.

Tools of My Trade

Good friends, good conversation, good food – these are the basic ingredients of successful entertaining. The best way to bring all these elements together is to keep kitchen duties to a minimum by collecting the kind of serving equipment and appliances best suited to your entertaining needs.

Until fairly recently, good cooking took time – lots of time – as well as patience and skill. Today we have many new kitchen aids – the electric blender, the food processor, the magic mixer, the microwave oven, the rotating radiant heat cooker and the electric frying pan – ready to perform what used to take hours of downright hard work.

Small wonder that today adventurous cooks with all the know-how of modern science at their fingertips can create fabulous *pâtés*, ethereal *quenelles* and smooth-as-smooth soups and *bisques* with just a touch of the switch of their electrical appliances.

And remember, a good deal of the smooth running of today's outdoor parties can be contributed by the portable electrical appliances that you can plug into sensibly located outdoor electrical outlets. Or for the less far-seeing, why not just rely on a long flex to attach to the electric frying pan or foldaway grill?

Three Basics I Could Not Do Without

BUTCHER'S BLOCK
One of the most used fitments in my kitchen is a butcher's regulation chopping block, four inches (10 cms) thick, placed next to the custom-built cooker top, ready for cutting meats, poultry and game. Thick enough to stand years of use without damage; large enough to hold foods that fall away from the knife – this is a cook's aid that a large kitchen should not be without. A CHOPPING BOARD, thick enough to withstand many washings without warping and large enough to be useful, makes an excellent substitute for a butcher's block in smaller kitchens.

CHOPPING BOWL
A small wooden chopping bowl with a knife which has a curved blade specially designed to fit it is a wonderful tool for chopping parsley, *fines herbes*, shallots and garlic. It is always in view, ready for use, in my kitchen.

MORTAR AND PESTLE
In France I learned to use a mortar and pestle – large size – for pounding dried breadcrumbs, herbs to make a sauce, or meats for a *pâté*. This age-old item of kitchen equipment is indispensable for pounding anchovies for a Provençal *anchoïade*, or poached salt cod for a *brandade de morue*.

Saucepans and Casseroles

Planning ahead for saucepans will save you money in the long run. The heavy metal ones are by far the best, and though they are expensive they will not dent or warp so easily, and the possibility of scorching is minimized. Food preparation for a family is more

---

easily accomplished with large saucepans. I choose those with straight sides.

DOUBLE SAUCEPAN
This combination of saucepans – the double boiler – is essential for the success of emulsion sauces such as Hollandaise or Béarnaise, and for the many sauces that require gentle heat over simmering water.

FRYING PAN
One of the great inventions for the kitchen, a heavy iron frying pan will last for ever. I keep two – a 6-inch (15 cm) frying pan for omelettes, and an all-purpose pan of larger size. These heavy-bottomed iron pans should be thoroughly treated before first using by heating, wiping dry of protective varnish, and then reheating with oil or lard over high heat. If, on use, the food still sticks, repeat the process. To keep an iron frying pan in best condition, do not clean with a metal knife or metal sponge, but clean it while hot with salt and a paper towel.

ENAMEL PAN
This is essential for boiling eggs. Never use an aluminium pan.

CASSEROLES
My advice here is to use restraint when choosing casseroles. They are beautiful and tempting, and since they are rather expensive, some thought should be given to sizes. If your kitchen storage space is limited, I suggest you begin with the following for large gatherings or buffets: two 8-pint (4.5 lit) or 12-pint (6.8 lit); two 6-pint (3.4 lit) for smaller dinners of four to eight; and several of smaller size for vegetables or dinners for two.

Once you decide on size, the range of design and material is immense. Imports from Sweden and France are now shown everywhere, along with the new English creations of coated cast iron, all lovely enough to be brought to the table.

Iron casseroles are now available in Britain. In America they have for years been known as 'Dutch ovens'. These are round, with a close-fitting lid, and are wonderful for pot roasts and chicken casseroles, and for stews that require prolonged and slow cooking. These iron casseroles, also imported from Finland in different shapes, require the same preparation and maintenance as the prosaic iron frying pan.

Cutting Tools

A carefully selected collection of kitchen knives is a good investment. The ones I use most frequently are kept in slots in the counter top. There are many fine imported kitchen knives on the market, and those with scalloped or serrated edges do, indeed, offer special advantages in cutting, and maintain their sharp cutting edge indefinitely. As a guide to a basic selection I suggest the following as the most practical:

HAM SLICER
A thin, 9-inch (23 cm)-bladed knife is perfect for making uniform slices of ham and is equally effective for poultry.

CARVING KNIFE
I recommend two – both about 9 inches (23 cms) in length; one with a serrated edge good for cold meats, cheeses, bread and pastry, and one with a straight edge for roasts and steaks.

FRENCH COOK'S KNIFE
Two of these should be included – a large one and a small one – to dice, chop or slice raw vegetables and fruit.

PARKING KNIFE
Choose one with a 3-inch (7 cm) blade and pointed tip for paring cucumbers, potatoes, onions and carrots.

CLEAVER
The cleaver is really a very useful addition to your kitchen for separating large sections of meat, cutting joints as well as game and lobster. I often use the flat side of mine as a meat tenderizer.

KITCHEN SHEARS
These culinary scissors are an absolute essential in a well-organized kitchen – for cutting through poultry joints, paring bacon rinds, trimming sliced cold meat and snipping the string off rolled meats.

Miscellany

COOKING FORK
One of the most useful of implements. Select one with a long wooden handle and stainless steel prongs. Hang it within easy reach of the stove.

WOODEN AND METAL SPOONS
Be sure your selection of cooking spoons corresponds to the sizes of your saucepans. A small spoon in a large casserole is a hazard simple to avoid.

SLOTTED METAL COOKING SPOON
Useful for making sauces and gravies smooth and for skimming stocks and gravies.

SPATULA
A flexible spatula of stainless steel for loosening food, icing cakes and turning omelettes.

LADLE
Used for soups, sauces and gravies, ladles come in a wide range of sizes.

WIRE WHISK
Round or flat, the wire whisk is best for use with sauces and eggs whites. A professional chef might need a dozen. Two or three different sizes are necessary for every kitchen.

METAL GRATER
Select one of the new ones in stainless steel with varied cutting edges for grating orange and lemon rind, cheese, nutmeg, etc.

PEPPER AND SALT MILLS
While not perhaps essential, these kitchen aids offer the indispensable advantage of freshly ground seasonings. I couldn't do without them.

SIEVES
A conical sieve used for the straining of sauces is one of the most useful kitchen utensils. A 6-inch (15 cm) sieve is a good size for all

purposes. I also find the ordinary round-bottomed sieves useful for the sieving and draining of vegetables.

MIXING BOWLS
Every kitchen should have a series of mixing bowls large enough to hold the ingredients to be used. I like a series of three bowls in assorted sizes, as well as a mammoth Swedish bowl with a lip, which I find most useful.

MEASURING EQUIPMENT
Accurate measurements are essential to any kind of cooking. If the equipment is kept within easy reach of cooking and preparation areas, measuring becomes automatic. A set of individual MEASUR-ING SPOONS in plastic or metal – 1 tablespoon, 1 dessertspoon, 1 teaspoon, ½ teaspoon and ¼ teaspoon – is ideal for measuring small quantities of ingredients. A PINT MEASURING CUP marked off in fluid ounces or tablespoons is also useful, as is a pair of KITCHEN SCALES.

ASBESTOS MAT
Useful for top-of-the-stove cooking in those casseroles that are not flameproof.

POT HOLDERS
A good selection of washable pot holders will save wear and tear on the hands when removing hot dishes from the oven or lifting saucepans with hot handles.

Some Basic Ingredients

Once upon a time – in order to buy certain vegetables and foreign foods in London – it was necessary to confine my shopping to the square mile of Soho and the food departments of one or two of the better stores.

Those were the days when to get wild rice for a special party I had to have it flown in from New York; when 'first pressing' olive oil from Provence and the tarragon wine vinegar prepared for me by Fifine in St Tropez were picked up personally each summer, and consequently had to be eked out carefully to last from one sunshine visit to the next; when bottled herbs and spices and 'hurry-up' packaged foods for the emergency shelf had to be ordered specially from America.

Now this picture has completely changed. Shops, stores and supermarkets the length and breadth of the land are full to bursting with foodstuffs from all over the world, fresh, packaged or frozen.

I am constantly amazed when I go into some little shop in the country and find the vegetable bins full of courgettes or zucchini, silver-green fennel, golden ears of corn, and red, green and yellow peppers. Garlic, of course, we have grown accustomed to, but once this most delectably potent bulb was looked upon as an almost sybaritic luxury. Shallots, however, I'd like to see more of.

The Aromatics

I love garlic – often called the noblest member of the onion tribe. This pungent bulb has been used in Mediterranean countries for thousands of years for its curative and healing properties as well as its culinary powers. A touch of garlic gives a particularly delicious flavour to a salad or a casserole. If you like a lot – as I do – chop a clove finely, and add it frankly to salads; or toss it in hot butter before adding it to your casserole or meat dish. Garlic has special affinities for kidneys and roast lamb and really comes into its own in the warm-blooded Mediterranean specialities of France and Italy.

I like to use garlic, shallots and onions – finely chopped and sautéed gently until transparent – as the base of many of my favourite casserole dishes. This combination of aromatics seems to bring out the superb flavour of meat, fish and poultry without overwhelming it with the taste of any one of these three ingredients.

Salt and pepper, found in every kitchen, are important cooks' aids, too. I prefer to use rough-ground sea salt, *gros sel*. I find food cooked with sea salt is far superior to food cooked with ordinary powdered salt, so I always have quantities of glistening white flakes on hand to grind into casseroles and salads. A salt mill for the table is essential here. Freshly ground black pepper is a must, too, for full flavour. Use a pepper mill to grind it as you use it.

Onions rank next to salt in my kitchen as an almost universal seasoner. Brought by French chefs to the starry heights of *haute cuisine*, this erstwhile peasant vegetable – first cousin of the lily and an important member of the pungent family of leeks, shallots, garlic and chives – has become almost a common denominator of classic cooking. Use it as a subtle seasoner for soups and sauces; simmer it in butter and olive oil for a sublime flavourer for casseroles and stews; sauté it to accompany liver; deep-fry it to accompany steak; and feature it on its own as the star performer in creamy onion tarts, creamed or baked onions, and French onion soup.

The delicate, violet-tinted shallot – a more polite member of the onion family – is usually finely chopped and sautéed in a little butter as a flavourful additive to casseroles, stews, sauces, and grilled or sautéed meat, fish and poultry. A grilled fillet steak, served with hot melted butter and sprinkled with finely chopped parsley and shallots is delicious. Chopped shallots in small game birds – quail, partridge, grouse – add greatly to the flavour; chopped shallots can also be used effectively in wine sauces and in stuffings for meat roasts. Fish dishes improve greatly with the addition of a little finely chopped shallot to the sauce.

Olive Oil

The olive – one of the symbols of Mediterranean cookery – not only provides the basic fat in which everything else is cooked, but is also the chief element of the dressing in which many raw foods and all salads are served. The olive trees of Provence – said to have been introduced by the Greeks over 2,000 years ago – produce many varieties of this fruit today: small, relatively dry and hard, medium-sized and moist, or large, soft and juicy.

Provençal olive oil is made of olives crushed to a pulp from which is pressed the fruity flavoured, golden-coloured, virgin oil, *l'huile vierge*, which adds so much to Provençal cookery and salads. Cold water is added to the remaining pulp after this first pressing to produce a second pressing, called *fine* or *extra fine* oil, more bland in flavour, but usually clearer in colour. A third pressing for manufacturing processes, or for the farmer's own use, is sometimes made with the addition of warm water to the almost dry olive pulp. Further pressings produce oil for use in soaps and fertilizers.

I like to serve a plate of wrinkled black olives – scooped fresh from a giant barrel with a black-stained olive scoop fashioned from olive wood – or green preserved olives flavoured with orange peel and fresh herbs, as a simple accompaniment to a glass of chilled *rosé* or white wine. It is a wonderful pre-lunch appetizer. Richly flavoured *tapénade*, a delicious mixture of pounded black olives, anchovy fillets, tuna fish and olive oil, flavoured with capers, mustard and a little cognac, makes a wonderful *hors-d'œuvre* when served with hard-boiled eggs (see page 279). Or try the famous *caviar du pauvre* (poor man's caviar) made of black olives, pitted and pounded with garlic and butter, and spread on canapés of toasted French bread.

I like, too, an even earthier version of olives and garlic which is the famous *frotte d'ail*, immortalized by Colette in her writings. To make Colette's *frotte d'ail*, just rub a stale piece of French bread with a cut clove of garlic, sprinkle with coarse salt and olive oil, and eat with gusto. It's basic, it's crude in flavour, perhaps, but to me it spells Provence on a sunny mid-morning, especially when washed down with a glass of chilled *rosé*.

Use olive oil in cooking to give earthy savour to stews, *ragoûts* and *daubes*. Always add a tablespoon or two (15–30 ml) of olive oil to butter when frying meat, fish or vegetables; it will keep the butter from browning. And add it, too, to the water in which you cook rice or spaghetti, to keep them glistening and separate. Use olive oil to keep frying pans and iron casseroles in top condition. And if you like a really fruity taste in your olive oil, put 2 or 3 black olives (the ones preserved in oil, not brine) in the bottom of your bottle. You will be delighted with the difference.

Butter

Some of the most delicious tastes in the world owe their particular flavour and attraction to fresh butter: the first asparagus of the season, served hot with melted butter, or melted butter and lemon juice; tiny new potatoes, cooked in their jackets and served with nothing but fresh butter, coarse salt and freshly ground black pepper; a Dover sole, cooked *à la meunière* in foaming butter; fresh mushrooms and cream – the mushrooms simmered in fresh butter with a little lemon juice, and then bathed in double cream – the whole encased in a butter-rich pastry case and served as the ambrosial accompaniment to poached chicken.

Butter does so many things: it adds flavour and unmatchable quality to pastry; it adds richness and body to sauces; blended with lemon juice, or finely chopped parsley and garlic, or Roquefort cheese, it provides an easy-to-make, easy-to-serve individual garnish for grilled steaks and chops, and poached or grilled sole, turbot or salmon.

I like to flavour slightly softened butter with lemon juice and finely chopped garlic, form it into marbled-sized balls, roll them in finely chopped parsley, and chill them in the refrigerator. Excellent with grilled beef steak, lamb chops, or grilled or poached sole, turbot or salmon. Or try blending equal amounts of softened butter and Roquefort cheese for an interesting 'butter' to serve with grilled beef steak. These, too, can be rolled in finely chopped parsley for added effect.

René Lasserre, owner of one of France's most elegant and most highly reputed restaurants, located just off the Rond Point des Champs Elysées in Paris, used butter to 'poach' the fillets of sole for his famous *casserolettes de filets de sole Lasserre*. This 'butter poaching' is so time-saving, so easy and so delicious, that I use it for fish of all kinds now. Here's how: remove fillets from sole; arrange them in a well-buttered *gratin* dish. Sprinkle with 2 finely chopped shallots and 4 finely chopped mushroom stalks; add salt and freshly ground black pepper, to taste, and cover with fish bones. Cover with generously buttered paper and 'poach' in hot oven (450°F/230°C/GM8) for 10 to 12 minutes.

Try this, too, with cod, salmon or turbot steaks. Delicious. Especially when served with a Fish Velouté Sauce.

For best results, make sure your butter is of the best quality. This is as true for an earthy *ragoût* of beef or veal as it is in the delicate realms of pastry-making.

For slow frying, mix equal quantities of butter and olive oil, putting the oil in the pan first to keep the butter from browning. For earthier casseroles, combine equal quantities of butter and oil in this way and then add diced cubes of fat salt pork or unsmoked bacon to create a richer emulsion with plenty of flavour.

Most country-style casseroles need no thickening and certainly no elaborate sauces to enhance their flavour. It is the slow, careful reduction of oil, butter and wine with shallots, garlic and the juices of meat, chicken or fish, cooked slowly *en cocotte* or *en casserole*, which gives to each of these dishes its own delicious flavour and texture.

There are times, however, when you will want to make sauces and gravies a little more full-bodied or substantial; then butter and flour play their part in the French chef's *beurre manié*.

TO MAKE A BEURRE MANIÉ

When the sauce should be very slightly thickened at the last moment, a *beurre manié* is indicated. Take a piece of butter (about 1 good tablespoon/15 ml) and knead it to a smooth paste in a cup or small bowl with the same amount of flour: stir *beurre manié* into the sauce bit by bit a few minutes before serving; but be sure to simmer long enough for the flour to be entirely cooked. Use a *beurre manié* to thicken any sauce or casserole dish.

Rely, too, on butter's affinity for flour to make super-smooth sauces by the *roux* method (see page 100).

Cream

The French respect cream for what it is – a luxurious complement to good cooking. More than any other single factor it has determined the nature of the fine, rich cooking of Normandy and Burgundy, two of France's most esteemed regional cuisines.

Norman cooks use the rich full beauty of cream mainly in the form of *sauce normande*, which begins with a *roux* made of butter and flour. To this is added a highly flavoured liquid obtained by boiling vegetables and herbs until the *bouillon* has become an essence of their flavours, enriched either by white wine or egg yolks, depending on the dish for which the sauce is being made. Rich Norman cream is added last, along with more butter and a dash of lemon. I like to serve this sauce with egg dishes, or as a flavourful accompaniment to poached fish or chicken.

In Burgundy, cream enters into a great many regional specialities: fish, shellfish, poultry and meats are cooked with cream; the famous hams of the Morvan region are often cooked in a *court-bouillon*, then sliced and served in a highly flavoured cream sauce; fresh *morilles* (earthy flavoured puff balls of the mushroom family) are a famous Burgundian speciality when served in a rich cream sauce; and *quenelles* (those featherlight dumplings of pounded pike and cream) are often served in the region around Lyons with a rich cream or Mornay sauce.

The French make the most delicious soups imaginable by simmering single vegetables – carrots, peas or potatoes – or combinations of vegetables – leeks and potatoes, leeks and carrots, or onions and celery – in a well-flavoured chicken stock. When the vegetables are tender, the mixture is put through the blender and then enriched with good butter and double cream, and flavoured with parsley or chervil. In simpler fashion, the combination of frozen spinach or frozen peas with a sliced onion, simmered in a little chicken stock, puréed in the blender and then enriched with double cream, is a wonderfully easy way to start a winter meal.

Use cream, as do the French, to add suavity to casseroles of veal, chicken or game. Fish and shellfish are enormously enhanced by the addition of a little double cream just before serving. Cream can be boiled; but remember, it must not be boiled too hard or too long, or it is liable to curdle or separate.

I like to use double cream as a sauce on its own for fish or vegetables. Just heat cream through; pour it into a serving bowl, add lemon juice, season to taste with salt and freshly ground black pepper, and stir in two or more tablespoons (30 ml) of finely chopped fresh parsley, tarragon or chives.

And remember, when adding cream to a casserole or vegetable dish, taste the dish just before serving. Nine times out of ten, it will need additional seasoning. Cream tends to soften flavours – a good thing to know if you have overseasoned a dish.

One of the most famous *liaisons* or thickening agents in the world is the addition of double cream mixed with egg yolks and a little lemon juice. The dish is then heated gently until the sauce thickens. On no account must you allow it to come to a boil, or your sauce will curdle.

And what would the majority of sweets and puddings be if the cook had not used rich, full cream in them or – failing this – if a jug of cream were not served with the dish in question? I love apple pie made of thick wedges of Bramley's famous seedlings, dusted with freshly grated orange and lemon peel, powdered cinnamon and nutmeg, baked in the oven and served with rich double cream.

Mustard

It is sometimes hard to believe – looking at the crusted mustard pots set out with salt and pepper shakers in small restaurants and cafés – that mustard is one of the noblest and most ancient flavourers of all.

Mustard is mentioned in the Bible. Hippocrates prescribed it for medicinal purposes. The early Egyptians used dried mustard seeds as a condiment much as we do pepper today. And Cleopatra is rumoured to have sprinkled it in her bath to 'invigorate' her! The Romans blended it and used it lavishly (Pliny the Elder gave a recipe which first blended mustard powder and vinegar). Even vegetables, combined with eggs to make a soufflé, or more simply simmered in oil with fresh herbs, were often dressed with a mustard sauce.

Mustard was brought to Gaul by the Roman legions. It became so popular that there was a guild of mustard-makers in the fifteenth century and Dijon became one of the greatest mustard-producing centres in the world.

In France, mustard is usually blended with wine vinegar or verjuice (the must of sour and immature grapes) and tarragon or *fines herbes*, and never with anything so basic as water. The result is that French mustard is deliciously subtle in flavour, yet full of a tart, piquant hotness that is the perfect accompaniment to meats and a wonderful flavour additive for sauces, gravies and pickles, chutneys and relishes.

There are two schools of mustard in France: the Dijonnais and the Bordelais. The original Dijon mustard – very light in colour, usually unflavoured by herbs – is generally the hotter of the two. Blended with verjuice, this mustard is, to my taste, the finer in flavour. In more recent years, a selection of herb-flavoured Dijon mustards has been marketed, and mustard fanciers now have some six different flavours to choose from. Bordeaux mustard – darker in colour and flavour, and blended with wine vinegar and various herbs and flavourings – is less hot. Wholegrain mustards have now become popular.

Do not keep prepared mustards too long. Store them in the refrigerator to keep loss of flavour and aroma at a minimum.

The English and Chinese have always preferred dry mustard mixed with water just before serving. The aroma or pungency of the mustard remains locked in the powder until it comes in contact with water. After three minutes, it is at its pungent best.

English mustard – produced in Britain since 1720, when it was first ground and sifted commercially – is a blend of powdered white and black mustards, with a little turmeric added to give the mustard powder a rich, golden-yellow colour. It is very hot in flavour.

Herbs and Spices

The Italians, the Spaniards and the French use finely ground spices and aromatic herbs – both fresh and dried – in the preparation of many of their most famous dishes. The peoples of the East have used finely ground barks, seeds, roots and berries in their cooking for centuries.

Today, these riches are at our fingertips, fresh or dried, ground or whole, ready to impart a magic touch to even the simplest dishes. For it is a mistake to think that simple cookery requires nothing more than a pinch of pepper and salt to make it palatable. There are so many more aromatics that we can call on to bring out the utmost in flavour in our everyday fare. So take a note from the ancients: use herbs and spices to enhance, blend or accent the flavours in a dish, to stimulate appetite, aid digestion and add aroma, colour and texture to today's mass-produced foods.

Spices are invariably stronger in flavour than herbs and so must be used with more discretion – our familiar standby, black pepper, is a case in point. Fresh herbs are always very mild; dried herbs, more concentrated in flavour. In general. I like to add most herbs towards the end of cooking. In this way, they cannot cook too long, losing savour or imparting a bitter taste to the food. Dried herbs have about twice the strength of fresh herbs and should be used in half measure to fresh green leaves.

Use herbs and spices imaginatively. These magic powders, leaves, berries and seeds are the secret of fine cooking. But use them sparingly until you have become accustomed to their effects in cooking. It is always easy to add extra seasoning, but it is very difficult to subtract. When trying out a new recipe in which you use herbs and spices, use half-quantities only, and then – if you like the flavour – add the rest towards the end of the cooking time. A good rule of thumb for using dried herbs and spices: use one generous pinch (or ¼ level teaspoon/1.25 ml) for each four servings.

HOW TO KEEP HERBS AND SPICES
Always buy herbs and spices in small jars or packets, never more than 2 oz (50 g) at a time. Do not keep them near the stove: heat will cause loss of flavour. Keep them away from strong light; colours will fade. And do not keep them too long; they lose their flavour and aroma.

Test herbs and spices occasionally and if they are stale, replace them with a fresh supply.

HOW TO USE HERBS AND SPICES
Be selective. Unless you are following a tested recipe, do not combine too many at one time. And remember, the correct herb or spice combination for any food is the one that tastes right to you. There are no rules. The use of seasoning is an art, not a science.

ALLSPICE
A delicately fragrant flavour, pungent and aromatic, that tastes like a blend of cinnamon, nutmeg and mace, strongly spiced with

---

cloves. Excellent for game, poultry stuffings and sausage mixtures. Use it ground or whole in stews, *ragoûts*, sauces and gravies. Use it whole for pickles and marinades; add 2 or 3 berries to a fresh pea soup; flavour chutneys, ketchup and spiced fruits with it. Use it with a light hand to flavour delicate sauces for fish and eggs; let its fragrance accent hot puddings, fruit pies and certain cakes.

ANISEED
A light, pleasantly liquorice flavour when used with a gentle touch in cooking. Used widely in confectionery and cake- and pastry-making. Sprinkle aniseed on cakes and cookies; pound it with sugar to flavour cakes, custards and creams. Use it in the Oriental manner to add flavour and excitement to fish and game.

BASIL
Fresh basil leaves and tender stems have a delightful odour and mildly pungent flavour when bruised. Combine chopped snippets of basil with oregano, chives and melted butter, and serve with spaghetti; sprinkle a teaspoon (5 ml) of finely chopped basil leaves and parsley on sliced, chilled tomatoes. Use it in salads, soups, stews and sauces; try its permeating flavour with grilled lamb chops.

BAY LEAF
The leaf of the bay tree, not properly speaking a 'herb', has been used so consistently since early times, that I shall include it here. Pungent, mildly aromatic, with a slightly bitter flavour when dried, bay leaves are an essential ingredient in a *bouquet garni*, and are thus to be found in most recipes for stews, casseroles, marinades, *court-bouillons* and soups. Crumbled bay leaves add much to pickling spices and vinegars, poultry stuffings, *pâtés* and *terrines*. Add a bay leaf to tomato sauce, tomato soup, and to stewed tomatoes.

BOUQUET GARNI
A *bouquet garni* is a bunch of herbs, either tied together or bound into a tiny cheesecloth sack, and cooked with the food. To make a simple *bouquet*: combine a few sprigs of parsley, chives and a bay leaf, and tie securely. A more important *bouquet garni* can be made up of 2 sprigs parsley, 2 sprigs thyme, 1 branch celery, 1 sprig

marjoram, 1 bay leaf and 1 sprig rosemary. I like to cut the celery into 2 equal pieces about 2½ inches (65 mm) in length, and place the herbs between them. When tied securely, this makes a firm little bundle of aromatics, full of savour.

CARDAMOM
Similar in flavour to ginger, allspice and black pepper, but with a fresher, almost citrus, flavour. It is used in India as one of the prime ingredients of hot curry powders and sauces. Use cardamom seeds whole for pickling and for curries; use it finely ground in pastries, sweet sauces and cakes.

Cardamom goes particularly well with orange. Try a little, too, sprinkled on melon, or just a hint of this fragrant spice to give a touch of the East to after-dinner coffee.

CHERVIL
A delicate, feathery herb, similar to parsley in flavour, but milder. A little finely chopped chervil is excellent in a delicate butter sauce such as a *sauce hollandaise*. Finely chopped chervil, parsley, chives and tarragon make up the subtle combination of fresh herbs necessary for an *omelette aux fines herbes*. Chervil alone makes a cheese omelette very special. Very good with most soups and stews. An excellent garnish for salads. Try chopping chervil finely and sprinkling it on grilled fish just before removing it from under the grill.

CHILI POWDER
A blend – like curry – of several ingredients, chili powder (not to be confused with powdered chilli) is a delicious combination of the finely ground pods of several kinds of hot pepper, paprika, cumin seed, dried garlic and oregano.

Rich in colour and flavour, chili powder is widely used in Mexican and Southwestern American cooking, as well as in tropical countries, to flavour native dishes, stews, meats, sauces and soups.

CHIVES
A light, delicate, onion flavour. This most refined member of the onion family is delicious in salad dressings, and as a garnish for vegetables. Try it on boiled potatoes, carrots or leeks. It is a necessary ingredient of *vichyssoise*, but try it also with cream of

asparagus or bean soup. Mix with butter and lemon juice – or cream cheese and sour cream – as a cocktail spread. Chop into meat sauces. When the slender leaves and young tops of the plant are cut close, others will grow in rapid succession, and a bed of chives can last for three to four years.

CINNAMON

When used in moderation, its fragrant odour and sweet spicy flavour are the perfect foil to fish and fish sauces. Combine cinnamon with pepper, ginger, cloves and mace. Use this mixture as a 'dry marinade' to rub on pork chops and game before cooking. Add a hint of cinnamon and cloves to Dijon mustard to flavour baked ham.

Spice mulled wines with cinnamon. Let this spice add interest to sweets, cakes and puddings. Sprinkle it over coffee, sliced fresh fruits and puddings.

Its highly fragrant odour and sweet aromatic flavour are a must for apple pies, dumplings, sauces and puddings.

CLOVES

The clove has a hot spicy flavour and a highly aromatic scent. Use whole cloves for pickling, for pork and ham, and for fruit dishes. Take advantage of the clove's natural affinity for onion, pork and ham.

Use ground cloves in spice cakes, gingerbreads, puddings and sweets. No apple pie is considered complete without a faint hint of clove, but be careful not to overdo it.

CORIANDER

Sweet yet tart in flavour, coriander is a favourite ingredient for hot curries and sauces. Rub coriander on pork before roasting, or on pork chops before cooking. Use dried coriander to flavour Moroccan dishes, with dried bean soups, and in poultry stuffings. Try this spice with meats, cheeses and pickles; use it sparingly in puddings and pastries.

Fresh coriander is used in practically all cooking in Mexico and South America, where it is called *ciantro*. It is also used extensively in China and Japan, where it is known as Chinese parsley. Its exotic flavour is the highlight in *ceviche* (raw fish salad), *guacamole* (mashed avocado salad) and other Mexican dishes. In Britain, coriander leaves or seeds are used in chutneys, with lemon sauce

---

for venison, and with braised celery or cream of celery soup. Its flavour seems to bring out the celery taste.

CUMIN SEED

Its strong aromatic scent and pungent flavour (similar to caraway seed but much stronger in flavour) are made use of extensively in Mexican cookery, Indian curries, and as a delicious flavourer for meat loaf, lamb and chicken dishes, and anything made with dried beans.

Use the seeds whole as an attractive and flavourful 'wrapping' for cubes of cream cheese.

CURRY POWDER

Commonly known as a spice, curry powder is in reality a blend of many herbs and spices. Commercial varieties may contain eight to thirty-eight different sorts. Connoisseurs of curry have special formulæ of freshly ground herbs and spices for various dishes. The following list – which reads like a complete herb and spice index – will give you some idea of the principal ingredients it is possible to include in a well-blended curry powder: allspice, aniseed, bay leaves, cardamon, cinnamon, cloves, coriander, cumin, dill, fennel, garlic, ginger, mace, mustard, nutmeg, black pepper, white pepper, red pepper, paprika, poppy seeds, saffron, turmeric, etc. The relative strength of the blend depends, of course, on how much hot pepper or ginger is used.

DILL

A lacy, delicately flavoured herb. Use fresh sprigs of dill in vegetable and fish salads. Try cucumbers with sour cream and fresh dill; new potatoes with lemon butter and fresh dill; potato salad with crumbled bacon and fresh dill in the dressing. Good with all grilled or poached fish.

FENNEL

This feathery herb, which looks something like dill, is excellent in fish sauces and in salad dressings. Fennel seeds – famous for their use in liqueurs of the *anisette* variety – add a subtle flavour and texture to pastries.

Dried fennel stalks are used by the French for flaming *loup de mer*, and as an aromatic in *bouillabaisse* and *soupe de poisson*.

The bulbs of fresh fennel (*finocchio* in Italy, *fenouil* in France) are also eaten as a salad. In this case the thickened stalk or bulb is sliced thinly and dressed with olive oil, lemon, salt and pepper. Eaten this way, it has a delightful anise or liquorice flavour.

GINGER

One of the earliest Oriental spices to be known to Europe, ginger originally came from Southern China, where the ripe roots were carefully selected, boiled in several waters to remove some of their fire, and then preserved in thick syrup.

This extremely pungent spice should be creamy white in colour when ground. It is smooth-skinned and light buff in colour when whole.

Ground ginger adds much to apple sauces, chutneys and stewed fruits. Try blending ground ginger, black pepper and crushed salt, and rubbing this over steaks and chops before grilling. Also good with lamb. Sprinkle ground ginger lightly on fish before grilling. Add lightly to fruit and wine sauces.

MACE

The dried outer sheath of the kernel of the fruit of the nutmeg tree, and similar, if stronger, in flavour. Use ground mace for pickling and for marinades, brines and game sauces. Use it with a lighter hand in cakes, sweets and puddings. Add mace with impunity to any sweet in which chocolate plays a leading part.

Oyster stew – a great favourite in New England – would not be the same without a dash of mace. Try mace with fish, shellfish, eggs and vegetables in a rich cream sauce. Cauliflower and carrots particularly, take kindly to a hint of mace, and puréed potatoes, enriched with cream and butter, are all the better for a dash of this versatile spice.

MARJORAM

Very pungent – a little goes a long way. Stews, soups, braised meats, sausages, pork roasts and chops all call for interesting uses of marjoram. This herb is also very good with fish. Try a little finely chopped with buttered carrots, spinach or turnips for a subtle new flavour. Its aromatic, slightly bitter taste is excellent in poultry stuffings.

MINT

There are about fourteen varieties of mint grown in Britain alone. Spearmint, the most popular, is used for flavouring peas and potatoes, and in the preparation of mint sauce to accompany roast lamb. Try it, too, in salads and salad dressings. Fresh pea soup, whether served hot or cold, is the better for the clean, clear flavour of fresh mint, as are pot cheeses, ices, wine cups and, of course, mint julep.

Try the other mint varieties – you can grow them in your garden or on the window sill – for further flavour flourishes: pineapple and *eau-de-Cologne* mint snipped into salads, or crystallized for cakes, or tied in bunches to flavour wine cups and *tisanes*; apple mint for poultry stuffings, fruit cups, and for jellies made from crab-apples and gooseberries.

MUSTARD
The French moisten powdered white and black mustards with verjuice (to make Dijon mustard), or with wine (for Bordeaux mustard), and add herbs for various special mustard blends.

English mustard is a blend of powdered white and black mustards with a little turmeric added to give the mustard powder a rich golden colour. It is very hot in flavour.

I like to use mustard to flavour sauces and gravies for meats and game, in pickles, chutneys and relishes and, of course, in salad dressings. See also page 698.

NUTMEG
Delicate and at the same time very aromatic, nutmeg is usually used as a substitute for, or as an adjunct to, mace. The whole nut keeps its flavour almost indefinitely. Ground nutmeg, however, soon loses its flavour, so it is much better to keep it in nut form and grate it as you need it.

OREGANO
Closely related to marjoram and sometimes called wild marjoram, oregano seems to go especially well with tomatoes and tomato sauces – hence a natural for pasta sauces. A touch of this herb makes grilled tomatoes delicious. Try oregano when baking onions or roasting pork or lamb. This herb is much used in Italy to flavour the many recipes for pizza. Use oregano in stuffing for meat or fowl, in basting sauces and in marinades.

PAPRIKA
Warmly aromatic and a rich red in colour, paprika is used a great deal in French, Spanish, Moroccan and Hungarian cookery. Use

this mild sweet cousin of the red pepper to add colour and flavour to eggs, seafood and vegetables. Fish dishes, cream soups and cooked cheese dishes all benefit from a sprinkling of paprika, and, of course, it is a prime ingredient of chicken or veal paprika, and of the Hungarian national dish, *goulash*.

PARSLEY

The best known and most generally used of all herbs, it is invariably thought of as a garnish for meat, fish and vegetables. Use finely chopped parsley to enhance the flavours of sauces, soups, stews, fish and meat salads, and stuffings, and as an intrinsic part of the traditional faggot of mixed herbs (the French call it a *bouquet*) which adds such a wonderful something to French country cooking. Parsley sauce is an excellent accompaniment to boiled or steamed fish, and boiled chicken.

PEPPER

This is our most widely used spice. BLACK PEPPER – one of the first spices to be introduced to Europe – is the dried unripe fruit of the *Piper nigrum* found in the East Indies. This spice lends flavour and excitement to most foods. It quickly loses flavour and aroma when ground. I prefer to grind it as I need it in a pepper mill. WHITE PEPPER – less pungent and less aromatic than black pepper – is the same seed freed from its outer skin. It is perfect for lighter sauces and in any dish where specks of black pepper would be unsightly. RED PEPPER – the most pungent of all spices – is very hot, pungent and biting. Use it sparingly to lend excitement to fish, shellfish, *canapé* spreads and salad dressings. Perfect for curry and barbecue sauces, and for the hot stews and *ragoûts* of Africa and the Caribbean.

ROSEMARY

A sprinkling of fresh rosemary leaves complements the flavour of lamb. For a delightful change, add chopped fresh rosemary, blended with chopped parsley and butter, to any baked chicken dish. The fresh, sweet, pine-woods flavour of this herb, used since biblical times, adds an indescribable taste to sauces, stews and cream soups. Try it on its own with steak or veal chops, using finely chopped rosemary leaves as you would pepper for a steak *au poivre*. Rosemary is better fresh than when dried.

SAFFRON

Once so greatly esteemed in this country as a flavourer of breads, cakes, soups and stews, saffron is now more or less forgotten. Not so in Italy, where it lends its special flavour and colour to *risotto alla milanese* (saffron rice); in France, where it is an integral part of *bouillabaisse* and Provençal fish soups; and in Spain, where it is one of the main ingredients of *paella*, Spain's national dish of chicken, sausage, seafood and saffron-flavoured rice. Use saffron to add colour and zest to rice dishes and fish soups of all kinds. Try it in baking, in saffron buns and saffron bread.

SAGE

Sage is used a good deal in Italian and Provençal dishes. *Saltimbocca* has thin slices of veal rolled with *prosciutto* (Parma ham) and a sage leaf, and fried gently in butter. In Provence, *daurade au sauge* (sea-bream cooked with sage) and *carré de porc au sauge* (roast pork with sage) are well-known specialities. Because of its strong bold flavour, it must be used with great care – especially in stuffings for chicken, duck and goose, where it is apt to swamp other more delicate flavours. It is fragrant, though a little bitter; good with pork and sausage.

TARRAGON

Known to most as a flavouring for wine vinegar, this fresh green herb is delicious when chopped finely and combined with melted butter and a little lemon juice as a sauce for fish. The delicate pungent taste of this difficult-to-grow herb – and its delightful perfume – make it a must in any herbal story. Add chopped fresh tarragon to any salad; use it to add special interest to a fricasséed or roast chicken. Use it in aspics with chicken, eggs or shellfish. Tarragon is an indispensable ingredient of a *sauce béarnaise* and adds its inimitable savour to green mayonnaise. Its faintly anise flavour is good in marinades for meat and fish.

THYME

Pungent, aromatic and popular, thyme is used to flavour stews, soups and sauces; it goes particularly well with dishes in which wine is used. There are many varieties of this herb, wild and cultivated. Lemon thyme adds zest and flavour to scrambled eggs, egg sandwich spreads and creamed eggs. Mix thyme to taste with salt and freshly ground black pepper, and rub over beef, lamb or veal before roasting. Casseroles of meat or poultry are greatly enhanced in flavour if a little thyme is added shortly before cooking time is up. Try this herb warmed in butter, with grilled lobster, shrimps and prawns. Add it to butter to dress carrots, mushrooms, onions and potatoes.

Cooking With Wine

Frrench cooks are famous for their superb casseroles of meat, fish and poultry, enhanced with the subtle flavour of aromatic herbs and simmered gently in a sauce made rich with good stock, cream or wine. It is perhaps just this use of herbs and wines, and the words so often called on to describe these dishes – rich, unctuous, exotic, sophisticated – that have made the less adventurous cook too intimidated to attempt them.

For the uninitiated to whom cooking with wine may seem as extravagant as it is difficult, the well-known author and gourmet, Paul Gallico, set down this golden rule to dispel once and for all any misunderstanding: 'The only different between cooking with wine and not cooking with wine is that you pour some wine in.'

My first contact with French food and wine was as dramatic and complete as any I have had since. It was in the winter of 1944, in the little river town of Duclair, just a few miles from Rouen. The dimly lit windows of a riverside inn beckoned the four travel-stained soldiers of the US Army standing on the *quai*. We were young – not one of us over twenty-one – weary of the training, travel and camp life that were to prepare us for the push ahead, and hungry for food other than our army rations, for faces other than our camp companions, and for that something else which we all felt was waiting for us somewhere in this war-spoiled terrain of Northern France – the spirit of France itself.

This was to be our first meal in France, not perhaps as it should have been, but as the fortunes of war and of the pot would permit. The innkeeper, surprised to find soldiers asking for anything other than beer or Calvados, claimed at first that he had nothing to serve us. Then, taking pity on our youth and the fact that we had journeyed thousands of miles for this encounter, he disappeared for a moment or two into the cellars, to return with a slim white earthenware terrine and two dust-covered bottles – all that he could find to offer us – the *pâté* made for himself and his wife, and the wine hidden from the Germans behind bricked-over walls in the cellar.

The *pâté* was a home-made terrine of duck, its top covered with the rich golden-white fat of its own body, which had simmered slowly in the oven with a little wine to cover; the fillets of its breast and liver marbling the rich red-stained meat as we cut into it. Crusty bread and glasses of cellar-cooled claret completed this unforgettable meal, the perfect introduction to the pleasures of French food and wines, for *pâté de canard*, as made in Duclair, is one of the most famous dishes of Normandy, and Chantemerle, the wine he found for us that night, one of the noblest wines of all France.

Good food and wine have been the symbols of French living since they emerged together from the monasteries at the end of the Dark Ages. And they have been linked inextricably ever since.

Guardians of the pleasures of the table as much as of the learning of the past, the monks kept the secrets of the gourmets safe for a thousand years after the Roman Empire collapsed. The kings of those days were merely chiefs; the barons taken up with wars. Not for them the fine points of the table.

But the traditions of good living persisted behind monastery walls. The strictest orders, though fasting themselves, provided hospitality for the great on pilgrimages or on their way to the wars, and for merchants traversing the ancient trade routes of Europe from the South to the Hanseatic Ports.

In their guests' refectories, a more sophisticated cuisine persisted, and wine played its part in full. For as the great Cistercian and Benedictine monasteries cleared the wooded lands presented to them over the centuries, they planted them with vines. Some of the most famous vineyards in Burgundy – Clos Vougeot, for instance, belonged to the Abbey of Citeaux – were tended by monks forbidden by their rule to drink the wines they produced. But they were not forbidden to sell them, and strategic gifts of their finest vintages to popes and kings often led to miraculous advancements for the clergy.

Equal miracles can be produced today by the marriage of the right wine with the right food. For the balance is important. In the districts where wine is grown and where cooking reaches its peak, a rustic cuisine accompanies the coarser wines; subtle cooking, the light wines; and rich full fare, the full-bodied vintages.

During the past two decades there has been a revolution at our tables: the British are becoming a nation of wine drinkers. Not just for special occasions and holidays, but for everyday living. It is no longer the hallmark of the connoisseur to have a bottle of wine on the table. And British cooks are catching up with their French counterparts, who have known this little kitchen secret all along: to make an everyday dish an event, just add a little wine.

The bouquet and flavour of a good table wine will vastly improve the quality of your cooking. Learn to cook with the same quality wines that you like to drink. There is no such thing as a good cooking wine; any wine that is fit to cook with is fit to drink. And a note to teetotallers . . . the cooking evaporates the alcohol in the wine and only the wonderful flavour remains.

Use wine to tenderize as well as flavour the type of dish that has made France famous – superb slow-cooking casseroles of meat, poultry and game, seized in a little butter or olive oil, enhanced with the flavour of aromatic herbs, and then simmered gently for hours in a sauce enriched with good stock and fine wine.

Let wine add flavour to soups, sauces, stews and salads. Lace a thick soup with dry sherry or Madeira; add a little dry white wine to a salad dressing for fish or potatoes; combine white wine with powdered saffron and a well-flavoured French dressing for a Spanish-style salad of fish and shellfish cooked in a *court-bouillon* of white wine and water, spiked with vinegar and flavoured with onion, carrots, lemon peel and bay leaf.

Sauces with a red wine base can add distinctive savour to delicious hurry-up dishes too; try *œufs en meurette*, poached eggs served on *croûtons* of fried bread and covered with a red wine sauce, or roast beef *à la bordelaise*, thin slices of rare roast beef simmered in butter and then bathed in a red wine sauce. Hard-boiled eggs, sliced and combined with thin strips of sautéed onions, and served with this sauce in individual casseroles, is an easy-to-prepare luncheon dish with a difference, and beefsteak *à la bordelaise*, rare beefsteak served with a red wine sauce, is a wonderful variation on the grilled meat theme. Even hamburgers and meat loaf are greatly improved by the addition of this simple sauce.

A Short Guide to Culinary Terms

À LA: In the manner of.

    À L'ALLEMANDE: German style. Often means garnished with sauerkraut, sausages or noodles.

    À L'ALSACIENNE: Alsatian style. Usually garnished with sauerkraut and sausages; sometimes with *foie gras*.

    À L'AMÉRICAINE: Usually dressed with a sauce containing tomatoes, dry white wine and brandy. Sometimes means dish cooked American style.

    À L'ANDALOUSE: Usually dresses fish, poultry and meat dishes with aubergines (eggplants), peppers and tomatoes.

    À L'AURORE: Usually garnished with a rose-coloured sauce.

    À LA BARIGOULE: Usually contains artichokes, mushrooms and a brown sauce.

    À LA BORDELAISE: Bordeaux style. With a rich wine sauce.

    À LA BOURGUIGNONNE: Burgundy style. With button mushrooms, button onions, and a rich wine sauce.

    À LA CRÈME: Served with cream or cooked in a cream sauce.

    À L'ESPAGNOLE: Spanish style. With tomatoes and peppers.

    À LA FINANCIÈRE: With truffles and Madeira sauce.

    À LA FLAMANDE: Flemish style. Usually with chicory.

    À L'INDIENNE: Indian style. With curry.

    À L'ITALIENNE: Italian style. With pasta, or with a rich brown sauce garnished with tomatoes, mushrooms and garlic.

    À LA JARDINIÈRE: Gardener's style. With mixed cooked vegetables.

    À LA MEUNIÈRE: Usually sautéed in butter, or a combination of butter and oil.

À LA NORMANDE: Norman style. With a fish-flavoured *Sauce Velouté* garnished with mussels, shrimps, etc. Or with apples.

À LA PAYSANNE: Country style.

À LA POLONAISE: Polish style. With buttered breadcrumbs, finely chopped parsley and hard-boiled eggs.

À LA PORTUGAISE: Portuguese style. With tomatoes, onions or garlic.

À LA PROVENÇALE: Provençal style. With tomatoes, garlic and olive oil.

À LA BROCHE: Roasted slowly on a revolving spit.

ABAISSE: French pastry-making term to describe a sheet (or layer) of pastry rolled out to a certain thickness.

ABATIS: Heart, liver, gizzard, neck and wing tips of fowl.

ACIDIFY: To add lemon juice or vinegar to a sauce or cooked dish.

ACIDULATED WATER: (1) Water mixed with an acidifying agent – lemon juice or vinegar – used to blanch sweetbreads, veal or chicken. (2) Lemon juice and water in equal quantities, added to sliced apples, pears or bananas to prevent them from turning brown.

AIGUILLETTE: Thin, vertically cut strips of prime cuts of meat. Usually cut from breasts of poultry and game.

ASPIC: The culinary term for calf's foot jelly, or jelly made with bones of meat, fish or poultry. Any meat, fish, poultry, game or vegetable may be served 'in aspic'.

BAIN-MARIE: A French kitchen utensil designed to keep liquids at simmering point without coming to a boil. It consists of a saucepan standing in a larger pan filled with boiling water. A *bain-marie* is a great help in keeping sauces, stews and soups hot without overcooking. In domestic kitchens, a double saucepan can do double duty as a *bain-marie*.

BAKE: To cook in dry heat in the oven. This term is usually used only for breads, cakes, cookies, biscuits, pies, tarts and pastries. When meats are cooked in the oven, the term used is 'to roast'.

TO BAKE 'BLIND': To bake a pastry shell without a filling. In order to keep the sides of pastry shells from collapsing and the bottom from puffing up during baking, place a piece of foil or waxed paper in the bottom of the pastry case, and weight this with dried beans or rice, or a combination of the two. When pastry shells have been baked according to recipe directions, the foil or paper is removed, and the beans and rice are returned to a storage jar, to be used again and again.

BARBECUE: To cook meat, poultry, game or fish in the open on a grill or spit over charcoal. Originally this term meant cooking a whole animal over an open fire or in a pit. Barbecued foods are usually basted with a highly seasoned sauce while cooking.

BARD: To cover meat, poultry, game and sometimes fish with thin strips of pork fat or unsmoked bacon before roasting or braising.

BASTE: To pour or spoon liquid over food as it cooks in order to moisten and flavour it.

BATTER: Something that is beaten. Usually means the mixture from which pancakes, puddings and cakes are made. The batter used for pancakes and for coating purposes is made of eggs, flour and milk (or sometimes water), and is fairly liquid in consistency.

BEAT: To mix with a spoon, spatula, whisk, rotary beater or electric blender; to make a mixture smooth and light by enclosing air.

BEURRE MANIÉ: Equal quantities of butter and flour kneaded together and added bit by bit to a stew, casserole or sauce to thicken it. See page 28.

BIND: To thicken soups or sauces with eggs, cream, etc.

BISQUE: A rich cream soup made of puréed fish or shellfish.

BLANCH: To preheat in boiling water or steam. This can be done for several reasons: (1) to loosen outer skins of fruits, nuts or vegetables; (2) to whiten sweetbreads, veal or chicken; (3) to remove excess salt or bitter flavour from bacon, gammon, ham, Brussels sprouts, turnips, endive, etc.; (4) to prepare fruits and vegetables for canning, freezing or preserving.

BLEND: To mix two or more ingredients thoroughly.

BOIL: To cook in any liquid – usually water, wine or stock, or a combination of the three – brought to boiling point and kept there.

BOILING POINT: The temperature at which bubbles rise continually and break over the entire surface of a liquid.

BONE: To remove the bones from fish, chicken, poultry or game.

BOUILLON: A clear soup, broth or stock made with beef, veal or poultry, and vegetables. Strained before using.

BOUQUET GARNI: Bunch or 'faggot' of culinary herbs. Used to flavour stews, casseroles, sauces. A *bouquet garni* can be small, medium or large, according to the flavour required for the dish and, of course, according to what the cook has at hand. See page 33.

BREAD: To roll in, or coat with, breadcrumbs before cooking.

BROCHETTE: See 'skewer'.

BROIL: See 'grill'.

BRUNOISE: Finely diced vegetables – carrots, celery, onions, leeks and sometimes turnips – simmered in butter and stock until soft. Used to flavour soups, stuffings, sauces and certain dishes of fish and shellfish.

CARAMELIZE: To melt sugar in a thick–bottomed saucepan, stirring continuously until it is a golden–brown syrup.

CHAUDFROID: A jellied white sauce made of butter, flour, chicken stock, egg yolks, cream and gelatine. Used to give a handsome shiny white glaze to chicken, ham, etc.
  BROWN CHAUDFROID is used to glaze meat and game.

CHILL: To place in refrigerator or other cold place until cold.

CHOP: To cut into very small pieces with a sharp knife or a chopper.

CHOWDER: A fish, clam or oyster stew.

CLARIFY: (1) To clear a stock or broth by adding slightly beaten egg whites and crushed egg shells, and bringing liquid to a boil. The stock is then cooled and strained before using. (2) To clarify butter: melt butter and pour off clear liquid, leaving sediment behind.

COAT: To dust or roll in flour until surface is covered before the food is cooked.

COCOTTE: (1) A round or oval casserole with a cover. Usually made of iron or enamelled iron. (2) Individual heatproof dishes used for baking eggs. Usually of earthenware or heatproof china.

COOL: To allow to stand at room temperature until no longer warm to the touch. *Not* to put in the refrigerator.

COURT-BOUILLON: The liquid in which fish, poultry or meat is cooked to give added flavour. A simple *court-bouillon* consists of water to which you have added 1 bay leaf, 2 stalks celery, 1 Spanish onion, 2 carrots, and salt and freshly ground black pepper, to taste. Other additives: wine, vinegar, stock, olive oil, garlic, shallots, cloves, etc.

CREAM: To work one or more foods with a heavy spoon or a firm spatula until the mixture is soft and creamy. To cream butter and sugar: beat softened butter with electric mixer or rub against sides of bowl with a wooden spoon until smooth and fluffy. Gradually beat or rub in sugar until thoroughly blended.

CROÛTE: The pastry case for *pâtés*, e.g. *pâté en croûte*. Usually a *brioche* or rich *brioche* dough.

CROÛTON: Bread trimmed of crusts, cut to shape (triangles, hearts, dice), rubbed with garlic (optional) and sautéed in oil or butter.

CUT IN: To combine fat and dry ingredients with two knives, scissor-fashion, or with a pastry blender. When making pastry.

DEEP-FRY: To cook in deep hot fat until crisp and golden. Also known as 'French-fry'.

DEVIL: (1) To grill food with a mixture of butter, mustard, chutney or Worcestershire sauce, and fresh breadcrumbs. (2) To cook or serve with a hot 'devil' sauce.

DICE: To cut into small even cubes.

DISJOINT: To cut poultry, game or small animals into serving pieces by dividing at the joint.

DISSOLVE: To mix a dry ingredient with liquid until it is absorbed.

DREDGE: To coat with a fine-particled substance by dusting, sprinkling or rolling the food in flour, cornflour, cornmeal, sugar, etc.

DUST: To sift over or sprinkle lightly with a fine-particled substance such as flour, sugar or seasonings.

DUXELLES: Finely chopped mushrooms and onion (or shallots), sautéed in butter until soft. Mixture should be quite dry. Used to flavour poached fish and shellfish, to dress a fillet of beef or leg of baby lamb before it is wrapped in pastry, or to garnish a *papillote*.

FILLET: (1) Special cut of beef, lamb, pork or veal; breast of poultry and game; fish cut off the bone lengthwise. (2) To cut any of the above for use in cooking.

FISH FUMET: A highly concentrated fish stock, made by reducing well-flavoured fish stock. Used to poach fish, fish fillets or fish steaks. Corresponds to essence for meats.

FLAKE: To break into small pieces with a fork.

FLAME: To pour or spoon alcohol over a dish and ignite it.

FOLD IN: When a mixture has been beaten until light and fluffy, other ingredients must be 'folded in' very gently with a spatula, so that the air will not be lost. Blend in new ingredients little by little, turning mixture very gently. Continue only until the ingredients are evenly blended.

FRICASSÉE: To cook chicken or veal in fat until golden, and then in a sauce. Fricassée is, in fact, a form of braising.

FRY: To cook in a little fat or oil in a frying pan.

GARNITURE: The garnish or trimming added to a cooked dish (or served at the same time on a separate dish): vegetables, rice, pasta, pastry shapes, *croûtons*, etc.

GLAZE: A thin coating of syrup or aspic – sometimes coloured with caramel – which is brushed over sweets, puddings or fruits (syrup), or cooked ham, tongue, chicken, beef, pork, veal, etc. (aspic). Food must be cold and quite dry before aspic will set.

GRATE: To reduce to small particles with a grater.

GRATIN: To cook '*au gratin*' is to brown food in the oven – usually covered in a sauce and dotted with breadcrumbs, cheese and butter – until a crisp, golden coating forms. A '*gratin* dish' is the heatproof dish used for cooking *au gratin*. Usually oval-shaped, in earthenware or enamelled iron.

GREASE: To rub lightly with butter, margarine, oil or fat.

GRILL: To cook by direct heat such as an open fire. In our day, by charcoal, gas or electricity.

JULIENNE: Cut into fine strips the length of a matchstick.

KNEAD: To work dough with hands until it is of the desired elasticity or consistency.

LARD: (1) Common cooking fat obtained by melting down of pork fat. (2) Culinary process by which *lardons* of pork fat or unsmoked bacon are threaded through meat, poultry, game (and sometimes fish), to lend flavour and moisture to food.

LARDONS: (1) Strips of fat or unsmoked bacon used as above. (2) Diced pork fat or unsmoked bacon, blanched and sautéed, used to add flavour and texture contrast to certain stews, *daubes*, *ragoûts* and casseroles.

LIAISON: To thicken a sauce, gravy or stew: (1) by the addition of flour, cornflour, arrowroot, rice flour, potato flour, or a *beurre manié* (flour and butter); (2) by stirring in egg yolk, double cream or, in the case of certain dishes of poultry or game, blood.

MACÉDOINE: (1) A mixture of raw or cooked fruit for a fruit salad. (2) A mixture of cooked diced vegetables, garnished with a cream sauce, mayonnaise or aspic, usually served as an *hors-d'œuvre* salad, or as a garnish.

MARINADE: A highly flavoured liquid – usually red or white wine or olive oil, or a combination of the two – seasoned with carrots, onion, bay leaf, herbs and spices. Marinades may be cooked or uncooked. The purpose of a marinade is to impart flavour to the food and to soften fibres of tougher foods.

MARINATE: To let food stand or steep in a marinade. See above.

MASK: To cover cooked food with sauce.

MINCE: To reduce to very small particles with a mincer, chopper or knife.

MIREPOIX: Finely diced carrots, onion, celery, and sometimes ham, simmered in butter until soft. Used to add flavour to dishes of meat, poultry, fish and shellfish.

OVEN-FRY: To cook meat, fish or poultry in fat in the oven, uncovered, basting food with fat from time to time.

POMMADE: A thick, smooth paste.

PARBOIL: To precook, or boil until partially cooked.

PARE or PEEL: (1) To cut off outside skin or covering of a fruit or vegetable with a knife or parer. (2) To peel fruits such as oranges or bananas without using a knife.

PAPILLOTE: To cook '*en papillote*' is the culinary term for cooking food enclosed in an oiled paper or foil case (*papillote*).

POACH: To cook gently in simmering (not boiling) liquid (water or syrup) so that the surface of the liquid barely trembles.

PIT: To remove pit, stone or seed, as from cherries.

POUND: To reduce to very small particles or a paste with a mortar and pestle.

PURÉE: To press through a fine sieve or food mill to produce a smooth, soft food.

QUENELLE: The finely pounded flesh of fish, shellfish, veal, poultry or game, mixed with egg whites and cream, and pounded over ice to a velvety smooth paste. These feather-light dumplings are then poached in a light stock or salted water.

RAGOÛT: A stew made from regular-sized pieces of meat, poultry or fish, sautéed in fat until brown, and then simmered with stock, meat juices or water, or a combination of these, until tender. *Navarin de mouton* is an example of a 'brown' *ragoût*; Irish stew is a typical 'white' *ragoût*, in which meat is not browned before stewing.

RAMEKIN: A small, earthenware dish for cooking individual portions: eggs, vegetable and seafood *gratins*, etc.

REDUCE: To cook a sauce over a high heat, uncovered, until it is reduced by evaporation to the desired consistency. This culinary process improves both flavour and appearance.

RENDER: To free tissue of fat by melting at a low temperature.

ROAST: To cook meat by direct heat on a spit or in the oven; although 'baking' would be a better term in the latter case, for when meat is cooked in a closed area (oven), vapour accumulates and changes texture and flavour of true roast.

ROUX: The gentle amalgamation of butter and flour over a low heat: capable of absorbing at least six times its own weight when cooked. (1) To make a white *roux*: melt 2 tablespoons (30 ml) butter in the top of a double saucepan; add 2 tablespoons (30 ml) sieved flour, and stir with a wire whisk for 2 to 3 minutes over water until the mixture amalgamates but does not change colour. (2) A pale *roux*: cook as above, stirring continuously, just a little longer (4 to 5 minutes), or until the colour of *roux* begins to change to pale gold. (3) A brown *roux*: cook as above until mixture acquires a fine, light brown colour and nutty aroma.

SALMIS: To cook jointed poultry or game in a rich wine sauce after it has been roasted until almost ready. Often done in a chafing dish at the table.

SALPICON: Finely diced meat, poultry, game, fish, shellfish or vegetables, bound with a savoury sauce, and used to fill *canapés* and individual *hors-d'œuvre* pastry cases. Also used to make rissoles, croquettes, and stuffings for eggs, vegetables and small cuts of poultry or meat.

SAUTÉ: To fry lightly in a small amount of hot fat or oil, shaking the pan or turning food frequently during cooking.

SCALD: To heat to just below boiling point. I use a double saucepan to scald cream or milk. This prevents scorching.

SCORE: To make evenly spaced, shallow slits or cuts with a knife.

SEAR: To brown and seal the surface of meat quickly over high heat. This prevents juices from escaping.

SIFT: To put through a sifter or a fine sieve.

SIMMER: To cook in liquid just below boiling point, with small bubbles rising gently to the surface.

SKEWER: (1) To keep in shape with skewers. (2) The actual 'skewer' – made of metal or wood – which is used to keep meats, poultry, game, etc., in shape while cooking. (3) The 'skewer' – piece of metal or wood – sometimes called '*brochette*', used to hold pieces of chicken, fish, poultry, etc., to be grilled over charcoal, or under gas or electricity.

SLIVER: To cut or shred into long, thin pieces.

STEAM: To cook food in vapour over boiling water. This process is often used in Oriental cooking.

STEEP: To let food stand in hot liquid to extract flavour or colour.

STIR: To mix with a spoon or fork with a circular motion until ingredients are well blended.

WHISK: To beat rapidly with a whisk, rotary beater or electric mixer, in order to incorporate air and increase volume.

ZEST: The finely grated rind of lemon or orange.

CHAPTER ONE

Time to Take Stock

I spent some of the happiest holidays of my childhood in my grandmother's Colonial house in the green hills of the Hudson River Valley, and on grey winter days my mind often goes back to the snug country kitchen where, with her usual Yankee thrift, she used to make her famous soups even more delicious with the special stocks she kept in huge glass candy jars with tight-fitting lids. She had two, I remember, one for beef stock and the other for a mixture of chicken and veal. She used to make the stocks from trimmings and scraps of meat for which she had no other use, and from the extra bones she always made a point of asking the butcher to give her with each order. These she would slowly simmer in a large stockpot on the back of her wood-burning range with a few carrots and onions, a leek or two and some pot herbs, until all the flavours were extracted. The beef stock was used for soups such as oxtail, *pot-au-feu*, or black bean, and for her more highly flavoured sauces. The chicken and veal stock she always used as part of the liquid in cream soups (no wine used in cooking for that household) and to enrich white sauces for eggs, chicken or vegetable dishes.

She was not a great cook, by any means, but she certainly could turn simple, homely soup into something more nearly approaching majesty than anyone that I have since met.

Indeed it is from her that my love stems for the great country soups – long-simmered concoctions of black beans, lentils or dried peas, made flavoursome with a ham hock, aromatics and stock; oyster stew, rich with cream and butter; fish chowders and chicken-in-the-pot – meals in themselves.

Every New Year's Eve – it was one of her traditions when all the family were together – she used to serve a special 'good luck' soup made of lentils and a knuckle of ham, simmered for hours in a rich beef stock. This we would have without fail on the stroke of midnight, served with crusty slices of home-baked bread and fresh country butter, the whole washed down with a glass of red wine – children included; all part and parcel of her private good luck ceremony. And woe betide any of her loved ones – one of my uncles or older brothers – if they had plans of their own for that evening.

I never go back there now, and all the happy times I spent there are just memories . . . but I keep on thinking about the house, hoping that one day – next year, next week, tomorrow perhaps – I will return to taste again the peace of that verdant valley, to visit the barn, the few acres of farm land, and the family cemetery on the hill, and go up the country road (probably a state highway now) to the lake where I caught my first bass. Any soups made there now will, of course, have to be made by me, for my grandmother has been dead for over fifty years. But the old country farmhouse with its gabled roof and 'revolutionary' windows will be the same, I know, and its kitchen will be just as I remember it.

The Stockpot

In a country kitchen like my grandmother's, where serious cooking was done every day, there were enough scraps and bones left over from daily meals – along with those obtained from the butcher – to furnish delicious stock for family soups and sauces without my grandmother having to buy fresh meat or use expensive meat extracts for the purpose.

Her stockpot was made of tinned copper, fitted with a tap to allow liquids to be drawn off when required without disturbing the fat at the top. For smaller kitchens a large enamelled saucepan or earthenware casserole can be used for making stocks, but be sure your saucepan is large enough to contain comfortably the bones, meat, water and vegetables necessary for making the stock, and still allow liquids to come not more than 4 inches (10 cms) from the top, so that you can skim it easily.

All scraps of meat, cooked or uncooked bones, pieces of vegetable, poultry giblets and bacon rinds can be kept for making stock. Meat juices can serve as well; but no thickened sauce – or rice, potatoes or bread – should be added, for they will cloud the stock.

Make sure that all scraps are clean and wholesome before adding them to the stockpot. Do not add scraps of game that are high. The greater variety of meat and vegetables used, the better will be the flavour of your stock.

To Make Stock

Break up the bones; remove any fat from the meat, and cut both meat and vegetables into small pieces. Put meat and bones in the stockpot and cover well with cold water. There should be double the weight of water that there is of meat. Instead of plain water, the liquid in which meat or vegetables have been boiled may be used, but avoid using the water in which cabbages or potatoes have been cooked, or that to which soda has been added, or any liquid that is too salty. A few washed and crushed egg shells put into the stock will help to clear it.

Cover the saucepan and bring the contents slowly to a boil. Lower the heat and keep the stock slowly simmering for 4 to 5 hours, or at most a whole day, taking off the lid from time to time to remove the scum. Strain stock through a fine sieve, or through a cloth stretched over a colander, into a large bowl; set aside to cool. Stock must never be allowed to remain in the saucepan overnight, nor should it be allowed to stand for hours at the side of the fire without cooking.

Always wash the stockpot thoroughly before it is used again.

On the following day, the bones and any useful pieces of meat should be put back into the stockpot along with any fresh scraps there may be. Do not return the vegetables to the pan if they have boiled for long as they are valueless. It is a mistake to put too many vegetables into a stock of this kind as they tend to make the stock ferment. Vegetables should never be left in the stock when it is not actually cooking. Neither should bits of meat, bones or vegetables be added to the pot at odd times. What is not ready when the stock is started should be kept for the next day's use.

TO KEEP STOCK

If stock has to be kept for some time, or if the weather is very hot, it is really better to make it without vegetables, as it will not turn sour so readily. Diced vegetables can be simmered in the stock to add savour to it for a soup or a sauce.

Stock will keep unrefrigerated if it is brought to a boil every day in warm weather or every second day in winter, and then poured into clean bowls. I keep my stock in covered jars in the refrigerator, where it keeps perfectly if brought to a boil every seventh day. If you have made too much stock, the surplus should be converted into a glaze.

TO REMOVE FAT FROM STOCK

Skim fat off the surface of the stock with a perforated spoon. When as much as possible has been taken off, dip the end of a clean cloth into boiling water and wipe the stock with it until stock is free from grease. If the stock has not jellied, use a paper towel instead of a cloth to remove the fat.

It is best not to remove fat from stock or soup until it is about to be used as it keeps out the air and helps to preserve it.

TO MAKE A MEAT GLAZE

Home-made glaze is very easily made in kitchens where there are large quantities of stock and bones at disposal. Any good brown stock can be used, and the second boiling from meat and bones is almost preferable to freshly made stock, as it is more gelatinous. Free the stock from fat and put at least 2 pints (1.1 lit) into a saucepan. Allow this to boil quickly, uncovered, skimming when necessary, until it is reduced to about ½ pint (300 ml). Strain through a very fine sieve or a piece of muslin placed over a colander. Then put stock into a smaller saucepan and reduce again until the glaze becomes syrupy, when it will be ready for use.

If not required at once, the glaze should be poured into a jar, and if a little melted butter or lard is poured over the surface, it will keep for weeks in the refrigerator. Use glaze to enrich soups and sauces as well as to coat meat, etc.

Basic Stocks

Stock – the liquid into which the juice and flavour of various nutritive substances have been drawn by means of long, slow cooking – serves as a foundation for most soups, stews, gravies and sauces.

Stock can be made from various ingredients and although meat and bones, cooked or uncooked and flavoured with vegetables, are the usual ones, poultry, game or fish with vegetables, and even vegetables alone, may all be utilized for the purpose.

Stock – especially meat stock – should always be made the day before it is to be used, as best results can be obtained only by long, slow cooking; it is only if the stock is cold that fat can be easily skimmed off the surface.

FLAVOURING THE STOCK
Do not let the flavour of vegetables overpower the flavour of the meats used in a meat, poultry or game stock; one flavour must not predominate over another. Onions, shallots, carrots, turnips and celery are the vegetables generally used, but leeks, tomatoes, parsnips and mushrooms may also be used for the darker stocks.

Vegetables are usually diced or left whole for stocks. They must not be allowed to cook too long in the stock, for after a certain time they tend to absorb flavours instead of adding to them. If a large quantity of meat is used and the stock is likely to cook for many hours, the vegetables should not be put in at the beginning of cooking time, or they should be lifted out before the stock has finished cooking. Stock vegetables may be served as a separate vegetable dish on their own, or made into vegetable purée with a little butter and cream added.

Different Kinds of Stock

Brown stock: Beef, beef bones and vegetables, with sometimes a little veal or some chicken or game bones added.

White stock: White meat such as veal, rabbit, chicken or mutton, and vegetables, with sometimes a calf's foot added for extra flavour.

Fish stock: Fish or fish trimmings with vegetables, and sometimes shellfish trimmings for added flavour.

Game stock: Game, or game bones and trimmings, and vegetables.

Vegetable stock: Made from vegetables alone, either dried or fresh or a mixture of the two. For vegetarian soups and dishes.

Glaze: A stock which is so much reduced in quantity that it forms an almost solid substance when cold. It is a means of preserving any surplus stock.

Different Kinds of Soups

Broth differs from a clear soup in that it is unclarified. The meat or poultry or game with which it is made is served either in the soup or after it, as a separate course. A broth is usually garnished with rice or barley and diced vegetables. Sometimes the vegetables are cut into larger pieces and served as an accompaniment to the meat.

Thickened soups can be made of fish, meat or vegetables. They generally have some stock as their basis – brown, white, fish or vegetable – according to the kind of soup it is, and sometimes a mixture of two or more of these. The soups are thickened with flour, arrowroot, cornflour, tapioca or sago. In some of the richer soups, a *liaison* (thickening agent) or combination of eggs and cream is used. Portions of the ingredients from which these soups are made are often served in them.

Purée is perhaps the simplest and most economical kind of soup. It differs from other thickened soups in that its thickness is caused by puréeing the meat, fish, vegetables or other ingredients of which it is composed.

Purées can be made of almost any vegetable, both fresh and dried, and of meat, game and fish. They sometimes have farinaceous substances such as rice, barley or macaroni added.

Farinaceous vegetables such as potatoes, peas, beans and lentils require no additional thickening to make a smooth, even purée. But the more watery vegetables – celery, carrots, turnips and vegetable marrow – require a *liaison* or thickening agent to make them cohere.

All purées can be made richer by adding double cream and 1 or 2 egg yolks just before serving. A small amount of diced butter is often added at the very last.

But remember, a purée should not be *too* thick. About the consistency of cream is just right. It is usually served with fried *croûtons*.

TO ADD EGGS AND CREAM TO SOUP

When a whole egg is added to soup to enrich it, it should be beaten with a fork and poured into the soup tureen; then pour the hot soup gradually over it, stirring all the time.

If only the yolk is used, beat it with a tablespoon (15 ml) of milk or water and add it in the same way.

When egg yolks and cream are used as a thickening (*liaison*), they should be beaten together. Always remove the saucepan containing the soup from the heat, and allow it to cool a little before the eggs and cream are stirred into it. Then return saucepan to heat and reheat very carefully, stirring continuously being careful not to let the soup boil again or it will curdle.

Beef Stock

Choose meat with a good proportion of bone and very little fat. Shin of beef is gelatinous and produces a good jelly, but the neck is also good and makes a better flavoured stock. Add veal to the beef for a more delicate flavour.

Uncooked chicken or game bones may be added to make a good stock, but scraps of cooked meat must never be used.

BASIC BEEF STOCK

3 lb (1.4 kg) shin or neck of beef
1 lb (450 g) shin of veal
4 oz (100 g) lean ham or 1 small ham bone
6 pints (3.4 lit) water
1 level tablespoon (15 ml) salt
3 large carrots, chopped and browned in butter
2 turnips, chopped and browned in butter
2 onions, chopped and browned in butter
2 leeks, sliced
2 stalks celery, sliced
1 *bouquet garni* (3 sprigs parsley, 1 sprig thyme,
1 bay leaf)
9 peppercorns
3 cloves

Trim meat of excess fat and remove marrow from the bones with the blade of a sharp knife. Bone meat; cut into large pieces and tie together. Break the bones in small pieces so that all the goodness can be extracted from them. Put the bones in a baking tin; sprinkle with fat and brown them in oven; then put bones, meat and ham or ham bone in a large saucepan with cold water and salt. Let them soak for ½ hour, or until the water is well coloured. Then put the saucepan on the heat and bring the contents slowly to a boil. Simmer gently for 30 minutes, and then remove any scum that may be on the top. When the stock has cooked about an hour and is clear of scum, add the prepared vegetables, *bouquet garni*, peppercorns and cloves.

Simmer stock gently for 4 to 5 hours longer, skimming when necessary. Then strain through a fine sieve, or a clean cloth stretched over a colander, into a large bowl. Cool. If well made, the stock should be clear, dark in colour and transparent, and form a stiff jelly when cold. When used for clear soup or consommé it is generally further cleared with raw beef or the whites and shells of eggs. (See consommé recipe page 64.)

Do not throw away meat after straining stock; it may be used again, with fresh vegetables and water, to make a second stock.

BASIC BEEF STOCK (QUICK METHOD)

1 lb (450 g) veal knuckle
1 lb (450 g) beef knuckle
4 tablespoons (60 ml) beef, veal or pork dripping
2 lb (900 g) lean beef
2 chicken feet (optional)
2 leeks (white parts only)
1 large onion stuck with 2 cloves
2 stalks celery, tops included
2 carrots, coarsely chopped
4 sprigs parsley
1 fat clove garlic
6 pints (3.4 lit) water
Salt and freshly ground black pepper

Have veal and beef knuckles coarsely chopped by your butcher. Brush with meat dripping and brown them in the oven. Place in a large stockpot with lean beef, chicken feet (if you have any), leeks, onion, celery, carrots, parsley and garlic. Cover with cold water and bring slowly to a boil, removing the scum as it accumulates on the surface. Simmer gently for 1 hour; season to taste with salt and pepper, and continue to simmer for another hour, or until the meat is tender. Correct seasoning and strain the stock through a fine sieve. Cool, remove the fat, and reheat or store in the refrigerator for later use.

BEEF CONSOMMÉ

4–5 pints (2.25–2.8 lit) beef stock
1 lb (450 g) minced lean beef
2 leeks, chopped
2 stalks celery, chopped
2 carrots, chopped
½ Spanish onion, chopped
Freshly ground black pepper
Whites and shells of 2 eggs

Strain beef stock and combine in a large saucepan with minced beef, chopped leeks, celery, carrots, onion, pepper to taste, and the whites and shells of 2 eggs. Simmer for 1 hour; strain through a fine cloth and cool. Skim grease from the surface and pour stock carefully into storage jars, taking care not to disturb any sediment which lies at bottom of stock. Stock will keep in the refrigerator for weeks, ready for use, if you bring it to a boil once every 7 days.

POT-AU-FEU

4 lb (1.8 kg) lean beef
2 lb (900 g) shin of beef (meat and bone)
1 lb (450 g) shin of veal (meat and bone)
4 oz (100 g) ox liver
2 chicken livers
1 bay leaf
Few sprigs parsley
Thyme
8–10 pints (4.8–6 lit) water, or
water and stock
Coarse salt
4–5 carrots
4–5 leeks
2 turnips
2 stalks celery
2 fat cloves garlic
2 Spanish onions stuck with 2 cloves
Cabbage and potatoes (optional)

Have your butcher bone the meat – chosen from the silverside, shoulder, top rib or top round, or a combination of two of these, plus some shin of beef and shin of veal, using the bone for its gelatinous content as well as the meat; ask him to cut the meat into large pieces, tie it up securely and break the bones for you.

Put the bones in the bottom of a large stockpot; place the meat on top, add livers, herbs and 8–10 pints (4.8–6 lit) of water, or water and stock, and put the stockpot on the lowest possible heat so that the water comes very slowly to a boil.

When the liquid barely begins to simmer in the pot, add a little salt to help the scum disengage itself, but be careful not to use too much, for the liquid of your *bouillon* will reduce by about a third in the long cooking process.

Skim scum from stock with a perforated spoon, being careful to scrape away any remaining at the sides of the pot. When the water begins to tremble, add half a glass of cold water to stop the boiling and bring a new rise of scum to the surface. Skim and repeat this several times until the scum is just a white froth which will of its own accord be consumed in the cooking.

Then add the carrots, leeks, turnips, celery and garlic, and the two onions each stuck with a clove. Skim carefully once again and put the lid on the stockpot, tilted so that the steam can escape. Keep heat as low as possible so that the stock just trembles gently at one point only. The cooking time for your *pot-au-feu* varies a little with the size of the pieces of meat. But as none should weigh more than 2 lb (900 g), 3 hours from the time you add the vegetables to the *bouillon* will be about right.

Cabbage, not usually a part of the classic *pot-au-feu*, can be cooked separately, in water at first and then in a little of the *bouillon*, and served with the meat and vegetables. Potatoes, too, are sometimes boiled or steamed separately and served with a *pot-au-feu*.

To prepare *bouillon*: bring 3½ pints (2 lit) of the *bouillon* to a fast boil; dip soup ladle into the *bouillon* at the point where the boiling is most active. The fat will be forced to the side of the pot and your resultant *bouillon* will be less greasy. Pour the *bouillon*, ladle by ladle, through a fine muslin laid over sieve into a clean saucepan. Allow it to cool for a few minutes; skim any remaining fat from the surface; pour *bouillon* into a clean saucepan and reheat.

To serve: remove the beef and vegetables carefully from the stockpot; drain. Cut the string from the meat and remove any small bones separated in cooking. Cut the meat to facilitate serving and place it in the centre of a large hot serving platter. Surround with cooked vegetables, grouping them by colour. If you have added cabbage, place it in a sort of *bouquet* at one side of the dish. Potatoes may be served with the other vegetables, or apart.

You can serve the *bœuf bouilli* alone '*au gros sel*', or you can accompany it with one or two kinds of mustard, small bowls of pickled gherkins and cocktail onions, and small carrots, pimentos and green tomatoes in vinegar. I personally like to serve a sauce made of whipped cream and grated horseradish with it, or as in Italy, with a piquant green sauce – *salsa verde*. Serves 8 to 12.

SOUPE À L'OIGNON GRATINÉE

6 medium-sized onions
3 tablespoons (45 ml) butter
3 tablespoons (45 ml) olive oil
Sugar
2½ pints (1.1 lit) beef stock
4–6 tablespoons (60–90 ml) cognac
½ teaspoon (2.5 ml) Dijon mustard
Salt and freshly ground black pepper
4–6 rounds toasted French bread
Grated Gruyère cheese

Peel and slice onions thinly. Heat butter and olive oil in a large saucepan with a little sugar; add the onion rings and cook them very, very gently over a low heat, stirring constantly with a wooden spoon, until the rings are an even golden brown. Add beef stock gradually, stirring constantly until the soup begins to boil. Then lower the heat, cover the pan, and simmer gently for about 1 hour.

Just before serving, stir in cognac and mustard; taste for seasoning, pour into a heatproof soup tureen or into individual heatproof serving bowls, each one containing toasted buttered rounds of French bread heaped with grated Gruyère cheese. Bake in a preheated hot oven (450°F/230°C/GM8) until cheese is bubbling and golden brown. Serves 4 to 6.

COLD BORSCH

1½ lb (675 g) lean beef
1 veal knuckle or duck's carcass
4 pints (2.25 lit) salted water
3 sprigs parsley
2 leeks, sliced
2 carrots, sliced
2 turnips, sliced
2 stalks celery, sliced
1 bay leaf
1 clove garlic
6 peppercorns
2 cloves
1 lb (450 g) cooked beetroot, coarsely grated
½ red cabbage, coarsely grated
2 potatoes, sliced
2 Spanish onions, sliced
4 oz (100 g) mushrooms, sliced
4 tablespoons (60 ml) red wine
½ pint (300 ml) sour cream

Put lean beef into soup kettle with veal knuckle or duck's carcass. Cover with 4 pints (2.25 lit) of salted water. Bring the water slowly to a boil, skim carefully, and add parsley, sliced leeks, carrots, turnips and celery; then add bay leaf, garlic, peppercorns and cloves.

Simmer, covered, for 1½ to 2 hours, skimming from time to time. Remove the meat from the soup, reserving it to serve as boiled beef. Strain soup into a saucepan and add coarsely grated beetroot and red cabbage, and sliced potatoes, onions and mushrooms. Bring to a boil, skim, and simmer, uncovered, for 1 to 1½ hours. Strain through a sieve, chill, and stir in red wine and sour cream before serving. Serves 8.

White Stock

The best white stock is that made from veal and chicken, with a little ham – or a ham bone – added for extra flavour. Rabbit, chicken or calf's foot, or even a piece of calf's head, if available, may be added to this basic stock.

BASIC WHITE STOCK

3 lb (1.4 kg) knuckle of veal or 2 lb (900 g) knuckle
of veal and 1 lb (450 g) neck of mutton
1 small ham bone
6 pints (3.4 lit) water
1 carrot
1 turnip
1 Spanish onion
1 leek
1 stalk celery
1 *bouquet garni*
2–4 cloves
8 white peppercorns
1 level tablespoon (15 ml) salt

Ask your butcher to bone meat; trim meat of excess fat; break the bones and chop the meat. Place the meat and bones in a large saucepan or stockpot together with ham bone and water, and bring slowly to a boil. Simmer, with the water barely bubbling, for at least 1 hour, skimming the scum from the surface frequently. Add vegetables, *bouquet garni*, cloves, peppercorns and salt, and continue to cook, skimming from time to time, for 1½ to 2 hours, or until meat is tender and stock well flavoured. Remove fat from surface; correct seasoning and strain stock through a fine sieve, or a clean cloth stretched over a colander, into a large bowl. Cool and store in the refrigerator.

BASIC CHICKEN STOCK

1 boiling fowl (about 4 lb/1.8 kg)
1 large veal knuckle
2 chicken feet
6 pints (3.4 lit) water
Salt
6 peppercorns
2 leeks
6 carrots
1 Spanish onion stuck with 2 cloves
2 stalks celery
1 *bouquet garni* (parsley, 1 sprig thyme,
1 bay leaf)
1 clove garlic

Place boiling fowl in a large stockpot with veal knuckle and chicken feet (for their extra gelatine content), and cover with water. Add salt and peppercorns, and bring slowly to a boil. Simmer, with the water barely bubbling, for at least 1 hour, skimming the scum from the surface frequently. Then add leeks, carrots, onion stuck with cloves, celery, *bouquet garni* and garlic, and continue to cook for 1½ to 2 hours longer, or until the chicken is tender. Remove fat, correct seasoning and strain through a fine sieve. Cool and and store in the refrigerator.

BASIC CHICKEN STOCK
(QUICK METHOD)

1 chicken (about 4 lb/1.8 kg)
1 lb (450 g) veal knuckle
6 pints (3.4 lit) water
2 leeks (white parts only)
1 Spanish onion stuck with cloves
2 carrots, coarsely chopped
2 stalks celery, tops included
1 fat clove garlic
4 sprigs parsley
Salt and freshly ground black pepper

Place chicken and veal knuckle in a large stockpot with water and bring to a boil, skimming until the scum no longer rises to the surface. Simmer for 1 hour. Add leeks, onion, carrots, celery, garlic and parsley; season to taste with salt and pepper, and continue to simmer for 1 hour. Correct seasoning and strain the stock through a fine sieve. Cool, remove the fat, and reheat or store in the refrigerator.

CHICKEN CONSOMMÉ

4–5 pints (2.25–2.8 lit) chicken stock
Whites and shells of 2 eggs

Strain chicken stock into a large saucepan. Add egg whites and shells and bring to a boil. Simmer for 1 hour; strain through a fine cloth and cool. Skim and keep as directed on page 64.

CHICKEN SOUP WITH MATZOH BALLS

2½ pints (1.4 lit) well-seasoned chicken stock

MATZOH BALLS
2 egg yolks
½ level teaspoon (2.5 ml) salt
2 tablespoons (30 ml) melted chicken fat
2 tablespoons (30 ml) finely chopped parsley
2–3 tablespoons (30–45 ml) matzoh meal
2 egg whites, stiffly beaten

MATZOH BALLS
Beat egg yolks until light. Add salt and melted chicken fat, and beat again. Add finely chopped parsley and matzoh meal, and mix well. Then fold in beaten egg whites thoroughly. Chill dough for 15 minutes and form into very small balls.

Drop balls into boiling stock; cover and simmer for 20 minutes, or until tender. Serves 4 to 6.

CHICKEN IN THE POT

1 boiling fowl (5–6 lb/2.5–3 kg)
1 lb (450 g) lean pickled pork
1 small cabbage, quartered
1 large turnip
1 large onion stuck with 4 cloves
Freshly ground black pepper
Thyme
Water or stock
Bay leaf
Butter

STUFFING
Chicken liver
4 oz (100 g) Parma ham or cooked ham
4 oz (100 g) fresh pork
1–2 cloves garlic
4 oz (100 g) dry breadcrumbs
Milk, to moisten
2–3 tablespoons (30–45 ml) finely chopped parsley
½ level teaspoon (2.5 ml) dried tarragon or chervil
Generous pinch mixed spice
2 eggs
Salt and freshly ground black pepper

VEGETABLE GARNISH
12 small white onions
12 small carrots
12 small potatoes
1 lb (450 g) green beans

Clean, singe and truss boiling fowl. To make the stuffing, put chicken liver, ham, pork and garlic through the finest blade of the mincer. Moisten breadcrumbs with milk; combine with minced meats and add finely chopped parsley, dried tarragon or chervil, mixed spice and eggs, and season to taste with salt and pepper. Mix well, adding more milk if necessary to make a fairly loose mixture.

Wash the pickled pork thoroughly and slice it in half. Clean and quarter cabbage and turnip, and place the vegetables in the bottom of a large stockpot with an onion stuck with cloves.

Place the fowl and pickled pork on the vegetables, and sprinkle with freshly ground black pepper and a little thyme. Add enough hot water or water and stock barely to cover; place a bay leaf on top of the fowl and cover with a piece of buttered paper. Bring the stock slowly to a boil; skim; reduce heat; place a lid tightly on the stockpot and simmer gently for about 2 hours. Garnish with small onions, carrots, potatoes, and green beans tied in bundles, and cook for about 45 minutes longer, or until the fowl is tender and the vegetables are cooked through.

To serve: place the fowl in the centre of a very large hot platter, place a piece of pork on each side, and surround the meat with the vegetables, grouped according to colour. Reserve the broth for soup. Serves 6 to 8.

GREEK LEMON SOUP

2½ pints (1.4 lit) well-seasoned chicken stock
6 tablespoons (90 ml) cooked rice
3 eggs
Juice of 1 large lemon
Salt and freshly ground black pepper

Heat chicken stock to boiling point; remove from the heat and add cooked rice to the stock.

Beat eggs with lemon juice; add some of the hot stock to this mixture little by little, stirring constantly, and when quite smooth pour this back into the soup and cook over the lowest possible heat for a few minutes, stirring briskly to incorporate the egg mixture thoroughly into the stock. Correct seasoning and serve. Serves 4 to 6.

Game Stock

Any kind of game may be used, provided it is not high. Uncooked game is better than cooked game, but both may be used.

BASIC GAME STOCK

---

2 lb (900 g) trimmings or pieces of game
1 lb (450 g) shin or neck of beef
3 oz (75 g) bacon
6 pints (3.4 lit) water
1 level tablespoon (15 ml) salt
2 large carrots, diced
1 large turnip, diced
1 Spanish onion, diced
2 stalks celery, diced
2–3 tomatoes, sliced
2–3 mushrooms, sliced
6–8 peppercorns
4–6 cloves
1 *bouquet garni* (3 sprigs parsley, 1 sprig thyme, 1 bay leaf)

Cut game and beef into small pieces; chop bones. Dice the bacon and melt it slowly in a large thick-bottomed saucepan. Add the prepared game, meats and bones, and sauté gently until lightly browned. Then add water and bring slowly to a boil. Add salt; skim well and simmer slowly for an hour, skimming from time to time. Add the vegetables, peppercorns, cloves and *bouquet garni*, and simmer together for about 3 hours longer. Strain and set aside until cold. If cooked slowly and kept well skimmed, the stock should be clear, but if a perfectly clear soup is wanted, it may be further clarified, as for chicken or beef consommé.

GAME SOUP

1 lb (450 g) trimmings of game or remains
of cooked game
8 oz (225 g) lean beef
2 oz (50 g) lean ham
2 tablespoons (30 ml) butter
1 small carrot, diced
1 small turnip, diced
1 onion, diced
1 stalk celery, diced
3½ pints (2 lit) beef stock
1 *bouquet garni*
Salt and freshly ground black pepper
3–4 juniper berries
½ glass dry sherry
8 oz (225 g) cooked breast of game

Cut game into small pieces. Slice beef thinly across the grain and
cut ham into small pieces. Melt butter in a saucepan and add
game, ham and diced vegetables. Brown meats and vegetables,
and then add stock and sliced raw beef. Add *bouquet garni*, salt,
freshly ground black pepper and juniper berries, and simmer
gently for 1 to 2 hours.

If the liquid reduces too much, add more water. Strain through
a fine sieve and remove grease from the top. Return soup to a
clean saucepan; add sherry and small tender strips of cooked
breast of game, and simmer gently until heated through. Serve
immediately. Serves 8.

Vegetable Stock

Vegetable stock – useful for so many vegetable soups and vegetarian dishes – can be made of almost any kind of vegetable; the
greater the variety, the better. The quantities below are given as a
guide, but any vegetable trimmings and parings may be utilized in
this way if they are clean and fresh. The best proportion is 1 lb
(450 g) of cut-up vegetables to 2 pints (1.1 lit) water.

BASIC VEGETABLE STOCK

4 pints (2.25 lit) water or light vegetable stock
6 large carrots
2 turnips
1 Spanish onion
2 large leeks
4 stalks celery
3–4 trimmings from a cauliflower
2 tablespoons (30 ml) butter or margarine
2 tablespoons (30 ml) olive oil
2 oz (50 g) dried beans, soaked overnight
1 *bouquet garni* (3 sprigs parsley, 1 sprig thyme,
1 bay leaf)
Sugar
Salt and freshly ground black pepper

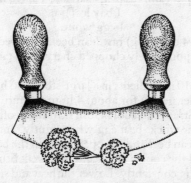

Liquid in which any vegetable has been boiled may be used for
making the stock.

Wash, pare and dice vegetables; drain. Melt butter or margarine
in a saucepan, add olive oil and fresh vegetables, and simmer,
stirring continuously, for 10 to 15 minutes, or until they start to
take on a little colour. Add ½ pint (300 ml) water or light stock,
and continue cooking until all the liquid is absorbed. Add soaked
beans and remaining water or light stock; stir well and bring to a
boil. Then skim; add *bouquet garni*, and sugar, salt and freshly
ground black pepper, to taste. Simmer for at least 2 hours. More
water may be added if the liquid becomes too reduced. Strain
before using.

Aspics

BASIC MEAT ASPIC

8 oz (225 g) beef bones
Duck or chicken carcass, if available
1 calf's foot or 4 cleaned chicken feet
1 Spanish onion, sliced
1 large leek, sliced
2 large carrots, sliced
2 stalks celery, chopped
2 pints (1.1 lit) water
Salt and freshly ground black pepper
1 *bouquet garni* (2 sprigs parsley, 1 sprig thyme,
1 bay leaf)
1 egg white
4 oz (100 g) raw lean beef, chopped
1 teaspoon finely chopped chervil and tarragon

Combine first 10 ingredients in a large stockpot; bring slowly to a boil and simmer gently for about 4 hours, removing scum from time to time. Strain and cool before skimming off the fat.

To clarify the stock: beat egg white lightly, and combine with chopped raw lean beef and chopped herbs in the bottom of a large saucepan. Add the cooled stock and mix well; bring stock slowly to a boil, stirring constantly. Lower the heat and simmer the stock very gently for about 15 minutes. Strain through a flannel cloth while still hot. Allow stock to cool and then stir in one of the following:

Sherry aspic: Stir in 4 tablespoons (60 ml) dry sherry.
Madeira aspic: Stir in 4 tablespoons (60 ml) Madeira.
Port aspic: Stir in 4 tablespoons (60 ml) port wine.
Tarragon aspic: When clarifying aspic, add 6 additional sprigs of tarragon.

This recipe will make 2 pints (1.1 lit) of jelly and will keep for several days in the refrigerator.

BASIC GAME ASPIC

Prepare game aspic in the same way as basic meat aspic, reinforcing its flavour with 4 oz (100 g) lean chopped beef and 4 oz (100 g) lean dark meat from the particular game the aspic is to be served with – partridge, pheasant, grouse, etc. – when you add egg white and fresh herbs to clarify the stock. I always add a tablespoon or two (15–30 ml) of *fine champagne* to game aspic after it has been clarified to improve the flavour further.

BASIC CHICKEN ASPIC

Chicken aspic can be made from well-flavoured chicken stock in the same way as meat or game aspic. Add 4 oz (100 g) raw lean chopped beef and a raw neck of chicken (or crushed chicken bones which have been well dried in the oven) with egg white and herbs. Proceed as above.

Fresh Vegetable Soups

FOUQUET'S CRÈME ELYSÉES

2½ pints (1.4 lit) chicken consommé
1 small packet frozen peas
2 tablespoons (30 ml) chicken stock
4 tablespoons (60 ml) butter
½ cucumber, peeled and seeded
2 egg yolks
¼ pint (150 ml) double cream
Salt and freshly ground black pepper

Defrost peas and simmer them in 2 tablespoons (30 ml) each chicken stock and butter until cooked through. Drain and purée in an electric blender or put through a fine sieve. Cut cucumber into matchstick-sized slivers and simmer in remaining butter until tender.

Beat eggs; add cream and purée of peas. Heat chicken consommé; stir in purée mixture and cook over a gentle heat, stirring continuously, until green-tinted soup is smooth and thick. Do not let soup come to a boil, or it will curdle. Just before serving, stir in *julienne* of cucumber sticks, and season to taste with salt and freshly ground black pepper. Serves 4 to 6.

POTAGE À LA BONNE FEMME

2 pints (1.1 lit) chicken stock
2 tablespoons (30 ml) butter
4–5 spring onions, thinly sliced
1 head lettuce, shredded
½ cucumber, peeled, seeded and sliced into
matchsticks
1 small packet frozen peas
4–5 sprigs tarragon, chervil or sorrel,
finely chopped
2 egg yolks
¼ pint (150 ml) cream
Salt and freshly ground black pepper
Fried croûtons of bread

Melt butter in a saucepan; add vegetables and herbs, and simmer gently for about 5 minutes.

Bring chicken stock to a boil; pour it over the vegetables and allow the soup to simmer gently for about 30 minutes, or until vegetables are quite tender.

Beat egg yolks and cream with a fork until well blended. Remove saucepan from the heat and strain egg and cream mixture into the soup, stirring constantly. Return pan to heat and simmer, stirring constantly, until the yolks thicken, but do not let it come to a boil, or your soup will curdle. Season to taste with salt and freshly ground black pepper. Serve with *croûtons*. Serves 4 to 6.

HOLLANDAISE SOUP

2 pints (1.1 lit) chicken stock
1 small turnip, diced
2 carrots, diced
½ cucumber, peeled, seeded and diced
1 small packet frozen peas
1 tablespoon (15 ml) butter
1 tablespoon (15 ml) flour
2 egg yolks
¼ pint (150 ml) single cream
1 teaspoon (5 ml) finely chopped parsley or tarragon
Sugar
Salt and freshly ground black pepper

Cook vegetables in separate saucepans of boiling salted water until just tender. Drain.

Melt the butter in a saucepan; add the flour and cook, stirring with a wooden spoon, until smooth. Pour in the stock and simmer, stirring constantly, until soup is slightly thickened. Skim if necessary. Remove saucepan from heat; mix egg yolks and cream together, and strain into soup, stirring constantly. Simmer gently over a low heat until the yolks thicken, but do not allow the soup to boil again, or it will curdle.

Just before serving: add the chopped parsley or tarragon and a pinch of sugar, and season to taste with salt and freshly ground black pepper. Put the prepared vegetables into a hot soup tureen; pour the soup over them and serve immediately. Serves 4 to 6.

FRESH LETTUCE SOUP I

2 heads lettuce
8 oz (225 g) spinach leaves
6 spring onions
2 tablespoons (30 ml) butter
2 pints (1.1 lit) well-flavoured chicken stock
Salt and freshly ground black pepper
1 egg yolk
3–4 tablespoons (45–60 ml) double cream
Fried *croûtons* of bread

Step 1: Remove hard stalks and discoloured leaves from lettuce and spinach. Wash the leaves well and drain. Trim roots and most of the green from onions. Slice vegetables thinly.

Step 2: Melt butter in a saucepan and simmer sliced vegetables gently for 15 minutes, stirring from time to time. Add stock; bring to a boil; reduce heat, cover and simmer gently for 35 minutes. Correct seasoning.

Step 3: Whisk egg and cream in a soup tureen; add hot soup, stirring all the time. Serve with *croûtons*. Serves 4 to 6.

FRESH LETTUCE SOUP II

2 heads lettuce
8 oz (225 g) spinach leaves
3–4 spring onions
2 tablespoons (30 ml) butter
1 pint (600 ml) well-flavoured chicken stock
Salt and freshly ground black pepper
½ pint (300 ml) Béchamel Sauce (page 104)
¼ pint (150 ml) cream
2–4 tablespoons (30–60 ml) finely chopped chervil or parsley
Fried *croûtons* of bread

Steps 1 and 2 as above.

Step 3. Add Béchamel Sauce and simmer for 10 minutes. Press through a fine sieve or blend in an electric blender. Return purée to a clean saucepan. Stir over a high heat until boiling; add cream and finely chopped chervil or parsley, and serve with *croûtons*.

CRÈME GERMINY

4 leaves sorrel
2 tablespoons (30 ml) butter
1 pint (600 ml) well–flavoured chicken consommé
8 egg yolks
4 tablespoons (60 ml) double cream
Salt and freshly ground black pepper

Wash and drain sorrel; shred finely. Simmer gently in butter until soft. Add chicken consommé and bring to a boil.

Combine egg yolks, double cream, and salt and freshly ground black pepper, to taste, in a large mixing bowl, and whisk with an egg beater until smooth. Pour hot consommé on to the egg mixture and mix well. Pour mixture into a clean saucepan and simmer gently over a very low heat, stirring constantly, until smooth and thick. Do not let soup come to a boil, or it will curdle. Serves 4.

FRESH MUSHROOM SOUP

4 tablespoons (60 ml) butter
3 tablespoons (45 ml) flour
1 pint (600 ml) chicken stock
½ pint (300 ml) milk
8 oz (225 g) mushrooms, washed and sieved
2 tablespoons (30 ml) chopped parsley
Juice of 1 lemon
¼ pint (150 ml) double cream
Salt and freshly ground black pepper

Melt butter; add flour and cook gently for 3 to 4 minutes. Add chicken stock; blend well and bring to a boil, stirring all the time. Add milk, sieved mushrooms, parsley and lemon juice, and cook for 5 minutes. Stir in cream and season to taste with salt and freshly ground black pepper. Serve hot or cold. Serves 4 to 6.

Chilled Summer Soups

SUMMER PEA SOUP

8–12 oz (225–350 g) shelled peas
1 medium potato, sliced
1 medium onion, sliced
1 lettuce, cut into quarters
1 pint (600 ml) chicken stock
½ pint (300 ml) double cream
Juice of ½ lemon
Salt and freshly ground black pepper

Place peas, potato, onion, lettuce and half the chicken stock in a saucepan, and bring to a boil. Cover and simmer for 15 minutes. Transfer contents of saucepan to the container of an electric blender and blend until vegetables are puréed, or press through a fine sieve.

Return to saucepan; add the remaining stock and simmer for 5 minutes. Add cream and lemon juice, and season to taste with salt and pepper. Chill. Serves 4.

SUMMER TOMATO SOUP

2 lb (900 g) ripe tomatoes
1 tablespoon (15 ml) sugar
2 teaspoons (10 ml) salt
½ teaspoon (2.5 ml) onion juice
Juice and grated rind of ½ lemon
8 tablespoons (120 ml) double cream
2 slices cooked ham, diced
¼ cucumber, peeled and diced
Finely chopped fresh parsley

Purée washed tomatoes in an electric blender; pass through a fine sieve. There should be a little over 1 pint (600 ml) of purée. Chill thoroughly in refrigerator, and just before serving add sugar, salt, onion juice and the juice and grated rind of ½ lemon. Beat well until smooth; stir in cream and add diced ham and cucumber. Garnish with finely chopped fresh parsley, and serve chilled. Serves 4.

VICHYSSOISE

6 large leeks
4 tablespoons (60 ml) butter
4 medium potatoes
1½ pints (900 ml) chicken stock
Salt, freshly ground black pepper and nutmeg
½ pint (300 ml) double cream
Finely chopped chives

Cut the green tops from the leeks and cut the white parts into 1-inch (25 mm) lengths. Sauté the white parts gently in butter until soft. Do not allow to brown.

Peel and slice potatoes and add to leeks with chicken stock, and salt, pepper and finely grated nutmeg, to taste, and simmer until vegetables are cooked.

Force the vegetables and stock through a fine sieve, or blend in an electric blender until smooth. Chill. Just before serving, add cream and serve sprinkled with chives. Serves 4 to 6.

GAZPACHO

6 large ripe tomatoes
½ Spanish onion, thinly sliced
1 green pepper, seeded and thinly sliced
½ cucumber, peeled and thinly sliced
1 clove garlic, finely chopped
Salt, Tabasco and freshly ground black pepper
6 tablespoons (90 ml) olive oil
3 tablespoons (45 ml) wine vinegar
¼–½ pint (150–300 ml) chilled chicken consommé
Finely chopped chives or parsley
Gazpacho accompaniments

Seed tomatoes and dice coarsely; combine in a salad bowl with thinly sliced Spanish onion, green pepper and cucumber. Season to taste with finely chopped garlic, salt, Tabasco and freshly ground black pepper, and marinate in olive oil and wine vinegar in the refrigerator for at least ½ hour.

Just before serving, add chilled chicken consommé and finely chopped chives or parsley. Serve with traditional *gazpacho* accompaniments: diced tomato, green pepper, onion, cucumber and garlic *croûtons*. Serves 4.

CHILLED SPANISH SOUP

2 slices white bread
8 large ripe tomatoes
1 cucumber
1½ pints (900 ml) chicken broth
1 teaspoon (5 ml) salt
Freshly ground black pepper
2 tablespoons (30 ml) olive oil
2 tablespoons (30 ml) lemon juice
1–2 cloves garlic, finely chopped
4 tablespoons (60 ml) finely chopped parsley
Garlic *croûtons*
1 green pepper, seeded and chopped
4–6 spring onions, finely chopped
2 hard-boiled eggs, finely chopped

Trim crusts from bread and soak in cold water. Peel, seed and chop 4 tomatoes; peel, seed and dice cucumber. Combine chopped vegetables (saving a little cucumber for garnish) with soaked bread and well-flavoured chilled chicken broth. Season to taste with salt, freshly ground black pepper, olive oil, lemon juice and finely chopped garlic and parsley. Purée in an electric blender or pass through a fine sieve. Chill.

Serve with small accompanying bowls of garlic *croûtons*, finely chopped green pepper, spring onions, tomatoes, cucumber and hard-boiled eggs. Serves 6 to 8.

CHILLED ASPARAGUS SOUP

1 bunch fresh asparagus
¼ Spanish onion, thinly sliced
4 tablespoons (60 ml) chicken stock
4 tablespoons (60 ml) butter
2 tablespoons (30 ml) flour
¾ pint (450 ml) chicken stock
Salt and freshly ground black pepper
½ pint (300 ml) double cream
1 tablespoon (15 ml) finely chopped parsley
Grated rind of ½ lemon

Cut the tips off asparagus and reserve for garnish. Break off tough white ends. Wash stalks and slice into 1-inch (25 mm) segments. Combine segments in a saucepan with finely chopped onion, chicken stock and butter, and simmer, covered, until tender. Remove cooked asparagus segments; stir in flour until well blended; add chicken stock and cook, stirring continuously, until soup reaches boiling point. Season to taste with salt and freshly ground black pepper.

Return asparagus segments to thickened soup and purée in an electric blender or press through a fine sieve. Allow to cool; then chill. Just before serving: add double cream and garnish with asparagus tips which you have cooked until tender and then chilled. Sprinkle with finely chopped parsley and grated lemon rind. Serves 4 to 6.

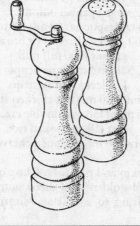

Blender Soups

FRESH SPINACH SOUP

2 lb (900 g) fresh spinach leaves
4 tablespoons (60 ml) butter
Salt and freshly ground black pepper
½ pint (300 ml) double cream
½ pint (300 ml) chicken stock

Wash the spinach leaves, changing water several times; drain them thoroughly. Put spinach in a thick-bottomed saucepan with butter, and simmer gently, stirring continuously, until spinach is soft and tender.

Whisk in electric blender or put through a wire sieve. Season to taste with salt and freshly ground black pepper. Combine with cream and chicken stock, and heat through. Serve immediately. Serves 4.

VERNON JARRATT'S LEEK AND PUMPKIN SOUP

1 lb (450 g) pumpkin
8 oz (225 g) potatoes
1 Spanish onion
4 tablespoons (60 ml) butter
4 oz (100 g) fresh haricot or broad beans
1 pint (600 ml) milk
Salt and cayenne pepper
1–2 leeks, cut in strips
1 pint (600 ml) hot chicken stock
¼ pint (150 ml) double cream
4 oz (100 g) boiled rice
2 tablespoons (30 ml) chopped chervil or parsley

Peel and dice pumpkin and potatoes. Chop onion and simmer in half the butter until golden; add diced pumpkin and potatoes, beans and milk. Bring to a boil and simmer for 45 minutes, stirring from time to time to prevent scorching. Strain through a fine sieve into a clean saucepan or put through blender: season to taste with salt and cayenne pepper.

Cut leeks into fine strips and 'melt' them in the remaining butter. Add to the soup along with hot chicken stock, and bring slowly to a boil. Just before serving, stir in cream, boiled rice and chopped chervil or parsley. Serves 4 to 6.

TRADER VIC'S BONGO BONGO SOUP

9 fresh oysters
4 tablespoons (60 ml) cooked spinach
¼ pint (150 ml) cream
2 tablespoons (30 ml) butter
1½ teaspoons (7.5 ml) monosodium glutamate
Dash of garlic salt
1 teaspoon (5 ml) HP sauce
Salt and freshly ground black pepper
¾ pint (450 ml) milk
1 tablespoon (30 ml) cornflour
Whipped cream (optional)

Blend oysters, spinach, cream, butter and seasoning in blender. Heat milk; add spinach and oyster mixture, and bring gently to simmering point; do not boil. Add cornflour which you have mixed to a smooth paste with warm milk and cook, stirring constantly, until thickened.

Before serving: top with whipped cream and glaze under grill (optional).

CARROT VICHYSSOISE 'FOUR SEASONS'

5 potatoes, sliced
7 large carrots, sliced
2 large leeks, sliced
1 ham bone
2½ pints (1.4 lit) chicken stock
1 teaspoon (5 ml) sugar
1 level tablespoon (15 ml) salt
Freshly ground black pepper
1 pint (600 ml) double cream
Raw carrot, cut in fine strips

Cook sliced vegetables and ham bone in stock until potatoes and carrots are tender. Put vegetables and stock through blender, or purée through a fine sieve. Season to taste with sugar, salt and a pinch of freshly ground black pepper. Stir in cream; heat through, but do not allow to come to a boil. Serve with a garnish of fine strips of raw carrot. Serves 6.

Peasant Soups

MOROCCAN HARIRA

1½ lb (675 g) diced raw lamb
Chicken giblets and trimmings (if available)
1 Spanish onion, finely chopped
4 oz (100 g) chick peas, soaked overnight
¼ level teaspoon (1.25 ml) powdered ginger
⅛–¼ level teaspoon (0.6–1.25 ml) powdered saffron
¼ level teaspoon (1.25 ml) paprika
Salt and freshly ground black pepper
Water
4 tablespoons (60 ml) butter
4 oz (100 g) rice
Salt
1 level tablespoon (15 ml) dried yeast
4 tablespoons (60 ml) finely chopped parsley
4 ripe tomatoes, peeled, seeded and chopped

Put diced lamb, chicken giblets and trimmings, finely chopped onion, soaked chick peas, powdered ginger, saffron and paprika, and salt and freshly ground black pepper, to taste, in a large saucepan. Add water to cover, about 4 pints (2.25 lit); bring to a boil and add 2 tablespoons (30 ml) butter. Turn down heat and simmer soup, covered, for 1½ to 2 hours, adding more water if necessary.

Combine rice, remaining butter and 1 pint (600 ml) salted water, and cook in the usual manner until rice is tender; drain rice, reserving liquid, and add cooked rice to soup.

Dilute yeast in reserved rice liquid; return to saucepan; add finely chopped parsley and tomatoes, and simmer, stirring from time to time, for 15 minutes. Add yeast mixture to soup; correct seasoning and serve. Serves 6 to 8.

OLD-FASHIONED MUTTON BROTH

1½ lb (675 g) neck or knuckle of mutton
2–3 leeks
2 small carrots
1 small turnip
1 stalk celery
3 pints (1.7 lit) cold water
Salt
1 tablespoon (30 ml) rice or barley
1 tablespoon (30 ml) finely chopped parsley
Freshly ground black pepper

Wipe the meat with a damp cloth. Cut it in small pieces away from the bone, removing all superfluous fat. Slice vegetables thinly.

Combine meat, bones and water in a saucepan; add salt, to taste. Cover and bring slowly to a boil. Skim well; add the rice, well washed, and the vegetables. (If barley is used, it should be soaked overnight and blanched before being added to the soup.) Simmer the soup for 2 to 3 hours, or until meat and vegetables are well cooked. Just before serving: remove the bones and any grease from the top of the broth; add finely chopped parsley, freshly ground black pepper, and more salt if necessary. Serves 6 to 8.

THOURINS

1 lb (450 g) Spanish onions, thinly sliced
2 tablespoons (30 ml) olive oil
1 tablespoon (15 ml) flour
1 glass dry white wine
2 pints (1.1 lit) beef consommé, boiling
6–8 slices stale rye bread
6–8 tablespoons (90–120 ml) freshly grated Gruyère

Simmer sliced onions in olive oil until they are a pale golden colour. Sprinkle with flour; stir until well blended; then moisten with a glass of dry white wine. Remove from heat and add boiling consommé. Cut stale rye bread into thin slices; place a layer of bread in a large soup tureen and sprinkle with a layer of grated Gruyère; continue until the bread is used up. Finish with a layer of Gruyère. Bring the *bouillon* to a boil and pour over the bread. Leave for a few minutes before eating. Serves 4.

MULLIGATAWNY SOUP

1½ lb (675 g) lean mutton or 1 rabbit
2 tablespoons (30 ml) butter or dripping
2 onions, diced
1 carrot, diced
1 small turnip, diced
1 cooking apple, diced
1 tablespoon (15 ml) curry powder
1–2 tablespoons (15–30 ml) flour
3 pints (1.7 lit) cold water
1 small *bouquet garni*
Salt and freshly ground black pepper
Squeeze of lemon juice
½ pint (300 ml) hot milk or cream
Boiled rice

Wipe the meat and cut it in small pieces away from the bone. (If using a rabbit, wash it well and let it soak for ½ hour in cold water with a little salt. Lift it out, dry, and cut into small joints.) Melt the butter or dripping in a saucepan; add diced vegetables and apple; sauté until onion is transparent and soft. Sprinkle with curry powder and flour, and mix well. Add meat, water, *bouquet garni*, and salt and freshly ground black pepper, to taste; stir soup and allow to simmer slowly for 1½ to 2 hours, skimming when necessary.

Just before serving: strain through a fine sieve into a clean bowl. Lift out the best pieces of meat to serve in the soup, and rub as much as possible of the remainder through the sieve. Rinse out the saucepan and return the soup to it with the meat. Correct seasoning; add a little lemon juice and hot milk or cream just before serving. Serve the soup in a hot soup tureen and serve boiled rice separately. Serves 6 to 8.

COCK-A-LEEKIE

1 cock or, failing this, 1 boiling fowl
2–3 bunches large leeks
Salt and freshly ground black pepper
Well-flavoured veal or beef stock
6–12 soaked whole prunes (optional)

Clean, singe, but do not truss cock; place it, with neck, feet, liver and gizzard, in the bottom of a well-greased iron or thick-bottomed saucepan.

Wash leeks; cut off roots and green tops to within an inch (25 mm) of the white. Split leeks; cut into inch-long (25 mm) segments and wash thoroughly under running water.

Pack leeks around chicken; season to taste with salt and freshly ground black pepper. Add enough cold veal or beef stock to cover: bring slowly to a boil and simmer gently for about 4 hours, or until chicken fairly drops from the bones and the leeks have disintegrated into the soup.

If you really want to be in the old Scots tradition, add 6 to 12 soaked whole prunes ½ hour before serving, and continue to simmer until tender. Serves 6 to 8.

OXTAIL SOUP

1 oxtail
2 tablespoons (30 ml) flour
2 tablespoons (30 ml) dripping
4 pints (2.25 lit) light stock
Salt
2 carrots, diced
1 turnip, diced
1 Spanish onion, diced
1–2 stalks celery, diced, or ½ teaspoon (2.5 ml) celery seed
3 tablespoons (45 ml) butter
1 *bouquet garni*
6 black peppercorns
1–2 tablespoons (15–30 ml) ketchup
1–2 tablespoons (15–30 ml) lemon juice
2–4 tablespoons (30–60 ml) dry sherry or Marsala

Cut oxtail into small joints, halving the larger joints. Remove all superfluous fat and wash the pieces well. Put them in a large saucepan with cold water to cover; bring to a boil and pour off the water.

Rinse out the saucepan and rinse and dry the pieces of tail. Put half the flour on a plate and coat the pieces of tail with it. Melt dripping in a large saucepan, and when hot, brown tail segments well on all sides. Add the stock and a little salt; bring to a boil and skim well.

Sauté diced vegetables in 2 tablespoons (30 ml) butter until golden, and add them with the *bouquet garni* and peppercorns when soup has ceased to throw up any scum. Simmer slowly for about 4 hours until oxtail is tender without falling to pieces. Then strain through a fine sieve into a bowl and if possible let stand until cold. Remove all fat from the top of the soup and reserve some of the best pieces of tail for serving in it. Then melt remaining butter in a saucepan and let it brown. Add remaining flour and cook, stirring continuously, until brown. Pour in strained soup and stir over the heat until boiling. Add the pieces of oxtail, ketchup, lemon juice, and sherry or Marsala, and simmer for a few minutes longer. Serves 8.

Mediterranean Fish Soups

Along the southern reaches of Provence from Marseilles to Monte Carlo the fish soup reigns supreme. I give you here a recipe for one of the best *soupes de poissons* to be found along the coast, and a recipe for a more delicate *bourride*, as well as a selection of shellfish soups and *bisques*. The first two recipes unless you are lucky enough to be preparing them on the Mediterranean are impossible to repeat exactly in this country, as the many little fishes that give them their unique savour are not available here. I suggest that in following these recipes you use whatever small bony fish you find available in your local markets, to capture some of the sunny warmth and flavour of Provence for your menus.

SOUPE DE POISSONS 'FIFINE'

2½–3 lb (1.1–1.4 kg) fish for soupe de poissons (see method)
2–3 tablespoons (30–45 ml) olive oil per person
2–3 Spanish onions
2–3 cloves garlic
6–8 ripe tomatoes, seeded and coarsely chopped
1 *bouquet garni* (parsley, thyme, rosemary, dried fennel)
1 bay leaf
5 pints (2.5 lit) salted water
½ teaspoon (2.5 ml) powdered saffron
1 small dried hot red pepper
Freshly grated cheese
Stale French bread, rubbed with garlic

Heat olive oil (2 to 3 tablespoons (30–45 ml) per person) in a large thick-bottomed casserole, and sauté sliced onions in the oil until transparent. Add garlic, chopped and seeded tomatoes, *bouquet garni* and bay leaf, and simmer, stirring frequently, until lightly browned. Then add fish (Fifine recommends *girelles*, *rascasses*, *roucaous*, *perches*, small crabs and a slice or two of eel) and continue to cook, stirring constantly, until the fish are soft.

Add salted water, saffron and red pepper, and bring to a boil; skim and cook over a fairly high heat for 20 minutes. Strain well, pressing all fish and vegetable juices through a sieve. Reheat and serve the soup in a large soup bowl, accompanied by bowls of freshly grated cheese and rounds of stale French bread rubbed with garlic. Serves 4 to 6.

LA BOURRIDE RAPHAELOISE À LA ROUILLE DE 'LA VOILE D'OR'

1 leek, sliced
1 Spanish onion, sliced
3 cloves garlic, crushed
Olive oil
4 large tomatoes, peeled, seeded and chopped, or
2 tablespoons (30 ml) tomato concentrate
¼ teaspoon (1.25 ml) powdered saffron
1 *bouquet garni*
Salt and freshly ground black pepper
2 lb (900 g) fish for soup
1 *daurade* or sea bass, filleted
Fried *croûtons* of bread
2–4 tablespoons (30–60 ml) Aïoli Sauce (page 558)
Rouille (see method)

Sauté sliced leek and onion and crushed garlic in olive oil until transparent; then add tomatoes (or tomato concentrate), saffron, *bouquet garni*, salt and freshly ground black pepper, to taste, and the fish for soup (any bony fish, or cod, whitefish, etc. and fish bones and heads). Add water to cover and cook for 30 minutes.

Then pass this very thick *soupe de poissons* through a fine sieve. Pour it into a clean saucepan and cook the fillets of *daurade* or sea bass in it until tender. Remove fillets from soup; drain; arrange on *croûtons* in a large shallow soup bowl. Whisk *Aïoli* into soup over a gentle heat until well blended. Do not boil. Serve with *Rouille*.

ROUILLE
Place 4 cloves garlic in a mortar with 1 or 2 dried hot red peppers, 3 egg yolks, and a pinch of powdered saffron. Add olive oil drop by drop, stirring with a pestle as you would for mayonnaise. Continue until sauce is thick and smooth.

MEDITERRANEAN FISH SOUP

A delicious *soupe de poissons* can be made in Britain using the recipe on the preceding page, with a combination of whiting, haddock and cod, and 1 mackerel, 1 herring and 3 or 4 sprats or pilchards, cut in 2-inch (50 mm) pieces, instead of Mediterranean fish. Serves 4 to 6.

MEDITERRANEAN SHELLFISH SOUP I

1 lb (450 g) onions, finely chopped
6 tablespoons (90 ml) olive oil
1 bay leaf
4–6 tablespoons (60–90 ml) finely chopped parsley
4–6 tablespoons (60–90 ml) finely chopped celery leaves
2 cloves garlic, finely chopped
1 lb (450 g) tomatoes, chopped
1 small can tomato concentrate
Salt and freshly ground black pepper
¼ pint (150 ml) dry white wine
1½ pints (900 ml) fish stock (made from 1 slice cod and
1 lb (450 g) fish trimmings from your fishmonger)
8–12 oz (225–350 g) cooked shellfish
2 tablespoons (30 ml) butter
Generous pinch of saffron
1 clove garlic
Grated rind of ½ lemon
2 tablespoons (30 ml) finely chopped parsley

Sauté finely chopped onions in olive oil until transparent. Add bay leaf and finely chopped parsley, celery leaves and garlic, and simmer until vegetables begin to take on colour. Add chopped tomatoes and tomato concentrate, salt and freshly ground black pepper, to taste, and dry white wine, and simmer for 10 minutes, stirring from time to time. Then add water and cook for 20 minutes longer. Strain. Bring stock to a boil; add cooked shellfish (one or more of the following: cockles, mussels, prawns, scallops, sliced lobster or *langouste*), sautéed in butter with saffron and garlic. Sprinkle with freshly grated lemon rind and finely chopped parsley, and serve immediately. Serves 4 to 6.

MEDITERRANEAN SHELLFISH SOUP II

Prepare as above. Just before serving: add 2 egg yolks beaten with juice of ½ lemon and heat through, stirring constantly. Do not allow soup to boil after eggs are added, or it will curdle.

POTAGE BISQUE DE HOMARDS

2 small lobsters (about 1 lb (450 g) each)
4 tablespoons (60 ml) finely chopped carrot
4 tablespoons (60 ml) finely chopped onion
1 bay leaf, crumbled
Thyme
3–4 sprigs parsley, chopped
Butter
Cognac
½ pint (300 ml) dry white wine
1½ pints (900 ml) light white stock or water
Salt and freshly ground black pepper
4 oz (100 g) washed rice
6–8 tablespoons (90–120 ml) double cream

Prepare a *mirepoix* by sautéeing finely chopped carrot and onion in butter with 1 bay leaf, thyme and parsley, until onion is soft and transparent.

Cut lobsters in two and add to *mirepoix*; brown them for a few minutes, stirring continuously; then add 3 to 4 tablespoons (45–60 ml) warmed cognac, and flame. Moisten with dry white wine and light white stock (chicken, fish, water, or a combination of all these). Season to taste with salt and freshly ground black pepper. Cook for 20 minutes. Remove the lobsters and reserve. Add washed rice, and simmer for a further hour.

When ready to serve: press *bouillon* and rice through a fine sieve; add double cream and 4 tablespoons (60 ml) butter, diced, stirring rapidly until thoroughly incorporated. Correct seasoning and add a few tablespoons cognac.

Dice lobster meat and add to *bisque*. Serves 6.

To make a *bisque d'écrevisses*, proceed in the same way. Twenty-five live *écrevisses* (crayfish) will replace the lobsters in this recipe.

CRÈME DE POISSONS AU CARI

2 lb (1 kg) white fish or fish trimmings
2 tablespoons (30 ml) butter
1 Spanish onion, sliced
1 carrot, sliced
1 turnip, sliced
1 tablespoon (15 ml) curry powder
2 tablespoons (30 ml) flour
3 pints (1.7 lit) well-flavoured fish stock
Salt and freshly ground black pepper
¼ pint (150 ml) double cream
Lemon juice
Boiled rice

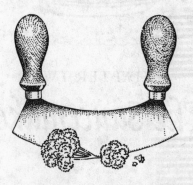

Wash the fish and cut it into small pieces. Melt the butter in a saucepan, add sliced vegetables and sauté them until onion is transparent. Add curry powder and flour, and stir until well blended. Then add fish and fish stock, and stir until boiling. Season with salt and freshly ground black pepper. Lower heat and simmer gently for 10 minutes. Lift out most attractive fish pieces and reserve them to serve in the soup. Simmer soup for 1½ hours longer, skimming when necessary.

Strain soup through a fine sieve, rubbing through a little of the fish and vegetables without allowing any bones to pass through. Reheat soup in a clean saucepan; add cream and cooked fish, and lemon juice, to taste. Serve with plain boiled rice on a separate dish. Serves 6 to 8.

CHAPTER TWO

The Saucemaker

Louis Diat, who was master chef of the famous Ritz–Carlton Hotel in New York, and creator of the world's most delicious chilled soup, *vichyssoise*, claimed that 'French housewives – or their *cuisinières* – can easily and consistently serve magnificent meals from simple ingredients and with few utensils because they get the most out of what they have.' Not the least of the French housewife's skills is her ability to turn out exquisite sauces that make a really distinguished dish from ingredients as simple as eggs, poached or grilled fish, or sliced cooked meat or poultry.

Saucemaking has been the key to French cuisine ever since the days of the great Carême, and today it ranks first among the many skills that any aspiring cook must learn, practise and finally master. It is perhaps just this importance in professional circles that has made the province of saucemaking a veritable no man's land for the home cook. Now I want to explode the theory that a saucemaker is born, not made, for, given a basis of good ingredients – fresh butter, flour, home-made stock, eggs, milk and cream – a little patience and the love of good food, any cook can learn to make a sauce.

Saucemaking ought to be pure pleasure, bringing simple food into the gourmet realm, and not the terrible *travail* fraught with dangers that most people imagine it to be. First of all, let us destroy a legend. There are only two main varieties of savoury sauce known to culinary art: brown sauce and white sauce. And both these basic sauces have two characteristics in common: (1) the *roux*; and (2) the reduction of liquid to improve flavour and texture.

The Roux

Almost every classic sauce recipe starts off with the recipe phrase: 'Make a *roux*', which is nothing more than the combination of equal quantities of butter and flour over a *low* heat so that the starch grains contained in the flour may burst their cells, combine completely with the butter and form a flavoursome mass which will absorb at least six times its own weight when cooked. This is the technical explanation of what happens when you make a *roux*. But all that is necessary for you to do is melt the butter in a saucepan; stir in an equal amount of flour until it is well blended; and then cook over a very low heat until the raw flour taste has gone, before adding the liquid and aromatics that complete the sauce.

Secret number one in easy saucemaking is to cook the *roux* over water in the top of a double boiler or double saucepan. In this way the flour can be cooked long enough to lose its raw flavour without running the danger of cooking too quickly or burning.

There are three kinds of *roux*: white – for making white sauces, cream sauces and Béchamel Sauce; pale – for making *veloutés*, Suprême Sauce and Allemande Sauce; brown – for making brown sauces.

To make white roux: Melt 2 tablespoons (30 ml) butter in the top of a double saucepan, and when it just begins to bubble, add 2 tablespoons (30 ml) sieved flour and stir with a wire whisk for 2 to 3 minutes until the mixture is smooth but has not changed colour.

To make pale roux: As above, but cook the mixture, stirring constantly with the whisk, just a little longer (4 to 5 minutes), until the colour of the *roux* just begins to change.

To make brown roux: Continue cooking until the mixture acquires a fine, light brown colour, and gives off a light nutty aroma as when you bake flour.

The Reduction of Liquid

The heart of every sauce is its flavoursome stock, which is made by reducing home-made meat, poultry or fish broths to a concentrated essence. This liquid ingredient of the sauce – whether it is home-made beef stock, stock made from veal, fish or poultry, or more simply milk or cream – is most important to the final quality and flavour of your finished sauce. It is no secret that French chefs use more liquid in their sauces – almost twice as much – and consequently cook them longer than do most other cooks; and as a result of this concentration and blending of flavours, their sauces are more suave, more transparent, and consequently more delicious.

Secret number two in easy saucemaking, therefore, is the careful reduction of liquid by slow simmering over a low heat, leaving the sauce thicker in consistency, smoother in texture and more concentrated in flavour.

After the liquid is added, sauces must be stirred constantly until boiling point, or they are apt to be lumpy. Incorrectly made sauces often have a raw taste because the flour in them is not properly cooked. It is best to remember that no sauce is ready as soon as it thickens, and even the simplest sauce must be cooked for at least 5 minutes after it thickens to avoid this. More important sauces should be cooked longer to allow flavours to improve by careful reduction.

The thickness of any sauce can be varied according to the purpose for which it is to be used by adding more or less liquid. When it is required for coating a piece of meat or fish, it should be just thick enough to coat the back of the spoon with which it is stirred. When the sauce is to be poured, it should be thin enough to flow smoothly.

If wine is used, it is advisable to boil the sauce for 2 or 3 minutes after it is added, to blend flavours. If cream is added, boil sauce for 1 or 2 minutes. Before adding egg yolks to a sauce, remove the saucepan from the heat; then add egg yolks; return to a very low heat and whisk them thoroughly into the sauce, but do not allow the sauce to come to a boil again or it will curdle. When lemon juice is to be added to any sauce containing milk or cream, add it last and do not allow sauce to boil again.

TO STRAIN SAUCE

Always strain all sauces before serving, except, of course, those which have chopped ingredients in them. A conical strainer is best, as it is easier to direct the flow of the liquid. For a finer sauce, cover strainer with a clean cloth to give a smooth, glossy appearance.

TO CLARIFY BUTTER

Butter always contains a little milk which, when brought to a high heat, is apt to make a sauce 'gritty' or slightly discoloured. I usually clarify butter before using it for the more delicate sauces by melting it in a small, thick-bottomed, enamelled saucepan over a very low heat. The butter foams; the foam falls gently to the bottom of the saucepan, leaving the clarified butter as clear as oil. Be careful when you decant this transparent liquid not to disturb any of the white sediment at the bottom. Use as directed.

TO ADD BUTTER TO A SAUCE

French chefs often incorporate finely diced butter into a sauce just before serving. The butter is usually whisked into the sauce with a wire whisk after the sauce has been taken off the heat. This makes the sauce thicker and more flavoursome. The sauce must not be returned to the heat after this butter has been whisked into it, or it will separate and become fatty.

TO MAKE A BUTTER POMMADE

Dice butter and put into a bowl which you have heated with boiling water and then carefully dried. Then mash butter with a spatula or wooden spoon until it is a smooth paste.

TO KEEP SAUCES WARM

When a sauce has to stand for some time before serving, place the saucepan containing it in a larger one with hot, not boiling, water, or in a *bain-marie*, and cover the saucepan to prevent a skin forming. With thicker sauces, a spoonful of liquid – water, stock or milk – or melted butter may be run over the top. Just before serving, whisk this protective covering into the sauce.

Basic Sauces

The three basic sauces – Béchamel, Velouté and Fish Velouté – and the basic brown sauce – Espagnole – are the foundation sauces for a host of glamorous side sauces, or *sauces composées*, as they are known in French kitchen terminology.

Names such as *soubise*, *poulette*, *mornay*, *bordelaise* and *yonnaise* lose their frightening complexity if we look at them as basic sauces with one or two simple additions.

The basic white sauces – Béchamel, Velouté and Fish Velouté – are made in the following manner:

Béchamel sauce: White *roux* plus milk, or milk and veal, or milk and ham.

Velouté sauce: White *roux* plus veal or chicken stock.

Fish Velouté: White *roux* plus fish stock.

It is from these three sauces that the following classic side sauces are made:

Cream sauce: Béchamel plus cream.

Mornay sauce: Béchamel plus egg yolks, cream, butter and grated cheese.

Aurore sauce: Béchamel plus tomato concentrate and butter.

Nantua sauce: Béchamel plus crayfish or lobster butter.

Soubise sauce: Béchamel plus onions and butter.

Supréme sauce: Velouté plus mushrooms and cream.

Allemande sauce: Supreme plus egg yolks and cream.

Basic Brown Sauce – known as Espagnole Sauce in professional parlance – makes the following side sauces:

Madeira sauce: Brown Sauce plus Madeira.

Bordelaise sauce: Brown Sauce plus shallots, red wine and beef marrow.

Sauce Fines Herbes: Brown Sauce plus shallots, white wine and fresh herbs.

Lyonnaise sauce: Brown Sauce plus onions, white wine and parsley.

To Keep Sauces

Velouté, Brown and Tomato Sauces, like stocks, can be kept in covered jars in the refrigerator for 1 week. Seal jars by pouring a little melted fat over the sauce. If you want to keep your sauces longer, bring to a boil after 7 days and return to the refrigerator in a *clean* covered jar.

Sauces containing milk, cream or eggs should be stored in the refrigerator for only 1 or 2 days.

White Sauces

Louis de Béchamel – Lord Steward of the household of Louis XIV – is often credited with the creation of *sauce béchamel*, the mother sauce of all white sauces. This famous sauce, dating back to the seventeenth century, is exceedingly easy to prepare. A simple Béchamel can be made with just flour, butter, milk and a little minced onion, but I think you will find that the following recipe which includes chopped veal adds greatly to the savour of this delicious sauce. The secret of making a good white sauce – and most other sauces – is to cook it slowly.

BÉCHAMEL SAUCE

Butter
½ onion, minced
2 tablespoons (30 ml) flour
1 pint (600 ml) hot milk
2 tablespoons (30 ml) lean veal or ham, chopped
1 small sprig thyme
½ bay leaf
White peppercorns
Freshly grated nutmeg

In a thick-bottomed saucepan, or in the top of a double saucepan, melt 2 tablespoons (30 ml) butter and cook onion in it over a low heat until transparent. Stir in flour and cook for a few minutes, stirring constantly, until mixture cooks through but does not take on colour.

Add hot milk and cook, stirring constantly, until the mixture is thick and smooth.

In another saucepan, simmer finely chopped lean veal or ham in 1 tablespoon (15 ml) butter over a very low heat. Season with thyme, bay leaf, white peppercorns and grated nutmeg. Cook for 5 minutes, stirring to keep veal from browning. Add veal to the sauce and cook over hot water for 45 minutes to 1 hour, stirring occasionally. When reduced to the proper consistency (two-thirds of the original quantity), strain sauce through a fine sieve into a bowl, pressing meat and onion well to extract all the liquid. Cover surface of sauce with tiny pieces of butter to keep film from forming.

For a richer Béchamel, remove the saucepan from the heat, add 1 or 2 egg yolks, and heat through. Do not let sauce come to a boil after adding eggs or it will curdle.

Béchamel Sauce was not always so simple. According to the archives, it was a much more complicated recipe three hundred years ago. I give it here just to show you how rich and exciting recipes of seventeenth-century France could get in royal circles.

CLASSIC BÉCHAMEL SAUCE

1½ lb (675 g) shin of veal
½ boiling fowl (minus breast)
4 pints (2.25 lit) well-flavoured white stock
1 Spanish onion
2 large carrots
1 *bouquet garni* (3 sprigs parsley, 1 sprig thyme, 1 bay leaf)
Salt and freshly ground white pepper
6 tablespoons (90 ml) clarified butter
6 tablespoons (90 ml) flour
1 pint (600 ml) double cream

Combine first 7 ingredients in a large saucepan or stockpot; bring to a boil; skim; lower heat and simmer for 1½ hours, skimming surface of stock from time to time. Strain stock; pour back into clean saucepan and cook over a high heat, stirring from time to time, until strained stock is reduced to half the original quantity.

Make a *roux* with clarified butter and flour; cook until well blended; pour in strained stock and simmer, stirring from time to time, until sauce is cooked. Stir in double cream; correct seasoning and use as required. Makes 3 pints (1.7 lit) of velvety Béchamel Sauce which will keep in a covered jar in the refrigerator for 7 days. This sauce is excellent – when combined with chicken and veal – for croquettes, *pains*, mousses, etc.

QUICK BÉCHAMEL SAUCE

2 tablespoons (30 ml) butter
½ onion, minced
2 tablespoons (30 ml) flour
1 pint (600 ml) hot milk
1 small sprig thyme
½ bay leaf
White peppercorns
Freshly grated nutmeg

Melt butter for the *roux* in a thick saucepan, or in the top of a double saucepan. Cook onion in it over a low heat until onion is soft but not browned. Remove pan from heat, stir in flour, return to heat and cook gently for 3 to 5 minutes, stirring constantly, until flour is cooked through. Add a quarter of the milk, heated to boiling point, and cook over water, stirring vigorously. As the sauce begins to thicken, add the remainder of the milk, stirring constantly with a wooden spoon. When the entire pint (600 ml) has begun to bubble, add thyme and bay leaf, season to taste with pepper and nutmeg, and let it cook very slowly for at least 10 minutes, so that the ingredients will be well blended. Strain through a fine sieve.

Using any versions of the Béchamel Sauce above, you can make a variety of sauces to accompany meat, fish, eggs and vegetables.

WHITE CHAUDFROID SAUCE

¾ pint (450 ml) Velouté Sauce (page 108)
1 tablespoon (15 ml) gelatine
¼ pint (150 ml) cold water
¼–½ pint (150–300 ml) double cream
2 egg yolks
Salt and white pepper

Soften gelatine in cold water. Bring Velouté Sauce to a boil in the top of a double saucepan; remove sauce from heat and dissolve softened gelatine in it. Whisk double cream and egg yolks, and whisk into sauce; season to taste with salt and white pepper. Strain sauce through a fine sieve, and cool. When the sauce is cool but not yet set, use it to coat cold eggs, chicken or game.

CREAM SAUCE

Add ¼ pint (150 ml) fresh cream to 1 pint (600 ml) Béchamel Sauce and bring to boiling point. Add a few drops lemon juice. For fish, poultry, eggs and vegetables.

MORNAY SAUCE

Mix 2 slightly beaten egg yolks with a little cream and combine with 1 pint (600 ml) hot Béchamel Sauce. Cook, stirring constantly, until it just reaches boiling point. Add 2 tablespoons (30 ml) butter and 2 to 3 tablespoons (30–45 ml) grated cheese (Parmesan or Swiss cheese is best). For fish, vegetables, poultry, poached eggs, noodles and macaroni mixtures.

AURORE SAUCE

Add 2 to 3 tablespoons (30–45 ml) tomato concentrate to 1 pint (600 ml) Béchamel Sauce and 'finish' with 1 tablespoon (15 ml) butter. Excellent with eggs, chicken or shellfish.

SAUCE NANTUA

Add 4 tablespoons (60 ml) fresh cream to ½ pint (300 ml) hot Béchamel Sauce. Blend well and strain through a fine sieve. Heat without boiling, season to taste with salt and white pepper, and stir in 2 to 3 tablespoons (30–45 ml) crayfish butter (shrimp or lobster butter will do) and 2 tablespoons (30 ml) chopped shellfish. The latter may be omitted. Wonderful with poached or coddled eggs and fish.

SAUCE SOUBISE

Slice 1 large onion, cover with hot water, and parboil for 3 to 5 minutes. Drain onion slices and cook in a saucepan with a little butter until they are soft but not brown. Add 1 pint (600 ml) hot Béchamel Sauce and cook for approximately 15 minutes longer.

Strain through a fine sieve, pressing the vegetables well to extract all the juice; return to the heat and gradually add ½ pint (300 ml) cream. Correct seasoning with salt and white pepper, and serve. For fish, lamb, veal or sweetbreads.

SAUCE POULETTE

Melt 1 tablespoon (15 ml) butter in a saucepan, add 6 finely chopped mushrooms, and cook until they start to brown. Add 2 shallots, finely chopped, mix well and add ¼ pint (150 ml) cream. Cook this mixture until it has reduced to half the original quantity and add ½ pint (300 ml) Béchamel Sauce. Bring to a boil and add 2 slightly beaten egg yolks mixed with a little cream. Bring to boiling point again, stirring constantly, but do not boil. Add the juice of ½ lemon, and 1 teaspoon (5 ml) chopped parsley. A wonderful sauce for fish, calf's brains or poultry.

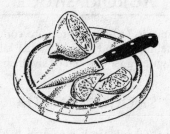

VELOUTÉ SAUCE (CHICKEN VELOUTÉ)

2 tablespoons (30 ml) butter
2 tablespoons (30 ml) flour
1 pint (600 ml) chicken stock
Salt
White peppercorns
Mushroom peelings or stems
Lemon juice

Melt butter in the top of a double saucepan; add flour and cook for a few minutes to form pale *roux*. Add boiling stock, salt and pepper, and cook, stirring vigorously with a whisk until well blended. Add mushroom peelings or stems; reduce heat and simmer gently, stirring occasionally and skimming from time to time, until the sauce is reduced to two-thirds of the original quantity and is thick but light and creamy. Flavour with lemon juice and strain through a fine sieve.

Note This sauce forms the foundation of a number of the best white sauces, which take their distinctive names from the different ingredients added. It can be used by itself, but in that case it is much improved by the addition of a little double cream and egg yolk.

FISH VELOUTÉ SAUCE

Proceed as for Velouté Sauce above, substituting 1 pint (600 ml) fish stock or canned clam juice for chicken stock, and omitting mushroom peelings or stems.

Note: Fish Velouté – like Chicken Velouté above – makes an excellent sauce on its own when a little double cream and 1 or 2 egg yolks are added.

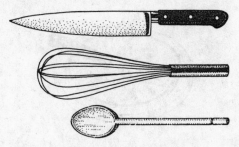

SAUCE SUPRÊME

3 tablespoons (45 ml) butter
2 tablespoons (30 ml) flour
1 pint (600 ml) boiling chicken stock
2 button mushrooms, finely chopped
¼ pint (150 ml) cream
Lemon juice
Salt and cayenne pepper

Melt 2 tablespoons (30 ml) butter in the top of a double saucepan and blend in the flour thoroughly, being very careful not to let it colour. Remove saucepan from heat and pour in the boiling stock. Cook over water, stirring constantly, until it thickens slightly; add finely chopped mushrooms and simmer for 10 to 15 minutes, stirring from time to time. Strain sauce; reheat and add cream and lemon juice. Season to taste with salt and a little cayenne. Remove sauce from the heat and whisk in the remaining butter, adding it in small pieces. Excellent for eggs, chicken and vegetables.

If the sauce is not to be used immediately, put several dabs of butter on top to prevent a skin forming.

SAUCE ALLEMANDE

Mix 2 slightly beaten egg yolks with a little cream, combine with 1 pint (600 ml) hot Suprême Sauce, and cook until it reaches boiling point, stirring constantly, but do not let it boil. 'Finish' sauce by swirling 2 tablespoons (30 ml) fresh cream into it.

Allemande Sauce is just a very rich Suprême Sauce, excellent with boiled chicken.

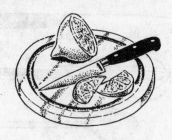

SAUCE NORMANDE

2 tablespoons (30 ml) butter
2 tablespoons (30 ml) flour
1 pint (600 ml) white stock
Fish liquor
2 egg yolks
Lemon juice
Salt and freshly ground black pepper

This sauce is usually served with sole or other fish cooked *à la normande*. Make a sauce in the usual way with 2 tablespoons (30 ml) butter, flour and stock. Add ½ pint (300 ml) liquor from the cooked fish and simmer 12 to 15 minutes longer, skimming when necessary. Remove saucepan from the heat and stir in egg yolks; then whisk in 2 tablespoons (30 ml) diced butter. Add lemon juice, salt and freshly ground black pepper, to taste. Strain before serving.

SHRIMP SAUCE

1 tablespoon (15 ml) butter
1 tablespoon (15 ml) flour
½ pint (300 ml) well-flavoured fish stock
¼ pint (150 ml) buttered shrimps
4 tablespoons (60 ml) double cream
Salt, white pepper and cayenne pepper
Lemon juice

Melt butter in a small saucepan and blend in the flour with a wooden spoon. Simmer *roux* for a minute or two, stirring continuously. Remove from heat and add fish stock.

Return to heat and simmer, stirring constantly, until sauce comes to a boil. Mash buttered shrimps slightly with a fork and add them to the sauce. Just before serving, add cream, and salt, white pepper, cayenne and lemon juice, to taste.

RICH AURORE SAUCE

½ pint (300 ml) Chicken Velouté (page 108)
4 tomatoes, sliced
4–6 tablespoons (60–90 ml) dry white wine
4–6 tablespoons (60–90 ml) white stock
2 tablespoons (30 ml) finely chopped cooked ham
2 tablespoons (30 ml) finely chopped cooked tongue

Combine tomatoes, wine and stock in a small saucepan, and reduce them to a pulp. Purée through a fine sieve and add purée to Chicken Velouté (or a well-flavoured Béchamel Sauce). Add chopped ham and tongue, and warm through.

PRAWN AND LOBSTER SAUCE

1 small lobster
¾ pint (450 ml) fish *fumet* or rich fish stock
3 tablespoons (45 ml) butter
3 tablespoons (45 ml) flour
½ pint (300 ml) double cream
8 oz (225 g) frozen prawns, coarsely chopped
2 tablespoons (30 ml) butter
Salt, freshly ground black pepper and cayenne pepper
2 tablespoons (30 ml) cognac

Shell lobster and boil chopped shells in fish *fumet* for a minute or two. Melt butter in the top of a double saucepan; stir in flour and cook over water for 3 minutes, stirring continuously until smooth. Strain fish *fumet* and add to *roux*, stirring continuously until sauce is rich and creamy. Simmer gently for 20 minutes; then add cream and continue cooking, uncovered, stirring from time to time to keep skin from forming, until the sauce is reduced to the desired consistency.

Dice lobster meat and sauté with chopped prawns in butter until heated through; season to taste with salt, freshly ground black pepper and cayenne. Flame with cognac and add to sauce. Makes about 1 pint (600 ml). Good for poached fish, and fish and shellfish soufflés.

Brown Sauces

There is only one basic brown sauce – *sauce espagnole* – and it is the foundation for many other famous French sauces. But there is nothing basic about this divinity among sauces. A good brown sauce depends entirely upon its ingredients. It can be only as good as the beef stock that went into it. No short cuts here; no beef stock cubes or canned consommés. You must use the best stock you can make from quality beef and the added savour of onions, carrots, turnips, herbs and tomatoes. As this sauce keeps very well, make 2 pints (1.1 lit) and store it in the refrigerator in a covered jar for future use. Sauce Espagnole, or Basic Brown Sauce, will keep indefinitely in the refrigerator if it is boiled up again once a week, and returned to the refrigerator in a clean jar.

Use Sauce Espagnole as a base for many exciting sauces, and as it is to lend interest to braised onions, carrots and celery, or to add to the butter that steaks and chops have been cooked in.

SAUCE ESPAGNOLE
(CLASSIC BROWN SAUCE)

2 tablespoons (30 ml) fat (unsalted beef, veal or pork
drippings)
2 oz (50 g) fat salt pork, diced
2 carrots, diced
1 onion, diced
2 tablespoons (30 ml) flour
3 pints (1.7 lit) brown stock
1 *bouquet garni* (1 stalk celery, 2 sprigs parsley,
1 sprig thyme, 1 bay leaf)
1 clove garlic
6 tablespoons (90 ml) French Tomato Sauce (page 124) or 2
tablespoons (30 ml) canned tomato concentrate

Melt fat in a large heavy saucepan, add diced salt pork, carrots and
onion, and cook until they start to turn golden, shaking the pan so
that they cook evenly. Sprinkle flour over this mixture and cook
gently on a very low heat, stirring frequently, until it takes on
a good golden brown colour. Add one-third of the boiling
stock together with *bouquet garni* and garlic, and cook, stirring
frequently, until the sauce thickens.

Add half of the remaining stock and cook very slowly over a
very low heat, stirring occasionally, for about 1½ to 2 hours, or
until the mixture is reduced to approximately half the original
quantity. As it cooks, skim off scum and fat rising to surface. Add
Tomato Sauce (or concentrate), and cook for a few minutes
longer. Then strain through a fine sieve into a bowl, pressing the
vegetables against the sieve to extract all their juice.

Clean the saucepan, return the mixture to it, add remaining
stock, and continue cooking slowly until the sauce is reduced to
about 2 pints (1.1 lit), skimming the surface from time to time as
needed.

Strain again. Cool, stirring occasionally. Store Sauce Espagnole in a covered jar in the refrigerator until ready to use. A little
butter melted over the top will seal it and help it to last even
longer. This recipe makes 2 pints (1.1. lit).

BASIC BROWN SAUCE

2 tablespoons (30 ml) butter
1 small onion, thinly sliced
2 tablespoons (30 ml) flour
1¼ pints (750 ml) well-flavoured brown stock
1 small carrot
1 small turnip
1 stalk celery or ¼ teaspoon (1.25 ml) celery seed
4 mushrooms
2–4 tomatoes or 1–2 tablespoons (15–30 ml) tomato
concentrate
1 *bouquet garni* (3 sprigs parsley, 1 sprig thyme, 1 bay leaf)
2 cloves
12 black peppercorns
Salt

Heat butter in a thick-bottomed saucepan until it browns. Add thinly sliced onion and simmer, stirring constantly, until golden. Stir in flour and cook, stirring constantly, for a minute or two longer.

The good colour of your sauce depends upon the thorough browning of these ingredients without allowing them to burn. When this is accomplished, remove saucepan from the heat and pour in the stock; return to heat and stir until it comes to a boil. Allow to boil for 5 minutes, skimming all scum from the top with a perforated spoon.

Wash and slice carrot, turnip, celery, mushrooms and tomatoes, and add them with the *bouquet garni*, cloves and peppercorns, and salt, to taste. Simmer the sauce gently for at least ½ hour, stirring occasionally and skimming when necessary. Strain through a fine sieve; remove fat; reheat before serving.

Side Sauces made from Espagnole or Brown Sauce

There are many side sauces made from Espagnole or Brown Sauce: *sauce demi-glace*, *Madeira*, *bordelaise*, *bourguignonne*, *chasseur*, *bigarade* and *lyonnaise*, to mention just a few. I give you here a selection of recipes from some of the most useful in everyday cooking. The others can be found in any good French cookbook.

SAUCE MADEIRA

Reduce 1 pint (600 ml) Espagnole or Brown Sauce to half the original quantity. Add 6 tablespoons (90 ml) Madeira. Heat the sauce well, but do not let it boil, or the flavour of the wine will be lost.

MADEIRA SAUCE WITH MUSHROOMS

Clean and dry caps of 8 oz (225 g) mushrooms and slice them thickly. Melt 2 tablespoons (30 ml) butter in a saucepan, add mushrooms, and salt and pepper, to taste, and cook, shaking pan from time to time, until mushrooms are golden brown. Add to Madeira Sauce and simmer for 5 minutes.

SAUCE LYONNAISE

Finely chop 2 medium-sized onions and sauté in 2 tablespoons (30 ml) butter until golden brown. Add 6 tablespoons (90 ml) dry white wine and simmer until reduced to half the original quantity. Add ½ pint (300 ml) Espagnole or Brown Sauce and cook gently for 15 minutes; add 1 teaspoon (5 ml) chopped parsley, and 'finish' by swirling in 1 tablespoon (15 ml) butter.

SAUCE 'FINES HERBES'

Remove leaves from 3 sprigs each of parsley, tarragon and chervil. Reserve them to garnish sauce. Chop stems and simmer gently in 6 tablespoons (90 ml) dry white wine for 5 minutes. In another saucepan, melt 2 tablespoons (30 ml) butter, and add 1 finely chopped shallot and the strained liquid in which herb stems were cooked. Cook this mixture until it is reduced to half the original quantity. Add Espagnole or Brown Sauce and cook for 10 to 15 minutes. Take off heat, and add juice of 1 lemon, and 'finish' by swirling in 1 tablespoon (15 ml) butter. When butter has been completely incorporated into the sauce, add herb leaves. Serve with meat, eggs or poultry.

BROWN CHAUDFROID SAUCE

1 tablespoon (15 ml) gelatine
8 tablespoons (120 ml) cold water
¾ pint (450 ml) Brown Sauce
½ pint (300 ml) stock
4–6 tablespoons (60–90 ml) Madeira or dry sherry

Soften gelatine in cold water. Combine Brown Sauce with stock and bring to a boil. Skim well; remove sauce from heat and dissolve gelatine in it. Add Madeira or dry sherry, to taste, and strain sauce through a fine sieve.

SAUCE BORDELAISE

½ pint (300 ml) Brown Sauce
2 shallots, finely chopped
1 clove garlic, finely chopped
1 glass red Bordeaux
1 bay leaf
2 tablespoons (30 ml) finely sliced beef marrow
Salt
1 teaspoon (5 ml) finely chopped parsley
A squeeze of lemon juice
Freshly ground black pepper

Simmer finely chopped shallots and garlic in a small saucepan with wine and bay leaf until wine is reduced to half the original quantity. Add Brown Sauce and simmer for 20 minutes, carefully removing any scum that rises. Strain the sauce and return it to the saucepan.

Poach finely sliced marrow in boiling salted water for 5 minutes; drain and add to the sauce with finely chopped parsley, lemon juice, and salt and freshly ground black pepper, to taste.

SAUCE DEMI-GLACE

1 pint (600 ml) Brown Sauce
Chopped stems and peelings of 6 mushrooms
6 tablespoons (90 ml) dry sherry or Madeira
1–2 tablespoons (15–30 ml) meat glaze

Simmer chopped mushroom stems and peelings in dry sherry or Madeira until liquid is reduced by half.

Reduce Brown Sauce to half the original quantity. Then add meat glaze, mushrooms and juices to this mixture, and simmer over a low heat for 15 minutes. Strain before serving.

SAUCE ROBERT

½ pint (300 ml) Brown Sauce
½ Spanish onion, finely chopped
2 tablespoons (30 ml) butter
1 glass white wine or 2 tablespoons (30 ml) vinegar
1 teaspoon (5 ml) Dijon mustard
¼ teaspoon (1.25 ml) sugar
1 or 2 red pimentos, cut in strips (optional)

Sauté finely chopped onion in butter until transparent; add wine or vinegar, mustard and sugar, and boil until liquids are reduced to half the original quantity. Then add Brown Sauce and simmer for 10 to 15 minutes longer.

Skim sauce well and strain before using. One or two red pimentos cut in strips may be added after straining. Serve with pork, goose, lamb cutlets or steak.

SAUCE PÉRIGUEUX

¼ pint (150 ml) Brown Sauce
¼ pint (150 ml) French Tomato Sauce (page 124)
2–3 truffles, finely chopped
1 glass Madeira
Salt and freshly ground black pepper

Combine finely chopped truffles and Madeira in a small saucepan, and simmer gently until the wine is reduced to half the original quantity. Add Brown and Tomato Sauces, and simmer for a few minutes longer, skimming sauce if necessary. Season to taste with salt and freshly ground black pepper.

SAUCE PIQUANTE

½ pint (300 ml) Brown Sauce
4–6 tablespoons (60–90 ml) vinegar
1 level tablespoon (15 ml) finely chopped shallots
1 tablespoon (15 ml) finely chopped capers
1 tablespoon (15 ml) finely chopped gherkin
Salt and freshly ground black pepper
1 tablespoon (15 ml) chopped parsley

Combine vinegar, finely chopped shallots, capers and gherkin in a saucepan, and simmer gently until the shallot is soft and the vinegar reduced to half the original quantity. Add Brown Sauce and bring to a boil. Just before serving, add salt and freshly ground black pepper if necessary, and finely chopped parsley. Serve with boiled mutton, veal or calf's head.

SAUCE ITALIENNE

½ pint (300 ml) Brown Sauce
2 tablespoons (30 ml) olive oil
2 shallots, finely chopped
½ glass dry white wine
6 Italian dried mushrooms
1 sprig thyme
1 bay leaf

Heat oil in a small saucepan and sauté finely chopped shallots until transparent. Add wine, mushrooms (which you have soaked until soft, pressed dry and chopped finely), thyme, bay leaf and Brown Sauce. Simmer sauce gently for 20 minutes, skimming when necessary. Just before serving, remove thyme and bay leaf.

Emulsion Sauces

MAYONNAISE

2 egg yolks
Salt and freshly ground black pepper
½ level teaspoon (2.5 ml) Dijon mustard
Lemon juice
½ pint (300 ml) olive oil

Place egg yolks (make sure gelatinous thread of the egg is removed), salt, pepper and mustard in a bowl. Twist a cloth wrung out in very cold water round the bottom of the bowl to keep it steady and cool. Using a wire whisk, fork or wooden spoon, beat the yolks to a smooth paste. Add a little lemon juice (the acid helps the emulsion), and beat in about a quarter of the oil, drop by drop. Add a little more lemon juice to the mixture and then, a little more quickly now, add more oil, beating all the while. Continue adding oil and beating until the sauce is of a good thick consistency. Correct seasoning (more salt, pepper and lemon juice) as desired. If you are making the mayonnaise a day before using it, stir in 1 tablespoon (15 ml) boiling water when it is of the desired consistency. This will keep it from turning or separating.

Note: If the mayonnaise should curdle, break another egg yolk into a clean bowl and gradually beat the curdled mayonnaise into it. Your mayonnaise will begin to 'take' immediately.

If mayonnaise is to be used for a salad, thin it down considerably with dry white wine, vinegar or lemon juice. If it is to be used for coating meat, poultry or fish, add a little liquid aspic to stiffen it.

If sauce is to be kept for several hours before serving, cover the bowl with a cloth wrung out in very cold water to prevent a skin from forming on the top.

CORAL MAYONNAISE

Wash and dry lobster coral; pound it to a paste in a mortar; rub it through a fine sieve. Add to mayonnaise.

SAUCE VERTE (GREEN MAYONNAISE)

½ pint (300 ml) well-flavoured mayonnaise
1 handful each sprigs of watercress, parsley and chervil
Salt
1 tablespoon (15 ml) finely chopped watercress leaves
1 tablespoon (15 ml) finely chopped chervil
2 tablespoons (30 ml) finely chopped parsley
1 tablespoon (15 ml) finely chopped tarragon leaves
Lemon juice
Freshly ground black pepper

Wash sprigs of watercress, parsley and chervil; pick them over carefully and put them in a saucepan with a little salted boiling water. Allow greens to boil for 6 to 7 minutes; drain and press as dry as possible. Pound greens in a mortar: rub through a fine sieve and add green purée to mayonnaise.

Whirl green mayonnaise and finely chopped watercress leaves and herbs in an electric blender, or blend well with a whisk; add lemon juice, salt and freshly ground black pepper, to taste. Serve this sauce chilled with fish and shellfish, poached and grilled salmon, or fish mousse.

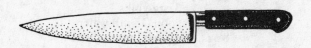

SAUCE TARTARE

½ pint (300 ml) mayonnaise
1 teaspoon (5 ml) chopped capers
1 teaspoon (5 ml) chopped gherkins
1 teaspoon (5 ml) each chopped parsley, tarragon and chervil
Pinch of sugar

Combine ingredients. Chill. I sometimes add a little finely chopped garlic. Good with grilled and poached fish. Almost a 'must' with deep-fried mussels, oysters or prawns.

SAUCE RÉMOULADE

½ pint (300 ml) well-flavoured mayonnaise
1 tablespoon (15 ml) finely chopped fresh tarragon,
and basil or chervil
1 tablespoon (15 ml) finely chopped parsley
1 clove garlic, finely chopped
1 level teaspoon (5 ml) dry mustard
1 teaspoon (5 ml) capers
2 small pickles, finely chopped

Combine ingredients and chill. Serve with grilled fish, prawns and lobster. Excellent with cold pork.

SAUCE BÉARNAISE

3 sprigs tarragon, coarsely chopped
3 sprigs chervil, coarsely chopped
1 tablespoon (15 ml) chopped shallots
2 crushed peppercorns
2 tablespoons (30 ml) tarragon vinegar
¼ pint (150 ml) dry white wine
3 egg yolks
1 tablespoon (15 ml) water
8 oz (225 g) soft butter, diced
Salt
Lemon juice
Cayenne pepper

Combine coarsely chopped herbs, chopped shallots, crushed peppercorns, vinegar and white wine in a saucepan. Cook over a high heat until liquid is reduced to two-thirds of the original quantity. Strain and return juices to the top of a double saucepan.

Beat egg yolks with water and add to the juices in the top of the double saucepan; stir briskly over hot, but not boiling, water with a wire whisk until light and fluffy. Never let water in bottom of boiler begin to boil, or sauce will not 'take'. Gradually add butter to egg mixture, whisking briskly all the time as sauce begins to thicken. Continue adding butter and stirring until sauce is thick.

Season to taste with salt, lemon juice and cayenne. Strain through a fine sieve and serve. Excellent with grilled, poached or fried fish.

SAUCE CHORON

Make a Béarnaise Sauce as above, and flavour to taste with tomato concentrate.

SAUCE HOLLANDAISE

1 teaspoon (5 ml) lemon juice
1 tablespoon (15 ml) cold water
Salt and white pepper
4 oz (100 g) soft butter
4 egg yolks
Lemon juice

Combine lemon juice, water, salt and white pepper in the top of a double saucepan or *bain-marie*. Divide butter into 4 equal pieces. Add the egg yolks and a quarter of the butter to the liquid in the saucepan, and stir the mixture rapidly and constantly with a wire whisk over hot, but not boiling, water until the butter is melted and the mixture begins to thicken. Add the second piece of butter and continue whisking. As the mixture thickens and the second piece of butter melts, add the third piece of butter, stirring from the bottom of the pan until it is melted. Be careful not to allow the water over which the sauce is cooking to boil at any time. Add rest of butter, beating until it melts and is incorporated in the sauce.

Remove top part of saucepan from heat and continue to beat for 2 to 3 minutes. Replace saucepan over hot, but not boiling, water for 2 minutes more, beating constantly. By this time the emulsion should have formed and your sauce will be rich and creamy. 'Finish' sauce with a few drops of lemon juice. Strain and serve.

If at any time in the operation the mixture should curdle, beat in 1 to 2 tablespoons (15–30 ml) cold water to rebind the emulsion.

MUSTARD HOLLANDAISE

Make a Hollandaise Sauce as shown in previous recipe, and flavour to taste with Dijon mustard.

SAUCE MOUSSELINE

Make in the same way as Hollandaise Sauce, adding 4 to 6 tablespoons (60–90 ml) whipped cream just before serving.

Other Sauces

FRENCH TOMATO SAUCE

2 tablespoons (30 ml) butter
2 tablespoons (30 ml) finely chopped ham
1 small carrot, finely chopped
1 small turnip, finely chopped
1 onion, finely chopped
1 stalk celery, finely chopped
6–8 ripe tomatoes, sliced
2 tablespoons (30 ml) tomato concentrate
1 tablespoon (15 ml) flour
1 *bouquet garni* (1 sprig each thyme, marjoram and parsley)
½ pint (300 ml) well-flavoured beef stock
Salt and freshly ground black pepper
Lemon juice
Sugar

Melt butter in a thick-bottomed saucepan; add finely chopped ham and vegetables, and sauté mixture until onion is transparent and soft. Stir in sliced tomatoes and tomato concentrate; simmer for a minute or two; sprinkle with flour and mix well. Then add *bouquet garni* and beef stock, and simmer gently, stirring continuously, until sauce comes to a boil. Season to taste with salt and freshly ground black pepper, and simmer gently for 30 minutes, stirring from time to time. If the sauce becomes too thick, add a little more stock. Strain through a fine sieve; reheat, and add lemon juice and sugar, to taste.

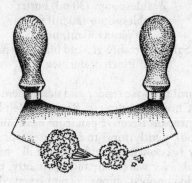

ITALIAN TOMATO SAUCE

2 Spanish onions, finely chopped
2 cloves garlic, finely chopped
4 tablespoons (60 ml) olive oil
6 tablespoons (90 ml) Italian tomato concentrate
1 large can Italian peeled tomatoes
2 bay leaves
4 tablespoons (60 ml) finely chopped parsley
¼ teaspoon (1.25 ml) oregano
1 small strip lemon peel
6 tablespoons (90 ml) dry white wine
Salt and freshly ground black pepper
1–2 tablespoons (15–30 ml) Worcestershire sauce

Sauté finely chopped onions and garlic in olive oil in a large, thick-bottomed frying pan until transparent and soft but not coloured. Stir in tomato concentrate and continue to cook for a minute or two, stirring constantly. Pour in Italian peeled tomatoes; add bay leaves, parsley, oregano and lemon peel. Add dry white wine, an equal quantity of water, and salt and freshly ground black pepper, to taste, and simmer gently, stirring from time to time, for 1 to 2 hours. Just before serving, stir in Worcestershire sauce, to taste.

ENGLISH ONION SAUCE

2 Spanish onions
2 tablespoons (30 ml) butter
2 tablespoons (30 ml) flour
¼ pint (150 ml) milk
Salt and freshly ground black pepper
Pinch of nutmeg

Boil onions until they are tender and drain them well, reserving onion liquor. Chop onions finely. Reserve. Melt butter in the top of a double saucepan. Remove pan from heat; stir in flour; return to heat and cook gently for 3 to 5 minutes, stirring constantly, until the flour is cooked through. Add milk, heated to boiling point, and cook over water, stirring constantly, until sauce starts to thicken. Add chopped onions, ¼ pint reserved (150 ml) onion liquor and salt, freshly ground black pepper and nutmeg, to taste.

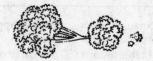

ENGLISH PARSLEY SAUCE

1 tablespoon (15 ml) butter
1 tablespoon (15 ml) flour
½ pint (300 ml) milk
2 tablespoons (30 ml) finely chopped parsley
Salt and white pepper
Lemon juice

Melt butter in the top of a double saucepan; stir in the flour and mix with a wooden spoon until smooth. Cook for a few minutes over water but do not allow *roux* to colour. Add milk, heated to boiling point, and cook, stirring constantly, until boiling. Add finely chopped parsley, season to taste with salt and white pepper, and simmer for 2 to 3 minutes longer. Just before serving, add lemon juice, to taste.

Note: A richer sauce can be made by using Béchamel or Velouté Sauce as a foundation.

ENGLISH BREAD SAUCE

½ pint (300 ml) milk
½ onion stuck with 1–2 cloves
2 oz (50 g) freshly grated breadcrumbs
2–3 tablespoons (30–45 ml) butter or double cream
Salt and white pepper
Pinch of cayenne pepper

Simmer milk and onion stuck with cloves until the milk is well flavoured. Remove onion and cloves, and add the breadcrumbs, which you have made fine by rubbing them through a wire sieve. Simmer sauce gently, stirring continuously, until the breadcrumbs swell and thicken the sauce. Add the butter or cream, and season to taste with salt, white pepper and a pinch of cayenne. Excellent with roast poultry and game.

BONANZA BARBECUE SAUCE

2 cloves garlic, crushed
1 Spanish onion, finely chopped
¼ pint (150 ml) corn oil
4 tablespoons (60 ml) stuffed olives, chopped
8 oz (225 g) peeled tomatoes, finely chopped
6 tablespoons (90 ml) dry white wine
Juice and grated rind of 1 orange
6 tablespoons (90 ml) lemon juice
2 tablespoons (30 ml) Worcestershire sauce
6 tablespoons (90 ml) brown sugar
1–2 teaspoons (5–10 ml) flour
Salt and freshly ground black pepper
Dash of Tabasco

Sauté crushed garlic and finely chopped onion in corn oil until they are golden but not brown. Add chopped olives and tomatoes, white wine, the juice and grated rind of 1 orange, lemon juice, Worcestershire sauce and brown sugar. Bring mixture to a boil and simmer gently for 20 to 30 minutes. Thicken slightly with flour, add salt and freshly ground black pepper, to taste, and a dash of Tabasco. Strain and use for basting charcoal-grilled meats, poultry and game.

GREEN PEPPER SAUCE

4 green peppers
4 tablespoons (60 ml) corn oil
1 clove garlic
¼ pint (150 ml) dry white wine
½ teaspoon (2.5 ml) salt
Freshly ground black pepper
2 tablespoons (30 ml) wine vinegar
2 tablespoons (30 ml) butter

Wash and seed green peppers; cut in very thin slices. Heat corn oil; toss in garlic and cook until golden but not brown. Remove garlic; add pepper slices and white wine, and cook slowly until tender, stirring frequently. Season with salt, freshly ground black pepper and vinegar. Keep warm, and just before serving, stir in 2 tablespoons (30 ml) butter. Excellent for all barbecued red meats.

CREOLE BARBECUE SAUCE

1 Spanish onion, finely chopped
1 clove garlic, crushed
1 green pepper, finely chopped
6 tablespoons (90 ml) butter
1 pound peeled tomatoes
6 tablespoons (90 ml) tomato concentrate
6 tablespoons (90 ml) red wine
2 tablespoons (30 ml) lemon juice
4 tablespoons (60 ml) brown sugar
Salt and freshly ground black pepper
Dash of Tabasco

Sauté chopped onion, garlic and green pepper in butter until lightly browned. Add tomatoes, tomato concentrate, red wine, lemon juice and sugar.

Bring sauce to a boil; simmer gently for 20 minutes; season to taste with salt and freshly ground black pepper, and add a dash of Tabasco. Serve hot with barbecued meat or fish.

Butters

BEURRE NOISETTE

4 oz (100 g) butter
Juice of ½ lemon

Melt butter and cook to a light hazelnut colour. Add lemon juice. Serve with eggs and fish.

BEURRE NOIR

4 oz (100 g) butter
1 tablespoon (15 ml) finely chopped parsley
1 tablespoon (15 ml) capers
1 tablespoon (15 ml) white wine vinegar

Melt butter and brown it. Stir in finely chopped parsley, capers and white wine vinegar. Serve with fish, brains and (minus capers) with certain egg dishes.

SHRIMP BUTTER

4 oz (100 g) butter
2–3 tablespoons (30–45 ml) chopped shrimps
1 teaspoon (5 ml) anchovy paste
Lemon juice
Salt and cayenne pepper

Pound butter, chopped shrimps and anchovy paste to a smooth paste in a mortar. Season to taste with lemon juice, salt and cayenne pepper. Press through a fine sieve. Chill.

WATERCRESS BUTTER

2–3 tablespoons (30–45 ml) finely chopped watercress
4 oz (100 g) butter
Lemon juice
Salt and freshly ground black pepper

Wash watercress very carefully, removing stalks and any discoloured leaves; chop finely. Dry chopped watercress in a cloth and pound it in a mortar with butter. Season to taste with lemon juice, salt and freshly ground black pepper. Chill.

PARSLEY BUTTER

Prepare as above, substituting finely chopped parsley for watercress.

GARLIC BUTTER

4 oz (100 g) butter
1–2 cloves garlic, finely chopped
1 tablespoon (15 ml) finely chopped parsley
Salt and freshly ground black pepper

Soften butter slightly, and pound together with finely chopped garlic and parsley. Season to taste with salt and freshly ground black pepper. Chill.

MAÎTRE D'HÔTEL BUTTER

4 oz (100 g) butter
1 tablespoon (15 ml) finely chopped parsley
1 tablespoon (15 ml) lemon juice
Salt and freshly ground black pepper

Cream butter with finely chopped parsley and lemon juice. Season to taste with salt and freshly ground black pepper. Chill.

Sweet Sauces

VANILLA CUSTARD SAUCE

¾ pint (450 ml) milk
½ teaspoon (2.5 ml) vanilla extract
4 tablespoons (60 ml) sugar
4 egg yolks
¼ teaspoon (1.25 ml) salt

Simmer milk for 5 minutes; stir in vanilla extract. Combine sugar, egg yolks and salt, and beat until fluffy and lemon-coloured. Pour a little of the hot milk into the egg and sugar mixture; blend well, and then stir into the hot milk. Heat slowly in the top of a double saucepan, stirring constantly, until the mixture coats a spoon. Serve warm over cake, sweet soufflé or ice cream.

RICH VANILLA SAUCE

¼ pint (150 ml) Vanilla Custard Sauce
¼ pint (150 ml) double cream, whipped until stiff
2–4 tablespoons (30–60 ml) Grand Marnier

Add whipped cream, and Grand Marnier, to taste, to Vanilla Custard Sauce.

BRANDY SAUCE

2 egg yolks
4–6 tablespoons (60–90 ml) each double cream,
water and brandy
1 tablespoon (15 ml) sugar

Combine ingredients in the top of a double saucepan and whisk with a small wire whisk over hot, but not boiling, water for 6 to 8 minutes, or until sauce is thick and frothy. Do not allow sauce to boil, or it will curdle.

RICH CARAMEL SAUCE

¾ pint (450 ml) Vanilla Custard Sauce
3 tablespoons (45 ml) castor sugar
3 tablespoons (45 ml) water

Put the castor sugar in a saucepan, stir it until melted, and let it take on a nice brown colour. Then add water, mix until smooth, and pour this caramel into ¾ pint (450 ml) Vanilla Custard Sauce.

ORANGE RUM SAUCE

3 tablespoons (45 ml) butter
6 oz (175 g) icing sugar
½ pint (300 ml) sour cream
1 teaspoon (5 ml) grated orange rind
2 tablespoons (30 ml) orange juice
1 tablespoon (15 ml) lemon juice
2 tablespoons (30 ml) rum

Cream butter and sugar until the mixture is smooth. Combine sour cream, grated orange rind, orange and lemon juice, and rum. Mix all well together and serve cold with cake or hot puddings.

APRICOT SAUCE

6–8 canned apricot halves
Sugar
1 teaspoon (5 ml) cornflour
¼ pint (150 ml) water
1–2 tablespoons (15–30 ml) Grand Marnier
2–3 drops red food colouring

Make apricot purée by forcing canned apricots through a fine sieve, and add sugar to taste. Combine purée with cornflour which you have dissolved in cold water, and stir in the top of a double saucepan until it boils and thickens. Add Grand Marnier and a few drops of red food colouring, and simmer for 2 to 3 minutes longer.

APPLE SAUCE

8 oz (225 g) cooking apples
4–6 tablespoons (60–90 ml) water
1 tablespoon (15 ml) brown sugar
Pinch of nutmeg
2 tablespoons (30 ml) butter

Peel, core and slice apples thinly into a bowl of acidulated water (water with a little lemon juice) to keep colour fresh. Drain apple slices and combine with the water, sugar and nutmeg in a small saucepan. Simmer, stirring frequently, until apples are reduced to a pulp. Add the butter and mash until smooth, or press through a fine sieve.

Serve with pork, roast duck, goose or suckling pig.

LEMON OR STRAWBERRY HARD SAUCE

4 oz (100 g) butter
12 oz (350 g) icing sugar
Juice and grated rind of 1 lemon or
½ cup mashed strawberries

Work butter until soft; stir in sugar gradually and smoothly. Stir in juice and grated rind of 1 lemon, or ½ cup mashed strawberries, and mix until smooth. Add more sugar if desired. Should sauce separate after standing, beat until well blended.

HOT CHOCOLATE SAUCE

2 oz (50 g) bitter chocolate
½ pint (300 ml) water
8 oz (225 g) sugar
1 tablespoon (15 ml) cornflour
Salt
2 tablespoons (30 ml) butter
2 tablespoons (30 ml) cognac
½ teaspoon (2.5 ml) very finely grated orange rind

Combine chocolate with water; heat, and when smooth, add combined sugar, cornflour and salt; cook, stirring continually, until sugar is dissolved and sauce is thick. Allow to boil for 3 minutes, then add butter and cognac. Stir and remove from heat. Add finely grated orange rind.

FRENCH ORANGE SAUCE

Grated rind and juice of 1 orange
1 tablespoon (15 ml) sugar
1 tablespoon (15 ml) butter
1 tablespoon (15 ml) cornflour
½ pint (300 ml) water
2 egg yolks
1–2 tablespoons (15–30 ml) Grand Marnier

Grate orange rind finely and rub it into the sugar with the back of a wooden spoon. Melt butter in the top of a double saucepan and stir in cornflour to make a *roux*. Then add the water and stir until boiling. Add orange juice to orange-flavoured sugar; pour into sauce and simmer for 2 to 3 minutes. Remove saucepan from the heat; allow to cool a little and stir in the egg yolks. Add Grand Marnier to taste.

CRÈME PÂTISSIÈRE 'TOUR D'ARGENT'

5 egg yolks
4 oz (100 g) icing sugar
1 tablespoon (15 ml) flour
8 fluid oz (225 ml) milk
½ teaspoon (2.5 ml) vanilla extract
8 fluid oz (225 ml) whipped cream
Castor sugar

Whisk egg yolks with icing sugar; then beat in flour. Bring milk to a boil; add vanilla extract, and then add to egg and sugar mixture; cook over water, stirring continuously, until smooth and thick. Remove from heat and cool. Then add whipped cream, sweetened to taste with sugar.

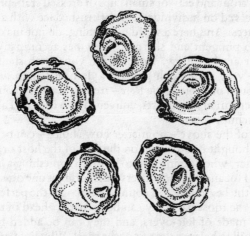

CHAPTER THREE

Hot and Cold Appetizers

There are almost unlimited numbers of appetizers, but the preparation of a large number of them requires the skill of a professional chef, to say nothing of a great amount of time and expensive ingredients.

Heading the list of simpler ones, though not the least expensive, are oysters on the half-shell, six or nine freshly opened natives of Colchester or Whitstable served on ice with coarse black pepper and a wedge or two of lemon. Try them, too, with tiny sausages, piping hot, as they do in Northern France; or roll them in fresh breadcrumbs and fry them in oil and butter. Serve immediately with a Béarnaise Sauce, or more simply, with wedges of lemon.

I like, too, great oiled platters of smoked fish – salmon, sturgeon, trout and eel – or small cups of dressed crab, prawns and lobster, served on individual trays of crushed ice with a choice of subtle sauces. And here a word of warning: do not make seafood sauces too pungent and sharp if fine wines accompany the first course, or are to follow. Better serve your fresh shellfish very plain and very cold, with perhaps a dash of lemon juice or, at most, a touch of *crème Marie Rose* – freshly made mayonnaise and whipped cream in equal parts, enlivened by a dash of Tabasco and a little ketchup.

But all of the above – no matter how choice – can be prepared without thought or attention on the part of the host or hostess. I much prefer, when dining out, to be given something a little more personal. Hot and cold appetizers – the sort that one often meets in France as the beginning to a country meal – are the perfect answer here. For the most part they can be prepared ahead of time; they are often made of left-overs; and they can be added to or subtracted from to balance the rest of the meal. Why not try a popular French dish from the Mediterranean – *caviar d'aubergines*, a chilled 'poor man's caviar' which, while quite unlike its namesake, is quite delicious: bake 1 or 2 large aubergines (eggplants) in a moderately hot oven (400°F/200°C/GM6) until soft (about 1 hour). Peel and chop 1 Spanish onion, 1 small green pepper, 4 tomatoes and 1 clove garlic, and sauté them until golden in 6 to 8 tablespoons (90–120 ml) olive oil. Peel baked aubergine, chop the flesh finely and add to other ingredients. Simmer vegetables gently, stirring from time to time, until the mixture is fairly thick. Season to taste with salt and freshly ground black pepper, and allow to cool. Then stir in 1 or 2 tablespoons (15–30 ml) each of dry white wine, olive oil and finely chopped parsley. Chill, and serve with thin slices of French bread.

Again from Provence is the well-known hot appetizer, *petits pâtés à la provençale* (shortcrust pastry rounds filled with minced cooked ham or veal, flavoured with finely chopped anchovy, onion and garlic). I often serve these piping hot with drinks, or with an inexpensive dry *vin rosé* on-the-rocks at cocktail parties. You will find my recipe on page 157. Try them, too, with tuna fish instead of veal.

Mushrooms *à la grecque* is one of my favourite ways of starting a

---

meal. Try vegetables – cauliflower, carrots and beans – prepared this way for a trio of vegetable appetizers that could lend freshness and flavour to a rustic meal. The secret here is to blanch the vegetables slightly before cooking them in wine. Be sure not to overcook them or they will be tasteless and soggy.

Lentils *en salade* is a highly decorative country salad of dried lentils, with its hearty sauce flavoured with finely chopped onion, garlic, parsley and mustard; it is garnished with anchovy fillets, tomato wedges and black olives for a Mediterranean effect.

Salade de bœuf is another appetizer-salad favourite of mine. This favourite stand by of French bistros is a wonderful way of making good use of left-over boiled beef.

Two of France's most famous restaurants – the Pyramide at Vienne and the Bonne Auberge at Antibes – make a speciality of serving course after course of hot and cold appetizers with great *panache*. At Antibes some people make their whole meal of these delicious *hors-d'œuvre*. You, too, can make this an easy entertaining pattern for your own parties.

Party Canapés and Appetizers

RUMAKI

To make 24 *rumaki* (Japanese hot canapés), you will need 12 oz (350 g) chicken livers, 24 half-slices of bacon, 8 water chestnuts and 24 cocktail sticks or toothpicks. Cut livers in half. Slice water chestnuts into 3 rounds each. Arrange bacon slices on a tray and grill in oven until they are translucent and a good deal of the fat has cooked off. Drain on absorbent paper; place half a liver and 1 slice water chestnut on each half-slice of bacon. Roll and secure with a cocktail stick. Keep in refrigerator until ready to use. Just before serving, grill until bacon is crisp.

OLIVE-ALMOND CANAPÉS

To make 24 of these canapés, you will need 24 large stuffed olives, 24 blanched almonds, 24 half-slices of bacon and 24 cocktail sticks. Insert a blanched almond into each olive and wrap each in a half-slice of bacon which you have grilled in the oven until transparent and fat-free (as above). Secure each canapé with a cocktail stick and just before serving, grill until bacon is crisp.

STUFFED PRUNES IN PORT

To make 24 canapés, boil 24 prunes in water for 15 minutes; drain and soak overnight in port wine. Drain and dry them; stone them and stuff with chutney. Wrap each chutney-stuffed prune in a half-slice of bacon (as above) and secure with a cocktail stick. Just before serving, grill until bacon is crisp.

CELERY STUFFED WITH RED CAVIAR

Cream 8 oz (225 g) cream cheese with ½ small grated onion, 2 tablespoons (30 ml) finely chopped parsley and 4 tablespoons (60 ml) red caviar. Season to taste with salt and freshly ground black pepper. Wash and trim celery, and cut into 2-inch (50 mm) sections. Stuff each section with red caviar mixture and serve on a bed of crushed ice.

CUCUMBER AND RED CAVIAR ROUNDS

1 cucumber
Vinegar
Salt
6 oz (175 g) cream cheese
1 carton sour cream
Red caviar

Peel cucumber and cut into 1-inch (25 mm) rounds. Scoop out the centre seeds, leaving the sides and bottom to form a 'basket'. Soak in a weak vinegar and salt solution for several hours in the refrigerator. Drain and dry. Whisk cream cheese with sour cream until smooth. Fill cucumber rounds with this mixture and top with red caviar.

JAVANESE STEAK SATÉS

1½ lb (675 g) rump steak
2 tablespoons (30 ml) soy sauce
6 tablespoons (90 ml) olive oil
2 tablespoons (30 ml) lemon juice
¼ Spanish onion, finely chopped
1 clove garlic, finely chopped
1 level tablespoon (15 ml) powdered cumin
Freshly ground black pepper

Cut 1-inch-thick (25 mm) steak into thin strips 3 inches (75 mm) long, and marinate for at least 4 hours in a mixture of soy sauce, olive oil, lemon juice, finely chopped onion and garlic, and powdered cumin.

Thread the beef on skewers; brush with marinade and grill over charcoal or under the grill until done, turning the skewers from time to time. Season to taste with freshly ground black pepper. Serves 4.

JAPANESE TERIYAKI
'PAN AMERICAN AIRLINES'

1½ lb (675 g) rump steak
2–4 tablespoons (30–60 ml) soy sauce
4 tablespoons (60 ml) *sake*, or medium sherry diluted with
water
4 tablespoons (60 ml) chicken stock
Honey
Freshly ground black pepper

Cut steak into 1-inch (25 mm) cubes and marinate for at least 30 minutes in a mixture of soy sauce, *sake* (or medium sherry diluted with a little water) and chicken stock, flavoured to taste with honey.

Thread the beef on skewers; brush with marinade and grill over charcoal or under the grill until meat is cooked to your liking, turning the skewers from time to time. Season to taste with freshly ground black pepper. Serves 4.

PASTRY CROUSTADES

Make shortcrust pastry (page 754); roll dough out thinly and stamp out rounds with a cutter. Butter small round tins deeper in shape than those used for tartlets, and line them with the pastry. Prick the pastry at the bottom and line each pastry round with waxed paper or foil; fill them with rice or beans, and bake 'blind' in a moderately hot oven (400°F/200°C/GM6) until pastry is golden brown. Remove the paper and rice, and fill with a purée or savoury mixture.

PASTRY BOUCHÉES

Make puff pastry (page 760) or use a frozen puff paste; roll out, and cut rounds or ovals 1½ to 2 inches (35–50 mm) in diameter. Bake in a fairly hot oven (425°F/220°C/GM7) and fill with a purée or savoury mixture.

BREAD CROUSTADES

1 loaf white bread, unsliced
Butter
Olive oil

Cut the bread into ¾-inch (20 mm) slices and cut out rounds with a 2 to 2½-inch (50–65 mm) pastry cutter or glass. Then, with a smaller cutter, cut down the centre of these rounds to about ¼ inch (6 mm) from the bottom. Scoop out centre part and discard. Fry in butter and olive oil until crisp, or brush with melted butter and bake in the oven. Drain well on paper towels.

Appetizer Salads

TOMATO SALAD

4–6 ripe tomatoes
6–8 tablespoons (90–120 ml) olive oil
2–3 tablespoons (30–45 ml) wine vinegar
Salt and freshly ground black pepper
Finely chopped parsley and garlic

Wipe tomatoes clean and slice crosswise into even slices. Place slices in a flat *hors-d'œuvre* dish; mix olive oil, wine vinegar, and salt and freshly ground black pepper, to taste, and pour over salad. Sprinkle to taste with finely chopped parsley and garlic. Serves 4.

TOMATO SALAD 'FINES HERBES'

8 large ripe tomatoes
8 tablespoons (120 ml) finely chopped parsley
4 tablespoons (60 ml) finely chopped onion
1 tablespoon (15 ml) finely chopped garlic
2 tablespoons (30 ml) finely chopped basil
2 tablespoons (30 ml) finely chopped tarragon
6–8 tablespoons (90–120 ml) olive oil
2–3 tablespoons (30–45 ml) wine vinegar
Salt and freshly ground black pepper
Vinaigrette Sauce (page 691)

Place large, firm, ripe tomatoes in boiling water for a few minutes. Peel and cut each tomato in even-sized thick slices. Re-form tomatoes and place them in a rectangular or oval *hors-d'œuvre* dish.

Mix the next 8 ingredients to form a thick, green, well-flavoured dressing. Sandwich three-quarters of the dressing carefully between layers of each tomato. Chill.

Dilute remaining dressing with a well-flavoured Vinaigrette Sauce; spoon over herb-stuffed tomatoes and serve. Serves 4.

MARINATED MUSHROOM APPETIZER

2 lb (900 g) small button mushrooms
Juice of ½ lemon
Salt
½ pint (300 ml) wine vinegar
¼ pint (150 ml) olive oil
4 cloves garlic, crushed
1 sprig thyme
2 sprigs parsley
1 bay leaf
4–6 peppercorns
12 coriander seeds

Trim stems and wash mushrooms thoroughly. Drain and place in a saucepan with cold water, lemon juice and salt, to taste. Bring gently to a boil; lower heat and simmer for 10 minutes. Place blanched mushrooms in a shallow earthenware dish.

Combine the remaining ingredients in an enamelled saucepan; bring to a boil; lower heat and simmer for 20 minutes. Pour marinade over mushrooms and allow to marinate in the refrigerator for 24 hours. Serves 4.

CELERIAC SALAD

1 celery root
Salted water
½ pint (300 ml) well-flavoured mayonnaise (page 120)
Freshly ground black pepper
Mustard, curry powder or paprika

Trim and wash celery root. Cut into matchstick-sized strips and blanch until tender in boiling salted water. Drain; cool and dry. Dress with mayonnaise seasoned to taste with freshly ground black pepper and mustard, curry powder or paprika. Serves 4.

CUCUMBER-STUFFED TOMATOES

8 large ripe tomatoes
Salt and freshly ground black pepper
½ large cucumber

DRESSING
6 tablespoons (90 ml) olive oil
6 tablespoons (90 ml) wine vinegar
Salt and freshly ground black pepper
Sugar

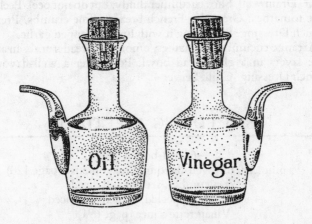

Cut tops off tomatoes and scoop out pulp and seeds. Sprinkle with salt and freshly ground black pepper, to taste. Turn upside down on a plate and chill.

Cut unpeeled cucumber into very thin slices. Place slices on a plate and salt them generously; cover with another plate and place a weight on top. Leave them for 2 hours; then rinse cucumber with cold water; place in a clean towel and press to rid cucumber slices of all liquids.

Make a salad dressing with equal parts of olive oil and wine vinegar; flavour to taste with salt, freshly ground black pepper and a little sugar, and fold sliced cucumber into dressing.

To serve: turn tomato cases right side up; fill with cucumber and serve as an appetizer, or as an accompaniment to poached salmon. Serves 4.

GAZPACHO SALAD

1 Spanish onion
Iced water
1 large cucumber
12 ripe tomatoes
4–6 tablespoons (60–90 ml) dry French breadcrumbs
¼ pint (150 ml) garlic-flavoured French Dressing
(page 691)

Peel and slice Spanish onion thinly and soak in iced water for 1 hour. Drain well. Slice cucumber thinly, but do not peel. Peel and slice tomatoes. Grate dry French bread to fine crumbs. Prepare French Dressing, flavouring it with finely chopped garlic.

Arrange cucumber, tomatoes, onion and breadcrumbs in alternate layers in a glass salad bowl. Pour over a well-flavoured French Dressing. Chill. Serves 4.

SLICED EGG APPETIZER

4–6 hard-boiled eggs
½ pint (300 ml) well-flavoured mayonnaise (page 120)
½ cucumber, seeded and diced
4–6 tomatoes, peeled, seeded and diced
Vinaigrette Sauce (page 691)

Shell eggs and cut into even slices. Place a bed of well-flavoured mayonnaise on a flat *hors-d'œuvre* dish. Cover with 2 rows of overlapping slices of egg. Garnish with a ring of diced cucumber and a ring of diced tomato. Sprinkle vegetables only with a well-flavoured Vinaigrette Sauce. Serves 4 to 6.

GRILLED PEPPERS EN SALADE

4–6 green, red or yellow peppers
Well-flavoured French Dressing (page 691)
Lettuce leaves
Anchovy fillets

Grill or roast peppers as close to the heat as possible, turning them until the skin is charred on all sides. Rub off skins under running cold water. Core, seed and slice peppers into thick strips and marinate in a well-flavoured French Dressing.

Serve as an appetizer salad on a bed of lettuce leaves with a lattice of anchovy fillets for garnish. Or serve in an *hors-d'œuvre* dish with French Dressing only.

Peppers prepared in this way will keep a long time under refrigeration if packed in oil in sterilized airtight jars.

ITALIAN ANTIPASTO PLATTER

1 head lettuce
4 tomatoes, cut in wedges
4 fennel, cut in wedges
1 small can tuna fish or sardines
1 small can artichokes in oil or brine
8 slices Italian salame
4 slices mortadella or prosciutto
8 radishes
8 ripe olives
1 tablespoon (15 ml) finely chopped parsley or capers

ITALIAN DRESSING
¼ pint (150 ml) olive oil
2 anchovy fillets, finely chopped
Lemon juice
Salt and freshly ground black pepper
Capers

Wash and trim lettuce. Dry leaves thoroughly. Cut tomatoes into wedges and toss lightly in Italian Dressing. Clean and trim fennel, and cut into thin wedges; toss lightly in dressing. Drain oil from tuna fish (or sardines); drain oil from artichokes. Chill vegetables.

Arrange lettuce leaves on a large serving dish. Place sliced meats, fish, vegetables, radishes and ripe olives in colourful groups on lettuce. Sprinkle with finely chopped parsley or capers. Serve with crusty bread and butter. Serves 4.

ITALIAN DRESSING

Warm ¼ pint (150 ml) olive oil slightly and add 2 anchovy fillets, finely chopped, mashing them with a fork until they are well blended with the oil. Add lemon juice and salt, pepper and capers, to taste.

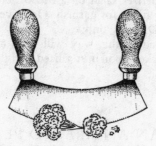

CŒURS DE CÉLERI EN SALADE

2 heads celery
1 chicken stock cube
1 level tablespoon (15 ml) salt
½ pint (300 ml) well-flavoured Vinaigrette Sauce (page 691)
½ level teaspoon (2.5 ml) paprika
Cayenne pepper
¼ pint (150 ml) double cream
4 hard-boiled eggs
4 tablespoons (60 ml) finely chopped parsley

Trim heads of celery, cutting off top third of branches and outside stalks; cut each head in half; put celery in a saucepan with trimmings, chicken stock cube and salt; cover with cold water and bring slowly to a boil. Simmer for 10 minutes; remove from heat and leave in hot water for 5 minutes; drain and cool. Arrange celery in a flat serving dish; spoon over half of the Vinaigrette Sauce and allow celery to marinate in this mixture for at least 1 hour.

Combine remaining Vinaigrette Sauce with paprika, a pinch of cayenne pepper and the double cream; mix well. Separate yolks from white of eggs, and rub each separately through a wire sieve.

To serve: place blanched celery hearts on a serving dish; cover each celery half with dressing; garnish one-third of each portion with sieved egg white, one-third with sieved egg yolk, and remaining third with finely chopped parsley. Serve immediately. Serves 4.

LENTIL SALAD

8 oz (225 g) lentils
1 Spanish onion, finely chopped
2 tablespoons (30 ml) olive oil
1 clove garlic
1 bay leaf
1 tablespoon (15 ml) salt
2½ pints (1.4 lit) water
4 tablespoons (60 ml) olive oil
2 tablespoons (30 ml) wine vinegar
Salt and freshly ground black pepper
Anchovy fillets, tomato wedges and black olives

DRESSING
½ Spanish onion, finely chopped
4 tablespoons (60 ml) finely chopped parsley
1 teaspoon (5 ml) prepared mustard
Salt and freshly ground black pepper
Olive oil
Juice of ½ lemon

Soak lentils overnight in water to cover. Drain. Sauté finely chopped onion in olive oil until transparent. Add garlic, bay leaf, salt and water, and simmer lentils in this stock for about 2 hours, or until tender. Drain and cool; then add olive oil and wine vinegar, and season to taste with salt and freshly ground black pepper.

Prepare dressing; pour over lentils and mix thoroughly; garnish with anchovy fillets, tomato wedges and black olives. Serves 4 to 6.

DRESSING
Combine finely chopped onion, parsley, mustard, salt and freshly ground black pepper in a bowl. Mix well and then pour in olive oil little by little, beating the mixture continuously, until sauce thickens. Flavour to taste with lemon juice.

GEORGE'S INSALATA 'LA MORRA'

8 oz (225 g) raw potatoes
Water
White wine vinegar
8 oz (225 g) cooked breast of chicken
1 slice cooked ham, ¼ inch (6 mm) thick
1 slice cooked tongue, ¼ inch (6 mm) thick
2 oz (50 g) Fontina, Caerphilly or Double Gloucester cheese
6 tablespoons (90 ml) well-flavoured mayonnaise
(page 120)
6 tablespoons (90 ml) whipped cream
Salt and freshly ground black pepper
Canned white truffles

Cut raw potatoes into matchsticks and boil them for 15 to 20 minutes in a mixture of water and white wine vinegar, three-fifths vinegar to two-fifths water. Drain and chill.

Cut chicken, ham, tongue and cheese into matchsticks, combine with potatoes, and dress with mayonnaise and whipped cream seasoned to taste with salt and freshly ground black pepper.

Just before serving, grate truffles over top of salad. Serves 4.

Note: Fontina cheese is firm, not crumbly, and slightly piquant without being strongly flavoured. Caerphilly or Double Gloucester are probably the nearest English equivalents.

Vegetable Appetizers

BAKED AVOCADOS CALIFORNIA

1 pint (600 ml) thick Béchamel Sauce (page 104)
2 tablespoons (30 ml) tomato concentrate
1 tablespoon (15 ml) grated onion
1 tablespoon (15 ml) butter
1 tablespoon (15 ml) curry powder
1 lb (450 g) cooked crabmeat, flaked
2 ripe avocado pears
Salt
Juice of 1 lemon

To 1 pint (600 ml) thick Béchamel Sauce, add 2 tablespoons (30 ml) tomato concentrate and 1 tablespoon (15 ml) each grated onion, butter and curry powder. Fold in flaked crabmeat and heat mixture just to boiling point, but do not let it boil.

Halve 2 avocado pears lengthwise: remove the stones and score flesh with a knife; sprinkle with salt and lemon juice to preserve colour. Pile avocado halves high with crabmeat mixture and arrange in a baking dish; add 1 inch (25 mm) boiling water and cover dish with foil. Bake in a slow oven (350°F/180°C/GM4) for about 20 minutes. Serves 4.

FONDS D'ARTICHAUTS AU FOIE GRAS 'LA MÈRE BRAZIER'

8 large artichokes
Juice of 1 lemon
Boiling water, salted
¼ pint (150 ml) Vinaigrette Sauce (page 691)
Salt and freshly ground black pepper
Green salad
8 thin rounds *pâté de foie gras*

To prepare artichokes: cut off stalks and tough outer leaves; slice through leafy part down to 2 last rows of leaves nearest stalk. Then pare off remaining leaves until only artichoke heart is left.

Remove 'choke' with the sharp edge of your knife and place artichoke hearts in cold water with the juice of lemon added to preserve colour.

Poach artichoke hearts in boiling salted water for about 30 minutes; cool, drain and dry.

Marinate artichoke hearts in a well–flavoured Vinaigrette Sauce for ¾ hour. When ready to serve, arrange on a bed of seasoned salad. Place 1 slice of *pâté de foie gras* on each artichoke heart, and serve. Serves 4.

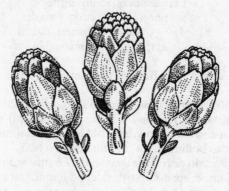

COURGETTE APPETIZER

2 tablespoons (30 ml) finely chopped onion
2 tablespoons (30 ml) finely chopped carrot
2 tablespoons (30 ml) butter
¼ pint (150 ml) dry white wine
¼ pint (150 ml) water
2 crushed garlic cloves
1 *bouquet garni* (2 sprigs parsley, 1 sprig thyme,
1 bay leaf)
12 courgettes (zucchini), sliced and unpeeled

Combine finely chopped onion, carrot and butter in a saucepan with dry white wine and water. Add crushed garlic cloves and *bouquet garni*, and simmer for 15 minutes. Add sliced unpeeled courgettes, and simmer until tender.

Transfer courgettes to an earthenware dish; pour *court-bouillon* over; chill and serve. Serves 4 to 6.

MOROCCAN CARROT APPETIZER

1 lb (450 g) carrots, cut in quarters lengthwise
4 tablespoons (60 ml) water
4 tablespoons (60 ml) olive oil
2 cloves garlic
1–2 tablespoons (15–30 ml) vinegar
Salt and freshly ground black pepper
Cayenne pepper
Paprika
Cumin powder
2 tablespoons (30 ml) finely chopped parsley

Blanch quartered peeled carrots in water to cover until water boils. Drain; add 4 tablespoons (60 ml) each water and olive oil, and the garlic, and simmer until carrots are tender. Drain; add vinegar, salt and pepper generously, and flavour to taste with cayenne, paprika and cumin powder. Garnish with finely chopped parsley. Serve cold as an appetizer. Serves 4.

COLD AUBERGINE
AND TOMATO APPETIZER

4 aubergines (eggplants)
Salt
6–8 ripe tomatoes
2 Spanish onions
Freshly ground black pepper
Olive oil

Peel aubergines and slice thinly. Sprinkle with salt and place slices under a weight for ½ hour. Rinse thoroughly with cold water, drain and dry. Slice tomatoes and onions thinly. Keep separate.

Arrange a thin layer of onion slices in the bottom of a shallow baking dish, then a layer of aubergine slices, then one of tomato slices. Season with freshly ground black pepper. Repeat until all the vegetables are used up, ending with a layer of onion. Pour in olive oil until vegetables are barely covered. Bake in a very slow oven (250°F/130°C/GM½) for about 3 hours, or until vegetables are cooked through. Chill and serve. Serves 6.

PETITS OIGNONS À L'ORIENTALE
'GRAND VENEUR'

2 lb (1 kg) small onions
1 pint (600 ml) water
½ pint (300 ml) white vinegar
5 oz (150 g) sugar
5 oz (150 g) sultanas
4 tablespoons (60 ml) tomato concentrate
4 tablespoons (60 ml) olive oil
Salt and freshly ground black pepper
Cayenne pepper

Combine ingredients in a saucepan and simmer for about ¾ hour.
Serve cold.

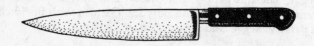

SALADE DE BŒUF

1½ lb (675 g) boiled beef
6 gherkins, thinly sliced
4 tablespoons (60 ml) finely chopped onion
6–8 tablespoons (90–120 ml) olive oil
2–3 tablespoons (30–45 ml) wine vinegar
Salt and freshly ground black pepper
1 tablespoon (15 ml) chopped gherkins
2 tablespoons (30 ml) finely chopped parsley

Trim fat from beef and cut in small, thin slices. Add thinly sliced
gherkins and finely chopped onion, and dress with olive oil, wine
vinegar, and salt and freshly ground black pepper, to taste. Toss
well and marinate in this mixture for at least 2 hours before
serving. Garnish with coarsely chopped gherkins and finely
chopped parsley. Serves 4 to 6.

POTATO SALAD

2 lb (900 g) long thin salad potatoes
6–8 tablespoons (90–120 ml) olive oil
6–8 tablespoons (90–120 ml) dry white wine or
beef consommé
2–3 tablespoons (30–45 ml) wine vinegar
4 tablespoons (60 ml) finely chopped shallots
2 tablespoons (30 ml) finely chopped parsley
Salt and freshly ground black pepper

Boil long thin salad potatoes in their skins until cooked through. Peel and cut into thick slices. While still hot, pour over marinade of olive oil, dry white wine (or beef consommé) and wine vinegar. Add finely chopped shallots and parsley; season to taste with salt and freshly ground black pepper. Serves 4 to 6.

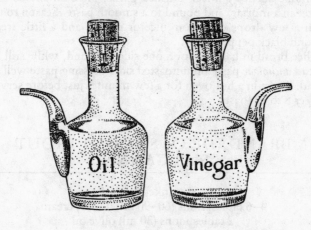

POTATO SALAD NIÇOISE

Prepare Potato Salad as above. Arrange anchovies in a lattice-work on top and place a black olive in the centre of each square. Garnish salad with a ring of tomato slices. Serves 4 to 6.

Bread or Pastry-based Appetizers

L'ANCHOÏADE – HOT ANCHOVY CANAPÉS

1 can anchovy fillets in oil
1 large clove garlic, crushed
1 tablespoon (15 ml) olive oil
1 tablespoon (15 ml) softened butter
Few drops lemon juice or cognac
Freshly ground black pepper
4–6 thick slices white bread

Combine anchovy fillets, crushed garlic, olive oil and softened butter in a mortar, and pound to a smooth paste. Season to taste with a few drops of lemon juice or cognac and a little freshly ground black pepper.

Slice bread in half; toast on one side only and, while still hot, spread *anchoïade* paste on untoasted side, pressing paste well into bread. Toast in a hot oven for a few minutes just before serving. Makes 8 to 12 toasts.

BRANDADE OF SMOKED TROUT SUR CANAPÉ

4 smoked trout
4–6 tablespoons (60–90 ml) double cream
2 tablespoons (30 ml) olive oil
Juice of ½ lemon
Salt and freshly ground black pepper
Sliced white bread
Softened butter
Finely chopped radishes or parsley

Remove skin and bones from smoked trout and pound fillets to a smooth paste in a mortar with double cream and olive oil. Season to taste with lemon juice, salt and freshly ground black pepper. Chill.

Toast white bread and cut rounds of toast with a glass or biscuit cutter. Spread each round with softened butter and then cover generously with smoked trout mixture. Sprinkle with finely chopped radishes or parsley, or a combination of the two.

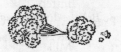

SWISS BACON AND MUSHROOM TOASTS

12 thin slices white bread
8 oz (225 g) grated Swiss cheese
¼ pint (150 ml) double cream
4 eggs
¼ pint (150 ml) milk
8 tablespoons (120 ml) butter

FILLING
12 slices bacon
12–14 mushrooms
2 tablespoons (30 ml) butter
2 tablespoons (30 ml) lemon juice

Trim crusts from bread. Mix Swiss cheese and cream, and spread on all bread slices. Add a filling (see below) to half the bread slices; top with remaining slices, cheese side down. Beat eggs and milk with a fork. Dip sandwiches into egg mixture, coating both sides. Heat butter till bubbling in a large frying pan; brown sandwiches on both sides over moderate heat. Serve with knife and fork or cut into bite-sized pieces. Serves 6.

FILLING
For 6 sandwiches, use 12 slices bacon, and 12 to 14 finely sliced mushrooms sautéed in 2 tablespoons (30 ml) each butter and lemon juice. Fry bacon over moderate heat. Drain on paper towel. Use about 1 tablespoon (15 ml) mushrooms and 2 slices trimmed bacon to fill each sandwich.

BRIOCHE DE FOIE GRAS

8 oz (225 g) *pâté de foie gras*
2 peeled truffles, cut in slivers
Slices of fat salt pork
6 tablespoons (90 ml) Madeira
2 tablespoons (30 ml) cognac
Butter
½ recipe *Brioche* dough (page 802)
1 egg yolk
Milk

Remove fat from *pâté de foie gras* and stud *pâté* with thin slivers of peeled truffle. Wrap the *pâté* in paper-thin slices of fat salt pork and place in a heatproof dish just large enough to hold it comfortably. Pour Madeira wine and cognac over it, and bake in a moderate oven (375°F/190°C/GM5) for 20 minutes. Cool the *pâté* in the dish.

Butter a large *brioche* mould and line it with a sheet of *brioche* dough 1 inch (25 mm) thick and a little larger than necessary to line the mould. Place the *pâté de foie gras* upright in the mould and cover with the overhanging edge of the dough.

Make a ball of the remainder of dough and place it on top of the *brioche*. Stand mould for 20 minutes in a warm place for the dough to rise; brush with egg yolk diluted in a little milk and bake in a hot oven (450°F/230°C/GM7) until the *brioche* is a golden-brown colour, and a wire tester inserted into the dough comes out clean. Cool *brioche*; place on serving dish and serve hot or cold as an *hors-d'œuvre*. Serves 6 to 8.

BRIOCHES FARCIES

8 tiny *brioches* or 4 normal-sized ones
2 smoked sausages, finely chopped
2 oz (50 g) ham, finely chopped
4 tablespoons(60 ml) milk
4 tablespoons (60 ml) cream
4 tablespoons (60 ml) freshly grated Gruyère
Freshly ground black pepper
Salt
1 tablespoon (15 ml) cognac

Cut caps off *brioches* and empty them. Pick apart interiors and combine with finely chopped meat of smoked sausages and cooked ham. Add milk, cream and grated Gruyère, and cook over a very low heat, stirring all the while, until you get a very thick paste. Add pepper, and a very little salt (sausages and ham are already rather salty). All this can be prepared in advance.

When ready to serve: reheat the mixture, stirring constantly. When it is very hot, remove from heat and stir in cognac; fill *brioches* with this mixture, replace caps and heat in the oven for a few minutes until warmed through. Serves 4.

PETITS PÂTÉS LA PROVENÇALE

1 recipe Shortcrust Pastry (page 754)
8 anchovy fillets, finely chopped
1 small onion, finely chopped
1 clove garlic, finely chopped
2–4 tablespoons (30–60 ml) olive oil
2 tablespoons (30 ml) finely chopped parsley
8 oz (225 g) cooked ham or veal, finely chopped
1–2 egg yolks
Salt and freshly ground black pepper

Prepare shortcrust pastry; cut 24 small circles of dough with a biscuit cutter or the top of a glass. Pound the finely chopped anchovy fillets, onion and garlic to a smooth paste in a mortar with olive oil. Blend in finely chopped parsley, ham or veal, and 1 or 2 egg yolks. Mixture must not be too wet. Season to taste with salt and freshly ground black pepper. Place 1 tablespoon (15 ml) of this mixture in the centre of each of the 12 pastry rounds, wet the edges of the dough and cover with remaining pastry rounds, pressing the edges well together. Brush with egg yolk and bake in a moderate oven (375°F/190°C/GM5) for about 20 minutes, or until the crust is golden. Makes 12.

LA CROÛTE LANDAISE

4 fat slices *brioche*
8 oz (225 g) button mushrooms, sliced
4 tablespoons (60 ml) butter
4 tablespoons (60 ml) double cream
Salt and freshly ground black pepper
4 thin rounds *mousse de foie gras*
¼ pint (150 ml) Cream Sauce (page 107)
1 egg yolk
2 tablespoons (30 ml) freshly grated Parmesan

Simmer sliced mushrooms in butter until soft. Purée them with cream; season to taste with salt and freshly ground black pepper. Toast *brioche* slices. Spread each slice thickly with mushroom purée and place on a baking sheet. Top each 'toast' with a slice of *foie gras* and spoon hot Cream Sauce, to which you have added an egg yolk, over each 'toast'. Cover with freshly grated Parmesan and grill until golden. Makes 4.

DÉLICES AU GRUYÈRE

4 tablespoons (60 ml) butter
4 tablespoons (60 ml) flour
¾ pint (450 ml) boiling milk
8 tablespoons (120 ml) freshly grated Gruyère
Freshly grated nutmeg
2 egg yolks
Salt and freshly ground black pepper
1 egg beaten with 2 tablespoons (30 ml) milk and
1 tablespoon (15 ml) olive oil
Fresh breadcrumbs
Oil, for frying

Melt butter in the top of a double saucepan; stir in 4 tablespoons (60 ml) flour and cook over water, stirring continuously with a wooden spoon, until smooth. Pour in boiling milk and mix with a whisk to make a thick sauce.

Simmer sauce for a few minutes longer; add grated Gruyère and a little grated nutmeg, and continue cooking, stirring continuously, until cheese is completely blended into sauce.

Remove sauce from heat; stir in egg yolks; season to taste with salt and freshly ground black pepper, and more nutmeg if desired. Continue to cook over water, stirring continuously, for 2 or 3 minutes, being careful not to let mixture boil. Spread in a rectangular baking tin and allow to cool. Cover with paper or foil and chill in refrigerator for 3 hours, or until needed.

Just before serving, cut into rectangles; flour lightly and dip in egg beaten with milk and olive oil; drain, roll in fresh breadcrumbs and fry in hot oil until golden. Serve immediately. Serves 4 to 6.

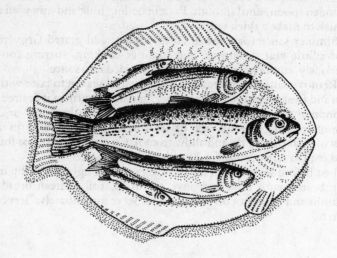

CHAPTER FOUR
Fish

O ne fish, at least, has had as devastating an effect on the history of the world as any conqueror, even Genghis Khan or Alexander the Great.

For the herring once swarmed in their millions up the east coast of the British Isles, to be scooped out of the sea with ease by the least daring of fishermen, and as a result became a staple part of the British diet, fresh, salted or dried.

Then, for some reason – a change in the ocean currents, a chilling of the coastal waters, the change brought about by the inundation of the Wash itself – the herring changed its habits and swam up the centre of the North Sea, midway between England

and Scandinavia, far out, where daring and skill – and a new kind of boat – were necessary. And it was this boat, basically a small fishing craft, that was to smash the naval power of Europe, based on the lumbering galleons that had held the Mediterranean since Roman times, and win for England the greatest empire the world has ever known.

Fish are as ever-present in our lives today; for nowhere in Britain are we more than sixty miles from the sea. Great catches from Newfoundland, Iceland and the Baltic are brought into our markets. But somehow, the great variety available does not find its way into markets throughout the country as it still does in Spain, France and Italy. And when upon occasion it does, fishmongers tell me, Britain's cooks seem loath to take advantage of the less familiar forms of sea life, preferring to stick to the familiar – if expensive – standbys of salmon, sole, trout, turbot, halibut and haddock.

How to Choose Fresh Fish

A fish is fresh when its eye is rounded and bright, when the body is firm, almost stiff, and leaves no imprint when you touch it, and if its scales are close-fitting.

Do not buy fish if it has too pungent an odour; if the scales come off easily; if the eye is sunken in its socket; if the fish droops lazily over the counter; if the area over the stomach or around the vent is green or blackish in colour.

In choosing cut fish such as cod, halibut or salmon, the flesh should have a firm appearance with a close grain. If it looks fibrous and watery, it has been held in storage for too long.

Many cooks think that there is nothing in the world as difficult to cook really well as fish, for its delicate flavour is so easily lost, and its light, creamy flakiness so quickly destroyed. Yet if we follow the simple and elementary rules for its preparation, we can all cook fish to perfection.

Fish Stock from Trimmings

A well-flavoured fish stock can be made at little expense or effort from fish trimmings. This stock can be used for cooking the fish or for making a sauce to accompany it. There is no comparison between a sauce made with a well-flavoured fish stock and one in which milk or water forms the liquid part. So if you have your fish filleted by your fishmonger, ask for the fish trimmings to be included with the fish.

To make the stock: wash the trimmings, discarding any black-looking skin, and break the bones in pieces. Put them in an enamelled saucepan with just enough water to cover them, and add a few parsley stalks, a sliced onion, a few white peppercorns and a little salt. Simmer for at least ½ hour and then strain ready for use. White wine may be added with the water.

Any white fish or the trimmings of white fish – haddock, cod, halibut or flounder – may be used for fish stock. Mackerel, herring and salmon are too oily and too strong in flavour. Uncooked trimmings, however, make a better stock than those which have already been cooked. A cod's head is an economical foundation for a well-flavoured fish stock. And always ask your fishmonger for heads and bones of sole. I also like to add a lobster shell, or the heads and shells of prawns and shrimps, when available.

BASIC FISH STOCK

2 lb (900 g) white fish or
2 lb (900 g) fish heads and bones
4 pints (2.25 lit) cold water
Salt
2 large carrots, diced
1 large turnip, diced
2 stalks celery, diced
2–3 parsley stalks
1 bay leaf
12 white peppercorns
Rind and juice of ½ lemon

Make sure that fish or trimmings are fresh and free from odour. Wash them thoroughly in cold water; cut them in pieces and put them in a saucepan with water and salt; bring slowly to a boil. Add more salt, and skim well. Then add diced vegetables, parsley stalks, bay leaf, peppercorns and thinly peeled lemon rind. Do not use too many vegetables as they will not only darken the stock, but also overpower the flavour of the fish. Allow to simmer slowly for from 1 to 1½ hours; add the lemon juice and strain, ready for use. Fish stock must not be allowed to cook as long as meat stock, or it will become bitter.

Fish stock may be cleared in the same way as meat stock by using raw fish and the whites and shells of eggs, but clear fish soup is rarely seen. When fish stock is used for sauces, it is usually mixed with milk, or made with milk and water.

BASIC COURT-BOUILLON

8 pints (4.5 lit) water
¼ pint (150 ml) wine vinegar
4 oz (100 g) carrots, sliced
4 oz (100 g) onions, sliced
1 handful parsley stalks
1 bay leaf
1 sprig thyme
Coarse salt
12 peppercorns

Combine *court-bouillon* ingredients in a large saucepan or fish kettle and bring to a boil; skim, and boil for 45 minutes. Strain and cool.

To Boil Fish

Whole fish or thick pieces of fish such as salmon, halibut, cod, ling, hake or turbot are best for boiling. If small fish or thin slices, steaks, or fillets are to be cooked in liquid, they should be steamed or poached.

Always put all fish – except salt fish – into water that is very hot but not bubbling too hard, to which you have added ½ oz (15 g) salt and 1 or 2 tablespoons (15–30 ml) vinegar or lemon juice per 4 pints (2.25 lit) water.

A simple *court-bouillon* (quickly made stock) can be made to lend extra savour by the addition of a *bouquet garni* (thyme, bay leaf and parsley), sliced carrots, onion and celery to the water, as well as salt and vinegar or lemon juice. For a more flavoursome *court-bouillon*, add ½ bottle inexpensive dry white wine instead of vinegar, or half white wine and half water may be used. And if the fish tends to be dry, add 2 (30 ml) or more tablespoons olive oil.

A *court-bouillon au bleu* is made by substituting claret for the white wine to give the fish a bluish tinge.

A long solid fish kettle, with a drainer to allow fish to be lifted out easily without being broken, is the best utensil to use for boiling fish. My kettle is 2 feet (70 cm) long, which is just large enough to hold a salmon trout comfortably. When boiling smaller fish or a centre cut of a larger fish, I always fasten the fish to the drainer with a piece of string to prevent it being knocked about during cooking. A large saucepan can be used for boiling fish if a plate is placed on the bottom of the saucepan and the fish tied in a piece of muslin or cheesecloth, with the ends of the cloth hanging over the sides of the pan so that the fish can be raised out of the water easily without being broken.

Do not use too much liquid to cook the fish or the skin will in all probability break. Just enough liquid to cover the fish by 2 inches (50 mm) is a good rule. Allow the liquid to come to a boil again after the fish is put in; then reduce heat to a bare simmer and cook for the required time. If the fish is cooked too quickly, the outside will crack and break before the inside is ready. Remove all scum that rises, for if allowed to remain, it will spoil the appearance of the fish.

Test the fish by flaking it with a fork before it is lifted from the water; the flesh ought to have lost its clear appearance and to have become white and opaque. It should also come away from the bone easily; a wooden skewer may be pushed in gently to try this. Overcooked fish is flavourless.

As soon as the fish is ready, lift it out of the cooking liquid and drain it well. If it cannot be served at once, keep it warm on the drainer placed across the fish kettle and covered over with a hot clean cloth. Garnish with fresh parsley and lemon wedges, and serve sauce separately. Boiled or steamed potatoes are usually served with boiled fish.

To Steam Fish

Fish steaks or fillets – salmon, cod, sole, turbot – or whole small fish can be cooked to perfection by steaming. If only a small quantity of fish is required – enough for 1 to 2 persons – you can steam it very simply between two plates. Butter one plate generously; place the fish on it and season to taste with salt, freshly ground black pepper and lemon juice. Add a little finely chopped mushroom and onion for extra savour, or, for a more exotic flavour, a little finely chopped green onion and a mixture of equal parts *sake* (or dry sherry) and soy sauce.

Cover with a piece of well-buttered paper and invert a second plate over top. Place plates on a saucepan of boiling water and allow fish to steam for 20 to 30 minutes, or until the fish flakes easily with a fork. The liquids in the plate should be served with the fish or slightly thickened with a *beurre manié* and then poured over the fish.

For larger fish – or a greater number of servings – a steamer is necessary. I use a special oval steamer which consists of a double saucepan with a perforated bottom to allow the steam to rise. This is big enough to steam 4 to 6 trout; a good centre cut of salmon; several lobsters; a capon; or a large platter of meat and vegetables in the Chinese manner.

To steam fish: plate fish in a well-buttered oval baking dish; sprinkle with 1 to 2 tablespoons (15–30 ml) each finely chopped onion and mushrooms; moisten with 4 to 6 tablespoons (60–90 ml) dry white wine, canned clam juice or well-flavoured fish stock; season to taste with salt and freshly ground black pepper, and place over boiling water to which you have added a clove or two of garlic for a flavour of the sea. Cover tightly and steam until fish flakes easily with a fork.

To Poach Fish

One of the most delicate ways of cooking fish fillets and small fish steaks or cutlets is to poach them in equal quantities of well-flavoured fish stock and dry white wine. Butter a shallow heat-proof *gratin* dish and place the fillets of fish in it; season with salt, freshly ground black pepper and a little lemon juice, and barely cover them with fish stock and wine. Place a piece of well-buttered waxed paper over fish and cook in a hot oven (450°F/ 230°C/GM8) or on top of the stove until the fish is tender and opaque (about 8 to 12 minutes for the more delicate fish).

To serve: lift dish out carefully, draining it well, and place it on a heated serving dish. Keep warm. Thicken pan liquids slightly with a *beurre manié* or with an egg yolk mixed with a little double cream and lemon juice, to taste. Serve with the fish. This manner of cooking fish is guaranteed to bring out the utmost in flavour of the most delicate fish.

To Grill Fish

Wash and clean fish; dry them lightly and score the skin across diagonally on both sides to prevent it cracking during cooking. Season with salt and freshly ground black pepper, and brush with olive oil or melted butter. Or marinate fish for 2 hours before cooking in equal quantities of olive oil and dry white wine with a little finely chopped garlic and a crumbled bay leaf or two. Or the fish may be split open, the bones removed, and then lightly coated with flour, egg and breadcrumbs, or fine oatmeal.

Always heat the grid thoroughly and grease it well before you place the fish on it. Keep the fish rather close to the fire while cooking or it will become flabby. Cook fish for 8 to 12 minutes according to its thickness, and turn it at least once during cooking time. I like to serve grilled fish with lemon quarters and *maître d'hôtel* or *fines herbes* butter.

To Bake Fish

The simplest method of baking fish is to place it in a well-buttered heatproof baking dish with a little finely chopped onion and mushroom, and salt and freshly ground black pepper, to taste; cover it with buttered waxed paper or foil, and cook in a moderate oven (375°F/190°C/GM5) until fish flakes with a fork. The fish may be served with or without sauce.

Otherwise the fish may be first poached for a few minutes in a little fish stock and then baked *au gratin* with butter, finely chopped parsley, mushrooms and shallots, and sprinkled with freshly grated breadcrumbs and Parmesan cheese; or a little Béchamel or Velouté Sauce may be poured around the fish before it is dotted with butter and sprinkled with chopped parsley, mushrooms, shallots and cheese.

To Fry Fish

When properly fried, fish should be a light golden brown and dry and crisp in texture, as free from fat as if it had never touched it. I like to deep-fry fish in a combination of lard and oil to give added flavour; for pan-frying or oven-frying I use butter or olive oil, or a combination of the two.

Small fish are better fried whole, large ones should be filleted or cut into steaks or cutlets.

To fry well, fish should be perfectly dry. Always pat fish dry with a clean cloth or paper towel before coating it with seasoned flour, fine oatmeal or cornmeal, beaten egg and dry breadcrumbs, or a frying batter. This serves two purposes: (1) to keep fat from entering the fish while it is immersed in the hot cooking fat or oil; and (2) to add a flavoursome crunchy coating to the fried fish, which adds enormously to the delicately flavoured flesh within.

If seasoned flour or flour and milk are used as a coating, apply it just before the fish is to be cooked, or the flour will become moist and the fish will not fry well. Batter, too, should be applied only at the last moment. But the fish may be coated with egg and dry breadcrumbs some time before it is to be fried – even the night before if the fish is to be served for breakfast.

PAN-FRYING

This method of cooking sautés delicately flavoured fish such as sole, plaice, brill or trout in ⅛ inch (3 mm) butter in a frying pan. Finely chopped parsley, lemon juice or slivered almonds are sometimes added to the sauce obtained. It is a good idea to add a little olive oil to the butter first to keep it from browning during the cooking process. Allow it to sizzle; lay in the prepared fish and cook gently, making sure that the entire bottom surface of the fish is in contact with the butter. When the fish begins to take on colour, add more butter. Then turn the fish with a fish slice or a palette knife and continue to cook until it flakes easily with a fork.

OVEN-FRYING

Heat the oven to 400°F/200°C/GM6. Cover the bottom of a shallow baking dish with butter and a little olive oil (about ¼ inch (6 mm)), and heat the dish in the oven until the butter sizzles. Brush fish with olive oil or melted butter and roll it in dry breadcrumbs mixed with chopped fresh herbs (parsley, chervil, chives, etc.) and a little grated lemon rind. Cook in the oven until tender, turning once during cooking time. See Plaice à la niçoise (page 201) for a Mediterranean variation of this simple cooking method.

DEEP-FRYING

Deep-fried fish should never be greasy. Thus the temperature of the fat or oil used for frying is of prime importance. It must be hot enough to seal the protective coating of flour, oatmeal, cornmeal, egg and breadcrumbs, batter or pastry at the very moment of immersion. This prevents grease from penetrating the food and keeps in the flavour and juices of the fish.

Deep-frying is simple when you know how. Vegetable fats and oils are the most pleasant to use – with a little lard added for extra flavour. Test the heat of your fat with an inch (25 mm) cube of day-old bread. If the temperature is right for deep-frying, the bread will brown on one side in about 40 seconds.

Do not put too many pieces of fish into the fat or oil at one time, or it will cool down so much that it will soak through the coating or batter. If you use a frying basket, do not let pieces overlap or the fish will not cook through. Cook until fish are golden brown; then lift out and drain on paper towels. If a frying basket is not used, a perforated spoon or skimmer is best for lifting out fish.

1. Use enough fat or oil to cover fish completely.
2. Do not allow fat to smoke or boil.
3. The temperature of the fat should vary as little as possible during cooking.
4. If fat becomes too hot or begins to smoke, drop a slice of raw potato into it to reduce temperature.
5. Always allow the fat or oil to reheat before adding a fresh lot of fish.
6. If you plunge fish into the fat a second time, the temperature of the second cooking should be higher than that of the first.

The Herring Family

The herring is a superb fish. Highly nutritious, rich in flavour, and incredibly cheap, this silvery fish is ample proof – if proof were needed – that the British react oddly to plenty.

For years, oysters – so prized by the Romans that they carried them all the way from Thames to Tiber – were inextricably linked with poverty, like winkles today. Rabbits were ignored while they bounded over the countryside, whereas the French have revelled for centuries in the delicacy of their meat. Salmon, being common, was refused even by the servants; while the herring, one of the richest and most succulent of fishes, made the great error of swarming round our shores, with the result that it was eaten only for breakfast or at most grilled and served with a mustard sauce as a luncheon appetizer. Madame Prunier astounded London between the wars by serving this non-U denizen of the deep, superbly cooked, for lunch and dinner at her elegant restaurant in St James's.

'The herring is one of the most delicious of marine fishes and would certainly be considered one of the greatest delicacies of the table if rare and costly,' wrote André Simon despairingly many years ago. So let us make the most of the herring. The most widely distributed of all types of fish, a member of the same family as the sprat, the pilchard and the shad, the herring is a delight when fresh. And because it swarms so near our shores, it can be sold fresher than almost any other fish we can buy, its taste – un-iced – more delicate than that of cousins brought in from the distant ocean fishing grounds.

When fresh, the herring has a bright and silvery appearance; if red about the gills, it has been dead some time. It should be plump in form and well covered with scales.

The herring is dried and cured in a great variety of ways around the world. Britain produces the kipper, the bloater, the salt – and the red herring. Almost every country has its own method of curing.

Sprats

These are fish of the same family as the herring, only much smaller in size, their ordinary length being 4 to 5 inches (10–13 cm). Like the herring they are oily in nature, but they are delicious when fresh, and usually very cheap.

Sprats are bright and silvery when very fresh. Clean them carefully and draw insides out through the gills without opening the fish. Fresh sprats may be grilled, fried, baked, or 'soused' like herrings.

The young of both sprats and herrings are sold as whitebait.

In season from October to March, they are dried on the Continent and are delicious when eaten as an *hors-d'œuvre* – skinned and raw.

Pilchards or Sardines

The pilchard is the aristocrat of the herring family. When young, they are canned by the French and the Portuguese as sardines, their quality depending largely on the olive oil they are packed in, and on the length of time they are left to mature in the can. As they move north, they grow larger. Still slightly smaller than the herring, they are caught off the coasts of Devon and Cornwall between July and December, and are excellent fresh, salted or canned.

Whitebait

A very small fish with a silvery appearance, whitebait is actually the small fry of the sprat or the common herring. It is considered a great delicacy on account of its delicate flavour and tenderness. It is a special favourite with the Londoner and is caught in large quantities near the mouth of the Thames. It makes its first appearance in March and is at its best from May to August. It is usually fried (see recipe on page 173) and served hot with lemon wedges.

GRILLED HERRINGS I

Step 1: Clean and scale fresh herrings, taking care not to break the delicate skin underneath; cut off heads; wash and dry carefully.
Step 2: Make 2 shallow incisions on sides of each fish with a sharp knife.
Step 3: Dip herrings in seasoned flour and then in melted butter; sprinkle with lemon juice and grill on a well-oiled baking sheet for 5 to 8 minutes on each side, or until they are cooked through.

Serve immediately with lemon wedges or with Hollandaise or Mustard Hollandaise (page 123).

GRILLED HERRINGS II

Step 1: As in first version.
Step 2: Split fish and brush generously with melted butter. Sprinkle with salt and freshly ground black pepper, to taste.
Step 3: Place fish skin side down on a well-oiled sheet, and grill them 4 or 5 inches (10 or 13 cms) from the heat for 10 to 15 minutes, or until the flesh is golden brown and flakes readily at the touch of a fork. Serve immediately with lemon wedges or with sauce as above.

FRIED HERRINGS

Step 1: As above.
Step 2: Make 2 or 3 shallow incisions on sides of each fish with a sharp knife.
Step 3: Dip herrings in well-seasoned flour and fry them on both sides in equal quantities of lard and butter in a large thick-bottomed frying pan. Serve with lemon wedges or with Hollandaise or Tartare Sauce (page 120 or 121).

BAKED HERRINGS

Step 1: As above.
Step 2: Remove roes; detach skin and pound roes with an equal amount of softened butter. Force mixture through a fine sieve; mix in 2 to 4 tablespoons (30–60 ml) fresh breadcrumbs, flavour with finely chopped parsley, and season to taste with salt and freshly ground black pepper.
Step 3: Slit herrings down backbone with a sharp knife and remove backbone carefully, snipping both ends free with kitchen scissors.
Step 4: Stuff herrings with roe mixture and place fish in a lightly buttered shallow ovenproof dish. Sprinkle lightly with breadcrumbs, finely chopped parsley and melted butter.

Step 5: Cover fish with buttered paper and bake in a moderately hot oven (400°F/200°C/GM6) for 15 to 20 minutes, or until cooked through. Just before serving, brown under grill. Serve with lemon wedges.

GRILLED HERRINGS WITH MUSTARD

4 fresh herrings
2 tablespoons (30 ml) flour
Salt and freshly ground black pepper
Olive oil
French mustard
Freshly grated breadcrumbs
4 tablespoons (60 ml) melted butter
Boiled new potatoes

Clean and scale fresh herrings, taking care not to break skin underneath. Cut off heads, and wash and dry fish carefully.

Make 3 shallow incisions on sides of each fish with a sharp knife. Dip herrings in seasoned flour; brush them with olive oil and grill on a well-oiled baking sheet for 3 to 4 minutes on each side.

Arrange herrings in a shallow ovenproof *gratin* dish; brush them liberally with French mustard; sprinkle with freshly grated breadcrumbs and melted butter, and put in a very hot oven (475°F/240°C/GM9) for 5 minutes. Serve in the *gratin* dish with boiled new potatoes. Serves 4.

SOUSED HERRINGS

12 fresh herrings
1 Spanish onion, finely chopped
¼ pint (150 ml) double cream
Salt and freshly ground black pepper
2 tablespoons (30 ml) pickling spice
Dry cider or dry white wine
¼ pint (150 ml) sour cream
½ cucumber, thinly sliced

Split herrings down the back; remove backbones carefully and stuff with their soft roes mixed with half the finely chopped onion, double cream, and salt and freshly ground black pepper, to taste.

Sprinkle half remaining chopped onion on the bottom of a shallow heatproof baking dish, season with 1 tablespoon (15 ml) pickling spice and arrange the fish on this bed, head to tail.

Cover with remaining spice and finely chopped onion; pour in dry cider or dry white wine to cover, and bake in a moderate oven (375°F/190°C/GM5), covered, until fish flakes easily with a fork. Cool; then remove fish; strain cooking liquids and blend with sour cream. Season to taste with salt and freshly ground black pepper. Arrange fish on a serving dish; pour over cream sauce and garnish with thinly sliced cucumber. Serves 6.

WHITEBAIT FRIED IN LARD

Whitebait
Iced water
Flour
Lard, for deep-frying
Salt and freshly ground black pepper
Lemon wedges

Put whitebait in a shallow bowl with ice cubes and a little water. Just before frying, spread fish on a clean tea cloth to dry. Place on paper liberally dusted with well-seasoned flour and dredge with more flour; place in a wire basket and shake off surplus flour. Then plunge the basket into very hot lard and fry quickly for 3 to 5 minutes, shaking basket continually to keep fish apart while cooking.

Lift basket from fat and shake it well before transferring fish to paper towels to drain. Place whitebait on a heated serving dish in a warm oven and repeat until all the whitebait are fried. Season with salt and freshly ground black pepper, and serve with lemon wedges.

Cod

The very word 'cod' seems to have an aura of dullness about it. But if it is usually a boring fish, the fault lies with the cook, not with the fish itself. A little imagination applied to the cod has produced marvellous meals all round the world, or at least all round the Atlantic, where it abounds. In Norway, or the United States where the fish has given its name to one of the most fashionable places on the whole East Coast, Cape Cod, the flavour of fresh cod is a revelation.

It was at the Cape that I first encountered the pleasures of fresh cod. As a boy, I used to spend my summers with the family in a small beach cottage right in the dunes by the water's edge. There the holidays were spent fishing, clamming and swimming: wonderful carefree weeks of sun and sea, with driftwood fires burning on foggy and rainy days, and with the ever-present smell of the sea around us. Clams dug from the sandy waters right at the door, fresh lobsters, grilled or steamed, and served with melted butter, dried bluefish and steamed cod were the foods I most looked forward to.

Steamed cod was our great discovery at the Cape, perhaps the easiest kind of cooking I know. We used to place the spanking-fresh cod steaks – large slices from near the shoulder – in a buttered *gratin* dish; season them to taste with salt, pepper, a little finely chopped onion and some clam juice, now available canned in Britain; dot them with butter and steam them over 1 pint (600 ml) of water lightly seasoned with 1 clove of garlic to give a subtle flavour and bring out the taste of the sea. Drawn butter flavoured with a little lemon juice was always served with the cod.

Almost every part of the cod is used in some way or other. Cod's roe, usually sold separately, is the inexpensive basis for many light *hors-d'œuvre* and appetizers; smoked roe is used for Greek taramasalata. Cod's tongues, both fresh and salted, and cod's liver, when made into a richly flavoured *pâté*, are much prized by the French.

And salt cod is a world-wide favourite – from New England, where it is made into delicious codfish balls for breakfast, to Provence, where it is served at its creamy best in a *brandade* (literally, a beating up) *de morue* (salt cold). This traditional Lenten dish combines poached salt cod with cream, olive oil and lemon juice, beats it to a smooth, highly flavoured purée, and serves the delicious end-result surrounded with crisp-fried *croûtons* of bread and pitted black olives.

Salt cod choice number two, from Provence, is *bouillabaisse de morue* (a robust sea chowder from the hill towns, for this is one *bouillabaisse* which needs no fresh fish). Here the basic cod is backed by onions, leeks, tomatoes, potatoes and the aromatics of Provence: saffron, fennel, thyme, orange peel and garlic.

To Buy Cod

Look for a short, plump fish with the head and tail small in proportion to the size of the body. Fresh cod can be bought whole, in steaks or centre cuts, or in fresh or frozen fillets. Salt cod can be bought by the half fish or 'flake', or in packaged fillets.

To Cook Cod

FRESH COD
Fresh cod may be steamed, poached, grilled, sautéed or baked.

Never overcook cod. It should be cooked to just that point of doneness when the flesh is still moist but flakes easily with a fork. When baking cod uncovered, baste frequently with light stock and butter, or dry white wine and butter, or lemon juice and butter. Add a bay leaf and a pinch of fresh or dried herbs to the basting liquor.

To marinate fresh cod: I like to marinate cod steaks or fillets for added flavour. Marinated cod may be cooked in any of the above ways.

Marinade 1: Equal parts of olive oil and dry white wine, flavoured with finely chopped garlic and parsley, crumbled bay leaf, and salt and freshly ground pepper, to taste. Marinate fish in this mixture for at least 4 hours, turning fish from time to time.

Marinade 2: Combine 1 sliced onion, ½ sliced lemon, 2 table-spoons (30 ml) chopped parsley, 1 crumbled bay leaf, 1 level teaspoon (5 ml) peppercorns, ½ level teaspoon (2.5 ml) each

thyme and allspice, 3 tablespoons (45 ml) vinegar, 1 level tablespoon (15 ml) salt and ½ pint (300 ml) water in a porcelain bowl.
Marinate fish in this mixture for at least 4 hours, turning it from
time to time.

   After use, the marinade will keep for 2 weeks if placed in a
covered container in the refrigerator.

TO COOK SALT COD
Soak overnight in a bowl under gently running water. Drain; put
salt cod in a saucepan, cover with cold water and bring to a boil;
drain and return to saucepan; cover with cold water and bring to
boil again; turn off heat and allow to steep in hot water for 10
minutes. Use as directed.

MEG DODS'S COD'S HEAD AND SHOULDERS

Cod's Head and Shoulders – a famous Norwegian speciality to
this day – used to be a favourite with cooks in this country, as this
interesting old recipe shows.

'Have a quart of good stock ready for the sauce, made of beef or
veal, seasoned with onion, carrot, and turnip. Rub the fish with
salt overnight, taking off the scales, but do not wash it. When to
be dressed, wash it clean, then quickly dash hot water over the
upper side, and with a blunt knife remove the slime which will
ooze out, taking care not to break the skin. Do the same to the
other side of the fish; then place it on the drainer, wipe it clean, and
plunge it into a turbot-kettle of boiling water, with a handful of
salt and a half-pint of vinegar. It must be entirely covered, and
will take from thirty to forty minutes' slow boiling. Set it to
drain, slide it carefully on a deep dish, and glaze with beaten eggs,
over which strew fine bread-crumbs, grated lemon-peel, pepper
and salt. Stick numerous bits of butter over the fish, and set it
before a clear fire, strewing more crumbs, grated lemon-peel and
minced parsley over it, and basting with the butter. In the
meanwhile thicken the stock with butter kneaded in flour, and
strain it, adding to it half a hundred oysters nicely picked and
bearded, and a glassful of their liquor, two glasses of Madeira or
sherry, the juice of a lemon, the hard meat of a boiled lobster cut

down and the soft part pounded. Boil this sauce for five minutes, and skim it well; wipe clean the edges of the dish in which the fish is crisping, and pour half of the sauce around it, serving the rest in a tureen.'

BROCHETTES OF COD AND SOLE WITH MUSTARD SAUCE

2 thick cod steaks
2 small sole, filleted
Salt
Flour
Oil, for frying

MUSTARD SAUCE
1 tablespoon (15 ml) butter
1 tablespoon (15 ml) olive oil
1 onion, coarsely chopped
1 bunch parsley stalks
Salt and freshly ground black pepper
1 tablespoon (15 ml) flour
½ pint (300 ml) canned clam juice
¼ pint (150 ml) dry white wine
1 tablespoon (15 ml) mustard

MUSTARD SAUCE
Heat butter and oil in a saucepan; add chopped onion and parsley stalks, season to taste with salt and freshly ground black pepper, and sauté, stirring continuously, until onion is transparent. Sprinkle with flour and stir until well blended; add clam juice and wine, and simmer gently for 20 minutes.

Place mustard in the top of a double saucepan and strain stock over it, pressing onion and parsley stalks well against sieve with a wooden spoon. Mix well over water and continue to cook until sauce is thick and smooth.

When ready to serve: cut fish into 1-inch (25 mm) squares and arrange them on small skewers. Salt and flour them, and deep-fry in very hot oil until golden. Serve *brochettes* immediately, accompanied by sauce. Serves 4.

MARINATED COD STEAKS

4 slices fresh cod, about 1 inch (25 mm) thick
Onion
Canned clam juice or well-flavoured fish stock
Salt and freshly ground black pepper
4 large peeled potatoes

SAUCE
1 tablespoon (15 ml) butter
1 tablespoon (15 ml) flour
¼ pint (150 ml) canned clam juice or
well-flavoured fish stock
Salt and cayenne pepper
1 egg yolk
¼ pint (150 ml) double cream
Juice of ¼ lemon

GARNISH
8 heart-shaped *croûtons*
4 slices grilled bacon
2 tablespoons (60 ml) finely chopped parsley

Marinate cod slices for at least 4 hours in Marinade 1 or 2 (page 175). Place marinated cod steaks in (1) a well-buttered *gratin* dish with 1 tablespoon (15 ml) finely chopped onion and 2 to 4 tablespoons (30–60 ml) clam juice; place in double steamer; cover and steam until tender (10 to 15 minutes); or (2) in a saucepan on a bed of sliced onion; add ¼ pint (150 ml) clam juice and just enough water to cover fish; season to taste with salt and freshly ground black pepper; cover pan, bring to a boil; lower heat and simmer gently for 15 to 20 minutes, or until fish flakes easily with a fork.

Scoop balls from potatoes with a potato scoop; boil them in salted water for 15 minutes. Drain and reserve.

SAUCE
Heat butter in the top of a double saucepan; add flour and cook over water, stirring, until sauce is smooth and thick. Add canned clam juice or stock; season to taste with salt and cayenne pepper, and simmer until smooth. Stir in egg yolk, cream and lemon juice, and simmer until thickened, being careful not to let sauce

come to a boil. Strain through a fine sieve into a clean saucepan. Add potato balls to sauce and heat for 3 minutes, stirring from time to time.

To serve: place fish on a heated serving dish; garnish with *croûtons*, grilled bacon and finely chopped parsley, and serve accompanied by sauce. Serves 4.

BRANDADE DE MORUE
(CREAM OF SALT COD)

1 lb (450 g) salt cod fillets (smoked haddock
fillets may be used in another delicious
version of this dish)
1–2 cloves garlic, crushed
6 tablespoons (90 ml) double cream
¼ pint (150 ml) olive oil
1–2 boiled potatoes (optional)
Juice and finely grated rind of ½ lemon
Freshly ground black pepper
Toast triangles fried in butter

Soak cod fillets overnight in a bowl under gently running water. Drain; put salt cod in a saucepan, cover with cold water and bring to a boil; drain and return to saucepan; cover with cold water and bring to a boil again; turn off heat and allow to steep in hot water for 10 minutes. Strain cod, remove skin and bones, and flake fish with a fork.

Place cod fillets in electric blender with crushed garlic, 2 tablespoons (30 ml) cream and 4 tablespoons (60 ml) olive oil, and blend (or work mixture to a smooth paste with a mortar and pestle), from time to time adding remainder of cream and olive oil alternately until they are completely absorbed and the *brandade* has the consistency of puréed potatoes. If mixture is too salty, add more potatoes, to taste.

Simmer mixture in a double saucepan or over water until heated through. Stir in lemon juice and grated peel, and season to taste with freshly ground black pepper.

Brandade de morue may be served hot or cold. If hot, place in a mound on a warm serving dish and surround with toast triangles fried in butter.

MEDAILLONS OF COD

12 oz (350 g) cod
Court-bouillon (flavoured with thyme, parsley
bay leaf, ½ Spanish onion, salt, peppercorns and
2 tablespoons (30 ml) olive oil)
1 large Spanish onion, finely chopped
Butter
4 potatoes, puréed
2 eggs, beaten
1 level tablespoon (15 ml) cornflour
4 tablespoons (60 ml) cold milk
Salt and freshly ground black pepper
Freshly grated nutmeg
Flour
Oil, for frying
4–6 tablespoons (60–90 ml) melted butter
Juice of ½ lemon

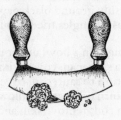

Simmer cod in 1 pint (600 ml) *court-bouillon* (water, thyme, parsley, bay leaf, ½ Spanish onion, salt, peppercorns and 2 tablespoons (30 ml) olive oil) for 20 minutes. Drain, and remove skin and bones.

Sauté finely chopped onion in butter until transparent and soft. Pound cod in mortar until smooth; add onion, puréed potatoes and eggs, and mix to a smooth paste.

Mix cornflour in milk until smooth and blend thoroughly into fish mixture. Season to taste with salt, freshly ground black pepper and nutmeg, and form mixture into cakes. Dust lightly with flour and fry in hot oil until golden. Drain on folded paper towels, and serve with a sauce of melted butter and lemon juice. Serves 4.

NEW ENGLAND FISH BALLS

12 oz (350 g) cooked salt cod, flaked
1 tablespoon (15 ml) grated onion
4 tablespoons (60 ml) milk
Freshly ground black pepper
12 oz (350 g) cooked potatoes, mashed
2 eggs
Flour
Butter or olive oil
Tomato Sauce (page 124)

Soak cod overnight in a bowl under gently running water. Drain and place in a saucepan; cover with cold water and bring slowly to a boil. Drain and return to saucepan; cover with cold water and bring to a boil again. Remove from heat and allow to steep in hot water for 10 minutes. Drain, and remove skin and bones.

Combine grated onion, milk, freshly ground black pepper, cod and mashed potatoes. Bind with raw egg. If mixture is too dry, add a little more milk.

Shape mixture into small balls, flour them and brown on both sides in a little hot butter or oil, or a combination of the two. Serve with Tomato Sauce.

STEAMED SALT COD IN THE ITALIAN MANNER

2 lb (900 g) salt cod

SAUCE
2 tablespoons (30 ml) finely chopped Spanish onion
4 tablespoons (60 ml) finely chopped parsley
2 cloves garlic, finely chopped
8 tablespoons (120 ml) olive oil
Juice of ½ large lemon
Salt, freshly ground black pepper and
monosodium glutamate

To cook salt cod: soak cod overnight in a bowl under gently running water. Drain; put salt cod in a saucepan; cover with cold water and bring to a boil; drain and return to saucepan; cover with cold water and bring to a boil; turn off heat and allow to steep in hot water for 10 minutes. Strain, and remove skin and bones.

Combine sauce ingredients and chill. When ready to serve, pour sauce over poached (or steamed) salt cod. Serves 4 to 6.

BOUILLABAISSE DE MORUE

1½ lb (675 g) salt cod
2 Spanish onions, sliced
2 leeks (white parts only), sliced
4 tablespoons (60 ml) olive oil
4 tomatoes, peeled, seeded and diced
2 tablespoons (30 ml) butter
2 pints (1.1 lit) water
1 *bouquet garni* (2 sprigs thyme, 1 sprig fennel, 1 bay leaf)
1 strip orange peel
2 cloves garlic, crushed
¼ teaspoon (1.25 ml) powdered saffron
Freshly ground black pepper
2 lb (900 g) potatoes, peeled and sliced
Stale French bread, garlic, grated cheese
Finely chopped parsley

Soak salt cod overnight. Drain and cut into large cubes.

Sauté sliced onions and leeks in olive oil until transparent. Simmer tomatoes in butter until smooth. Fill a large saucepan with water; add vegetables with *bouquet garni*, orange peel, crushed garlic and saffron, and season to taste with freshly ground black pepper.

Bring to a boil; add sliced potatoes, and when they are half cooked, add cubed salt cod. Lower heat and simmer *bouillabaisse* until cod is tender.

To serve: place slices of stale French bread rubbed with garlic and sprinkled with grated cheese in individual soup dishes; pour over *bouillon*; serve cod and potatoes on a separate serving dish, sprinkled with finely chopped parsley. Serves 6 to 8.

Haddock

One of our most useful fish, fresh haddock (a smaller version of the cod) is obtainable all the year round, but is at its best from October until the beginning of January.

To Buy Haddock

The average market size weighs 2½ to 3 pounds (1.1–1.4 kg). The flesh is white and firm with a delicate flavour, and can be prepared in a variety of ways. Choose medium-sized haddock, as the flesh is inclined to be coarse when the fish grows to a large size.

To Cook Haddock

FRESH HADDOCK
Fresh haddock may be steamed, poached, grilled, sautéed or baked.

SMOKED HADDOCK
In Britain, smoked haddock is a traditional breakfast dish grilled, boiled or served with *maître d'hôtel* butter. I like to serve this excellent fish creamed (poached in water and milk until tender and then folded into a rich sauce made of equal quantities of double cream and stock from the haddock, and cooked with a *roux* until thick and creamy). Try smoked haddock, too, made into a creamy *brandade*.

FRESH HADDOCK WITH LEMON BUTTER

4 fillets fresh haddock
Salted water
Sprigs of fresh parsley
Boiled potatoes
4 oz (100 g) butter, melted
Juice of ½ lemon
Salt and freshly ground black pepper

Cut fillets into manageable portions and poach them gently in simmering salted water for about 20 minutes, or until fish flakes easily with a fork. Serve on a heated serving dish, garnished with sprigs of parsley and boiled potatoes. Serve with melted butter seasoned to taste with lemon juice, salt and freshly ground black pepper. Serves 4.

BAKED FRESH HADDOCK

1 small fresh haddock (about 3 lb (1.4 kg))
¼ Spanish onion, finely chopped
8 button mushrooms, finely chopped
2 tablepoons (30 ml) butter
2 tablespoons (30 ml) finely chopped parsley
Salt and freshly ground black pepper
¼ pint (150 ml) double cream or dry white wine

Sauté finely chopped onion and mushrooms in butter until onion is transparent. Have fish cleaned and scaled. Wipe it well with a damp cloth and place it in a well-buttered shallow baking dish in which you have sprinkled half the onion and mushroom mixture.

Cover fish with remaining onions and mushrooms; season with finely chopped parsley, and salt and freshly ground black pepper, to taste, and add ¼ pint (150 ml) double cream or dry white wine. Bake in a moderate oven (375°F/190°C/GM5) until fish flakes easily with a fork. Serve immediately in the casserole. Serves 4 to 6.

SMOKED HADDOCK IN COURT-BOUILLON

2 lb (900 g) smoked haddock fillets
Water and milk, to cover
Melted butter
Thin lemon slices

Soak haddock in water for 2 hours. Drain fish and put in a saucepan; cover with equal amounts of water and milk, and bring to a fast boil. Remove from heat and allow to stand for 15 minutes. Drain haddock, reserving stock for some other use (see below). Serve with melted butter and thin lemon slices. Serves 4 to 6.

CREAMED HADDOCK

2 lb (900 g) smoked haddock, cooked as above
3 tablespoons (45 ml) butter
3 tablespoons (45 ml) flour
¾ pint (450 ml) double cream
½ pint (300 ml) haddock stock (see above)
Freshly ground black pepper and grated nutmeg
Triangles of bread sautéed in butter

Melt butter in the top of a double saucepan; stir in flour and cook over water for 3 minutes, stirring continuously until smooth. Add cream and ½ pint (300 ml) haddock stock (see above), and continue to cook, stirring from time to time. Season to taste with freshly ground black pepper and a little grated nutmeg.

Fold haddock pieces (with skin and bones removed) into sauce and simmer gently until ready to use. Serve in a shallow casserole, surrounded by triangles of bread sautéed in butter. Serves 4 to 6.

SMOKED HADDOCK AU FOUR

2 lb (900 g) smoked haddock fillets
Butter
Hot milk
Boiled new potatoes
Lemon quarters

Soak haddock fillets in water for 2 hours. Drain fish and arrange in a well-buttered shallow baking dish. Add barely enough hot milk to cover fish. Dot with butter and bake in a moderate oven (375°F/190°C/GM5) until fish flakes with a fork. Serve in the baking dish, accompanied by boiled new potatoes and lemon quarters. Serves 4 to 6.

Hake

The hake is a large fish, somewhat resembling the cod in appearance, but with a hook-shaped fin on the back of its head. The flesh is tender and white, and flakes easily. When very fresh, hake has a most delicate flavour, infinitely finer than cod. It is a useful fish for sauced dishes, as its bones are so easy to remove. The French call this versatile fish *colin* in Paris; *merlan* in Provence; and *saumon blanc* on menus everywhere. Generally moderate in price, it can be cooked according to any of the recipes given for cod, haddock or halibut, but is perhaps most successful poached, baked or sautéed.

I like hake poached in *court-bouillon* and served hot with a delicate *sauce mousseline*; or cold with a mayonnaise or a *sauce verte*.

FISH TURBAN

1½ lb (675 g) hake or halibut
Well-flavoured *court-bouillon* (page 163)
½ pint (300 ml) milk
8 oz (225 g) freshly grated breadcrumbs
4 egg yolks
4 tablespoons (60 ml) double cream
4 egg whites
Salt, freshly ground black pepper and cayenne pepper
Butter
Scallops, crab, prawns or mussels

Poach fish in a well-flavoured *court-bouillon* until flesh flakes easily with a fork; remove from *court-bouillon* and drain. Remove skin and bones, and flake fish. Bring milk to boil; pour over fresh breadcrumbs and mix well with flaked fish; pound in a mortar until smooth. Add egg yolks and cream, and mix well into mixture. Beat egg whites until stiff and fold gently into fish mixture. Season to taste with salt, freshly ground black pepper and a pinch of cayenne. Spoon mixture into a buttered ring mould; place mould in a tin of boiling water and bake in a slow oven (325°F/170°C/GM3) for 1 hour.

To serve: unmould turban on to a heated serving dish and fill ring with curried scallops or crab, or more simply, mussels in a lightly curried cream sauce. Serves 6 to 8.

Whiting

A well-known member of the cod family, whiting is best remembered for being served with its tail in its mouth. The flesh is tender and very easy to digest, and for this reason it is a great favourite for invalids. It is sometimes called 'the chicken of the sea'. At its best from October to March, it is unfortunately not a good keeping fish and must be eaten absolutely fresh.

Besides the recipes given below, whiting may be cooked according to any of the recipes given for haddock.

FRIED WHITING

4–6 whiting
Milk
Salt and freshly ground black pepper
Flour
2 eggs, well beaten
Breadcrumbs
Butter or oil, for frying

PARSLEY AND LEMON BUTTER
3 tablespoons (45 ml) softened butter
1 tablespoon (15 ml) finely chopped parsley
Juice of ¼ lemon
Salt and freshly ground black pepper

Have whiting cleaned and skinned. Make a slit down the back of each fish on either side of the backbone to make a pocket. Snip off bone at each end with scissors and carefully lift it out. Dip fish in milk seasoned to taste with salt and freshly ground black pepper; then in flour; then in beaten egg, and finally in breadcrumbs, pressing the breadcrumbs on evenly with a spatula to give the fish a neat shape.

Fry the fish in butter in a frying pan or in deep fat until golden brown. Just before serving, open each pocket and stuff with a pat of chilled Parsley and Lemon Butter. Serve immediately. Serves 4 to 6.

PARSLEY AND LEMON BUTTER
Combine softened butter with finely chopped parsley and lemon juice. Add salt and freshly ground black pepper, and chill until ready to use.

BAKED WHITING IN PORT

4–6 whiting
Softened butter
Salt and freshly ground black pepper
¼ pint (150 ml) port
4–6 tablespoons (60–90 ml) double cream

Have whiting cleaned and skinned. Lay prepared fish in a well-buttered baking dish just large enough to hold them. Spread fish with softened butter; season to taste with salt and freshly ground black pepper, and pour over port. Cover fish with buttered paper or foil, and bake in a moderate oven (375°F/190°C/GM5) until fish flakes easily with a fork.

Just before serving: transfer fish to a heated serving dish; stir cream into pan juices; correct seasoning and pour over fish. Serve immediately. Serves 4 to 6.

4–6 whiting
3 tablespoons (45 ml) finely chopped mushrooms
3 tablespoons (45 ml) finely chopped parsley
1 tablespoon (15 ml) finely chopped onion
1 tablespoon (15 ml) butter
Milk
Water
Salt and freshly ground black pepper
½ pint (300 ml) well-flavoured Mornay Sauce (page 107)
3 tablespoons (45 ml) freshly grated Gruyère

Have whiting cleaned and skinned. Make a slit down the back of each fish on either side of the backbone to make a pocket. Snip off the bone at each end with scissors and carefully lift it out.

Sauté finely chopped mushrooms, parsley and onion in butter until onion is transparent and cooked through. Stuff each fish with a little of this stuffing; close the fish carefully, and poach in equal quantities of milk and water, seasoned with salt and freshly ground black pepper.

Transfer poached fish to a heated serving dish; cover with hot Mornay Sauce; sprinkle with freshly grated Gruyère and glaze under a preheated grill until golden and bubbly. Serves 4 to 6.

Mackerel

A regal and richly flavoured fish, the mackerel comes to British shores in large quantities during the spring and early summer. It is at its best from March to July.

Mackerel is a close-textured, rather oily fish, difficult for some digestions to cope with, except when perfectly fresh and in season. It spoils more quickly than almost any other fish and can become dangerous if not properly refrigerated as soon as it is caught. Avoid limp mackerel as they can be quite dangerous.

Choose stiff, opalescent, medium-sized mackerel, with bright protruding red eyes, and markings that are bright and distinct. Mackerel come in sizes up to about 16 inches (45 cm) long.

Mackerel may be eaten fresh, salted or marinated.

MAQUEREAUX BASQUAISE
'CHEZ MICHEL'

12 small fresh mackerel
2 lb (900 g) fresh tomatoes
8 oz (225 g) green peppers
2 oz (50 g) shallots, finely chopped
3 lemons, thinly sliced
¾ pint (450 ml) dry white wine
⅓ pint (200 ml) vinegar
6–8 tablespoons (90–120 ml) olive oil
Salt and freshly ground black pepper
1 *bouquet garni*
Half-rounds of lemon

Clean and empty 12 small fresh mackerel and arrange fish in a
large heatproof baking dish. Peel, seed and chop tomatoes; seed
and chop peppers, and combine with finely chopped shallots in a
saucepan. Slice lemons into thin rounds and add to vegetable
mixture with dry white wine, vinegar and olive oil. Season to
taste with salt, freshly ground black pepper and a *bouquet garni*.

Cook for 20 minutes, and then pour boiling mixture over the
mackerel. Place pan containing fish over a medium heat; bring to
a boil; lower heat and cook fish for 10 to 15 minutes. This dish is
eaten cold, decorated with half rounds of lemon. Serves 12.

MAQUEREAUX AU VIN BLANC
'LE PETIT ST BENOÎT'

6 small mackerel
1 lemon, thinly sliced
4 carrots, thinly sliced
1 Spanish onion, thinly sliced
2 sprigs thyme
2 bay leaves
8 black peppercorns
4 cloves
1 pint (600 ml) water
½–¾ pint (300–450 ml) dry white wine
Salt

Ask your fishmonger to clean mackerel and remove heads. Make a *court-bouillon* with heads of fish, sliced lemon, carrots, onion, thyme, bay leaves, peppercorns, cloves, water and dry white wine. Salt generously and cook for ½ hour.

Place fish in a flat heatproof dish; pour hot *court-bouillon* over them and cook fish in *court-bouillon* for 10 to 15 minutes, or until they flake easily with a fork. Serve the fish cold in their liquor. Serves 6.

MACKEREL BAKED WITH HERBS

4–6 fresh mackerel
2–3 tablespoons (30–45 ml) finely chopped parsley
Butter
Thyme
Flour
Salt and freshly ground black pepper

Have your fishmonger clean, head and tail the fish. Combine finely chopped parsley with 2 to 3 tablespoons (30–45 ml) softened butter and as many pinches of powdered thyme. Lay the fish in a well-buttered baking dish and dust lightly with flour. Season to taste with salt and freshly ground black pepper; dot with butter; cover with a well-buttered piece of paper or foil and bake in a hot oven (450°F/230°C/GM8) until fish flakes easily with a fork. The roes should be lightly floured and cooked in the dish with the fish. Serve immediately. Serves 4 to 6.

Sole and Lemon Sole

There must be more ways of cooking sole than any other single fish in the world. Greatly popular with chefs in top restaurants, it is considered – along with the turbot – to be the finest of all white fish.

Its flesh is firm and delicate in flavour, and it lends itself to a variety of modes of cooking. It is definitely at its best when eaten fresh.

There are two different kinds of sole: the real or black sole, which is long and narrow in shape, with a dark and roughish upper skin, and the lemon sole, which is rounder and more like the plaice in appearance, with a smoother and reddish brown upper skin. The lemon sole is decidedly inferior in quality to the real sole and is, in consequence, cheaper.

FILETS DE SOLE BONNE FEMME

2 sole (about 1 lb (450 g) each)
Salt and freshly ground black pepper
Butter
2 tablespoons (30 ml) finely chopped shallots
2 tablespoons (30 ml) finely chopped mushrooms
¼ pint (150 ml) dry white wine
Fish stock made from fish trimmings
1 *bouquet garni* (bay leaf, thyme, 4 sprigs parsley)
12 button mushroom caps
1 tablespoon (15 ml) lemon juice
Flour

Ask your fishmonger to fillet sole; keep heads, bones and trimmings for stock. Season fillets generously with salt and freshly ground black pepper, and put them in the bottom of a buttered earthenware baking dish. Sprinkle with finely chopped shallots and mushrooms, and add ⅛ pint (75 ml) dry white wine and just enough fish stock to cover fish. Add *bouquet garni*; bring to a boil; cover with buttered paper and bake in a moderate oven (375°F/ 190°C/GM5) for 10 minutes. Sauté mushroom caps in 2 tablespoons (30 ml) butter and lemon juice until tender.

Arrange poached fillets on a heated serving dish; put fish liquor into a small saucepan; add remaining dry white wine and reduce over a high heat to two-thirds of the original quantity. Thicken sauce if necessary with a *beurre manié* (made by mixing equal quantities of butter and flour to a smooth paste). Bring sauce to a boil and cook until it is as thick as cream.

Place 3 mushroom caps on each portion of sole; pour sauce over and glaze for a minute or two under grill before serving. Serves 4.

SOLES AU CHABLIS
'HÔTEL DE LA CÔTE D'OR'

2 sole (about 1 lb (450 g) each)
¼ pint (150 ml) water
Salt and freshly ground black pepper
1 *bouquet garni* (bay leaf, thyme, 4 sprigs parsley)
Butter
2 shallots or small white onions, finely chopped
¼ pint (150 ml) dry white Chablis

Have fishmonger fillet the sole, but ask him for the bones, head and trimmings to make a fish *fumet*. Simmer bones and trimmings for 15 minutes in ¼ pint (150 ml) water flavoured to taste with salt, freshly ground black pepper and a *bouquet garni*. Strain and reserve liquid.

Place fillets of sole in a well-buttered heatproof *gratin* dish or shallow casserole. Sprinkle with finely chopped shallots (or onions) and add Chablis (or other dry white Burgundy), fish *fumet* and salt to taste. Cover with buttered paper and bake in a moderate oven (375°F/190°C/GM5) for about 15 minutes.

Arrange poached fillets on a heated serving dish; put fish liquor into a small saucepan and reduce over a high heat to half the original quantity. Whisk in 2 to 4 tablespoons (30 to 60 ml) butter; correct seasoning and strain sauce over sole. Serve immediately. Serves 4.

FILETS DE SOLE AU VERMOUTH

2 sole (about 1½ lb (675 g) each), filleted
6 tablespoons (90 ml) dry vermouth
6 tablespoons (90 ml) melted butter
1–2 teaspoons (5–10 ml) tomato concentrate
Salt and freshly ground black pepper
6 tablespoons (90 ml) cream
1 truffle, or parsley, finely chopped
Crescents of flaky pastry

Place fillets of sole in a well-buttered flameproof *gratin* dish or shallow casserole. Blend vermouth, melted butter and tomato concentrate, and pour over fish. Season to taste with salt and freshly ground black pepper. Cook over a high heat until fish flakes easily with a fork.

Add cream and simmer gently for a minute or two, shaking the pan continuously so that the sauce will thicken gradually.

To serve: place fish fillets on a heated serving dish; pour over sauce; sprinkle with finely chopped truffle or parsley, and garnish with several crescents of flaky pastry. Serve immediately. Serves 4.

SOLE EN PAPILLOTE 'FESTA DEL MARE'

4 small sole, filleted
Flour
Salt and freshly ground black pepper
2 tablespoons (30 ml) butter
1 tablespoon (15 ml) olive oil
4 tablespoons (60 ml) mushrooms, thinly sliced
4 tablespoons (60 ml) frozen prawns
4 tablespoons (60 ml) cockles
1 clove garlic, finely chopped
1 tablespoon (15 ml) finely chopped parsley
¼ pint (150 ml) dry white wine
¼ pint (150 ml) double cream

Flour fillets and season to taste with salt and freshly ground black pepper. Sauté fillets gently on each side in butter and olive oil. Add sliced mushrooms, prawns, cockles, finely chopped garlic and parsley, and dry white wine. Bring to a boil; reduce wine to half the original quantity; add cream; lower heat and simmer gently for about 10 minutes, or until fish flakes with a fork.

To make *papillotes*: cut 4 pieces of paper (or foil) in pieces approximately 8½ inches by 11 inches (21 by 28 cms); fold in half and cut into heart shapes. Open paper (or foil); brush with oil and place 4 fish fillets on each piece; garnish with mushroom–prawn–cockles mixture and pour over sauce. Fold paper or foil shapes over and seal edges well by crimping them firmly together.

Place *papillotes* in a fireproof dish; pour over a little olive oil and bake in a moderately hot oven (400°F/200°C/GM6) for 10 minutes. Arrange on a serving platter; slit edges of *papillotes*; roll back and serve immediately. Serves 4.

CASSOLETTE DE SOLES 'MIRABELLE'

8 oz (225 g) puff pastry (page 760)
2 sole (1 lb/450 g each), filleted
2 shallots
Butter
12 mussels
4 oysters, shelled
Salt and freshly ground black pepper
1 glass dry white wine
½ pint (300 ml) cream

Take 4 flan moulds 4 inches (10 cm) across, roll the pastry out very thinly and line the moulds. Bake 'blind'. Fold fillets over; chop shallots finely, and put fish and shallots in a saucepan with a good-sized piece of butter, mussels, oysters, salt, freshly ground black pepper, wine and cream. Allow to cook for 12 minutes, and then remove the fish and shellfish. Take the mussels out of their shells. Reduce the sauce until thick and add 2 tablespoons (30 ml) butter. Warm the pastry cases in the oven for 2 minutes, fill with fish and shellfish, and pour the sauce over the top. Serves 4.

POACHED FILLET OF SOLE WITH GRAPES

Butter
3 shallots, finely chopped
8 fillets of sole
Salt and freshly ground black pepper
¼ pint (150 ml) dry white wine
¼ pint (150 ml) fish stock made with fish trimmings and
½ chicken stock cube
¼ pint (150 ml) thick Cream Sauce (page 107)
1 egg yolk
1 cup seedless white grapes
2–4 tablespoons (30–60 ml) whipped cream

Spread 2 tablespoons (30 ml) butter in a shallow fireproof pan and sprinkle with finely chopped shallots (1 small onion may be substituted). Season fillets of sole to taste with salt and freshly ground black pepper; roll them up; fasten with toothpicks and arrange in the pan. Moisten with dry white wine, and stock made with fish trimmings and ½ chicken stock cube. Cover fish with a circle of buttered greaseproof paper cut the size of the pan, with a small hole in the middle. Bring to a boil; cover the pan and poach gently for 10 to 12 minutes.

Remove wooden picks from fillets and arrange fish on a heated dish.

Cook the fish liquor until it is reduced to about a quarter of the original quantity; strain, add Cream Sauce mixed with egg yolk, and warm through until smooth. Do not allow to boil.

Simmer small seedless white grapes in a little water for a few minutes. Drain, and simmer in 1 tablespoon (15 ml) butter; pour around fish. Fold whipped cream into the sauce; pour it over the fish and brown under a hot grill until golden. Serves 4.

SOLE ST ANDRÉ AU WHISKY

4 small sole
Flour
8 oz (225 g) butter
4 oz (100 g) prawns in their shells
4 tablespoons (60 ml) whisky
6 fluid oz (175 ml) double cream
Salt, freshly ground black pepper and cayenne pepper
4 crescents of flaky pastry (optional)

Trim sole, sprinkle them with flour and simmer in a little butter until fish flakes easily with a fork. Do not let them take on colour.

Shell prawns and reserve. Put prawn shells through the finest blade of a mincer or a *moulinette*, and cream thoroughly with remaining butter. Reserve prawn butter thus obtained.

When sole are cooked, arrange them on a heated serving dish; pour off the cooking butter and pour whisky into the pan, scraping all the crusty bits from bottom and sides of pan. Add cream and the prawn butter, and cook, stirring continuously, until sauce is reduced. Season to taste with salt, freshly ground black pepper and cayenne pepper, and strain sauce over the sole.

Sprinkle with shelled prawns and garnish, if desired, with crescents of flaky pastry. Serves 4.

FILETS DE SOLE DU PAYS NORMAND

2 Dover sole (1–1¼ lb (450–550 g) each)
2 shallots, finely chopped
½ pint (300 ml) reduced fish *fumet* (see next page)
½ pint (300 ml) dry white wine
¼ pint (150 ml) double cream
4 mushroom stalks, finely chopped
1–2 egg yolks
Salt, freshly ground black pepper, and cayenne
pepper or freshly grated nutmeg

FISH FUMET
Bones and trimmings from sole
Butter
1 small piece turbot with bone
4 sprigs parsley
2 sprigs thyme
2 bay leaves
1 shallot, finely chopped
¼ pint (150 ml) dry white wine
¼ pint (150 ml) water
2 mushrooms, sliced
⅛ teaspoon (0.6 ml) fennel seed
6 peppercorns
Salt

GARNISH
12 poached mussels
24 small cooked prawns
4 mushroom caps simmered in butter and
lemon juice
Crescents of flaky pastry (optional)

Ask your fishmonger to fillet Dover sole. Reserve bones and trimmings.

FISH FUMET

Butter the saucepan; combine bones and trimmings from sole with small piece of turbot, parsley, thyme, bay leaves, finely chopped shallot, dry white wine, water, sliced mushrooms, fennel seed and peppercorns, and salt, to taste. Bring to a boil; skim and simmer for 10 to 15 minutes. Strain fish *fumet* and reduce to half the original quantity (there should be about ½ pint/ 300 ml).

To prepare fish: poach fillets of sole with finely chopped shallots in equal quantities of fish *fumet* and dry white wine until fish flakes easily with a fork (about 7 to 8 minutes). Remove fillets and keep warm in a low oven.

To make sauce: reduce poaching liquid until syrupy. Bring cream to a boil with finely chopped mushroom stalks and add reduced poaching liquid little by little, stirring briskly with a wooden spatula or whisk until sauce is well blended. Remove saucepan from heat and stir in egg yolks which you have first mixed with a little hot sauce. Whisk well, return to heat and simmer, stirring continuously, until sauce is smooth and thick. Do not allow the sauce to boil after the eggs have been added. Correct seasoning, adding a little more salt, freshly ground black pepper, and cayenne or freshly grated nutmeg, if necessary.

To serve: place sole fillets on a heated serving dish and pour sauce over them. Garnish with poached mussels, prawns, and mushroom caps which you have poached in a little butter and lemon juice. Add crescents of flaky pastry, if desired. Serves 4.

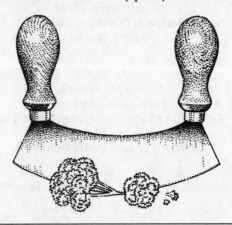

SOLE WITH CAVIAR

2 lb (900 g) fillets of sole

COURT-BOUILLON
Butter
Bones and trimmings of sole
Juice of 1 lemon
4 sprigs parsley
1 bay leaf
½ Spanish onion, finely chopped
4 mushrooms, finely chopped
Salt and freshly ground black pepper
Water and dry white wine

SAUCE
4 tablespoons (60 ml) butter
4 tablespoons (60 ml) flour
½ pint (300 ml) reduced *court-bouillon* (see page 163)
½ pint (300 ml) double cream

GARNISH
Black caviar
6 baked 1-inch (25 mm) tart shells (page 753)
Sour cream

COURT-BOUILLON

Butter an enamelled saucepan or baking dish; lay half the fish
bones and trimmings on bottom of pan; add lemon juice, parsley,
bay leaf, onion, mushrooms, salt and freshly ground black pepper, and enough water and dry white wine in equal quantities to
cover fish. Bring to a boil; add fish fillets; cover with remaining
bones and simmer gently, covered with a piece of buttered paper,
for 10 to 15 minutes, or until fish flakes easily with a fork.

Remove fish fillets from *court-bouillon* and keep warm. Cook
court-bouillon over a high heat until reduced to about ½ pint (300
ml). Strain.

SAUCE

Melt butter in the top of a double saucepan; stir in flour and cook
over water, stirring continuously, until smooth. Add strained
court-bouillon and cook, stirring from time to time, until thick and

smooth. Add double cream and continue cooking until sauce is reduced to the desired consistency.

To serve: place fish fillets on a heated serving dish: pour over sauce; garnish with a sprinkling of black caviar. Surround with tiny tartlets filled with sour cream and topped with black caviar. Serves 6.

SOLE NORMANDE GRATINÉE

2 Dover sole, filleted
Salt
¼ pint (150 ml) fish *fumet* (¼ pint (150 ml) water,
fish trimmings and 1 small onion, finely chopped)
1 wine glass white wine
Freshly ground black pepper
4–6 button mushrooms, sliced
2 tablespoons (30 ml) butter
1 tablespoon (15 ml) lemon juice
½ small packet frozen prawns
½ pint (300 ml) Hollandaise Sauce (page 123)
2 tablespoons (30 ml) double cream
Crescents of flaky pastry (optional)

Poach fillets of sole in a very little salted water for a very short time until fish loses its translucency.

Make a fish *fumet* (a concentrated fish stock) by simmering fish trimmings in ¼ pint (150 ml) water with 1 small onion, finely chopped. Add liquid from poached sole fillets, and dry white wine. Season to taste with salt and freshly ground black pepper.

Sauté sliced mushrooms in butter and a little lemon juice; stir in prawns and heat through. Place mushrooms and prawns in the bottom of a well-buttered *gratin* dish; set poached fillets on top; moisten fish with fish *fumet* and cook in the oven until heated through.

Make ½ pint (300 ml) Hollandaise Sauce; stir in cream; pour over fish and glaze under grill until golden. If desired, garnish with crescents of flaky pastry. Serves 4.

Plaice

It is difficult to spot the difference between the various flat fish in the shops. Sole, of course, stands out immediately, but plaice, lemon sole, megrims, dabs, witches and flounders are often all lumped together. Plaice is the best of this category of flat fish and can be recognized by the yellow to reddish-brown spots on its dark side, the underside being white. When these spots turn dark in colour, it is a sign that the fish is no longer fresh.

At its best from June to December, plaice is apt to be tasteless at other times, because it is the spawning season.

OVEN-FRIED PLAICE À LA NIÇOISE

4–6 plaice, filleted
1 level tablespoon (15 ml) salt
½ pint (300 ml) milk
4 oz (100 g) dry breadcrumbs
2–4 tablespoons (30–60 ml) finely chopped parsley
2 cloves garlic, finely chopped
Freshly grated peel of ½ lemon
¼ teaspoon (1.25 ml) thyme
4 tablespoons (60 ml) melted butter
Paprika
Lemon wedges

Preheat oven to very hot (450°F/230°C/GM8). Add salt to the milk. Dip plaice fillets in the milk and then in the breadcrumbs, which you have mixed with finely chopped parsley and garlic, grated lemon peel and thyme.

Arrange the fish pieces in a well-buttered baking dish and pour the melted butter over them. Place the dish on the top shelf of the oven for about 12 minutes. Garnish with Paprika. Serve with lemon wedges. Serves 4 to 6.

8–12 fresh fillets of plaice
Salt and freshly ground black pepper
Flour
1 egg, well beaten
Fresh breadcrumbs
Hot lard or oil, for frying
Lemon wedges
Chips

Season plaice fillets with salt and freshly ground black pepper. Dip first in flour, then in beaten egg, and then in breadcrumbs, pressing breadcrumbs into fillets with a spatula to make them adhere well. Shake off loose crumbs and fry in hot lard or oil (temperature 375°F/190°C.) until golden brown. Serve with lemon wedges and crisp-fried chips. Serves 4.

CURRIED PLAICE WITH RICE

8–12 fillets of plaice
½ Spanish onion, finely chopped
Butter
1½ level tablespoons (22 ml) curry powder
Salt and freshly ground black pepper
½ pint (300 ml) dry white wine
½ pint (300 ml) well-flavoured Béchamel Sauce (page 104)
Juice of ¼ lemon
Boiled rice

Slice each fillet into 3 pieces. Sauté finely chopped onion in 2 tablespoons (30 ml) butter until transparent. Stir in 1 level tablespoon (15 ml) curry powder, and season to taste with salt and freshly ground black pepper. Spread onion mixture over the bottom of a shallow heatproof casserole; arrange fish pieces on top; dot with butter; cover casserole and cook for 10 minutes over a medium heat. Remove cover; sprinkle with remaining curry powder; moisten with dry white wine and cook over a high heat until sauce is reduced to a third of the original quantity. Flavour Béchamel Sauce with lemon juice; cover fish with sauce and simmer over a low heat for 15 minutes. Arrange fish pieces and sauce in a heated serving dish, and serve with boiled rice. Serves 4.

Turbot

The best of all flat fish, turbot surpasses even the sole in delicacy of flavour. The flesh is firm, rich and of a creamy white colour; if it has become bluish in colour, it should be rejected. The thick part of the fins is particularly favoured by the epicure. Turbot is usually poached in *court-bouillon* and served with a good sauce, its name varying with the sauce which accompanies it. Small turbots are called 'chicken' turbots; they may be cooked according to any of the recipes for sole. When cooking whole turbots or chicken turbots, have the spine cut in one or two places in the middle of the back where the flesh is thickest. This prevents the fish from curling up during cooking and also helps it to cook more quickly.

Turbot is at its best during the summer, from April to August, and has excited the attention of the greatest gastronomes from Grecian times onwards. Carême matched it with a lobster sauce. Perfection!

TURBOT AU BEURRE BLANC

1 turbot (about 5 lb/2.5 kg)
Well-flavoured *court-bouillon* (page 163)

BEURRE BLANC
3 shallots, finely chopped
¼ pint (150 ml) white wine vinegar
Dry white wine
4–8 oz (100–225 g) diced butter
A few drops lemon juice
Salt and freshly ground black pepper

Place a small whole turbot (cleaned and prepared by your fishmonger) in a well-flavoured simmering *court-bouillon*. Bring gently to a boil; skim; lower heat until the liquid barely simmers, and poach for 25 to 35 minutes, or until flesh flakes easily with a fork. Remove fish from *court-bouillon*; drain and arrange on a hot serving dish. Serve immediately with *Beurre Blanc*. Serves 8.

Note: Few houses today have a fish kettle or pan large enough to deal with a whole turbot. If this is the case, have your fishmonger cut turbot into more manageable portions.

BEURRE BLANC
Simmer chopped shallots in wine vinegar for 1 hour, adding a little dry white wine if it becomes too dry. Strain this reduced sauce into a small saucepan and whisk in diced butter over a high heat until sauce becomes thick and smooth. Do not let sauce separate, or all you will have is melted butter. Add a few drops of lemon juice, and season to taste with salt and freshly ground black pepper.

TURBOT AU GRATIN

2 lb (900 g) poached turbot, flaked
½–¾ pint (300–450 ml) well-flavoured Cream Sauce (page 107)
Butter
4 tablespoons (60 ml) freshly grated
Parmesan

Bring well-flavoured Cream Sauce to a boil in the top of a double saucepan; add flaked turbot and heat through.

Pour turbot and sauce into a well-buttered, shallow, ovenproof baking dish; sprinkle with grated cheese; dot with butter and glaze under a preheated grill until sauce is golden and bubbly. Serve immediately. Serves 4.

TURBOT BAKED IN CREAM

4 thick slices turbot
Butter
Salt and freshly ground black pepper
1 pint (600 ml) double cream
Lemon juice
Dijon mustard
Worcestershire sauce

Place turbot slices in a well-buttered ovenproof baking dish or shallow casserole, and season generously with salt and freshly ground black pepper

Season cream to taste with lemon juice, Dijon mustard and Worcestershire sauce. Pour over fish; cover with buttered paper or a piece of foil and place baking dish in a pan of boiling water in a preheated moderate oven (375°F/190°C/GM5) for 15 to 20 minutes, or until fish flakes easily with a fork.

To serve: transfer turbot to a heated serving dish; correct seasoning of sauce and strain over fish. Serve immediately. Serves 4.

Halibut

A large flat fish resembling the turbot in appearance, halibut – little known in France – is a great favourite on this side of the English Channel. Obtainable all the year round, halibut is best during the autumn and winter months. Its flesh is inclined to be dry and rather flavourless unless it is carefully cooked. Halibut is at its best cooked *en court-bouillon* and served with a good sauce. Besides the recipes given below, it may be cooked according to any of the recipes given for turbot, brill, sole and lemon sole, to which family it belongs.

In America, this fish – called flounder – is very popular, replacing the Dover sole and the turbot, which are not fished in American waters.

Halibut is usually sold in steaks, sometimes in fillets. For a large party – and if you have a classic-shaped fish kettle large enough to hold it – you can order a whole fish from your fishmonger.

HALIBUT WITH GREEN BUTTER

3 lb (1.4 kg) halibut, cut in serving portions
Butter
1 Spanish onion, thinly sliced
2–4 carrots, thinly sliced
1 *bouquet garni* (thyme, bay leaf, parsley, celery, rosemary)
Dry white wine
Water
Salt and freshly ground black pepper

GREEN BUTTER
8 oz (225 g) softened butter
2 hard-boiled eggs, sieved
2 tablespoons (30 ml) olive oil
1–2 cloves garlic, mashed
12 spinach leaves
6 lettuce leaves
6 sprigs watercress
6 sprigs parsley
2 shallots, chopped
2 tablespoons (30 ml) capers
½ level teaspoon (2.5 ml) French mustard
Lemon juice
Salt and freshly ground black pepper

Wipe halibut with a damp cloth and place in a shallow well-buttered baking pan. Add sliced onion, carrots and *bouquet garni*. Cover fish with dry white wine and water in equal quantities, and season to taste with salt and freshly ground black pepper. Poach gently for 30 minutes, or until the fish flakes easily with a fork. When done, drain well, place on a heated serving dish and garnish each portion with a slice of Green Butter. Serves 4 to 6.

GREEN BUTTER
Place softened butter, sieved hard-boiled eggs, olive oil and mashed garlic in an electric blender, and blend until creamy. Add more oil if mixture seems too dry.

Blanch spinach leaves (with stems removed), green lettuce leaves, watercress, parsley and chopped shallots. Drain well, chop and add to butter mixture with capers and French mustard.

When well blended, add lemon juice, salt and freshly ground black pepper, to taste, and chill until ready to serve. This is also delicious with grilled salmon.

BAKED HALIBUT IN BATTER

1½–2 lb (675–900 g) cooked halibut,
turbot or fresh haddock
Butter
Salt and freshly ground black pepper
Grated lemon rind
1 tablespoon (15 ml) finely chopped parsley
1 tablespoon (15 ml) finely chopped fresh chervil,
tarragon or basil, when in season
4 tablespoons (60 ml) melted butter
Prawns and/or mussels (optional)

BATTER
4 oz (100 g) sifted plain flour
2 eggs
1 pint (600 ml) milk
Salt

Remove skin and bones from fish; break fish into bite-sized chunks or flakes, and arrange in a well-buttered pie dish. Season to taste with salt, freshly ground black pepper and a little grated lemon rind, and sprinkle with finely chopped fresh parsley and herbs. (If fresh herbs are not available, substitute ¼ teaspoon (0.6 ml) each dried crushed tarragon and rosemary.) Pour melted butter over the fish and toss lightly until fish pieces are well coated. Sprinkle with cooked prawns and/or steamed mussels if desired.

BATTER
Sieve flour into a mixing bowl and make a well in the centre. Break 1 egg into the well and mix it into the flour with a wooden spoon. Stir in half the milk; season to taste with salt, add the remaining egg and beat until batter is smooth. Then gradually beat in remaining milk. Let batter stand for at least 1 hour.

Pour batter over the fish and bake in a moderate oven (375°F/190°C/GM5) until the batter is well risen, browned and firm to the touch. Serve immediately. Serves 6.

KEDGEREE

4 oz (100 g) rice
Salted water
1 lb (450 g) poached halibut, turbot or salmon
4 tablespoons (60 ml) butter
1 teaspoon (5 ml) curry powder
2 hard-boiled eggs
Salt and freshly ground black pepper
½ pint (300 ml) hot Cream Sauce (page 107)

Cook rice in boiling salted water until tender but not mushy. Drain and keep warm.

Dice or flake fish, removing any bones and skin. Melt butter in saucepan; blend in curry powder; add fish and sauté gently.

Finely chop whites of hard-boiled eggs and combine with rice and fish. Season to taste with salt and freshly ground black pepper. Fold in hot Cream Sauce.

Serve on a platter, with yolks of hard-boiled eggs, pressed through a sieve or finely chopped, sprinkled over the top. Serves 4.

JAPANESE SASHIMI

1 lb (450 g) fresh halibut, sea bass or mackerel

SHOYU SPICE SAUCE
1 teaspoon (5 ml) grated horseradish
1 teaspoon (5 ml) dry mustard
Pinch of ginger
1 tablespoon (15 ml) vinegar
1 tablespoon (15 ml) corn oil
¼ pint (150 ml) soy sauce

In Japan, *sashimi* (raw fish ribbons) is served as an appetizer on individual plates or small bowls, accompanied by a Shoyu Spice Sauce.

SHOYU SPICE SAUCE
Combine horseradish, mustard, ginger and vinegar, and mix to a smooth paste. Add corn oil and soy sauce.

Fillet the fish, taking care to remove all bones. Cut the fillets diagonally across the grain into thin ribbons ½ inch (12 mm) wide.

To serve: place fish ribbons on each plate. Accompany with a small bowl of Shoyu Spice Sauce. Fish slices are picked up one by one with chopsticks and dipped into the sauce. Serves 4.

Salmon and Salmon Trout

Guided by instinct, the salmon will return after years at sea to the river of its birth to spawn – leaping over any obstacles in its way, braving weirs and waterfalls, hurling itself many feet out of the water until it surmounts the obstacle or dies of exhaustion in the attempt; there is no turning back.

At its best from January to September, salmon is definitely party fare. For no other fish combines so many gastronomic qualities. It is a meaty fish, with meat that is at once firm and flaky; it has few bones; it is rich in natural fat so that even the most inexperienced cook has difficulty in drying it out; and its fine flavour is unsurpassed. Whether it is prepared whole or cut into thick steaks, served hot or cold, this king of the sea spells luxury living at its best.

Generally caught in rivers, it is both a salt- and fresh-water fish, first cousin to the trout, salmon trout, char, whitefish, grayling and smelt. Salmon is of such great commercial value that special game laws have been passed to regulate salmon fishing and protect the fish. It is illegal to sell fresh salmon during the closed season, although Dutch and other imported salmon may be had all year round.

When choosing salmon, select one with a small head and tail, and a broad, plump body. The scales should be bright and silvery, and the flesh rich and rose-coloured.

Freshly caught salmon should be cooked as soon as possible after it is caught, although it will keep, and be quite good for several days, if refrigerated.

The most frequent method of cooking salmon is to poach it. But it may also be steamed, grilled, sautéed, cooked on the spit, braised or baked. Perhaps the most regal treatment of this royal fish I ever tasted was the *tronçon de saumon à la Metternich* served to me in Paris by a friend noted for the excellence of his table. This was a thick centre cut of fresh salmon poached in a *court-bouillon*; placed on a pedestal of moulded cooked rice; masked with a highly flavoured sauce, and surrounded with tiny cups made of inverted mushrooms caps and hollowed-out truffles, mounted on diminutive golden pedestals of fried bread. Each truffle and mushroom was filled with a *macédoine* of truffles and prawns in a rich sauce. It was extraordinary – an experience, in fact – but I am afraid that when it comes to cooking this delicious fish, the simplest methods are still the best. I like to poach a whole salmon or a thick centre piece in a lightly flavoured *court-bouillon* and then serve it hot with Hollandaise Sauce or *Sauce Choron* (a tomato-flavoured Béarnaise Sauce); or cooled in its own liquid, drained, and served cold with a well-flavoured mayonnaise sauce or *Sauce Verte* (mayonnaise flavoured and tinted with fresh green herbs).

Fresh salmon steaks are delicious braised in white wine (*au vin blanc*) or, for that matter, in red wine (*à la bourguignonne*). I like, too, to make its tender meat into rustic croquettes, sophisticated soufflés and mousses or ethereal *quenelles*. Try it diced and served in individual soufflé dishes or scallop shells with a Normande, Béchamel or Mornay Sauce. Thread inch-square (25 mm) cubes on a skewer; brush with melted butter, or olive oil and lemon juice, and grill until cooked through.

The cardinal rule is never, never overcook it. Cook it quickly and gently (no boiling here), to the proper point of doneness. The flesh should be tender and flaky, but still moist. Overcooked fish is dry fish. Fish boiled too rapidly in aggressive water is a fish spoiled, both in flavour and in texture. And no matter how you cook it, serve it with a chilled white wine, always dry: a Muscadet, Meursault or Sancerre, a noble Rhine wine, or a Pouilly Fumé or Fuissé.

Salmon Trout

A more delicately flavoured fish than the salmon – and smaller in size – the salmon trout is served whole. It is cooked in much the same way as salmon and served with similar accompaniments. Whole salmon trout, weighing from 3 to 6 lbs (1.4–3 kg), may be poached in the same way as salmon, but sometimes their length causes inconvenience if no fish kettle is available. In this case, the fish may be poached in the oven, preferably in a heatproof dish, in *court-bouillon* or wine. Or wrap the fish in greaseproof paper or foil; place on a baking sheet, and bake for 1 hour for a 2- to 3-lb (900 g–1.4 kg) fish. Unwrap greaseproof paper or foil, and carefully slide the fish and its juices off on to a heated serving dish. A hot salmon trout cooked to perfection needs nothing more than its own juices and a simple sauce made of fresh melted butter and lemon juice. If salmon trout is to be served cold, always remove skin while the fish is still warm. A cold salmon trout eaten several hours after it is cooked is much more delicate in flavour and texture than one cooked and kept until the following day. I like to serve cold salmon trout with *Sauce Verte*, well-flavoured mayonnaise flavoured and coloured with finely chopped herbs steeped for a minute or two in a little boiling water. Salmon trout is available from May to July.

MARINATED SALMON STEAKS

4 fresh salmon steaks
Butter
Salt and freshly ground black pepper
Paprika
1 tablespoon (15 ml) dry breadcrumbs

MARINADE
1 Spanish onion, sliced
2 cloves garlic, finely chopped
2 stalks celery, sliced
2 bay leaves
4 tablespoons (60 ml) red wine vinegar
4 tablespoons (60 ml) olive oil
4 peppercorns

MARINADE
Combine sliced onion, finely chopped garlic, sliced celery, bay leaves, red wine vinegar, olive oil and peppercorns in a large bowl. Place salmon steaks in the marinade mixture and marinate for at least 2 hours.

Remove steaks from marinade; drain and place in a well-buttered ovenproof *gratin* dish. Brush with melted butter; sprinkle with salt, freshly ground black pepper and paprika. Sprinkle lightly with breadcrumbs, place under a preheated grill and grill for 5 minutes. Then bake in oven for 5 to 10 minutes longer, or until fish flakes easily with a fork. Serves 4.

GRILLED SALMON STEAKS

4 large salmon steaks
Salt and freshly ground black pepper
4 tablespoons (60 ml) melted butter
Lemon wedges

LEMON AND PARSLEY BUTTER
4 oz (100 g) slightly softened butter
2 tablespoons (30 ml) finely chopped parsley
Lemon juice
Salt and freshly ground black pepper

Season both sides of salmon steaks to taste with salt and freshly ground black pepper, and leave to stand at room temperature for 15 minutes.

Place steaks on a buttered, preheated baking sheet; brush with 2 tablespoons (30 ml) melted butter and grill for 3 to 5 minutes about 3 inches (8 cm) from heat. Turn steaks, brush with remaining butter and grill until fish flakes easily with a fork (3 to 5 minutes). Serve with Lemon and Parsley Butter and lemon wedges. Serves 4.

LEMON AND PARSLEY BUTTER
Pound slightly softened butter in a mortar with finely chopped parsley, and lemon juice, salt and freshly ground black pepper, to taste.

SAUTÉED SALMON STEAKS

4 fresh salmon steaks
Flour
4 tablespoons (60 ml) butter
¼ pint (150 ml) dry white wine
Bay leaf
Salt
White pepper
Pinch of celery seed
2 tablespoons (30 ml) finely chopped parsley

Choose centre cuts of salmon about ¾ inch (18 mm) thick. Rub steaks well on both sides with flour. Melt butter in a heavy frying pan or French casserole, and when hot, sauté steaks lightly. When steaks are light brown, add white wine and seasonings. Cover and simmer, with frequent basting, on top of stove until cooked (about 30 minutes). When salmon is cooked, sprinkle with finely chopped parsley and serve. Serves 2 to 4.

COLD SALMON WITH WATERCRESS MOUSSELINE

4 fresh salmon steaks
1 pint (600 ml) water
½ Spanish onion, sliced
1 stalk celery, sliced
1 bay leaf
Juice of 1 lemon
Salt and freshly ground black pepper

WATERCRESS MOUSSELINE
2 bunches watercress
¼ pint (150 ml) double cream
Salt and freshly ground black pepper

Combine water, sliced onion, celery, bay leaf and lemon juice, and salt and freshly ground black pepper, to taste, in a wide saucepan. Bring to a boil; then reduce heat and simmer gently for 15 minutes. Add salmon steaks to the simmering liquid, carefully placing them on the bottom of the pan without letting them overlap. Cover pan and simmer for 10 minutes, or until fish flakes easily with a fork.

Chill the steaks in their own liquid. Just before serving, drain. Serve with Watercress Mousseline. Serves 4.

WATERCRESS MOUSSELINE
Remove leaves from watercress; place them in cold water; bring to a boil and then simmer for 10 minutes. Rinse well in cold water; drain and pass through a fine sieve.

Bring double cream to a boil in a saucepan; add sieved watercress, and season to taste with salt and freshly ground black pepper. Chill. Just before serving, whisk until thick and smooth.

SALMON BROCHETTES

2–3 fresh salmon steaks (about 1½ inches/38 mm thick)
6 tablespoons (90 ml) olive oil
2 tablespoons (30 ml) lemon juice
¼ Spanish onion, finely chopped
4 tablespoons (60 ml) finely chopped parsley
Salt and freshly ground black pepper
4 small onions, sliced
4 tomatoes, sliced
16 small bay leaves
Lemon juice

Cut fresh salmon steaks into bite-sized cubes and marinate for at least 2 hours in olive oil, lemon juice, finely chopped onion and parsley, and salt and freshly ground black pepper, to taste. Place fish cubes on a skewer alternately with a slice of onion, a slice of tomato and a bay leaf. Grill over charcoal or under the grill, turning frequently and basting from time to time with marinade sauce.

To serve: remove cooked fish from skewer on to serving plate and sprinkle with lemon juice. Serves 4.

SALMON POACHED IN COURT-BOUILLON

1 whole salmon (about 6 lb/3 kg)
Lemon slices
Cucumber slices
Fresh watercress or parsley
Mousseline Sauce, *Sauce Choron* or *Sauce Verte*
(pages 121–124)

COURT-BOUILLON
3 pints (1.7 lit) water
1 bottle dry white wine
1 large Spanish onion, sliced
4 carrots, sliced
2 stalks celery, sliced
2 bay leaves
1 *bouquet garni*

Combine elements of *court-bouillon* in a kettle large enough to hold salmon; bring to a boil; skim; lower heat and simmer for 30 minutes. Let *court-bouillon* cool slightly; lower the cleaned salmon, wrapped in muslin, into it. Simmer gently for 45 to 60 minutes, or until fish flakes easily with a fork.

Remove fish carefully from the *court-bouillon* with the help of the muslin and carefully remove the skin. Arrange the salmon on a hot platter and garnish with lemon slices, cucumber slices, and fresh watercress or parsley. Serve with Mousseline Sauce, *Sauce Choron* or *Sauce Verte*.

POACHED SALMON IN ASPIC

1 salmon poached in *court-bouillon*
1 egg white and shell
2–2¼ tablespoons (30–33 ml) gelatine
¼ pint (150 ml) cold water
Mayonnaise or *Sauce Verte* (pages 120–124)

Poach salmon as above; remove carefully from *court-bouillon* to a large board or platter and let it cool. Remove the skin carefully, cutting it at the tail and stripping it to the head.

Reduce *court-bouillon* to 2 pints (1.1 lit). Clarify it with the crushed shell and the white of an egg, and strain it through a clean cloth. Dissolve gelatine in water and prepare an aspic using the hot *court-bouillon*. Brush salmon with cooled aspic. Decorate as desired and brush with aspic again.

Serve with mayonnaise or *Sauce Verte*.

SALMON SOUFFLÉ MOUSSE

1¼ lb (550 g) fresh salmon
4 tablespoons (60 ml) cognac
2 egg whites
1 teaspoon (5 ml) onion juice
3 tablespoons (45 ml) lemon juice
Salt and freshly ground black pepper
Cayenne pepper
¾ pint (450 ml) double cream
4 egg whites
Butter
Prawn and Lobster Sauce (page 109)

Remove bones and skin from salmon; dice and marinate in cognac for 2 hours.

Place 2 egg whites in blender; then add diced salmon, the marinade, onion juice and lemon juice, season to taste with salt, freshly ground black pepper and cayenne pepper, and blend at low speed until fish and eggs form a smooth paste. Turn to high speed and blend until very smooth.

Put purée in a bowl surrounded with cracked ice; cool. Whip cream until thick and whisk into fish purée. Beat whites of 4 eggs very stiff but not dry, and gently fold into mixture; correct seasoning; remove bowl from ice and pour mixture into a buttered soufflé dish. Stand in a pan of hot but not boiling water and bake in a slow oven (350°F/180°C/GM4) until firm enough to turn out – 45 to 60 minutes. Turn out on to a heated serving dish and serve with Prawn and Lobster Sauce. Serves 4.

BRANDADE DE SAUMON

1½ lb (675 g) fresh salmon
1 clove garlic, crushed
6 tablespoons (90 ml) double cream
¼ pint (150 ml) olive oil
Juice of ½ lemon
Salt and freshly ground black pepper
Toast triangles fried in olive oil or butter

Poach salmon until tender. Remove from water; drain and flake, removing bones and skin.

Place salmon flakes in electric blender with crushed garlic, 2 tablespoons (30 ml) cream and 4 tablespoons (60 ml) olive oil, and blend, adding remainder of cream and olive oil alternately from time to time, until the oil and cream are completely absorbed and the *brandade* is creamy smooth.

When ready to serve: simmer mixture in top of a double saucepan; stir in lemon juice, and season to taste with salt and freshly ground black pepper.

Brandade de saumon may be served hot or cold. If hot, place in a mound on a warm serving dish and surround with toast triangles fried in olive oil or butter. Serves 4.

MARINATED SMOKED SALMON WITH DILL

8 oz (225 g) sliced smoked salmon
1 teaspoon (5 ml) whole black peppers
½ teaspoon (2.5 ml) dill seed
Bay leaf
½ pint (300 ml) dry white wine
¼ pint (150 ml) sour cream
1 level tablespoon (15 ml) prepared mustard
Salt
Lemon juice
1 tablespoon (15 ml) chopped chives
1 dill pickle, thinly sliced

Place salmon in a covered glass dish. Sprinkle with whole peppers and dill seed. Add bay leaf and cover with dry white wine. Place in refrigerator and allow salmon to marinate in this mixture overnight.

Just before serving, drain wine and spices from salmon. Place spices and half of the wine in a mixing bowl. Add sour cream and prepared mustard, and flavour to taste with salt and lemon juice.

Place salmon on a serving dish; cover with sauce and garnish with chopped chives and sliced pickle. Serves 4.

SALMON TROUT 'CAPRICE'

1 salmon trout (2–2½ lb/900 g– 1.1 kg)
1 Spanish onion, sliced
1–2 carrots, sliced
½ bay leaf
1 sprig thyme
¼ bottle champagne
Fish stock
Salt and freshly ground black pepper
¼ pint (300 ml) double cream
Flour
Butter
4 oz (100 g) button mushrooms, simmered in butter
and lemon juice
2 oz (50 g) butter, diced
8 crescents of flaky pastry
Truffles, thinly sliced (optional)

Spread onion and carrot slices over the bottom of a heatproof baking dish large enough to hold salmon trout; place fish on top. Add ½ bay leaf, sprig of thyme, champagne and a little fish stock. Season with salt and freshly ground black pepper, and bring to a boil. Cover fish with greaseproof paper and place dish in a moderate to moderately hot oven (375°–400°F/190°–200°C/GM5–6) for approximately 15 to 20 minutes, basting fish occasionally with pan juices to keep it moist.

When cooked, transfer fish to a heated serving dish and keep warm. Drain off liquor and reduce until almost evaporated, adding double cream, and a little fish stock thickened with a *roux* of flour and butter.

To prepare fish: remove all the skin and dark outer flesh, scraping it off gently with a knife. Place mushrooms down centre of fish.

'Finish' sauce by adding diced butter, piece by piece, shaking pan gently just off the heat so that sauce does not boil. Correct seasoning. Pour sauce over salmon trout, and serve garnished with flaky pastry crescents, and thinly sliced truffles if desired. Serves 4.

Trout

A member of the same royal family of fish as the salmon and the salmon trout, the trout is the perfect fish – exquisite in shape, delicate in colouring, seemingly dappled with sunlight. Its flavour makes its appearance on any table an occasion – a feast, not just a meal.

Trout are at their best in spring and summer.

TROUT EN PAPILLOTE

4 small trout
2 tablespoons (60 ml) finely chopped onion
8 oz (225 g) button mushrooms, finely chopped
2 tablespoons (60 ml) finely chopped parsley
Butter or olive oil
Salt and freshly ground black pepper
4 thin slices lemon
4 tablespoons (60 ml) dry white wine

Clean and prepare 4 small trout. Sauté finely chopped onion, mushrooms and parsley in 4 tablespoons (60 ml) butter until onion is transparent; season to taste with salt and freshly ground black pepper, and stuff fish with this mixture.

Cut 4 rectangles of foil large enough to envelop fish completely. Brush foil with melted butter or olive oil and place fish in centre of each piece of foil.

Sprinkle each fish with salt and freshly ground black pepper, top with a slice of lemon, and pour over 4 tablespoons (60 ml) each melted butter and dry white wine.

Bring the foil up over the top of fish and double-fold the edges to form a tight pocket. Close the ends of the foil by folding them over and turning them up so the juices will not run out.

Place on a baking sheet and bake in a moderate oven (375°F/190°C/GM5) for 15 to 20 minutes. Arrange on serving dish. Slit edges of foil and roll back. Serves 4.

TROUT 'AU GRATIN'

4 fresh trout, filleted
¼ pint (150 ml) dry white wine
¼ pint (150 ml) water
Salt and freshly ground black pepper
Butter
8 button mushrooms, quartered
4 oz (100 g) frozen prawns
¼ pint (150 ml) double cream
2 egg yolks
4 tablespoons (60 ml) freshly grated Gruyère

Poach trout fillets in a *court-bouillon* made of equal parts dry white wine and water, and seasoned to taste with salt and freshly ground black pepper.

Transfer fillets to a well-buttered ovenproof dish and keep warm. Add 4 tablespoons (60 ml) butter, quartered mushrooms and half the prawns to the sauce, and bring to a boil. Cook over a high heat until sauce is reduced to half the original quantity. Remove from heat.

Combine double cream and egg yolks in a small bowl; stir in a little of the hot sauce; then pour egg and cream mixture into hot sauce and cook over a medium heat, stirring constantly, until mixture thickens. Do not let it come to a boil, or eggs will curdle.

Pour sauce over trout fillets; sprinkle with freshly grated Gruyère and glaze under preheated grill until sauce is bubbly and golden. Serves 4.

BAKED ENGLISH TROUT WITH BACON

4 fresh trout
8 slices trimmed bacon
Salt and freshly ground black pepper
2 tablespoons (30 ml) finely chopped parsley
2–4 tablespoons (30–60 ml) melted butter

Clean trout; split them open and remove backbones. Cover the bottom of a fireproof *gratin* dish or shallow baking dish with bacon slices. Lay the split fish on the bacon cut sides down and sprinkle with salt, freshly ground black pepper and finely chopped parsley. Dribble with 2 to 4 tablespoons (30–60 ml) melted butter and bake in a moderate oven (375°F/190°C/GM5) for 20 to 30 minutes, or until fish flakes easily with a fork. Serve from baking dish. Serves 4.

BAKED TROUT WITH CREAM

4 fresh trout
Butter
2 tablespoons (30 ml) finely chopped shallots
¼ pint (150 ml) dry white wine
Juice of 1 lemon
2 tablespoons (30 ml) finely chopped parsley
Salt and freshly ground black pepper
¼ pint (150 ml) double cream
2 tablespoons (30 ml) freshly grated breadcrumbs

Clean trout. Butter a fireproof *gratin* dish or shallow baking dish generously; sprinkle with finely chopped shallots and arrange the fish in it side by side. Add dry white wine and strained lemon juice; sprinkle with finely chopped parsley and season to taste with salt and freshly ground black pepper. Place fireproof *gratin* dish over a high heat and bring liquid to a boil; transfer to a preheated moderate oven (375°F/190°C/GM5) and bake for 12 to 15 minutes, or until fish are done.

Bring cream to a boil and pour it over the trout. Sprinkle with freshly grated breadcrumbs; return to the oven until crumbs are brown. Serve immediately from baking dish. Serves 4.

STUFFED TROUT WITH WHITE WINE

4–6 fresh trout
8 oz (225 g) cod or hake
4 large mushrooms, finely chopped
2 tablespoons (30 ml) butter
1 egg white
Salt and freshly ground black pepper
¼–½ pint (150–300 ml) double cream
½ pint (300 ml) fish stock or canned clam juice
½ pint (300 ml) dry white wine
4 shallots, finely chopped

SAUCE
¼ pint (150 ml) fish stock
2 tablespoons (30 ml) butter
1 tablespoon (15 ml) flour
½ pint (300 ml) double cream
1 egg yolk
Few drops lemon juice
Flour
Butter

Slit trout carefully down the back, and bone and empty them.
Remove bones and skin from cod or hake. Sauté finely chopped
mushrooms in butter. Pound cod or hake to a smooth paste in a
mortar; pass through a wire sieve and pound in mortar again with
raw egg white. Season to taste with salt and freshly ground black
pepper. Place mixture in a bowl over ice for 1 hour, gradually
working in cream by mixing with a spatula from time to time.
Add sautéed mushrooms to this mixture, and stuff fish.

Just before serving: poach stuffed trout in fish stock (or canned
clam juice) and dry white wine with shallots, and salt and freshly
ground black pepper, to taste.

When trout are cooked, place on a heated serving dish and pour
sauce over them. Serves 4 to 6.

SAUCE
Reduce cooking liquid over a high heat to a quarter of the original
quantity. Melt 1 tablespoon (15 ml) butter in the top of a double
saucepan; add flour and make a *roux*; add fish stock and simmer

until thickened. Stir in double cream and egg yolk. Whisk in a few drops of lemon juice and remaining butter. If sauce seems too thin, thicken with a *beurre manié*, made by mixing equal quantities of flour and butter to a smooth paste. Heat until sauce is smooth and thick, stirring constantly. Strain sauce over fish and serve immediately.

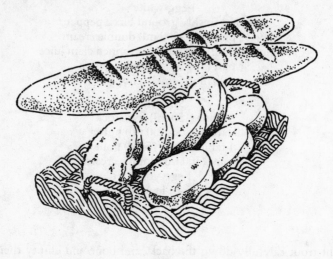

Pike

The Water-wolf, the Lord of the Stream, the Freshwater Shark – such are the names justly given to the pike, a savage and voracious fish, dangerous to fishermen and its own kind alike, but pardoned for all its faults by the gourmet because it can be transmuted into the perfection of *quenelles de brochet*. Unlike so many freshwater fish, its flesh is very delicate when young and makes excellent eating, but beware of the bones, for they are sharp and so hard in texture that they do not dissolve in the stomach.

The best pike are those weighing from 2½ to 4 lb (1.1–1.8 kg). Use the tender flesh of pike to make the featherweight 'fish dumplings' of French *haute cuisine*, one of the most famous dishes of Burgundy and the region around Lyons – *quenelles de brochet*. I give you recipes for *quenelles* and *mousseline* of pike.

QUENELLES DE BROCHET 'MIRABELLE'

PÂTE À CHOUX MIXTURE
6 tablespoons (90 ml) milk
6 tablespoons (90 ml) water
1 tablespoon (15 ml) butter
Salt
6 tablespoons (90 ml) sifted plain flour
2 eggs

QUENELLE MIXTURE
1¼ lb (550 g) pike (after skin and bones
have been removed)
4 tablespoons (60 ml) softened butter
2 egg yolks
6–8 tablespoons (90–120 ml) double cream
2 egg whites
Salt, white pepper and nutmeg
Cognac
Flour

POACHING MIXTURE
Butter
Flour
Salted water

SAUCE
Nantua or Mornay Sauce (page 107)

PÂTE À CHOUX MIXTURE
Bring milk and water to a boil; add the butter, and salt to taste, and cook, stirring constantly, until butter melts. Remove saucepan from the heat and gradually stir in sifted flour. Then add eggs one at a time, beating well after each addition. Stir the mixture over the heat until the paste comes away from the sides of the saucepan and forms a ball. Spread on a plate and allow to cool.

QUENELLE MIXTURE
Put boned and skinned fish twice through the finest blade of your mincer. Combine in a large mixing bowl with cooled *pâte à choux* mixture and softened butter, and mix well. Place bowl in a larger bowl filled with ice and leave for 5 minutes. Then beat for 5

minutes. Add egg yolks and double cream, and beat for 5 minutes more.

Whisk egg whites until stiff and fold gently into *quenelle* mixture. Season to taste with salt, white pepper and nutmeg. Then stir in 1 tablespoon (15 ml) cognac.

Form *quenelles* by rolling 1 tablespoon (15 ml) of the mixture at a time on a floured board into small sausage or cork shapes. Continue until mixture is used up. Keep firm in refrigerator until ready to use.

TO POACH QUENELLES

Butter a large shallow saucepan or baking tin generously. Dust *quenelles* lightly with flour again, and place in pan in rows; add boiling salted water to cover and poach over a low heat for about 20 minutes, or until puffed, without allowing the water to boil again. Remove and drain on a cloth.

Serve *quenelles* with Nantua or Mornay Sauce. Serves 6.

Note: When pike is difficult to find, use turbot, halibut, sole, salmon or trout.

MOUSSELINE DE BROCHET HOMARDINE

12 oz (350 g) fresh pike (after skin and bones
have been removed)
1 small lobster (about 12 oz/225 g)
Olive oil
2 shallots, finely chopped
½ pint (300 ml) dry white wine
¼ pint (150 ml) Madeira
Salt and freshly ground black pepper
1 tablespoon (15 ml) flour
Butter
¾ pint (450 ml) double cream
1 lb (450 g) spinach
4 tablespoons (60 ml) chicken stock
4 large mushrooms
Freshly grated breadcrumbs
Crescents of flaky pastry (optional)

Cut lobster tail (shell and all) into slices; cut remaining body in half lengthwise and remove the coral. Carefully remove the intestinal tube. Sauté lobster pieces in olive oil over a high heat for 3 minutes; add finely chopped shallots and moisten with dry white wine and Madeira. Season to taste with salt and freshly ground black pepper, and cook for 15 minutes. Remove lobster pieces from pan. Add flour and 2 tablespoons (30 ml) butter to lobster coral; mix well and add to pan juices, stirring until sauce is well blended. Pour sauce into the top of a double saucepan; add ¼ pint (150 ml) double cream and allow to simmer over water until ready to serve.

To make *mousseline*: mince pike through the finest blade of your mincer. Place minced pike in a mortar, season to taste with salt and freshly ground black pepper, and pound it to a smooth paste, adding remaining double cream gradually to create a smooth, firm mousse. Oil 4 pieces of waxed paper. Divide pike mousse into 5 equal parts and put 1 portion of the mixture on each of 4 pieces of paper together with a *medaillon* of lobster tail (with shell removed). Fold each packet into a 'finger' 4 inches (10 cm) long and 2 inches (5 cm) thick. Poach them in simmering salted water for 15 minutes.

To make spinach *mousses*: wash spinach carefully; drain and cook with 4 tablespoons (60 ml) each butter and chicken stock. Drain until fairly dry. Put through the mincer with remaining pike *mousseline*. Season with salt and freshly ground black pepper, and mix well. Butter 4 individual aspic moulds and line with spinach mixture, placing remaining lobster meat, finely chopped, in the centre. Cover with the remaining spinach and poach in a *bain-marie* for 20 minutes.

To stuff mushroom caps: wash mushroom caps. Finely chop the stalks. Mix chopped stalks with 4 tablespoons (60 ml) softened butter, and stuff mushroom caps with this mixture. Sprinkle with freshly grated breadcrumbs and bake in a moderate oven (375°F/190°C/GM5) on a buttered baking sheet.

To serve: unfold the *mousselines* of pike; arrange them in the centre of a long hot serving dish; mask with half the sauce (putting the rest in a sauceboat) and keep warm.

Remove lobster-filled spinach mousses carefully from the moulds and garnish the dish with them together with the mushroom caps. Add flaky pastry crescents if desired. Serves 4.

Carp

'The Carp is the queen of rivers,' said Izaak Walton; 'a stately, a good, and a very subtle fish; that was not at first bred, nor hath been long in England, but is now naturalized.' In fact, the carp is an Asiatic fish that only reached Europe, along with its cousin the goldfish, in the Middle Ages. Because of the great size it can attain – nearly five feet (15 m) in some cases – carp are credited with extreme longevity, and hopeful visitors to Fontainebleau imagine that they are feeding the self-same fish that took bread from the hand of Marie Antoinette. But a carp twenty years old is at its finest in flavour, and we would do well to copy the French, who esteem this fish as a great delicacy of the table and not just an ornamental addition to a garden pool.

The carp requires careful cleaning. It should be soaked for an hour or two in salt and water, and then washed in vinegar and water before being cooked.

CARP WITH WINE BUTTER

1 carp (2–3 lb/900 g–1.4 kg), cooked in *court-bouillon*
(see page 163)
4–6 tablespoons (60–90 ml) butter
2–3 tablespoons (30–45 ml) cognac
4 tablespoons (60 ml) finely chopped parsley

WINE BUTTER
¼ pint (150 ml) Beaujolais
1 tablespoon (15 ml) finely chopped shallots
Salt and freshly ground black pepper
½ teaspoon (2.5 ml) sugar
Grated rind of ½ lemon
4 oz (100 g) butter, diced

Cook carp in *court-bouillon*. Skin and trim carefully.

Place fish in a long oval ovenproof dish with a cover; heat butter until it just begins to turn colour and pour it over the fish. Heat cognac; sprinkle over fish and flame. Then baste fish with combined pan juices; cover and keep warm in a low oven.

WINE BUTTER

Combine Beaujolais and chopped shallots, salt, freshly ground black pepper, sugar and grated lemon rind in a frying pan, and reduce it over a high heat until only 3 to 4 tablespoons (45–60 ml) of liquid remain. Add a little diced butter to the pan and cook over a high heat, shaking the pan continuously and adding remaining butter gradually, until a thick red sauce results.

Mask fish with sauce; sprinkle with finely chopped parsley and serve immediately. Served 4 to 6.

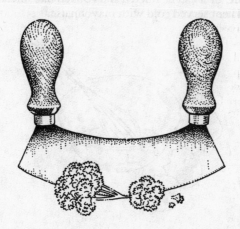

CARP IN COURT-BOUILLON

1 carp (2–3 lb/900 g–1.4 kg)
1 recipe *Court-bouillon* (page 163)
Melted butter
Lemon juice
Boiled new potatoes

Prepare *court-bouillon* as directed. Strain and cool.

Put carp in strained *court-bouillon* and bring gently to a boil; lower heat and simmer fish until flesh flakes easily with a fork. Remove carp carefully from *court-bouillon*; drain; skin and trim. Serve immediately with melted butter flavoured to taste with lemon juice. Garnish with boiled new potatoes. Serves 4 to 6.

Brill

The brill – a flat sea fish of good quality and flavour – is similar in appearance to the turbot, but smaller in size. The skin is smoother and of a pale yellowish-brown colour with reddish spots. When fresh, the brill's flesh has a yellow tinge; if bluish in colour, it is not good. Its flesh is very delicate, more fragile in body than that of the turbot.

Brill may be poached in *court-bouillon* like turbot and served with a sauce, or it can be filleted and cooked like filleted sole.

It is excellent served cold with mayonnaise.

BAKED FILLETS OF BRILL

2 small brill
Butter
1 tablespoon (15 ml) finely chopped shallots
Salt and freshly ground black pepper
4 tablespoons (60 ml) dry white wine
4 tablespoons (60 ml) fish *fumet* (made from bones and trimmings of brill)
¼ pint (150 ml) double cream
1 egg yolk, beaten
Lemon juice
8 button mushrooms, thinly sliced and simmered in a little lemon juice and butter

Ask your fishmonger to skin and fillet brill. Reserve fish bones and trimmings to make a concentrated fish *fumet*.

Butter a shallow baking dish generously and sprinkle with finely chopped shallots. Arrange brill fillets in baking dish and season generously with salt and freshly ground black pepper.

Moisten with dry white wine and fish *fumet*, and bake in a 350°F/180°C/GM4 oven for 20 to 25 minutes, or until fish flakes easily with a fork. Pour pan juices into a small saucepan; add double cream mixed with beaten egg yolk and bring almost to a boil; lower heat and cook, stirring constantly, until sauce is thick. Correct seasoning with salt and pepper, and a little lemon juice if desired, and pour over fish. Garnish with thinly sliced mushrooms which you have simmered in a little lemon juice and butter. Serves 4.

BARBUE AU PÊCHEUR

2 lb (900 g) brill
3 potatoes
8 oz (225 g) mushrooms
4 tablespoons (60 ml) butter
Salt and freshly ground black pepper
1–2 tablespoons (15–30 ml) flour
Lemon juice
2 tablespoons (30 ml) finely chopped parsley

Dice and parboil potatoes. Wash and dice mushrooms. Melt 2 tablespoons (30 ml) butter in a thick-bottomed frying pan; add the potatoes and let them cook slowly with the lid on until almost done. Then add diced mushrooms, season to taste with salt and freshly ground black pepper, and cook until tender.

Cut brill in thick slices; remove bones and skin. Season pieces with salt and freshly ground black pepper, and coat them lightly with flour. Melt remaining 2 tablespoons (30 ml) butter and sauté fish until golden brown on each side.

To serve fish: arrange the pieces on a hot serving dish and place potato and mushroom garnish in little heaps around the dish. Add a little lemon juice to the butter in which the fish was cooked and let it turn a golden brown. Strain over the fish and sprinkle with finely chopped parsley. Serves 4.

General Fish Recipes

BAKED FISH WITH MUSTARD SAUCE

1 white fish (3 lb/1.4 kg)
½ pint (300 ml) dry white wine
¼ pint (150 ml) water
2 tablespoons (30 ml) olive oil
3 tablespoons (45 ml) finely chopped parsley
6 tablespoons (90 ml) finely chopped shallots
2 teaspoons (10 ml) dry mustard
Salt and freshly ground black pepper

Combine dry white wine, water, olive oil, finely chopped parsley and shallots with dry mustard that has been mixed with a little hot water. Season to taste with salt and freshly ground black pepper, and pour liquid over a 3-pound (1.4 kg) fish which has been cleaned and scored. Bake in a slow oven (350°F/180°C/GM4) for 30 to 40 minutes, or until the fish flakes easily at the touch of a fork, basting it every 10 minutes. Remove the fish to a heated serving platter, pour the basting sauce over the fish and serve. Serves 4 to 6.

ROUGETS EN PAPILLOTE 'BAUMANIÈRE'

4 small *rougets* (red mullet), 4–5 oz (100–150 g) each
Olive oil
Salt and freshly ground black pepper
4 bay leaves
4 thin slices grilled bacon
4 slices lemon
4 anchovy fillets

SAUCE
4–5 egg whites
½ pint (300 ml) double cream
4–5 anchovy fillets, mashed
Salt and freshly ground black pepper
Freshly grated nutmeg

Rougets are not emptied before cooking. Just sprinkle each fish with olive oil; season to taste with salt and freshly ground black pepper; place 1 bay leaf on one side of fish and a thin slice of grilled bacon on the other side.

Cut 4 pieces of greaseproof paper approximately 8½ inches by 11 inches (21 by 27 cm); fold in half and cut in heart shapes. Open; brush with oil, and place prepared fish, bay leaf and bacon on one half. Fold paper shape over and seal edges well by crimping them together. Sauté *papillotes* in deep fat or olive oil for about 18 minutes.

Arrange *papillotes* on a serving dish; open each one carefully; decorate *rougets* with lemon and anchovy. Serve with the following sauce. Serves 4.

SAUCE
Beat egg whites until stiff; whip cream; combine the two, add mashed anchovy fillets, and season to taste with salt, freshly ground black pepper and grated nutmeg. Cook over boiling water, skimming constantly, until heated through. Strain; serve hot.

ITALIAN FISH CASSEROLE

1¼ pints (750 ml) well-flavoured chicken stock
8 oz (225 g) long-grained rice
½ pint (300 ml) well-flavoured Italian Tomato Sauce
(page 124)
1½ lb (675 g) different fish, cut in pieces
Butter
4 tablespoons (60 ml) finely chopped parsley
Salt and freshly ground black pepper
2 tablespoons (30 ml) freshly grated Parmesan
Green salad

Bring chicken stock to a boil; add rice and simmer until cooked through. Prepare well-flavoured Tomato Sauce. Cut fish; remove bones; add fish pieces to sauce and simmer until fish flakes easily with a fork.

Butter a shallow heatproof *gratin* dish. Fill with rice mixed with finely chopped parsley; season to taste with salt and freshly ground black pepper, and dot with knobs of butter. Arrange pieces of cooked fish on this bed; mask with sauce; sprinkle with grated cheese and put in a moderate oven (375°F/190°C/GM5) for 10 minutes. Serve with a green salad. Serves 4.

SEA BASS 'YAKHNI'

2 sea bass, filleted (8 fillets)
Juice of 2 lemons
Salt and freshly ground black pepper
¼ teaspoon (1.2 ml) powdered cumin seed
Pilaff rice

YAKHNI SAUCE
4 tablespoons (60 ml) olive oil
1 large Spanish onion, finely chopped
2 bay leaves
4–6 tablespoons (60–90 ml) finely chopped parsley
4 tablespoons (60 ml) finely chopped celery leaves
2 cloves garlic, finely chopped
1 lb (450 g) tomatoes, peeled, seeded and
finely chopped
1 tablespoon (15 ml) tomato concentrate

Combine lemon juice, salt, freshly ground black pepper and powdered cumin in a bowl, and marinate fish fillets in the mixture for at least 1 hour, turning fillets occasionally.

YAKHNI SAUCE

Heat oil in a shallow pan and sauté onion until transparent. Add bay leaves and finely chopped parsley, celery leaves and garlic, and simmer until vegetables begin to take on colour. Add tomatoes and tomato concentrate, and simmer for 30 minutes longer, stirring from time to time. Serves 4.

To cook fish: 30 minutes before serving, spread half of the Yakhni Sauce over the bottom of a large ovenproof dish. Remove the fish fillets from the marinade juices; drain and arrange on the sauce. Pour over remaining sauce; cover with a piece of oiled paper and bake in a moderate oven (375°F/190°C/GM5) for ½ hour, or until fish flakes with a fork. Serve hot with pilaff rice.

SARDINES FARCIEUS AUX ÉPINARDS

18 fresh sardines (heads, tails and
backbones removed)
3 lb (1.4 kg) fresh spinach
Olive oil
2 cloves garlic
1 Spanish onion, finely chopped
Salt and freshly ground black pepper
Freshly grated breadcrumbs

Wash spinach carefully and remove stems. Drain well and cook until limp. Place in a saucepan with 2 tablespoon (30 ml) olive oil, stirring constantly. Drain spinach and then chop finely with garlic.

Sauté finely chopped onion in 4 tablespoons (60 ml) olive oil until golden; add finely chopped spinach and season to taste with salt and freshly ground black pepper. Mix well. Spread two-thirds of spinach mixture in the bottom of a *gratin* dish.

Place prepared sardines (with heads, tails and backbones removed) open side up on a clean towel. Place a tablespoon (15 ml) of reserved spinach mixture on each sardine half; roll fish up tightly (starting at the head) and place them in rows on the bed of spinach. Sprinkle with breadcrumbs and then with olive oil, and bake in a moderate oven (375°F/190°C/GM5) for 20 minutes, or until done. Serves 6.

EGYPTIAN FISH TAGUEN

3 tablespoons (45 ml) olive oil
1 small onion, finely chopped
1 clove garlic, finely chopped
4 oz (100 g) risotto rice
1 fillet of sea bass, turbot or halibut, weighing
about 8 oz (225 g)
Salt and freshly ground black pepper
½–¾ pint (300–450 ml) well-flavoured fish stock
1–2 Italian canned tomatoes, chopped
Lemon slices

Heat the oil and add the onion and garlic. When the vegetables start to take on colour, add the rice and cook until it turns golden brown. Place half the rice in a small earthenware casserole and top with the fish. Season to taste with salt and freshly ground black pepper. Add remainder of rice and pour over all the fish stock and chopped tomato. Cover casserole and cook in a moderately hot oven (400°F/200°C/GM6) until rice is done – 45 minutes to 1 hour. Serve garnished with lemon slices. Serves 1.

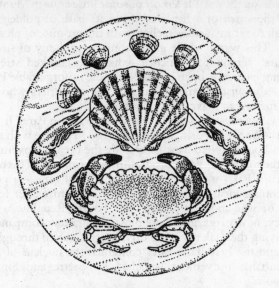

CHAPTER FIVE
Shellfish

C ooking – like *couture* – is a national art, reflecting the personality, moods and tastes of a people, creating the indefinable aura of a country. The very atmosphere of Paris, when I went to live there just after the war, seemed to be made up of tantalizing odours, escaping from the numberless casseroles simmering on kitchen stoves in every back street. I used to love the sharp, acrid aroma of coffee beans roasting near the Bourse; the sudden, sensual whiff that would waft across the table as the lid was lifted from a golden-crusted *cassoulet* in my favourite little restaurant round the corner from the École des Beaux-arts; or the saffron-scented goodness of a rich *bouillabaisse* bubbling in a huge cauldron on the outside *terrasse* of some little *bistro* in Montmartre. Even the smell of a fish sizzling in its bath of golden oil was enough to set my senses reeling with the promise of pleasures to come. This was a whole gastronomic symphony of smells and flavours, certain to influence – like the crooked streets, the winding *quais*, the open markets and the unforgettable Paris sky itself – the writers, artists, painters and couturiers who had the good fortune to make Paris their home.

I was twenty-two when I first went to live in Paris. It was just after the Second World War. I had been in France with the OSS and had been invited back in 1946 by the French Government to head their dramatic radio programmes to America. This post-war period in Paris was an exciting, wonderful time – a period of burgeoning ideas and new hopes for the future after four long years of war and occupation. The Fourth Republic was in its infancy; new magazines were blossoming; new companies were displaying their talents in the tiny theatres dotted throughout the city; and the Left Bank cafés contained the nucleus of the new existentialist movement launched by Sartre and Simone de Beauvoir.

There was no central heating in those days of post-war restrictions; we shivered all day in unheated offices and studios, sustained momentarily by a hot rum grog in an equally unheated café. At home I worked at my typewriter with the back legs of my chair literally charring in the fireplace in a vain attempt to keep warm. And at night, every night, I went to the theatre. The theatres of Paris were unheated too, and as the curtain went up on the play of the evening, a current of icy wind poured out over the audience. For some unknown reason, bravado probably, all French plays of the time were set in Ancient Greek or Roman times, with the actors and actresses gallantly nude in the wintry atmosphere. The plays were wonderful, and night life was, too. It was during this period that Mark Doelnitz launched the vogue for the twenties at the Bœuf sur le Toit just off the Champs Elysées; Inez Cavanaugh sang in her inimitable way in one of the little Left Bank bars for the new wave of Americans; restaurants were beginning to function again as restrictions gradually eased . . . and I learned to love to cook *à la française* with the goods that we had at hand.

It was a wonderful experience to see Paris grow and change after its years of occupation and hardship; to feel the excitement each relaxation of war-time restrictions would bring. I soon got to know the street markets at the Odéon, the Place de l'Alma, and in the Rue des Pyrenées; to visit the great central market of Les Halles, an experience in itself; and to enjoy the simple great dishes of a returning economy: *harengs à l'huile, coq-au-vin, bœuf à la bourguignonne*, and *canard aux navets*.

After one or two attempts to find a daily – the first divided her working hours between my apartment and that of Edwige Feuillère just down the street, and seemed by far to prefer the lovely Edwige; the second lived only for the kitchen, completely ignored dusting and the care of my clothes, and was apt to invite my friends, and often just stray business acquaintances, to stay on for sumptuous dinners at my expense – I was third-time lucky. A wonderful, pink-cheeked, silver-haired lady came from her native Burgundy one day in answer to an advertisement I had put in the evening paper. Naomi had, until shortly before her appearance on my doorstep, been a *cordon bleu* cook to a famous French Marquis. Increasing years and a tendency to migraines made her feel that she wanted an occupation that was a little less strenuous than the Marquis's kitchen. And so she came to stay with me for the five years that I lived in Paris.

Naomi was an unforgettable addition to my life; a treasure such as one can only dream about, a wonderful cook, an unparalleled shopper, and a friend I shall never forget. I think it is in large part thanks to her that I am so interested in food today. Watching her at work in my small and far from perfect kitchen, seeing the attention she would give to a sauce or a *ragoût*, how lovingly she would pare meat of all sinews before cooking it, how finely she would chop vegetables for a *brunoise*, a *mirepoix*, a *duxelles*, taught me more than I can say about the positive joys of cooking.

It is from her that I learned how delicious fish and shellfish could be when served with a subtle sauce in which the concentrated *fumet* – the very essence of the fish preserved in a distillation of its own valuable stock – added its indefinable aura to the finished dish. It was she who first taught me how to cook fish in a *court-bouillon* to bring out its full flavour; how to make a delicately flavoured fish aspic to show it off to its greatest advantage; how to prepare a subtle fish *velouté*, then add a 'butter' of pounded prawn, crayfish or lobster shells, as the *point de départ* for a host of delicious soups, sauces and soufflés based on shellfish. But best of all, perhaps, she introduced me to that ethereal series of *mousses*, *pains* and *quenelles*, made up of the pounded meats of fish or shellfish with egg whites and cream, that forms the basis of so many *haute cuisine* specialities of her native France. I never prepare Naomi's prawn or crayfish *quenelle* mixture today without stopping for a moment to remember with gratitude all that she meant to that young American setting out with faltering steps on the way to one of the greatest pleasures of life: the preparation and the enjoyment of good food. Naomi, I bless you. And thank you.

Clams

Most French cooks disapprove of canned food. Tongues in glass and canned truffles they allow as stand-bys, but canned food to them is no substitute for the real thing.

Admittedly, many canned foods are still a poor substitute for fresh foods. But others have been so altered in the canning process that they have become new varieties, new species almost, in their own right. It is time to take a look at some of these positive successes: canned pears, for instance, bear so little resemblance to the tree-grown variety that another fruit has been added to our larder. Canned tomato juice and Italian peeled tomatoes and tomato concentrate are another case in point. How many delicious Italian dishes would be denied us without their invaluable assistance. And baked beans have been transmuted into a new dish, a new taste, that would take the ordinary cook days of effort to counterfeit.

Some canned foods bring us the real taste of foods that are impossible to get in Britain. Ask for pineapple juice on the islands of Hawaii, which are almost sinking under the weight of their pineapple crops, and immediately a can will be opened. No attempt is made to crush fresh for you the ever-present pineapple. The canned juice is exactly what a fresh-picked pineapple tastes like. For in the last few days before cutting, a pineapple left on the stalk changes physically from anything we can ever get in this country. The fibrous core, left growing in the sunlight, suddenly changes into almost pure sugar, soft, sweeter than you would imagine possible, giving to the whole fruit a completely new character.

Clam juice, too, is another of those perfect products. In restaurants and homes all along the New England coasts, cans of clam juice are being opened to serve, with a spark of fresh lemon juice, as a freshener before the meal, so near to the actual flavour is it. And canned whole clams, minced clams and clam juice can add a new dimension and savour to a multitude of fish dishes. Try a fresh, well-iced clam juice cocktail, to bring you for a tenth of the price the rare delight of the liquor that rests in the shell of a newly opened fresh clam or oyster – the veritable taste of the sea. Use this precious broth to add flavour to fish soups, stews and sauces. Thicken it with a *roux*, made by combining 1 tablespoon (15 ml) each butter and flour; add ¼ pint (150 ml) double cream, and lemon juice to taste, and you have a superbly easy Clam Velouté Sauce for poached or grilled fish. And use the clams themselves, either whole or minced, for a variety of fish dishes – soufflés, and sauces for fish, pasta and mousses. Make minced clams the feature of the easy-to-make version of New England Clam Chowder (see overleaf). And use whole clams for one of the best clam soups I ever tasted, served to me in New York by well-known American food writer, James Beard (see recipe overleaf).

BAKED EGGS WITH CLAMS

1 can minced clams
2 tablespoons (30 ml) butter
1 tablespoon (15 ml) dry sherry
4 mushrooms, diced
4–6 tablespoons (60–90 ml) cream
Salt and freshly ground black pepper
Lemon juice
4 eggs

Melt butter; add sherry, and sauté diced mushrooms in this mixture until tender – about 3 minutes. Add drained clams and cream, and continue cooking until the mixture thickens a little. Add salt, freshly ground black pepper and lemon juice, to taste, and divide the mixture between 4 individual baking dishes. Break 1 raw egg into each dish, and bake for 5 minutes in a hot oven (450°F/230°C/GM8). Serves 4.

EASY NEW ENGLAND CLAM CHOWDER

2 cans minced clams
1 can clam juice
1 large potato, diced
4 oz (100 g) salt pork or unsmoked bacon, in 1 piece
1 tablespoon (15 ml) butter
½ Spanish onion, finely chopped
1 bay leaf
½ pint (300 ml) milk
½ pint (300 ml) cream
Beurre manié
Salt and freshly ground black pepper

Peel and dice potato; put in a saucepan and cover with cold water; bring slowly to a boil. Drain.

Dice salt pork or unsmoked bacon. Put diced meat in a small saucepan; cover with cold water and bring slowly to a boil. Drain, and sauté in 1 tablespoon (15 ml) butter until golden. Add onion and sauté until onion is transparent.

Add parboiled potato, bay leaf and clam juice, and bring to a boil. Reduce heat and simmer for 15 minutes. Add minced clams, milk, cream, *beurre manié* (1 tablespoon (15 ml) butter mashed to a smooth paste with 1 level tablespoon (15 ml) flour), season to taste with salt and freshly ground black pepper, and simmer for 15 minutes. Serves 4 to 6.

JAMES BEARD'S CLAM SOUP

2 7-oz (200 g) cans whole clams in juice
¾ pint (450 ml) double cream
2 tablespoons (30 ml) butter
Salt and freshly ground black pepper
Paprika

In a blender, blend whole clams in juice until the mixture is thick. Pour it into the top of a double saucepan. Add double cream and butter, and season to taste with salt and freshly ground black pepper. Heat the soup to boiling point over hot water, and serve it with a dash of paprika. Serves 4 to 6.

Crab

Found both in salt and fresh water, crabs are available all the year round, but are at their best from May to August. Crabs contain less meat for their size than lobsters, but the meat is a good deal sweeter and, according to many, more delicate in flavour.

Soft-shelled crabs are those which have just shed their old shells, and are markedly blue on top. They are particularly famous in Maryland, and in San Francisco, where Fisherman's Wharf, with its row of giant steaming crab cauldrons and its cluster of seafood restaurants, has become a world-famous tourist attraction in its own right.

Choose heavy crabs of medium size; the light ones tend to be watery. The male crab – recognized by its large claws – is considered the best for table use.

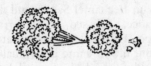

POTTED CRAB

1 cooked crab
6 tablespoons (90 ml) softened butter
Lemon juice
Anchovy paste
Cayenne pepper
Melted butter
Finely chopped parsley

Pick all the meat from the crab and pound it in a mortar with softened butter, flavouring the mixture to taste with lemon juice, anchovy paste and cayenne pepper. The mixture should be quite smooth. Pass through a fine sieve and pack the mixture into little pots. Pour melted butter over the top of each pot and bake in a moderate oven (375°F/190°C/GM5) for 20 minutes. Cover again with melted butter and allow to cool. Serve in the pot, garnished with finely chopped parsley.

CREAMED CRAB RAMEKINS

1½ lb (675 g) cooked crabmeat, flaked
2 stalks celery, thinly sliced
½ Spanish onion, finely chopped
Butter
4 oz (100 g) button mushrooms, finely sliced
¾ pint (450 ml) Béchamel Sauce (page 104)
1 tablespoon (15 ml) Worcestershire sauce
Dash of Tabasco
1 wine glass dry sherry
Salt and freshly ground black pepper
2–3 hard-boiled eggs, sliced
Freshly grated cheese

Sauté celery and onion in 2 tablespoons (30 ml) melted butter until onion is transparent. Add sliced mushrooms and continue to cook for 1 minute. Stir in Béchamel Sauce, and flavour to taste with Worcestershire sauce, Tabasco, dry sherry, salt and freshly ground black pepper. Fold in flaked crabmeat and sliced eggs, and bring to a boil. Pour mixture into individual buttered casseroles; sprinkle with freshly grated cheese and bake in a slow oven (350°F/180°C/GM4) for 20 minutes, or until golden brown. Serves 4 to 6.

CRAB LOUIS

½ pint (300 ml) well-flavoured mayonnaise (page 120)
2 tablespoons (30 ml) tomato ketchup
Tabasco or Worcestershire sauce
3 tablespoons (45 ml) olive oil
1 tablespoon (15 ml) wine vinegar
2 level tablespoons (30 ml) finely grated onion
2 tablespoons (30 ml) finely chopped parsley
6 tablespoons (90 ml) double cream, whipped
Salt, freshly ground black pepper and cayenne pepper
1–2 tablespoons (15–30 ml) chopped, stuffed or ripe olives
1 lb (450 g) cooked crabmeat, flaked
4–6 large tomatoes
Lettuce and sliced hard-boiled eggs, for garnish

Blend together mayonnaise, tomato ketchup, Tabasco or Worcestershire sauce, olive oil, wine vinegar, finely grated onion, finely chopped parsley and whipped cream. Season to taste with salt, freshly ground black pepper and a dash of cayenne. Stir in chopped, stuffed or ripe olives, and chill for 1 or 2 hours before serving. Add flaked crabmeat.

Slice tomatoes in half; place on salad plates; pile crab salad on tomatoes and garnish with lettuce and sliced hard-boiled eggs. Serves 4 to 6.

This sauce is delicious for all seafood cocktails.

CRAB ALBERT STOCKLI

Clarified butter
2 thin slices French bread
4 slices lemon
4–6 oz (100–175 g) cooked crab
Juice of ½ lemon
1 tablespoon (15 ml) cognac
4 tablespoons (60 ml) dry white wine
4 tablespoons (60 ml) concentrated fish stock
Chopped parsley
Chopped chives
Salt and freshly ground black pepper
1 raw carrot, grated

Heat 3 tablespoons (45 ml) clarified butter in a small frying pan. Place slices of French bread in middle of pan and arrange slices of lemon around them; sauté until bread is golden brown on both sides. Transfer *croûtons* to a plate and keep warm. Press lemon slices lightly in the butter and transfer to plate with *croûtons*.

Place crab pieces in pan juices and squeeze lemon juice over them. Sauté carefully so that crab pieces do not disintegrate in cooking. Flame with cognac; add white wine, fish stock, finely chopped parsley and chives. Allow mixture to simmer until it has reduced a little. Season to taste with salt and freshly ground black pepper.

To serve: place *croûtons* in middle of dinner plate with lemon slices around them. Spoon crabmeat mixture over *croûtons* and top with grated raw carrot. Serves 1.

MOUSSE OF CRABMEAT
'RAINBOW ROOM'

8 oz (225 g) fillet of pike
8 oz (225 g) fillets of white fish
6 oz (175 g) fresh butter, diced
2 eggs
2 egg yolks
½ level tablespoon (7.5 ml) chopped fresh chervil
1 tablespoon (15 ml) finely chopped parsley
Salt and freshly ground black pepper
Generous pinch of nutmeg
½ pint (300 ml) whipped cream (measured after whipping)
2 tablespoons (30 ml) cognac
5 oz (150 g) crabmeat, flaked

Make sure that pike and white fish fillets are free of bones, and put them through the mincer. Pound in a mortar until smooth. Then force the pounded fish through a strainer and work it again in the mortar. Gradually incorporate diced fresh butter, eggs and additional egg yolks, and chopped chervil and parsley; season to taste with salt, freshly ground black pepper and nutmeg. Work for 15 minutes with a wooden spatula in a bowl placed on ice. Stir in whipped cream, cognac and flaked crabmeat. Turn mixture into a well-buttered ring mould and poach over hot water for 35 minutes. Serves 6.

Langouste

SPINY LOBSTER OR CRAYFISH

The spiny lobster or crayfish is often looked down on in Britain, where it is compared disparagingly with the lobster. But it is one of the best of the English shellfish, particularly along the Devon and Cornish coasts, and, despite its lack of claws, its body is very tender and there is more of it than there is of the lobster. So it depends on what consistency you like – the extreme smoothness of the flesh of a lobster's claw, or the textured sweetness of its body. I prefer the body-flesh, and delight in using crayfish in the classic lobster dishes, as well as cooking them in their own right.

LANGOUSTE AMOUREUSE

1 live langouste or lobster (about 2½ lb/1.1 kg)
Salt and freshly ground black pepper
6–8 tablespoons (90–120 ml) olive oil
2½ tablespoons (38 ml) fresh butter
Mirepoix bordelaise (2 carrots, 4 shallots and
1 Spanish onion, browned in butter)
¼ pint (150 ml) dry white wine
White stock
6 tomatoes, peeled, seeded and chopped
2 cloves garlic
Dash of cayenne pepper
1 *bouquet garni* (3 sprigs parsley, 1 sprig thyme,
1 bay leaf)
Beurre manié
4 tablespoons (60 ml) fresh cream
Finely chopped tarragon or parsley

Cut *langouste* or lobster tail in pieces and split body in half
lengthwise. Remove coral and reserve; remove the sandy pocket.

Season tail pieces and body with salt and freshly ground black
pepper. Heat oil in a large thick-bottomed frying pan; add tail
pieces and body, and sauté, stirring from time to time, until
coloured; drain; add butter and *mirepoix bordelaise*.

Moisten with dry white wine and enough white stock (chicken
or veal) to cover pieces. Add tomatoes, garlic, cayenne and
bouquet garni. Simmer gently for about 20 minutes. Remove and
drain tail pieces only, and place them on a heated serving dish.

Reduce cooking liquid over a high heat, and blend coral
together with *beurre manié* (1 tablespoon (15 ml) butter mashed
with 1 tablespoon (15 ml) flour) and fresh cream. Add to sauce;
correct seasoning and strain through a fine sieve over tail pieces,
pressing body and vegetables well to extract juices. Sprinkle with
chopped tarragon or parsley. Serves 3 generously.

Écrevisses

FRESHWATER CRAYFISH OR CRAWFISH

This freshwater shellfish used to abound in English streams, but it has almost died out now, and the British have stopped even thinking about it. Pollution and over-fishing have caused crayfish to begin to disappear from French streams, but the gourmets cannot be denied, and great tanks bring the crayfish in live from Eastern Europe to cope with the demand.

There are several kinds of crayfish, as I once saw dramatically demonstrated at the Restaurant Dubern in Bordeaux, where a shipment of *écrevisses* from Yugoslavia was unfortunately tipped into the ornamental pool inhabited by *écrevisses* from Poland, and a full-scale battle broke out between them.

SOLE AND CRAYFISH TARTS

12 crayfish, cooked in *court-bouillon*
¼ pint (150 ml) liquid in which crayfish were cooked
1 medium onion, finely chopped
Butter
2 tablespoons (30 ml) flour
½ pint (300 ml) double cream
2 sole, filleted
6 baked shortcrust or fingertip pastry shells
(page 754 or 760)

Pound cooked crayfish while still warm in a mortar with ¼ pint (150 ml) of the liquid in which they were cooked. Press through a fine sieve and reserve.

Simmer finely chopped onion in 1 tablespoon (15 ml) butter until transparent.

Melt 2 tablespoons (30 ml) butter in the top of a double saucepan. Stir in flour and cook over water, stirring constantly, until mixture is pale brown in colour. Add onion; moisten with crayfish mixture and continue to cook over water, stirring from time to time, until it forms a smooth paste. Add double cream gradually and cook for a further 20 minutes, stirring from time to time. If sauce is too thick, add more cream. The flavour and texture of the sauce depends on the trouble you take making it.

Cut fillets of sole into thin strips and poach in *court-bouillon*; drain and place in individual pastry shells. Pour crayfish sauce over the sole, and serve immediately. Serves 6.

ÉCREVISSES À LA BORDELAISE
'BOIS JOLI'

8 shallots
4 carrots
4 sprigs parsley
1 bay leaf
6–8 tablespoons (90–120 ml) butter
24 live crayfish
4 tablespoons (60 ml) cognac
8 tablespoons (120 ml) double cream
8 tablespoons (120 ml) chicken stock
8 tablespoons (120 ml) dry white wine
1 teaspoon (5 ml) tomato concentrate
Salt and freshly ground black pepper
Cayenne pepper
2 tablespoons (30 ml) finely chopped parsley

Chop shallots and carrots finely; add parsley and bay leaf, and simmer in butter until vegetables are soft. Add crayfish and cook over a high heat, stirring constantly, until shells redden. Flame with cognac; moisten with double cream, chicken stock and dry white wine in which you have diluted the tomato concentrate. Season to taste with salt, freshly ground black pepper and cayenne pepper, and reduce over a high heat for 15 minutes, or until sauce has reduced to the proper consistency. Serve immediately with finely chopped parsley. Serves 4.

Lobster

The heavier a lobster is in relation to its size, the more tender and succulent its flesh will be. Lobsters hold on strongly to life and can live off their own flesh for weeks, sometimes, before being sold. You can see no difference by looking at their shells, although their movements slowly become more languid, but the one sure test is weight – lightness in proportion to size is a defect, no matter what the size may be.

The lobster must be bought and used as fresh as possible. If bought alive, the lobster should be strong and active in its movements. If already cooked, the tail should be pressed tightly against the body and should spring back sharply when pulled out straight with the fingers.

Ali-Bab, nom-de-plume of a famous French cookery writer, advocates cooking lobster in boiling sea-water.

My grandmother, who lived as a child on the New England coast where 'a lobster is a lobster', liked to boil them in this way too. She used to serve them steaming hot, right out of the bubbling pot of sea-water, with plenty of melted butter. Very few cooks, she claimed, knew how to grill a lobster without cooking away the sea-water that gives it taste and flavour. She used to like them served whole, with the shell unopened.

A lobster cooked in a *soupe de poissons* mixture is delicious. Serve it with home-made mayonnaise – to which you have added a little lemon pulp, lobster coral, freshly grated horseradish, or *fines herbes*.

HOT BOILED LOBSTER

2 live lobsters (about 2 lb/900 g each)
Boiling salted water or *court-bouillon*
Melted butter
Salt and paprika
Lemon juice

Fill a large saucepan three-quarters full of salted water (1 tablespoon (15 ml) to 2 pints (1.1 lit)) or a well-flavoured *court-bouillon*. Plunge in the lobsters head first and boil quickly for 1 minute;

then lower heat and simmer slowly until lobster is cooked through. A lobster of 2 lb (900 g) requires about 25 minutes. Remove any scum that rises during cooking. When cooked, lift out lobster; drain well, and rub shell with a little melted butter to make it shine. Crack claws; split body in half down the middle, removing intestine, the stomach (near the head) and the spongy looking gills. Brush with melted butter and serve immediately with additional melted butter, flavoured to taste with salt, paprika and lemon juice. Serves 4.

COLD LOBSTER MAYONNAISE

4 small live lobsters
Boiling salted water or *court-bouillon*
Olive oil
Lettuce leaves
Mayonnaise (page 120)

Boil the lobsters as above; drain, and rub shells with a little olive oil. When cold, remove the two large claws from the body and crack them. Split each lobster in half down the middle, removing inedible parts as above. Garnish with lettuce leaves and serve with home-made mayonnaise. Serves 4.

GRILLED LOBSTER

2 live lobsters (1½–2 lb/675–900 g each)
Salt and freshly ground black pepper
6 tablespoons (90 ml) butter
Cayenne pepper
Paprika

Plunge lobsters for 3 minutes in boiling water to which you have added salt and a generous amount of freshly ground black pepper. Drain and slice in half lengthwise. Keep warm.

Melt butter gently in a saucepan, and season to taste with cayenne pepper and paprika. Pour over lobster and grill until golden. Serves 4.

LOBSTER NEWBURG

4 small cooked lobsters
4 tablespoons (60 ml) butter
4 tablespoons (60 ml) heated cognac
2 egg yolks, beaten
½ pint (300 ml) double cream
Salt and freshly ground black pepper
Cayenne pepper and paprika
Rice or individual *vol-au-vent* cases (page 762)

Cut lobsters in half lengthwise. Crack claws. Remove lobster meat from the shells and cut into large cubes. Sauté lobster pieces in butter for a few minutes. Add heated cognac and flame

Combine beaten egg yolks and cream in the top of a double saucepan and cook over water, stirring continuously, until the mixture coats the spoon. Add lobster meat and pan juices, and heat through, being careful the sauce does not curdle. Season to taste with salt, freshly ground black pepper, cayenne and paprika. Serve on a bed of rice or in individual *vol-au-vents*. Serves 4.

QUICK LOBSTER THERMIDOR

4 small cooked lobsters
¾ pint (450 ml) rich Cream Sauce (page 107)
Dry sherry
1 level teaspoon (5 ml) dry mustard
Pinch of cayenne pepper
Worcestershire sauce
Salt and freshly ground black pepper
4 tablespoons (60 ml) grated Parmesan
Paprika
Butter

Cut lobsters in half lengthwise. Crack claws. Remove lobster meat from the shells and cut into large cubes. Reserve shells. Heat Cream Sauce; season to taste with a little dry sherry, dry mustard, cayenne pepper, Worcestershire sauce, salt and freshly ground black pepper. Simmer gently for 2 minutes; add diced lobster meat and heat through.

Fill lobster shells with mixture; sprinkle grated Parmesan cheese over the top; dust with paprika; dot with butter and brown under grill. Serves 4.

LOBSTER COLBERT

2 medium-sized live lobsters
Well-flavoured wine *court-bouillon*
Butter
½ pint (300 ml) champagne
4 oz (100 g) finely sliced mushrooms, cooked in butter
¼ pint (150 ml) double cream
2 tablespoons (30 ml) meat glaze
1 freshly baked *vol-au-vent* case (page 762)

Cook lobsters in a well-flavoured wine *court-bouillon*. After 25 minutes of slow cooking, remove shells, and cut tails and claws into thin rounds. Just before serving, warm them through in foaming butter and then add champagne. When the wine is reduced to three-quarters of the original quantity, add finely sliced mushrooms cooked in butter. Cover these with cream mixed with meat glaze. Then dress them in a *vol-au-vent* case which has just come out of the oven. Serves 4.

ALBERT STOCKLI'S LOBSTER AROMATIC

2 lb (900 g) freshly cooked lobster meat
1 tablespoon (15 ml) finely chopped shallots
8 oz (225 g) butter
3 tablespoons (45 ml) Pernod
6 tablespoons (90 ml) brandy
6 tablespoons (90 ml) sherry
¼ level teaspoon (1.25 ml) paprika
⅛ level teaspoon (0.6 ml) thyme
½ level teaspoon (2.5 ml) curry powder
¼ level teaspoon (1.25 ml) ground fennel
⅛ level teaspoon (0.6 ml) cayenne pepper
¾ level teaspoon (4 ml) salt
Juice of 1 lemon
¾ pint (450 ml) *Sauce Américaine* (below)
½ pint (300 ml) double cream, whipped stiff
Cooked white rice

SAUCE AMÉRICAINE
1½ lb (675 g) fish and fish trimmings
4 tablespoons (60 ml) butter
½ Spanish onion, finely chopped
Lobster shells, crushed
1 bay leaf
8 tablespoons (120 ml) brandy
6 tablespoons (90 ml) flour
4 tablespoons (60 ml) tomato concentrate
6 tablespoons (90 ml) water
¼–½ pint (150–300 ml) fish stock

Sauté finely chopped shallots in butter until golden. Slice lobster meat; add to pan and stir gently in butter and shallot mixture. Add Pernod, brandy and sherry, and flame, stirring continuously until flames die out. Mix paprika, thyme, curry powder, fennel, cayenne and salt, and sprinkle lightly over lobster. Add lemon juice and mix well. Blend in *Sauce Américaine*. Do not stir. Fold in whipped cream a little at a time with a gentle 'turning' motion. Do not allow mixture to boil.

Make a ring of cooked white rice on serving plate and spoon lobster meat and part of sauce into centre of ring. Spoon remainder of sauce around the rice ring. Serves 4.

SAUCE AMÉRICAINE
Dice fish and sauté in butter with finely chopped onion and crushed lobster shells, stirring constantly, until onion is transparent. Add bay leaf and brandy, and flame. Stir in flour, then tomato concentrate and water. Cover saucepan and simmer gently for 20 minutes. Strain sauce into a bowl and add hot fish stock. Makes ¾ to 1 pint (450–600 ml) .

LOBSTER IN PERNOD

2 medium–sized live lobsters
Cold dry white wine
Tarragon
3 tablespoons (45 ml) butter
2 tablespoons (30 ml) flour
Salt and white pepper
2 tablespoons (30 ml) finely chopped chervil
4 tablespoons (60 ml) Pernod, slightly heated
Finely chopped parsley

Cover lobsters with dry white wine and 8 to 10 sprigs tarragon. Bring to a boil and simmer for 20 minutes. Let cool in wine. Remove from pan and cut tails in sections 1½ inches (38 mm) long.

Remove green liver and coral, and put them in a small saucepan with 2 tablespoons (30 ml) each butter and flour. Heat mixture gently, blend to a smooth paste, and add enough of the strained wine *bouillon* to make a smooth creamy sauce. Season lightly with salt and white pepper. When sauce is smooth, blend in 2 table-spoons (30 ml) each finely chopped chervil and tarragon leaves.

Place lobster pieces in a deep heatproof casserole; add remaining butter, cover and reheat gently. When butter foams, pour slightly heated Pernod over the lobster sections. Set aflame, and when spirit has burned out, add the sauce. Lift lobster pieces gently with a spoon to let sauce penetrate completely.

Cover the casserole and set in a very slow oven (250°F/130°C/GM½) for 10 minutes to let lobster become imbued with the various flavours. Serve in the casserole, sprinkled with chopped tarragon or parsley. Serves 4.

Mussels

Mussels are a nuisance to clean, but that is no reason why they should be almost totally ignored by the British. *Moules à la marinière* dangles French delight at us from the fancier restaurant menus, but good English mussel stew, which is its equivalent, is rarely considered as a dish for even a meal at home, or even on holiday by the seaside, where the mussels are there for the picking.

These magical molluscs can be cooked in every way that you can cook an oyster, and they are a marvellous substitute for those elusive American clams, French *clovisses* and Spanish *almejas*, that keep appearing in foreign cookbooks.

I like to simmer mussels in dry white wine with a little finely chopped parsley and a shallot, strip them of their shells, roll them in egg yolk and breadcrumbs, and then slip them on metal skewers alternately with cubes of fat unsmoked bacon, and deep-fry them in hot fat until golden. Prepare mussels as above and fold them in a fat, creamy omelette; use them in a rich Italian spaghetti sauce; or serve them by themselves on the half-shell with a garlic butter dressing. You'll enjoy their fine savour.

To clean mussels: Place mussels in a bowl and wash well under running water. Scrape each shell with a knife, removing all traces of mud, seaweed and barnacles. Discard any mussels with cracked, broken or opened shells: they are dangerous. Rinse again in running water and remove 'beards'.

To open mussels: Combine ½ pint (300 ml) dry white wine, 2 to 3 tablespoons (30–45 ml) finely chopped parsley, 2 sprigs thyme, 1 bay leaf and freshly ground black pepper in a saucepan; add mussels; cover saucepan and steam mussels, shaking the pan constantly until shells open.

To keep cooked mussels: Wrap mussels in a damp towel and put them on one of the lower shelves of your refrigerator. Strained mussel liquor may also be kept in the refrigerator, to be used the following day for a *sauce velouté* or a *soupe aux moules*.

MOULES À LA MARINIÈRE

4–6 dozen mussels
4 shallots, finely chopped
Butter
½ pint (300 ml) dry white wine
Finely chopped parsley
2 sprigs thyme
1 bay leaf
Freshly ground black pepper
1 tablespoon (15 ml) flour

Moules à la marinière is not the elegant dish that we often encounter in restaurants, thickened with double cream, egg yolks or a *beurre manié*. It is basic, rustic and utterly delicious.

Scrape, beard and wash mussels as directed.
Sauté finely chopped shallots in 1 tablespoon (15 ml) butter until transparent but not coloured. Add wine, 2 to 3 tablespoons (30–45 ml) parsley, thyme and bay leaf, and freshly ground black pepper, to taste, and simmer gently for 10 minutes. Add mussels to this mixture; cover saucepan and steam, shaking constantly, until mussel shells open. Remove top shells and arrange mussels in a large, deep, heated serving platter. Keep warm.
Reduce the cooking liquid to half the original quantity. Thicken, if you must, by adding a *beurre manié*, made by creaming together 2 tablespoons (30 ml) butter and 1 tablespoon (15 ml) flour. Correct seasoning and pour sauce over mussels. Sprinkle with a little finely chopped parsley and serve immediately. Serves 4 to 6.

MUSSELS AU GRATIN

4 dozen fresh mussels
¾ pint (450 ml) dry white wine
½ Spanish onion, finely chopped
4 tablespoons (60 ml) finely chopped parsley
4 tablespoons (60 ml) butter
Freshly grated breadcrumbs
Finely chopped chives

Clean fresh mussels. Place in saucepan with dry white wine, finely chopped onion and 2 tablespoons (30 ml) finely chopped parsley. Cover and steam for 4 or 5 minutes, or until shells open. Remove mussels, reserving liquor. Remove one half-shell from each; place mussels in their half-shells in 4 individual ovenproof dishes. Add butter to mussel liquor; cook for 3 minutes, or until reduced to half the original quantity. Pour this sauce over mussels; sprinkle each one lightly with equal parts freshly grated breadcrumbs, chives and remaining finely chopped parsley. Grill for 2 or 3 minutes. Serve as appetizer. Serves 4.

BROCHETTES DE MOULES

4 pints (2.25 lit) mussels
2 tablespoons (30 ml) finely chopped shallots
2 sprigs thyme
2 sprigs parsley
1 bay leaf
Salt
¼ pint (150 ml) dry white wine
8 oz (225 g) unsmoked bacon, in 1 piece
Freshly ground black pepper
Melted butter
Béarnaise Sauce (page 122)

Scrape, beard and wash mussels, and place them in a saucepan with finely chopped shallot, thyme, parsley and a bay leaf. Season lightly with salt and moisten with dry white wine. Cover saucepan and steam for 4 to 5 minutes, or until shells are well opened.

Remove mussels from their shells; dice unsmoked bacon and place mussels on small skewers with squares of bacon between them. Season to taste with freshly ground black pepper. Brush with a little melted butter and cook under grill until bacon is golden, turning skewers from time to time. Serve with Béarnaise Sauce. Serves 4.

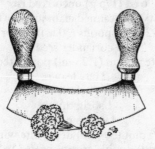

SALADE DE MOULES

4 dozen mussels
2 tablespoons (30 ml) chopped shallots
2 sprigs thyme
2 sprigs parsley
1 bay leaf
Salt
¼ pint (150 ml) very dry white wine
Wine vinegar
Olive oil
Freshly ground black pepper
4 tablespoons (60 ml) chopped parsley

Scrape, beard and wash mussels. Place in a saucepan together with chopped shallots, thyme, parsley and a bay leaf. Season lightly with salt and moisten with dry white wine. Simmer until the mussels are fully opened. Remove them from their shells.

Prepare a dressing made of one part liquid in which the mussels were cooked, one part wine vinegar and one part olive oil. Season to taste with salt and freshly ground black pepper; pour dressing over mussels while they are still warm. Sprinkle with chopped parsley. Mussels should be moist, but without excess dressing. Serve cold as *hors-d'œuvre*. Serves 4.

MUSSEL PILAFF

4 dozen mussels
4 tablespoons (60 ml) olive oil
1 Spanish onion, finely chopped
6 oz (175 g) uncooked rice
½ pint (300 ml) canned clam juice or fish stock
2 tablespoons (30 ml) butter
4 coriander seeds
¼ level teaspoon (1.25 ml) powdered saffron
2 bay leaves
1 clove
1 sprig thyme
4 sprigs parsley
½ pint (300 ml) dry white wine
½ pint (300 ml) double cream, heated to boiling point
Salt and freshly ground black pepper
Finely chopped parsley

Heat olive oil in a thick-bottomed saucepan; stir in half of the finely chopped onion and 6 oz (175 g) rice; simmer gently, stirring, until rice becomes semi-transparent. Add clam juice or well-flavoured fish stock and simmer gently, stirring from time to time with a wooden fork and adding a little hot water if necessary, until rice is tender but not soft – 20 to 25 minutes.

Heat butter in a saucepan; add remaining chopped onion, and coriander, saffron, bay leaves, clove, thyme, parsley and dry white wine, and cook over a high heat until liquid is reduced to half the original quantity. Strain into heated cream, and add mussels which you have steamed open and removed from their shells. Season to taste with salt and freshly ground black pepper. Arrange hot rice in a ring on a large heated serving dish; pour mussels and sauce into centre of ring; sprinkle with finely chopped parsley and serve immediately. Serves 4 to 6.

Oysters

Raced across the Alps from Britain, the oyster was one of the greatest luxuries of Imperial Rome. You can almost measure the spread of Roman civilization by the oyster shells they left behind – Verulanium near St Albans is swarming with them – and the industry the Romans founded during their 400 years' occupation of the Isles satisfied British needs up to the middle of the last century.

Then man had to come to the oyster's aid to prevent it being eaten out of existence. And now the baby brood oysters are tenderly protected from their marine enemies, so that they can plump up enough to fall victim to man's insatiable demands.

Great snobbery surrounds the oyster: and why should it not, when some of the finest of them are reared in beds owned by the Prince of Wales himself? I agree that the native oysters of Colchester and Whitstable should be eaten raw on the half-shell, their flavour enhanced by nothing but the fresh liquor in the shell, unspoilt by cayenne, or vinegar, or more than a drop of lemon. I agree that they should be left their closed season, when R is out of the month and they are busily engaged in providing us with offspring for future years. But I do insist that oysters from the Continent should be enjoyed all the year round; that they should be cooked in a hundred delicious ways (it is the shortness of the cooking time that is all-important in keeping them tender and flavourful); that we should overcome our fear of them, stand up to them, and use them as we want to.

OYSTERS WITH BLACK CAVIAR

2 dozen fresh oysters
4 tablespoons (60 ml) black caviar
Crushed ice
Lemon halves

Spread each oyster in its half-shell with ½ teaspoon (2.5 ml) black caviar. Serve the oysters with lemon halves, on beds of crushed ice. Serves 4.

FRIED OYSTERS

2–3 dozen oysters
2 eggs, beaten
Milk
Salt and freshly ground black pepper
Cornmeal, biscuit crumbs, or fresh breadcrumbs
4 oz (100 g) butter
¼ pint (150 ml) olive oil
Lemon wedges

Shell oysters. Combine beaten eggs and a little milk in a bowl. Season to taste with salt and freshly ground black pepper. Dip oysters in egg mixture, then in cornmeal or crumbs, and allow to set on paper towel or foil for about 5 minutes before cooking.

Melt butter in a large thick-bottomed frying pan or deep-fryer. Add olive oil; bring to frying temperature and cook oysters in fat until they are golden brown. Serve immediately with wedges of lemon. Serves 4 to 6.

STUFFED OYSTERS AND MUSSELS WITH GRUYÈRE BUTTER

12 fresh oysters
24 fresh mussels
4 cloves garlic, finely chopped
4 shallots, finely chopped
½ pint (300 ml) dry white wine
4 oz (100 g) freshly grated Gruyère
4 tablespoons (60 ml) butter
2 tablespoons (30 ml) finely chopped parsley
Cayenne and freshly ground black pepper
Fresh breadcrumbs

Combine washed and 'bearded' mussels (see page 256) with finely chopped garlic, shallots and dry white wine in a small saucepan. Cover and steam open. Remove top shells from mussels and arrange mussels on a baking tray with fresh raw oysters from which you have removed the top shells.

Reduce wine and shallot mixture to half the original quantity over a high heat. Cool and mix to a smooth paste with freshly grated Gruyère, butter and finely chopped parsley. Season to taste with cayenne and freshly ground black pepper.

Loosen each oyster and mussel from shell with a sharp knife. Place a knob of Gruyère stuffing on each; sprinkle lightly with freshly grated Gruyère and breadcrumbs, and place under grill until sauce is melted and sizzling. Serve immediately. Serves 4.

OYSTERS ROCKEFELLER

24 freshly opened oysters
4 tablespoons (60 ml) finely chopped shallots
8 oz (225 g) butter
4 tablespoons (60 ml) fine breadcrumbs
1 bunch watercress
4 tablespoons (60 ml) chopped celery leaves
4 tablespoons (60 ml) chopped parsley
1 teaspoon (5 ml) finely chopped chervil
1 teaspoon (5 ml) finely chopped tarragon
4 tablespoons (60 ml) Pernod
Salt, freshly ground black pepper and
cayenne pepper
Rock salt

Sauté shallots in 4 tablespoons (60 ml) butter until transparent; add breadcrumbs and stir over a low heat until lightly browned.

Put watercress leaves, separated from their stems, through the fine blade of a food chopper with celery and parsley. Combine shallot and breadcrumbs mixture and minced greens in a large bowl or mortar; add finely chopped chervil and tarragon, and Pernod, and season with salt, freshly ground black pepper and cayenne pepper. Add the remaining butter and pound to a smooth paste. Keep this green herb butter cool until ready to use.

Place a bed of rock salt in a baking tin large enough to hold the oysters comfortably, or in 4 small tins; dampen salt slightly and place oysters in their half-shells on this bed. Place 1 tablespoon (15 ml) of green herb butter on each oyster and bake in a hot oven (450°F/230°C/GM8) for 4 to 5 minutes, or until butter has melted and oysters are heated through. Serve immediately. Serves 4.

OYSTER PIE

Puff or shortcrust pastry, to cover dish
(page 760 or 754)
12 oysters and their liquor
6 tablespoons (90 ml) dry white wine
12 oz (350 g) turbot, poached and diced
Salt and freshly ground black pepper
Grated nutmeg
½ pint (300 ml) hot Béchamel Sauce (page 104)
2 tablespoons (30 ml) double cream
1 level tablespoon (15 ml) finely chopped onion
2 tablespoons (30 ml) finely chopped parsley
Butter

Make pastry; roll out to fit top of deep oval or round baking dish.
Preheat oven to fairly hot (425°F/220°C/GM7). Remove oysters
from shells and cook them in their liquor and dry white wine until
edges curl. Drain and reserve liquor. Combine oysters with
poached and diced turbot in deep pie dish. Season to taste with
salt, freshly ground black pepper and grated nutmeg.

Prepare Béchamel Sauce, and add oyster and wine stock. Stir in
cream, finely chopped onion and finely chopped parsley, and
pour over oysters and turbot. Mix well; dot with butter.

Fit pastry top in place, moisten the edges of pastry with water
and fit well to edges of dish. Cut vents in top to let steam escape,
and bake for about 15 to 20 minutes, or until pastry is golden and
done. Serves 4 to 6.

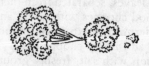

Prawns, Shrimps and Scampi

Just whisper the word '*tempura*' to a Japanese and watch his eyes
light up with pleasure. This great dish from Japan is an exciting
newcomer to Western tables.

I first tasted *tempura* in San Francisco's elegant Mingei-Ya, one
of the most popular of the city's restaurants, where one sits on the

floor at low tables in Japanese fashion, in a serene setting of Japanese *shoji* screens and architectural plants. Our meal began with *sashimi* (Japanese raw fish with *wasabi* sauce), followed by *tempura* (large prawns dipped in batter and deep-fried with vegetables), *sukiyaki* (Japanese beef and vegetables sautéed to order at the table) and *misu* (a deliciously light-flavoured Japanese soup).

Tempura is always based on seafood – usually Pacific prawns, lobster or sliced fish – dipped in a gossamer-light batter, and deep-fried until pale golden in sesame or peanut oil, or a combination of the two. To this main staple is added a variety of batter-dipped and deep-fried vegetables: quartered mushroom caps, green pepper rings, diced aubergine, sliced carrots, blanched string beans, or sprigs of fresh watercress and parsley.

The whole dish is magnificently light; the foods are fried to *al dente* tenderness, the outside coating of delicate batter to a crisp pale gold.

JAPANESE TEMPURA

4 large sprigs parsley
2 small green peppers
8 mushrooms, halved
½ Spanish onion, sliced
16–20 raw Pacific prawns, shelled
Peanut oil, for frying

TEMPURA BATTER
3 oz (75 g) sifted flour
1 egg yolk
¼ pint (150 ml) cold water

TEMPURA SAUCE
¼ pint (150 ml) Japanese *dashi* (a fish stock made with
dried bonito flakes); canned clam juice or a rich
homemade fish stock will substitute
4 tablespoons (60 ml) soy sauce
½ level teaspoon (2.5 ml) sugar
4 tablespoons (60 ml) water
4 tablespoons (60 ml) *sake* or dry sherry
Pinch of powdered ginger

Wash and prepare vegetables; cut green pepper into rings; halve mushrooms; slice onion. Peel and clean prawns, leaving on tails.

TEMPURA BATTER
Sift flour 3 times. Beat egg yolk and water together. Gradually add the flour, stirring lightly from the bottom with a spoon. Flour should not be mixed in too thoroughly.

TEMPURA SAUCE
Combine *dashi* (or clam juice or fish stock) with soy sauce, sugar and water. Bring to a boil and simmer for 5 minutes. Stir in *sake* (or dry sherry) and powdered ginger. Serve in individual bowls.

When ready to serve: heat oil in a deep frying pan to 300°–325°F/ 150°–170°C/GM2–3. Dip prawns in batter and fry in hot oil until golden. Remove with perforated spoon and set on paper towel to drain. Dip green pepper rings, parsley sprigs, mushroom halves and onion slices in batter, and fry separately in hot oil until golden. Drain. Serve Tempura immediately with accompanying small bowls of Tempura Sauce. Guests dip each batter-encased ingredient into sauce bowl before eating. Serves 4.

SHRIMPS OR PRAWNS WITH MUSHROOMS

1 lb (450 g) shrimps or prawns
2 tablespoons (30 ml) oil
½ teaspoon (2.5 ml) salt
8 oz (225 g) mushrooms, sliced
¼ pint (150 ml) chicken stock
2 tablespoons (30 ml) cornflour
2 teaspoons (10 ml) soy sauce
¼ cup water

Shell the shrimps or prawns, cutting prawns into 2 or 3 pieces, depending on size. Put them in a frying pan in which the oil and salt have been heated, and cook for 4 minutes, or until they are pink. Add the sliced mushrooms and the chicken stock. Cover the pan and cook over a low heat for 5 minutes.

Make a sauce of the cornflour, soy sauce and about ¼ cup of water. Pour this over the shrimps or prawns and mushrooms, and cook for 3 or 4 minutes until the sauce thickens. Stir throughout the cooking process. Serve hot. Serves 4 if served with 2 or more other Chinese dishes.

FRIED PRAWNS WITH WATER CHESTNUTS

8 oz (225 g) shelled prawns – fresh or frozen
1 clove garlic, finely chopped
2 spring onions, finely sliced
10 water chestnuts, finely sliced
4 oz (100 g) mushrooms, finely sliced
8 sprigs chicory
4 tablespoons (60 ml) peanut oil

SAUCE
1 teaspoon (5 ml) cornflour
½ level teaspoon (2.5 ml) salt
Pinch of sugar
2 teaspoons (10 ml) soy sauce
1 teaspoon (5 ml) vinegar
1 tablespoon (15 ml) sake, or sherry and water
¼ pint (150 ml) chicken or fish stock

Combine finely chopped garlic, sliced spring onions, water chestnuts, mushrooms and chicory in a large bowl. Add with the prawns to hot oil and sauté until prawns are cooked through. Remove prawns and vegetables to a hot serving dish and keep warm.

SAUCE
Mix all sauce ingredients smoothly together and add to the oil in the frying pan. Simmer gently for 3 minutes then pour over the prawns and serve hot.

This dish serves 4 if served with 2 or more other dishes.

CHINESE STEAMED SCAMPI

1½ lb (675 g) frozen scampi
Cornflour
4 shallots, finely chopped
4 oz (100 g) mushrooms, finely sliced
2 oz (50 g) cucumber, finely sliced
2 tablespoons (30 ml) soy sauce
4 tablespoons (60 ml) dry white wine
Coarse black pepper
Steamed rice
Tomatoes

Defrost scampi, roll in cornflour, and place on a large dish in steamer with finely chopped shallots, sliced mushrooms and cucumber, soy sauce and white wine. Season with a little coarsely ground pepper and cook over 2 inches (50 mm) of fast-boiling water, covered, so that the dish is entirely confined in steam, until tender – about 15 minutes.

Serve hot on a bed of steamed rice, garnished with sliced fresh tomatoes. Serves 4.

PRAWN BISQUE

8 oz (225 g) cooked prawns
¼ pint (150 ml) canned clam juice
¾ pint (450 ml) double cream
¼ teaspoon (1.25 ml) paprika
Salt and freshly ground black pepper
4–6 tablespoons (60–90 ml) dry sherry
1 tablespoon (15 ml) finely chopped parsley
1 tablespoon (15 ml) finely chopped chives

Place cooked prawns (saving 1 or 2 for garnish) and clam juice in the container of electric blender, and blend for 1 minute. Remove to the top of a double saucepan, add cream and paprika, and season to taste with salt and freshly ground black pepper. Cook over hot water, stirring from time to time, until soup comes to a boil. Thin to taste with additional clam juice. Add sherry, and serve immediately in individual cups, garnished with chopped prawns and finely chopped parsley and chives. Serves 4 to 6.

PRAWNS IN RED WINE

1½ lb (675 g) large prawns, shelled
4 tablespoons (60 ml) olive oil
2 tablespoons (30 ml) chopped shallots
½ pint (300 ml) red Burgundy
1 clove garlic, crushed
1 bay leaf
Peppercorns, crushed
2 tablespoons (30 ml) butter
4 tablespoons (60 ml) each chopped onion, carrot and leek
1 tablespoon (15 ml) tomato concentrate
2 tablespoons (30 ml) cornflour
¾ pint (450 ml) strong chicken stock
Rice

Heat 2 tablespoons (30 ml) olive oil in a frying pan. Add shallots and cook gently until transparent. Add Burgundy, garlic, bay leaf and peppercorns, and simmer for 10 to 15 minutes.

Heat the butter and remaining oil in another pan; add mixed vegetables and cook until they turn golden. Mix tomato concentrate and cornflour, and blend into vegetable mixture, add chicken stock and stir until it boils. Add Burgundy mixture and simmer until thick. Strain the sauce. Add prawns and simmer until cooked through. Serve with rice. Serves 4.

SCALLOPS IN PORT WINE

8 scallops
8 tablespoons (120 ml) dry white wine
8 tablespoons (120 ml) fish stock or water
2 tablespoons (30 ml) finely chopped shallots
4 tablespoons (60 ml) double cream
Salt and freshly ground black pepper

SAUCE
2 tablespoons (30 ml) butter
½ Spanish onion, finely chopped
2 carrots, finely chopped
½ clove garlic, finely chopped
2 tablespoons (30 ml) flour
Stock from scallops
2–4 tablespoons (30–60 ml) port

Wash scallops well in cold water. Separate coral from scallops and remove any membranes attached.

Combine scallops and coral in a saucepan with dry white wine, fish stock or water, shallots and cream, and season to taste with salt and freshly ground black pepper. Cover pan and simmer for 5 minutes. Strain sauce over scallops. Heat through and serve immediately. Serves 4.

SAUCE
Melt butter in the top of a double saucepan; add finely chopped onion, carrots and garlic; simmer until vegetables are browned. Sprinkle with flour; add stock from scallops and cook over water, stirring continuously, until sauce is smooth and thick. Add port to taste; correct seasoning.

SEAFOOD BOUQUET WITH WHISKY

12 fillets of sole
Flour
2 tablespoons (30 ml) butter
2 tablespoons (30 ml) olive oil
12 large prawns, shelled
24 shelled mussels
1 can whole clams
1 tablespoon (15 ml) finely chopped parsley
1 level teaspoon (5 ml) rosemary leaves
8 tablespoons (120 ml) whisky
¼ pint (150 ml) double cream
¼ pint (150 ml) clam juice
Boiled rice

Lightly flour fillets of sole, and fry them in butter and olive oil until golden brown. Remove carefully and keep warm. Lightly flour prawns, mussels and canned clams. Add to frying pan and fry in remaining fat until golden. Remove. Add finely chopped parsley and rosemary to pan; add whisky, and flame. Combine double cream and clam juice; stir into pan juices and whisk until well blended. Add sole, prawns, mussels and clams to sauce; heat through and serve over rice. Serves 4 to 6.

AMERICAN SEAFOOD CASSEROLE

8 oz (225 g) lobster, sliced
8 oz (225 g) prawns, shelled
8 oz (225 g) fillets of sole, sliced
8 oz (225 g) scallops, cut in quarters
24 mussels, removed from their shells
4 shallots, finely chopped
4 tablespoons (60 ml) butter
¼ pint (150 ml) dry white wine
8 oz (225 g) fresh mushrooms, thinly sliced
1 pint (600 ml) thick Béchamel Sauce (page 104)
Salt and freshly ground black pepper
Rice or individual pastry cases

Cook and have ready for use: lobster, prawns, sole, scallops and mussels.

Simmer finely chopped shallots in 2 tablespoons (30 ml) butter until transparent; add dry white wine and simmer gently until shallots are cooked through. Sauté thinly sliced mushrooms in remaining butter and add to wine and shallot mixture.

Make Béchamel Sauce in the usual way in the top of a double saucepan. Stir in seafood and mushroom-onion mixture, and heat through. Season to taste with salt and freshly ground black pepper, adding a little more white wine if the mixture is too thick. Serve with rice or in individual pastry cases. Serves 6 to 8.

PRAWNS IN ASPIC

1½ lb (675 g) prawns
White wine *court-bouillon*
2 egg whites, lightly beaten
Salt and freshly ground black pepper
2 tablespoons (30 ml) gelatine
¼ pint (150 ml) dry white wine
Lemon peel
Truffles
Watercress
Mayonnaise (page 120)
Lemon juice

Cook prawns in a white wine *court-bouillon* for 5 minutes. Cool the prawns, then shell and de-vein them. Reduce the *court-bouillon* to 2 pints (1.1. lit); strain it, and clear it by adding 2 lightly beaten egg whites. Bring liquid slowly to a boil, stirring continuously. When liquid reaches boiling point, let it stand for 10 minutes over a very low heat, barely simmering. Strain through a sieve lined with a wet flannel cloth and cool. Correct seasoning.

To make aspic: soften gelatine in white wine. Reheat the *court-bouillon* and dissolve the gelatine in it. Allow to cool. Coat a mould with a thin layer of the aspic and arrange thin cut-outs of lemon peel and truffles on it. Chill until firm; add the cooked prawns and fill the mould with the remaining aspic. Chill until aspic is firmly set; turn out the mould on a serving dish and garnish with watercress. Serve cold with mayonnaise, flavoured to taste with additional lemon juice. Serves 4.

Scallops

There are many ways of cooking scallops. In America, tiny bay scallops – ½ to 1 inch (13–25 mm) in diameter – are rolled in egg and breadcrumbs and fried in hot fat or oil, or brushed with paprika-flavoured butter and cooked under the grill in heatproof ramekins. In Britain and France, we prefer our scallops large, at least 2 inches (50 mm) in diameter complete with coral tongues, and they are cooked in a variety of ways. My favourite way of cooking these delicious shellfish is the following.

COQUILLES ST JACQUES AU GRATIN

8–12 scallops (with shells)
6–8 tablespoons (90–120 ml) dry white wine
2 tablespoons (30 ml) butter
Paprika
Salt and freshly ground black pepper
6 oz (175 g) mushrooms, and 2 oz (50 g) onion and
shallot, finely chopped and softened in butter
1 tablespoon (15 ml) finely chopped parsley
2–4 tablespoons (30–60 ml) reduced Velouté Sauce (page 108)
Freshly grated Parmesan
Breadcrumbs and melted butter

Wash and trim scallops. Drain. Simmer scallops and coral for 5 minutes in dry white wine and butter, flavoured with paprika, salt and freshly ground black pepper. Add mushrooms, onion and shallot mixture, and finely chopped parsley. Moisten with reduced Velouté Sauce; correct seasoning. Garnish cleaned scallop shells or individual heatproof dishes with this mixture. Sprinkle with grated cheese, breadcrumbs and melted butter, and put under the grill until brown. Serves 4 to 6.

SEAFOOD SALAD WITH MEDITERRANEAN DRESSING

8 oz (225 g) cooked crabmeat, flaked
8 oz (225 g) cooked and shelled prawns
12 oz (350 g) cooked lobster meat, diced
12 oz (350 g) sole or turbot, cooked in
court-bouillon and diced
Mixed salad greens: lettuce, watercress,
cos lettuce, endive, etc.
4–6 tomatoes, cut in wedges
12 black olives
12 green olives

MEDITERRANEAN DRESSING
½ pint (300 ml) olive oil
6 tablespoons (90 ml) wine vinegar
Salt and freshly ground black pepper
2 cloves garlic, finely chopped
2 tablespoons (30 ml) each finely chopped
parsley, chives and tarragon

Prepare cooked crabmeat, prawns, lobster and fish, and place each in an individual bowl. Combine Mediterranean Dressing ingredients and pour 2 to 3 tablespoonfuls (30–45 ml) into each bowl. Place bowls in refrigerator to marinate for at least 2 hours. Reserve remainder of salad dressing.

Just before serving, prepare salad greens. Arrange in a large salad bowl; place marinated seafood in centre of greens; garnish with tomato wedges and olives. Pour remaining dressing over greens. Serves 4 to 6.

CHAPTER SIX

Eggs and Omelettes

For close on a thousand years the Romans began almost every meal with eggs. 'From eggs to apples' was their equivalent of 'from soup to nuts'. The Greeks before them based a large part of their cuisine on eggs, as did early Eastern civilizations such as the Chinese.

To the ancients, the egg was almost sacred. Gods were hatched from them, witches hid in their empty shells, and philosophers held them up as symbols of the world and its elements: the shell, earth; the white, water; the yolk, fire; and the space under the shell, air. St Thomas Aquinas went even further in the Middle Ages, when he used the egg as evidence of the unity of life itself.

One of the basic foods from the start of human history, eggs have now been relegated by the British almost wholly to the breakfast table. But, like the Romans, I believe that eggs can be served with almost everything, from honey to rose petals, from herbs and cheese to meat and fish and game. So besides the simple boiled, poached or fried eggs of nursery days, think of eggs as the French do, in terms of feathery soft omelettes drooping moist with savoury fillings, or aristocratic soufflés, creamy rich concoctions puffed to insubstantial lightness under golden crusts.

The greatest virtue of the egg to most of us today is that it is always there – handy in the refrigerator – ready to lend its sophisticated magic to fantastically light and insubstantial soufflés and moistly golden omelettes whenever there are unexpected guests.

We depend on the egg – one of the great basics of all cookery – to enrich and flavour chicken soups and sauces; to bind croquettes, meat loaves, and stuffings for meat, poultry and game; to coat meat, fish and vegetables for deep-frying; to add substance to batters and richness to cakes and pastry, and to act as the foundation for sauces made from butter and oil – mayonnaise, Hollandaise and Béarnaise. I like to use raw eggs to dress a salad, and to add colour and quality to a spaghetti sauce. Even the shell can be used to clarify consommés and jellies.

No single food is more essential to good cooking than the homely egg.

Boiled Eggs

Soft-Boiled Eggs

1. Slip the eggs gently with a spoon, one by one, into a saucepan with just enough boiling water to cover them. If only half the egg is immersed in the water, it will not cook evenly. Lower heat until water is just barely bubbling and allow 3 minutes for a classic soft-boiled egg – the white coagulated but still on the soft side and the golden yolk runny – or ½ to 1 minute more if it is to be set pretty firm.

2. Or place the eggs in boiling water as above. When the water reboils, remove the saucepan from the heat, cover it and allow eggs to stand for 10 minutes. You will find the whites have set without being tough, and the yolk will be creamy.

3. Or place the eggs in cold water over the heat, and remove them as soon as the water boils.

Soft-boiled eggs can be reheated by standing them for 3 or 4 minutes in hot (not boiling) water. (Once cooked and removed from the heat, no amount of subsequent heating will harden them.) If the egg is cracked, rub it over with a cut lemon just before you put it in the water, or cover the crack with a piece of gummed paper. The paper will come off, but not before the white of the egg is sufficiently coagulated to prevent it escaping into the water.

Hard-Boiled Eggs

Put the required number of eggs into a saucepan of boiling water, lowering them in carefully with a spoon to avoid breaking the shells. Allow the water to come to a boil again, and then boil the eggs for exactly 10 minutes. Lift eggs out and plunge them at once into cold water. They will shell more easily.

To shell hard-boiled eggs: tap the egg all round with the back of a knife. The shell can then be removed easily without damaging the white. Do not overcook the eggs, or the yolks will have a circle of green round them.

EGGS MAYONNAISE WITH CUCUMBER AND TOMATOES

4–6 hard-boiled eggs
½–¾ pint (300–450 ml) well-flavoured mayonnaise
(page 120)
½ large cucumber, seeded but not peeled, diced
4–6 ripe tomatoes, peeled, seeded and diced
Ripe olives
Olive oil and wine vinegar
Salt and freshly ground black pepper
Finely chopped parsley or tarragon

Shell hard-boiled eggs and cut in even slices. Arrange slices in overlapping rows on a bed of well-flavoured mayonnaise. Garnish serving dish with a ring of mixed diced cucumber and tomatoes, arranged in clusters of green and red. Dot with ripe olives; then sprinkle with a dressing of 3 parts olive oil to 1 part wine vinegar, and season to taste with salt, freshly ground black pepper and finely chopped parsley or tarragon. Serves 4.

STUFFED EGGS WITH GREEN MAYONNAISE

4–6 hard-boiled eggs
4 tablespoons (60 ml) pounded buttered shrimps
4 tablespoons (60 ml) mayonnaise
Lemon juice
½–¾ pint (300–450 ml) Green Mayonnaise (page 120)
2 tablespoons (30 ml) finely chopped fresh herbs

Shell hard-boiled eggs and cut them in half lengthwise. Remove yolks and mash them to a smooth thick paste with pounded buttered shrimps, mayonnaise and lemon juice, to taste.

Stuff each egg white with shrimp mixture, piling it up to re-form egg shape.

Arrange stuffed eggs on a bed of Green Mayonnaise in an *hors-d'œuvre* dish. Sprinkle with finely chopped herbs. Serves 4 to 6.

EGG AND ANCHOVY BARRELS

4 hard-boiled eggs
8 anchovy fillets
2 tablespoons (30 ml) mayonnaise
¼ teaspoon (1.25 ml) paprika
Salt and freshly ground black pepper
Watercress
Capers

Shell eggs and cut tops and bottoms off with a sharp knife dipped in cold water. Carefully remove yolks from broad end of eggs, being careful not to split whites. Mash yolks to a smooth paste with 4 anchovy fillets, mayonnaise and paprika. Season with salt and freshly ground black pepper, and stuff eggs with this mixture. If mixture is too stiff, add more mayonnaise.

To serve: place eggs, broad end up, on a bed of watercress. Split remaining anchovy fillets and wrap around centre of each egg. Top each barrel with capers. Serves 4.

EGG AND ONION CASSEROLE

6 eggs
4 onions
2 tablespoons (30 ml) butter
½ pint (300 ml) light Béchamel Sauce (page 104)
Salt and freshly ground black pepper

Hard-boil the eggs for 15 minutes in boiling water. Remove shells and slice eggs. Slice onions and sauté in butter until they are soft and golden; do not let them brown. Add onions and butter to hot Béchamel Sauce; stir well; fold in the egg slices and season to taste with salt and freshly ground black pepper. Heat through in an ovenproof casserole and serve hot. Serves 4.

ŒUFS À LA TAPÉNADE

8–10 stoned ripe olives
4–5 anchovy fillets
2 tablespoons (30 ml) tuna fish
1 teaspoon (5 ml) Dijon mustard
1–2 tablespoons (15–30 ml) chopped capers
4–6 tablespoons (60–90 ml) olive oil
1 tablespoon (15 ml) cognac
Freshly ground black pepper
4–6 hard-boiled eggs
Lettuce

Pound stoned ripe olives, anchovy fillets and tuna fish in a mortar with mustard and capers. When the mixture has been blended to a smooth paste, put it through a fine sieve and whisk olive oil into it. Add cognac, and season to taste with freshly ground black pepper.

Cut hard-boiled eggs in half lengthwise and remove yolks. Blend yolks with *tapénade* mixture, adding a little more olive oil if necessary. Fill egg hollows with mixture and serve on a bed of lettuce. Serves 4 to 6.

Note: The *tapénade* mixture keeps well in a covered jar and is excellent as a highly flavoured canapé spread.

Poached Eggs

Half-fill a shallow saucepan with water and bring to a boil. Add vinegar or lemon juice in the proportion of 1 teaspoonful (5 ml) to 1 pint (600 ml) of water, and a good pinch of salt. When the water is simmering gently, break 1 egg into a cup, and from this slip it gently into the pan. Gather the white lightly together with a spoon and pour some of the acidulated water over it. Repeat this with each egg, and let them cook for 3 minutes, or until the white is nicely set without being hard. Lift each egg out separately with a perforated spoon and trim off any ragged edges of white, letting the egg drain over the pan. Place poached eggs on rounds of hot buttered toast, and arrange them symmetrically on a dish garnished with parsley, or serve them in any number of other ways.

ŒUFS MOLLETS

If, like me, you find attractively turned out poached eggs difficult to make successfully, turn your attentions to the *œuf mollet*. *Oeuf mollet* is the French culinary term for a shelled soft-boiled egg, with the white delicately firm and the yolk deliciously runny. To make *œufs mollets*, boil the eggs as usual, but for 5 minutes only. Then put them in cold water for 5 minutes before removing the shells carefully under cold water. If eggs are not to be used at once, put them back in the cold water. If they are to be served hot, reheat them in hot, slightly salted water, or in hot chicken stock or milk. *Oeufs mollets* may be served in any of the following recipes for poached eggs.

EGGS IN ASPIC

Madeira Aspic (page 76)
8 fresh tarragon leaves
1 slice cooked ham, cut *en julienne*
4 poached eggs
2 teaspoons (10 ml) each cooked peas, diced cooked
turnip and diced cooked carrot (optional)

Coat the bottom of small individual moulds with Madeira Aspic;
allow to set. Pour boiling water over tarragon leaves; dry and
arrange on aspic. Place 2 to 4 thin strips of ham across leaves, and
dribble a little aspic over them to hold them in place.

Trim poached eggs with scissors and place in mould. Pour aspic
over them to cover. Garnish, if desired, with cold cooked peas
and diced cooked turnip and carrot. Cover with aspic. Chill.
Unmould just before serving. Serves 4.

POACHED EGGS HOLLANDAISE

4 poached eggs
1 recipe Fingertip Pastry (page 760)
Salt and freshly ground black pepper
Butter
8 tablespoons (120 ml) Hollandaise Sauce (page 123)

Bake 4 individual pastry cases; remove from tins. Place 1 poached
egg in each case; season to taste with salt and freshly ground black
pepper, and dot with butter; warm through for a few minutes in a
moderate oven (375°F/190°C/GM5). Top each egg with 2 tablespoons (30 ml) Hollandaise Sauce and serve immediately. Serves
4.

ŒUFS BÉNÉDICTINE I

4 eggs
4 slices cooked ham
Butter
4 slices white bread
8 tablespoons (120 ml) Hollandaise Sauce (page 123)

Poach eggs and keep warm. Cut 4 rounds of sliced ham just large enough to fit individual egg dishes. Warm in butter. Toast bread and cut rounds of the same size. Butter toast rounds and place 1 in each heated egg dish. Cover each round with warmed ham and top with a poached egg. Spoon over Hollandaise Sauce and serve immediately. Serves 4.

ŒUFS BÉNÉDICTINE II

4 eggs
4 slices white bread
Butter
8 tablespoons (120 ml) *Brandade de Morue* (page 179)
8 tablespoons (120 ml) Hollandaise Sauce (page 123)

Poach eggs and keep warm. Toast bread and cut rounds to fit individual egg dishes. Butter each round and spread it with 2 tablespoons (30 ml) hot *brandade de morue*. Place in individual egg dishes. Top with a poached egg and spoon over Hollandaise Sauce. Serve immediately. Serves 4.

Baked Eggs

ŒUFS EN COCOTTE

A popular first course today, basically this very simple recipe butters individual *cocottes*, ramekins or soufflé dishes, breaks 1 or 2 eggs into each, flavours the eggs to taste with salt and freshly ground black pepper, covers each egg with a little hot cream, and bakes them in a preheated slow oven (325°–350°F/170°–180°C/ GM3–4) until the whites just begin to set and the yolks are still runny. The variations on this simple dish are infinite. I like the following: (1) place a spoonful of lightly sautéed diced chicken liver, Italian sausage or ham in the bottom of each *cocotte* before adding eggs; (2) sprinkle eggs with finely grated cheese before adding cream; (3) set eggs on a bed of creamed spinach; add eggs and cream, and serve with a little tomato sauce.

BAKED EGGS IN TOMATO CUPS

4 large tomatoes
Salt and freshly ground black pepper
4 eggs
Butter

HOT CURRY SAUCE
2 tablespoons (30 ml) butter
2 tablespoons (30 ml) flour
¼ pint (150 ml) milk
¼ pint (150 ml) single cream
Salt and white pepper
1 level teaspoon (5 ml) curry powder

Cut tops from tomatoes, remove pulp, and drain. Season insides of tomato cases with salt and a little freshly ground black pepper. Break an egg into each tomato case; dot with butter, and season with salt and freshly ground black pepper. Bake in individual baking dishes in a moderate oven (375°F/190°C/GM5) until the eggs are firm. Serve topped with Hot Curry Sauce. Serves 4.

HOT CURRY SAUCE
Melt butter in a thick-bottomed saucepan. Add flour and cook, stirring constantly, until well blended. Add milk and cream slowly, stirring constantly. Season to taste with salt, white pepper and curry powder. Cover and simmer gently for 8 minutes.

BAKED EGGS AND BACON

8 eggs
4–6 tablespoons (60–90 ml) diced Cheddar
4 slices bacon, grilled and diced
Salt and freshly ground black pepper
8 tablespoons (120 ml) double cream

Butter 4 individual *cocottes* or soufflé dishes; sprinkle a quarter of
the diced cheese and diced grilled bacon over bottom of each dish.
Break 2 eggs into each dish; season to taste with salt and freshly
ground black pepper, and top with 2 tablespoons (30 ml) double
cream. Bake in a slow oven (350°F/180°C/GM4) for 15 minutes,
or until egg whites are firm. Serves 4.

SURPRISE EGGS

4 eggs
Salt and white pepper
Butter
4 tablespoons (60 ml) double cream
4 tablespoons (60 ml) grated Parmesan

Separate eggs. Beat the whites very stiff, and season generously
with salt and white pepper. Butter individual ramekins or *cocottes*,
and spoon an egg white into each. Use rather large dishes, as egg
whites tend to rise like a soufflé. Make a depression with the back
of your spoon for each egg yolk. Place yolks in hollows (1 to each
ramekin); cover each yolk with 1 tablespoon (15 ml) cream, and
sprinkle with grated cheese. Bake in a hot oven (450°F/230°C/
GM8) for 8 to 10 minutes. Serves 4.

BAKED EGGS LORRAINE

4 eggs
Butter
2 slices bacon, cut in half
Salt and freshly ground black pepper

Place 1 teaspoon (5 ml) butter and a half-slice of bacon in each of 4 individual heatproof *cocottes*, and cook in a moderate oven (375°F/190°C/GM5) until bacon is soft. Turn bacon and break an egg into each *cocotte*. Season to taste with salt and freshly ground black pepper, and return to oven for a few more minutes until egg whites are set. Serves 4.

Oeufs Moulés

A sort of *œuf en cocotte* in reverse, this was a fashionable first-course egg in nineteenth-century France. Nothing more or less than eggs baked in *dariole* moulds and then turned out before serving, these little egg turrets make a decorative first course, especially if served with an appropriate sauce and placed in individual pastry cases, cooked artichoke hearts, mushroom caps or tomato cases.

Here again, the method is simplicity itself: butter individual *dariole* moulds generously. Break an egg into each mould; place moulds in a baking tin of hot water and cook in a slow oven (350°F/180°C/GM4) for 15 minutes. The insides of the moulds may be sprinkled with finely chopped parsley, finely chopped chives blanched in boiling water, or finely chopped mushrooms simmered in butter.

To serve: turn out moulds into individual pastry cases and pour any one of the following sauces over them: (1) a purée of peeled, seeded and chopped tomatoes softened in butter with a hint of finely chopped shallot, thyme, salt and freshly ground black pepper; (2) a purée of poached artichoke hearts enriched with Chicken Velouté Sauce (page 108) and double cream; (3) a purée of poached asparagus tips enriched with Chicken Velouté (page 108) and cream.

Or set each *œuf moulé* on a base of poached artichoke hearts, baked mushrooms caps or tomato cases, and mask eggs with a little well-flavoured Béchamel or Hollandaise Sauce (page 104 or 123).

Scrambled Eggs

Most of us think of scrambled eggs today as a breakfast dish to be served with crisp slices of bacon or diminutive sausages sautéed until golden. But in France, scrambled eggs can be a dish of creamy perfection, worthy of being served as a first course on its own at a luncheon party of distinction. I remember a remarkable luncheon at the elegant Plaza-Athénée in Paris, which started off with a delicious version of scrambled eggs (3 eggs per person cooked in butter until soft and moist) mixed with diced truffles and asparagus, and piled into a golden *croustade* of flaky pastry garnished with individual moulds of ham mousse and asparagus tips. Elegant and different, and yet, except for the diced truffles and the ham mousses, not too difficult or extravagant to make.

Taking a leaf from the Plaza-Athénée's book, I have often served small hot pastry cases filled just before serving with scrambled eggs lightly flavoured with a little grated Parmesan, and tossed with diced ham and mushrooms simmered in butter. Try this, too, with thin slivers of sliced smoked salmon or flaked smoked trout and sliced radishes.

SCRAMBLED EGGS

5 good-sized eggs
Salt and freshly ground black pepper
Butter
4 tablespoons (60 ml) double cream

Break eggs into a bowl and season to taste with salt and freshly ground black pepper. Mix eggs lightly with a fork, but do not beat them. Heat butter in the pan until it is sizzling but has not changed colour. Pour eggs into pan; allow them to set slightly; then stir them constantly with a wooden spoon, running edge of spoon round the pan and drawing the eggs into the centre of the pan. Cook until creamy. Then, with a wire whisk, whip double cream and a little diced butter into egg mixture until eggs are fluffy. Serve immediately on hot plates. Serves 2.

Good scrambled eggs need care and attention. Always heat the pan before adding butter. Use plenty of butter and make sure it is hot (but not coloured) before adding the eggs.

Scrambled eggs with cheese: Combine beaten eggs with grated Gruyère, Parmesan and double cream, to taste. Cook as in basic recipe above.

Scrambled eggs with buttered shrimps: Warm shrimps through in their butter and fold into scrambled eggs cooked as in basic recipe above.

Scrambled eggs with mushrooms: Sauté thinly sliced button mushrooms in butter until soft; season generously with salt and freshly ground black pepper, and fold into scrambled eggs when they are half cooked. Continue to cook as in basic recipe above. Garnish with sautéed mushroom caps.

Scrambled eggs with artichokes: Dice cooked artichoke hearts; toss in butter; season generously with salt and freshly ground black pepper, and fold into scrambled eggs when they are half cooked. Continue to cook as in basic recipe above. Garnish with finely chopped parsley.

SCRAMBLED EGG CROUSTADES

1 recipe Shortcrust Pastry (page 754)
12 eggs
4 tablespoons (60 ml) butter
4 oz (100 g) cooked ham, diced
6 quartered button mushrooms, sautéed in butter

Line individual *brioche* moulds thinly with pastry and bake until golden. Keep warm.

Scramble eggs (3 per person) in butter until creamy but still quite moist. Toss with diced cooked ham and mushrooms sautéed in butter.

Fill pastry cases and serve immediately. Serves 4.

Variation: Bake twice as many pastry cases as you will need: pile eggs, ham and mushrooms high in half of the cases, and top with remaining cases, inverted to form pastry covers.

Fried Eggs

FRIED EGGS

2 eggs
1 tablespoon (15 ml) butter
Salt and freshly ground black pepper

Melt butter in a small frying pan. Break 1 egg at a time into a cup; season with salt and freshly ground black pepper; slide eggs quickly into the sizzling butter and cook for 1 to 2 minutes, or until done as you like them. Lift out with a spatula or a perforated spoon; drain and serve immediately. Serves 1.

ŒUFS SUR LE PLAT

8 eggs
2 tablespoons (30 ml) butter
Salt and freshly ground black pepper

Lightly butter 4 flat heatproof dishes and break the eggs into them without breaking the yolks. Season with salt and freshly ground black pepper, and place the remaining butter in a small pieces on the top. Bake in a preheated slow oven (325°F/170°C/GM3) for 4 to 5 minutes, or until the whites are set but not hard. Serve hot in the dishes in which the eggs were cooked. Serves 4.

DEEP-FRIED EGGS IN PASTRY

4–6 eggs
Salt and freshly ground black pepper
Puff pastry
Yolks of 2 eggs, well beaten
Breadcrumbs
Fat, for deep-frying

Soft-boil eggs and place them in cold water. Shell eggs carefully, and spinkle to taste with salt and freshly ground black pepper.

Roll out pastry very thinly and cut out oblong-shaped pieces large enough to enfold each egg. Wrap each egg in pastry, sealing the joins with a little beaten egg. Trim superfluous pastry edges with scissors, making sure it is not too thick in any one part.

When ready to serve: brush eggs with beaten egg yolks; toss them in fine breadcrumbs and fry them in hot fat until golden brown. Drain well and serve immediately. Serves 4 to 6.

The Omelette

Brillat-Savarin, giving a recipe for an omelette made with blanched carp's roe, tuna, shallot, parsley, chives and lemon juice, recommends: 'This dish should be reserved for breakfasts of refinement, for connoisseurs in gastronomic art – those who understand eating – and where all eat with judgment; but especially let it be washed down with some good old wine, and you will see wonders.'

It might seem a trifle banal after that to give a recipe for an ordinary omelette, for every cook thinks he knows how to make one, but the number of people who have never eaten a really good one is quite surprising. For although omelettes are quite easy to make once you have acquired a *tour de main*, they are also easy to spoil. It is really child's play to make a perfect omelette, yet one false move and the dish is ruined – and you might as well throw it away.

The most important thing to remember in omelette-making as well as in all preparations based on eggs is that only strictly fresh eggs should be used, and the butter must be of the best quality.

Below is my favourite formula for an especially light omelette for 2 people.

BASIC OMELETTE

5 good–sized eggs
Salt and freshly ground black pepper
1 tablespoon (15 ml) water
1 tablespoon (15 ml) butter
2 tablespoons (30 ml) whipped egg white
A little freshly grated Gruyère or Parmesan

Break eggs into a bowl and season to taste with salt and freshly ground black pepper. Heat the omelette pan gradually on a medium heat until it is hot enough to make butter sizzle on contact. Add water to eggs and beat with a fork or wire whisk just enough to mix yolks and whites. Add butter to heated pan and shake until butter coats bottom of pan evenly. When butter is sizzling, pour in the beaten eggs all at once.

Quickly stir eggs for a second or two in the pan to assure even cooking just as you would for scrambled eggs. Then, if you want your omelette to be supremely light, stir in 2 tablespoons (30 ml) whipped egg white and a sprinkling of freshly grated Gruyère or Parmesan cheese – not enough to give it a cheesy flavour, but just enough to intensify the eggy taste of your omelette.

And now is the time to start working: as eggs begin to set, lift edges with a fork or palette knife so that the liquid can run under. Repeat until liquid is all used up but the eggs are still moist and soft, keeping eggs from sticking by shaking pan during the above operation.

Remove eggs from heat and, with one movement, slide the omelette towards the handle. When a third of the omelette has slid up the rounded edge of the pan, fold this quickly towards the centre with your palette knife. Raise the handle of the pan and slide opposite edge of omelette one-third up the side farthest away from the handle. Hold a heated serving dish under the pan, and as the rim of the omelette touches the dish, raise the handle more and more, until the pan is turned upside down and your oval-shaped, lightly browned omelette rests on the dish.

French chefs usually 'finish' their omelettes by skimming the surface lightly with a knob of butter on the point of a knife. Serve immediately. Serves 2.

After one or two tries to achieve your cook's *tour de main*, you should be able to produce a delicious omelette every time, golden on the outside and as juicy as you could wish inside.

The Omelette Pan

The first essential of successful omelette-making is a good pan. I keep a pan exclusively for eggs. It is a pan expressly designed for omelettes alone – one of good weight, with rounded sides so that the eggs can slide easily on to the plate when cooked. The best omelette pans are made of copper, steel or aluminium.

The size of the pan is important. It must not be too small or too large for the number of eggs used in the omelette. For unless it is well proportioned to the number of eggs generally used, the omelette will either be unmanageably thick or too thin. I find a pan 7 or 8 inches (17 or 20 cm) in diameter is just about right for a 4- to 5-egg omelette.

Never wash your omelette pan. Instead, just rub it clean after use with paper towels and a few drops of oil, then rub it dry with a clean cloth. If any egg adheres to the pan, it can be rubbed off with a little dry salt.

Once you have mastered the recipe for the basic omelette – *omelette nature*, the French call it – you are ready to try some of the many exciting variations on the omelette theme. Some of the most delicious are the easiest to make; but always remember to prepare the omelette filling before you make the omelette itself. In this way your omelettes can come to the table crisply cased, with a wonderfully moist interior and filling. And always serve your omelette as soon as it is cooked, as the most successful omelette will spoil and toughen if kept waiting. It is far better to let your guests wait for the omelette than to let the omelette wait for the guests.

Savoury Omelettes

INDIVIDUAL FRENCH OMELETTES

2 eggs
1 tablespoon (15 ml) water
Salt
Butter
1 tablespoon (15 ml) whipped egg white
1 tablespoon (15 ml) freshly grated Gruyère

Beat eggs with water until well mixed. Add salt to taste. Heat butter until sizzling in a preheated omelette pan. Remove pan from heat and pour in egg mixture. Return to heat and, shaking pan with one hand, stir egg mixture with fork in the other hand until eggs just begin to set. Add whipped egg white; sprinkle with freshly grated Gruyère and quickly stir eggs with a wide circular motion, shaking pan all the time to keep the omelette from sticking.

When eggs are set but surface is still moist, roll omelette on to a hot plate by tilting pan, starting it away from edge at one side with a fork and letting it roll over itself. Serves 1.

Portuguese omelette: Peel, seed and coarsely chop 4 ripe tomatoes. Simmer gently in butter until soft. Season to taste with salt and freshly ground black pepper. Make omelette as above and fill with tomatoes.

Florentine omelette: Wash fresh spinach leaves several times in cold water; drain. Simmer with a little butter until soft, stirring continuously. Press dry, and add butter, salt and freshly ground black pepper, to taste. Make omelette as above and fill with spinach.

Omelette with chicken livers: Slice 4 to 6 button mushrooms and 4 chicken livers, and sauté quickly in butter. Season generously with salt and freshly ground black pepper; add a little gravy or Brown Sauce (page 114). Make omelette as above and fill with liver and mushroom mixture. Sprinkle with finely chopped parsley.

ANCHOVY OMELETTE

4–6 good-sized eggs
1 tablespoon (15 ml) water
4–6 anchovy fillets, finely chopped
1 tablespoon (15 ml) finely chopped parsley
1 tomato, peeled, seeded and chopped
Olive oil
1 tablespoon (15 ml) freshly grated Gruyère
Butter

Beat eggs with water until well mixed. Add chopped anchovy fillets, parsley and tomato. Heat olive oil until sizzling in a preheated omelette pan. Remove pan from heat and pour in egg mixture. Return to heat and, shaking pan with one hand, stir egg mixture with fork in the other hand until eggs just begin to set. Sprinkle with freshly grated Gruyère and quickly stir eggs with a wide circular motion, shaking pan constantly to keep omelette from sticking.

When eggs are set but surface is still moist, roll omelette on to a hot plate by tilting pan, starting it away from edge at one side with a fork and letting it roll over itself. Pick up a small piece of butter on the point of a sharp knife and rub it over omelette. Serve immediately. Serves 2.

OMELETTE BÉNÉDICTINE

4–6 good-sized eggs
1 tablespoon (15 ml) water
Butter or olive oil
4–6 tablespoons (60–90 ml) *Brandade de Morue* (page 179)

CREAM SAUCE
1 tablespoon (15 ml) butter
1 tablespoon (15 ml) flour
¼ pint (150 ml) dry white wine
¼ pint (150 ml) double cream
Salt and freshly ground black pepper

This is an excellent luncheon omelette if you have left-over *brandade de morue*.

Beat eggs with water until well mixed. Heat butter or olive oil until sizzling in a preheated omelette pan. Remove pan from heat and pour in egg mixture. Return to heat and, shaking pan with one hand, stir egg mixture with fork in the other hand until eggs just begin to set. When eggs are still soft, spread warmed *brandade de morue* over centre; fold omelette; transfer to a heated dish; pour Cream Sauce over it and serve at once. Serves 2 to 3.

CREAM SAUCE
Melt butter in the top of a double saucepan; stir in flour and cook, stirring constantly, until smooth. Add dry white wine and double cream, and stir until boiling; reduce heat and cook, stirring from time to time, until smooth. Season to taste with salt and freshly ground black pepper.

OMELETTE PROVENÇALE

2 tomatoes, peeled, seeded and finely chopped
1 clove garlic, finely chopped
1 small onion, finely chopped
8 sprigs fresh parsley, chopped
2 sprigs fresh tarragon, chopped
Salt and freshly ground black pepper
2 tablespoons (30 ml) olive oil
4 eggs
1 tablespoon (15 ml) butter

Combine finely chopped tomatoes, garlic, onion, parsley and tarragon. Season with salt and freshly ground black pepper, and sauté in olive oil in a frying pan for about 10 minutes. Keep warm.

Beat eggs lightly, season with salt and pepper, and cook in butter as for Basic Omelette (page 290). When eggs are still soft, spread tomato and herb mixture in centre, fold omelette and serve at once on a heated dish. Serves 2.

OMELETTE BASQUE

1 sweet green pepper, sliced
Pork fat or olive oil
1 onion, coarsely chopped
3 ripe tomatoes, peeled, seeded and coarsely
chopped
1 clove garlic, mashed
2 tablespoons (30 ml) *jambon de Bayonne* or
cooked ham, diced
Salt and freshly ground black pepper
4 eggs

Sauté green pepper very slowly in pork fat or olive oil. Add onion
and tomatoes with garlic and ham. Season to taste with salt and
freshly ground black pepper, and simmer mixture slowly until
the vegetables are rather soft.

Beat 4 eggs lightly, season to taste and stir gently into hot
vegetable mixture. Be sure not to let them overcook, for this
Basque omelette should be soft and wet, almost the consistency of
scrambled eggs. Serve on a hot platter. Serves 2.

OMELETTE PAYSANNE

1 tablespoon (15 ml) butter
4 tablespoons (60 ml) diced salt pork
4 tablespoons (60 ml) diced cooked potato
1 teaspoon (5 ml) finely chopped parsley
1 teaspoon (5 ml) finely chopped chives
Salt and freshly ground black pepper
4 eggs

Melt butter in omelette pan and add diced salt pork. When meat is
browned, remove to a plate and keep warm. Add potato to fat in
the pan and sauté until soft and golden. Return salt pork to pan,
add finely chopped parsley and chives, and season to taste with
salt and pepper. Beat eggs lightly and pour over mixture; then
proceed to cook as for Basic Omelette (page 290). *Omelette
paysanne* is served flat, browned on both sides. Serves 2.

EGGS FOO YUNG

4 tablespoons (60 ml) finely chopped onion
2 tablespoons (30 ml) butter
2 tablespoons (30 ml) peanut oil
2–4 tablespoons (30–60 ml) chopped roast pork
4–6 tablespoons (60–90 ml) chopped cooked shrimps
1 can bean sprouts
Freshly ground black pepper
Soy sauce
4 eggs
Water

Sauté finely chopped onion in butter and oil until transparent; add chopped roast pork and cooked shrimps, and continue cooking until golden. Add bean sprouts, and season to taste with pepper and soy sauce.

When ready to serve, beat 4 eggs in a large bowl with a little water, and stir in meat and vegetable mixture. Divide mixture into 4 equal parts and make 4 separate flat omelettes, browned on both sides in oil. Serves 4.

CUCUMBER AND HAM OMELETTE

3 tablespoons (45 ml) peeled, seeded and
diced cucumber
Salt
Butter
3 tablespoons (45 ml) diced cooked ham
1 teaspoon (5 ml) finely chopped parsley,
chives or chervil
Freshly ground black pepper
4–6 eggs, well beaten

Drop diced cucumber into boiling salted water and boil for 3 minutes. Drain well and dry with a clean towel.

Melt butter, and sauté diced cucumber and ham for 5 minutes, stirring constantly. Add finely chopped parsley, chives or chervil, or a combination of all three, and salt and freshly ground black pepper, to taste.

Combine the mixture with well-beaten eggs and make omelette in the usual way. Serves 2 to 3.

Sweet Omelettes

INDIVIDUAL FRENCH DESSERT OMELETTES

2 eggs
1 tablespoon (15 ml) water
Small pinch of salt
1 level tablespoon (15 ml) castor sugar
Butter
1 tablespoon (15 ml) whipped egg white
Heated rum, cognac or Kirsch, for flaming

Beat eggs with water, salt and sugar until well mixed. Heat butter until sizzling in a preheated omelette pan. Remove pan from heat and pour in egg mixture. Return to heat and, shaking pan with one hand to keep omelette from sticking, stir egg mixture with a fork in the other hand as you would for scrambled eggs. Add whipped egg white and stir it quickly into egg mixture.

When eggs are set but surface is still moist, roll omelette on to a hot plate by tilting pan, starting it away from edge at one side with a fork and letting it roll over itself. Pour a little heated rum, cognac or Kirsch over omelette, and flame. Serves 1.

Cherry omelette: Remove stems and pits from 20 cherries, and sauté cherries for a few minutes in butter. Flame with a little heated rum. Make omelette as above for 4, and fold in cherries and juices. Serves 4.

Pear omelette: Peel, core and slice 2 ripe pears, and sauté slices for a few minutes in butter. Add a little Kirsch. Make omelette as above for 4, and fold in sliced pears and juices. Serves 4.

Strawberry omelette: Wash and hull 20 ripe strawberries, and marinate in a little Kirsch. Make omelette as above for 4, and fold in strawberries and juices. Serves 4.

OMELETTE AU RHUM

4–6 eggs
Salt
3 tablespoons (45 ml) castor sugar
2 tablespoons (30 ml) butter
4–6 tablespoons (60–90 ml) heated apricot jam
4 tablespoons (60 ml) heated rum

Beat eggs with a pinch of salt and 2 tablespoons (30 ml) sugar. Heat butter in a preheated omelette pan. Remove from heat and pour in the eggs. Return to heat and continue to cook as for Individual French Dessert Omelettes above. When omelette is cooked, spread with heated apricot jam. Fold on to a hot platter, sprinkle with remaining sugar and flame with heated rum. Serve immediately. Serves 4.

FRENCH APPLE OMELETTE

4–6 eggs
Salt
5 tablespoons (75 ml) castor sugar
2 apples, peeled, cored and sliced
5 tablespoons (75 ml) butter
3 tablespoons (45 ml) double cream
2 tablespoons (30 ml) Calvados or brandy

Beat eggs with a pinch of salt and 2 tablespoons (30 ml) sugar.

Sauté sliced apples gently in 3 tablespoons (45 ml) butter until lightly browned, turning them from time to time. Add double cream, Calvados or brandy, and 2 tablespoons (30 ml) sugar. Keep warm.

Heat remaining butter in a preheated omelette pan. Remove from heat and pour in the eggs. Return to heat and continue to cook as for Individual French Dessert Omelettes above.

When the omelette is cooked, fill it with apple mixture and fold it on to a hot platter. Sprinkle with remaining sugar and serve immediately. Serves 4.

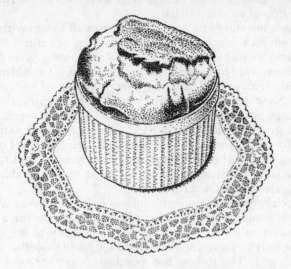

CHAPTER SEVEN
Soufflé Sorcery

Why is it, I wonder, that simple things seem so appallingly complicated before one tries them? And why does one often try the more difficult things first, looking with awe at the people who dare to attempt the easy?

We struggle with water-colours, never dreaming of attempting the easier oil paints; we teach our children languages, Latin and Greek for the very young, French when they are older; and the very same thing holds true when we turn our attention to the ubiquitous egg. Soufflés, for instance, hold no terrors for me. I have always found it more difficult to soft-boil or poach an egg to perfection. But a soufflé . . . give me an oven I can trust, a timer, and the requisite number of fresh eggs, and I can turn out a marvel at the drop of a proverbial hat.

That is my story . . . or at least it was until I was invited to a Paris 'pot luck' luncheon on the very last day of a trip to Paris – 'pot luck' because it was a Monday and all the shops were shut. I had been warned by my host that in all probability I would have to make do with a soufflé and that everything would be *tout-à-fait simple*. So when Monday and the hour of luncheon came, I arrived – dressed in sports jacket and slacks – to find myself in a drawing-room in the French grand manner, complete with nine floor-to-ceiling windows overlooking the Seine and the Louvre, some of the most beautiful furniture I have ever seen, and a group of sparkling Parisians, gathered for what was to be the most memorable meal of that Paris visit.

Lunch began with a superb *soufflé au turbot* . . . served with all possible pomp and pride in a large flat oval Pyrex dish on a Louis XIII silver salver . . . the smooth golden body of the soufflé broken only by the oven-crisped head and tail of the turbot visible at each end. The turbot, first poached in a white wine *court-bouillon*, had been carefully boned, leaving just the head and tail, and then gently deposited on its bed of cheese-flavoured soufflé mixture. The body of the fish was then covered with another layer of soufflé; the whole baked in the oven; and served with a delicate, pink-tinted *Sauce Choron* (Béarnaise with a little tomato added for colour and flavour).

Rôti de bœuf à la périgourdine – a great platter of rose-red slices of rare beef, surrounded by stuffed *champignons de Paris* and served with a fabulously rich sauce made of beef stock, Madeira and fresh black truffles from Périgord – provided the main course of this 'hastily organized' luncheon. Then followed a great dish of *primeurs de Paris* (tiny fresh peas, baby carrots, new-season *haricots verts* and the smallest of *pommes rissolées*), a French salad spiked with a hint of shallot and tarragon, a platter of cheeses, and a *tarte alsacienne*, thin slices of eating apple set in spirals on a layer of *crème pâtissière* in a crumbly *pâte sablée* crust. Coffee was served . . . with gold spoons. The whole meal was perfection. But it is the soufflé I shall remember. And it is the soufflé that I have determined – after an unsuccessful attempt, unenthusiastically aided by my host, to extract the secret from his cook – to recreate for myself one day.

The thing that still puzzles me is how the weight of the turbot could have been supported in the soufflé, for a soufflé is built, like Ben Johnson's dream castles, of air. To transform air into a building material sounds next to impossible, but all you need for it is one simple implement; an egg beater. For after all, the most awe-inspiring of soufflés is nothing more than a simple air mixture of eggs, butter, flour, and a purée of fruit, vegetables, meat, fish or fowl. And the last – unglamorous and unpretentious as the case may be – are very often left-overs.

Soufflés, technically speaking, can be divided into three definite categories: the *soufflé de cuisine* – the famous savoury soufflé of France – makes the perfect beginning to a meal, whether it is a simple cheese affair (try a combination of Gruyère and Parmesan), a concoction of fish or shellfish, or one made with a well-seasoned base of puréed vegetables (endive, onion, or mushroom and cheese). Savoury soufflés also make light-as-air entrées to dramatize a luncheon or supper party. For here you can let your imagination run riot. I remember one superb duck soufflé, served to me in Rome, whose creamy interior was studded with olives stuffed with *pâté de foie gras*.

Why not experiment? What do you risk? The basic soufflé mixture of flour, butter, milk, eggs and grated cheese remains just the same whether you add a breakfast-cupful of diced kippers, chicken, lobster or sole.

Category number two in our soufflé line-up is the *soufflé d'entremets*. I give you a selection on the following pages; but the choice is limitless. Chocolate, coffee, vanilla; *soufflé aux liqueurs*; or the whole gamut of sweet soufflés based on purées of fresh or cooked fruits (strawberries, raspberries, cherries, cranberries, or the sharp tang of lemon and orange, and the more muted note of mandarins).

A well-known soufflé in France is the *soufflé arlequin* or *soufflé panaché*. This is simply a soufflé made by combining two different variations of the basic sweet soufflé mixture – chocolate and vanilla – and spooning them in gently side by side, so that each half of the soufflé is a different colour and flavour when cooked. *Soufflé aux fruits confits* is another favourite French classic for you to try. Simply add chopped *fruits glacés* and a little coarsely chopped praline to the basic sweet soufflé mixture which you have flavoured with a little Jamaica rum.

Our third category, the *soufflé froid*, is not really a soufflé at all, but a moulded mousse made with a base of whipped cream and gelatine, and served in round moulds or soufflé dishes. Cover the bottom of the dish with a layer of gelatine, tie a strip of paper round the top of the dish to permit the mixture to be piled high above the edge, and *voilà*, when the paper is removed, it gives the illusion of a real soufflé.

Soufflés are perfectly easy to make if you follow a few basic rules.

1. A rich smooth sauce is the basis of all soufflé – a thick Béchamel Sauce for a savoury soufflé; a *crème pâtissière* for a sweet soufflé.
2. The egg yolks must be beaten one by one into the hot sauce after the saucepan is removed from the heat, or they will curdle.
3. Egg whites must be beaten until stiff but not dry. In separating the eggs, be sure there is no speck of yolk left in the whites, or you will not be able to beat your whites stiff.
4. A slow to medium oven (325°–350°F/170°–180°C/GM3–4) is an essential for a perfect soufflé. If your oven is too hot, the soufflé will be well cooked on the top and undercooked inside.
5. Sweet soufflés should be softer than entrée or vegetable soufflés.
6. A soufflé must never be too liquid before it goes into the oven. I find that the proportion of egg whites, when well beaten, should just about equal the bulk of the basic mixture. With the addition of the beaten egg whites you double the volume of your mixture. Cooking will double it again.
7. Finally, a soufflé must be eaten immediately.

If you are partial to soufflés – and I believe the whole world is – you will find that you can mix the major ingredients in advance and store them in the refrigerator. This is a trick used in many French restaurants. You just add the beaten egg whites before baking. I have had some wonderful soufflés made this easy way. Of course, if you are a novice cook, there are a certain number of culinary operations to master before you can be sure of turning out a perfect soufflé each and every time. You have to know how to regulate your oven heat, how to make a smooth white sauce, how to fold in stiffly beaten egg whites without making them lose their lightness, and how to keep your eggs from curdling when making a sauce. But these are the simple, everyday techniques of the kitchen. You will need them for any type of cookery.

Savoury Soufflés

CHEESE SOUFFLÉ

2 tablespoons (30 ml) butter
2 tablespoons (30 ml) flour
½ pint (300 ml) hot milk
5 egg yolks
4–6 oz (100–175 g) grated cheese
Salt and freshly ground black pepper
6 egg whites

Melt 2 tablespoons (30 ml) butter in the top of a double saucepan; add flour gradually and mix to a smooth paste, stirring constantly. Add hot milk and cook until sauce is smooth and thick. Remove from heat and add egg yolks one by one, alternately with grated cheese. Mix well and return to heat. Cook until cheese melts. Add generous amounts of salt and freshly ground black pepper. Remove from heat and allow to cool slightly.

Beat egg whites until they are stiff but not dry, and then gently fold into warm cheese mixture. Pile mixture in a buttered soufflé dish or casserole. Bake in a preheated slow oven (350°F/180°C/GM4) for 35 to 40 minutes, or until soufflé is golden. Serve immediately. Serves 4.

CHEESE SOUFFLÉ PUDDING

4–6 slices white bread
Softened butter
3 egg yolks
¼ pint (150 ml) double cream
6 oz (175 g) freshly grated Gruyère
¼ teaspoon (1.25 ml) dry mustard
Salt and freshly ground black pepper
3 egg whites

Remove crusts from bread and cut each slice into triangles. Butter both sides of bread and line a soufflé dish with triangles so that the points stick out above the rim of the dish.

Beat egg yolks lightly with cream, mix in grated cheese and mustard, and season to taste with salt and freshly ground black pepper.

Beat egg whites until stiff and fold gently into cheese mixture. Spoon mixture into the bread-lined soufflé dish and bake in a moderate oven (375°F/190°C/GM5) for 25 minutes, or until puffed and golden. Serve immediately. Serves 4.

EASY SALMON SOUFFLÉ

4 tablespoons (60 ml) butter
3 tablespoons (45 ml) flour
½ pint (300 ml) milk
8 tablespoons (120 ml) grated Parmesan
1 can salmon
A little cream
Salt and cayenne pepper
4 egg yolks
5 egg whites

Melt 4 tablespoons (60 ml) butter in the top of a double saucepan; add 3 tablespoons (45 ml) flour and stir until well blended. Add milk and continue cooking, stirring continuously, until the sauce has thickened. Stir in grated cheese and heat until cheese has melted into the mixture. Add canned salmon, pounded to a smooth paste with a little cream to make soufflé smooth. Heat through. Season generously with salt and cayenne pepper.

Beat egg yolks in a bowl and pour hot salmon mixture over them, stirring until well blended. Beat egg whites until stiff and gently fold them into mixture, a little at a time. Pour into a buttered and floured soufflé dish and set in a pan of hot water.

Bake in a preheated slow oven (350°F/180°C/GM4) for 25 to 30 minutes. Serve at once. Serves 4 to 6.

HERRING SOUFFLÉ

4 tablespoons (60 ml) butter
2 tablespoons (30 ml) flour
½ pint (300 ml) milk
½ Spanish onion, finely chopped
1 tablespoon (15 ml) finely chopped parsley
1 level tablespoon (15 ml) anchovy paste
Salt, nutmeg and cayenne pepper
6 oz (175 g) cooked herring fillets, finely chopped
4 egg yolks, lightly beaten
5 egg whites

Melt 3 tablespoons (45 ml) butter in the top of a double saucepan; add flour and stir until smooth. Add milk and stir over low heat until thick. Remove from heat. Sauté finely chopped onion in remaining butter until transparent; combine with parsley and stir into sauce; add anchovy paste, and salt, nutmeg and cayenne pepper, to taste. Stir finely chopped cooked herring fillets into soufflé mixture. Remove saucepan from heat and allow mixture to cool slightly. Stir in lightly beaten egg yolks; blend well.

Beat whites until they are stiff but not dry, and fold gently into sauce. Pour into an 8-inch (20 cm) soufflé dish around which you have tied greaseproof paper to make a high 'collar'. Preheat oven to 350°F/180°C/GM4 and bake soufflé for 45 minutes. Serve immediately. Serves 4.

MUSSEL SOUFFLÉ

24 mussels, prepared as for *Moules à la Marinière* (page 257)
2 tablespoons (30 ml) butter
2 tablespoons (30 ml) flour
½ pint (300 ml) hot milk
2 tablespoons (30 ml) grated Parmesan
Salt and freshly ground black pepper
4 tablespoons (60 ml) mussel liquor
4 eggs

Prepare and cook the mussels as directed. Shell, reserving liquor, and chop coarsely. Melt butter in a saucepan; add flour and stir until smooth. Add hot milk and stir over low heat until thick. Remove from heat. Add grated Parmesan and season to taste with salt and freshly ground black pepper. Stir in chopped mussels and mussel liquor, and allow mixture to cool slightly.

Separate eggs; beat yolks lightly and stir into sauce. Beat whites until they are stiff but not dry, and fold into sauce. Pour into an 8-inch (20 cm) soufflé dish around which you have tied greaseproof paper to make a high 'collar'. Preheat oven to 350°F/180°C/GM4 and bake soufflé for 45 minutes. Serve immediately. Serves 4.

CHICKEN SOUFFLÉ

6 oz (175 g) cooked chicken
2 oz (50 g) cooked ham or tongue
2 tablespoons (30 ml) butter
¼ pint (150 ml) Béchamel Sauce (page 104)
A little grated lemon rind
Salt and freshly ground black pepper
Pinch of mace or nutmeg
4 eggs, separated

Mince the chicken and ham (or tongue) together, then blend until smooth in an electric blender with 2 tablespoons (30 ml) butter and ¼ pint (150 ml) Béchamel Sauce. The sauce must be thick, or the mixture will be too moist. Season the mixture with grated lemon rind, salt and freshly ground black pepper and a pinch of mace or nutmeg.

Work in egg yolks and then rub mixture through a wire sieve. Beat egg whites until stiff and fold them lightly into the mixture.

Pour the purée into a well-buttered soufflé dish, filling it not more than two-thirds full, and bake in a slow oven (350°F/180°C/GM4) until well risen and firm to the touch. Serve the soufflé at once in the dish in which it was baked. A sauce may be served separately if wished, but it is not necessary. Serves 4.

INDIVIDUAL GAME SOUFFLÉS

3 oz (75 g) cooked game
3 oz (75 g) cooked ham
2 tablespoons (30 ml) butter
1 tablespoon (15 ml) flour
¼ pint (150 ml) well-flavoured game stock
(page 73)
Salt and freshly ground black pepper
Cayenne pepper
Lemon juice
3 eggs
6 fresh mushrooms, grilled

Chop the game and ham finely or put them through the finest blade of your mincer. Melt 2 tablespoons (30 ml) butter in a small saucepan; add the flour and then the game stock. Stir over the heat until a smooth paste is formed and the mixture draws away from the sides of the pan.

Remove saucepan from the heat; stir in the minced meats; season generously with salt, freshly ground black pepper, cayenne and lemon juice. Separate eggs and beat in egg yolks one at a time. Whip the egg whites to a stiff froth and fold them into soufflé mixture. Butter 6 individual ramekins or soufflé dishes; fill them three-quarters full with the mixture and bake in a slow oven (350°F/180°C/GM4) for 12 to 15 minutes, or until well risen and firm to the touch. Serve at once with a grilled mushroom on the top of each soufflé. Serves 6.

LANGOUSTE SOUFFLÉ

2 live *langoustes* or lobsters (about 2 lb (900 g) each)
Boiling salted water or *court-bouillon*
½ pint (300 ml) Béchamel Sauce (page 104)
Fresh butter
Paprika, salt and freshly ground black pepper
¼ pint (150 ml) double cream
4 egg yolks
5 egg whites, stiffly beaten

Cook *langoustes* or lobsters in boiling salted water or a *court-bouillon* of your choice for 25 minutes. Allow them to cool in their own juices.

Cut shells in half and remove flesh. Pound flesh in a mortar with 2 to 3 tablespoons (30–45 ml) each thick Béchamel Sauce and butter. Season to taste with paprika, salt and freshly ground black pepper.

Combine remaining Béchamel and double cream in the top of a double saucepan; add pounded *langouste* or lobster and cook over water, stirring constantly, until sauce is smooth and thick.

Beat egg yolks in a bowl until well blended; stir in a little of the hot Béchamel Sauce and then return egg mixture to remaining sauce. Cook over water, stirring from time to time, until sauce is thick. But do *not* allow sauce to boil, or it will curdle.

Remove from heat and beat until slightly cooled. Then fold stiffly beaten egg whites into the sauce; correct seasoning and fill empty *langouste* shells with mixture. Arrange buttered foil around shells to form a 'collar' so that mixture will not run over; place shells in a pan with a little hot water and cook in a preheated slow oven (350°F/180°C/GM4) for about 20 minutes, or until soufflés are puffed and golden. Serves 4.

INDIVIDUAL PARTRIDGE SOUFFLÉS

1 partridge, roasted
1 chicken liver, cooked
2 tablespoons (30 ml) butter
2–4 tablespoons (30–60 ml) cold Brown Sauce (page 114)
Salt and freshly ground black pepper
3 egg yolks
4 egg whites

Put cooked partridge meat and chicken liver through mincer. Then pound in a mortar with 2 tablespoons (30 ml) butter and the cold Brown Sauce. Season to taste with salt and freshly ground black pepper. Strain through a fine sieve.

About 20 minutes before serving, heat this purée in the top of a double saucepan without letting it come to a boil, stirring constantly. Remove from heat and beat in egg yolks one by one. Whisk egg whites until stiff and then fold gently into the mixture.

Brush interiors of 6 individual soufflé dishes with melted butter and fill with the partridge mixture; place moulds on a baking tin and bake in a slow oven (350°F/180°C/GM4) for 12 to 15 minutes. Serves 6.

CHICORY SOUFFLÉ

8 oz (225 g) braised chicory
1 tablespoon (15 ml) butter
Freshly grated Parmesan
2 tablespoons (30 ml) lemon juice
5 egg yolks
1 tablespoon (15 ml) grated onion
Salt and freshly ground black pepper
6 egg whites

Pass braised chicory through a sieve and dry it out over a low heat in 1 tablespoon (15 ml) butter, stirring all the time with a wooden spoon to keep it from sticking. Stir in 2 oz (50 g) freshly grated Parmesan and 2 tablespoons (30 ml) lemon juice.

Remove from the heat and stir in egg yolks one at a time. Season rather strongly with grated onion, and salt and freshly ground black pepper. Beat egg whites until stiff but not dry and fold into soufflé mixture. Butter a soufflé dish, dust with a little grated Parmesan and fill with the mixture. Place in a preheated slow oven (350°F/180°C/GM4) and bake for 25 to 35 minutes. Serves 4.

SOUFFLÉ OF GREEN BEANS

1 lb (450 g) green beans
Salt
2 tablespoons (30 ml) butter
1½ tablespoons (22 ml) flour
½ pint (300 ml) hot milk
Freshly ground black pepper
4 tablespoons (60 ml) grated Parmesan
2 eggs, separated

Cook beans in boiling salted water until tender – about 20 minutes. Drain.

Place 2 tablespoons (30 ml) butter in the top of a double saucepan and melt it over water. Stir in flour until smooth; add hot milk and cook over a low heat, stirring constantly, for 10 minutes. Season to taste with salt and freshly ground black pepper. Remove from heat and stir in cheese and egg yolks.

Sauté drained beans in frying pan with 2 tablespoons (30 ml) butter for about 3 minutes. Put through fine sieve, or blend in electric blender, and stir purée into sauce. Beat egg whites with a little salt until stiff. Fold into mixture. Spoon into a well-buttered baking dish (or soufflé dish) and bake in a low oven (350°F/180°C/GM4) for 30 to 35 minutes. Serve immediately as a vegetable. Serves 4.

COLD SMOKED SALMON SOUFFLÉ

2 tablespoons (30 ml) butter
2 tablespoons (30 ml) flour
½ pint (300 ml) hot milk
1 tablespoon (15 ml) gelatine
4 tablespoons (60 ml) water
1 packet (3 oz (75 g)) cream cheese, mashed
2 tablespoons (30 ml) freshly grated Parmesan
Salt and freshly ground black pepper
Cayenne pepper
3 egg yolks
6 oz (175 g) smoked salmon, minced
¼ pint (150 ml) double cream, whipped
4 egg whites
Crushed walnuts, finely chopped
parsley or paprika

Melt 2 tablespoons (30 ml) butter in the top of a double saucepan; stir in flour until smooth. Add hot milk, stirring constantly until sauce begins to boil. Then reduce heat and simmer for 5 minutes, stirring from time to time. Remove from heat and stir in gelatine, which you have softened in 4 tablespoons (60 ml) cold water. Stir sauce until gelatine is completely dissolved. Then stir in mashed cream cheese and grated Parmesan, and season to taste with salt, freshly ground black pepper and cayenne pepper. Beat egg yolks in one by one and allow the sauce to cool a little. Mix in minced smoked salmon and whipped cream.

Beat egg whites until stiff but not dry. Fold them gently into soufflé mixture. Pour mixture into a soufflé dish which you have prepared in the following manner: butter a strip of waxed paper or foil and tie it around the outside of a well-buttered soufflé dish so that the paper extends 2 inches (50 mm) above the edge of the dish.

Chill soufflé in refrigerator for at least 3 hours. Remove paper or foil 'collar' carefully before serving, and sprinkle top of soufflé with crushed walnuts, finely chopped parsley or paprika. Serves 4 to 6.

Dessert Soufflés

VANILLA SOUFFLÉ

4 tablespoons (60 ml) butter
2 tablespoons (30 ml) flour
½ pint (300 ml) hot milk
Pinch of salt
5 egg yolks
4 tablespoons (60 ml) sugar
½ teaspoon (2.5 ml) vanilla extract
6 egg whites

Melt 4 tablespoons (60 ml) butter in the top of a double saucepan; add flour and cook, stirring, until well blended. Add hot milk and salt. Cook the sauce, stirring constantly, until smooth and thick, and continue cooking and stirring for a few more minutes. Let sauce cool slightly.

Beat egg yolks well with 4 tablespoons (60 ml) sugar and vanilla extract, and mix well with batter. Beat egg whites until they are stiff but not dry, and fold gently into the batter mixture. Pour the batter into a buttered and lightly sugared soufflé mould, and bake in a slow oven (350°F/180°C/GM4) for 35 to 45 minutes, or until the soufflé is puffed and golden. Serve at once. Serves 4.

CHOCOLATE SOUFFLÉ

2½ oz (65 g) chocolate
¼ pint (150 ml) milk
4 tablespoons (60 ml) castor sugar
3 egg yolks
Vanilla extract
1 tablespoon (15 ml) cornflour
2 tablespoons (30 ml) double cream
4 egg whites

Break chocolate into small pieces and put it in an enamelled saucepan with half the milk. Cook gently, stirring from time to time, until the chocolate is melted and quite free from lumps. Combine sugar, egg yolks and desired amount of vanilla extract in a mixing bowl, and work them together with a wooden spoon until they are of a creamy consistency. Mix remaining milk with cornflour and add it by degrees to the egg mixture, together with the chocolate. Pour into a saucepan and cook until almost boiling. Remove from heat; add cream and cook for a few minutes, stirring occasionally.

Beat egg whites to a stiff froth and fold them into chocolate mixture. Pour into a well-buttered soufflé dish and bake in a slow over (350°F/180°C/GM4) for 30 to 40 minutes, or until well risen and firm to the touch. Should the soufflé become too brown, put a piece of paper over the top. Sprinkle with a little sugar just before serving. Serves 4.

CHOCOLATE RUM SOUFFLÉ

2 oz (50 g) bitter chocolate, cut in small pieces
½ pint (300 ml) hot milk
2 tablespoons (30 ml) butter
2 tablespoons (30 ml) flour
4 oz (100 g) sugar
4 eggs yolks
Salt
1–2 tablespoons (15–30 ml) Jamaica rum
5 egg whites
Whipped cream

Melt chocolate in the milk in the top of a double saucepan and beat until smooth and hot. Do not allow it to come to a boil. Melt butter in a saucepan and blend in flour and sugar. Add chocolate mixture and stir over a low heat until the mixture starts to boil. Remove from heat.

Beat egg yolks and stir 2 tablespoons (30 ml) of the hot chocolate mixture into them. Then pour the egg yolks into the chocolate mixture. Add salt and Jamaica rum, and beat over a low heat until mixture thickens slightly. Remove from heat, and when cool, fold in stiffly beaten egg whites. Pour mixture into an 8-inch (20 cm) soufflé dish; set dish in a pan of boiling water and cook in a slow oven (325°F/170°C/GM3) for 45 minutes, or until soufflé is puffed and golden. Serve immediately with whipped cream. Serves 4.

APRICOT SOUFFLÉ

2 tablespoons (30 ml) butter
2 tablespoons (30 ml) flour
½ pint (300 ml) hot milk
Pinch of salt
3 egg yolks
4 oz (100 g) sugar
4 tablespoons (60 ml) Kirsch
Apricots, cooked in syrup and diced
4 egg whites

Melt 2 tablespoons (30 ml) butter in the top of a double saucepan; add flour and cook, stirring, until well blended. Add hot milk and salt. Cook the sauce, stirring constantly, until smooth and thick, and continue cooking and stirring a little longer. Cool slightly.

Beat egg yolks well with 4 oz (100 g) sugar and combine them with the sauce. Flavour with 2 tablespoons (30 ml) Kirsch and add diced cooked apricots which have been well drained and then soaked in the remaining Kirsch. Let the mixture get cold, then add egg whites, beaten until they are stiff but not dry. Fill the soufflé dish (lightly buttered and sprinkled with sugar) up to three-quarters full and cook in a slow oven (350°F/180°C/GM4) for 35 minutes, or until well-puffed. Serves 4.

SOUFFLÉ AU GRAND MARNIER

2 tablespoons (30 ml) butter
2 tablespoons (30 ml) flour
½ pint (300 ml) hot milk
Pinch of salt
5 egg yolks
4 tablespoons (60 ml) sugar
½ teaspoon (2.5 ml) vanilla extract
2 tablespoons (30 ml) Grand Marnier
6 egg whites

Melt 2 tablespoons (30 ml) butter in the top of a double saucepan; add flour and cook, stirring, until well blended. Add hot milk and salt. Cook the sauce, stirring constantly, until smooth and thick, and continue cooking and stirring for a few more minutes. Let sauce cool slightly.

Beat egg yolks with sugar and vanilla extract, and mix well with sauce. Stir in Grand Marnier.

Butter a soufflé dish. Beat the egg whites until stiff but not dry, and fold into the cooled mixture. Pour into the prepared soufflé dish. Bake in a preheated slow oven (350°F/180°C/GM4) for 35 minutes, or until soufflé is well puffed and golden. Serves 4.

SOUFFLÉ AUX FRUITS CONFITS

4 tablespoons (60 ml) crystallized fruits, coarsely chopped
4 tablespoons (60 ml) cognac
4 egg yolks
1 tablespoon (15 ml) flour
3 tablespoons (45 ml) sugar
½ pint (300 ml) double cream
½ teaspoon (2.5 ml) vanilla extract
4 tablespoons (60 ml) Grand Marnier
5 egg whites
Pinch of salt
Butter
Whipped cream

Marinate coarsely chopped crystallized fruits in cognac for at least 2 hours. Beat egg yolks, flour and sugar together in the top of a double saucepan. Add the cream. Place over hot water and cook, stirring constantly, until thick and smooth. Do not allow to come to a boil. Stir in vanilla extract and Grand Mariner. Allow to cool, stirring occasionally.

Beat the egg whites and salt until stiff but not dry, and fold into the cooled mixture. Pour half the mixture into a buttered soufflé dish. Scatter cognac-soaked fruits over soufflé mixture and then cover with remaining mixture. Bake in a preheated slow oven (350°F/180°C/GM4) for 35 minutes, or until soufflé is well puffed and golden. Serve immediately with whipped cream. Serves 4.

NORMANDY SOUFFLÉ

2 ripe apples
1 tablespoon (15 ml) butter
1 tablespoon (15 ml) sugar
2 ripe pears
Sugar and lemon juice
2 tablespoons (30 ml) Calvados or cognac
5 egg whites

CRÈME PÂTISSIÈRE
4 egg yolks
4 oz (100 g) sugar
2 tablespoons (30 ml) sifted flour
½ pint (300 ml) milk
½ teaspoon (2.5 ml) vanilla extract

CRÈME PÂTISSIÈRE
Beat egg yolks and sugar together until mixture is lemon-coloured. Mix in flour, then add milk and vanilla extract, and mix thoroughly. Place mixture in top of a double saucepan and cook over water, stirring constantly, until smooth and thick. Remove from heat; put mixture through a sieve and allow to cool.

Peel, core and slice apples; add 1 tablespoon (15 ml) each butter and sugar, and bake in the oven until soft. Peel and core pears. Mash pears and cooked apples; drain off excess liquid if necessary, and flavour to taste with sugar, lemon juice and Calvados or cognac.

Whisk egg whites until stiff and fold into custard (*crème pâtissière*). Spread a well-buttered soufflé dish with half the custard mixture; cover with a layer of fruit purée and top with remaining custard mixture. Bake in a slow oven (350°F/180°C/GM4) for 40 minutes. Serve at once. Serves 4 to 6.

SOUFFLÉ PUDDINGS

8 tablespoons (120 ml) butter
4 oz (100 g) icing sugar
4 oz (100 g) sifted plain flour
⅔ pint (400 ml) boiled milk
½–1 teaspoon (2.5–5 ml) vanilla extract
5 egg yolks
6 egg whites

SABAYON SAUCE
4 egg yolks
4 oz (100 g) sugar
6 fluid oz (175 ml) Marsala
1 tablespoon (15 ml) cognac

Work 8 tablespoons (120 ml) softened butter into a *pommade* in a mixing bowl. Add icing sugar and sifted flour, beating well between each addition. Dilute with hot milk flavoured with vanilla extract.

Cook over a high heat, stirring continuously, until mixture dries out and leaves the sides of the pan (like a *pâté à choux*). Remove from heat; thicken with egg yolks, one by one, then carefully fold in the beaten egg whites. Pour into well-buttered soufflé moulds; place moulds in a baking tin filled with hot water, and cook in a slow oven (350°F/180°C/GM4) until puddings are done. Serve with Sabayon Sauce. Serves 4.

SABAYON SAUCE
Beat egg yolks and sugar until yellow and frothy in the top of a double saucepan. Add the Marsala; place over hot water and cook, stirring constantly, until thick and foamy. Stir in cognac; chill.

Variations:
Orange Curaçao Soufflé Puddings
Kummel Soufflé Puddings
Benedictine Soufflé Puddings

Make puddings as above, but flavour with the liqueur of your choice. Serve with Sabayon Sauce flavoured with the same liqueur instead of Marsala and cognac as in above recipe.

Cold Dessert Soufflés

BASIC COLD SOUFFLÉ

½ pint (300 ml) milk
A 1-inch (25 mm) vanilla bean
3 egg yolks
3 level tablespoons (45 ml) sugar
1 level tablespoon (15 ml) gelatine
3 tablespoons (45 ml) water
6–8 tablespoons (90–120 ml) double cream, whipped
4 egg whites

Heat milk with vanilla bean. Remove bean and keep milk hot. Whisk egg yolks and sugar until thick and lemon-coloured. Add hot milk and cook over hot water without allowing mixture to boil. Dissolve gelatine in water and add to custard; strain and cool.

Stir custard mixture over ice, and when it begins to set, fold in whipped cream, followed by egg whites, beaten until stiff but not dry. Tie a band of greaseproof paper around a large soufflé dish; pour in the mixture and allow to set in refrigerator. Serves 4.

COLD LEMON SOUFFLÉ

6 egg yolks
6 oz (175 g) castor sugar
Juice of 2 lemons
Grated rind of 1 lemon
6 egg whites, stiffly beaten
½ oz (15 g) gelatine
¼ pint (150 ml) water
Redcurrant jelly

Beat egg yolks thoroughly with sugar, lemon juice and grated lemon rind. Transfer mixture to the top of a double saucepan and cook over water, stirring constantly with a whisk, until mixture thickens. Remove from the heat; let it cool slightly and then fold in the stiffly beaten egg whites. Dissolve gelatine in water and add to egg mixture. Pour the mixture into a serving bowl and chill. Whisk redcurrant jelly and serve separately. Serves 4 to 6.

ICED COFFEE SOUFFLÉS

4 eggs
4 oz (100 g) sugar
2 tablespoons (30 ml) powdered coffee
2 oz (50 g) chocolate
2 tablespoons (30 ml) water
2 tablespoons (30 ml) rum
½ pint (300 ml) cream
Grated chocolate, for decoration

Separate eggs and beat yolks with sugar and powdered coffee until mixture is thick and creamy. Melt chocolate and water in a small saucepan; add rum, and stir into egg and coffee mixture.

Whip cream and fold into soufflé mixture. Whisk egg whites and fold into mixture. Pour into individual soufflé dishes or custard cups and freeze for 4 hours. Decorate with grated chocolate. Serves 6 to 8.

SOUFFLÉ GLACÉ PRALINÉ 'EAST ARMS'

Water
3½ oz (90 g) sugar
4 egg yolks, well beaten
4 oz (100 g) loaf sugar
4 oz (100 g) chopped almonds
12 fluid oz (350 ml) cream, whipped
6 egg whites, stiffly beaten
Crystallized violets (optional)

Boil 4 tablespoons (60 ml) water and 3½ oz (90 g) sugar in the top of a double saucepan until sugar is dissolved. Allow to cool; add beaten egg yolks. Whisk over simmering water until mixture is thick and light. Allow to cool.

Boil loaf sugar and 4 tablespoons (60 ml) water until sugar is caramel-coloured. Stir in almonds and pour into an oiled baking tin. When cool, crush with rolling pin.

Mix custard mixture, whipped cream and crushed almond mixture until smooth, and then carefully fold in stiffly beaten egg whites. Pour soufflé mixture into 2 soufflé dishes with paper collars. Allow to set in refrigerator for 5 to 6 hours. Decorate with crystallized violets if desired. Serves 8 to 10.

SOUFFLÉ GLACÉ AU COINTREAU

⅔ pint (400 ml) whipped cream
Fruits confits
Cointreau

CRÈME PÂTISSIÈRE
8 egg yolks
8 oz (225 g) castor sugar
⅔ pint (400 ml) milk
1 vanilla bean, opened

MERINGUE ITALIENNE
8 egg whites
1 lb (450 g) sugar
6–8 tablespoons (90–120 ml) water

CRÈME PÂTISSIÈRE

Beat egg yolks and sugar together until mixture is lemon-coloured. Then add milk and vanilla bean, and mix thoroughly. Place mixture in top of a double saucepan and cook over water, stirring constantly, until smooth and thick. Remove from heat, put through sieve and allow to cool.

MERINGUE ITALIENNE

Beat egg whites until stiff but not dry. Then cook sugar with water until you can pull it to a fine thread with a spoon; allow to cool. Pour syrup over egg whites gradually, beating well as you pour.

Add *crème pâtissière* to the cold meringue, together with whipped cream, some *fruits confits*, and Cointreau, to taste.

Tie a band of waxed paper around a porcelain soufflé dish so that the band is higher than the dish. Pour the mixture into the soufflé dish and let it come about 2 to 3 inches (5–8 cm) above the rim of the dish (it will be held in place by the paper).

Chill in the refrigerator, and just before serving, remove the paper band. The *soufflé glacé*, overflowing the dish, will give the appearance of a hot soufflé. Serves 6.

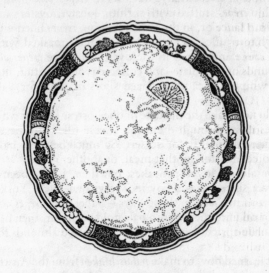

CHAPTER EIGHT
Pancakes and Fritters

W hat is the symbolic significance of the pancake? Raced
with through the streets in one part of the country;
stiffened with horsehair and tossed high in the air before being
scrambled for in another; but on one day of the year only. Shrove
Tuesday alone is Pancake Day for the British. For the rest of the
year they seem a little out of place – a dessert without a reason.
Perhaps it is exactly this that is the clue, for pancakes are not
desserts any more than omelettes are sweets.

Pancakes – one of the great basics of cookery and the root of a
thousand dishes – are good throughout the meal. Try tiny ones no
bigger than a 50p coin, stuffed with caviare and sour cream, as

finger food at a cocktail party; serve *crêpes aux fruits de mer*, wafer-thin *crêpes* stuffed with shrimp, lobster, oysters and clams in a shrimp sauce or, in the Italian fashion, *crêpes* filled with diced ham, white truffles and a thick Béchamel, masked with a rich tomato sauce and baked in the oven. Or make *crêpes au mocha*, crisp rounds of chocolate- and coffee-flavoured batter, filled with chilled whipped cream or glazed slices of pear, for a delicious dessert.

But do not make the mistake of one hostess I know who served pancakes right through the meal, cheese-filled as a first course, then flamed in brandy for dessert. So much better to have saved the pyrotechnics for another meal, or another guest.

I have always loved pancakes; but then, I have been making them ever since I was a boy in Tarrytown, New York. *Palatschinken* was my *forte* in those days – paper-thin *crêpes* cooked in butter or oil until they were a pale golden colour, then filled with home-made apricot jam sparked with toasted almonds for added crunch.

I first learned how to make *palatschinken* from the Austrian wife of my music teacher who came every Thursday evening without fail to give me lessons on the violin and the clarinet. Needless to say, I have never forgotten how to make the crisply golden *palatschinken*; but any fragmentary knowledge that I might have gained of either instrument has completely escaped me.

The pancake has always been a part of America's heritage. Many an early settler was saved from starvation by a meal of acorn and beechnut pancakes eaten by the light of an Indian fire.

Pancakes have always figured, too, in the wonderful buffet 'guest-breakfasts' held throughout the hospitable South during the racing season. Traditional chicken hash and meltingly tender 'flannel cakes' hot off the griddle provided the earthy backbone for those rustic feasts – with home-made sausages flavoured with a hint of sage, and eggs stirred gently with cream and soft-scrambled in farmhouse butter, close runners-up for favour.

Western America is famous for its pancakes made with yellow cornmeal . . . called *tortillas* by the Mexican Indians. There is a host of names along the Mexican borders for these concoctions – *tacos*, *enchiladas*, *chalupas*, what you will.

But, taking America as a whole, the pancake habit is primarily a breakfast habit. Fluffy griddle cakes, flapjacks, sourdough pancakes, 'johnny cakes', or just plain pancakes, are the highlight of

Sunday home breakfasts throughout the fifty states. And I must say, even when made with a mix, these pancakes, served with fresh butter and lashings of Vermont maple syrup, are a welcome sight.

In Russia, buckwheat pancakes are served as appetizer *blini*, the ultimate in pancake sophistication when topped with shining black caviar and sour cream, or, more prosaically, with thin slices of smoked salmon and cottage cheese. In France, *crêpes Suzette* reign supreme for late-night brilliance. Sweden prides itself on its elegant dessert of pancake stacks dressed with lingonberries. And even China has its pancake – the crisp-fried egg roll without which no Chinese meal is complete.

The delights of the pancake are endless if you think of it with imagination. Easy to make once you get the hang of it; inexpensive to serve if you don't go overboard for *blini* with caviar; and with the basic ingredients always on hand in the larder, the pancake is a boon for the hostess with unexpected guests. Eggs, milk, flour, a little sugar, a dash of salt, and the merest drop of cognac, rum, wine or beer, and you are there.

You will have to get used to your pan, of course. I like to keep a thick-bottomed omelette pan just for *crêpes*. It is not too big, about 6 inches (14 cms) in diameter at the bottom, with sloping sides bringing it to about 7½ inches (15 cms) at the top. This is perfect for swirling a tiny knob of butter round the sides of the pan on the point of a knife . . . the sloping edge lets just enough butter slip down under the edges of the *crêpe* as it cooks to prevent sticking.

Then there is the cooking time. I like my batter thin, about as thick as top of milk or light cream, so that the *crêpes* will be crisp and thin. When the batter is as thin as this, the *crêpe* takes under a minute to cook to golden perfection on each side.

If your pan is well tried – *and* you do not use it for anything else but *crêpes* (even though you make *crêpes* only once a month or once a year), *and* you never wash it but just wipe it out between *crêpes* with a piece of well-buttered paper – you will find that they are quite easy to make.

Golden Rules for Golden Crêpes

1. Buy a special thick-bottomed frying pan for *crêpes* and never use your pancake pan to cook any other food.
2. Do not wash the pan . . . wipe it out after use with a paper towel.
3. Keep your batter extremely liquid, like light cream. If your batter is too thick, add a little cold liquid just before using.
4. Make *crêpes* very thin.
5. Always include a tablespoon or two (15–30 ml) of melted fresh butter or light oil in the batter.
6. Swirl a bit of butter with a knife around the edge of the pan to keep *crêpes* from sticking.
7. Keep pancakes hot – in the oven if you want them crisp, between two plates over boiling water if you want them softly tender.

Experiment with fillings – almost anything goes. Try *crêpes au Roquefort*, the basic *crêpes* mixture filled with a Roquefort cheese-flavoured thick Béchamel. Try kipper supper cakes; sauté coarsely chopped kipper fillets in butter, add a thick Béchamel flavoured with a little cognac or lemon juice, and pass the mixture through a fine sieve. Fill pancakes and glaze in a hot oven. Delicious for late-night suppers.

Or try strawberry pancakes . . . sliced fresh strawberries delicately flavoured with Kirsch and folded into a lemon *crêpe*. I like *crêpes au fromage*, too, for a hot beginning to a cold outdoor meal. To try these cheese-filled *crêpes*, use an electric frying pan and cook them for guests on an outdoor table. I first tasted this dish on the sun-filled terrace of the Club de l'Ancre in Ramatuelle just outside St Tropez, and I cannot think of it without a dash of sunshine in the recipe.

Pancakes have been enjoyed around the world for centuries. Let them come to your aid when you entertain today.

Savoury Pancakes

BASIC FRENCH CRÊPES
(FOR SAVOURY FILLINGS)

6 tablespoons (90 ml) plain flour
½ level teaspoon (2.5 ml) salt
2 eggs
¾ pint (450 ml) milk
Butter or oil
2 tablespoons (30 ml) cognac (optional)

Sift flour and salt into a mixing bowl. Beat eggs and add them to dry ingredients. Mix in the milk and 2 tablespoons (30 ml) melted butter or oil gradually to avoid lumps. Add cognac if desired. Strain batter through a fine sieve and let it stand for at least 2 hours before cooking the *crêpes*. Batter should be as thin as cream. Add a little water if too thick.

For each *crêpe*, spoon about 2 tablespoons (30 ml) batter into buttered pan, swirling pan to allow batter to cover entire surface thinly; brush a piece of butter around edge of hot pan with the point of a knife. Cook over a medium heat until just golden but not brown (about 1 minute each side). Repeat until all *crêpes* are cooked, stacking them on a plate as they are ready. Makes 20 to 24 golden *crêpes*.

AMERICAN BREAKFAST PANCAKES

5 oz (150 g) plain flour
Generous pinch of salt
1 level tablespoon (15 ml) sugar
1 level tablespoon (15 ml) baking powder
3 eggs
¾ pint (450 ml) milk
4 tablespoons (60 ml) melted butter

Sift flour, salt, sugar and baking powder into a mixing bowl. Separate eggs; beat egg yolks into dry ingredients with a wooden spoon. Add milk and melted butter, and mix well.

Beat egg whites until stiff and fold into pancake batter. When ready to use, drop by spoonfuls on a hot, oiled, electric griddle (450°F/230°C.). Brown on both sides, and serve with grilled sausages and unsmoked bacon, butter and maple syrup. Serves 4.

JEWISH BLINTZES

4 tablespoons (60 ml) plain flour
Generous pinch of salt
2 eggs, well beaten
6 tablespoons (90 ml) milk
6 tablespoons (90 ml) water
Butter
Cheese or Lox Filling
Cinnamon-flavoured sugar
Chilled sour cream

Sift flour and salt into a mixing bowl. Beat in eggs, milk, water, and 1 tablespoon (15 ml) melted butter. Let stand for 2 hours. Brush 8-inch (20 cm) frying pan with butter and pour 3 tablespoons (45 ml) batter into heated pan. Cook as usual for *crêpes*. Top each *blintz* with filling of your choice (see below). Fold over 2 sides and roll up into a small package. Repeat until batter mixture or filling is used up.

Just before serving, crisp the filled *blintzes* in hot butter; dust with cinnamon sugar and serve hot with chilled sour cream. Makes 12.

CHEESE FILLING
Combine 1 carton cottage cheese with 2 tablespoons (30 ml) cream cheese, 1 beaten egg and 1 to 2 tablespoons (15–30 ml) sugar.

LOX FILLING
Combine 1 carton cottage cheese with 4 oz (100 g) smoked salmon, diced. Flavour with lemon juice and a little finely chopped raw onion or chives, to taste.

1 pint (600 ml) milk
1 level tablespoon (15 ml) yeast
8 oz (225 g) buckwheat flour (or half buckwheat
and half plain flour)
½ level teaspoon (2.5 ml) salt
3 egg yolks
Melted butter
1 level tablespoon (15 ml) sugar
3 egg whites, stiffly beaten
Sour cream
Caviar and lemon wedges (optional)

Heat half the milk until lukewarm and combine in a warm bowl with yeast. Sift flour together with salt, and add enough of this to the liquid to make a thick 'sponge' (see page 810). Cover bowl. Stand in a warm place and let sponge rise for about 2½ hours.

Beat egg yolks and whisk into remaining milk. Add 2 tablespoons (30 ml) melted butter and the sugar, and add to raised sponge mixture with remaining sifted flour. Beat well and let stand, covered, for 30 minutes more.

When ready to serve, fold in stiffly beaten egg whites. Cook on a buttered griddle (I use an iron Swedish *plattar* pan with indentations for cakes). *Blini* should not be more than 3 inches (8 cms) in diameter. Makes about 30 *blini*.

Serve *blini* hot with melted butter and sour cream, or for special occasions, with sour cream, caviar and lemon wedges.

ITALIAN SPINACH PANCAKES

½ recipe Basic French Crêpes (page 325)
12 oz (350 g) frozen spinach
Butter
Salt and freshly ground black pepper
8 oz (225 g) Ricotta or cottage cheese
3 eggs, lightly beaten
Freshly grated Parmesan
6 tablespoons (90 ml) double cream
Freshly grated nutmeg
½ pint (300 ml) well-flavoured Italian Tomato Sauce
(page 124)

Make 8 to 12 *crêpes* before making the spinach and cheese filling.

Cook spinach with 2 tablespoons (30 ml) butter, and season to taste with salt and freshly ground black pepper. Drain thoroughly, and add Ricotta or cottage cheese, the beaten eggs, 1 to 2 oz (25–50 g) grated Parmesan, cream and nutmeg, to taste.

Spread each pancake generously with spinach and cheese filling. Roll pancakes and put them in a well-buttered rectangular baking dish. Chill until 1 hour before using.

When nearing time to serve, brush each pancake with melted butter and sprinkle with freshly grated Parmesan cheese; bake for 20 minutes in a slow oven (350°F/180°C/GM4). Serve with well-flavoured Tomato Sauce. Serves 4.

ITALIAN HAM AND CHEESE PANCAKES

½ recipe Basic French Crêpes (page 325)
8–12 oz (225–350 g) Mozzarella cheese
4 thin slices prosciutto (raw Parma ham)
Butter
2 tablespoons (30 ml) plain flour
½ pint (300 ml) hot milk
Salt and cayenne pepper
½ level teaspoon (2.5 ml) ground nutmeg
½ pint (300 ml) double cream
2 egg yolks, well beaten
¼ pint (150 ml) well-flavoured Italian Tomato Sauce
(page 124)

Make 8 to 12 *crêpes* before making ham and cheese filling. Cut 8 to 12 thin slices Mozzarella cheese and put aside for later use. Dice the remaining cheese and the ham.

Melt 2 tablespoons (30 ml) butter in the top of a double saucepan; stir in flour and cook over water, stirring constantly, until smooth. Add hot milk and continue to cook, stirring constantly, until thickened. Season to taste with salt, cayenne pepper and nutmeg.

Combine cream and beaten egg yolks in a bowl; pour in some of the hot sauce and whisk until smooth. Return cream and egg mixture to the saucepan; add diced cheese and ham, and cook over water until sauce is smooth, thick and golden. Do not let sauce boil after eggs are added or it will curdle. Let mixture cool.

Spread a thin coating of well-flavoured Tomato Sauce over each pancake and then cover generously with cheese and ham filling. Roll pancakes and put them in a well-buttered rectangular baking dish. Chill until 1 hour before using.

When nearing time to serve, spoon a little Tomato Sauce over each pancake and top with a thin strip of Mozzarella cheese. Bake for 20 minutes in a low oven (350°F/180°C/GM4). Serves 4.

CRÊPES AU FROMAGE

1 recipe Basic French Crêpes (page 325)
4 tablespoons (60 ml) butter
4 tablespoons (60 ml) plain flour
1 pint (600 ml) milk
9 oz (250 g) Gruyère, diced
Salt and freshly ground black pepper
Paprika
3 egg yolks
Oil
1 whole egg, beaten
Breadcrumbs
Fat, for frying

Melt butter in the top of a double saucepan; stir in flour and cook the *roux*, stirring constantly, for 5 minutes, or until well blended. Gradually add milk and stir the sauce with a whisk over boiling water until thick and smooth.

Add cheese and continue cooking until cheese is melted. Season to taste with salt, freshly ground black pepper and paprika. Remove mixture from the heat and beat in the yolks of 2 eggs. Pour batter into an oiled baking dish and allow to cool. When ready to use, cut mixture into 1–inch by 3–inch (25 mm by 75 mm) rectangles.

Make *crêpes* according to Basic French Crêpes recipe. Fold each *crêpe* around a cheese rectangle. Dip cheese *crêpes* in beaten egg and then in breadcrumbs, and fry in deep hot fat (375°F/190°C) until golden brown. Serve as hot *hors-d'œuvre*. Serves 6.

CRÊPES AUX FRUITS DE MER

½ recipe Basic French Crêpes (page 325)
1–2 tablespoons (15–30 ml) each freshly grated
Gruyère and Parmesan

SEAFOOD FILLING
2 tablespoons (30 ml) each finely chopped onion
and shallots
2 tablespoons (30 ml) butter
2 tablespoons (30 ml) finely chopped raw veal or
cooked ham
2 tablespoons (30 ml) plain flour
Salt and freshly ground black pepper
¼ level teaspoon (1.25 ml) nutmeg and cayenne mixed
1 bay leaf, crumbled
2 tablespoons (30 ml) chopped parsley
1 pint (600 ml) warm milk
2 egg yolks, well beaten
2 tablespoons (30 ml) double cream
2 tablespoons (30 ml) lemon juice
4–6 tablespoons (60–90 ml) dry white wine
2 tablespoons (30 ml) freshly grated Parmesan
1 lb (450 g) diced freshly cooked lobster, crab or
mussels, or a combination of the three

Make *crêpes* and cover them with waxed paper or foil to prevent
them drying out.

SEAFOOD FILLING
Sauté finely chopped onion and shallots in butter until transparent; add finely chopped veal or ham and continue to cook,
stirring constantly, for 2 to 3 minutes. Sprinkle with flour and
cook, stirring, for 2 to 3 minutes more. Season to taste with salt,
freshly ground black pepper, nutmeg and cayenne pepper. Add
crumbled bay leaf, chopped parsley and half the warm milk, and
stir until well blended. Transfer contents to the top of a double
saucepan; add remaining milk and cook over water for 1 hour,

stirring from time to time. Strain into a bowl in which you have whisked egg yolks, double cream, lemon juice and white wine. Return to heat and cook until thickened. (Do not allow sauce to boil or eggs will curdle.) Stir in grated cheese and diced shellfish, and heat through.

To serve: top each *crêpe* with 2 tablespoons (30 ml) prepared filling, and roll loosely; place in rows in a rectangular baking dish. Top with remaining sauce and 1 or 2 tablespoons (15–30 ml) each freshly grated Gruyère and Parmesan cheese. Place under a preheated grill and cook until golden brown. Serves 4.

TRADER VIC'S CRAB CRÊPES BENGAL

CRÊPES
¾ pint (450 ml) milk
3 oz (75 g) sifted plain flour
3 eggs
1 egg yolk
Salt
Slivers of truffle (optional)

DEVILLED CRAB FILLING
8 oz (225 g) crabmeat
2 level teaspoons (10 ml) finely chopped shallots or onion
1 tablespoon (15 ml) butter
½ level teaspoon (2.5 ml) curry powder
Salt and freshly ground black pepper
Monosodium glutamate
2 dashes Worcestershire sauce
1 dash Tabasco
¼ pint (150 ml) dry white wine
½ pint (300 ml) thick Cream Sauce (page 107)

GLAZING SAUCE
4 tablespoons (60 ml) Cream Sauce, reserved from Filling ingredients
4 tablespoons (60 ml) Hollandaise Sauce (page 123) or 2 egg yolks
4 tablespoons (60 ml) whipped cream

CRÊPES

Mix milk and flour well but quickly, then add the eggs and egg yolk, and mix well, adding a dash of salt. Cook *crêpes* as usual. They should be about 5½ inches (14 cms) in diameter.

Spoon 2 tablespoons (30 ml) Devilled Crab Filling on to each *crêpe* and roll. Glaze with sauce (below) and brown under the grill until golden. Garnish with a thin slice of truffle. Serve 2 *crêpes* per person as a main course, and 1 *crêpe* as an appetizer.

DEVILLED CRAB FILLING

Sauté crabmeat and finely chopped shallots or onion lightly in butter. Add curry powder, salt, freshly ground black pepper and monosodium glutamate, to taste, and Worcestershire and Tabasco sauces. Add wine and cook over medium heat for about 3 minutes; then add Cream Sauce (reserving 4 tablespoons (60 ml) for glazing sauce), and mix well.

GLAZING SAUCE

Mix ingredients together well, and use as directed above.

Sweet Pancakes

BASIC FRENCH CRÊPES
(FOR SWEET FILLINGS)

6 tablespoons (90 ml) plain flour
½ level teaspoon (2.5 ml) salt
1–2 tablespoons (15–30 ml) sugar
2 eggs
¾ pint (450 ml) milk
Butter or oil

Sift flour, salt and sugar into a mixing bowl. Beat eggs and add them to dry ingredients. Mix in milk and 2 tablespoons (30 ml) melted butter or oil gradually to avoid lumps. Strain through a fine sieve and leave batter to stand for at least 2 hours before cooking the *crêpes*. Batter should be as thin as cream. (Add a little water if too thick.)

Spoon about 2 tablespoons (30 ml) batter into heated and buttered pan, swirling pan to allow batter to cover entire surface thinly; brush a piece of butter around edge of hot pan with the point of a knife and cook over a medium heat until just golden but not brown (about 1 minute each side). Repeat until all *crêpes* are cooked, stacking them on a plate as they are ready. Makes 20 to 24 golden *crêpes*.

RICH DESSERT CRÊPES
(FOR SWEET FILLINGS)

Prepare as above, adding 1 beaten egg and 2 tablespoons (30 ml) cognac or rum to Basic French Crêpes recipe.

CRÊPES AUX MARRONS GLACÉS

½ recipe Basic French Crêpe (page 333)
¼ pint (150 ml) double cream
Vanilla extract
Icing sugar
8 *marrons glacés*, chopped

Make about 12 *crêpes*, transferring them to a warm plate as you cook them. Whip cream, flavoured to taste with vanilla extract and icing sugar, adding a little iced water to make mixture lighter. Fold in chopped *marrons glacés* with syrup. Fill *crêpes* with this mixture and roll up. Dust with icing sugar. Serves 4.

CRÊPES AUX FRUITS

½ recipe Basic French Crêpe (page 333)
3 eating apples, peeled, cored and diced
Butter
Juice of ½ lemon
3 tablespoons (45 ml) apricot jam
3 tablespoons (45 ml) chopped almonds
6 tablespoons (90 ml) whipped cream
2–3 tablespoons (30–45 ml) Calvados
Crushed macaroons
Sugar

Make about 12 *crêpes*, transferring them to a warm plate as you cook them.

Cook diced apples in 3 tablespoons (45 ml) butter and lemon juice until tender. Stir in apricot jam and chopped almonds. Then fold in whipped cream flavoured with Calvados. Cover *crêpes* with mixture; fold in four and place them in a buttered ovenproof dish. Sprinkle with crushed macaroons and sugar, and glazed for a minute or two under grill. Serves 4.

CRÊPES AUX MANDARINES

½ recipe Basic French Crêpe (page 333)
Grated peel of 1 mandarin orange
2–4 tablespoons (30–60 ml) Curaçao

BEATEN MANDARIN BUTTER
8 oz (225 g) fresh butter
Juice of 1 mandarin orange
A little grated mandarin orange peel
2–4 tablespoons (30–60 ml) Curaçao

Make *crêpes* as in Basic French Crêpes recipe, adding grated mandarin peel and Curaçao, to taste, to basic recipe. Keep very hot in oven in a heatproof dish. At the table, place a spoonful of Beaten Mandarin Butter on each *crêpe*; fold in four and serve immediately. Serves 4.

BEATEN MANDARIN BUTTER

Soften fresh butter and beat it at a low speed in electric mixer until smooth; then add mandarin juice, a little mandarin peel and Curaçao, and beat at high speed until butter is fluffy and a delicate light yellow in colour – 8 to 10 minutes.

PFANNKUCHEN (GERMAN PANCAKES)

3 eggs, beaten
½ pint (300 ml) milk
Generous pinch of salt
1 level teaspoon (5 ml) sugar
3 oz (75 g) plain flour
Butter
Strawberry jam, cooked apples or thick
Chocolate Sauce (page 133)
Cinnamon-flavoured sugar

Beat eggs, milk, salt, sugar and flour together. Let stand for ½ hour. Brush thick-bottomed 10-inch (26 cm) frying pan with butter; pour in 5 to 6 tablespoons (75–90 ml) batter at a time; tilt pan to make batter spread to form large, flat pancake, and cook over medium heat until batter bubbles. Turn and bake other side. Stack on plate in heated oven. Coat each pancake with butter and strawberry jam, cooked apples or thick Chocolate Sauce, and roll up. Cut each pancake in half. Sprinkle with cinnamon sugar. Serves 4.

SWEDISH PANCAKES

4 oz (100 g) plain flour
1 tablespoon (15 ml) sugar
½ teaspoon (2.5 ml) salt
2 egg yolks
¾ pint (450 ml) warm milk
2 tablespoons (30 ml) melted butter
2 egg whites, stiffly beaten
Preserved lingonberries
Beaten butter (see method)

Sift flour, sugar and salt into mixing bowl. Beat egg yolks and add them to dry ingredients. Combine warm milk and melted butter, and beat in gradually to avoid lumps. Strain through a fine sieve and leave batter to stand for at least 2 hours. Before cooking, beat again, and fold in stiffly beaten egg whites. Bake on a griddle, a large iron frying pan, or a special Swedish *plattar* pan with indentations for pancakes. The pancakes should be about 3 inches (8 cms) in diameter. Serve with preserved lingonberries and beaten butter. (Soften fresh butter and beat it in electric mixer on low speed until smooth; then beat on highest speed until butter is fluffy and a delicate light yellow colour – 8 to 10 minutes. If you store it in refrigerator, allow to soften again at room temperature.)

CRÊPES AU KÜMMEL

8 oz (225 g) plain flour
Icing sugar
4 eggs
3 egg yolks
Vanilla extract
1 pint (600 ml) milk
6–8 tablespoons (90–120 ml) double cream
2 tablespoons (30 ml) butter
1 small glass Kümmel
Finely crushed macaroons

Sift flour and 3 oz (75 g) icing sugar into a mixing bowl; then beat in eggs and egg yolks one by one, until mixture is thick and lemon-coloured. Add vanilla extract to milk, and heat. Combine with double cream and beat gradually into batter mixture. Add butter, which you have cooked until it is light brown in colour, and Kümmel (cognac or rum may be substituted); strain through a fine sieve and let stand for 1 to 2 hours.

Cook *crêpes* in usual way.

Place *crêpes* one on top of the other as they are cooked, sprinkling each with icing sugar and finely crushed macaroons.

CRÊPES DES OLIVIERS

5 oz (150 g) plain flour
4 oz (100 g) sugar
⅓ pint (200 ml) warm milk
4 eggs, beaten
Butter
Grated rind and juice of 2 oranges
Grand Marnier

Combine flour and 2 tablespoons (30 ml) sugar in a mixing bowl, and gradually beat in warm milk, beaten eggs and 4 oz (100 g) melted butter. Add finely grated rind of 1 orange to flavour the *crêpes* mixture and allow to stand for 2 hours before using.

Make a syrup with remaining sugar, grated rind of remaining orange and juice of 2 oranges. Flavour to taste with Grand Marnier.

Make pancakes in usual way and fold in four. Place on a well-buttered ovenproof dish and heat through with the syrup. Serves 4.

Fritters

The golden world of fritters, croquettes, doughnuts and crullers is a closed book for many of today's hostess-cooks, who seem to feel that these old-fashioned sweets and 'batter cakes' have no part to play in modern menu planning. How many realize, I wonder, that fritters can make a delicious and highly personal sweet at small cost. Some fritters are made of a dough-like mixture to which some sweet ingredient or fruit is added; others are made of a soft cream-like mixture and covered with a coating of egg and breadcrumbs. When fruit is used, sprinkle it first with sugar and a little liqueur; or marinate it in wine, brandy, or liqueur as well. The fruits can then either be coated with batter, or chopped and mixed into the batter itself. A good fritter batter should be smooth and light, yet thick enough to coat the morsel without running off.

To fry fritters, the fat must not be less than 2 or 3 inches (50 to 75 mm) in depth. Your fat should be hot enough to make the fritters puff out and become crisp and light. If the fat has not reached the proper temperature, it will soak into the batter, and the fritters will be soggy, heavy and indigestible. Make sure your fat is boiling before it is used. Test this by dropping a small piece of the fritter batter or dough into the hot fat. If it is sufficiently hot, the piece will rise to the surface immediately and sizzle briskly.

Do not put too many fritters into the fat at one time, or your fat will cool, and the fritters won't have enough room to puff. Reheat the fat to the correct temperature between each relay of fritters. Let one side of the fritters brown before turning them to the other. When both sides are brown, lift them out with a perforated spoon and drain on paper towels. Sprinkle with sugar flavoured with vanilla, cinnamon or grated lemon or orange rind. Sauce or additional sugar and lemon wedges are served separately.

BATTER I

4 oz (100 g) plain flour
Pinch of salt
¼ pint (150 ml) warm water or milk
1 tablespoon (15 ml) oil or melted butter
2–3 egg whites

Sift flour and salt into a mixing bowl, and make a well in the centre. Pour water or milk into the well gradually, beating with a wooden spoon to make batter smooth and free from lumps. Add oil or melted butter and beat again for a few minutes. Whisk egg whites to a stiff froth and fold them lightly into the batter.

BATTER II

8 oz (225 g) plain flour
Pinch of salt
2 eggs, well beaten
2 tablespoons (30 ml) oil or melted butter
1 tablespoon (15 ml) brandy
½ pint (300 ml) light beer

Sift flour and salt into a mixing bowl, and make a well in the centre. Stir beaten eggs into the well and then beat in the other ingredients little by little until batter is perfectly smooth. Cover the bowl and let batter stand for at least 6 hours in a very cool place before using.

Savoury Fritters

HARD-BOILED EGG FRITTERS

4 hard-boiled eggs
1 slice bacon, ¼ inch (6 mm) thick
½ Spanish onion, finely chopped
4 tablespoons (60 ml) butter
2 tablespoons (30 ml) finely chopped parsley
¾ pint (450 ml) cold well-flavoured Béchamel Sauce
(page 104)
Salt and freshly ground black pepper
1 egg, beaten
Breadcrumbs
Oil or fat, for frying
Lemon wedges

Shell and chop eggs coarsely. Chop bacon and sauté with finely chopped onion in butter until onion begins to take on colour. Combine chopped eggs, bacon, onion and finely chopped parsley. Mix well and then stir into cold Béchamel Sauce. Season to taste with salt and freshly ground black pepper.

Form mixture loosely into balls and chill. When ready to cook, remove from refrigerator and re-form into more perfect shapes – patties, balls or cork shapes; dip in beaten egg and then in breadcrumbs.

Fry in hot oil until golden. Drain well and serve very hot with lemon wedges. Serves 4 to 6.

MUSHROOM FRITTERS

4 oz (100 g) plain flour
¼ teaspoon (1.25 ml) salt
2 egg yolks
1 tablespoon (15 ml) melted butter
¼ pint (150 ml) white wine, cider or ale
¼ pint (150 ml) milk or water
2 egg whites, stiffly beaten
8 oz (225 g) button mushrooms
Juice of 1 lemon
Salt and freshly ground black pepper
Oil, for frying

Sift flour and salt together, make a well in the centre, and into this pour the egg yolks and cool melted butter; stir briskly, drawing the flour in by degrees and adding the white wine, cider or ale, a little at a time. Let it stand for 1 hour.

When ready to cook, stir in the milk or water and fold in the stiffly beaten egg whites. Wash the mushrooms and sprinkle with the lemon juice and seasoning. Dip each mushroom in the batter and fry in hot oil until golden. Drain well and serve very hot. Serves 4 to 6.

CORN AND CLAM FRITTERS

½ Spanish onion, finely chopped
4 tablespoons (60 ml) butter
1 can minced clams
1 small can corn niblets
2 tablespoons (30 ml) finely chopped parsley
¾ pint (450 ml) cold well-flavoured Béchamel Sauce
(page 104)
Salt and freshly ground black pepper
1 egg, beaten
Fresh breadcrumbs
Oil or fat, for frying
Lemon wedges

Sauté finely chopped onion in butter until onion begins to take on colour. Stir in drained minced clams and drained corn niblets, and continue to cook, stirring constantly, for 2 minutes. Stir in finely chopped parsley and combine with cold Béchamel Sauce. Season to taste with salt and freshly ground black pepper.

Form mixture loosely into balls and chill. When ready to cook, remove from refrigerator and re-form into more perfect shapes – patties, balls or cork shapes; dip in beaten egg and then in breadcrumbs.

Fry in hot oil until golden. Drain well and serve very hot with lemon wedges. Serves 4 to 6.

Sweet Fritters

APPLE FRITTERS

4 ripe apples
Sugar
Lemon or orange juice
Rum or cognac
1 recipe Batter I or II (page 339)

Peel, core and chop the apples. Sprinkle them with sugar and a little lemon or orange juice, and rum or cognac, to taste. Let them stand for a few minutes, and then mix them with Batter I or II. Take up a spoonful of the mixture at a time, and fry in boiling fat until puffed and golden brown in colour. Do not make fritters too

large or they will not cook through. Test the first one before lifting the others from the fat. Sprinkle with sugar and serve immediately. Serves 4 to 6.

AMERICAN APPLE FRITTERS

1 tablespoon (15 ml) butter
2 tablespoons (30 ml) sugar
2 eggs, separated
6 oz (175 g) sifted plain flour
1–2 tablespoons (15–30 ml) milk
1 teaspoon (5 ml) baking powder
Pinch of salt
3 ripe apples, peeled, cored and finely chopped
Fat, for frying
Icing sugar

Cream butter and sugar until smooth. Beat egg yolks into mixture, then add the sifted flour and milk little by little, beating well. Add baking powder and salt; then fold in finely chopped apple. Beat egg whites until stiff and fold them gently into the mixture. Form the mixture into small balls the size of a walnut; drop them into boiling fat, and fry until golden. Drain, sprinkle with icing sugar and serve immediately. Serves 4.

FRESH PEACH FRITTERS

4 ripe peaches
Sugar
Maraschino or Kirsch
Macaroon crumbs
1 recipe Batter I or II (page 339)
Fat, for frying
Lemon wedges

Peel and stone peaches, and cut into quarters. Sprinkle the pieces with sugar and a few drops of Maraschino or Kirsch, and roll in macaroon crumbs. Allow to stand for a few minutes.

Dip prepared quarters one by one in Batter I or II, lifting each one out with a skewer and dropping it into a saucepan of hot fat.

Fry fritters, turning them from time to time, until golden brown on all sides. Lift fritters out of fat with a skewer or perforated spoon and dry on sugared paper in a moderate oven. Continue until all are cooked. Serve with additional sugar and lemon wedges. Serves 4 to 6.

PEAR FRITTERS

4 ripe pears
Sugar
White wine
Kirsch
Macaroon or cake crumbs
1 recipe Batter I or II (page 339)
Fat, for frying
Lemon wedges

Peel and core pears, and cut into quarters or eighths. Sprinkle slices with sugar and marinate in dry white wine with a little Kirsch for at least 15 minutes. Roll in macaroon or cake crumbs, and dip in batter, lifting each piece out with a skewer.

Fry fritters in deep hot fat as above until golden. Serve with additional sugar and lemon wedges. Serves 4 to 6.

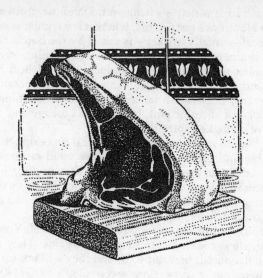

CHAPTER NINE

All About Beef

When one mentions beef in Britain, one naturally thinks of the lusty Beef of Old England – charred on the outside, rose-red inside, running with juices when cut – and the galaxy of recipes in which prime beefsteak plays its kingly part. I love the noble sirloin, the majestic porterhouse, the sophisticated *tournedos*, and the fine fat fillets and rump steaks with which British cuisine abounds. But I love, too, the simpler fare that comes from this versatile animal. After all, if 45 per cent of a carcass gives pieces for rapid cooking, there is still 55 per cent left with economical cuts for slow cooking. One of my favourite dishes is corned beef and cabbage – not out of a can, but the fresh, moist, rich Irish variety – a hangover, I suppose, from my many visits to New York restaurants, where it is a regular standby.

The beef – usually brisket – is salted by the butcher and then slowly simmered in water with onions, turnips, carrots and peppercorns until it is moistly tender. Corned beef is always served with its homely partner, cabbage, a boiled potato or two, and a creamy horseradish sauce. When served steaming hot like this, thick-cut slices of pink beef, green cabbage and the fluffy white potato make a splendid dish.

I like, too, to serve the more economical cuts – thin flank, thick flank, shin and brisket – for earthy stews and casseroles in the French and Italian manner, where long, slow cooking brings out the utmost in flavour and tenderness. French *pot-au-feu* is a case in point: here a combination of shin of beef, brisket and a piece of square-cut thin flank makes for delicious eating.

So be adventurous in trying out new cuts of beef. You will find the long, slow-cooking cuts are good bargains. They are moist and well flavoured, they cut well, and they will not turn stringy if simmered in a very slow oven (280°–300°F/140°–150°C/GM½–1) for at least 3 hours, or cooked slowly in a casserole on top of the stove, so that the liquid in which they are cooking barely bubbles.

Generally, the best beef is that taken from beef cattle about 18 months to 2 years old. The lean of good quality beef should be bright cherry red in colour when freshly cut; the fat, a creamy white; the suet, hard and dry. Beef, of course, darkens in colour when exposed to the air.

The flesh should be firm and moist to the touch, smooth in texture with a rather open grain. Tender beef is usually marbled with fat. There should be little or no gristle between the fat and the lean, as gristle indicates that it is the flesh of an old animal. The interior of the bones should be rosy white.

Beef should be well hung before it is used. To be really tender it should 'ripen' in the cold room at the butcher's for at least 8 days before it is sold. Some restaurants which specialize in steaks keep their meat for 2 to 3 weeks. A black crust forms on the exterior, which means a big loss in profits (because it is cut off), but a steak thus obtained reaches perfection. Do not try this in your own refrigerator, however, for your meat will only spoil. To hang properly, beef must be hung without any covering in a well-ventilated atmosphere kept at a constant low temperature.

Some Different Cuts of Beef

Sirloin: This is the best cut for roasting, but it is somewhat expensive. The chump end (adjoining the rump) is considered the best, as it has the largest amount of undercut. The wing rib makes an excellent smaller joint for roasting.

Porterhouse steak: Cut from the wing end.

T-bone steaks (so popular in New York) are cut directly across the sirloin.

Baron of beef: The sirloin from both sides of the animal when not separated. This joint was the highlight of the banquets of our ancestors, but it is rarely seen nowadays.

Fillet or undercut of the sirloin is the tenderest part for entrées or fillets of beef.

Tournedos is an inch-thick (25 mm) slice from the fillet, usually encircled by a thin strip of fat.

Ribs: The cuts from the ribs are also good for roasting, those nearest the sirloin being the best. These better cuts are slightly less expensive than sirloin. Various sizes of joint can be cut according to special requirements. It is more economical to have the bone removed and the meat itself rolled. The bone can be used for soup. Two to three ribs make a good roast for a small family. When roasting a large cut whole, it is better to have the thin end cut off and used for a separate dish, otherwise it will overcook before the thicker part is ready. Back and top ribs are not so tender. They are better stewed or braised than roasted.

Rump: This is an excellent piece of fleshy meat. Some of the best steaks are cut from this part. It is a first-rate cut, if expensive, for pies, rolled beef, or a tender *carbonade* or stew.

Topside, buttock or round: This is another very fleshy piece of meat with little bone. It is one of the best pieces for braising or boiling,

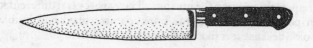

and is often salted. It can also be roasted, but, though economical, it is not as fine in flavour as the ribs or sirloin. The topside and the silverside are both cut from the buttocks.

Aitch bone: This is one of the cheaper cuts of meat, containing a large proportion of bone. It is an awkwardly shaped joint and difficult to carve. It is generally boiled and sometimes salted.

Brisket: This cut – principally for boiling or stewing – is a good buy. It is rather fat, but is excellent when salted and boiled, and then served cold. It can also be used for pot roasts.

Flank: The thick flank (or top rump) is one of the most economical cuts to buy, as it contains no bone and very little fat. Suitable for slow roasting, braising, stewing and boiling, for pies and puddings. The thin flank contains much more fat, and is best salted and boiled, and eaten cold, or used for a moist, well-flavoured *pot-au-feu*.

Clod is suitable for soups, stews and long-simmered *ragoûts*.

Shin is coarse-grained and very gelatinous. It is excellent for stocks and soups. When simmered slowly, the top part makes a very good stew, rich in flavour.

Cheek: Suitable for stews and for making soup, it contains a high proportion of bone.

Cow heel is very gelatinous, and is used principally for making jelly or, along with meat, as a foundation for soups. It is also good when carefully boiled or stewed, and served with a *sauce piquante*.

Oxtail is used for making soups, and can also be stewed or braised.

Heart: Rather coarse and indigestible, the heart can be made palatable by stuffing and very careful roasting or braising.

Tongue is usually salted and boiled, and served hot with a *sauce piquante*, or cold.

Tripe: The inner lining of the stomach, usually sold partially cooked. It is very tender and easily digestible, and for this reason is frequently ordered for invalids. They are several different kinds of tripe, popularly known as 'honeycomb', 'blanket', 'double', or 'book' (because it is like the leaves of a book).

How Much Beef to Buy

Boneless meat: Allow 4 to 6 oz (100–175 g) of meat per person for boneless steak, liver, stewing meats, minced beef and rolled roasts.

Meat with average amount of bone: Allow 6 to 10 oz (175–275 g) per person for roasts and steaks.

Meat with large amount of bone: Allow 10 to 12 oz (275–350 g) per person.

How to Refrigerate Beef

Unwrap meat, put it in the special meat compartment in the refrigerator, or on a plate near the bottom of the refrigerator; cover loosely with waxed paper or foil.

Large pieces (roasts, pot roasts, etc.) may be kept for 5 to 8 days in the refrigerator; steaks for 3 to 5 days; stewing meats, liver, heart, etc., for 2 days; minced meat for 1 to 2 days.

Roast Beef

ROAST PRIME RIBS OF BEEF

1 rib roast of beef (5–8 lb/2.5–3.8 kg)
4–6 tablespoons (60–90 ml) butter or fat
Freshly ground black pepper
1 flattened piece of beef suet, to cover roast
4–6 tablespoons (60–90 ml) red wine or water
Salt

Spread beef with butter or fat and sprinkle with freshly ground black pepper. Tie a flattened layer of beef suet over the top.

When ready to roast, place the meat on a rack over a roasting pan, resting meat on the bone ends, and roast in a preheated fairly hot oven (425°F/220°C/GM7) for 15 minutes. Reduce oven to 325°F/170°C/GM3; add warmed red wine or water to pan and continue to roast, basting frequently, allowing 15 to 18 minutes per pound (450 g) if you like your beef rare, 20 to 24 minutes per pound (450 g) for medium, and 25 to 30 minutes per pound (450 g) if you prefer it well done.

When meat is cooked to your liking, season to taste with salt and additional pepper, remove to a warm serving platter and let it stand for 15 to 20 minutes at the edge of the open oven before carving. During this time the beef sets, the cooking subsides, and the roast is ready for carving. In the meantime, pour off the fat in the roasting pan and use the pink juices that pour from the roast as it sets; stir all the crusty bits into it to make a clear sauce. Bring to a boil, reduce heat and simmer for 1 or 2 minutes. Strain and serve in a sauceboat with roast. Serves 8 to 10.

ROAST BEEF 'REDBRIDGE'

4 thick slices rare roast beef
2 tablespoons (30 ml) butter
Meat juices left over from roast, skimmed of fat
1 tablespoon (15 ml) Dijon mustard
4–6 tablespoons (60–90 ml) red wine
Freshly ground black pepper
Finely chopped chives

Melt butter in a large frying pan and sauté beef slices until warmed through. In the meantime, whisk meat juices with mustard until well blended. Pour over meat and allow to sizzle for a moment; then pour in red wine and turn up heat to reduce sauce. Season to taste with a little freshly ground black pepper and finely chopped chives. Serves 4.

ROAST FILLET OF BEEF

1 fillet of beef (4–6 lb/1.8–3 kg), stripped of fat
Olive oil or melted butter
Freshly ground black pepper
Salt
Mushrooms, sautéed in butter
Baked potatoes

Fillet of beef, the most tender of all beef cuts, cooks in a short time. At its best when served crusty brown outside and pink to rare inside, it should be roasted in a hot oven (450°F/230°C/GM8) for 45 to 60 minutes.

To roast fillet: place fillet on rack in a shallow roasting pan, tucking narrow end of fillet under to make the roast evenly thick. Brush generously with olive oil or melted butter and season with freshly ground black pepper. Roast in preheated oven for 45 to 60 minutes, or until beef is cooked to your liking. Slice in 1-inch (25 mm) slices; season with salt, and serve with sautéed mushrooms and baked potatoes. Serves 8 to 12.

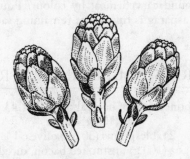

CARNE ASSADA
(PORTUGUESE POT ROAST)

4 lb (1.8 kg) rolled beef (round or rump), in 1 piece
¾ pint (450 ml) red wine
Juice of ½ lemon
6 tablespoons (90 ml) olive oil
2 cloves garlic, finely chopped
1 level teaspoon (5 ml) salt
1 level teaspoon (5 ml) paprika
½ level teaspoon (2.5 ml) freshly ground black pepper
2 bay leaves
2 cloves
1 tablespoon (15 ml) flour

GARNISH
Fried potatoes
Asparagus tips
Halved hard-boiled eggs

Marinate beef overnight in red wine, lemon juice and 2 table-spoons (30 ml) olive oil, flavoured with garlic, salt, paprika, freshly ground black pepper, bay leaves and cloves. Drain, reserving the juices; brown meat in a heatproof casserole in the remaining olive oil. Add marinade juices. Cover casserole; cook in a slow oven (325°F/170°C/GM3) for 2½ hours. Uncover casserole; baste meat with pan juices and continue to cook until meat is tender – about ½ hour.

To serve: remove beef to a heated serving dish and keep warm. Thicken pan juices with flour; correct seasoning and strain. Arrange fried potatoes, cooked asparagus tips and halved hard-boiled eggs around carved meat by colour. Pour a little sauce over meat and asparagus tips; serve remaining sauce separately. Serves 6.

BRAISED BEEF IN PASTRY

1 boned loin of beef (about 3 lb/1.4 kg)
4 oz (100 g) butter
2 tablespoons (30 ml) olive oil
4 oz (100 g) unsmoked bacon, diced
½ pint (300 ml) dry white wine
½ pint (300 ml) well-flavoured beef stock
1 beef bone, sawn in pieces
1 calf's foot, split
Salt and freshly ground black pepper
1 Spanish onion, finely chopped
1 lb (450 g) button mushrooms, finely chopped
½ pint (300 ml) well-flavoured Béchamel Sauce
(page 104)
Puff pastry (page 760)
1 egg, beaten

Melt half the butter in a thick-bottomed heatproof casserole; add olive oil and diced bacon, and sauté meat in this amalgamation of fats until it is well browned on all sides. Add dry white wine, stock, beef bone, calf's foot and barely enough hot water to cover the meat. Season to taste with salt and freshly ground black pepper. Cover casserole and simmer gently for 3½ to 4 hours. Remove the meat from the liquid; raise heat, and boil the stock with bones and calf's foot until the sauce is reduced to a third of the original quantity.

Sauté finely chopped onion and mushrooms in remaining butter until onion is transparent. Add vegetable mixture to well-flavoured Béchamel Sauce and allow to cool.

Cut beef into slices and spread each slice thickly with Béchamel Sauce. Re-form the spread slices into a roast, slip a metal skewer as a marker between each slice and place roast on a sheet of pastry. Cover with remaining sheet of pastry, allowing handles of skewers to pierce through pastry, and seal edges well with beaten egg. Decorate with pastry leaves. Bake in a moderately hot oven (400°F/200°C/GM6) for about 40 minutes, or until pastry is cooked through and golden brown. Strain sauce and serve with roast.

To carve roast: remove metal skewer markers from roast one by one, and slice pastry through where skewer was. In this way each piece of pre-sliced meat will have its own pastry shell. Makes 12 servings.

Steak

GRILLED STEAK

---

1 rump steak (about 1½ inches/38 mm thick)
Freshly ground black pepper
2–4 tablespoons (30–60 ml) softened butter
Salt

Remove steak from refrigerator at least 30 minutes before cooking; slit fat in several places around side to prevent meat from curling during cooking. Preheat grill for 15 to 20 minutes. Sprinkle both sides of steak with freshly ground black pepper and spread with softened butter.

Rub hot grill with a piece of suet; place steak on grid, and grill for 8 minutes on each side for a rare steak; grill a few minutes longer if you prefer steak to be medium rare. Sprinkle with salt, to taste. Serves 4.

PLANKED STEAK

1 rump steak (about 1½ inches/38 mm thick)
Freshly ground black pepper
2–4 tablespoons (30–60 ml) softened butter
Salt
Olive oil
Glazed onions
Grilled tomatoes
Buttered peas
Pommes de Terre Duchesse
Sprigs of watercress

Grill steak as above. Place it on a plank or wooden platter that has been oiled thoroughly with olive oil and heated in the oven. Arrange glazed onions, grilled tomatoes and buttered peas around steak, and garnish with a ring of *pommes de terre duchesse*. Brown under grill and garnish with fresh watercress. Serves 4.

GRILLED STEAK 'FINES HERBES'

Make a sauce of 6 tablespoons (90 ml) melted butter combined with 1 tablespoon (15 ml) each chopped chives and chopped parsley.

Transfer thick steak, grilled as above, to a heated serving platter, and pour sauce over it. Top with slices of beef marrow poached for 4 minutes in salted water.

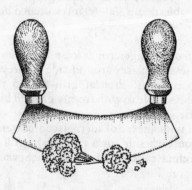

GRILLED STEAK WITH MUSHROOMS

Sauté 8 oz (225 g) button mushrooms in 4 tablespoons (60 ml) butter and a little lemon juice. Season with salt, freshly ground black pepper and a little finely chopped garlic. Transfer thick steak, grilled as above, to a heated serving platter, and top with mushrooms.

GRILLED STEAK WITH ROQUEFORT BUTTER

Cream 1 oz (25 g) Roquefort cheese and 2 oz (50 g) butter with the juice of ½ lemon and 2 tablespoons (30 ml) finely chopped parsley, chervil or chives. Season to taste with salt and freshly ground black pepper.

Transfer thick steak, grilled as above, to a heated serving platter, and top with Roquefort butter.

PEPPER STEAK

4 fillet steaks
Salt
1–2 tablespoons (15–30 ml) crushed peppercorns
3 tablespoons (45 ml) butter
1 tablespoon (15 ml) olive oil
Dash of cognac
8 tablespoons (120 ml) well-flavoured veal stock
2 tablespoons (30 ml) double cream

Flatten steaks; season to taste with salt, and press crushed peppercorns well into each side of meat. Sauté steaks on each side in 2 tablespoons (30 ml) butter and 1 tablespoon (15 ml) olive oil until tender. Remove and keep warm.

Add a dash of cognac to the pan; pour in veal stock and cook over a high heat, stirring occasionally, until stock is reduced to half the original quantity. Add remaining butter and shake pan vigorously until butter is amalgamated into sauce; then add cream, and continue to shake pan until sauce is rich and smooth. Pour over steaks and serve immediately. Serves 4.

FILLET 'HARE AND HOUNDS'

4 fillet steaks
Salt and freshly ground black pepper
4 tablespoons (60 ml) butter
2 tablespoons (30 ml) olive oil
1 tablespoon (15 ml) Dijon mustard
2 tablespoons (30 ml) brown sugar

Season steaks generously with salt and freshly ground black pepper.

Heat butter and olive oil in a thick-bottomed frying pan. Sauté steaks on each side until tender. Spread mustard over top of steaks; sprinkle with brown sugar; transfer steaks to a *gratin* dish and glaze under preheated grill for a few minutes until golden brown.

Pour off fat from pan juices; heat remaining juices and pour over steak. Serve immediately. Serves 4.

BEEFSTEAK WITH OYSTER SAUCE

1 thick rump steak
Freshly ground black pepper
Softened butter

OYSTER SAUCE
1 dozen oysters
1 tablespoon (15 ml) butter
1 tablespoon (15 ml) lemon juice
Salt and cayenne pepper
2 egg yolks
4–6 tablespoons (60–90 ml) double cream
Worcestershire sauce

Remove steak from refrigerator at least 30 minutes before cooking and slit fat in several places around sides to prevent meat from curling during cooking. Preheat grill for 15 minutes. Sprinkle both sides of steak with freshly ground black pepper and spread with butter. Grill on both sides until steak is cooked as you like it – 8 to 10 minutes on each side. In the meantime, make sauce.

OYSTER SAUCE

Remove oysters from shells, saving the liquor; combine oysters and liquor in a saucepan with butter and lemon juice, and salt and cayenne pepper, to taste. Simmer gently for 2 or 3 minutes until the oysters begin to curl up, then add egg yolks beaten with cream, and a little Worcestershire sauce. Heat through but do not allow to come to a boil again. Keep sauce warm over hot water.

To serve: place steak on hot serving dish and surround with Oyster Sauce. Serves 4 to 6.

ENTRECÔTES BERCY

2 sirloin steaks (about 1 lb/450 g each)
Sprigs of fresh watercress

BERCY SAUCE
4 oz (100 g) beef marrow, diced
4 shallots, finely chopped
½ pint (300 ml) dry white wine
8 oz (225 g) softened butter, diced
2 tablespoons (30 ml) finely chopped parsley
2 tablespoons (30 ml) lemon juice
Salt and freshly ground black pepper

Grill steaks in the usual manner and serve on a heated serving dish; garnish with sprigs of fresh watercress. Serve immediately with Bercy Sauce. Serves 4.

BERCY SAUCE

Poach diced beef marrow in boiling water; drain and cool. Simmer finely chopped shallots in white wine until the liquid is reduced to a third of the original quantity. Remove from heat and whisk until slightly cooled, then with pan over hot but not boiling water, gradually whisk in diced softened butter, stirring continuously until sauce is thickened. Stir in diced beef marrow, finely chopped parsley and lemon juice, and season to taste with salt and freshly ground black pepper.

TOURNEDOS 'EN BOITE'

4 thickly cut tournedos
4 tablespoons (60 ml) butter
6 finely chopped shallots
French mustard
Worcestershire sauce
Pinch of rosemary
Salt and freshly ground black pepper
4 tablespoons (60 ml) cognac

Place well-trimmed *tournedos* in 4 individual heatproof casseroles with butter and finely chopped shallots, flavoured to taste with French mustard and Worcestershire sauce. Cover and cook in a moderately hot oven (400°F/200°C/GM6) for about 5 minutes; then drain fat; turn *tournedos* over; add 1 pinch each of rosemary, salt and freshly ground black pepper to each casserole. Pour cognac over meat; cover and continue cooking for a few minutes longer. Serve in casseroles. Serves 4.

TOURNEDOS EN CROÛTE

4 tournedos
4 tablespoons (60 ml) butter
4 mushrooms, finely chopped
4 oz (100 g) *pâté de fois gras*, crumbled
Salt and freshly ground black pepper
2–4 tablespoons (30–60 ml) dry sherry or Madeira
Flaky pastry (page 759)
1 egg, separated

Sauté *tournedos* in 2 tablespoons (30 ml) butter for about 3 minutes on each side. Remove from pan and allow to cool.

Sauté mushrooms in the remaining butter until golden. Add crumbled *pâté de foie gras* and sauté the mixture until lightly browned. Season to taste with salt and freshly ground black pepper, and add enough sherry or Madeira to bind the mixture (about 2 tablespoons (30 ml)). Spread the top of each *tournedos* thinly with this mixture and allow to cool.

Cut 4 rounds of flaky pastry 1 inch (25 mm) larger in diameter than the meat, and the same number about 1½ inches (38 mm) larger in diameter.

Lay *tournedos* on the smaller rounds and cover them with the larger ones. Paint pastry edges with lightly beaten egg white and press together firmly. Decorate pastry tops with cut out leaves, etc., and paint with lightly beaten egg yolk. Bake in a moderately hot oven (400°F/200°C/GM6) for 15 to 20 minutes, or until the pastry is golden. Serves 4.

Note: For a more inexpensive version of this dish, substitute for *foie gras* ½ Spanish onion and 2 thin slices of cooked ham, both finely chopped and sautéed in butter until golden.

RARE FILLET STROGANOFF 'FOUR SEASONS'

8–12 slices fillet of beef
4 tablespoons (60 ml) melted butter
Paprika
Rich beef stock or *jus de viande*
1 tablespoon (15 ml) brandy
½ tablespoon (8 ml) dry sherry
¼ pint (150 ml) sour cream
Lemon juice
Salt and freshly ground black pepper

Sauté beef in melted butter for a minute or two on each side. Sprinkle with paprika; add rich beef stock or *jus de viande*; cover and simmer gently until meat is done to your liking. Remove meat and keep warm; add brandy and sherry to juices, and reduce sauce to the desired consistency. Add sour cream (be careful not to bring sauce to a boil after sour cream is added). Sprinkle lemon juice to taste into sauce; add salt and freshly ground black pepper if necessary. Serves 4 to 6.

FONDUE BOURGUIGNONNE

2 lb (900 g) fillet steak
8 oz (225 g) butter
¼ pint (150 ml) corn or olive oil

Dice raw meat into bite-size pieces, cutting off all bits of fat or gristle. Combine butter and oil in *fondue* cooker or chafing dish, and keep it simmering gently in centre of table. Dip each beef cube in hot fat with a fork, and cook to taste. Flavour by dipping cooked beef into the sauce of your choice.

Individual bowls of two or more of the following sauces should be served as a garnish: mayonnaise (page 120); finely chopped garlic, parsley and capers; Béarnaise Sauce (page 122); Anchovy Butter (page 129) or Garlic Butter (page 130). Serves 6.

CHINESE STEAK WITH GREEN PEPPERS

1 lb (450 g) rump steak
4 tablespoons (60 ml) corn or peanut oil
1 small clove garlic
¼ Spanish onion, diced
1 green pepper, diced
Salt and freshly ground black pepper
¼ teaspoon (1.25 ml) ginger
1 level tablespoon (15 ml) cornflour
¼ pint (150 ml) well-flavoured stock
1–2 teaspoons (5–10 ml) soy sauce
Rice

Cut steak diagonally across the grain into thin slices, then cut into strips about 2 inches (5 cms) long. Heat oil in frying pan over medium heat. Place garlic clove in hot oil. Remove after 3 minutes. Add meat to oil and stir-fry over medium heat until meat starts to brown. Mix in onion, green pepper, salt, freshly ground black pepper and ginger, and cook over medium heat, stirring constantly, until just tender – about 3 minutes. Blend cornflour with stock and soy sauce. Stir mixture into frying pan; bring to a boil and cook, stirring constantly, until liquid is thickened. Serve over rice. Serves 2 to 4.

CHINESE STEAMED BEEF

1 lb (450 g) beefsteak
1 teaspoon (5 ml) cornflour
Salt and freshly ground black pepper
2 teaspoons (10 ml) soy sauce
1 tablespoon (15 ml) oil
2 tablespoons (30 ml) sherry
1 teaspoon (5 ml) wine vinegar
2 spring onions

Slice beefsteak across the grain into thin strips. Place them in a bowl. Blend cornflour, salt, freshly ground black pepper, soy sauce, oil, sherry and vinegar, and pour over beef. Chop the onions very finely and sprinkle over top. Cover tightly and let stand for at least 1 hour.

When ready to cook: place bowl of beef on a stand over a saucepan of boiling water; cover saucepan and steam until beef is tender. Serve immediately. Serves 2 to 4.

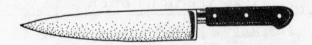

STEAK POELE 'PAUL CHÊNE'

4 thick steaks
Salt and freshly ground black pepper
2 tablespoons (30 ml) butter
2 tablespoons (30 ml) hot beef stock
Juice of ½ lemon
1 tablespoon (15 ml) finely chopped parsley
1 tablespoon (15 ml) finely chopped chervil

Season steaks generously with salt and freshly ground black pepper, and sauté on both sides in butter until done as you like them.

Place steaks on a heated dish; add hot stock and lemon juice to pan juices, and pour over the meat; sprinkle with finely chopped herbs, and serve immediately. Serves 4.

ISLAND PAPER-WRAPPED BEEF

12 oz (350 g) tender beefsteak
3 tablespoons (45 ml) *sake* or dry sherry
3 tablespoons (45 ml) soy sauce
1 level tablespoon (15 ml) cornflour
1 Spanish onion, finely chopped
Oiled paper
Peanut oil, for frying

Slice beef thinly across the grain; marinate in *sake* (or dry sherry), soy sauce, cornflour and finely chopped onion for 10 to 15 minutes, stirring from time to time. Divide the beef into equal portions on 4-inch (10 cm) squares of oiled paper (18 to 20 squares) and fold securely into little packets. Deep-fry the packages in hot oil for 2 minutes and serve hot, just as they are in their little paper jackets. Serves 4 to 5 as an appetizer, if 1 or 2 other dishes are served.

STEAK IN BEER

1 thick rump steak (2–2½ lb/900 g–1.1 kg)
4 tablespoons (60 ml) olive oil
1 clove garlic, finely chopped
Salt and freshly ground black pepper
1 lb (450 g) button mushrooms, sliced
4 tablespoons (60 ml) butter
Juice of ¼ lemon
1 tablespoon (15 ml) flour
½ pint (300 ml) beer
1–2 teaspoons (5–10 ml) soy sauce

Brush steak with olive oil, sprinkle with ½ clove garlic, finely chopped, and season to taste with salt and freshly ground black pepper. Allow steak to absorb these flavours for at least 1 hour. Grill until medium rare.

A few minutes before the steak is done, sauté sliced mushrooms in butter and lemon juice until tender. Add flour and stir until well blended; then pour in beer. Bring the mixture to a boil. Add soy sauce and remaining finely chopped garlic, and season to taste with freshly ground black pepper. Place steak on a heated serving dish; pour bubbling mushroom and beer sauce over meat and serve immediately. Serves 4.

Minced Beef

GRILLED BEEFBURGERS

2 lb (900 g) rump steak, minced
4 tablespoons (60 ml) chopped beef marrow
4 tablespoons (60 ml) double cream or cold water
4 tablespoons (60 ml) finely chopped parsley
4 tablespoons (60 ml) finely chopped onion
Salt and freshly ground black pepper
4 tablespoons (60 ml) melted butter

Combine first 5 ingredients; season to taste with salt and freshly ground black pepper, and form mixture into 8 patties. Brush patties with melted butter and grill for 4 to 5 minutes on each side. Serves 4.

HAM-AND-BEEFBURGERS

1 lb (450 g) freshly minced beef
French mustard
Salt and freshly ground black pepper
4 thin slices ham
Butter
Olive oil

ANCHOVY BUTTER
2 tablespoons (30 ml) softened butter
Anchovy paste

Form beef into 8 thin, oval-shaped patties. Spread 4 patties with French mustard, and season generously with salt and freshly ground black pepper. Place a slice of cooked ham on each patty, trimming away excess ham. Place ham scraps on top of ham slice and top with remaining patties, pressing meat firmly together.

Sauté patties in equal quantities of butter and olive oil for 2 or 3 minutes on each side. Serve patties with knobs of Anchovy Butter, made by combining butter with anchovy paste, to taste. Serves 4.

BEEF AND PORK LOAF

2 lb (900 g) each lean beef and pork
1 Spanish onion, quartered
4 oz (100 g) fresh breadcrumbs
Milk
1 small can Italian tomatoes
3 eggs, well beaten
2 bay leaves, crumbled
Salt and freshly ground black pepper
Thyme
6–8 tablespoons (90–120 ml) heated stock
Tomato Sauce (page 124)

Put beef, pork and quartered onion through mincer twice; mix well with fresh breadcrumbs which you have moistened with a little milk. Then add canned tomatoes, well-beaten eggs, crumbled bay leaves, and salt, freshly ground black pepper and thyme, to taste. Mix well.

Put mixture in a well-greased baking dish, or pat into a loaf shape on a greased baking sheet or oiled board. Bake in a slow oven (325°F/170°C/GM3) for at least 1 hour, basting occasionally with a little hot stock. Serve with Tomato Sauce. Serves 8.

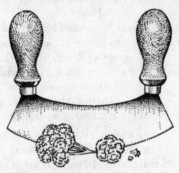

MRS BEETON'S COTTAGE PIE

2 lb (900 g) minced raw beef
1½ Spanish onions, chopped
Butter
6 medium-sized carrots, minced
1 tablespoon (15 ml) tomato concentrate
1 tablespoon (15 ml) finely chopped herbs
(parsley, thyme, bay leaf, chervil, sage, etc.)
Beef stock
Salt and freshly ground black pepper
Cooked potatoes

Sauté chopped onions in butter until transparent; add minced beef and sauté, stirring continuously, until brown. Stir in minced carrot, tomato concentrate and finely chopped herbs. Add beef stock, to cover; season to taste with salt and freshly ground black pepper, and simmer for 30 to 40 minutes, or until meat is tender. Place meat mixture in a well-buttered deep oval pie dish.

Mash cooked potatoes; season to taste with clarified butter, salt and freshly ground black pepper; pile mixture on meat and brown in oven for 8 to 10 minutes, or until golden. Serves 4 to 6.

Beef Stews

BEEF STEW WITH PARSLEY DUMPLINGS

3½ lb (1.6 kg) stewing beef
Flour
Salt and freshly ground black pepper
2 tablespoons (30 ml) butter or lard
2 tablespoons (30 ml) olive oil
1 pint (600 ml) hot water, or stock made with 1 beef cube
12 button onions
12 small carrots
1 tablespoon (15 ml) cornflour, dissolved in a little stock

PARSLEY DUMPLINGS
4 oz (100 g) sifted plain flour
2 level teaspoons (10 ml) baking powder
½ teaspoon (2.5 ml) salt
2 tablespoons (30 ml) butter
1 egg, beaten
2 tablespoons (30 ml) finely chopped parsley
¼ pint (150 ml) milk

Cut meat into 2-inch (5-cm) cubes. Dredge in flour seasoned to taste with salt and freshly ground black pepper. Heat fat and oil in a thick-bottomed heatproof casserole, and sauté meat until well browned on all sides. Add hot water or stock; cover casserole tightly and simmer gently for 1½ to 2 hours, or until beef is tender. About 30 minutes before the end of cooking time, add onions and carrots, and more liquid if necessary. Cover and continue to cook for 15 minutes. Drop Parsley Dumplings gently on top of stew; cover casserole and finish cooking.

To serve: arrange meat, vegetables and dumplings on a heated serving dish and keep warm. Thicken gravy with cornflour which you have dissolved in a little stock. Serves 4 to 6.

PARSLEY DUMPLINGS
Combine sifted flour, baking powder and salt in a mixing bowl. Cut in butter with a pastry blender or with 2 knives. Combine beaten egg, parsley and milk, and stir into flour to make a soft dough.

To make dumplings: scoop out dumpling batter with a wet serving spoon, and drop quickly by the spoonful on to meat and vegetables in casserole, leaving a little space at sides for steam to circulate. Cover casserole and steam gently for 15 minutes.

BŒUF SAUTÉ À LA BOURGUIGNONNE 'ALEXANDRE DUMAINE'

2½ lb (1.1 kg) beef
½ bottle red wine
8 oz (225 g) carrots, sliced
1 oz (25 g) shallots, finely chopped
2 oz (50 g) onion, finely chopped
1–2 sprigs thyme
1–2 bay leaves
8 oz (225 g) unsmoked bacon
12 button onions
12 baby carrots
1 tablespoon (15 ml) flour
1 glass water
2–4 cloves garlic
Bouquet garni (celery, thyme, bay leaf, parsley)
Salt and freshly ground black pepper
12 button mushrooms
Butter

Cut beef into bite-sized pieces and marinate overnight in red wine with carrots, shallots, onion, thyme and bay leaves. Drain well and dry lightly with a clean cloth.

Dice bacon and brown in a *cocotte* with small onions and carrots. When these are lightly coloured, remove them together with the bacon, and sauté drained beef in remaining fat until brown. Sprinkle with flour, and add red wine from marinade and a glass of water.

Return diced bacon, onions and carrots to the pan, and add garlic and a *bouquet garni*; season to taste with salt and freshly ground black pepper. Simmer gently until meat is tender and the sauce reduced to half the original quantity – about 2¾ to 3 hours. Brown mushrooms in butter and add to meat about 10 minutes before end of cooking. Serves 4.

BŒUF EN DAUBE

3 lb (1.4 kg) lean top rump of beef
3 cloves garlic
4 oz (100 g) fat salt pork
3 tablespoons (45 ml) olive oil
4 shallots, finely chopped
4 tomatoes, peeled, seeded and coarsely chopped
2 cloves garlic, finely chopped
12 button onions
4 oz (100 g) button mushrooms, quartered
4 sprigs parsley
½ pint (300 ml) rich beef stock
Flour and water

MARINADE
3 slices lemon
1 bay leaf
Pinch of thyme
3 teaspoons (15 ml) finely chopped herbs
(chives, tarragon, parsley)
¼ pint (150 ml) dry white wine
3 teaspoons (15 ml) olive oil
Salt and freshly ground black pepper

Make 6 small incisions in top rump of beef with a sharp knife and bury half a clove of garlic in each.

Combine ingredients of marinade mixture in a mixing bowl, and marinate meat in this mixture, turning occasionally, for 12 hours.

Remove rind from piece of fat salt pork; dice pork and sauté in olive oil until golden; remove pork bits, and brown beef well on all sides in the resulting amalgamation of fats.

Place pork rind in the bottom of an ovenproof casserole; place beef on it and surround with sautéed pork bits, finely chopped shallots, peeled, seeded and coarsely chopped tomatoes, garlic, button onions, quartered button mushrooms and parsley. Strain the marinade juices over the meat and add beef stock.

Seal the casserole hermetically (make a thick paste of flour and water; shape it into a long, narrow roll and fit it round the edge of the casserole; press lid of casserole firmly into this pastry band and seal). Cook in a very slow oven (250°F/130°C/GM½) for 4 to 5 hours. Serve from the casserole. Serves 6.

BEEF MARINATED IN BEER

4 lb (1.8 kg) beef (rump or round)
4 tablespoons (60 ml) olive oil
2 tablespoons (30 ml) brown sugar
2 tablespoons (30 ml) flour
4 tablespoons (60 ml) red wine
4 tablespoons (60 ml) double cream

BEER MARINADE
1 bottle beer (pale or brown ale)
1 pint (600 ml) water
4 tablespoons (60 ml) olive oil
1 Spanish onion, sliced
6 carrots, sliced
2 bay leaves
6 peppercorns
2 cloves
1 level teaspoon (5 ml) allspice
Salt

BEER MARINADE
Combine beer, water, olive oil, sliced onion and carrots, and seasonings in a large mixing bowl. Place beef in this marinade and marinate in the refrigerator for 2 or 3 days, turning meat once or twice each day.

When ready to cook; remove meat from marinade and drain, reserving marinade. Heat olive oil in heatproof casserole just large enough to hold beef. Add meat, and brown on all sides. Pour ½ pint (300 ml) marinade juices with vegetables and seasonings over meat. Cover casserole and cook for 1¾ hours in a very slow oven (300°F/150°C/GM2), adding more marinade juices during cooking if necessary.

Remove casserole from oven; sprinkle meat with brown sugar and simmer on top of the stove, uncovered, for 15 minutes longer, turning meat until sugar has melted and browned.

Stir flour into remaining marinade juices. Add red wine and pour over meat. Return casserole to oven, uncovered, for 30 minutes, or until sauce has thickened. Remove meat to dish; strain sauce and skim fat. Stir in double cream and pour over meat. Serve immediately. Serves 6 to 8.

PAMPAS BEEF WITH OLIVES

4 lb (1.8 kg) lean beef
4 tablespoons (60 ml) flour
4 tablespoons (60 ml) melted butter
4 tablespoons (60 ml) olive oil
Salt and freshly ground black pepper
8 oz (225 g) bacon, diced
2 cloves garlic
2 carrots, sliced
1 lb (450 g) button onions
2 tablespoons (30 ml) chopped parsley
2 bay leaves
2 sprigs thyme
1 small piece orange peel
1 bottle good red wine
Beurre manié
12 ripe olives, pitted
12 mushrooms, sliced

Cut beef into large cubes; roll them in flour, and brown on all sides in melted butter and olive oil. Transfer to a casserole, and season to taste with salt and freshly ground black pepper.

Sauté diced bacon, garlic, carrots and onions in remaining fat until bacon is crisp and vegetables are golden. Transfer to casserole with meat; add parsley, bay leaves, thyme and orange peel; gradually moisten with 1 bottle of good red wine and cook in a slow oven (300°F/150°C/GM2) for 1½ to 2 hours until meat is almost done. Correct seasoning; stir in, little by little, a *beurre manié* made with 1 tablespoon (15 ml) flour blended to a paste with the same amount of butter; add pitted ripe olives and sliced mushrooms; cover and allow to simmer in a slow oven or on the charcoal grill until mushrooms are cooked and meat is tender. Serves 6.

BŒUF À L'AIL

4 lb (1.8 kg) beef (rump or top round)
4 tablespoons (60 ml) butter
2 tablespoons (30 ml) olive oil
1 lb (450 g) tomatoes, peeled, seeded and chopped
2 tablespoons (30 ml) tomato concentrate
2 sprigs thyme
2 bay leaves
Salt and freshly ground black pepper
4 cloves garlic
Water, stock or dry white wine
Noodles or boiled new potatoes

Cut beef into cubes about 2 inches (5 cms) square. Sauté cubes in butter and olive oil until well browned. Add tomatoes, tomato concentrate, thyme and bay leaves, and season to taste with salt and freshly ground black pepper.

Do not peel the garlic; just smash cloves with the heel of your hand and add them to casserole. Simmer beef gently for about 3 hours, adding a little hot water, stock or dry white wine if meat becomes dry. Serve with noodles or boiled new potatoes. Serves 6.

STUFATINO DI MANZO

2½ lb (1.1 kg) lean beef, cut into bite-sized pieces
1 tablespoon (15 ml) lard
1 tablespoon (15 ml) olive oil
8 oz (225 g) fat salt pork, diced
1 onion, sliced
2 cloves garlic, chopped
Salt and freshly ground black pepper
Generous pinch of marjoram
Generous pinch of rosemary
¼ pint (150 ml) red wine
4 tablespoons (60 ml) tomato concentrate, diluted in water

Heat lard and olive oil in a thick-bottomed pan or flameproof casserole; when fat begins to bubble, add diced salt pork, sliced onion and garlic, and sauté until golden. Add pieces of beef seasoned with salt, freshly ground black pepper, marjoram and rosemary, and cook, stirring frequently, until meat is well browned on all sides. Now add red wine (one of the rougher Italian ones) and continue cooking until the wine is reduced to half the original quantity. Add diluted tomato concentrate, and enough boiling water to cover the meat. Cover the pan and simmer slowly for about 2 hours, or until the meat is tender and the sauce thick and richly coloured. A tablespoon or two of red wine just before serving will add extra bouquet to this dish, which should be served directly from the casserole. Serves 4.

BŒUF À LA CORSE 'CHEZ VICTOR, AUX DEUX MARCHES'

2½ lb (1.1 kg) lean beef
½ calf's foot
8 oz (225 g) unsmoked bacon, in 1 piece
2 tablespoons (30 ml) olive oil
2 tablespoons (30 ml) butter
2 tablespoons (30 ml) cognac
2 tablespoons (30 ml) tomato concentrate
1 Spanish onion, quartered
2 cloves garlic
Bouquet garni
Salt and freshly ground black pepper
1 bottle red wine
4½ oz (115 g) dried mushrooms
3–4 oz (75–100 g) green olives, pitted
2 tablespoons (30 ml) finely chopped parsley

Cut beef into cubes about 2 inches (5 cms) square. Put calf's foot and bacon in a pan of cold water and bring to a boil; drain and dry well. Heat olive oil and butter in a large thick-bottomed fireproof casserole. Add beef, calf's foot and bacon, and sauté until meats are golden brown. Add cognac, and flame. Then add tomato concentrate, onion, garlic and *bouquet garni*, and season to taste with salt and freshly ground black pepper. Add just enough red wine to cover the meat; cover casserole and simmer gently for 1½ hours, adding a little hot water from time to time if necessary.

Then add dried mushrooms which you have soaked for ½ hour in warm water, and olives which you have pitted. Continue to cook for 15 minutes. Remove *bouquet garni*; sprinkle with finely chopped parsley and serve in the casserole. Serves 4 to 6.

HOCHEPOT DE QUEUE DE BŒUF

1 large oxtail
8 oz (225 g) butter
4 medium-sized onions, sliced
3 large carrots, sliced
3 cloves garlic, crushed
1 glass good brandy
1 bottle Chablis
1 pint (600 ml) rich beef stock
Salt and freshly ground black pepper
Bouquet garni
24 button mushrooms
4 oz (100 g) fat salt pork, diced
24 tiny onions
Sugar
Finely chopped parsley
Purée of peas or chestnuts

Cut large oxtail into 4-inch (10 cm) segments and blanch in cold water for at least 6 hours. Drain well and dry lightly with a clean towel.

Melt 4 tablespoons (60 ml) butter in a large thick-bottomed saucepan or flameproof casserole, and sauté the pieces of oxtail with sliced onions and carrots until golden. Then add crushed garlic. Cover casserole for 2 minutes; pour in brandy, and flame. Put out the flames with a bottle of dry Chablis. Add just enough rich beef stock to cover the pieces of oxtail; add salt, freshly ground black pepper, and a *bouquet garni*, and simmer for 3 hours.

Strain sauce into a bowl through a fine sieve. Place pieces of oxtail in a clean casserole and garnish with mushrooms which you have sautéed lightly in 2 tablespoons (30 ml) butter, diced fat salt pork which you have sautéed in 2 tablespoons (30 ml) butter, and onions which you have simmered until tender in a little water with the remaining butter and a little sugar.

Skim fat from surface of sauce; pour sauce over the meat and vegetables. Bring slowly to a boil; cover the casserole and cook in a slow oven (325°F/170°C/GM3) for 1 hour. When the *hochepot* is done, the meat should be meltingly tender and the sauce rich and smooth, and slightly thick without the aid of flour or a *beurre manié*.

Sprinkle with finely chopped parsley and serve from the casserole with a purée of peas or chestnuts. Serves 4 to 6.

Boiled and Spiced Beef

ELIZA ACTON'S SPICED BEEF

'For twelve pounds of the round, rump, or thick flank of beef, take a large teaspoonful of freshly-pounded mace, and of ground black pepper, twice as much of cloves, one small nutmeg, and a quarter of a teaspoonful of cayenne, all in the finest powder. Mix them *well* with seven ounces of brown sugar, rub the beef with them and let it lie three days; add to it then half a pound of fine salt, and rub and turn it once in twenty-four hours for twelve days. Just wash, but do not soak it; skewer, or bind it into good form, put it into a stewpan or saucepan nearly of its size, pour to it a pint and a half of good beef broth, and when it begins to boil, take off the scum, and throw in one small onion, a moderate-sized faggot of thyme and parsley, and two large, or four small carrots. Let it simmer quite softly for four hours and a half, and if not wanted to serve hot, leave it in its own liquor until it is nearly cold. This is an excellent and far more wholesome dish than the hard, bright-coloured beef which is cured with large quantities of salt and salt-petre: two or three ounces of juniper-berries may be added to it with the spice, to heighten its flavour.

'Beef, 12 lbs. [6 kg]; sugar, 7 oz. [200 g]; mace and black pepper, each, 1 large teaspoonful [7 ml]; cloves, in powder, 1 large dessertspoonful [10 ml]; nutmeg, 1; cayenne, ¼ teaspoonful [1.25 ml]: 3 days. Fine salt, ½ lb [225 g]: 12 days. Beef broth (or bouillon), 1½ pints [900 ml]; onion, 1 small; bunch of herbs; carrots, 2 large or 4 small: stewed 4½ hours.

'Obs. – We give this recipe *exactly* as we have often had it used, but celery and turnips might be added to the gravy; and when the appearance of the meat is much considered, three-quarters of an ounce of saltpetre may be mixed with the spices; the beef may also be plainly boiled in water only, with a few vegetables, or baked in a deep pan with a little gravy. No meat must ever be left to cool in the stewpan or saucepan in which it is cooked; it must be lifted into a pan of its own depth, and the liquor poured upon it.'

IRISH SPICED BEEF

1 round of beef (about 20 lb/10 kg)
Salt
Saltpetre
½ oz (15 g) whole cloves
8 oz (225 g) allspice
8 oz (225 g) black peppercorns
8 oz (225 g) coarse brown sugar
3 Spanish onions, thickly sliced
6 bay leaves
6 sprigs thyme
6 cloves
8 pints (4.5 lit) water
4 pints (2.25 lit) porter

An old recipe from the family of Muriel Chenevix Trench:

'Place meat in a large shallow recipient big enough to hold it. Rub with equal quantities of salt and saltpetre once daily for 4 days. Grind cloves, allspice and peppercorns, and combine with coarse brown sugar.

Rub beef with this mixture every second day for 3 weeks, turning it occasionally.

When ready to cook beef: bruise onion slices and place around meat with bay leaves, thyme and cloves. Wrap them to meat with strips of bandage or muslin.

Combine water and porter; bring to the boil; add meat and if necessary more water to cover, and simmer gently for about 6 hours. Cool and serve as required.'

FRESH OR SALT BRISKET WITH HORSERADISH SAUCE

3–4 lb (1.4–1.8 kg) fresh or salt beef brisket
2 Spanish onions
4 large carrots
2 bay leaves
Water
Salt and freshly ground black pepper

HORSERADISH SAUCE
1 tablespoon (15 ml) butter
1 tablespoon (15 ml) flour
½ pint (300 ml) hot milk
1 small jar grated horseradish
1 tablespoon (15 ml) lemon juice
Salt and freshly ground black pepper

Place meat in a casserole with onions, carrots and bay leaves, and cover with water. Season with salt (no salt if salt beef is used) and freshly ground black pepper, and simmer gently for 3 to 4 hours, or until meat is tender. Cool in stock. Slice meat thinly and reheat in stock just before serving. Serve with Horseradish Sauce. Serves 6 to 8.

HORSERADISH SAUCE

Melt butter in the top of a double saucepan: add flour and cook, stirring constantly, until smooth. Add hot milk, stirring constantly until mixture comes to a boil. Drain horseradish, add it to sauce with lemon juice, and season to taste with salt and freshly ground black pepper.

MR PICKWICK'S BOILED DINNER

4 lb (1.8 kg) shoulder of beef
1 lb (450 g) salt pork
2 bay leaves
6 peppercorns
1 boiling chicken
1 loin of pork
8 large carrots, scraped
8 medium onions, peeled
8 large potatoes, peeled
8 small turnips, peeled and quartered
1 medium head cabbage, cut in eighths

HORSERADISH CHANTILLY
Whipped cream
Salt
Freshly grated horseradish

Have your butcher bone and tie beef; place it in a large stockpot or heavy-bottomed saucepan with just enough cold water to cover, and bring to a boil; add salt pork, bay leaves and peppercorns; cover and simmer over the lowest of heats for 3 to 4 hours, or until meat is tender, adding chicken and fresh pork after first hour.

Cool slightly; skim excess fat, and add carrots, onions, potatoes and turnips. Cook for about 20 minutes; then add cabbage wedges; cook until cabbage and vegetables are tender but crisp.

Serve the beef, pork, salt pork and chicken on a platter, garnished with vegetables. Accompany with Horseradish Chantilly: salted whipped cream into which you have stirred freshly grated horseradish, to taste. Serves 8 to 10.

CHAPTER TEN
All About Veal

Veal is one of the most versatile of meats. Almost every part of the calf can be used to advantage, from its head (calf's head *à la vinaigrette*) to its toes (calf's feet *à la poulette*). Indeed, a famous Scot, a nobleman and judge, once gave a dinner at which every course was veal: the meal began with veal broth, followed by a roasted fillet of veal, veal cutlets, a veal pie and a calf's head, and ended with calf's foot jelly. 'When we kill a beast,' he explained to his astonished guests, 'we just eat up ae side and down the tither.'

I am not suggesting that you go as far as the noble judge in your enthusiasm for veal. But the kidneys, with the rich fat that surrounds them, and the sweetbreads are well-known delicacies. The breast and shoulder, boned, stuffed and rolled, are delicious roasted, poached or braised; the liver, the heart, and even the feet, make very good eating; and no meat is so generally useful for rich stocks, soups and sauces.

Veal is a delicate, young meat that requires careful cooking. Do not stew or braise it too long, or the juices will dry out and the meat will be tough and coarse. Always lard veal – or cover it with a protective layer of fat or bacon – before you roast it. Do not sear veal at a high temperature as you do beef. Cook it in a slow oven (325°F/170°C/GM3) for about 20 to 35 minutes per pound (450 g). Veal is at its succulent best when cooked to just the right point of moist tenderness – well cooked, yes, but with a delicate hint of pinkness still in evidence.

Ask your butcher to cut shin of veal into thick slices of marrow-filled bone and meat for a rich, robust *osso buco*. Spice diced shoulder or leg of veal with paprika and caraway for a regal *goulash* in the Hungarian manner. Slice thin escalopes in half to wrap around thin slices of cheese and *prosciutto*; dip them in egg and breadcrumbs, and sauté lightly in butter and oil as they do in Italy. Combine thin escalopes with *prosciutto* again; spike each one with a sage leaf; roll it up, and sauté in oil and butter, for *saltimbocca alla romana*.

Serve *blanquette de veau* country style – great chunks of tender meat (breast and shoulder) bathed in a creamy sauce in which the juices of the meat, egg yolk and just a hint of lemon juice play their part. Stuff breast of veal with spinach, fresh herbs, rice and just a touch of garlic in the Provençal manner, delicious served hot in thick slices, and equally good cold and thinly cut, the brilliant green of the stuffing contrasting wonderfully with the pink of the meat encasing it.

I like milk-fed veal in the Continental manner, slaughtered at a tender age (five to twelve weeks) when the flesh is pale, almost white, faintly tinged with pink. Young veal is fine-grained, firm and smooth; the fat is white and satiny. Other veal is darker in colour, and can be tough and stringy.

Flavour veal with tarragon, basil, rosemary, thyme, paprika and cayenne; onion, shallot, garlic, tomato and lemon: cheese, cream and sour cream; ham, sausage and bacon; dry white wine, dry vermouth and Marsala; and anchovies, prunes and olives.

Some Different Cuts of Veal

Fillet: Escalopes are cut across the grain from this expensive joint. When preparing for roasting, it is best to lard this joint or cover with a thin layer of fat to prevent it drying out.

Knuckle: Lower part of the leg. Excellent for boiling or for stewing pieces and pie pieces. It can also be boned and stuffed and then braised. The knuckle is full of marrow. Very good for stock or for jellied veal or veal moulds.

Shin: Wonderful for stocks and broths. This inexpensive cut can be sawn across the bone to make individual servings for Italian *osso buco*.

Loin: Sold as one joint with bone, or boned and stuffed, or as separate loin chops with or without kidney. I like to roast the loin until half done; then cut it into thick chump chops with kidney; flavour chops to taste with salt, pepper, rosemary and bay leaf; baste with olive oil and bake in the oven in small earthenware dishes. Deliciously tender and moist.

Best end of neck: May be roasted or braised. Can be divided into cutlets. Usually grilled, fried, braised or stewed.

Neck: Ideal for stews.

Shoulder: Sold on the bone, or stuffed and rolled. When knuckle is removed, the remaining 'oyster' makes a good roasting piece. This cut is excellent for *blanquette de veau*, or for a veal *goulash* or stew. Small pieces of boneless shoulder are used for pies, stews and fricassées.

Breast: The breast is not used often enough. I like this economical cut stuffed, and either roasted, braised or steamed. It is also suitable for stewing, pot-roasting and boiling. I also use it with an equal quantity of shoulder for a *blanquette de veau*.

Calf's kidney: Delicious sautéed with bacon, avocado pear or onions.

Pie Veal: Many butchers sell scraps of veal cut up ready to use for hot and cold veal pies. These are usually small pieces from the shoulder, breast and leg.

How Much Veal to Buy

Escalopes: Allow 4 to 6 oz (100–175 g) meat per person.

Other boneless meat: Allow 6 to 8 oz (175–225 g) meat per person

Meat with average amount of bone: Allow 10 to 12 oz (275–350 g) with bone for roasts and chops.

Meat with large amount of bone: Allow 12 to 14 oz (350–400 g) per person.

How to Refrigerate Veal

Veal does not keep as well as other meats and should be used soon after slaughtering. To keep it at its best: unwrap meat, place it in the special meat compartment in your refrigerator, or on a plate near the bottom of the refrigerator; cover loosely with waxed paper or foil.

Large pieces (leg, loin, shoulder and boned or unboned breast) may be kept up to 3 to 4 days in the refrigerator; chops for 2 to 3 days; cut-up stewing meats, pie pieces, etc., for 1 to 2 days; minced meat, 1 day only.

Roast Veal
ROAST LEG OF VEAL

1 leg of veal (4½–6 lb/1.8–3 kg), boned, and tied
Salt and freshly ground black pepper
Dried thyme
8 oz (225 g) unsmoked bacon, thinly sliced
2 cloves garlic
4 carrots, thinly sliced
1 Spanish onion, thinly sliced
2 bay leaves
4 oz (100 g) butter
½ pint (300 ml) dry white wine
2 tablespoons (30 ml) tomato concentrate
Beurre manié

Ask your butcher to bone the veal; lard it with fat and tie it securely into a neat roast.

Rub meat with salt, freshly ground black pepper and dried thyme. Cover it with thin bacon slices and place meat in a roasting pan. Surround the veal with garlic cloves, sliced carrots and onion, and bay leaves. Melt the butter; combine with wine and tomato concentrate, and pour over meat. Roast in a slow oven (350°F/180°C/GM4) for 2 to 2½ hours, or until veal is cooked through, basting frequently.

Skim fat from surface of pan juices and thicken gravy slightly with a *beurre manié*, made by mashing together 1 tablespoon (15 ml) butter and 1 tablespoon (15 ml) flour.

ROAST LOIN OF VEAL WITH BREADCRUMBS

1 loin of veal (5–6 lb/2.3–3 kg), boned rolled and tied
6 slices unsmoked bacon
2 tablespoons (30 ml) softened butter
1 Spanish onion, finely chopped
2 carrots, finely chopped
2 stalks celery, finely chopped
Salt and freshly ground black pepper
¾ pint (450 ml) well-flavoured stock
1 egg, well beaten
6 tablespoons (90 ml) breadcrumbs
2 tablespoons (30 ml) freshly grated Parmesan

Line roasting pan with slices of bacon and place rolled veal on the bacon. Spread meat with softened butter and surround it with chopped onion, carrots and celery. Season meat generously with salt and freshly ground black pepper, and roast it in a pre-heated hot oven (450°F/230°C/GM8) until well browned on all sides. Add stock; reduce oven heat to 325°F/170°C/GM3 and continue roasting the meat for 2 to 2½ hours, or until it is done, basting frequently.

Remove strings from roast, and brush top and sides with egg; sprinkle with breadcrumbs and Parmesan, and return to the oven for 15 minutes, or until crumbs are golden.

Reduce pan juices over high heat; strain and serve with roast.

VEAL WITH ROSEMARY

1 rump roast of veal, boned, rolled and tied
Salt and freshly ground black pepper
Dried thyme
Flour
2 tablespoons (30 ml) butter
2 tablespoons (30 ml) olive oil
¼ pint (150 ml) dry white wine
¼ pint (150 ml) water
2 cloves garlic, finely chopped
3 sprigs fresh rosemary
2 Spanish onions, quartered
6 carrots, quartered

Season roast generously with salt, freshly ground black pepper and thyme. Dredge with flour. Heat butter and olive oil in a thick-bottomed casserole, and brown meat on all sides.

Add dry white wine, water, finely chopped garlic and rosemary; cover casserole and cook in a slow oven (325°F/170°C/ GM3) for 1½ hours. Add quartered onions and carrots, and continue to cook until meat and vegetables are tender – 30 to 40 minutes more. Remove roast and vegetables to a heated serving dish. Slice meat and serve with pan juices. Serves 6.

ROAST LOIN OF VEAL

1 loin of veal
Salt and freshly ground black pepper
Crushed rosemary
2–3 tablespoons (30–45 ml) softened butter
¼ pint (150 ml) dry white wine

Have butcher bone and trim a loin of veal. Season to taste with salt, freshly ground black pepper and crushed rosemary. Spread with softened butter and roast the meat in a slow oven (325°F/ 170°C/GM3) for about 20 to 30 minutes per pound (450 g), or until it is well done, basting frequently. Add a little hot water if fat tends to scorch during cooking.

Remove veal from oven; add dry white wine and make sauce with the pan juices in the usual manner.

NOIX DE VEAU FARCIE

1 *noix de veau* (topside of leg), trimmed of fat
and tied
Salt and freshly ground black pepper
Crushed rosemary
Softened butter
8 button mushroom caps, sliced
¾ pint (450 ml) Suprême Sauce (page 109)
4 tablespoons (60 ml) freshly grated Parmesan
4 thin slices *pâté de fois gras*, diced
Thin slices of white truffle
Melted butter

Season veal with salt, freshly ground black pepper and crushed rosemary. Spread meat with softened butter and roast it in a moderate oven (375°F/190°C/GM5) for about 18 to 20 minutes per pound, or until it is well done, basting frequently. Add a little hot water if fat tends to scorch during cooking.

Cut a thin slice off the top and then carefully cut out the interior (as you would for a *brioche farcie* or a *vol-au-vent*), leaving a thin shell of meat.

Slice veal taken from *noix* thinly and sauté it in butter with sliced mushrooms; add ½ pint (300 ml) Suprême Sauce flavoured with freshly grated cheese, and fold in diced *pâté de foie gras* and sliced truffle.

Fill the meat shell with this mixture; replace the cover; brush with melted butter and return to the oven for several minutes to glaze. Serve immediately with remaining Suprême Sauce.

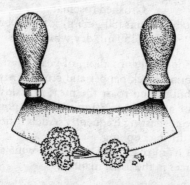

VEAL AVESNOISE

6 slices roast veal
Freshly ground black pepper
4 oz (100 g) Gruyère, finely grated
1–2 teaspoons (5–10 ml) strong mustard
¼ pint (150 ml) double cream

Place 6 fairly thick slices of roast veal in a baking pan. Sprinkle with freshly ground black pepper and spread liberally with a *pommade* made of finely grated Gruyère mixed with mustard to taste, and enough cream to make a smooth mixture of spreading consistency.

When ready to serve: glaze veal slices under a preheated grill for a few minutes until the sauce is golden in colour. Serve immediately. Serves 6.

Medaillons and Escalopes

COSTOLETTE DI VITELLO ALLA VALDOSTANA 'GEORGE'S'

6 large veal cutlets
6 oz (175 g) Fontina cheese, thinly sliced
Canned white truffles, thinly sliced
Salt and freshly ground black pepper
Flour
2 eggs, beaten
Breadcrumbs
Butter
1 tablespoon (15 ml) olive oil
Boiled rice
Freshly grated Parmesan

Slice the cutlets with a sharp knife to make a pocket with both parts still attached to the bone. Stuff this pocket with thin slices of Fontina cheese and white truffle. Season to taste with salt and freshly ground black pepper. Press the pocket shut, beating the edges so that they are properly sealed.

Flour the cutlets; roll them in beaten egg and then in breadcrumbs. Sauté cutlets gently in 3 tablespoons (45 ml) butter and 1 tablespoon (15 ml) olive oil until they are a rich golden brown. Serve with boiled rice dressed with butter and freshly grated Parmesan. Serves 6.

ITALIAN VEAL CUTLETS AU GRATIN

8 thin escalopes of veal
¼ pint (150 ml) double cream
2–4 tablespoons (30–60 ml) freshly grated Parmesan
4 oz (100 g) Mozzarella cheese, diced
4 oz (100 g) cooked ham, diced
2 eggs
Salt and freshly ground black pepper
2 tablespoons (30 ml) butter

Combine cream, grated Parmesan and diced Mozzarella cheese and ham in the top of a double saucepan, and cook over hot water, stirring constantly, until cheese melts.

Beat eggs in a bowl; then whisk in hot cheese mixture and season to taste with salt and freshly ground black pepper.

Melt butter in a thick-bottomed frying pan and brown veal escalopes on both sides. Season with salt and freshly ground black pepper; place 2 escalopes in each of 4 individual *gratin* dishes and spoon cheese mixture over them. Place under a hot grill until sauce is well browned and bubbling. Serves 4.

SALTIMBOCCA ALL'ALFREDO

4 thin slices veal
12 small fresh sage leaves or ½–1 level teaspoon (2.25–5 ml)
dried sage
Freshly ground black pepper
4 thin slices prosciutto (raw Parma ham)
Flour
Melted butter
2 tablespoons (30 ml) Marsala or dry white wine

Flatten veal into thin pieces and cut each slice into 2 or 3 pieces. Place 1 sage leaf (or a pinch of dried sage) on each slice and add freshly ground black pepper to taste (no salt, the *prosciutto* will flavour meat). Cover each slice of veal with *prosciutto* cut to the same size, form each one into a small roll and secure with a wooden toothpick. Dust veal and ham rolls with flour and sauté in melted butter until they are golden on all sides; then add Marsala or white wine. Let it cook for a moment, then cover the pan and simmer gently until the veal and ham rolls are quite tender. Remove toothpicks and transfer to a hot serving dish. Serve immediately. Serves 4.

VEAL PARMESAN 'FOUR SEASONS'

16 thin slices veal
Flour
3 eggs, well beaten
4 oz (100 g) fresh breadcrumbs
8 oz (225 g) freshly grated Parmesan
Grated rind of 5 lemons
Olive oil or butter

Dip thin slices of veal in flour, then in beaten egg, and finally in a mixture of breadcrumbs, cheese and lemon rind. Sauté veal slices on both sides in oil or butter until golden brown. Serve immediately. Serves 8.

VEAL BIRDS

12 thin slices veal cutlet
4 tablespoons (60 ml) butter
1 Spanish onion, finely chopped
4 oz (100 g) mushrooms, finely chopped
¾ pint (450 ml) well-flavoured stock
1 bay leaf
3–4 celery tops
3–4 sprigs parsley
Beurre manié
Salt and freshly ground black pepper

FORCEMEAT STUFFING
4 oz (100 g) fresh breadcrumbs
2 oz (50 g) suet, freshly grated
4 tablespoons (60 ml) finely chopped fresh parsley
½ level teaspoon (2.5 ml) each dried thyme, marjoram and basil
½ level teaspoon (2.5 ml) grated lemon rind
2 eggs
Salt and freshly ground black pepper
Water or dry white wine (optional)

FORCEMEAT STUFFING
Mix breadcrumbs, freshly grated suet, finely chopped fresh parsley, dried herbs, lemon rind and eggs. Season generously with salt and freshly ground black pepper. If mixture seems too dry, add a little water or dry white wine.

Beat thin slices of veal with a rolling pin to flatten and tenderize them. Spread forcemeat mixture on each piece of meat; roll up and secure with very fine string.

Heat 2 tablespoons (30 ml) butter in a thick-bottomed saucepan and sauté finely chopped onion and mushrooms until onion is transparent. Remove vegetables; add remaining butter to pan and cook veal 'birds' over a moderate heat until well browned. Pour in stock; add sautéed mushrooms and onions, bay leaf, celery tops and parsley; cover pan and simmer gently for 30 to 40 minutes, or until meat is tender.

Just before serving: remove strings from veal birds and thicken gravy with a *beurre manié*, made by mashing together 1 tablespoon

(15 ml) butter and 1 tablespoon (15 ml) flour. Correct seasoning and serve immediately. Makes 12 veal birds. Serves 4 to 6.

VEAL MEDAILLONS WITH POMMES DE TERRE MACAIRE

4–6 veal chops
Salt and freshly ground black pepper
Flour
2 tablespoons (30 ml) butter
1 tablespoon (15 ml) olive oil
4–6 tablespoons (60–90 ml) port
Stock (see method)
2 tablespoons (30 ml) sultanas

POMMES DE TERRE MACAIRE
2 lb (900 g) medium-sized potatoes
6 oz (175 g) softened butter
Salt and freshly ground black pepper

Trim bones from veal chops to make veal rounds. Season veal rounds with salt and freshly ground black pepper; dust with flour and sauté in butter and olive oil until tender.

Remove veal and keep warm; pour off excess butter and add port and a little well-flavoured stock (made with veal bones, 1 bay leaf, ½ chicken stock cube and a little water), stirring in all the crusty bits from the sides of the pan.

To serve: unmould potato cakes (*Pommes de terre Macaire*) on to a heated serving dish; top with veal *medaillons*; and mask with port sauce in which you have heated some sultanas, previously soaked overnight in a little port. Serve immediately. Serves 4 to 6.

POMMES DE TERRE MACAIRE
Bake potatoes in the oven; cut them in half and scoop out the pulp. Using a fork, mash this pulp up with the softened butter. Season to taste with salt and freshly ground black pepper.

Spread mixture in well-buttered individual tart tins just the size of the *medaillons*. Bake in the oven to form potato cakes.

MEDAILLONS DE VEAU
ORLOFF 'MAXIM'S'
(VEAL STEAKS WITH WINE SAUCE)

6 slices fillet of veal (about 4 oz/100 g each)
Salt and freshly ground black pepper
1 tablespoon (15 ml) flour
Butter
6 shallots
8 tablespoons (120 ml) dry white wine
8 tablespoons (120 ml) port
8 tablespoons (120 ml) stock

Season the steaks with salt and freshly ground black pepper; dust them lightly with flour, and sear on both sides in a shallow pan containing 4 tablespoons (60 ml) melted butter. Lower the heat and cook slowly for 10 to 12 minutes. Remove from pan and keep hot.

Chop the shallots and soften them in the pan juices; add the white wine and port. Reduce by half over a high heat and add the stock. When hot but not boiling, remove from the heat and stir in 2 to 4 tablespoons (30–60 ml) butter in small pieces. Pour sauce over the steaks. Serve immediately. Serves 6.

Veal Chops

CÔTES DE VEAU À MA FAÇON

4 thick veal chops
Salt and freshly ground black pepper
Flour
Butter
1 tablespoon (15 ml) olive oil
3 oz (75 g) fresh breadcrumbs
4 oz (100 g) freshly grated Gruyère
¼ pint (150 ml) slightly thickened veal stock

Season chops generously with salt and freshly ground black pepper. Dust with flour on both sides. Heat 3 tablespoons (45 ml) butter and the oil in a heatproof *gratin* dish just large enough to hold chops, and brown them on both sides. When browned, coat chops with a thick *pommade* made of breadcrumbs, Gruyère and 4 oz (100 g) softened butter, worked to a thick paste. Add veal stock to *gratin* dish and place in a moderate oven (375°F/190°C/GM5) for 10 to 15 minutes, or until *pommade* is golden and bubbling, glazing chops with veal stock from time to time. Serves 4.

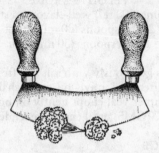

CÔTES DE VEAU GRAND'MÈRE 'PETITE AUBERGE'

4 thick veal chops
Salt and freshly ground black pepper
2 tablespoons (30 ml) butter
2 tablespoons (30 ml) olive oil
16 button onions
4 oz (100 g) diced bacon
8 button mushrooms, cut in quarters
4 tablespoons (60 ml) well-flavoured beef stock or
glace de viande
2 tablespoons (30 ml) finely chopped parsley

Season veal chops to taste with salt and freshly ground black pepper, and sauté in butter and olive oil until golden on both sides. Cover pan and simmer chops gently for about 10 minutes. Place button onions and diced bacon in cold water, and bring to a boil. Drain, and add to chops with quartered mushrooms. Simmer gently, uncovered, for about 5 minutes. Add well-flavoured beef stock or *glace de viande*. Sprinkle with finely chopped parsley and serve immediately. Serves 4.

VEAL CHOPS EN CASSEROLE

4–6 thick veal chops
Salt and freshly ground black pepper
2 tablespoons (30 ml) butter
2 tablespoons (30 ml) olive oil

VELOUTÉ SAUCE
½ pint (300 ml) well-flavoured stock
2 tablespoons (30 ml) butter
2 tablespoons (30 ml) flour

Season veal chops generously with salt and freshly ground black pepper. Heat butter and olive oil in a shallow earthenware casserole, and simmer veal chops gently on both sides in a slow oven (325°F/170°C/GM5) until chops are tender.

VELOUTÉ SAUCE
Melt butter in the top of a double saucepan; stir in flour and cook over water, stirring constantly, until smooth. Stir in hot stock and cook, stirring from time to time, until sauce is smooth and thickened.

Five minutes before serving, pour sauce over chops; correct seasoning and serve in casserole. Serves 4 to 6.

VEAL CHOPS AUX FINES HERBES

4–6 veal chops
Salt and freshly ground black pepper
Butter
2 tablespoons (30 ml) olive oil
6 tablespoons (90 ml) dry white wine
1 tablespoon (15 ml) finely chopped shallots
¼ pint (150 ml) well-flavoured veal or chicken stock
1 tablespoon (15 ml) flour
2 tablespoons (30 ml) mixed *fine herbes* (parsley, chervil and tarragon,), finely chopped

Season veal chops generously with salt and freshly ground black pepper. Sauté gently on both sides in 2 tablespoons (30 ml) each butter and olive oil until almost tender. Add dry white wine and finely chopped shallots, and continue cooking until done.

Transfer to a heated serving dish and keep warm. Reduce dry white wine and pan juices over a high heat to half the original quantity. Add to a sauce made with well-flavoured stock thickened with 1 tablespoon (15 ml) each butter and flour. Stir in finely chopped *fines herbes* and pour over chops. Serve immediately. Serves 4 to 6.

Casseroles, Braised Veal and Stews

VEAU À LA MENAGÈRE

2½ lb (1.1 kg) veal, in 1 piece
4 tablespoons (60 ml) butter
2 tablespoons (30 ml) flour
Hot water or light stock
1 bay leaf
Thyme
Salt and freshly ground black pepper
12 mushroom caps
1 small packet frozen peas
12 button onions, blanched
12 small carrots, blanched

Melt butter in the bottom of a heatproof casserole. Stir in flour and allow to colour, stirring continuously. Place veal in this and brown on all sides. Then add hot water or light stock and stir constantly until liquid comes to a boil. Add bay leaf, and thyme, salt and freshly ground black pepper, to taste, and simmer gently, covered, for 1 hour. Then add mushroom caps, peas, and button onions and small carrots which you have blanched in water. Continue to cook until meat and vegetables are tender. Serves 4 to 6.

BRAISED SHOULDER OF VEAL

1 shoulder of veal
Salt and freshly ground black pepper
2–3 tablespoons (30–45 ml) butter
2–3 tablespoons (30–45 ml) olive oil
4 oz (100 g) onions
4 carrots
2 stalks celery
3 cloves garlic
2–3 tablespoons (30–45 ml) flour
2 bay leaves
¾ pint (450 ml) water
¾ pint (450 ml) dry white wine
Watercress

Season veal generously with salt and freshly ground black pepper. Heat butter and olive oil in a large heatproof casserole, and brown veal on all sides in fat to seal in juices. Remove veal.

Chop onions, carrots, celery and garlic, and brown them in the pan, stirring constantly. Sprinkle with flour and stir until flour is absorbed by the *mirepoix* of vegetables. Return veal to the pan and add bay leaves, water and dry white wine. Cover the casserole and cook in a preheated slow oven (325°F/170°C/GM3) for 1½ hours. Turn the meat at least once during cooking time.

When veal is tender, strain pan juices into a clean saucepan and reduce the sauce over high heat to half the original quantity. Season the sauce to taste, adding a little more white wine (or cognac) if desired. The flavour of the sauce should be quite pronounced to enhance the rather mild taste of the veal.

Carve half the braised veal into rather thick slices. Arrange slices on a heated serving platter with remaining unsliced veal; spoon some of the sauce over the meat and garnish serving dish with sprigs of fresh watercress. Serve remaining sauce separately.

NOIX DE VEAU À LA BOURGEOISE

1 *noix de veau* (topside of leg) trimmed of fat and tied
Bacon, cut in thin strips
2 tablespoons (30 ml) cognac
2 tablespoons (30 ml) finely chopped parsley
Dried thyme
Salt and freshly ground black pepper
Pork fat
3–4 onions
3–4 large carrots
6–8 sprigs parsley
1 bouquet chives
½ pint (300 ml) beef, veal or chicken stock

SAUCE
1 tablespoon (15 ml) butter
1 tablespoon (15 ml) flour
4–6 tablespoons (60–90 ml) dry white wine
½ pint (300 ml) stock
4 tablespoons (60 ml) butter, diced

Marinate thin strips of bacon in cognac with finely chopped parsley, and dried thyme, salt and freshly ground black pepper, to taste, for at least 2 hours. Lard the veal with these pieces. Place several thin pieces of pork fat in a casserole (I use an oval Le Creuset casserole for this); place veal on top; surround with onions, carrots, parsley and chives, and moisten with well-flavoured stock.

Cook over a medium heat until liquid begins to boil; reduce heat; cover casserole and simmer for 1½ to 2 hours, or until veal is tender. Remove veal to a heated serving dish and keep warm. Reduce pan juices over high heat to a quarter of original quantity and glaze veal with several tablespoons of this sauce. Keep warm.

SAUCE
Melt butter in the top of a double saucepan; add flour and stir until smooth. Add dry white wine, the remaining pan juices and stock, and cook over water, stirring constantly, until smooth. Reduce sauce over a high heat, stirring from time to time. Whisk in diced butter. Serve with roast.

VEAL FRICASSÉE

3 lb (1.4 kg) rump or shoulder of veal
Lemon juice
Butter
2 Spanish onions, chopped
4 large carrots, sliced
2 tablespoons (30 ml) flour
¾ pint (450 ml) dry white wine
Well-flavoured veal or chicken stock
Salt and freshly ground black pepper
Bouquet garni
4 leeks, cut in thin strips
12 button mushroom caps
4 egg yolks
⅔ pint (400 ml) double cream
1 tablespoon (15 ml) each finely chopped tarragon,
chervil and parsley
Freshly grated nutmeg

Cut veal into 1½-inch (38 mm) cubes and soak for 12 hours in cold water with a little lemon juice. Change water 2 or 3 times.

Sauté blanched veal pieces in butter in a deep heatproof casserole until golden. Add onion and carrots, and continue to simmer, stirring from time to time, until onion is transparent. Sprinkle with flour and sauté a few minutes more. Add dry white wine and just enough well-flavoured stock to cover meat. Season with salt and freshly ground black pepper, and bring to a boil. Remove any scum that forms on the surface with a perforated spoon as you would for a *pot-au-feu*. Add *bouquet garni*; reduce heat; cover casserole and simmer gently over a very low heat or in a very slow oven (300°F/150°C/GM2) for 1½ hours, or until tender.

Cook strips of leek in a little salted water until tender. Drain and keep warm in a little butter. Simmer mushroom caps in a little butter and lemon juice, and keep warm.

Whisk egg yolks with double cream; pour a little of the hot stock into the cream and egg mixture, whisking to prevent eggs from curdling; then add mixture to hot stock in casserole and heat through, being careful not to let mixture come to a boil.

Stir mushroom caps, leeks and finely chopped herbs carefully into the fricassée; season with a little grated nutmeg and keep warm in oven until ready to serve. Serves 6.

VEAL IN SOUR CREAM

3 lb (1.4 kg) lean veal, cut from shoulder or leg
Salt and freshly ground black pepper
4 tablespoons (60 ml) butter
2 tablespoons (30 ml) olive oil
1 tablespoon (15 ml) flour
½ pint (300 ml) sour cream
¼ level teaspoon (1.25 ml) paprika
2 tablespoons (30 ml) finely chopped onion
8 oz (225 g) button mushrooms, quartered
Boiled rice

Cut veal into 1½-inch (38 mm) cubes. Season generously with salt and freshly ground black pepper, rubbing seasoning well into meat. Heat 2 tablespoons (30 ml) each butter and oil in a thick-bottomed frying pan, and sauté meat, 4 to 6 pieces at a time, until lightly browned on all sides. Place meat in a heatproof casserole; add flour to fat remaining in pan and cook, stirring constantly, until smooth. Then add sour cream and cook, stirring, until well blended. Season to taste with salt, freshly ground black pepper and paprika.

Melt remaining butter in a separate saucepan and simmer chopped onion until golden. Add quartered mushrooms and simmer over a low heat for 5 minutes. Combine mushroom-onion mixture with sour cream sauce; add a little hot water if necessary, and pour over veal; cover casserole and bake in a slow oven (325°F/170°C/GM3) for 1 hour, or until meat is tender. Serve with boiled rice. Serves 4 to 6.

POT-ROASTED VEAL WITH ANCHOVIES

1 leg of veal (about 6 lb/3 kg)
1 can anchovy fillets, cut in thin strips
2 cloves garlic, cut in thin strips
Softened butter
Salt and freshly ground black pepper
4–6 cloves
2 Spanish onions, sliced
2 bay leaves
¼ pint (150 ml) dry white wine
¼ pint (150 ml) water
4 tablespoons (60 ml) fine breadcrumbs
Beurre manié

Trim and wipe leg of veal. Make small incisions all over the surface with tip of a sharp knife; stuff incisions with thin anchovy and garlic strips. Rub with 2 tablespoons (30 ml) softened butter; sprinkle with salt and freshly ground black pepper, and insert cloves.

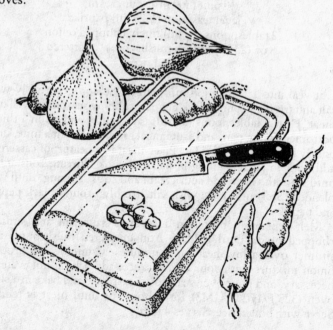

Place roast in an ovenproof casserole, and surround with sliced onions, bay leaves, dry white wine, water and 2 tablespoons (30 ml) butter.

Cover casserole and roast in a preheated slow oven (325°F/170°C/GM3) for about 3½ hours, basting with pan juices from time to time. Turn roast over; dust with breadcrumbs; dot with 2 tablespoons (30 ml) butter and roast 15 minutes longer, or until crumbs are browned.

Transfer veal to a heated serving dish; keep warm. Stir *beurre manié*, made by mashing 1 tablespoon (15 ml) each flour and butter, into pan juices, and cook, stirring constantly, until sauce is thick. Strain gravy around roast and serve immediately. Serves 12.

OSSO BUCO

4–6 thick slices shin of veal
Flour
Salt and freshly ground black pepper
4 tablespoons (60 ml) olive oil
3 cloves garlic, finely chopped
½ Spanish onion, finely chopped
¼ pint (150 ml) boiling chicken or veal stock
¼ pint (150 ml) dry white wine
4 tablespoons (60 ml) tomato concentrate
4 anchovy fillets, finely chopped
4 tablespoons (60 ml) finely chopped parsley
Grated rind of ½ lemon
Saffron rice

Choose shin of veal with plenty of meat and have it sawn into pieces 2 inches (5 cms) thick. Dredge pieces with flour, season generously with salt and freshly ground black pepper, and simmer in olive oil until lightly browned on all sides. Add 1 clove garlic and ½ Spanish onion, finely chopped; pour boiling stock, white wine and tomato concentrate over meat; cover the pan and simmer for 1½ hours. Then add anchovy fillets and the remaining garlic cloves, both finely chopped. Blend thoroughly, heat through, and serve sprinkled with finely chopped parsley and grated lemon rind. In Italy, saffron rice is always served with this richly coloured, highly flavoured dish. Serves 4 to 6.

TENDRONS DE VEAU EN TERRINE

2½ lb (1.1 kg) breast of veal, cut into cutlets
Lemon juice
4 tablespoons (60 ml) butter
2 tablespoons (30 ml) flour
¾ pint (450 ml) well-flavoured Velouté Sauce
(page 108)
Bouquet garni
4–6 peppercorns
8 button onions, blanched
4 sweetbreads, blanched and sliced
8 button mushrooms caps
2 egg yolks
2 tablespoons (30 ml) finely chopped parsley

Soak veal 'cutlets' overnight in water and the juice of 1 lemon. Drain and sauté in butter until they begin to stiffen. Sprinkle with flour and continue to cook, stirring constantly, until veal begins to take on a little colour. Moisten with Velouté Sauce; add *bouquet garni*, peppercorns and blanched button onions, and simmer, covered, for 1 hour. Then add sliced blanched sweetbreads and button mushroom caps, and continue to cook for 45 to 60 minutes longer. Strain, reserving sauce, and place veal, sweetbreads and vegetables in a clean *terrine*.

Mix egg yolks with juice of ½ lemon; add a little of the hot sauce to this mixture; pour egg mixture into rest of hot sauce and cook, stirring constantly, until thick and smooth. Do not allow the sauce to boil, or yolks will curdle. Pour sauce over veal and sweetbreads; sprinkle with finely chopped parsley and serve. Serves 4.

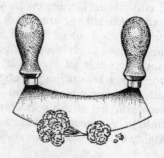

Liver, Sweetbreads, etc.

CALF'S LIVER WITH AVOCADO 'FOUR SEASONS'

12 thin slices calf's liver
12 thin slices avocado pear (2–3 avocados)
Juice of 3 lemons
Flour
Salt and freshly ground black pepper
8 oz (225 g) butter
8 tablespoons (120 ml) beef or veal stock
½ teaspoon (2.5 ml) thyme

Peel avocados and remove stones; slice thinly. Brush each slice with a little lemon juice to preserve colour. Slice calf's liver thinly. Dip sliced avocado and calf's liver in flour well seasoned with salt and freshly ground black pepper. Sauté very quickly in a little butter. Arrange on platter. Brown remaining butter in saucepan; add remaining lemon juice, beef or veal stock, and thyme. Pour over liver. Serves 6.

SWISS LIVER BROCHETTES

4 slices calf's liver, cut in rectangles
10 sage leaves
4–6 tablespoons (60–90 ml) butter
2–4 tablespoons (30–60 ml) olive oil
½ Spanish onion, finely chopped
4–6 baking potatoes
Salt and freshly ground black pepper

Cut each slice of liver into 5 rectangles; place each rectangle alternately with a sage leaf on metal skewers, 5 liver pieces to each skewer; heat a little butter and olive oil in a thick-bottomed frying pan, and sauté finely chopped onion until transparent. Add liver *brochettes* and sauté, covered, until brown and tender.

Peel potatoes and grate coarsely. Heat remaining butter and oil in frying pan. (I like to use an oval pan for this recipe as the *brochettes* look so attractive on an oval potato cake.) Add potatoes; season generously with salt and freshly ground black pepper, and simmer gently, covered, shaking pan from time to time to prevent sticking, until potato cake is crisp and brown on the bottom. Invert potato cake on to a plate and then slide cake into frying pan to brown other side.

To serve: arrange the *brochettes* on the potato cake. Serves 4.

LE FOIE CHAUD AUX POMMES

1½ lb (675 g) fresh calf's liver, sliced
2 lb (900 g) tart eating apples, cored,
peeled and quartered
1 glass white Alsatian wine
Dried currants, soaked in wine
¼ teaspoon (1.25 ml) cinnamon
Salt and freshly ground black pepper
Pinch of ground cloves
Pinch of powdered thyme
1 tablespoon (15 ml) flour
4 tablespoons (60 ml) butter
Finely chopped parsley

Simmer peeled and quartered apples with white Alsatian wine until tender. Add the currants, which you have soaked in wine, and the cinnamon; keep warm.

Season sliced liver with salt, freshly ground black pepper, ground cloves and powdered thyme. Sprinkle with flour, and brown in butter for 3 minutes.

Arrange the *compôte* of warm apples on a heated serving dish; place sautéed liver slices over this. Garnish with finely chopped parsley. Serves 4.

ROGNONS AU PORTO 'LA PAILLOTE'

4 calf's kidneys
2 tablespoons (30 ml) butter
½ Spanish onion, finely chopped
2–4 tablespoons (30–60 ml) parsley, finely chopped
Salt and freshly ground black pepper
4–6 button mushrooms, thinly sliced
1 teaspoon (5 ml) flour
2–4 tablespoons (30–60 ml) port
Baked pastry shell or cooked rice

Free kidneys of fibres and fat; slice thinly. Melt butter in a frying pan; when butter is sizzling, add sliced kidneys. Then add finely chopped onion and parsley, and sauté, stirring constantly, for a few minutes. Season to taste with salt and freshly ground black pepper. Add sliced mushrooms and continue cooking, stirring continuously. Add flour; stir in port; and cook until well blended. Serve in a baked pastry shell or ring of cooked rice. Serves 4.

SWEETBREADS À LA ROYALE

1 pair sweetbreads
Salt
Juice of ½ lemon
1 Spanish onion, coarsely chopped
2 carrots, coarsely chopped
Butter
1 tablespoon (15 ml) flour
Freshly ground black pepper
4 tablespoons (60 ml) heated cognac
8 tablespoons (120 ml) dry white wine
6 fluid oz (120 ml) well-flavoured veal stock
1 tablespoon (15 ml) double cream
8 tablespoons (120 ml) port
4 mushroom caps, sautéed in butter

Soak sweetbreads in cold water for 1 hour, changing water when it becomes tinged with pink. Blanch them for 15 minutes in simmering salted water to which you have added lemon juice. Drain and cool; then trim and cut into slices 2 inches (5 cms) thick.

Sauté chopped onion and carrots in a little butter until golden. Remove and keep warm. Flour sweetbreads lightly, add to pan with a little more butter, and sauté until golden. Spoon vegetables over sweetbreads; season to taste with salt and freshly ground black pepper; cover with buttered paper and place in a moderate oven (375°F/190°C/GM5) for 10 minutes. Remove paper; flame with cognac and remove sweetbreads to a heated serving dish. Keep warm.

Add dry white wine to the pan and cook over a high heat, stirring continuously and scraping all crusty bits from sides of pan, until sauce is reduced to half the original quantity. Add veal stock and simmer gently for 5 minutes; strain; then add cream and port. Correct seasoning and pour sauce over sweetbreads. Top with sautéed mushroom caps. Serves 4.

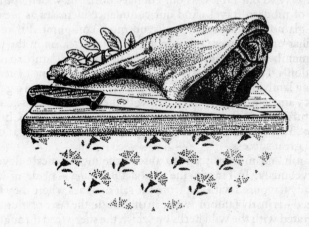

CHAPTER ELEVEN

All About Lamb and Mutton

Don't little lambs grow up any more? Mutton gets harder and harder to find, while butchers' shops and supermarkets all over Britain are full to bursting point with leg, shoulder, loin and chops of tender lamb, from this country and New Zealand. And yet Irish stew, Scots hotchpotch, and boiled mutton with caper sauce, rightfully take their places with grilled mutton chops – seared black on the outside, moistly tender within – among the finest dishes in the world. I like a boned leg of mutton, too – filled with a savoury stuffing, wrapped in suet pastry and simmered to full-flavoured perfection in a stock enriched with vegetables.

We look on lamb today with much more imagination than we did even a few years ago. Exotic recipes from the Middle East, North Africa, the Caribbean Islands and the Orient are making their way to our tables, as our culinary horizons widen with the ease of modern travel. And our confidence increases as we find that glamorous dishes are really no more complicated than the familiar ones we were often tempted to fall back on in the past. I remember enjoying highly spiced Indonesian lamb roast at London's Trader Vic's. This recipe marinates a joint of tender young lamb in a Javanese *saté* sauce (finely chopped onions, garlic, honey and lemon juice, flavoured with the Trader's own *saté* spice mixture) and grills it over an applewood fire in a special Chinese oven. This delicious dish can be cooked in an electric or gas oven with great success.

Lamb and mutton seem to absorb the most delicate flavours marvellously. In France, the *gigot des prés salés* – made of lamb already flavoured with salt from the salt marshes where they have grazed – is justly famous, while in the South, the taste of mutton is saturated with the wild herbs on which the sheep feed throughout their lifetime.

Spices also seem to go extremely well with lamb. Try Moroccan steamed lamb, which combines the flavours of powdered saffron and cumin to give a delicious new slant to a time-honoured recipe; season a leg of lamb in the Provençal manner with a savoury coating of finely chopped garlic, parsley and fresh breadcrumbs, mashed to a paste with softened butter and lemon juice. And for a more subtly seasoned lamb stew, serve easy-to-make *blanquette d'agneau* – tender chunks of lamb simmered in stock flavoured with vegetables, the sauce enriched just before serving with egg yolks, lemon juice and cream. These recipes are in my cookery book *Great Dishes of the World*; you will find many more on the following pages.

Some Different Cuts of Lamb and Mutton

Leg: Lean, with a small amount of bone, the leg is one of the most economical cuts for roasting, braising or poaching. When a joint is too large for a small family, ask your butcher to cut it into two pieces; one to roast or poach, the other to braise or stew; or take just one half of a leg. When the chump end of the loin is cut along with the leg it is called the haunch.

Loin: It is generally divided into two parts, the middle loin and the chump end, or cut into cutlets or chops. The loin makes one of the finest and most delicate roasts, but there is a large proportion of fat and bone. If ordering for a roast, it must be well jointed by your butcher, or it will be difficult to carve. Sometimes the chine bone, which runs down the centre of the back, is sawn off almost completely and removed altogether after cooking. The double loin, from both sides of the animal, is called the saddle, a wonderful joint for large dinner parties.

Best end of neck: An excellent piece for grilling and braising, it is tender and delicate in flavour. It is also used for cutlets.

Middle neck or scrag end lies nearer the head, and is a cheaper piece, containing a good deal of bone. It is very good for broth, or for stews, casseroles, hotpots and curries.

Shoulders: This is another good joint for roasting, preferred by some to the leg, as it is usually more delicate in flavour. Large shoulders are often cut into 2 or 3 strips. I like to braise, poach or steam the shoulder, or use it, cut in strips or cubes, for stews, pies and hotpots.

Breast: This is an inexpensive piece of lamb, rather inclined to be fatty. When boned, stuffed and rolled, it makes an excellent roast that is unbeatable for tenderness and flavour. Use the breast cut into an Irish stew, where the potatoes can absorb some of the fat.

Head makes an excellent broth. It can also be served as a dish by itself with a *sauce piquante*, or used for cold pies.

Pluck (sheep's heart, liver and lungs – sold together in Scotland) are the basics of haggis. The heart is sometimes sold by itself, and is good stuffed and roasted. The liver can also be bought separately, and is generally sautéed, or simmered in stock with bacon and fresh herbs.

Lamb's tongue and sweetbreads are usually sold separately; very delicate in flavour.

Kidneys are generally grilled or stewed, and used with beef in pies and stews. The loin roast often contains one of the kidneys.

Baby Lamb

When very young, lamb is cut in quarters. The forequarter consists of the best end of neck, neck, shoulder and breast, and the hindquarter is made up of the leg and the loin.

If the hindquarter proves to be too large a joint, the upper part may be cut into chops and served as one dish, while the lower portion makes a delicious small roast. I also like it steamed and served with a sauce. The forequarter may be divided in the same way, the breast piece being stewed or braised, and the shoulder roasted. The chops from the neck may be cut off separately, and either grilled, sautéed, breadcrumbed and deep-fried, or used for Scots hotchpotch.

Lamb's head: Prepare it in the same way as sheep's head. It is more delicate in flavour.

How to Cook Lamb and Mutton

Lamb should never be overcooked. It is at its succulent best – moist and richly flavoured – when it is a little pink on the inside. So do not roast it until it is a dull greyish-brown in colour, with the meat falling off the bones, the flesh dry and tough. Instead, treat lamb gently in the French fashion, roasting it until the juices run pink.

For maximum juiciness and minimum shrinkage, I like to cook it for 20 to 25 minutes per pound (450 g) at a relatively low temperature (300°–325°F/150°–170°C/GM2–3) for roasting, and a bare simmer for cooking in liquid. Mutton should be cooked at the same temperature for 40 minutes per pound (450 g). Serve lamb or mutton either really hot or really cold. Nothing is less appetizing than lukewarm lamb.

In selecting cuts of lamb, look for a high proportion of meat to the bone, creamy-white fat, and firm, fine-textured lean that is pinkish in colour. Mutton should be well hung to be tender. Its meat is a lighter red than beef, with a brownish tinge. Its fat is white and hard. A smooth covering of fat ensures succulence.

How Much Lamb or Mutton to Buy

Boneless meat: Allow 4 to 6 oz (100 g–175 g) per person for boned roasts, stewing meats, minced lamb, liver, etc.

Meat with average amount of bone: Allow 6 to 8 oz (175–225 g) per person for roasts and steaks.

Lamb chops: Baby lamb chops: 2 to 3 per person; lamb chops: 1 to 2 per person according to size; mutton chops: 1 per person.

Meat with large amount of bone: Allow 8 to 12 oz (225–350 g) per person.

How to Refrigerate Lamb or Mutton

Newly purchased lamb or mutton should be wrapped loosely in waxed paper or foil and stored as soon as possible in the coldest part of the refrigerator.

Lamb and mutton chops and lamb steaks (cut from the leg) will keep for 2 to 3 days; roasts and large joints, even longer. Diced or minced meat and offal should be used a day or two after being bought.

Roast Lamb

ROAST LEG OF LAMB

1 leg of lamb (about 6 lb (3 kg))
2 cloves garlic, slivered
1 teaspoon (5 ml) rosemary
Juice of 1 lemon
4 tablespoons (60 ml) softened butter
Salt and freshly ground black pepper

Cut small slits in the lamb and insert slivers of garlic. Combine rosemary with lemon juice, softened butter, and salt and freshly ground black pepper, to taste. Spread leg of lamb with this mixture and place on a rack in an open roasting pan. Roast meat, uncovered, in a preheated very slow oven (300°F/150°C/GM2) for 20 to 25 minutes per pound (450 g).

Transfer lamb to a heated serving dish and let stand for 20 minutes before carving. Serves 6 to 8.

CROWN ROAST OF LAMB

1 crown roast of lamb (made from rib sections of
two loins of lamb)
2 cloves garlic, slivered
1 teaspoon (5 ml) rosemary
Juice of 1 lemon
Salt and freshly ground black pepper
Creamed button onions or puréed peas
Finely chopped mint

Cut small slits in the lamb and insert slivers of garlic. Rub meat with rosemary and lemon juice, and sprinkle generously with salt and freshly ground black pepper.

Preheat oven to very slow (300°F/150°C/GM2). Cover tips of the crown's bones with foil to prevent them from burning as the roast cooks. Place the meat on a rack in an open roasting pan.

Cook crown of lamb until tender – it should be rare when served. Remove from oven; remove foil and replace with paper frills. Fill the centre of the crown with creamed button onions or puréed peas; sprinkle with finely chopped mint and serve immediately. Serves 6.

ROAST SADDLE OF LAMB

1 saddle of lamb
Softened butter
Salt and freshly ground black pepper
Crushed rosemary
¼ pint (150 ml) boiling water
¾ pint (450 ml) beef stock
Beurre manié
Puréed potatoes and peas

Spread saddle of lamb with softened butter and sprinkle with salt, freshly ground black pepper and crushed rosemary, to taste.

Place saddle in a moderately hot oven (400°F/200°C/GM6); pour water into roasting pan and roast lamb for 1 to 1½ hours, basting frequently.

Remove roast from oven and transfer to a heated serving dish. Discard fat from pan; add well-flavoured beef stock and a *beurre manié* (1 tablespoon (15 ml) butter kneaded to a smooth paste with 1 tablespoon (15 ml) flour); and cook over a high heat, stirring all crusty bits from sides of pan into sauce, until sauce is smooth and thick. Strain into sauceboat. Serve roast with puréed potatoes and peas.

SALLE D'AGNEAU AU ROMARIN

1 saddle of lamb
Salt and freshly ground black pepper
12 sprigs fresh rosemary
Olive oil

SAUCE
4 sprigs fresh rosemary
¼ pint (150 ml) water
¼ pint (150 ml) well-flavoured gravy
4 oz (100 g) softened butter, diced
2 tablespoons (30 ml) cognac
Salt and freshly ground black pepper

Season saddle of lamb with salt and freshly ground black pepper. Tie 12 sprigs of fresh rosemary to it and sprinkle lightly with olive oil. Roast lamb in usual way and serve with sauce.

SAUCE
Bring 4 sprigs fresh rosemary to a boil in ¼ pint (150 ml) water. Reduce water to about 4 tablespoons (60 ml) over a high heat.

Heat gravy in the top of a double saucepan; add 2 tablespoons (30 ml) reduced rosemary water to this and then, over hot but not boiling water, beat in diced softened butter until sauce is thick and smooth. Add cognac, and season to taste with salt and freshly ground black pepper.

ROAST STUFFED SHOULDER OF LAMB

1 shoulder of lamb
Olive oil
Salt and freshly ground black pepper
Lemon juice
Flour
2 tablespoons (30 ml) butter
2 tablespoons (30 ml) olive oil

STUFFING
8 oz (225 g) sausage meat
½ Spanish onion, finely chopped and sautéed in
2 tablespoons (30 ml) butter
1 tablespoon (15 ml) finely chopped parsley
1 egg, beaten
8 oz (225 g) spinach, chopped and sautéed in butter
Salt, freshly ground black pepper and spices

Have your butcher bone and trim a shoulder of lamb ready for rolling. Do not have him roll it.

Brush lamb with olive oil and sprinkle with salt and freshly ground black pepper, to taste. Sprinkle with lemon juice.

STUFFING
Combine the following ingredients in a large mixing bowl: sausage meat, finely chopped onion which you have sautéed in butter until transparent, finely chopped parsley, beaten egg, sautéed spinach, and salt, freshly ground black pepper and spices, to taste. Mix well. Lay this stuffing on meat; roll up and sew up with fine string.

Dust the lamb roll with flour; place it in a roasting pan with 2 tablespoons (30 ml) each butter and olive oil, and roast it in a slow oven (325°F/170°C/GM3) for about 1½ to 2 hours, basting frequently with fat.

ROAST SHOULDER OF LAMB WITH HERBS

1 shoulder of lamb
Olive oil
Salt and freshly ground black pepper
6 bay leaves
6 sprigs each thyme and rosemary

Have your butcher bone and trim a shoulder of lamb ready for rolling. Do not have him roll it.

Lay lamb out flat; brush with olive oil and sprinkle with salt and freshly ground black pepper, to taste. Place 2 bay leaves and 2 sprigs each thyme and rosemary on lamb; roll up neatly and tie securely. Place 4 bay leaves and 4 sprigs each thyme and rosemary around lamb and tie securely. Brush with olive oil and roast in a hot oven (450°F/230°C/GM8) for 20 minutes; lower heat to moderate (375°F/190°C/GM5) and cook until tender.

LEG OF LAMB IN PASTRY 'L'OUSTAU DE LA BAUMANIÈRE'

1 small leg of lamb (3–4 lb/1.4–1.8 kg)
2 lamb kidneys, diced
Butter
2½ oz (65 g) sliced mushrooms
1–2 truffles, diced (optional)
Thyme and rosemary
Salt and freshly ground black pepper
1–2 tablespoons (15–30 ml) Armagnac or good brandy
Flaky pastry (page 759)
1 egg yolk, slightly beaten

Have butcher bone lamb. Sauté kidneys in 2 tablespoons (30 ml) butter in a thick-bottomed frying pan for 1 minute. Add sliced mushrooms and diced truffles, and season to taste with thyme, rosemary, salt and freshly ground black pepper. Simmer, stirring constantly, for 1 or 2 minutes more. Sprinkle with Armagnac, or a good brandy.

Stuff leg of lamb with this mixture; reshape leg of lamb and stitch or tie opening with heavy thread. Sprinkle lamb with salt and freshly ground black pepper, and roast in a moderate oven (375°F/190°C/GM5) for 20 to 25 minutes, or until half cooked. Cool; rub with 2 tablespoons (30 ml) softened butter; wrap in thinly rolled flaky pastry. Brush with cold water and bake in a hot oven (450°F/230°C/GM8) for 15 to 20 minutes more. Brush with slightly beaten egg yolk and continue baking until the crust is browned. Serves 6 to 8.

TRADER VIC'S INDONESIAN LAMB ROAST

1 best end of lamb (about 8 ribs)

JAVANESE SATÉ SAUCE
1 large Spanish onion, finely chopped
½ level tablespoon (7.5 ml) salt
½ level tablespoon (7.5 ml) garlic salt
Pinch of monosodium glutamate
1 level tablespoon (15 ml) Trader Vic's Saté Spice (or ½ level tablespoon (7.5 ml) curry powder and ½ level teaspoon (2.5 ml) each powdered turmeric, coriander and chili powder)
Juice of 1 lemon
1–2 tablespoons (15–30 ml) honey
Freshly ground black pepper

Cut best end of lamb into 4 portions. Trim all the fat to the rib bones. Wrap the bone ends with foil to prevent burning. Marinate in Javanese Saté Sauce for at least 12 hours. To make sauce, combine all ingredients in a large porcelain bowl.

When ready to serve: barbecue lamb in a moderate oven (375°F/190°C/GM5) for 18 to 20 minutes, or until tender. Remove foil, and serve. Serves 4.

RACK OF LAMB WITH HAREM PILAFF
'RAINBOW ROOM'

2 racks of baby lamb, trimmed
Salt and freshly ground black pepper
2–3 teaspoons (10–15 ml) English mustard
3 tablespoons (45 ml) dry white wine
6 tablespoons (90 ml) fresh breadcrumbs
3 tablespoons (45 ml) finely chopped parsley
½ teaspoon (2.5 ml) finely chopped garlic

HAREM PILAFF
2 tablespoons (30 ml) finely chopped onion
4 oz (100 g) fresh butter
8 oz (225 g) rice
4 tablespoons (60 ml) white wine
1¼ pints (750 ml) beef stock
Salt
4 oz (100 g) button mushrooms, sliced
4 oz (100 g) diced avocado pear
½ level teaspoon (2.5 ml) finely chopped garlic
4 oz (100 g) tomatoes, peeled, seeded and diced
¼ level teaspoon (1.25 ml) oregano
Salt and freshly ground black pepper
3 oz (75 g) raw chicken livers, diced

Season trimmed racks of lamb generously with salt and freshly ground black pepper and roast in a moderately hot oven (400°F/ 200°C/GM6) for 20 minutes. Form a paste with English mustard and dry white wine. Brush racks of lamb with paste, then pat on mixture of breadcrumbs and finely chopped parsley and garlic. Return meat to oven and roast for 8 to 10 minutes. Serve with Harem Pilaff. Serves 4 to 6.

HAREM PILAFF
Sauté finely chopped onion in half the butter for 1 minute; add rice and stir for another minute. Pour white wine and beef stock over rice; season with salt. Bring to a boil; cover casserole and let simmer in oven for 18 minutes. Stir once only with a fork.

In the meantime, sauté mushrooms in 2 tablespoons (30 ml) butter for 3 minutes; add diced avocado and finely chopped garlic.

Sauté for 1 minute; add diced tomatoes and oregano, and season to taste with salt and freshly ground black pepper. Let simmer for 5 minutes.

In another pan, sauté chicken livers in remaining butter and add to the finished rice, stirring with a fork. Form rice into a ring, and fill opening with avocado and mushroom mixture.

Lamb Chops, Steaks and Cutlets

LAMB STEAKS WITH BÉARNAISE SAUCE

3 tender lamb steaks, cut from leg of baby lamb
Salt and freshly ground black pepper
3 tablespoons (45 ml) butter or lard
Watercress
Béarnaise Sauce (page 122)

Ask your butcher to cut 3 tender lamb steaks about 1 inch (25 mm) thick from the large end of a leg of lamb. (The remainder, boned and cut into 1-inch (25 mm) cubes, can be used for a curried lamb dish with rice.)

Flatten lamb steaks with a cleaver and season with salt and freshly ground black pepper; melt butter or lard in a thick-bottomed frying pan; place lamb steaks in pan and sauté in the hot fat for 6 minutes per side. Transfer to a heated serving dish; garnish with sprigs of fresh watercress and serve immediately with Béarnaise Sauce. Serves 6.

GRILLED LAMB CHOPS

8–10 tenderloin lamb chops
Suet
Lemon juice
Rosemary or oregano
Salt and freshly ground black pepper

Have your butcher trim a loin of baby lamb into 8 or 10 chops.

Preheat grill for 15 to 20 minutes; rub grid with a piece of suet; place chops on it; sprinkle with lemon juice and season to taste with rosemary or oregano, salt and freshly ground black pepper. Grill for 3 to 5 minutes on each side. Serve immediately. Serves 4 to 6.

GRILLED LAMB CUTLETS 'REFORME'

8 small lamb cutlets
Freshly ground black pepper
Softened butter
Salt

SAUCE
1–2 tablespoons (15–30 ml) vinegar
2 tablespoons (30 ml) sugar
1 oz (25 g) crushed peppercorns
1 onion, finely chopped
½ pint (300 ml) well-flavoured Brown Sauce
(page 114)
4 oz (100 g) tongue, cut *en julienne*
1 small beetroot, cut *en julienne*
White of 1 hard-boiled egg, cut *en julienne*
2 gherkins, cut *en julienne*

Remove lamb cutlets from refrigerator at least 30 minutes before cooking and trim fat. Preheat grill; sprinkle both sides of cutlets with freshly ground black pepper, and spread with softened butter. Grill over charcoal or under grill in usual manner. Sprinkle with salt, and serve immediately with the sauce. Serves 4.

SAUCE
Place vinegar, sugar, crushed peppercorns and finely chopped onion in a saucepan, and reduce over a high heat until onion is soft and highly flavoured. Add Brown Sauce; simmer for a few minutes. Strain and add slivers of tongue, beetroot, white of hard-boiled egg and gherkins. Serve hot with grilled chops or steaks.

LAMB CHOPS EN CROÛTE
'RAINBOW ROOM'

8 lamb chops, 1½ inches (38 mm) thick
Salt and freshly ground black pepper
Olive oil
10 oz (275 g) puff pastry (page 760)
1 egg, beaten

DUXELLES
1 tablespoon (15 ml) finely chopped shallots
4 tablespoons (60 ml) butter
10 oz (275 g) mushrooms, finely chopped
2 tablespoons (30 ml) Demi-glace or Brown Sauce
(page 118 or 114)
2 tablespoons (30 ml) finely chopped parsley
Breadcrumbs (optional)

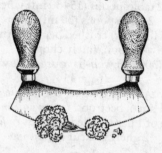

Trim all fat from lamb chops. Season with salt and freshly ground black pepper; brown on both sides in a hot pan with a little olive oil. Chops should remain very rare on the inside. Cool.

Roll out puff pastry into 8 circles big enough to encase chops. Spread *duxelles* of mushrooms on top of chops. Place 1 chop on each circle of dough and wrap in pastry, leaving bone out; moisten join with water and seal securely. Brush with beaten egg; bake for 15 minutes in a moderately hot oven (400°F/200°C/GM6). Serves 8.

DUXELLES
Sauté chopped shallots in butter until transparent. Add chopped mushrooms (stalks and peels will do) and stir over a medium heat until moisture has evaporated. Add Demi-glace or Brown Sauce,

and finely chopped parsley. Let simmer for 5 minutes. Bread-crumbs may be added to achieve desired consistency.

BREADED LAMB CHOPS

4–6 tender lamb chops
Salt and freshly ground black pepper
Flour
2 eggs, well beaten
Fresh breadcrumbs
4–6 tablespoons (60–90 ml) clarified butter
Béarnaise or Soubise Sauce (page 122 or 107)

Trim lamb chops and flatten with the side of a cleaver; season to taste with salt and freshly ground black pepper. Roll chops in flour; dip in beaten egg and then roll in breadcrumbs.

Heat clarified butter in a thick-bottomed frying pan and sauté chops for 5 minutes on each side, or until golden brown and tender. Serve chops with Béarnaise or Soubise Sauce. Serves 4 to 6.

HERB-BREADED LAMB CUTLETS

4–6 lamb cutlets or chops
4–6 oz (100–175 g) dry breadcrumbs
1 tablespoon (15 ml) finely chopped parsley
¼ level teaspoon (0.6 ml) dried thyme
¼ level teaspoon (0.6 ml) dried marjoram
Grated rind of ½ lemon
Salt and freshly ground black pepper
2 eggs, well beaten
4 tablespoons (60 ml) olive oil

Combine breadcrumbs, finely chopped parsley, dried thyme and marjoram, and freshly grated lemon rind. Mix well.

Season lamb cutlets generously with salt and freshly ground black pepper; dip in well-beaten egg and then coat with bread-crumb mixture.

Heat olive oil in a frying pan and sauté lamb cutlets over a low heat until they are well browned on both sides. Serves 4 to 6.

BREADED LAMB FINGERS SAINT GERMAIN

2–2½ lb (900–1.1 kg) breast of lamb
1 Spanish onion, quartered
4 large carrots, quartered
¾ pint (450 ml) well-flavoured veal or chicken stock
Salt and freshly ground black pepper
Flour
2 eggs, well beaten
Breadcrumbs
4–6 tablespoons (60–90 ml) clarified butter
Purée of green peas
Béarnaise Sauce (page 122)

Poach lamb with Spanish onion and carrots in well-flavoured veal or chicken stock until tender – 1½ to 2 hours.

Carefully pull out the bones and place the meat on a flat dish; top with another dish and weight it lightly. When cold, cut meat into thin strips about 1½ inches (38 mm) wide. Trim strips neatly; season to taste with salt and freshly ground black pepper. Roll strips in flour; dip in beaten egg and then roll in breadcrumbs.

Heat clarified butter in a thick-bottomed frying pan and sauté strips until golden brown. Arrange strips in a ring round a purée of green peas. Serve with Béarnaise Sauce. Serves 6.

Braised Lamb and Lamb Stews

BRAISED STUFFED SHOULDER OF LAMB

1 shoulder of lamb
Olive oil
Salt and freshly ground black pepper
Lemon juice
Flour
Butter
Beef, veal or chicken stock, or dry white wine
½ calf's foot (optional)

STUFFING
8 oz (225 g) sausage meat
½ Spanish onion, finely chopped
2 tablespoons (30 ml) butter
1 tablespoon (15 ml) finely chopped parsley
1 egg, beaten
8 oz (225 g) spinach, chopped and sautéed in butter
Salt, freshly ground black pepper and spices

Have your butcher bone and trim a shoulder of lamb ready for rolling. Do not have him roll this.

Brush lamb with olive oil, and season to taste with salt and freshly ground black pepper. Sprinkle with lemon juice.

STUFFING
Combine the following ingredients in a large mixing bowl: sausage meat, finely chopped onion which you have sautéed in butter until transparent, finely chopped parsley, beaten egg, sautéed spinach, and salt, freshly ground black pepper and spices, to taste. Mix well. Lay this stuffing on meat; roll up and sew up with fine string.

Dust the lamb with flour and brown meat slowly on all sides in equal quantities of olive oil and butter in an oval *cocotte* or casserole just large enough to hold it. Moisten the lamb with a little hot stock (beef, veal or chicken), dry white wine, or even hot water. Cover casserole; lower heat and cook for 1½ to 2 hours, adding a little more liquid from time to time if necessary. If thicker sauce is desired, add half a calf's foot after meat is browned.

SHOULDER OF LAMB CAMARGAISE

1 shoulder of lamb
Salt and freshly ground black pepper
Butter
Olive oil
Well-flavoured stock
2 tablespoons (30 ml) tomato concentrate
Mushroom stalks
Bouquet garni
Beurre manié (made by mashing equal quantities
of butter and flour)

MARINADE
3 tablespoons (45 ml) olive oil
¾ pint (450 ml) dry white wine
2 Spanish onion, chopped
4 large carrots, chopped
2 cloves garlic, smashed

RISOTTO STUFFING
8 oz (225 g) risotto rice
Salt
1 canned pimento, cut in thin strips
6 black olives, pitted and cut in strips
6 button mushroom caps, thinly sliced
3 tablespoons (45 ml) butter
Freshly grated Gruyère
Freshly ground black pepper

Ask your butcher to bone lamb; do not let him tie it. Ask for bones. Season boned shoulder of lamb generously with salt and freshly ground black pepper. Place lamb in a porcelain or earthenware casserole with marinade ingredients. Marinate lamb in this mixture for at least 8 hours, turning meat from time to time.

RISOTTO STUFFING
Cook risotto rice in boiling salted water until it is tender but not mushy. Drain well.

Simmer strips of pimento, black olives and sliced mushrooms in butter until soft. Combine with rice and season to taste with freshly grated Gruyère, salt and freshly ground black pepper.

To stuff: drain lamb, reserving vegetables and juices of marinade. Wipe lamb dry and lay out on table; season with salt and freshly ground black pepper, and lay risotto stuffing down centre of meat. Tie up meat.

Brown lamb well on all sides in butter and olive oil. Place it in a heatproof casserole with bones and vegetables of the marinade. Add marinade juices and well-flavoured stock to cover lamb. Stir in tomato concentrate, mushroom stalks and a *bouquet garni*. Bring to a boil; lower heat and cover casserole; simmer lamb gently for 2 hours. Remove lamb from casserole and keep warm. Bring stock to a boil and cook until reduced to half the original quantity. Strain through a fine sieve; thicken if necessary with a little *beurre manié*, and keep warm.

To serve: remove strings from lamb and place it on a heated serving dish. Pour a little sauce over lamb and serve immediately with the remaining sauce in a sauceboat. Serves 6 to 8.

LAMB EN COCOTTE

1 loin of lamb, boned and rolled
Thin strips of bacon
2 tablespoons (30 ml) butter
2 large carrots, sliced
2 Spanish onions, sliced
Salt and freshly ground black pepper
1 glass dry white wine or water
2–4 tomatoes, quartered

Order a rolled loin of lamb from your butcher. Lard roast with thin strips of bacon.

Melt butter in a thick-bottomed *cocotte* or casserole just large enough to hold lamb; add sliced carrots and onions; simmer, stirring, until onion is transparent. Add meat, and season to taste with salt and freshly ground black pepper; sauté lamb until golden on all sides. Transfer casserole to a slow oven (325°F/170°C/GM3) and cook, uncovered, for 1½ to 2 hours, or until lamb is tender, adding a little dry white wine or hot water if necessary, to prevent *cocotte* from scorching.

When meat is half cooked, add quartered tomatoes.

TIPSY LOIN OF LAMB

1 loin of lamb, prepared for roasting
Salt and freshly ground black pepper
½ level teaspoon (2.5 ml) nutmeg
1 level teaspoon (5 ml) dried sage
½ level teaspoon (2.5 ml) marjoram
2 tablespoons (30 ml) bacon fat
3 cloves garlic, finely chopped
4 tablespoons (60 ml) finely chopped parsley
Bouquet garni (1 bay leaf, 1 sprig thyme, 2 sprigs
green celery leaves)
Claret
¾ pint (450 ml) beef stock
1 tablespoon (15 ml) flour
1 tablespoon (15 ml) butter

Rub lamb well on all sides with salt and pepper, nutmeg, sage and marjoram. Sear meat in hot bacon fat with finely chopped garlic and parsley. Place roast in a heatproof oval casserole. Add *bouquet garni*, tied with heavy white thread. Cover meat with claret and cook uncovered in a moderate oven (375°F/190°C/GM5), allowing 30 to 35 minutes per pound (450 g); turn meat occasionally. When meat is done, the wine will have evaporated. Remove meat and keep warm; pour beef stock into casserole with pan juices, and reduce over a high heat to half the original quantity. Brown flour in butter and mix with a little stock until smooth. Stir this *roux* into remaining stock and cook, stirring constantly, until sauce is thick and smooth. Correct seasoning and serve with meat.

DAUBE DE MOUTON

1 leg of lamb
8 oz (225 g) bacon, thinly sliced, and 8 oz (225 g) bacon,
in 1 piece
Olive oil
Salt and freshly ground black pepper
Dried thyme, marjoram, crumbled bay leaf
Red wine
2 carrots, finely chopped
1 Spanish onion, finely chopped
4 cloves garlic, smashed
1 bay leaf
2 sprigs thyme
1 sprig rosemary
4 sprigs parsley
4 tablespoons (60 ml) finely chopped onion
Bouquet garni (parsley, thyme, celery, etc.)
1 strip dried orange peel
Well-flavoured stock
Flour and water paste

Bone leg of lamb and cut it into large pieces weighing about 3 oz (75 g) each. Cut half the bacon slices into ¼-inch (6 mm) strips. Lard each of the lamb pieces with 2 strips of bacon which you have rubbed with a little olive oil, salt, freshly ground black pepper, dried thyme, marjoram and crumbled bay leaf.

Note: If you do not have a larding needle, cut 2 holes in meat cubes with a thin-bladed knife and insert strips of well-seasoned bacon into holes with the point of a skewer.

To marinate meat: place prepared lamb cubes in a large earthenware bowl and add just enough red wine to cover meat. Add 4 tablespoons (60 ml) olive oil, finely chopped carrots and Spanish onion, garlic, a bay leaf, thyme, rosemary and parsley, and salt and freshly ground black pepper, to taste. Marinate for at least 4 hours.

To cook *daube*: dice uncut bacon and blanch it with remaining bacon slices. Cover the bottom of a large earthenware ovenproof casserole with a layer of lamb cubes; sprinkle with 4 tablespoons (60 ml) finely chopped onion and the diced blanched bacon, and season with a pinch of dried thyme and crumbled bay leaf. Cover with a layer of lamb; sprinkle with onions, bacon and dried herbs as above; drop in a *bouquet garni* (parsley, thyme, celery, etc.) and a strip of dried orange peel. Then cover with a final layer of lamb cubes right to the very top of the casserole. Pour in strained marinade juices and a little stock. Top with remaining thin bacon slices; cover casserole and wrap a band of paste (made with flour and water) around join to seal it completely.

Cook for 2½ to 3 hours in a very slow oven (300°F/150°C/GM2).

To serve: remove pastry seal and the cover; remove bacon strips and *bouquet garni*; skim; serve *daube* from casserole. Serves 6 to 8.

NAVARIN DE MOUTON AUX AROMATES

3 lb (1.4 kg) boned shoulder or breast of lamb
3 tablespoons (45 ml) lard
2 Spanish onions, quartered
2 tablespoons (30 ml) flour
Granulated sugar
Salt and freshly ground black pepper
4 small turnips, quartered
Bouquet garni
½ pint (300 ml) light stock
4 tablespoons (60 ml) tomato concentrate
12 small white onions
4 oz (100 g) unsmoked bacon, diced
12 small potatoes, peeled
4 oz (100 g) fresh peas
3 tablespoons (45 ml) finely chopped parsley
3 small cloves garlic, finely chopped
Grated rind of 1 lemon

Cut lamb into cubes and brown in lard with quartered onions. Remove some of the fat; blend in flour, stirring over low heat until slightly thickened; sprinkle with a generous pinch or two of granulated sugar to give a deeper colour to the sauce, and season to taste with salt and freshly ground black pepper.

Add quartered turnips and *bouquet garni*. Stir in stock and tomato concentrate diluted with a little water. Simmer, covered, in a slow oven (350°F/180°C/GM4) for 1 hour.

Drain the pieces of lamb in a sieve, reserving sauce, and remove bits of skin and bones which have separated from meat during cooking. Allow sauce to cool; skim off fat, and strain the sauce into a clean casserole. Add pieces of lamb. Then glaze button onions; blanch and sauté diced unsmoked bacon; peel potatoes; shell peas; and add all these to stew. Bring to a boil and cook, covered, in a slow oven (350°F/180°C/GM4) for 30 to 40 minutes, or until vegetables are cooked and lamb is tender. Sprinkle with parsley, garlic and lemon rind; serve from casserole. Serves 4 to 6.

LAMB STEW WITH COURGETTES

2½ lb (1.1 kg) boned shoulder of lamb
4 tablespoons (60 ml) olive oil
1 Spanish onion, finely chopped
1 large can Italian peeled tomatoes
2 tablespoons (30 ml) tomato concentrate
2 tablespoons (30 ml) finely chopped parsley
Oregano
Salt and freshly ground black pepper
2 lb (900 g) courgettes (zucchini)
4 tablespoons (60 ml) butter

Cut lamb into 2-inch (5 cm) cubes. Heat oil in a thick-bottomed heatproof casserole and brown lamb on all sides; add chopped onion and cook until lightly browned. Add tomatoes and tomato concentrate dissolved in a little water, and season to taste with chopped parsley, oregano, salt and freshly ground black pepper.

Bring to a boil; reduce heat and cover casserole; simmer gently for 1 hour. Then brown courgettes (zucchini) in butter; add them to casserole and continue cooking for 30 minutes longer, or until meat and vegetables are cooked. Serves 4 to 6.

IRISH STEW

3 lb (1.4 kg) shoulder of mutton
1 lb (450 g) onions
2 lb (900 g) potatoes
Salt and freshly ground black pepper
Light stock
2–3 tablespoons (30–45 ml) chopped parsley

Cut mutton in 2½-inch (65 mm) cubes; peel and slice onions and potatoes thickly. Place a layer of sliced onions on the bottom of a heatproof casserole; cover with a layer of meat, and then a layer of potatoes, and continue filling casserole in alternate layers, finishing with potatoes. Season each layer with salt and freshly ground black pepper. Add light stock, to cover; bring to a boil; skim; lower heat and simmer, covered, until tender – almost 3 hours. Just before serving, sprinkle with chopped parsley. Serves 4 to 6.

RICH IRISH STEW

Add 12 oz (350 g) carrots, peeled and sliced, and 4 stalks celery, sliced, to the layers in the above recipe, and cook as above.

LAMB CURRY

2½ lb (1.1 kg) boned shoulder of lamb cut into
2-inch (5 cm) cubes
2 tablespoons (30 ml) butter
2 tablespoons (30 ml) olive oil
2 Spanish onions, chopped
2 cloves garlic, finely chopped
½ pint (300 ml) yoghurt
1 tablespoon (15 ml) curry powder
¼ level teaspoon (1.25 ml) each ginger and turmeric
⅛ level teaspoon (0.6 ml) each paprika and cayenne pepper
1 tablespoon (15 ml) flour
Coarse salt
Freshly ground black pepper

Heat butter and olive oil in a thick-bottomed heatproof casserole. Add chopped onions and garlic, and sauté until vegetables are transparent. Remove vegetables and reserve.

Add the meat to the casserole and brown on all sides. Return the onion and garlic; add yoghurt, stir in spices and flour, and season to taste with salt and freshly ground black pepper. Simmer until tender – about 40 minutes. If desired, thin the sauce with a little light stock before serving. Serves 4 to 6.

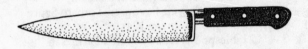

LAMB KORMA

2½ lb (1.1 kg) lamb
2 cloves garlic
½ oz (15 g) green ginger
1–2 Spanish onions, finely chopped
4 oz (100 g) butter
¼ pint (150 ml) yoghurt
2 tablespoons (30 ml) tomato concentrate
1 level tablespoon (15 ml) ground coriander
2 cloves
2 cardamoms
1 tablespoon (15 ml) ground turmeric
1 tablespoon (15 ml) cumin seed
1 small cinnamon stick
Chili powder and salt
Rice

Cut lamb into pieces. Smash garlic and green ginger in a bowl and add 1 pint (600 ml) cold water. Sauté finely chopped onion in half the butter until transparent; add yoghurt, tomato concentrate, spices and salt.

Sauté meat in remaining butter in another pan until golden. Stir into spice mixture; add a little garlic-ginger water and simmer, covered, until meat is tender, adding more garlic-ginger water as necessary from time to time. Correct seasoning and serve with rice. Serves 4 to 6.

HASH OF LAMB WITH POTATO BORDER

1 lb (450 g) cooked lamb, diced
6 large potatoes
2 tablespoons (30 ml) butter
1 egg, well beaten
Salt and freshly ground black pepper
½ Spanish onion, finely chopped
2 tablespoons (30 ml) olive oil
½ pint (300 ml) well-flavoured Tomato Sauce
(page 124)
2 tablespoons freshly grated Parmesan

Peel and boil potatoes in usual way. Mash 4 potatoes with butter and beaten egg, and season to taste with salt and freshly ground black pepper. Force a border of mashed potatoes through a piping bag round a shallow ovenproof dish.

Sauté finely chopped onion in olive oil until transparent; dice remaining 2 cold boiled potatoes and add with diced lamb to onion; continue cooking until golden. Moisten with well-flavoured Tomato Sauce and simmer gently for 10 to 15 minutes, stirring from time to time.

Spoon hash into centre of potato border; sprinkle with freshly grated Parmesan and cook in a hot oven (450°F/230°C/GM8) for about 12 minutes, or until golden brown. Serves 6.

Lamb Kidneys

LAMB KIDNEYS EN BROCHETTE

8–12 lamb kidneys
4–6 tablespoons (60–90 ml) melted butter
Salt and freshly ground black pepper
Fresh breadcrumbs
Garlic Butter (page 130)
4 slices grilled bacon
Sprigs of watercress
Boiled new potatoes

Split kidneys in half from rounded edge; remove thin outer skin; open them and run skewer through them to keep them open. Brush with melted butter; season with salt and freshly ground black pepper, and sprinkle generously with breadcrumbs. Grill in usual manner. Just before serving: place a knob of Garlic Butter on each kidney half. Garnish with grilled bacon and watercress. Serve with boiled new potatoes. Serves 4.

ROGNONS FLAMBÉS

8–12 lamb kidneys
4–6 tablespoons (60–90 ml) butter
2–4 tablespoons (30–60 ml) finely chopped onion
2 teaspoons (10 ml) Dijon mustard
Salt and freshly ground black pepper
6 tablespoons (90 ml) port
Cognac
2 tablespoons (30 ml) finely chopped parsley
Juice of ½ lemon
Boiled new potatoes

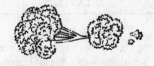

Remove thin outer skins from kidneys. Sauté quickly in half the butter with finely chopped onion until kidneys stiffen and begin to brown. Dice kidneys (the interiors will still be raw); melt remaining butter in a thick-bottomed frying pan and add diced kidneys, onion, Dijon mustard and salt and freshly ground black pepper. Stir over a high heat for a minute or two; add port. Reduce heat and allow to simmer, stirring continuously, until kidneys are tender.

Sprinkle kidneys with cognac and ignite; allow the flames to die down, stirring continuously. Do not allow sauce to boil at any time during its preparation, or kidneys will be tough. Just before serving, sprinkle with finely chopped parsley and lemon juice. Serve with boiled new potatoes. Serves 4.

ROGNONS AU PORTO

8–12 lamb kidneys
2 tablespoons (30 ml) butter
½ Spanish onion, finely chopped
2–4 tablespoons (30–60 ml) finely chopped parsley
Salt and freshly ground black pepper
4–6 button mushrooms, thinly sliced
1 teaspoon (5 ml) flour
4–6 tablespoons (60–90 ml) port
4 *croûtons* fried in butter, or rice

Clean kidneys of fibres and fat; slice thinly. Melt butter in a frying pan; add finely chopped onion and parsley, and sauté, stirring constantly, for a few minutes. Season to taste with salt and freshly ground black pepper. Add kidneys and sliced mushrooms, and continue to cook, stirring continuously, until tender. Stir in flour; pour over port. Serve with *croûtons* fried in butter, or rice. Serves 4.

ROGNONS SAUTÉS AU VIN ROUGE 'ÉTOILE'

8 lamb kidneys
4 oz (100 g) mushrooms, sliced
2 tablespoons (30 ml) butter
1 onion, finely chopped
¼ pint (150 ml) red wine
2–4 tablespoons (30–60 ml) Demi-glace or Brown Sauce
(page 118 or 114)
2 tablespoons (30 ml) finely chopped parsley

Sauté sliced mushrooms in butter until golden; remove and keep warm. Sauté chopped onion in pan until transparent; add kidneys, cut in small pieces, and simmer lightly for a minute or two. Pour red wine over meat and cook, stirring, until sauce bubbles. Reduce heat; stir in Demi-glace or Brown Sauce, and allow to simmer for a minute, until reduced to half the original quantity. Stir in cooked mushrooms; sprinkle with parsley and serve. Serves 4.

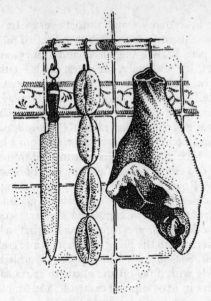

CHAPTER TWELVE
All About Pork

In the time of Marco Polo, it is said, lusty Chinese war lords preferred their pigs raw, and ate whole legs of uncooked pork at one sitting. The more fastidious preferred theirs baked in clay and then simmered in a rich broth of chicken, herbs and wine. Perhaps they ate it with their famous winter or sour cabbage (cabbage with rice wine added to preserve it during the winter months), a forerunner of our own sauerkraut, brought to Central Europe by the Tartar hordes. Pork – both fresh and smoked – goes wonderfully well with sauerkraut today, adding its smooth succulence and subtle flavour to the distinctive tartness of the *Kraut*.

Pork is eaten in so many ways: almost every part of the pig is used for some succulent food preparation. Stuffed pig's tail, pig's trotters, *tête de porc*, brawn, pig's liver and kidney, as well as the more usual loin, leg and belly, are eaten fresh – either roasted, grilled, fried, or simmered lovingly *en casserole*. Or they are smoked or salted, to be used in much the same way. Still other cuts are used for sausages of every description, and *pâtés* and pies.

I prefer pork as it is cooked in France. (1) *Carré de porc à la bonne femme*. Ask your butcher to remove the rind from a loin of pork, leaving the fat. Mix softened butter, crumbled thyme, bay leaf, salt and pepper to a smooth paste, and rub into pork several hours before roasting. Roast pork in usual way, fat side up, until half cooked; surround with peeled new potatoes, glazed button on-ions and sautéed mushroom caps, and continue cooking until tender. (2) *Carré de porc à la provençale*. Ask butcher to bone and tie loin of pork. Pierce with the point of a sharp knife and insert sage leaves into pork. Season with salt, pepper, crumbled thyme and bay leaf; sprinkle with olive oil and allow to stand for at least 12 hours. Place pork in an ovenproof casserole; add 6 tablespoons (90 ml) each water, dry white wine and olive oil, and 2 to 3 crushed garlic cloves; cook in a slow oven (350°F/180°C/GM4) until tender. (3) Marinated fillet, leg or loin of pork. Combine 2 glasses dry white wine, 2 tablespoons (30 ml) olive oil, 1 sliced Spanish onion, 2 bay leaves, 2 cloves and a little thyme, and marinate pork in this mixture for at least 12 hours. When ready to cook: remove from marinade; drain and dry; brush with olive oil and roast in the usual way, basting from time to time, and adding a little of the marinade if necessary.

How to Buy Pork

The lean should be pale pink, smooth in texture and finely grained. The skin should not be too thick. If it is too dark, the meat tends to be dry and tough. The fat should be pearly white. Pork meat should have no smell.

How to Cook Pork

All cuts of pork, provided they are tender and fairly fat, can be roasted. Cook pork slowly in an uncovered shallow pan or casserole. Maximum flavour is reached only when the pork is slowly and well cooked. Cook it until the meat has lost its pinkish tinge and is pale beige in colour. I like to roast pork in a slow oven (325°–350°F/170°–180°C/GM3–4) for about 35 minutes per pound (450 g).

To glaze pork roasts after cooking: increase oven temperature to 425°F/220°C/GM7; sprinkle fat with 2 to 3 tablespoons (30–45 ml) brown sugar; return meat to oven to glaze.

Flavour pork with honey, sage, soy sauce, thyme, bay leaf, ginger, onions, garlic, leeks, apples, or dried prunes and apricots; moisten it with cider, cream, dry white wine, tomato sauce, or pineapple, apple or orange juice. Serve with pickled peaches, baked apples, apple sauce, brandied or pickled pears, fresh or canned pineapple, sauerkraut, and almost any spicy chutney, pickle or relish.

Some Different Cuts of Pork

Fillet: This is the choicest cut of all and, naturally, the most expensive. There is, of course, no bone and practically no waste. The meat is exceptionally tender. Excellent for roasting or grilling.

Loin: This is generally scored and roasted. Pork chops are also cut from this part.

Spare ribs: The new interest in Chinese and outdoor cooking has brought this moderately priced joint into high favour. It is fairly lean, and excellent for roasting, braising, stewing or barbecuing.

Shoulder: May be purchased either with the bone, or boned and rolled. This cut makes an excellent roast when stuffed with a herb stuffing.

Leg: Another piece for roasting. The skin should always be scored by the butcher to make crackling. If left unscored, it is difficult to carve the joint. I also like it salted and then boiled.

Blade bone: Cut from behind the head, or top of foreleg. I like it for stuffing with bone removed. An inexpensive joint, delicious when roasted or braised.

Hand and spring: Well-flavoured joint cut from the foreleg. Can be boned (knuckle removed) and rolled. Inexpensive.

Belly: Often rather fatty, usually salted and boiled. The thicker end is sometimes rolled for an inexpensive roast.

Head: Usually salted. Can be made into brawn, or boiled and served cold. Pig's cheek – sometimes sold separately – can be used to make Bath chaps.

Feet (pettitoes): Very cheap; often sold already prepared. Can be cooked in various ways. Usually boiled or stewed. Often substituted for calf's feet to add succulence to country stews.

Tongue: Should be pickled and then served in the same way as sheep's tongue.

Pig's fry: The heart, lights, liver and sweetbreads are generally cut in slices and fried.

How Much Pork to Buy

Boneless meat: Allow 6 oz (175 g) meat per person for liver, minced pork, patties, sausage meat and rolled roasts.

Pork chops: Allow 1 per person.

Meat with average amount of bone: Allow 8 to 10 oz (225–275 g) meat with bone per person for roasts and casseroles.

Meat with large amount of bone: Allow 10 to 12 oz (275–350 g) per person.

How to Refrigerate Pork

Unwrap meat and rewrap it loosely in waxed paper, clean wrapping paper or foil.

Large pieces (leg, loin, shoulder, etc.) may be kept for 4 to 6 days in the refrigerator; pork chops for 3 days; pork sausage meat and sliced liver, 2 days; minced fresh pork, 1 day only.

Pork Loin and Fillet

ROAST LOIN OF PORK
(LOW HEAT METHOD)

1 loin of pork (7–8 cutlets)
4 tablespoons (60 ml) softened butter
Crumbled thyme and bay leaf
Dijon mustard
Salt and freshly ground black pepper
Flour
Butter
Watercress
Puréed potatoes

Have your butcher remove the rind without removing fat. Mix softened butter with crumbled thyme, bay leaf and mustard, to taste, to a smooth paste, and rub well into pork several hours before roasting. Season to taste with salt and freshly ground black pepper, and let stand at room temperature to absorb flavours. Arrange the meat fat side up and brown it in a hot oven (450°F/ 230°C/GM8) for 15 minutes. Reduce the oven heat to slow (350°F/180°C/GM4) and continue to roast until the meat is done.

Remove excess fat from the pan and thicken pan drippings with a little flour kneaded with an equal amount of butter. Garnish with sprigs of watercress, and serve with puréed potatoes.

ROAST LOIN OF PORK BOULANGÈRE
(HIGH HEAT METHOD)

1 loin of pork (7–8 cutlets)
Salt and freshly ground black pepper
Butter
2 tablespoons (30 ml) flour
6–8 large potatoes
1 Spanish onion, finely chopped
2 tablespoons (30 ml) finely chopped parsley
Hot light stock or water

Season pork generously with salt and freshly ground black pepper; place it on the rack of a roasting pan and roast it in a fairly hot oven (425°F/220°C/GM7) for 1 hour, or until pork is half cooked, basting it from time to time. Remove pork and roasting rack from pan; skim off excess fat. Thicken pan gravy with 2 tablespoons (30 ml) each butter and flour in the usual way. Pour into a small saucepan and reserve.

Peel and slice potatoes thinly, and place them in roasting pan with finely chopped onion and parsley, and salt and freshly ground black pepper, to taste. Spread potatoes with 4 tablespoons (60 ml) softened butter, and place pork roast on top, adding just enough hot stock (or water) to cover the potatoes. Bring the liquid to a boil; return pan to a moderately hot oven (400°F/200°C/GM6) and cook for 1 to 1½ hours longer, or until meat is done, the liquid has almost completely cooked away, and the potatoes are nicely browned on top. Reheat pan gravy and serve with roast and potatoes.

ROAST LOIN OF PORK NORMANDE

1 loin of pork (7–8 cutlets)
Salt and freshly ground black pepper
Dried thyme and nutmeg
4–6 tablespoons (60–90 ml) apple cider
4–6 tablespoons (60–90 ml) apple jelly
Flour and butter
Watercress
4 eating apples, cored and thinly sliced, sautéed in
4 tablespoons (60 ml) butter

Rub pork with salt, freshly ground black pepper, thyme, and a sprinkling of nutmeg. Arrange meat fat side up and brown in a hot oven (450°F/230°C/GM8) for 10 minutes. Reduce heat to slow (350°F/180°C/GM4) and continue to roast until meat is done, basting with blended cider and jelly for the first 1½ hours of cooking time.

Remove excess fat from the pan, adding a little water or cider if fat starts to scorch. Make gravy by thickening pan drippings with a little flour kneaded with an equal amount of butter. Serve with watercress and thinly sliced apples sautéed in butter.

BARBECUED LOIN OF PORK

1 loin of pork
¼ teaspoon (1.25 ml) dry mustard
¼ teaspoon (1.25 ml) ground coriander
¼ teaspoon (1.25 ml) ground cloves
2 cloves garlic, finely chopped
¼ teaspoon (1.25 ml) freshly ground black pepper
4 tablespoons (60 ml) olive oil
4 tablespoons (60 ml) soy sauce
4 tablespoons (60 ml) vinegar
6 tablespoons (90 ml) water
2 tablespoons (30 ml) sugar
1 small fresh pineapple

GARNISH
Diced fresh pineapple
Sliced cucumber
Watercress and parsley sprigs

Have your butcher cut backbone from ribs.

Mix mustard, coriander, cloves, garlic, freshly ground black pepper, olive oil, soy sauce, vinegar, water and sugar together in a saucepan; bring to a boil; lower the heat and simmer for ½ hour.

Peel pineapple, reserving flesh for garnish; place loin on a flat baking pan; brush with marinade; cover with pineapple skin, and roast meat in a slow oven (350°F/180°C/GM4) for about 2 hours, or until done, basting frequently with the hot barbecue sauce.

Garnish with diced fresh pineapple, sliced cucumber, watercress and parsley sprigs. Serves 6.

CHOUCROUTE GARNIE AU CHAMPAGNE

Fat salt pork, thinly sliced
2 Spanish onions, sliced
4 cloves garlic, coarsely chopped
4 lb (1.8 kg) sauerkraut, well washed
1 large piece salt pork
Freshly ground black pepper
4–6 juniper berries
Champagne (or white wine)
1 boned loin of pork
1 large Lorraine sausage, or 1 Cotechino sausage
and 4–8 other sausages (*Bratwurst, Knockwurst,*
frankfurters, *saucisses de Toulouse*)
Boiled potatoes

Line a deep earthenware casserole or stockpot with thinly sliced
fat salt pork; add half the sliced onions and chopped garlic. Place a
thick layer of well-washed and drained sauerkraut on top with a
large piece of salt pork. Grind plenty of black pepper over it;
sprinkle with juniper berries, and add remaining onions and
garlic. Cover with remaining sauerkraut and add just enough
champagne (or white wine) to cover the sauerkraut. Cover and
cook in a very slow oven (300°F/150°C/GM2) for 4 to 6 hours.
The longer it cooks the better.

A loin of pork, fresh or smoked, is excellent with *choucroute*.
Add it to the *choucroute* about 2½ hours before serving. Half an
hour later add a large Lorraine sausage (or a Cotechino sausage,
and a selection of small sausages as available: *Bratwurst, Knockwurst* and frankfurters are tasty additions, as are the famous
saucisses de Toulouse; use any or all of these meats).

To serve, heap the *choucroute* in the middle of a platter and
arrange slices of meat and sausages around it. For those with a
taste for the spectacular – place an unopened half-bottle of champagne, with only the wires removed, in the centre of the hot
sauerkraut just before bringing it to the table. Then watch the
warmed champagne gush out over the sauerkraut. Serve with
boiled potatoes. Serves 8.

PORK À LA BERRICHONNE

½ leg of pork, boned and rolled (about 4–5 lb/1.8–2.5 kg)
1 pint (600 ml) dry white wine
Salt and freshly ground black pepper
4 carrots, sliced
1 Spanish onion, finely chopped
2 cloves garlic, finely chopped
4 sprigs thyme
6 sage leaves
1 bay leaf
2 tablespoons (30 ml) butter
½ pint (300 ml) stock

Marinate pork overnight in a porcelain or glass bowl in dry white wine with salt, freshly ground black pepper, sliced carrots, finely chopped onion and garlic, and herbs. The next day, remove pork from marinade; wipe dry and sauté in butter in a thick-bottomed heatproof casserole until golden on all sides. Pour off butter and moisten with marinade juices. Simmer uncovered in a slow oven (325°F/170°C/GM3) for 2 hours until the liquid is reduced. Then add stock; cover casserole, and simmer until tender at 275°F/140°C/GM1. Remove roast and keep warm. Strain juices through a fine sieve; reheat the sauce and serve with roast.

CHINESE FRIED PORK PELLETS

1 lb (450 g) pork fillet
½ teaspoon (2.5 ml) salt
Dash of monosodium glutamate
1 tablespoon (15 ml) *sake*
Corn or peanut oil, for frying

BATTER
1 egg white
5 tablespoons (75 ml) cornflour
3 tablespoons (45 ml) soy sauce
2 tablespoons (30 ml) *sake*
2 tablespoons (30 ml) ginger juice

Cut pork into bite-sized pieces, place in a bowl, and season with salt, monosodium glutamate and *sake*.

BATTER

Beat egg white in a bowl until stiff; add cornflour mixed with soy sauce, *sake* and ginger juice, and mix well to make batter.

Heat oil for deep-frying to 350°F/180°C. Cover pork well with batter and fry until crisp and golden. Serves 4, if served with 2 or more other dishes.

FILET DE PORC EN CROÛTE

1 fillet of pork (about 14–16 oz/400–450 g)
Salt and freshly ground black pepper
1 recipe Puff Pastry (page 760)
2 oz (50 g) Parma ham, sliced very thinly
Beaten egg

DUXELLES

1 lb (450 g) button mushrooms, finely chopped
1 Spanish onion, finely chopped
4 tablespoons (60 ml) butter
Salt and freshly ground black pepper
Powdered thyme
2 tablespoons (30 ml) freshly chopped parsley
4 tablespoons (60 ml) freshly grated breadcrumbs
2 eggs, well beaten

Season fillet lightly with salt and freshly ground black pepper, and sear it quickly on all sides. Cool. Roll out puff pastry about ⅛ inch (3 mm) thick, in a shape 2 inches (5 cm) longer than the fillet and about 10 inches (25 cm) wide.

Place fillet in centre of pastry; spread evenly with the *duxelles* and top with thin slices of ham. Fold one side of pastry over the pork; spread a little beaten egg over the upper surface and then fold over the second side of the pastry, overlapping the first. Roll pastry ends out flat, spread with beaten egg on the upper side and fold the ends over the roll. Place pastry-wrapped fillet in a baking tin with the folded ends down. Brush the surface with beaten egg and decorate with lattice strips of leaves cut from pastry scraps. Brush pastry again with beaten egg; prick lightly with a fork and bake in a moderately hot oven (400°F/200°C/GM6) for about 40 minutes. Serves 4.

DUXELLES

Sauté finely chopped mushrooms and onion in butter; season to taste with salt, freshly ground black pepper and powdered thyme. Add freshly chopped parsley and freshly grated breadcrumbs. Stir in beaten eggs. Mix well and heat through. Turn out into a small pan and set aside to cool.

Note: This filling should be prepared in advance.

FILLET OF PORK WITH TURNIPS

1 fillet of pork
6 tablespoons (90 ml) water
Salt and freshly ground black pepper
18–24 small turnips
4 tablespoons (60 ml) butter
Fat from pork
2 tablespoons (30 ml) sugar
¼ pint (150 ml) beef stock flavoured with 1–2 tablespoons
(15–30 ml) tomato concentrate

Have butcher trim and tie a fillet of pork. Put it in a casserole with water, and season to taste with salt and freshly ground black pepper. Cook uncovered in a moderately hot oven (400°F/200°C/GM6) for 30 minutes, or until meat is nicely browned.

Blanch turnips in boiling water for 10 minutes; drain. Sauté turnips in a large thick-bottomed casserole with butter and a little fat from the roast. Sprinkle with sugar; season to taste with salt and freshly ground black pepper; simmer, shaking pan from time to time, until turnips are glazed.

When pork is three-quarters cooked: skim excess fat; surround with glazed turnips; moisten with tomato-flavoured stock; cover pan and simmer in a slow oven (325°F/170°C/GM3) until pork is tender, turning meat from time to time.

CHINESE PORK WITH WATERCRESS

4 bunches watercress
1 teaspoon (5 ml) salt
Juice of ½ lemon
4 tablespoons (60 ml) corn oil
1 small clove garlic, finely chopped
1 lb (450 g) fillet of pork, thinly sliced
2–3 tablespoons (30–45 ml) soy sauce
1 tablespoon (15 ml) *sake* or dry sherry

Trim watercress stems and wash well, picking out all yellowed or damaged leaves. Drain. Soak for 30 minutes in cold water to which you have added 1 teaspoon (5 ml) salt and the juice of ½ lemon. Drain, rinse in clean water and dry.

When ready to serve: heat oil in frying pan, add garlic and thin pork slices, and brown the meat quickly on all sides. Add the soy sauce, *sake* or dry sherry, and watercress, and cook, stirring constantly, until the juice begins to boil. Cover pan and cook for 2 minutes longer. Serve immediately. Serves 4 to 6, if served with 2 or more other dishes.

POLYNESIAN PORK SATÉ

2 lb (900 g) lean pork
6 Brazil nuts, grated
1 level tablespoon (15 ml) ground coriander seed
2 cloves garlic, finely chopped
1 level tablespoon (15 ml) salt
1 Spanish onion, grated
4 tablespoons (60 ml) lemon juice
1–2 tablespoons (15–30 ml) brown sugar
4 tablespoons (60 ml) soy sauce
1 teaspoon (5 ml) pepper
⅛ teaspoon (0.6 ml) crushed hot red pepper

Cut pork into 1-inch (25 mm) cubes. Combine remaining ingredients in a large mixing bowl. Add pork cubes and allow them to marinate in this mixture for at least 2 hours.

When ready to serve: thread pork on metal skewers and grill over charcoal or under a gas or electric grill until cooked through. Serves 4 to 6.

CHINESE FRIED PORK BALLS

1 lb (450 g) finely ground pork
Dash of ginger juice
2 tablespoons (30 ml) cornflour
1 teaspoon (5 ml) *sake*
½ teaspoon (2.5 ml) salt
¼ teaspoon (1.25 ml) monosodium glutamate
Oil, for frying

Mix first 6 ingredients in a bowl. Make balls 1¾ inches (45 mm) in diameter. Heat oil to 350°F/180°C. Fry until browned. Fry again just before serving. Serves 4, if served with 2 or more other dishes.

DANISH MEAT BALLS (FRIKADELLER)

8 oz (225 g) finely ground pork
8 oz (225 g) finely ground veal
4 oz (100 g) flour
¾ pint (450 ml) milk
1 egg
Salt and freshly ground black pepper
½ teaspoon (2.5 ml) ground cloves
1 medium-sized onion, finely chopped and sautéed in butter
Butter and oil, for frying

Combine finely ground meats and flour, mixing well. Add milk little by little, stirring well to make a smooth paste. Stir in egg and season to taste with salt, freshly ground black pepper, ground cloves, and finely chopped onion which you have sautéed in butter until transparent.

Form mixture into small balls about 1 inch (25 mm) in diameter and fry *frikadeller* evenly on all sides in butter and oil until cooked through. Serves 4 to 6.

PEARL BUCK'S SWEET AND SOUR SPARE RIBS

2½ lb (1.1 kg) spare ribs of pork
¾ pint (450 ml) water
4 tablespoons (60 ml) soy sauce
Salt
3 tablespoons (45 ml) sugar or honey
3 tablespoons (45 ml) vinegar
1 tablespoon (15 ml) cornflour
¼ pint (150 ml) water
2 tablespoons (30 ml) *sake*, or dry sherry and water
1 level teaspoon (5 ml) grated fresh ginger root

Cut ribs into separate pieces and cook in water with soy sauce and salt, to taste. Bring to a boil, turn down heat and allow to simmer for 1 hour. Transfer to a frying pan; add remaining ingredients and fry until gravy becomes translucent. Serves 4.

Pork Chops

PORK CHOPS IN RED WINE

4–6 good-sized pork chops
Salt and freshly ground black pepper
Flour
2 tablespoons (30 ml) butter
2 tablespoons (30 ml) olive oil
2 tablespoons (30 ml) finely chopped shallots
¼ pint (150 ml) red wine
2 tablespoons (30 ml) finely chopped parsley

Trim excess fat from pork chops; season them generously with salt and freshly ground black pepper; dust with flour and sauté gently in butter and olive oil until cooked through and brown on both sides.

Transfer the pork chops to a heated serving dish; pour excess fat from pan. Add finely chopped shallots and red wine to the pan, and cook slowly, stirring in all the crusty bits from sides and bottom of the pan. Skim fat and cook sauce until reduced to half the original quantity. Correct seasoning and pour over chops. Sprinkle with finely chopped parsley and serve immediately. Serves 4 to 6.

PORK CHOPS IN CIDER

4–6 pork chops
Salt and freshly ground black pepper
2 tablespoons (30 ml) butter
2 tablespoons (30 ml) olive oil
¼ teaspoon (1.25 ml) powdered basil
¼ teaspoon (1.25 ml) powdered marjoram
¼ teaspoon (1.25 ml) powdered thyme
2 Spanish onions, finely chopped
¼ pint (150 ml) cider
¼ pint (150 ml) water

Trim excess fat from pork chops; season them generously with salt and freshly ground black pepper, and sauté in butter and olive oil until brown on both sides. Transfer chops to an ovenproof baking dish and sprinkle with powdered basil, marjoram and thyme. Simmer finely chopped onions in remaining fat until transparent; add to pork chops, and moisten with cider and water. Cover the casserole and bake in a slow oven (350°F/180°C/GM4) for 45 to 60 minutes, or until tender. Serve from casserole. Serves 4 to 6.

FLEMISH PORK CASSEROLE

4 thick pork chops
4 tablespoons (60 ml) butter
4 tart eating apples
6 sprigs rosemary, chopped
Salt and freshly ground black pepper
Watercress

Trim excess fat from 4 good-sized pork chops; season chops and brown very slowly on both sides in 2 tablespoons (30 ml) butter. Peel apples and cut them into eighths. Put the half-cooked chops in a shallow casserole, sprinkle with rosemary, salt and freshly ground black pepper, and arrange mounds of apples around them. Sprinkle chops and apples with remaining butter, melted, and bake in a moderate oven (375°F/190°C/GM5) for about ½ hour, or until the pork is thoroughly cooked. Decorate the chops with paper ruffs; garnish with watercress and serve from the casserole. Serves 4.

PORK CHOPS 'AVESNOISE'

4 pork chops, cut from fillet
1 tablespoon (15 ml) olive oil
1 tablespoon (15 ml) butter
Salt and freshly ground black pepper
4 oz (100 g) finely grated Gruyère
1–2 level teaspoons (5–10 ml) Dijon mustard
Thick cream

Trim excess fat from 4 good-sized pork chops and sauté them gently with a little oil and butter in a thick-bottomed frying pan; season to taste with salt and freshly ground black pepper.

When cooked, spread with a *pommade* made of finely grated Gruyère (about 6 tablespoons/90 ml) mixed with mustard and just enough cream to make a smooth mixture of spreading consistency.

Spread chops generously with cheese *pommade* and glaze quickly under the grill until sauce is golden. Serve immediately. Serves 4.

Ham

MONSIEUR UDE'S RECEIPT, HAMS SUPERIOR TO WESTPHALIA

'Take the hams as soon as the pig is sufficiently cold to be cut up, rub them well with common salt, and leave them for three days to drain; throw away the brine, and for a couple of hams of from fifteen to eighteen pound weight, mix together two ounces of saltpetre, a pound of coarse sugar, and a pound of common salt; rub the hams in every part with these, lay them into deep pickling-pans with the rind downwards, and keep them for three days well covered with the salt and sugar; then pour over them a bottle of good vinegar and turn them in the brine, and baste them with it daily for a month; drain them well, rub them with bran, and let them be hung for a month high in a chimney over a wood-fire to be smoked.

'Monsieur Ude directs that the hams, when smoked should be hung as high as possible from the fire, that the fat may not be melted; a very necessary precaution, as the mode of their being cured renders it peculiarly liable to do so.'

THE FRENCH MANNER OF BOILING HAM

1 raw ham (about 10 lb/5 kg)
1 pint (600 ml) water or light stock
½ pint (300 ml) dry white wine
6 large carrots, sliced
2 Spanish onions, sliced
Bouquet garni
Peppercorns

Desalt ham overnight in cold water, changing water several times. Make a well-flavoured *court-bouillon* by bringing water (or light stock), dry white wine, sliced carrots and onions, *bouquet garni* and peppercorns to a boil. Skim and allow to simmer for 30 minutes. Wrap ham in a thin cloth and place it in the *court-bouillon*. Let it simmer gently for 3 hours. Allow to cool in *court-bouillon*. Drain. Slice thinly as needed.

HAM WITH MADEIRA

1 ham, cooked as above
½ pint (300 ml) Madeira
Madeira Sauce (page 116)

Cook the ham as above; remove the rind and a good part of the fat, and place the ham in a baking tin. Moisten with Madeira wine and cook for 30 minutes in a hot oven (450°F/230°C/GM8), basting frequently with Madeira. The ham will take on a good colour. Serve with Madeira Sauce.

JAMBON PERSILLÉ EN GELÉE

1 shin or knuckle of veal, coarsely chopped
2 calf's feet, coarsely chopped
Generous *bouquet garni* (4 sprigs parsley,
4 sprigs tarragon, 2 bay leaves, 2 sprigs thyme)
4 shallots
6 black peppercorns
1 bottle dry white wine
2–2½ lb (900–1.1 kg) ham (cut in 1 piece)
Finely chopped fresh parsley
1 tablespoon (15 ml) tarragon vinegar
4 tablespoons (60 ml) dry white wine

Place shin bone, or knuckle of veal with plenty of meat on it, and calf's feet in a saucepan with *bouquet garni*, shallots, peppercorns and white wine; add enough water to cover the bones. Bring slowly to a boil, removing scum as it rises; then cover pan and simmer stock over a low heat for about 3 hours.

Soak ham in cold water for the same length of time to remove some of the salt. Place ham slice in the stock and bring slowly to a boil, removing scum as it rises. When liquid is barely simmering, cover pan and simmer gently until ham is tender. Dice ham coarsely, meat and fat together, and press it gently into a wet glass bowl which you have dusted well with finely chopped parsley.

Strain stock through a fine sieve; cool. Skim all fat from surface and moisten ham with a little of the stock. Clarify stock; strain through a sieve lined with a wet flannel cloth. Cool until syrupy, then stir in tarragon vinegar, 4 tablespoons (60 ml) wine and a large amount of finely chopped parsley. Pour over pink ham chunks and leave to set in the refrigerator. Serve in slices from bowl. Serves 6 to 8.

JAMBON À LA CRÈME DU RELAIS FLEURI

4 thick slices ham
1 tablespoon (15 ml) butter
1 tablespoon (15 ml) flour
¼ pint (150 ml) port
Salt and freshly ground black pepper
1 egg yolk
¼ pint (150 ml) thick cream

Warm ham slices in a very slow oven.

In the meantime, prepare the following sauce: make a *roux blond* with butter and flour. Add port, and salt with freshly ground black pepper, to taste, and simmer until sauce is rich and thick. Remove from heat, and cool. When sauce is barely warm, whisk in egg yolk and cream. Correct seasoning. Heat through, but do not allow sauce to come to a boil.

To serve: arrange ham slices on a warm serving dish and pour sauce over them. Serve immediately. Serves 4.

COLD PARSLEYED HAM (simpler version)

2 lb (900 g) cooked ham (cut in 1 piece)
1 pint (600 ml) well-flavoured chicken or veal stock
¼ pint (150 ml) dry white wine
Freshly ground black pepper and nutmeg
6–8 tablespoons (90–120 ml) chopped fresh parsley
2 tablespoons (30 ml) gelatine
1–2 tablespoons (15–30 ml) tarragon vinegar

Dice ham; simmer gently for 5 minutes in chicken or veal stock and white wine, with freshly ground black pepper and nutmeg, to taste. Draining, reserving stock, and place diced ham in a wet glass bowl which you have dusted lightly with a little finely chopped parsley.

Soften gelatine in a little water. Stir into hot stock; add remaining parsley and tarragon vinegar. Allow to cool until syrupy and pour over diced ham, which should be covered. Allow to set for 12 hours before unmoulding. Serves 6 to 8.

HAM STEAKS STUFFED WITH SWEET POTATOES

4 thick slices ham (about 8 oz (225 g) each)
1 can small sweet potatoes
4 tablespoons (60 ml) melted butter
Grated rind of ½ lemon
Grated rind of ½ orange
¼ level teaspoon (1.25 ml) powdered cinnamon
2–4 tablespoons (30–60 ml) bourbon or rum
Salt and freshly ground black pepper
2 tablespoons (30 ml) brown sugar

Mash sweet potatoes with melted butter, and flavour with grated lemon and orange rind, cinnamon, bourbon or rum, and salt and freshly ground black pepper, to taste.

Spread the stuffing thickly on 2 ham steaks and top with remaining steaks. Sprinkle the steaks with brown sugar, and season with freshly ground black pepper. Wrap loosely in foil and bake in a slow oven (325°F/170°C/GM3) for 1 hour. Serves 4.

HAM STEAKS 'FORUM OF THE TWELVE CAESARS'

4–6 thick slices ham (about 8 oz/225 g each)
1 lb (450 g) Italian spiced mustard fruit
(*frutta di Cremona*)
½ pint (300 ml) liquid honey, heated
12 walnuts

Grill ham steaks on one side for about 3 minutes. Turn and grill other side for 1½ minutes. Arrange segments of mustard fruit on top of steaks and place under grill for 1 to 2 minutes more. Remove from grill; place steaks on a heated serving dish and pour heated honey over them. Garnish each steak with 2 or 3 walnuts. Serve immediately. Serves 6.

Sausages

SAUSAGES AND MASH

1 lb (450 g) pork sausages
2 tablespoons (30 ml) lard
Butter
Salt and freshly ground black pepper
¼ teaspoon (1.25 ml) powdered thyme
¼ teaspoon (1.25 ml) powdered sage
2 egg yolks
Milk or single cream
2 cups mashed potatoes
Beaten egg (optional)
2 tablespoons (30 ml) breadcrumbs

Blanch sausages by putting them in a saucepan with cold water and bringing them quickly to a boil. Drain them; remove their skins; cut them into 3 pieces each and sauté pieces in lard for a minute or two to brown them.

Place sausages in a buttered pie dish or heatproof baking dish and sprinkle them with salt, freshly ground black pepper, powdered thyme and powdered sage.

Combine yolks with 4 tablespoons (60 ml) milk or cream, and beat into potato mixture. Season to taste with salt and freshly ground black pepper. Spread potato mixture over sausages. Brush with milk or beaten egg; sprinkle with breadcrumbs and bake in a moderate oven (375°F/190°C/GM5) for 20 to 30 minutes, or until potatoes are golden brown. Serves 2 to 4.

SALSICCIE CON I FAGIOLI

8 Italian sausages
2 tablespoons (30 ml) olive oil
2 tablespoons (30 ml) butter
6–8 tablespoons (90–120 ml) tomato concentrate
6–8 tablespoons (90–120 ml) cold water
1 lb (450 g) dry white beans, cooked
Salt and freshly ground black pepper

Prick holes in sausages with a fine skewer or the point of a sharp knife; place in a frying pan just large enough to hold them and cover with water. Cook over medium heat until water evaporates. Remove sausages and brown in a little oil and butter, turning them from time to time, until they are cooked through and well coloured on all sides – 20 to 30 minutes. In this way, the sausages will be well cooked, but will remain soft and with their skins intact. Remove sausages. Then, in remaining fat, to which you should add a little olive oil (or lard), stir in tomato concentrate. Cook for a minute or two, stirring; then add 6 tablespoons (90 ml) water and simmer gently for 5 to 10 minutes.

Add cooked and drained white beans, season with salt and freshly ground black pepper, and simmer gently for a few minutes to allow beans to absorb flavour. Then add sausages and heat through. Serve beans on platter, topped by sausages. Serves 4.

Salt Pork

BOILED SALT PORK

2½–3 lb (1.1–1.4 kg) pickled or salted pork
2 Spanish onions
6 carrots
12 parsnips or 6 turnips

Choose a nice piece of pickled or salted pork; wash it, cover it with cold water and soak for 24 hours, changing water several times. When ready to cook, place meat in a saucepan with enough warm water to cover it. Bring slowly to a boil; skim well and then simmer gently until tender, allowing 25 minutes to the pound (450 g) and 25 minutes over.

After skimming, add onions, carrots, and parsnips or young turnips. When ready, place the meat on a hot serving dish; strain some of the liquid around it and garnish with vegetables. Use remaining liquid to make pea or lentil soup.

PETIT SALÉ AUX CHOUX

1½ lb (1.1 kg) pickled or salted pork
Bouquet garni
1 Spanish onion, stuck with 2 cloves
Peppercorns
1 medium-sized cabbage
Boiled potatoes (optional)

Wash pickled or salted pork and soak, covered, for 24 hours in cold water, changing water several times.

Put fresh water in a large heatproof casserole; add meat and bring gently to a boil. Skim well and add *bouquet garni*, onion stuck with cloves, and peppercorns.

Clean and prepare cabbage, and add it to boiling liquid. Reduce heat, and simmer meat and vegetables for about 2 hours. Remove cabbage and drain well; place it in a shallow serving bowl; place meat on top and surround, if desired, with boiled potatoes. The pot liquor will serve to make lentil or pea soup. Serves 4 to 6.

BOILED SALT PORK WITH
PEASE PUDDING

1 shoulder or breast of salt pork
6 large carrots
2 Spanish onions, stuck with 2 cloves
6 small leeks
6 parsnips

PEASE PUDDING
1 lb (450 g) split peas
1 Spanish onion, thinly sliced
Butter
3 eggs, beaten
Salt, freshly ground black pepper and
grated nutmeg

Place salt pork in water; bring to a boil; skim; add vegetables; bring to a boil and skim again. Then lower heat and simmer pork and vegetables gently until tender. Place the pork on a heated serving dish; surround with accompanying vegetables and serve with Pease Pudding.

PEASE PUDDING
Soak peas overnight in cold water. Place in a saucepan with sliced onion; cover with water and simmer gently for 2 to 4 hours, or until cooked. Purée. Combine purée with 4 oz (100 g) butter and

beaten eggs, and season to taste with salt, freshly ground black pepper and grated nutmeg. Mix well, put into a buttered pudding basin and cook in water in a moderately hot oven (400°F/200°C/GM6) until done; or place in a scalded, buttered and floured cloth, tie up and cook in the pot with the pork. Serves 6 to 8.

POTÉE BOURGUIGNONNE

1½ lb (1.1 kg) pickled or salted pork
6 sausages
4 oz (100 g) bacon
1 small cabbage
8 oz (225 g) turnips
8 oz (225 g) carrots
1 Spanish onion
Bouquet garni
Peppercorns
1 lb (450 g) small potatoes, peeled

Desalt meat by soaking for 24 hours. Put the salt pork, sausages and bacon in a heatproof casserole with cold water. Bring gently to a boil. Prepare cabbage, turnips, carrots and Spanish onion. Add to the *pot-au-feu* when it is boiling. And *bouquet garni* and peppercorns. Reduce heat and simmer for 1½ hours. Add peeled potatoes and cook for 40 to 50 minutes longer.

Drain vegetables. Place cabbage in a shallow serving bowl; place the salt pork on it and surround with sausages, bacon cut into thin slices, and vegetables. The *bouillon* will serve as the base for an excellent soup. Serves 6.

CHAPTER THIRTEEN
All About Poultry

The chicken has always been the symbol of prosperity. Politicians from Henry of Navarre to President Roosevelt have harped on its regular appearance at the dinner table as the ultimate aim for the masses.

Today, we have chickens *en masse*. New techniques of breeding and new methods of marketing have made this old-time luxury an everyday snack . . . but with the usual penalty. The birds we have now are far removed from the free-ranging chickens of Henri IV or even of Roosevelt's depression years. In plumping them up, mass production has removed some of the taste, a little of the pleasure . . . and it has faced us all with a new challenge. But with imagination and skill we can do much to give back to chicken dishes the splendour they had when they only reached the tables of kings.

One of the easiest foods to prepare, chicken is also one of the most versatile; it can be grilled, poached, braised, fried or roasted. You can barbecue it, curry it, serve it in red wine or white wine, in a cream sauce, or just plain roasted with a delicious stuffing.

Everything is good in the chicken – the neck, feet, wings, heart, liver, gizzard and fat. The French even eat cocks' combs as a deliciously delicate addition to a chicken casserole or fricassée. I am not suggesting that you go as far as this – cocks' combs are too hard to come by – but do use the fat to fry with; it would be very expensive if you had to buy it. And the other parts are excellent for making stocks, soups and gravies.

The flesh of broiler chickens, raised with special feeding in pens and not allowed to run, is very white and fine-textured. But I prefer those that are free ranging before being penned up for fattening. The meat has a firmer texture with much more flavour.

In judging a chicken, notice the bony lower legs and feet, which in a young bird are thick and heavy looking. As a bird ages, these become thin and dry. The breastbone of a young chicken is soft enough to break easily when pressed with the fingers.

Chickens are usually trussed for roasting. This is done to hold the legs and wings to the body to keep them from drying out during cooking. If they are not tied to the body, the heat spreads them out and they are apt to become dry and tough.

There are hundreds of different recipes for cooking chickens – every country has its own special chicken dishes – but in reality only five or six basic methods of cooking the bird are used in the preparation of all dishes: poaching, roasting, braising, sautéeing, frying and casseroling. Always ensure chicken is cooked throughly.

It was Naomi, my cook in Paris, who first revealed to me the possibilities of a chicken. I always remember her at work in my kitchen. Earthenware and terracotta casseroles, which she used for making *coq-au-vin* or for marinating fish and game, stood in neat rows on wooden shelves all along one wall. Against the opposite wall was a large, scrubbed, wooden table with a piece of marble cut in for pastry-making. The table came with the house, a gift, as it were, of the previous owners, and never before or since have I seen a piece of kitchen equipment so perfectly formed for its task. Over it, Naomi kept her large and small saucepans, copper and enamel for the most part, with one or two iron *cocottes*, hanging in rows. Whisks, wooden spoons and spatulas were kept in a large earthenware crock on the table, ready at hand to finish a sauce or whip up a mayonnaise. Naomi was most particular about her kitchen equipment and used to say that choosing the right casserole or saucepan was just as important as choosing the right ingredients.

My first introduction to the delights of French chicken cookery was *coq-au-vin à la beaujolaise* – a tender chicken sautéed until golden in butter and olive oil with a few *lardons* of fat salt bacon; flamed in cognac, and then simmered to tender perfection in red wine with tiny white onions and button mushrooms. I have since learned a whole gamut of chicken-in-wine dishes, specialities of the many wine-growing regions of France, but Naomi's will always linger in my memory as something very special. She also introduced me to *poulet à la MacMahon*, chicken poached in stock with celery, carrots, onions and herbs, served in a thickened Velouté Sauce to which she had added double cream, Madeira and a little freshly puréed tomato, to give a most delicate flavour and complexion. A richer relation of this dish was her chicken breast with *foie gras*. You will find the recipe on page 484.

But perhaps my favourite recipe of all was her *poule-au-pot*, chicken simmered 'in the pot' with pork and vegetables. This is a wonderful dish for a country luncheon or an informal winter dinner party. Naomi served it with a horseradish cream sauce, coarse sea salt and pickled gherkins.

Which Chickens To Buy

Broilers weigh from 1 to 2½ lb (450 g–1.1 kg). Half a broiler is usually considered a portion, except for the very large ones. Disjoint broilers for sautéeing.

Fryers weigh from 1 to 3½ lb (450 g–1.6 kg). The best ones have full, compact bodies and full breasts. They may be split, cut or disjointed for cooking, and are used for frying and sautéeing, and for roasting when a small bird is required.

Roasting chickens are used for roasting, for casserole dishes, and for most fricassées.

Boiling fowls are mature hens, the most flavourful of all chickens, although they require long, slow cooking. They range from 3 to 8 lb (1.4–3.8 kg) and are usually quite fatty.

Capons are unsexed male birds. They are large and delicately flavoured birds, used for roasting, braising, or poaching.

Poulardes are unsexed female birds with fine flesh and excellent flavour.

To Joint Poultry

Cut off the wings, taking a slice off the breast with them, and separating them at the joint. Remove the legs, cut them in two at the joint and chop off the ends of the bones. Then separate the breast, bone and all, from the back of the fowl. Cut the breast in half lengthwise right through the bone, and in half again if large. Then chop the back through in two pieces.

The number of joints depends very much on the size of the bird, but ten pieces at least should be procured from a good-sized chicken – two wings, four pieces from the legs, two from the breast and two from the back.

To Bone Poultry

Tell your butcher not to truss the bird as it will be firmer and easier to work on. Singe it, pick out any feather ends and remove the legs at the first joint, at the same time withdrawing the sinews. Cut off the neck close to the body, leaving a flap of skin to turn over in the usual way. Lay the bird on a chopping board breast down, and make a cut through the skin right down the middle of the back. Then, with the point of your boning knife, work down one side, raising the flesh as cleanly from the bones as possible, being careful not to break through the skin.

Disjoint legs and wings from the body, and continue removing the flesh from the carcass until the centre of the breastbone is reached. Then proceed with the other side of the bird in the same way, and lift the carcass out.

To bone the legs: take hold of the first bone where it was disjointed from the body and scrape the flesh off it until the next joint is reached. Crack the joint, and remove the first part of the bone. Remove the flesh from the other parts of the bone in the same way, turning the leg inside out. Bone the second leg, and then remove as much of the wingbone as possible, cutting off the lower joint entirely.

Spread the bird out on the table – skin side down – and remove any pieces of sinew or gristle. Trim off any discoloured bits at the neck or tail.

To Truss Poultry

Pluck bird and singe if necessary. Cut off the feet at the first joint. Cut the neck close to the body, leaving a piece of skin to tuck in. Draw the bird carefully, making sure that you do not break the gall bladder as you remove it. Wipe bird inside and out with a damp cloth. Reserve the feet, neck, liver, heart and gizzard for later use.

Lay the bird on its back and turn the wings under; bring the legs close to the body and pass a metal or wooden skewer first through flesh of the wing, the middle of the leg and the body; then out the other side through the other leg and the wing.

Pass a piece of string over each end of the skewer; bring it round the vent; fasten the legs tightly and tie securely.

BASIC BOILED CHICKEN

1 boiling chicken
½ lemon
Butter
Salted water or stock
1 Spanish onion stuck with cloves
2 carrots
2 stalks celery
1 bay leaf
½ pint (300 ml) Parsley or Chicken Velouté Sauce
(page 126 or 108) or a celery sauce
Bacon rolls or quartered hard-boiled eggs

Rub cleaned and trussed boiling chicken with cut side of ½ lemon and wrap it in a piece of well-buttered waxed paper to keep it a good colour. Put the chicken in boiling salted water, or better yet, a little light stock, with 1 Spanish onion stuck with cloves, and carrots, celery and bay leaf; allow it to simmer slowly until tender. Unless cooked slowly, the flesh will become hard and tasteless. The time will depend on the age and size of the chicken – from 2 to 3 hours.

When chicken is tender, remove from stock to a hot dish; remove paper and string from chicken, and mask it with Parsley or Chicken Velouté Sauce, or a celery sauce. Garnish with little rolls of bacon or quartered hard-boiled eggs. Serves 4.

BASIC STEAMED CHICKEN

1 roasting chicken
½ lemon
Salt and freshly ground black pepper
4 tablespoons (60 ml) butter
4 tablespoons (60 ml) chicken stock
2 tablespoons (30 ml) finely chopped onion
Parsley or Velouté Sauce (page 126 or 108)
or a celery sauce

Rub cleaned and trussed chicken with cut side of ½ lemon; sprinkle with salt and freshly ground black pepper, to taste; place it in a *gratin* dish just large enough to hold it. Add butter, chicken stock and finely chopped onion, place *gratin* dish in a large double steamer over 3 inches (7.5 cms) of rapidly boiling water, and steam for 1 to 2 hours, according to size of chicken.

Serve with pan juices, Parsley or Velouté Sauce, or a celery sauce. Serves 4.

GRILLED SPRING CHICKEN

2 tender poussins (young chickens)
Salt, freshly ground black pepper and paprika
Lemon juice
Melted butter
2 tablespoons (30 ml) browned breadcrumbs
Sprigs of watercress
Lemon wedges

Only very young and tender chickens can be cooked in this way. Split cleaned chickens open through the back, flatten and trim birds, cutting off feet and wingtips; wipe with a damp cloth, and season generously with salt, freshly ground black pepper, paprika and a little lemon juice. Skewer birds open; brush both sides with melted butter and sprinkle with fine browned breadcrumbs.

Grill over charcoal or under grill for 25 to 30 minutes, turning the birds occasionally and basting frequently with melted butter. Serve very hot, garnished with watercress and lemon wedges. Serves 4.

ROAST CHICKEN

1 roasting chicken
Stuffing
2 slices fatty bacon
Butter
1 tablespoon (15 ml) sifted flour
Watercress
Lemon juice
Salt
½ pint (300 ml) chicken stock
Freshly ground black pepper
½ pint (300 ml) English Bread Sauce (page 127)

Loosen the skin at the neck end of a cleaned and trussed roasting chicken as much as possible from the breast; insert stuffing over the flesh of the breast and fill the loose skin of the neck with as much as it will hold. Fold the skin over and fasten with 1 or 2 stitches. Stuff body cavity as well.

Tie 1 or 2 slices of fat bacon over the breast, making 1 or 2 slits in the bacon to prevent it from curling. Cover the bird with waxed paper and roast in a slow oven (325°F/170°C/GM3), basting frequently with butter, for 1 to 1½ hours, according to the size and age of the bird. Test it by feeling the flesh of the leg: if it gives way to pressure it is ready.

A few minutes before the end of cooking time, remove the paper and bacon; sprinkle the breast lightly with flour; baste well, and brown quickly.

To serve: put bird on a hot serving dish; remove the trussing string, and garnish with watercress seasoned with lemon juice and salt, to taste.

Pour away the fat from the roasting pan in which bird was roasted; add chicken stock and stir over a high heat until boiling, scraping in any brown bits from sides of pan. Season to taste with salt and freshly ground black pepper, and serve in a sauceboat.

Serve with English Bread Sauce. Serves 4.

ROAST CHICKEN WITH WATERCRESS STUFFING

1 roasting chicken (3½–4 lb/1.6–1.8 kg)

STUFFING
6 tablespoons (90 ml) finely chopped onion
6 tablespoons (90 ml) finely chopped celery
6 tablespoons (90 ml) butter
1 bunch watercress, finely chopped
Salt and freshly ground black pepper
4 oz (100 g) dry breadcrumbs

STUFFING
Simmer onion and celery in half the butter until soft. Add finely chopped watercress and season to taste with salt and freshly ground black pepper. Cook until all liquids evaporate.

Melt remaining butter, stir in breadcrumbs and add to watercress mixture.

Stuff chicken with this mixture and roast in usual manner.

BRAISED CHICKEN WITH TOMATOES

1 tender chicken
1 tablespoon (15 ml) olive oil
4 tablespoons (60 ml) butter
1 lb (450 g) tomatoes, peeled, seeded and coarsely chopped
1 clove garlic, finely chopped
4 tablespoons (60 ml) finely chopped onion
Salt and freshly ground black pepper
½ pint (300 ml) well-flavoured chicken stock
4–6 tablespoons (60–90 ml) dry sherry
1 tablespoon (15 ml) finely chopped parsley

Prepare and truss chicken. Melt olive oil and 2 tablespoons (30 ml) butter in a thick-bottomed casserole, and brown chicken in it on all sides. Melt remaining butter in a frying pan, and sauté tomatoes, garlic and onion until onion is soft. Add vegetables to the browned chicken; season with salt and freshly ground black pepper, and pour in the stock. Cover casserole; place in a slow oven (325°F/170°C/GM3) and simmer until chicken is tender. If necessary, a little more stock may be added during the cooking.

To serve: place chicken on a hot serving dish and remove trussing thread or string. Skim fat from tomatoes; add dry sherry; sprinkle with finely chopped parsley; correct seasoning and pour sauce around the chicken. Serves 4.

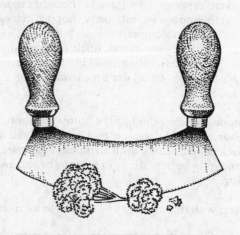

POULET SAUTÉ 'QUAGLINO'S'

1 tender chicken (2½–3 lb/1.1–1.4 kg)
Salt and freshly ground black pepper
2 tablespoons (30 ml) butter
Bouquet garni (2 parsley roots,
1 sprig thyme, 1 bay leaf)
1–2 tablespoons (15–30 ml) finely chopped onion
1 small clove garlic
1 glass dry white wine
1 lb (450 g) ripe red tomatoes, peeled, seeded and chopped
4 button mushrooms, simmered in
butter and lemon juice

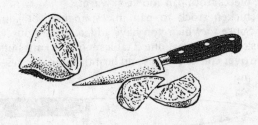

Cut chicken into serving pieces, reserving backbone. Season well with salt and freshly ground black pepper, and put chicken pieces, flesh side down, in a sauté pan or thick-bottomed frying pan just large enough to hold them comfortably. Add butter and sauté chicken pieces until they are browned on all sides – about 10 minutes.

Add backbone and *bouquet garni*; cover pan and simmer gently for 20 minutes. Remove wings and breasts after 15 minutes. They are the most delicate, and cook most quickly. Keep warm.

Remove remaining pieces and sauté finely chopped onion in pan juices until transparent. Add garlic and dry white wine, and continue cooking until wine is reduced to half the original quantity. Add tomatoes and simmer gently for 5 minutes more. Return sautéed chicken to the pan and allow it to steep gently, covered, over the lowest of heats for 5 minutes. Do not allow liquid to boil or your chicken will be tough. Garnish with button mushrooms which you have simmered in butter and lemon juice; serve immediately. Serves 4.

CHICKEN SAUTÉ ALEXANDRA

1 tender chicken (2½–3 lb/1.1–1.4 kg)
Salt and freshly ground black pepper
4 tablespoons (60 ml) butter
Bouquet garni (2 parsley roots, 1 sprig thyme, 1 bay leaf)
¼ pint (150 ml) chicken stock
¼ pint (150 ml) Chicken Velouté Sauce (page 108)
2 tablespoons (30 ml) cooked puréed onions
2 tablespoons (30 ml) double cream

Prepare chicken pieces, sauté in 2 tablespoons (30 ml) butter, and simmer as in basic recipe for Poulet Sauté on preceding page. Remove pieces from pan and keep warm.

Add chicken stock to pan juices; reduce. Stir in Chicken Velouté Sauce to which you have added cooked puréed onions, double cream and remaining 2 tablespoons (30 ml) butter. Strain the sauce over chicken pieces and heat through. Serves 4.

POULET SAUTÉ À LA CRÈME

1 tender chicken (2½–3 lb/1.1–1.4 kg)
Salt and freshly ground black pepper
4 tablespoons (60 ml) butter
Bouquet garni (2 parsley roots, 1 sprig thyme,
1 bay leaf)
½ pint (300 ml) double cream

Prepare chicken pieces, sauté in 2 tablespoons (30 ml) butter, and simmer as in basic recipe for Poulet Sauté on preceding page. Remove pieces from pan and keep warm.

Add cream to pan juices and reduce to half of the original quantity. Stir in remaining 2 tablespoons (30 ml) butter and strain. Add chicken pieces to strained sauce, heat through and serve. Serves 4.

POULET SAUTÉ À L'ESTRAGON

1 plump chicken
4 tablespoons (60 ml) olive oil
4 tablespoons (60 ml) finely chopped shallots
1 wine glass very dry white wine
1 glass water
Salt and freshly ground black pepper
1 lb (450 g) potatoes, diced
8 tablespoons (120 ml) butter
Finely chopped fresh tarragon
Finely chopped parsley

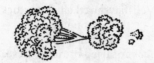

Clean a fine fat chicken and cut it in serving pieces (drumsticks, thighs, wings, and the carcass, cut into 4 to 6 pieces).

Sauté chicken pieces in olive oil in a heavy-bottomed heatproof casserole or iron *cocotte*, turning pieces often, until golden on all sides. Drain off surplus oil; add finely chopped shallots; stir well, cooking for another minute or two, until shallots are transparent. Add dry white wine and water (the water is to remove the acidity of the wine), and season to taste with salt and freshly ground black pepper. Cook, covered, for about 20 minutes, by which time the sauce should be reduced to half the original quantity. If not, reduce it over a high heat.

In the meantime, sauté diced potatoes in 4 tablespoons (60 ml) butter in a frying pan until they are golden.

Place chicken pieces on a warm serving dish; add diced cooked potatoes and keep warm. Add finely chopped tarragon and remaining butter to sauce in the casserole. Stir well; taste, and correct seasoning. Pour sauce over the diced potatoes and the chicken pieces. Sprinkle a little finely chopped parsley over it.

When you serve this dish, mix a little sauce into the potatoes so that they will be well moistened by it. Your sauce should not be too liquid, and there should only be about 2 tablespoons (30 ml) per person. Serves 4 to 6.

POULET À LA MARENGO

1 tender chicken
Salt and freshly ground black pepper
2 tablespoons (30 ml) butter
2 tablespoons (30 ml) olive oil
2 shallots, finely chopped
1 tablespoon (15 ml) flour
1 glass dry sherry
4 tablespoons (60 ml) tomato concentrate
Bouquet garni (4 sprigs parsley, 1 stalk celery,
1 bay leaf)
12 button mushrooms, sliced
Well-flavoured chicken stock
Lemon juice
Cayenne pepper
Croûtons of fried bread or crescents
of flaky pastry

Cut chicken into serving pieces, removing as much of the skin as possible. Season pieces with salt and freshly ground black pepper, and sauté in butter and olive oil until golden.

Sprinkle with finely chopped shallots and flour, and continue to cook, shaking pan, until shallots are transparent. Then add dry sherry, tomato concentrate, *bouquet garni*, sliced mushrooms and enough well-flavoured stock to cover. Cover the saucepan and simmer gently in a slow oven (325°F/170°C/GM3) until the chicken is tender.

To serve: arrange chicken pieces on a heated serving dish; skim fat from sauce; add lemon juice and cayenne pepper, to taste, and strain sauce over chicken pieces. Garnish with sliced mushrooms and *croûtons* or pastry crescents, and serve immediately. Serves 4 to 6.

FRIED CHICKEN STRIPS

1 lb (450 g) raw chicken breast
1 egg, beaten
2 tablespoons (30 ml) finely chopped onion
1 clove garlic, finely chopped
2 tablespoons (30 ml) cornflour
1 tablespoon (15 ml) soy sauce
1 tablespoon (15 ml) *sake*
1 teaspoon (5 ml) sugar
Salt
Fat, for deep-frying
Finely chopped parsley

Remove skin from chicken breast and slice across grain into
¼-inch (6 mm) wide strips. Place chicken strips in a bowl; add
beaten egg and finely chopped onion and garlic. Sprinkle with
cornflour, soy sauce, *sake* and sugar, and salt, to taste, and mix
well. Marinate chicken strips in this mixture for 10 to 15 minutes.
Then fry strips, one by one, in deep hot oil until golden. Drain.
Just before serving, fry again. Garnish with finely chopped
parsley and serve immediately. Serves 4 in Chinese meal; 2 as
main course on its own.

TWICE-FRIED CHICKEN

1 tender chicken (about 3½ lb/1.6 kg)
4 tablespoons (60 ml) soy sauce
8 tablespoons (120 ml) *sake*, or dry sherry diluted
with a little water
1 level teaspoon (5 ml) sugar
1 level teaspoon (5 ml) fresh ginger root,
finely chopped
Fat or oil, for frying
Cornflour, sifted

Bone chicken and cut the meat into 1-inch (25 mm) pieces.
Combine soy sauce, *sake* (or dry sherry diluted with a little
water), sugar and ginger. Marinate chicken pieces in this mixture
for at least 2 hours. Drain the chicken well, reserving marinade

juices. Dry the pieces and fry in deep fat until golden. Remove from fat and drain. Then add pieces to marinade juices, stirring well so that all pieces are coated by marinade. Allow to stand in marinade for at least 15 minutes.

Drain the chicken pieces; dust lightly with sifted cornflour and re-fry in deep fat until crisp and golden brown. Serves 4.

JAPANESE CHICKEN

1 tender chicken (about 3½ lb/1.4 kg)
2–4 tablespoons (30–60 ml) soy sauce
4–6 tablespoons (60–90 ml) *sake*, or dry sherry
diluted with a little water
1 tablespoon (15 ml) brown sugar
½ oz (15 g) ginger root, finely chopped
2 shallots, finely chopped
4 slices lemon, coarsely chopped
1 clove garlic, coarsely chopped
Cornflour
4 tablespoons (60 ml) peanut or olive oil

Combine soy sauce, *sake* (or sherry and water), sugar, chopped ginger root, shallots, lemon and garlic. Cut chicken into serving pieces; dust with a little cornflour and marinate in this mixture for at least 4 hours, turning chicken in juices from time to time. Place chicken in a shallow baking dish; sprinkle with peanut or olive oil and bake in a slow oven (325°F/170°C/GM3) for 1 to 1½ hours, basting from time to time. Serves 4.

EGYPTIAN LEMON CHICKEN

2 small chickens
4 tablespoons (60 ml) olive oil
1 clove garlic, finely chopped
Grated rind and juice of 1 lemon
¼ teaspoon (1.25 ml) dried thyme
Salt and freshly ground black pepper
4 oz (100 g) butter
2 tablespoons (30 ml) finely chopped parsley

Cut chickens into serving pieces and place in a shallow bowl. Sprinkle with olive oil, finely chopped garlic, grated rind and juice of 1 lemon, and thyme, and season to taste with salt and freshly ground black pepper. Marinate chicken pieces in this mixture for at least 2 hours, turning pieces from time to time.

When ready to cook: butter a rectangular ovenproof baking dish generously. Place chicken pieces and juices in dish and dot with butter. Cook in a slow oven (350°F/180°C/GM4) until tender, basting frequently. When tender, remove from oven, sprinkle with finely chopped parsley, and serve immediately. Serves 4 to 6.

POULET DU MARQUIS

2 small chickens (about 2 lb/900 g each)
2 strips bacon
Salt and freshly ground black pepper
4 tablespoons (60 ml) cognac
½ pint (300 ml) double cream
1 egg yolk
1 tablespoon (15 ml) butter

Truss birds; cover breasts with strips of bacon and place in a thick-bottomed casserole. Season to taste with salt and freshly ground black pepper. Roast in a moderate oven (375°F/190°C/GM5) for 30 to 40 minutes, or until breasts are tender when pierced with a fork.

Remove birds from casserole and slice off breast meat in single pieces. Keep warm. Remove remaining meat from carcasses and chop finely. Chop bones coarsely. Add chopped meat and bones to casserole, and simmer gently for 5 to 10 minutes, stirring from time to time. Skim off fat; add 2 tablespoons (30 ml) cognac and flame.

Whisk cream and egg yolk together and pour into casserole. Cook sauce gently, stirring continuously, until slightly thickened. Do not allow sauce to come to a boil or it will curdle.

Finish sauce by whisking in remaining cognac and butter. Correct seasoning, and strain sauce through a colander (to remove bones) on to chicken breasts. Serve immediately. Serves 4.

SPANISH FRIED CHICKEN

4 chicken breasts
Butter
2 leeks (white parts only), finely chopped
4 sprigs parsley
1 bay leaf
¼ pint (150 ml) dry white wine
¼ pint (150 ml) chicken stock
Salt and freshly ground black pepper
½ pint (300 ml) thick Béchamel sauce (page 104)
Flour
2 eggs, well beaten
Fine breadcrumbs
Oil, for frying

SPINACH PURÉE
2 lb (900 g) spinach
4 tablespoons (60 ml) butter
4 tablespoons (60 ml) chicken stock
Freshly ground black pepper
Thick Béchamel Sauce
2 egg yolks, well beaten
Salt

Place chicken breasts in a well-buttered shallow *gratin* dish with finely chopped leeks, parsley, bay leaf, equal parts dry white wine and chicken stock, and salt and freshly ground black pepper, to taste. Cover with a piece of well-buttered foil and 'poach' in a moderately hot oven (400°F/200°C/GM6) until tender. Allow chicken to cool in dish in which it was cooked; then drain.

Coat each breast with well-flavoured thick Béchamel Sauce and allow to cool on a wire rack until sauce is firm. Dip each breast in flour, then in beaten egg, and then in fine breadcrumbs, pressing breadcrumbs well against chicken breast with a spatula.

Just before serving: fry in deep hot oil until golden. Serve on bed of puréed spinach. Serves 4 to 6.

SPINACH PURÉE
Wash spinach several times in cold water. Combine in a large saucepan with butter and chicken stock, and freshly ground black

pepper, to taste, and cook over a high heat, stirring constantly, until spinach is tender – about 5 minutes. Drain and squeeze dry; chop and then purée in electric blender.

Combine spinach with a little thick Béchamel Sauce and beaten egg yolks; correct seasoning and reheat in the top of a double saucepan until ready to use.

CHICKEN WITH DUMPLINGS

1 large chicken (4–5 lb/1.8–2.5 kg)
2 pints (1.1 lit) water
1 teaspoon (5 ml) salt
4 carrots
1 Spanish onion stuck with 1 clove
2 stalks celery

SAUCE
3 tablespoons (45 ml) butter
3 tablespoons (45 ml) flour
½ pint (300 ml) milk

DUMPLINGS
8 oz (225 g) sifted plain flour
3 level teaspoons (15 ml) baking powder
½ teaspoon (2.5 ml) salt
3 tablespoons (45 ml) finely chopped parsley
¼ pint (150 ml) milk

To cook chicken: bring water to a boil in a large saucepan. Add salt, vegetables, and chicken, which you have cut into serving pieces. Bring to a boil again. Skim; reduce heat and simmer chicken gently for 1 hour, or until almost tender. Remove cooked chicken and vegetables from stock. Skim fat from stock, reserving 6 tablespoons (90 ml) for dumplings. Strain chicken stock and reserve.

SAUCE
Melt butter in a small saucepan; stir in flour until smooth; add milk and cook, stirring constantly, until sauce is smooth and creamy. Measure 1¼ pints (750 ml) of the chicken stock into a large casserole; bring to a boil and add cream sauce to stock,

stirring constantly; bring to a boil again and simmer for 5 minutes. Add chicken pieces to sauce.

DUMPLINGS
Sift flour, baking powder and salt into a mixing bowl. Stir in 6 tablespoons (90 ml) melted chicken fat and the finely chopped parsley with a fork. Add milk a little at a time, stirring with fork, until mixture is just dampened.

Drop a tablespoonful at a time on to chicken pieces in gently bubbling sauce. Cover and cook for 20 to 25 minutes, or until dumplings are cooked through. Serves 6.

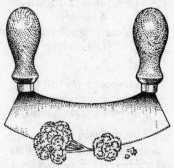

CHICKEN FRICASSÉE

1 tender chicken
Lemon juice
Salt
Chicken stock
Salt and freshly ground black pepper
Bouquet garni
Dry white wine
8 small white onions
2 tablespoons (30 ml) butter
2 tablespoons (30 ml) flour
8 button mushrooms, sliced
2 egg yolks
Double cream (optional)
2 tablespoons (30 ml) finely chopped parsley
Croûtons of bread fried in butter

To whiten chicken: clean and wash chicken; cut into serving pieces and put in a saucepan with juice of ½ lemon and enough cold salted water to cover. Bring to a boil; remove from heat and drain. Plunge into cold water for 5 minutes. Drain.

Place chicken in a saucepan with chicken stock to cover; add salt, freshly ground black pepper, *bouquet garni*, dry white wine and onions. Bring to a boil; skim; reduce heat and simmer gently until chicken is tender. Remove chicken pieces and onions to a clean casserole and keep warm in oven. Strain and reserve stock.

To make sauce: melt butter in the top of a double saucepan; add flour and stir until smooth. Pour in strained chicken stock and stir over water until boiling. Add sliced mushrooms and simmer gently for 15 minutes. Combine yolks with juice of ½ lemon (and a little double cream if desired), and stir in a little of the hot sauce. Pour egg and lemon mixture into double saucepan and stir until thick and smooth. Do not allow to boil or sauce will curdle.

To serve: place hot cooked chicken pieces and onions in a heated serving bowl; pour sauce over them and garnish with finely chopped parsley and *croûtons* of fried bread. Serve immediately. Serves 4.

CHICKEN PAPRIKA

2 young chickens (about 2½ lb/1.1 kg each)
Salt and freshly ground black pepper
4 oz (100 g) butter
1 large onion, chopped
1 tablespoon (15 ml) paprika
1 tablespoon (15 ml) flour
¾ pint (450 ml) good white stock
1 tablespoon (15 ml) tomato concentrate
¼ pint (150 ml) thick cream
Juice of ½ lemon

Rinse chickens and pat dry. Cut into serving pieces and season with salt and freshly ground black pepper.

Heat butter in a heatproof casserole or large iron frying pan; add onion and cook until transparent; stir in paprika. Add chicken and cook slowly until pieces are golden; then cover and cook 20 minutes longer, or until chicken is almost tender. Sprinkle with flour; add stock and tomato concentrate; stir well and cover. Bring to a boil and simmer for 20 minutes. Remove chicken to warmed serving dish. Stir cream and lemon juice into casserole; stir well, and cook for 5 minutes without allowing sauce to come to a boil. Pour sauce over chicken. Serves 4 to 6.

COQ-AU-VIN À LA BEAUJOLAISE

Young cock or roasting chicken (about 3 lb/1.4 kg)
3 tablespoons (45 ml) butter
2 tablespoons (30 ml) olive oil
4 oz (100 g) salt pork or unsmoked bacon, diced
12 button onions
12 button mushrooms
Salt and freshly ground black pepper
Flour
2 cloves garlic, finely chopped
1 sprig thyme
2 bay leaves
2 sprigs parsley
4 tablespoons (60 ml) cognac, warmed
½ bottle good Beaujolais
1 sugar lump
1 tablespoon (15 ml) flour
2 tablespoons (30 ml) finely chopped parsley

Cut the chicken into serving pieces. Heat 2 tablespoons (30 ml) each butter and olive oil in a heatproof casserole with the salt pork or bacon, cut in cubes. When the cubes begin to turn golden, add the onions and cook for a minute or two, and then add the mushrooms. Sauté the mixture gently until the onions begin to turn transparent and the mushrooms become brown; remove from casserole and keep warm.

Roll chicken pieces in seasoned flour and sauté them in the same fat for about 5 minutes, or until they turn golden brown on one side. Then, without piercing, turn chicken pieces over to brown on the other side. As each of the pieces begins to 'stiffen', remove it and put in a covered dish in a warm oven. When chicken pieces have been browned, return the onions, bacon, mushrooms, chicken segments and their juices to the casserole. Add salt,

pepper, finely chopped garlic, thyme, bay leaves and parsley:
cover casserole and cook in a slow oven (350°F/180°C/GM4) until
almost tender. Remove chicken pieces, bacon and vegetables
from the casserole and keep warm. Skim off excess fat from the
juices in casserole. Set casserole on a high heat, pour in cognac,
warmed in a soup ladle, and ignite. Allow to burn for a minute or
two and then extinguish by pouring in ½ bottle of good Beaujolais. Add a lump of sugar; bring to a boil and reduce the sauce
over a quick heat to half the original quantity. Thicken with a
beurre manié made of the remaining 1 tablespoon (15 ml) butter
and 1 tablespoon (15 ml) flour. Strain sauce into a clean casserole;
return chicken pieces, bacon and vegetables to the casserole; cover
and let simmer in a very low oven until ready to serve. Garnish
with finely chopped parsley. Serves 4 to 6.

CHICKEN EN COCOTTE

1 tender chicken
Salt and freshly ground black pepper
2 tablespoons (30 ml) butter
2 tablespoons (30 ml) olive oil
4 oz (100 g) fat bacon, diced
4 shallots, coarsely chopped
2 carrots, coarsely chopped
4 tablespoons (60 ml) cognac
4 tomatoes, peeled, seeded and chopped
Bouquet garni
½ pint (300 ml) red wine

Cut chicken into serving pieces and season to taste with salt and
freshly ground black pepper. Heat butter and oil in an iron *cocotte*
or a heavy casserole and sauté bacon pieces until golden. Remove
bacon; add coarsely chopped shallots and carrots; cook, stirring
constantly, until vegetables soften; add chicken pieces and brown
them on all sides. Return bacon bits to the pan; pour cognac over
and flame. Then add peeled, seeded and chopped tomatoes,
bouquet garni and red wine. Cover the casserole and let the chicken
simmer over a low heat until it is very tender. Add more wine or a
little chicken stock during the cooking if the sauce reduces too
quickly. Serves 4.

CHICKEN EN CASSEROLE

1 chicken
6 small white onions
4 carrots, diced
2 turnips, diced
2 stalks celery, sliced
2 bay leaves
½ pint (300 ml) well-flavoured chicken stock
Salt and freshly ground black pepper

Prepare and truss chicken. Put it in a heatproof casserole with peeled white onions, diced carrot and turnip, sliced celery and bay leaves. Heat chicken stock; add to casserole; cover and cook in a slow oven (325°F/170°C/GM3) for 1½ to 2 hours, or until the chicken is quite tender, basting occasionally with the stock. Season with salt and freshly ground black pepper. Cut chicken into serving pieces. Serve in casserole. Serves 4.

CHICKEN STUFFED WITH GRAPES

1 roasting chicken (4–5 lb/1.8–2.5 kg)
Salt and freshly ground black pepper
Butter
Dry white wine

STUFFING
4 slices dry crumbled bread
1 Spanish onion, finely chopped
4 cloves garlic, finely chopped
Butter
4–6 oz (100–175 g) white seedless grapes
6 tablespoons (90 ml) melted butter
1 tablespoon (15 ml) finely chopped parsley
¼ teaspoon (1.25 ml) dried sage
Salt and freshly ground black pepper

Rub chicken on the inside with salt and stuff it with the grape stuffing.

Skewer the opening. Truss the chicken and rub it with butter, salt and freshly ground black pepper. Roast the bird in a slow oven (325°F/170°C/GM3) for 1½ to 2 hours, or until done, basting from time to time with a little dry white wine. Serves 4 to 6.

STUFFING
Combine bread with onion and garlic which you have sautéed in a little butter, and grapes, melted butter, finely chopped parsley and sage; season to taste with salt and freshly ground black pepper.

POLLO ALLA ROMANA CON PEPERONI

2 small frying chickens
Salt and freshly ground black pepper
4–6 tablespoons (60–90 ml) olive oil
½ Spanish onion, finely chopped
½ pint (300 ml) dry white wine
1 lb (450 g) tomatoes, peeled, seeded and chopped
2 cloves garlic, mashed
2–4 green peppers, sliced

Cut chickens into serving pieces and season to taste with salt and freshly ground black pepper. Sauté chicken pieces in olive oil until golden brown on all sides. Add finely chopped onion and dry white wine, and cook over a high heat until wine is reduced to half the original quantity. Add chopped tomatoes and garlic; cover pan and simmer until chicken is tender.

In the meantime, sauté sliced green peppers in a little olive oil until tender. Serve with chicken. Serves 4 to 6.

ITALIAN CHICKEN WITH SAUSAGES

1 chicken (about 5 lb/2.5 kg)
2 tablespoons (30 ml) olive oil
1 Spanish onion, sliced
2 cloves garlic, sliced
2 oz (50g) sliced mushrooms
4 negroni or 8 chipolata sausages
1 medium can Italian peeled tomatoes
2 tablespoons (30 ml) tomato concentrate
6 tablespoons (90 ml) red wine
Salt and freshly ground black pepper

Heat olive oil in a thick-bottomed frying pan. Sauté onion and garlic in the oil until transparent. Add sliced mushrooms and sauté until golden. Remove and set aside. Sauté sausages in fat remaining in pan until golden. Remove; allow to cool and slice in 2-inch (5 cm) segments.

Cut chicken into serving pieces and brown in the fat. Return onion, garlic, mushrooms and sausages to the pan. Add tomatoes and tomato concentrate, and simmer gently for at least 45 minutes. Add the wine and cook for 5 minutes longer. Season to taste with salt and freshly ground black pepper. Serves 4 to 6.

POULARDE AU PORTO

1 plump chicken (about 3½ lb/1.4 kg)
4–6 tablespoons (60–90 ml) butter
8 oz (225 g) mushroom caps
4 tablespoons (60 ml) cognac
⅔ pint (400 ml) double cream
4–6 tablespoons (60–90 ml) port
1 level tablespoon (15 ml) cornflour
Salt and freshly ground black pepper

Cut chicken into 4 serving pieces and simmer gently in butter for 10 minutes, turning pieces from time to time so that chicken does not brown. Add mushroom caps; cover pan and continue cooking until tender, turning chicken pieces from time to time.

Place chicken and mushrooms on a hot serving dish; keep warm. Add cognac to pan, stirring well to scrape all crusty bits from sides of the pan. Stir in cream and port, mixed with cornflour, and continue cooking over a high heat until sauce is reduced to half the original quantity. Correct seasoning and pour sauce over chicken and mushrooms. Serve immediately. Serves 4.

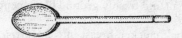

CURRIED CHICKEN

1 tender chicken
1 Spanish onion, finely chopped
1 clove garlic, finely chopped
2 tablespoons (30 ml) butter
1 tablespoon (15 ml) flour
1 tablespoon (15 ml) curry powder
¼ level teaspoon (1.25 ml) each ginger and turmeric
⅛ level teaspoon (0.6 ml) each paprika and cayenne pepper
Salt
1 level teaspoon (5 ml) sugar
1 tablespoon (15 ml) chutney
½ pint (300 ml) well–flavoured chicken stock
Juice of ½ lemon
6 tablespoons (90 ml) double cream
Plain or saffron rice

Cut the chicken into serving pieces and remove as much of the skin as possible. Sauté chopped onion and garlic in butter until transparent in a heatproof casserole. Coat chicken pieces with a mixture of flour, curry powder and spices, and sauté them with onion and garlic until golden. Sprinkle with salt to taste, sugar and chutney. Add a little chicken stock and cook for 10 minutes over a medium heat, stirring from time to time, adding a little more butter if necessary. Then pour in remaining stock and just enough water to cover chicken pieces. Cover casserole and simmer gently until the chicken is tender. Add lemon juice and double cream. Arrange chicken on a hot serving dish and pour the sauce over it. Serve with plain or saffron rice. Serves 4 to 6.

CHICKEN BREASTS WITH FOIE GRAS

Breasts of 2 young chickens
4 tablespoons (60 ml) butter
2 tablespoons (30 ml) olive oil
2 generous tablespoons (30 ml) *foie gras*
¾ pint (450 ml) double cream
Salt and freshly ground black pepper

Separate each half chicken breast into 2 *suprêmes* and sauté them gently in butter and olive oil, covered, until tender but not brown. In the meantime, rub *foie gras* smooth with 4 tablespoons (60 ml) double cream. Season generously with salt and freshly ground black pepper. Reserve.

To finish dish: remove chicken pieces from pan when cooked through. Keep warm. Add remaining cream to pan and bring to a boil. Blend *foie gras* mixture into the sauce and cook, stirring continuously, until smooth. Correct seasoning; pour sauce over chicken pieces and serve immediately. Serves 4.

Duck

There are three schools of thought on the cooking of ducks. One widely held theory is that for maximum flavour and succulence a duck should be roasted for 15 to 20 minutes per pound (450 g) at a high temperature (450°F/230°C/GM8). Another school of thought decrees that a slow oven (325°–350°F/170°–180°C/GM3–4) is the best means to bring about this end. The third school shambles about somewhere in between, starting the duck off in a hot oven (450°F/230°C/GM8) for 15 to 30 minutes, and then lowering the oven heat to 350°F/180°C/GM4, thereby getting the best, or worst, of all worlds. I find that cooking a duckling in a slow oven gives the best results, with a straight 350°F/180°C/GM4 temperature right through the cooking time.

Roast duckling usually served in Britain and America with garden peas and potatoes, or at most, with an orange sauce or *sauce bigarade* – is ennobled by the French into one of the great classics of all cookery: duckling *à la rouennaise*, sometimes called duckling *au sang* or *à la presse*. The original recipe dates back to the fourteenth century. The duckling is only about two-thirds cooked in the kitchen so that the process may be finished at the table before the diner. The partly cooked bird is cut into serving pieces at the table: the breast, cut into thin strips, is flamed in cognac and simmered in a wine sauce enriched with the duck's own blood, caught by crushing the carcass. The drumsticks and wingtips, scored lightly with a knife, brushed with mustard and grilled, are served separately.

To Choose a Duck

You can best judge the age of a duck by pressing its beak with your finger. A young duck's beak should be soft and flexible, while an older bird's beak will be hard and firm. The legs should be smooth and the webbing of the feet soft and easily torn. A duck is a very fatty bird, so you will need to use little additional fat when roasting. I usually cut all visible fat from openings before cooking, and pour off excess fat occasionally as it accumulates in the pan.

A good duck should have a plump breast, but it should not be over-fattened.

To Prepare Bird for Roasting

Singe and draw the duck, making a slit lengthwise above the vent to facilitate pulling out the inside. Then wash the bird quickly in warm water and dry it in a cloth. Cut off the feet and wings at the first joint, and season the bird with salt inside and out. It may now either be trussed and simply roasted, or filled with stuffing.

One of the simplest stuffings I know for duck is made of tart cooking apples and prunes. Take 3 to 4 apples according to size, and peel them; remove cores and cut them in small sections. Combine them in a bowl with 6 to 8 prunes which you have soaked and stoned. Season generously with salt, freshly ground black pepper and dried sage. Put this mixture into the body of the duck and sew up the opening. Then truss in the same way as you would a chicken, but do not cross the wings over the back.

To Roast Duck

Place duck, breast side up, on a rack in a roasting pan. Cover breast of the bird with buttered foil and roast in a slow oven (350°F/180°C/GM4) for 1½ to 1¾ hours. Remove foil from time to time and baste duck with pan juices. Remove foil 20 minutes before removing duck from the oven; dredge breast with flour and leave in oven until well browned. Transfer to a hot serving dish; remove trussing threads and strings, and keep duck warm while preparing gravy.

TO PREPARE GRAVY
Skim fat from juices in the roasting pan. Pour in stock made from duck giblets and stir in all crusty bits from sides of pan; add a little cornflour or a *beurre manié* to thicken sauce, and bring to a boil. Cook 2 to 3 minutes and season to taste with salt and freshly ground black pepper. Skim sauce and strain. Orange or lemon juice and the finely chopped cooked liver of the duck may be added just before serving. Garnish duck with a little watercress and serve the sauce separately.

ROAST DUCKLING FARCI À LA GRECQUE 'WHITE TOWER'

1 Aylesbury duckling (about 5 lb/2.5 kg)
1 cup *bourgourie* (Greek ground wheat)
Chicken stock
1 Spanish onion, unpeeled
Duck's liver, heart and gizzard, chopped
Butter
1 tablespoon (15 ml) finely chopped shallots
4 tablespoons (60 ml) blanched almonds, chopped
Sage, salt and freshly ground black pepper

Simmer *bourgourie* in chicken stock with 1 unpeeled Spanish onion until tender; drain. Peel onion and chop finely.

Chop liver, heart and gizzard, and sauté in butter with finely chopped shallots. Combine *bourgourie*, chopped onion, giblets and chopped almonds in a bowl, and mix well. Add sage, salt and freshly ground black pepper, to taste, and stir into *bourgourie* mixture.

Stuff duck with this mixture and roast as above. Serves 4 to 6.

CANARD BRAISÉ À L'ORANGE

1 tender duckling (5–6 lb/2.5–3 kg)
Salt and freshly ground black pepper
6 tablespoons (90 ml) butter
¼ pint (150 ml) Cointreau
1 tablespoon (15 ml) sugar
1 tablespoon (15 ml) vinegar
5 oranges
¼ pint (150 ml) beef stock
Watercress

Trim wingtips and cut off the neck of duckling. Wipe the bird with a damp clean cloth inside and out, and sprinkle the cavity with salt and freshly ground black pepper.

Melt butter in a deep heatproof casserole just large enough to contain duckling, and sauté duck until golden on all sides. Reduce heat; cover and simmer gently for 45 minutes, turning duck from time to time. Add two-thirds of the Cointreau and allow to simmer for a few more minutes.

Remove duck; add sugar, vinegar, juice of 1 orange and beef stock to pan juices; place casserole over a high heat and bring to a boil, stirring constantly, scraping all the crusty bits from sides of pan into sauce. Reduce to lowest possible heat and simmer gently for 10 minutes. Skim fat from surface and pass sauce through a fine sieve. Season generously with salt and freshly ground black pepper, and add remaining Cointreau. (Sauce may be thickened if desired.)

Peel 4 remaining oranges and separate into segments; place half of them in a saucepan; strain sauce over them and bring to a boil. Remove from heat.

To serve: place duckling on heated serving dish; pour a little sauce around it and garnish with remaining fresh orange segments and sprigs of watercress. Serve orange segments in sauce separately. Serves 4 to 6.

DUCK WITH TURNIPS

1 tender duck
2 tablespoons (30 ml) flour
Salt and freshly ground black pepper
4 tablespoons (60 ml) butter
4–8 young turnips, quartered
1 tablespoon (15 ml) castor sugar
1½ pints (900 ml) well-flavoured stock
Bouquet garni
1 Spanish onion, quartered

Prepare and truss the duck as for roasting. Dust with 1 tablespoon (15 ml) flour and season inside and out with salt and freshly ground black pepper. Melt the butter in a heatproof casserole; sauté duck on all sides until it is nicely browned. Remove the duck and add quartered turnips to juices in the casserole. Sprinkle with sugar and simmer turnips until lightly coloured. Remove and keep warm. Stir remaining flour into the fat left in the casserole until smooth, and pour in the stock. Bring to a boil and skim; add the *bouquet garni* and quartered onion, and season to taste.

Return duck to casserole; cover and cook gently for 30 to 45 minutes. Add turnips and continue cooking about 30 minutes longer, or until the duck and turnips are tender, turning duck occasionally during cooking time.

When ready to serve: transfer duck to a hot serving dish; remove strings, and arrange turnips around duck. Skim fat from pan juices; reduce sauce over a high heat, and strain over and round the duck. Serves 4.

DUCK EN DAUBE

1 tender duck
Salt and freshly ground black pepper
1 stalk celery, chopped
2 carrots, sliced
2 large onions, sliced
8 tablespoons (120 ml) cognac
¾ pint (450 ml) dry red wine
4 oz (100 g) fat bacon, diced
1 tablespoon (15 ml) olive oil
Bouquet garni
1 clove garlic
8 oz (225 g) mushrooms, sliced

Cut duck into serving pieces and place in a porcelain or earthenware bowl. Add salt and freshly ground black pepper, celery, carrots, sliced onions, cognac and red wine; marinate the duck in this mixture for at least 2 hours.

Remove duck pieces from the marinade; drain and dry with a clean cloth. Sauté diced bacon in olive oil until golden. Remove bacon bits, and brown duck pieces in fat. Place bacon bits and duck pieces with pan juices in a large heatproof casserole, cover, and simmer gently for 20 minutes.

Add the marinade, *bouquet garni*, garlic and mushrooms. Simmer over a very low heat for 1½ hours, or until duck is tender. Remove *bouquet garni*; skim fat; correct seasoning and serve from the casserole. Serves 4.

DEVILLED DUCK, CHICKEN OR TURKEY

6 portions cold roast duck, chicken or turkey
4 oz (100 g) softened butter
1 tablespoon (15 ml) Dijon mustard
1 teaspoon (5 ml) English mustard
1 tablespoon (15 ml) chutney
1 level teaspoon (5 ml) curry powder
1–2 tablespoons (15–30 ml) lemon juice
Salt and cayenne pepper

Score poultry with a sharp knife. Combine butter, mustards, chutney, curry powder and lemon juice in a mortar, and pound to a smooth paste. Season to taste with salt and cayenne pepper. Spread on cold duck, chicken or turkey, and grill until sizzling hot. Serves 6.

DUCK EN GELÉE

1 tender duckling
6 tablespoons (90 ml) butter
8 tablespoons (120 ml) dry white wine
1 pint (600 ml) veal stock
Salt and freshly ground black pepper
Bouquet garni (2 sprigs parsley, 2 sprigs thyme,
1 stalk celery, 2 bay leaves)
12 cubes fat bacon
12 young turnips
12 button mushrooms
12 button onions
2 tablespoons (30 ml) gelatine
Green salad

Clean duckling and sauté in 4 tablespoons (60 ml) butter in a heatproof casserole until golden on all sides. Moisten with dry white wine; bring to a boil; add veal stock. Add salt, freshly ground black pepper and a *bouquet garni*; reduce heat and simmer gently.

Sauté bacon cubes in remaining butter until golden; remove, and sauté turnips in resulting fat until golden. Combine sautéed bacon and turnips with button mushrooms and onions, and add to duckling. Simmer, covered, for about 1½ hours, or until duckling is tender and vegetables are cooked through, basting duckling from time to time. Remove duckling to an oval *terrine* just large enough to hold it, and surround with bacon cubes, turnips, mushrooms and onions. Strain stock through a sieve; cool and remove fat from surface.

Clarify the stock, and strain, while hot, through a sieve lined with a wet flannel cloth. Soften gelatine in a little cold water; stir into the hot stock, and pour over duckling, covering it. Allow to set for 12 hours before unmoulding. Serve with a green salad. Serves 4.

CANETON DE COLETTE

1 plump duck (about 5 lb/2.5 kg)
1–2 duck livers
Butter
Salt and freshly ground black pepper
Allspice
½ glass cognac
½ glass port
Stock (optional)

Clean, singe and truss a plump duck. Remove wishbone to help carving, and roast duck for 25 minutes, or until flesh is pink when cut. Sauté duck livers in butter for a minute or two until they stiffen but are not cooked through; add pan juices from duck, then mash livers with a fork and season generously with salt, freshly ground black pepper and allspice. Pour warmed cognac and port over sauce; ignite and reduce over a high heat to three-quarters of the original quantity.

Remove drumsticks and wings, and sauté in butter until cooked through. Remove breast of duck; cut into long fine strips; sauté in butter and arrange in centre of heated serving dish.

Cut carcass in half and press in a duck press to obtain as much blood and juices as possible (or cut duck carcass into 4 to 6 pieces and press each piece with pincers to obtain juices). Mix these juices with mashed livers, adding a little stock if necessary, and heat through until bubbling.

Arrange drumsticks and wings on serving dish; correct seasoning of sauce and strain through a fine sieve over strips of meat and drumsticks. Serves 4.

Goose

A plump, well-fattened goose is one of the most delectable birds there is. Like duckling, it needs slow roasting to bring it to the peak of succulent perfection. I like to place diced apple and onion, flavoured with a little finely chopped garlic and dried thyme or sage, in the cavity of the goose; rub it outside with coarse salt, dried thyme and freshly ground black pepper, and roast it in a moderately hot oven (400°F/200°C/GM6) for 15 to 20 minutes, or until fat starts to run, then reduce oven temperature to 300°F/150°C/GM2, and continue cooking for 25 minutes per pound (450 g), basting occasionally with a little white wine, butter and dried thyme. The skin should be pricked from time to time during cooking to release melted fat.

I once had a goose stuffed entirely with bruised garlic, and then roasted in the usual way. When I say usual way, this is an exaggeration, I am afraid, for this particular goose was spit-roasted over an open fire. It was absolutely delicious.

In Alsace, where goose-raising is one of the country's prime interests, I've watched true connoisseurs of roast goose stuff a bird with sausage meat seasoned with crushed juniper berries, and cook it in a wood-fired oven until its golden skin was drawn tight as a drum over the juicy succulence beneath. Served with sauerkraut and surrounded with slices of fatty pork and Strasbourg sausages, this was a dish fit for the gods.

I like, too, goose as it is prepared in Bordeaux; stuffed with a bread stuffing, seasoned with finely chopped onions, garlic and herbs, and served with sautéed wild mushrooms.

To Choose a Goose

A gosling – or 'green goose' as it used to be called in Britain – is a tender young bird, not more than six months old, with fine pink flesh and creamy skin. At their best from July to the end of August, goslings are very delicate in flavour.

A goose is an adult bird six months to one year old. The legs should be yellow and pliable, and the webbing of the feet easily torn. The bill should be yellow with few bristles and the underbill easily broken when bent. The breast should be plump, but without too much fat, and the skin smooth. A goose should not be eaten after it is a year old as the flesh becomes tough.

To Prepare a Goose for Roasting

Cut neck skin down the centre to the shoulder; free skin from neck and cut neck off as close to body as possible. Remove any pinfeathers. Singe bird if necessary, by holding it over a gas flame. Cut out oil sack over the tail. Then wash goose inside and out, and wipe dry. Rub neck and body cavities with salt and freshly ground black pepper; rub outside of body with a cut lemon.

Remove excess fat from goose in the following manner: lay cleaned goose on a rack in a roasting pan and place in a moderately hot oven (400°F/200°C/GM6). Cook for 15 minutes, or until fat begins to run, then remove goose from oven. Tip goose to let fat in body cavity run out, and pour off fat from pan. Return to oven, and repeat this process 2 or 3 times. The goose is now ready for stuffing. A goose really needs no trussing as wings are close to the body and the legs are too short to need trussing the way a chicken or a turkey does. After loosely stuffing neck and body cavities, tie a cord around leg ends to leave 3 or 4 inches (7.5–10 cms) between legs.

To Roast Bird

Place goose, breast side down, on a rack in a shallow roasting pan. Prick fatty parts of goose with a fork to help draw out remaining fat during cooking. Roast goose at 400°F/200°C/GM6 for 15 minutes, and then in a very slow oven (300°F/150°C/GM2) for 3 hours, pouring off fat during roasting as it accumulates. Then turn goose and cook for 1½ to 2 hours more, or until goose is nicely browned and the meat is very tender. You will find that long slow cooking at this temperature will cook out excess fat and leave meat juicy and tender.

ROAST STUFFED GOOSE

1 goose (8–10 lb/3.8–5 kg)
Melted butter
Salt and freshly ground black pepper
4–6 tablespoons (60–90 ml) Calvados or cognac
Dry breadcrumbs

STUFFING
1 Spanish onion, finely chopped
4 tablespoons (60 ml) butter
2 tablespoons (30 ml) olive oil
8 oz (225 g) sausage meat
2 tablespoons (30 ml) finely chopped parsley
Goose liver, heart and gizzard, cooked and chopped
2 eggs, well beaten
Juice of ½ lemon
Crushed dried thyme and sage
Salt and freshly ground black pepper
2–3 oz (50–75 g) dry breadcrumbs

STUFFING
Sauté finely chopped onion in butter and olive oil until transparent. Add sausage meat and sauté with onion until golden. Combine onion and sausage mixture in a bowl with finely chopped parsley, cooked and chopped liver, heart and gizzard. Stir in eggs and lemon juice, and thyme, sage, salt and freshly ground black pepper, to taste. Add breadcrumbs and mix well.

Stuff and tie goose; brush lightly with melted butter and season generously with salt and freshly ground black pepper. Roast in a preheated hot oven (400°F/200°C/GM6) for 15 minutes; reduce heat to 300°F/150°C/GM2, and continue roasting until goose is tender – about 25 minutes per pound (450 g).

Skim off fat several times during cooking and baste goose with pan juices. The reserved fat will keep indefinitely in a cool place.

If you cover goose with foil, remove foil at least ¾ hour before end of cooking time; 15 minutes before end of cooking time, flame goose with heated Calvados or cognac and sprinkle lightly with dry breadcrumbs; raise oven heat to 450°F/230°C/GM8 and cook for 15 minutes.

ROAST GOOSE WITH SAGE AND ONION STUFFING

1 goose
Apple Sauce (page 133)

STUFFING
8 oz (225 g) butter
1 lb (450 g) Spanish onions, chopped
6 oz (175 g) celery, chopped
1 loaf bread, freshly grated
2 eggs, well beaten
1 large cooking apple, peeled, cored and diced
1 tablespoon (15 ml) powdered sage
2 teaspoons (10 ml) salt
Freshly ground black pepper

STUFFING
Melt butter, and sauté onion and celery until golden. Combine with breadcrumbs, beaten eggs, diced apple, sage, and salt and freshly ground black pepper, to taste.

Lightly stuff the goose. Truss and place on a rack in a shallow roasting pan. Roast in a slow oven (325°F/170°C/GM3) for about 25 minutes per pound (450 g). Prick the skin occasionally to let the fat run out. Skim fat from pan from time to time. Serve goose with Apple Sauce. Serves 10 to 12.

'HOT OVEN' GOOSE WITH BAKED APPLES AND FRUIT TARTS

1 tender goose (8–10 lb/3.8–5 kg)
6 tablespoons (90 ml) butter
Crumbled dried sage leaves
Crushed juniper berries
Salt and freshly ground black pepper
8 cooking apples, peeled and cored
8 baked Fingertip Pastry tart shells (page 760)
Red or black currant preserve
4 tablespoons (60 ml) Calvados or cognac

Place the goose on a rack in a roasting pan and spread with 4 tablespoons (60 ml) butter which you have mixed with crumbled sage leaves and crushed juniper berries. Season generously with salt and freshly ground black pepper. Place bird in a preheated hot oven (450°F/230°C/GM8), and roast for 30 minutes. Spoon off excess fat and baste goose with pan juices. Return to oven and roast for 18 minutes per pound (450 g), removing excess fat from pan juices, and basting goose every 15 minutes.

Forty-five minutes before goose is done: place peeled and cored cooking apples around bird; dot each apple with remaining butter and continue to cook as above.

To serve: place goose on a large heated serving dish and surround alternately with baked apples and baked tart shells filled with currant preserve. Remove all fat from sauce; add Calvados or cognac; correct seasoning and spoon a little sauce over goose and each baked apple. Serve remaining sauce separately. Serves 8.

GARLIC GOOSE

1 tender young goose
2 Spanish onions, sliced
4 large carrots, sliced
Bouquet garni (2 stalks celery, thyme, parsley)
8 peppercorns
Coarse salt
4 tablespoons (60 ml) melted butter
2 tablespoons (30 ml) olive oil

GARLIC SAUCE
12 cloves garlic
¾ pint (450 ml) milk
4 egg yolks
¼ pint (150 ml) double cream
Salt and freshly ground black pepper

GARNISH
12 triangles bread, fried in butter
Black olives

Place cleaned and singed goose in water in a large thick-bottomed saucepan and bring to a boil. Remove scum from surface of boiling water; add sliced onions and carrots, *bouquet garni*, pepper-corns and salt, to taste. Skim again; reduce heat and simmer goose gently until tender. Remove from pan and drain; cut it into serving portions. Sauté the pieces gently in melted butter and olive oil until they are lightly browned on both sides. Keep warm.

GARLIC SAUCE

Cook 12 cloves garlic in milk until tender. Remove garlic, and mash 6 garlic cloves to a purée. Whisk yolks, cream and garlic purée in the top of a double saucepan until sauce begins to thicken. Add ½ pint (300 ml) of the hot milk and cook over hot water, stirring constantly, until sauce is thick and smooth, being careful not to let sauce boil, or it will curdle. Season to taste with salt and freshly ground black pepper; then add more mashed garlic if a more pungent flavour is desired.

To serve: place sautéed goose pieces on a heated serving platter and mask with Garlic Sauce. Garnish dish with fried *croûtons* and black olives. Serves 8.

GOOSE WITH SOUR SAUCE

1 tender young goose
2 Spanish onions, sliced
4 large carrots, sliced
Bouquet garni (2 stalks celery, thyme, parsley)
8 peppercorns
Coarse salt
4 tablespoons (60 ml) butter
2 tablespoons (30 ml) olive oil

SOUR SAUCE
12 oz (350 g) sorrel
6 tablespoons (90 ml) butter
4 tablespoons (60 ml) stock
8 oz (225 g) gooseberries
Sugar
4 tablespoons (60 ml) dry white wine
Salt and freshly ground black pepper

GARNISH
Sprigs of watercress

Poach goose. Cut it into serving portions and sauté pieces until lightly browned as in recipe for Garlic Goose on preceding page.

SOUR SAUCE
Wash and clean sorrel carefully; stew in 4 tablespoons (60 ml) each butter and stock until tender. Drain, reserving sorrel liquor. Cook gooseberries in a little water with sugar to taste until tender. Drain. Purée sorrel and gooseberries, and combine in a saucepan with remaining butter, dry white wine and ¼ pint (150 ml) sorrel liquor. Bring to a boil; reduce heat and simmer for 15 to 20 minutes. Season to taste with salt, freshly ground black pepper and sugar. Sauce should be tart.

To serve: place sautéed goose pieces on a heated serving dish. Garnish with sprigs of watercress and serve with Sour Sauce. Serves 8.

Turkey

Today, Americans chiefly regard Thanksgiving Day as an opportunity to display their prowess with turkey. How many realize, I wonder, that one of the earliest recorded New England Thanksgiving feasts included roast pork, deer, goose, pigeon, lobsters, oysters and clam chowder, as well as the traditional bird.

To Choose a Turkey

A good turkey can be recognized by the whiteness of its skin and flesh, and its smooth black legs. The wattles should be a bright red, the breast broad and plump, with the end of the bone tender. Beware of those long hairs and violet-tinted flesh. Turkeys are sold in three ways: oven-ready, frozen and dressed. Oven-ready birds are drawn and cleaned, individually packaged and ready for roasting, with cleaned giblets and neck in the cavity of the bird. They are often frozen. Dressed turkeys are not oven-ready. Sold with feathers removed, complete with head and feet, they are not drawn. Your butcher will prepare the bird for you; but ask him to weigh it again after it is drawn so that you can be certain of its weight for roasting times. Your dressed bird should weigh about a fourth more than an oven-ready bird, as you will lose a fifth to a quarter of its weight in drawing.

To Prepare Bird for Roasting

Remove any pinfeathers with strong tweezers or the back of a small kitchen knife. If necessary, singe bird by holding it over a gas flame. Then wash turkey inside and out, and wipe dry. Rub neck and body cavities with salt and freshly ground black pepper; wrap loosely in foil and store in refrigerator until ready to stuff.

Prepare stuffing just before you are ready to cook bird. Stuff body cavity loosely; stuffing will swell during cooking. Place a piece of dry stale bread in the vent of the bird after it is stuffed to help keep juices inside and avoid the bother of having to sew up the vent. Tie legs together with string and fasten the string around tail. Stuff neck cavity loosely; draw neck skin over cavity to the back and fasten with a metal skewer. Twist tip ends of wings behind back.

To Roast Bird

Rub turkey with softened butter and place, breast side up, in a roasting pan. Cover breast with thin strips of unsmoked bacon and then cover bacon with a piece of muslin brushed with melted butter to prevent bird drying out during roasting.

Roast stuffed turkey in a slow oven (325°F/170°C/GM3) for 3½ to 4 hours for a 10- to 12-pound (5–6 kg) oven-ready bird, allowing about 15 minutes per extra pound (450 g) of weight for larger birds. To let turkey brown and crisp, remove bacon and muslin 20 to 30 minutes before turkey is done.

TO MAKE GIBLET GRAVY
Wash giblets, and combine neck, heart and gizzard in a saucepan with 1 coarsely chopped Spanish onion, 1 bay leaf, 4 sprigs each celery leaves and parsley, salt and freshly ground black pepper, ¼ pint (150 ml) dry white wine and enough water to cover. Bring to a boil; skim; lower heat and simmer for 1½ hours, adding more water from time to time. Add liver and continue cooking for 30

---

minutes more. Remove heart, gizzard and liver, and chop pieces coarsely.

Skim fat from pan juices. Make a pale *roux* with 4 tablespoons (60 ml) butter and 4 tablespoons (60 ml) flour. Add ¼ pint (150 ml) dry white wine to roasting pan and cook over a high heat, stirring all crusty bits from bottom and sides of pan into sauce. Add enough stock (or stock and wine) to make 2 pints (1.1 lit) of liquid, and add to *roux*. Stir over water until sauce is smooth and thick. Chop prepared giblets and add to sauce. Correct seasoning and allow to simmer gently over water until you are ready to serve bird.

TURKEY WITH ORANGE SAUCE

1 medium-sized turkey (about 10 lb/5 kg)
1 orange
1 Spanish onion
2 tablespoons (30 ml) olive oil
Salt and freshly ground black pepper
¼ teaspoon (1.25 ml) dried rosemary
¼ teaspoon (1.25 ml) dried oregano
4 oz (100 g) butter, melted
4–6 slices unsmoked bacon
¼ pint (150 ml) dry white wine
Juice of 2 oranges
1 clove garlic, finely chopped
1 chicken stock cube

ORANGE SAUCE
Turkey giblets
2 tablespoons (30 ml) butter
2 tablespoons (30 ml) flour
Stock from giblets
Pan juices
Salt and freshly ground black pepper

Dice unpeeled orange; peel and dice onion. Toss in a mixing bowl with olive oil, salt, freshly ground black pepper, rosemary and oregano. Stuff bird loosely with this mixture. Brush bird with a little melted butter; season generously with salt and freshly ground black pepper, and place in a roasting pan, breast side up.

Cover breast with bacon slices and roast bird in a preheated slow oven (325°F/170°C/GM3) for 30 minutes. Baste turkey with basting sauce made of remaining melted butter, dry white wine and orange juice, seasoned with finely chopped garlic, chicken stock cube, and salt and freshly ground black pepper, to taste. Cover loosely with foil and continue to cook, basting frequently, until turkey is tender. Remove and discard orange and onion stuffing before serving. Serves 6 to 8.

ORANGE SAUCE
Cook giblets as in basic recipe on page 499. Chop. Melt butter in the top of a double saucepan. Add flour and stir until smooth. Add strained stock from giblets and pan juices (with fat removed), and cook over water, stirring constantly, until sauce is smooth and thick. Add chopped giblets; heat through; correct seasoning and serve with turkey.

TURKEY GALANTINE

1 medium–sized turkey (about 10 lb/5 kg)
Salt and freshly ground black pepper
1 level tablespoon (15 ml) mixed chopped herbs
(thyme, marjoram and rosemary)
1½ lb (675 g) veal
1 lb (450 g) fresh pork
8 oz (225 g) fatty bacon
8 oz (225 g) fresh breadcrumbs
Milk
Grated rind of 1 lemon
6 tablespoons (90 ml) finely chopped parsley
4–6 tablespoons (60–90 ml) dry sherry
2 tablespoons (30 ml) cognac
8 oz (225 g) cooked ham, cut in strips
4 hard–boiled eggs, quartered
¼ teaspoon (1.25 ml) mixed spice
4 tablespoons (60 ml) sliced pistachio nuts
Stock
Well–coloured aspic jelly (page 76)
Sprigs of watercress
Slices of orange and lemon

Bone turkey (see page 461) and spread it out on a board, skin side down; make it evenly thick by cutting off slices of breast and placing them over thinner parts of bird. Season generously with salt, freshly ground black pepper and mixed chopped herbs.

Put veal, pork and fatty bacon through the finest blade of your mincer twice, and mix with breadcrumbs which you have soaked in a little milk. Add grated lemon rind, 4 tablespoons (60 ml) finely chopped parsley, and sherry and cognac, and mix well. Spread this stuffing evenly over the boned turkey and then lay over it the cooked ham, cut in strips, and the quartered hard-boiled eggs. Sprinkle with remaining finely chopped parsley, mixed spice and sliced pistachio nuts, bring the two sides of the back together and sew up carefully. Wrap re-formed bird in a piece of muslin and tie securely at each end and around middle of bird. Simmer in a well-flavoured stock for 3 to 4 hours, or until tender.

When cooked, remove bird from stock and drain; roll bird into an attractive shape and then press it between 2 boards with a weight on top. When cold, remove muslin; wipe fat from turkey and glaze with well-coloured aspic jelly.

To serve: place galantine on a serving dish. Garnish with sprigs of fresh watercress, and orange and lemon slices.

CURRIED TURKEY

1½ lb (675 g) cooked turkey meat, diced
4 tablespoons (60 ml) butter
1 Spanish onion, finely chopped
2 stalks celery, thinly sliced
1 cooking apple, peeled, cored and diced
1 clove garlic, finely chopped
1 tablespoon (15 ml) curry powder
1 tablespoon (15 ml) flour
½ pint (300 ml) turkey or chicken stock
¼ pint (150 ml) dry white wine
2 tablespoons (30 ml) finely chopped parsley
Cooked rice

Melt butter and sauté finely chopped Spanish onion and sliced celery until onion is transparent; add diced apple, finely chopped garlic and curry powder mixed with flour; continue to cook, stirring constantly, until mixture begins to turn golden. Stir in stock and white wine, and cook the sauce, stirring, until it is smooth and thick. Add diced turkey and parsley, and simmer until heated through. Serve curried turkey in a ring of cooked rice. Serves 4.

DEVILLED TURKEY LEGS

2 turkey legs
Melted butter
1 teaspoon (5 ml) English mustard
½ teaspoon (2.5 ml) French mustard
¼ teaspoon (1.25 ml) curry powder
Cayenne pepper
Salt
Toasted breadcrumbs
Sauce Piquante, page 119 (optional)

Chop off the ends of the leg bones and trim each leg into 2 pieces. Score flesh several times, both along and across and fairly deep, and dip pieces into melted butter. Mix mustards with curry powder, cayenne pepper and salt, and spread this mixture over the legs, pressing it well into the cuts. Let legs stand for at least ½ hour before cooking.

When ready to cook, sprinkle with toasted breadcrumbs and grill for 7 to 8 minutes, or until nicely browned, basting turkey legs from time to time with a little more melted butter. Serve very hot. *Sauce Piquante* may be served separately if desired. Serves 4.

Guinea Fowl

The guinea fowl – in spite of its exotic appearance – is a domestic bird that lives in the barnyard with other poultry. Its plumage is dark grey dotted with white, and the flesh is darker in colour than that of the ordinary fowl. It really belongs to the pheasant family, and resembles that bird in flavour, except that it is inclined to be a little dry. Guinea fowl should always be larded before roasting, and requires careful basting. Roast in a slow oven.

Guinea fowl is often served in place of game when the latter is out of season. It can be cooked in almost any of the ways for chicken or pheasant.

ROAST GUINEA FOWL

2 guinea fowl
½ Spanish onion, halved
½ lemon, halved
6 juniper berries, crushed
½ teaspoon (2.5 ml) dried thyme
Salt and freshly ground black pepper
Melted butter

Place ¼ Spanish onion, ¼ lemon, 3 juniper berries and ¼ teaspoon (1.25 ml) dried thyme in the cavity of each bird. Skewer openings and truss birds; season with salt and freshly ground black pepper, and roast in a slow oven (325°F/170°C/GM3), basting birds with melted butter every 10 minutes. Serves 4.

GUINEA FOWL EN COCOTTE

2 guinea fowl
1 large cooking apple, coarsely grated
1 Spanish onion, coarsely grated
1 packet (3 oz (75 g)) Philadelphia cream cheese
6 juniper berries, crushed
Lemon juice
Salt and freshly ground black pepper
Butter
Olive oil
¼ pint (150 ml) dry white wine

Combine apple and onion with mashed cream cheese, crushed juniper berries, and lemon juice, salt and freshly ground black pepper, to taste. Stuff birds with this mixture. Skewer openings and truss birds; spread with well-seasoned softened butter. Place birds in casserole and sauté in a little butter and olive oil until golden on all sides; lower heat and add dry white wine. Cover casserole and simmer birds gently, turning them from time to time, until tender. Serves 4.

Pigeon

The pigeon is a very versatile bird which, when young, lends itself readily to many different ways of cooking, from the sophisticated elegance of boned squabs, stuffed with *pâté de foie gras*, set in a pastry case and glazed with Madeira-flavoured aspic, to the simpler homilies of pigeons *en cocotte*, the young pigeons braised in butter and a little dry white wine until meltingly tender, and garnished with diced sautéed potatoes and poached bacon.

To Choose Pigeon

The legs should be of a pinkish colour; when they are large and deeply coloured, the bird is old. The breast should be flat and plump. The tame pigeon – smaller than the wild species – is better for cooking. Tame pigeons should be cooked at once, as they soon lose their flavour, but wood pigeons may be hung for a few days.

For best results, cook delicate pigeons in a casserole or a covered baking dish in a slow oven (325°F/170°C/GM3). When they are very young and tender, they may be split and grilled.

PIGEONS WITH GREEN PEAS

2 young pigeons
4 tablespoons (60 ml) butter
8–10 small white onions, peeled
4 oz (100 g) bacon, diced
1 tablespoon (15 ml) flour
½ pint (300 ml) chicken stock
Bouquet garni
Salt and freshly ground black pepper
½ pint (300 ml) cooked green peas

Clean and truss pigeons as for roasting. Melt butter in a heatproof casserole and sauté pigeons, turning them over and over until browned on all sides. Remove pigeons; add onions and diced bacon to casserole, and sauté until golden; sprinkle with flour. When flour has combined with the butter, add stock and stir until mixture boils. Skim well and return pigeons to the sauce; add *bouquet garni*. Season to taste with salt and freshly ground black pepper; cover the casserole and simmer gently until the pigeons are tender.

When pigeons are cooked, transfer them to the centre of a hot serving dish and surround with peas and onions. Serves 4.

PIGEONS IN RED WINE

2 young pigeons
4 tablespoons (60 ml) butter
1 Spanish onion, finely chopped
1 tablespoon (15 ml) flour
½ pint (300 ml) red wine
Bouquet garni (thyme, parsley, bay leaf)
Salt and freshly ground black pepper
1 level tablespoon (15 ml) sugar
12 button mushrooms, sautéed in lemon juice
and butter
12 small white onions, simmered in red wine and
a little sugar
2 tablespoons (30 ml) finely chopped parsley

Clean pigeons and cut them in half. Melt butter in a large, thick-bottomed, heatproof casserole and sauté pigeons until well browned. Remove pigeons from pan and sauté finely chopped Spanish onion until golden brown. Return pigeons to casserole and sprinkle lightly with flour. When the flour is thoroughly mixed with the butter, add red wine and *bouquet garni*, and salt, freshly ground black pepper and sugar, to taste. Cover casserole and cook in a slow oven (325°F/170°C/GM3) for 2 hours. Fifteen minutes before serving, add cooked button mushrooms and small white onions to casserole.

When ready to serve: correct seasoning and sprinkle with finely chopped parsley. Serve from casserole. Serves 4.

PIGEONS WITH GREEN OLIVES

2 young pigeons
4 tablespoons (60 ml) butter
4 shallots, finely chopped
½ Spanish onion, finely chopped
4 oz (100 g) unsmoked bacon, diced
1 tablespoon (15 ml) flour
½ pint (300 ml) chicken stock
1 tablespoon (15 ml) finely chopped parsley
Salt and freshly ground black pepper
Thyme and marjoram
16 stoned green olives
4 tablespoons (60 ml) cognac

Clean and truss the pigeons as for roasting. Melt the butter in a heatproof casserole and sauté the pigeons, turning them over and over until browned on all sides. Remove pigeons; add finely chopped shallots and onion with diced unsmoked bacon to casserole, and sauté until golden; sprinkle with flour. When flour has combined with the butter, add stock and stir until mixture comes to a boil. Skim well, and return pigeons to the sauce with finely chopped parsley, and salt, freshly ground black pepper, thyme and marjoram, to taste. Cover casserole and simmer gently for about 2 hours, or until pigeons are tender. Twenty minutes before pigeons are done, add stoned green olives which you have blanched to remove salt and then soaked overnight in cold water and cognac. Remove cover and continue cooking.

To serve: arrange pigeons on a hot serving dish; surround with olives, and strain sauce over them. Serves 4.

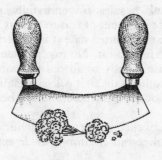

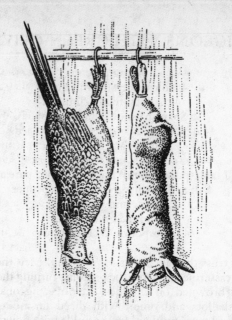

CHAPTER FOURTEEN
Game for Gourmets

I love game. I always have and I always will. I love it for two reasons, I think, besides its wonderfully special flavour. First of all: you cannot eat it out of season. On its appointed date it is shot. On its next appointed date it is preserved by law until it is once again perfect to eat. No eager restaurateur can ply you with early grouse in July or forced pheasant in June as he so triumphantly produces the first pale asparagus, and strawberries flown in from God knows where, months before they should be eaten.

To many city dwellers in our current civilization, the coming of spring and summer and autumn is made apparent only by the changing covers of their favourite magazines. The fruits and meats, the vegetables and herbs that marked their coming in the past and brought such constant fresh delights to the palate have now been so 'improved' by modern science that they are available all year round.

But game is game; the social stigma of eating it too early or too late has preserved it in all its glory. And with its coming, the second miracle happens: my favourite restaurants in France and Italy become renewed, revivified by its woodland delights for the precious months of the shooting season. It is in the autumn, not the spring, that chefs are reborn.

I have loved game since I was a child. My brother Jack was, in his own estimation, a great hunter. From the age of twelve he used to go out, equipped first with an air gun, later with a shotgun, and all through the season bring back bags of grey squirrel, wild rabbit, duck or pheasant. One of my earliest game memories was the squirrel pot pie which my mother used to make when he brought back a particularly rich bag of these small, smooth, firm-fleshed beasts. The flavour was exquisite: the squirrels – first carefully cleaned (the little oil sacs that give the squirrel its gamy flavour removed from back and forelegs) and then cut into serving pieces – were sautéed in butter until golden, perfumed with marjoram, bay leaf, shallots and garlic, moistened with red wine and tomatoes, and then simmered *en casserole* in the oven to just the right degree of moist tenderness. Perhaps the reason I liked this dish, and its preparation, best, was because I was often allowed a small glass of the red wine that went into it. And if Brother Jack's aim was sometimes a little wide off the mark, the dish was further improved, for me at least, by the little pieces of shot, like fugitive juniper berries, that could be found in the sauce.

As a boy, my father and brother used to let me tag along on weekend camping trips on which we used to subsist – except for emergency rations of baked beans, bacon, eggs and coffee – on the fish and game that were caught during the day. Butter-fried trout and 'sunnies' fresh from their natural habitat, served for breakfast with coffee made over an open fire, are the mouth-watering memories here; and once when Dad was host, home-made baking powder biscuits, cooked over the flames in a special tin oven brought along for the purpose, completed this outdoor meal.

It was on days such as these that I first learned how good a simple bird – wild pigeon, quail or pheasant – could be, freshly cleaned, rubbed inside and out with butter or oil and, for the sophisticated, a drop of whisky or brandy, and flamed over an open fire. The secret here was to baste them with melted butter in which any field herbs, rosemary, sage, etc., had been steeped.

In the country, in the early days of September, when it is still warm enough to enjoy the pleasures of eating in the open, I like to use an outdoor charcoal grill when cooking game. Grouse, partridge and pheasant are excellent when barbecued over the coals . . . as are tender young rabbits on the spit, and marinated venison steaks and chops.

BARBECUED GROUSE
Clean and split birds, and rub them well inside and out with seasoned butter. Grill over charcoal for 12 to 15 minutes, turning them once or twice during the cooking.

CHARCOALED PARTRIDGE
Clean and split the birds, and flatten them out. Brush with seasoned butter or oil. Cook for 15 to 20 minutes, basting occasionally.

WILD DUCK ON THE SPIT
Choose small ducklings. Rub well inside and out with a mixture of olive oil, soy sauce, crushed juniper berries and lemon juice. Spit birds on one long spit, side to side. Secure in place with long metal skewers and cook over a medium charcoal fire for about 20 to 30 minutes. Just before serving, flame with cognac.

I think the classic contention that all feathered game should be roasted or grilled often leads to disappointment with dry-fleshed game birds, for there is nothing so basic, nothing so difficult to do really well, simple though the process of roasting a piece of meat may seem to be. The very simplicity of the roast is what makes it so difficult. There is nothing to hide behind, no thick sauces with which to cover up mistakes, and the cook is limited to the most transparent of seasoning, the thinnest of gravies. If everything is not exactly right, the defects will stand out a mile.

So don't limit yourself to oven-roasted birds; serve them pot-roasted in a *cocotte* or casserole with a little butter and a choice of aromatics: the delicate flavour of shallots, finely chopped with a hint of garlic, fresh tarragon, wild marjoram, the ginny power of the juniper berry, the sharp tang of lemon or the earthy aroma of white truffles. For less tender birds, a *daube*, the age-old French manner of cooking meat, poultry or game, in which the flesh is cut into serving pieces, marinated in red or white wine with sliced onions, carrots, garlic and bay leaf, wiped dry and then sautéed in butter until golden. The marinade is then added to the casserole and the whole is simmered in the lowest of ovens until rich and moistly tender.

Cooking game in a casserole also has the advantage of allowing the host-cum-cook to entertain with no last-minute worries about serving and carving. I well remember one memorable dinner when the guests were called for seven-thirty and dinner was to be served at eight. One of the two guests of honour, through no fault of her own, did not arrive until eight-thirty, and pheasant cooked *à la souvarov* saved the day. This deliciously fragrant casserole combines pheasant, cut in serving pieces and sautéed in butter, with red wine, port, *foie gras* and truffles. It is then simmered gently in a hermetically sealed casserole in the lowest of ovens until ready to be called for.

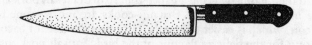

To Prepare Game

Whether you beg, bag or buy your game, it is best to leave the initial preparations to the skilled hands of the professional. Most butchers and poulterers will clean and pluck game for you for a nominal charge.

If you must pluck it yourself, do not scald the bird before plucking. Pluck it dry by pulling the feathers downwards in the direction they grow to avoid the skin being ripped. Start at the top with the neck and wings, then the body and tail. When plucked, pass the bird over a flame to remove any tiny feathers that remain . . . and if you have trouble picking these small feathers out, try the trick of a friend of mine, amateur hunter-cum-cook, who pours melted paraffin wax over the bird, allows it to cool and then removes it. All the down, he claims, adheres to the wax.

To Draw Game

Slit the neck skin from the breast towards the head, making an incision just large enough to remove the crop and windpipe. Then make another incision from the vent to the abdomen. Remove the innards, taking care not to break the gall bladder, which is attached to the liver. Wipe the abdominal and neck cavities with a damp cloth and then, just before cooking, clean the body and neck cavities again with a little cold water, cut off the wings at the second joint, and remove the oil glands at the base of the tail.

The most frequent crime committed by cooks against game birds is to allow the birds to dry out during cooking, which destroys their delicate wild flavour. All game, because of its natural life, is firmer, darker and less fatty than domestic meat, and requires 'larding' or 'barding' before cooking.

To Bard Game

To prevent game birds from drying out in cooking, French chefs bard their game by tying a paper-thin strip of fat salt pork around the body of the bird. In Britain, cooks are more prone to use bacon, which is easier to handle, but I find the taste of bacon too strong for the delicate flavour of the bird. Fat salt pork, used to bard game and to line game pâtés and *terrines*, is a far more subtle 'moisturizer'.

To Lard Game

Game, particularly rabbit, hare and venison, is much improved if long strips of fat salt pork are threaded through the meat to act as internal 'moisturizers' during cooking time. A professional larding needle is necessary for this operation.

Stuffing, too, can be used to advantage as an internal basting, but it must be moist enough to do this job to perfection. I like to grease my birds on the inside with a pastry brush dipped in melted butter or olive oil, before stuffing with a moist dressing in which onion or shallot, apple or lemon peel play their part. Of course, it would be unwise to stuff a small bird that takes only 15 minutes to cook with a long, slow-cooking stuffing. In this case I like to use the moistener suggested to me by the late Gilbert Harding, who used to pride himself on his cooking. A piece of raw steak and half an unpeeled apple made up his secret; particularly good with partridge.

To Joint Game Birds

Cut off the wings, taking a slice off the breast with them and separating them at the joint. Remove the legs, cut them in two at the joint and chop off the ends of the bones. Then separate the breast, bone and all, from the back of the birds. Cut the breast in half lengthwise, right through the bone, and in half again, if large. Then chop the back through in two pieces. The number of joints depends very much on the size of the bird.

To Bone Game Birds

Tell your butcher not to truss the bird as it will be firmer and easier to work on. Singe it, pick out any feather ends and remove the legs at the knee joint, at the same time withdrawing the sinews. Cut the neck off close to the body, leaving a flap of skin to turn over in the usual way. Lay the bird on a chopping board breast down, and make a cut through the skin right down the middle of the back. Then, with the point of your boning knife, work down one side, raising the flesh as cleanly from the bones as possible, and taking care not to break through the skin.

Disjoint legs and wings from the body, and continue removing the flesh from the carcass until the centre of the breastbone is reached. Then proceed with the other side of the bird in the same way, and lift the carcass out.

To bone the legs: take hold of the first bone where it was disjointed from the body, and scrape the flesh off it until the next joint is reached. Crack the joint and remove the first part of the bone. Remove the flesh from the other parts of the bone in the same way, turning the leg inside out. Bone the second leg, and then remove as much of the wingbone as possible, cutting off the lower joint entirely.

Spread the bird out on the table – skin side down – and remove any pieces of sinew or gristle. Trim off any discoloured bits at the back or tail.

To Truss Game Birds

Pluck bird; singe if necessary. Cut off the feet at the first joint. Cut the neck close to the body, leaving a piece of skin to tuck in. Draw the bird carefully, taking care not to break the gall bladder as you remove it. Wipe bird inside and out with a damp cloth. Reserve the feet, neck, liver, heart and gizzard for later use.

Lay the bird on its back and turn the wings under; bring the legs close to the body and pass a metal or wooden skewer through, first through the flesh of the wing, middle of the leg and the body; then out the other side through the other leg and wing.

Pass a piece of string over each end of the skewer; bring round the vent; fasten the legs tightly and tie securely.

Grouse

Grouse is the one succulent game bird that the British can really call their own. French gourmets are apt to lick their lips at the very mention of '*le grouse*', but unless they come over to shoot in Scotland or Northern England, chances are they have never tasted the real thing.

A mild-flavoured bird whose taste improves with hanging, its rich, dark meat needs only brief cooking. Some cooks like their grouse hung until it is quite high; I, for one, prefer it when it is not too ripe. The first grouse of the season marks the opening of a major culinary event in the gastronomic calendar . . . and gourmets feast on them as eagerly as they feast on the first strawberries or asparagus of the season.

Grouse shot from mid-August to mid-October of the year in which they have been bred are considered by many to be the best of all game birds. Young grouse need no great sauces. Plain roast, or at most planked, grilled, or cooked in a little butter *en cocotte*, is all the attention they need. Of course, if more grouse than we expect come our way, why say no to a grouse pie, potted grouse or a game pâté in which the distinctive flavour of a young grouse plays its part?

Grouse should never be overcooked. They should be larded or barded and carefully basted with fat during cooking time to keep them moist – 15 to 20 minutes cooking time for very young birds; 25 to 30 minutes for fatter ones.

The traditional accompaniment to roast grouse is a *croûton* of bread, cut in a rectangle just large enough to fit the grouse, and fried in clarified butter and a little olive oil. The grouse livers, drawn from the bird half-way through its cooking time and allowed to continue to cook in the pan juices, are pounded, spread on the *croûton* and seasoned with a little salt and cayenne pepper. Watercress, a little clear gravy, bread sauce or toasted bread-crumbs, and tart rowan or red currant jelly are often served as well.

Grouse are usually served whole. As the birds fatten – from mid-September to mid-October – they become large enough to split in two.

More mature birds are better pot-roasted in a *cocotte* or casserole with a little butter, some finely chopped shallots or onion and a hint of garlic. I sometimes add a little wild marjoram or crushed juniper berries for extra flavour; or, for more special occasions, sliced white truffles.

ROAST GROUSE

4 young grouse (¾–1 lb/350–450 g each)
4 tablespoons (60 ml) softened butter
Juice of 1 lemon
Salt and freshly ground black pepper
4 slices bacon
4 *croûtons* big enough to serve as base for grouse
Clarified butter
1 tablespoon (15 ml) olive oil
Cayenne pepper
Watercress, Bread Sauce (page 127) or
browned breadcrumbs, and redcurrant jelly

Combine softened butter and lemon juice in a mixing bowl, and add salt and freshly ground black pepper, to taste. Stuff birds with this mixture. Tie a thin slice of fat bacon over the breast of each bird and roast in a fairly hot oven (425°F/220°C/GM7) for 20 to 25 minutes. When birds are half cooked, remove livers; mash them slightly and place in pan to cook with grouse until birds are tender.

Just before serving, fry *croûtons* in a little clarified butter and olive oil until golden. Spread with mashed livers and crusty bits from pan, and season to taste with salt and cayenne pepper.

To serve: remove bacon and string; place 1 bird on each *croûton* and arrange on a heated serving dish. Serve with watercress, Bread Sauce or browned breadcrumbs, and red currant jelly. Serves 4.

SPATCHCOCKED GROUSE

Very tender, young grouse
Salt and freshly ground black pepper
Finely chopped parsley and shallots (optional)
Melted butter
Dried thyme or crushed juniper berries
Maître d'hôtel Butter (page 130)
Game potato chips or grilled mushrooms

Only very young and tender birds can be prepared in this way. Split them through the back without separating the halves, wipe the pieces carefully with a damp cloth and skewer them open. Season with salt and pepper and, if liked, a little finely chopped parsley and shallot. Brush birds on both sides with melted butter and season generously with salt, freshly ground black pepper and a little dried thyme or crushed juniper berries. Grease grid and make it very hot. Place the birds on it, and grill them over a high heat, turning them occasionally and brushing them with more butter when necessary. Cooking time will depend very much on the size and thickness of the grouse. When cooked to your liking (grouse should never be overcooked), place the birds on a very hot dish with a pat of Maître d'hôtel Butter on the top of each one. Garnish with game potato chips or grilled mushrooms.

GROUSE EN COCOTTE

2 tender grouse
6 oz (150 g) fatty bacon
Salt and freshly ground black pepper
2 tablespoons (30 ml) butter
2 tablespoons (30 ml) olive oil
4 shallots, coarsely chopped
2 carrots, coarsely chopped
2 tablespoons (30 ml) cognac
Bouquet garni
¼ pint (150 ml) red wine
¼ pint (150 ml) well-flavoured stock

Have your poulterer prepare birds for roasting. Place a layer of fat bacon over breasts. Season birds to taste with salt and freshly ground black pepper. Heat butter and oil in an iron *cocotte* or a heavy casserole, and sauté 4 oz (100 g) diced fat bacon until golden. Remove bacon; add chopped shallots and carrots, and cook, stirring constantly, until vegetables soften; then add grouse and brown well on all sides. Return bacon pieces to the pan; pour over cognac, and flame. Then add *bouquet garni*, red wine and well-flavoured stock. Cover the casserole and let the birds simmer over a low heat until tender. Add more wine or stock if the sauce reduces too quickly while cooking. Serves 4.

SALMIS OF GROUSE

3 grouse
6 tablespoons (90 ml) red or dry white wine
6 tablespoons (90 ml) rich beef stock
2 lemons
Salt, freshly ground black pepper and nutmeg
1–2 level tablespoons (15–30 ml) dry mustard
2½ oz (65 g) sliced mushrooms
1 tablespoon (15 ml) butter
1 tablespoon (15 ml) flour
2 tablespoons (30 ml) finely chopped parsley

Roast grouse slightly (until about half cooked) and cut them into serving pieces. Be sure to cut birds on a carving dish to catch blood and juices. Arrange pieces in a large shallow heatproof casserole.

Crush livers and giblets into serving dish with juices; add red or dry white wine, beef stock and juice of 2 lemons; stir in the finely grated peel of 1 lemon and season to taste with salt, freshly ground black pepper, nutmeg and mustard.

Add sliced mushrooms and pour this mixture over birds in casserole; cook until heated through, stirring so that each piece of meat is thoroughly moistened and is kept from sticking to the dish.

Do not let the *salmis* come to a boil. Just before serving, stir in a *beurre manié* made of butter and flour. Sprinkle with finely chopped parsley. Serves 6.

Partridge

The monks of the Grande Chartreuse, self-denying Carthusians who live on vegetables and are strictly forbidden the flesh of bird or beast, are credited with inventing a famous French recipe, the *chartreuse* of partridge, for days of feasting. This country dish, whether or not the partridges were concealed in the cabbage to satisfy the consciences of the fasting friars, is a delicious way of dealing with older birds.

But partridge is at its best when young. After the bird is one year old, its flesh becomes dry and hard. Young partridges, with their delicate, fragile, gamy flavour, should be hung for at least 4 days, then surrounded with a paper-thin strip of fat bacon or fat salt pork, and roasted or pot-roasted in a casserole until tender.

One of the best partridge dishes I ever had – and also one of the simplest – was a casserole of partridge cooked in lentils that I first tasted at Il Grande Ristorante Fagiano, at the back of the Piazza Colonna in Rome.

'Il Fagiano' – now defunct, alas – was a dimly lit, red-plush-banquetted hangover from another, more serious era, which catered, when I knew it, mainly for politicians and financiers, with an occasional editor from the neighbouring *Corriere della sera* and a pleasure-loving *monsignore* thrown in. It was, in fact, a restaurant for men who knew how to eat. And their greatest season was the autumn, when they could have their way with pheasant – after which the restaurant was named – and with partridge and woodcock and snipe. Il Fagiano's cooking – like its clientele and its décor – was serious, a little heavy perhaps, but filled with the lusty simplicity of the good things of living. I have passed many a memorable luncheon there, feasting on partridge with lentils or pheasant with white truffles, from time to time toasting the tall shaft of the column of Marcus Aurelius through the red sunlight of a Barbero Rosso or a Valpolicella.

ROAST PARTRIDGE
Clean bird carefully, wiping it both inside and out with a damp cloth, but do not wash it. Then take a piece of butter the size of a nutmeg, work it up with a little salt and freshly ground black pepper and a squeeze of lemon juice, and put this inside the body along with the liver. Truss bird; tie a slice of fat bacon over the breast; and roast in a fairly hot oven (425°F/220°C/GM7) for 25 to 45 minutes, basting frequently with butter or bacon fat, as the flesh of the partridge is inclined to be dry. Remove the slice of fatty bacon a few minutes before serving, dredge the breast with flour and roast again until nicely browned. The time required for roasting will depend very much on the age and size of the bird – a young and tender bird will be sufficiently cooked in 25 to 30 minutes, while an older one will require ¾ hour. When ready to serve, transfer the bird to a hot serving dish and remove the trussing thread or string.

Serve with watercress, Bread Sauce (page 127) or browned breadcrumbs, and a good brown gravy made in the roasting pan.

PARTRIDGES AU GRATIN
Cut 2 roasted partridges into serving pieces and warm through in a little hot stock. Drain pieces and sauté for a few moments in butter to which you have added breadcrumbs, finely chopped parsley, chives and shallots, and salt and freshly ground black pepper, to taste. Sprinkle with breadcrumbs and serve immediately.

STUFFED GAME CASSEROLE

2 partridges or pheasants
4 oz (100 g) lean veal, finely chopped
4 oz (100 g) lean ham, finely chopped
6 tablespoons (90 ml) cognac
Salt and freshly ground black pepper
Spices
Fatty salt pork or fatty bacon
4 tablespoons (60 ml) butter
2 tablespoons (30 ml) olive oil
2 shallots, finely chopped
1 lb (450 g) button mushrooms
2 cloves garlic
Juice of ½ lemon

Clean partridge and stuff with the following mixture: finely chopped livers and hearts of the birds combined with finely chopped veal and ham, moistened with cognac and flavoured with salt, pepper and spices.

Truss birds firmly and wrap each one in fatty salt pork or a slice of fat bacon; place in a fireproof casserole with 2 tablespoons (30 ml) butter, the olive oil and finely chopped shallots. Cover casserole and simmer partridges until tender.

Sauté mushrooms in remaining butter with garlic cloves. Season well and pour over partridges. Finish cooking on an asbestos mat on top of the stove or in a low oven; just before serving, sprinkle with lemon juice. Serves 4.

PARTRIDGE WITH CABBAGE

1 partridge (over 1 year old)
2 small cabbages
Salt
4 oz (100 g) ham or lean bacon
2 tablespoons (30 ml) butter or dripping
2 large carrots, coarsely chopped
1 Spanish onion
1–2 cloves
Bouquet garni
2 small smoked sausages
Freshly ground black pepper
Well-flavoured stock

Trim the cabbages; cut in pieces and wash well. Cook cabbage in boiling salted water for 10 to 12 minutes. Then strain and press out the water. Blanch ham or bacon for a few minutes to remove some of the salt. Melt butter or dripping in a casserole; put in the partridge, trussed as for roasting, and brown it on all sides. Remove partridge; add half the cabbage with the chopped carrots, the onion stuck with the cloves, and a *bouquet garni*. Lay the partridge, ham and sausages on top, and cover with remaining cabbage. Season with freshly ground black pepper; moisten with stock; cover and simmer gently, in the oven if possible, or at simmering point over a very low heat, until partridge is tender – 1½ to 2 hours.

To serve: remove the partridge, ham and sausages from the saucepan. Cut the partridge into neat joints, and slice the ham and sausages. Remove the carrot, onion and *bouquet garni*. Arrange cabbage on a hot serving dish; place the partridge pieces on top, and garnish with sliced ham and sausage. Serves 4.

CASSEROLED PARTRIDGE

2 partridges
4 tablespoons (60 ml) melted butter
Salt and freshly ground black pepper
4 tablespoons (60 ml) shredded bread
2 tablespoons (30 ml) finely chopped ham
4–6 juniper berries, crushed
Grated rind of ½ lemon
Marjoram
Fatty salt pork
6 tablespoons (90 ml) dry white wine
¼ pint (150 ml) rich chicken stock
1 carrot, finely chopped
1 small onion, finely chopped

Clean partridges inside and out. Brush cavities with a little of the melted butter, and season liberally with salt and pepper. Combine remaining melted butter, shredded bread, chopped ham, crushed juniper berries and grated lemon rind; season to taste with salt, freshly ground black pepper and marjoram, and stuff birds with this mixture.

Truss birds; wrap a thin piece of fat salt pork around each one and roast in a casserole in a moderate oven (375°F/190°C/GM5) with dry white wine, chicken stock, and finely chopped carrot and onion, basting from time to time, for about 1 hour, or until tender. Serves 4.

VEAL AND PARTRIDGE PIE

8 oz (225 g) lean veal
8 oz (225 g) lean pork
4 oz (100 g) fatty salt pork
Salt and freshly ground black pepper
Parsley, marjoram and thyme, finely chopped
1 plump partridge
4 oz (100 g) bacon, diced
¼ pint (150 ml) beef stock
Shortcrust pastry (page 754)
1 egg yolk

Pass veal, lean pork and fat salt pork twice through the finest blade of your mincer; season generously with salt, freshly ground black pepper and finely chopped parsley, marjoram and thyme. Cut the partridge into serving pieces. Line a deep pie dish with minced meat mixture; on this, place a layer of partridge pieces, then a few cubes of bacon and more minced meats. Continue to add these until the dish is well filled. Moisten with beef stock; cover with a short pastry crust; decorate and brush with yolk of egg. Bake in a moderate oven (375°F/190°C/GM5) for 1 to 1½ hours. Serve hot or cold. Serves 6.

PARTRIDGE WITH LENTILS

2 partridges
Salt and freshly ground black pepper
2 tablespoons (30 ml) butter
2 tablespoons (30 ml) olive oil
4 oz (100 g) fatty salt pork, diced
1 Spanish onion, sliced
2 carrots, sliced
¼ pint (150 ml) dry white wine
¼ pint (150 ml) chicken stock

LENTILS
12 oz (350 g) lentils
1 onion, stuck with 2 cloves
2 cloves garlic
1 sprig fresh thyme
2 sprigs fresh parsley
Salt and freshly ground black pepper

Clean and prepare partridges in the usual way: then sprinkle cavities with a little salt and freshly ground black pepper, and sauté the birds in a fireproof casserole in butter and oil with diced fat salt pork and sliced onion and carrots. When birds are golden on all sides, add dry white wine and cook until wine is reduced by half. Add chicken stock and season to taste with salt and freshly ground black pepper; cover casserole and cook over a low heat until partridges are tender, about 45 minutes.

To serve: place partridges on hot serving dish and surround with cooked lentils. Skim fat from pan juices; strain and pour over birds. Serves 4.

LENTILS
Soak lentils overnight. Drain and cover with water, adding onion, garlic, thyme and parsley, and salt and pepper, to taste. Bring to a boil; reduce heat and allow to simmer until tender but not too soft. Each lentil should be separate, not mushy. When cooked, drain lentils and remove onion, garlic and herbs.

PARTRIDGE EN SALADE

2 partridges
¼ pint (150 ml) olive oil
3 tablespoons (45 ml) finely chopped shallots
Wine vinegar
3 tablespoons (45 ml) finely chopped chervil or parsley
Salt, freshly ground black pepper and dry mustard
2 apples, peeled and diced
2 stalks celery, sliced

Roast partridges for 18 to 20 minutes. Cut into serving pieces. Slice breasts. Combine partridge pieces in a bowl with olive oil and shallots. Marinate in this mixture for at least 12 hours, turning pieces from time to time.

When ready to serve, remove partridges from marinade and arrange them in a serving bowl. Make a well-flavoured *vinaigrette* with the oil in the dish by adding wine vinegar, finely chopped chervil or parsley, and salt, freshly ground black pepper and dry mustard, to taste. Pour *vinaigrette* mixture over partridges; add diced apples and celery; toss and serve. Serves 6.

Pheasant

According to Brillat Savarin, who liked them well hung, the pheasant is the best of all game birds. So let us take advantage of their season, which starts with a flourish on 1 October and lasts through to 11 February. Roast them first, in the traditional manner, then, as we become more familiar with this delectable bird, let us be more daring in the time-honoured ways of cooking it.

Some gourmets like them hung by the legs until the weight of their bodies causes the birds to fall. But for my less demanding palate, 3 days to a week is enough to bring out the full rich flavour of this bird. I like pheasants served *en casserole* with brandy and cream; cooked in the Norman manner on a bed of tart apples, the sauce made rich with Calvados and cream; or pheasant with white truffles – 2 young pheasants, fat and tender, ready to be eaten 3 or 4 days from the time of their shooting, sautéed in butter with some finely chopped shallots and some thinly sliced fresh white truffles from Alba that I bring back from Italy every chance I have. There is something about the aroma of a white truffle that defies description. Its tender, lavender-hued whiteness adds more than just flavour to a dish, it adds history and the almost wicked savour of something rescued from antiquity. Whatever its magic, it smacks of sea, of earth and of tradition . . . and it is fabulous with game.

ROAST PHEASANT

2 tender pheasants (about 2½ lb/1.1 kg each)
Salt and freshly ground black pepper
2 slices fatty salt pork or fatty bacon
Chicken stock
Red wine
Watercress, Bread Sauce (page 127) or
browned breadcrumbs

STUFFING
1 cooking apple
4 tablespoons (60 ml) softened butter
Juice of ½ lemon
4 tablespoons (60 ml) finely chopped onion
2 tablespoons (30 ml) olive oil
Salt and freshly ground black pepper

GRAVY
¼ pint (150 ml) chicken stock
2 tablespoons (30 ml) red currant jelly
2 tablespoons (30 ml) freshly grated breadcrumbs

STUFFING
Grate apple coarsely and combine with softened butter, lemon
juice and finely chopped onion which you have softened in olive
oil. Season generously with salt and freshly ground black pepper.

Stuff birds with this mixture. Season with salt and pepper. Tie a
thin slice of fatty salt pork or bacon over the breasts and roast in a
slow oven (350°F/180°C/GM4) for about 1 hour, or until tender,
basting from time to time with chicken stock and red wine.

GRAVY
Skim fat from pan juices; combine ¼ pint (150 ml) of the pan
juices (made up, if necessary, with water and red wine) with
chicken stock, red currant jelly and freshly grated breadcrumbs:
simmer gently, stirring continuously, until thickened.

To serve: remove bacon and string; transfer birds to a heated
serving dish. Garnish with watercress and serve with gravy and
Bread Sauce or browned breadcrumbs. Serves 4 to 8.

CASSEROLE OF PHEASANT

2 young pheasants
6 oz (175 g) cooked ham, finely chopped
6 tablespoons (90 ml) cooked rice
6 tablespoons (90 ml) cognac
1 egg
Salt and freshly ground black pepper
Powdered thyme and marjoram
Fatty salt pork
4 tablespoons (60 ml) butter
4 tablespoons (60 ml) olive oil
2–4 shallots, finely chopped
2 tablespoons (30 ml) cognac, warmed
1 lb (450 g) button mushrooms
2 cloves garlic
Juice of ½ lemon

Clean birds and stuff with the following mixture: finely chopped
livers of the birds combined with finely chopped ham and cooked
rice, moistened with cognac and egg, and flavoured to taste with
salt, freshly ground black pepper and powdered thyme and
marjoram.

Truss birds firmly, wrap each one in fatty salt pork and brown
them on all sides in a fireproof casserole with 2 tablespoons (30
ml) each of butter and olive oil, and the finely chopped shallots.
Pour 2 tablespoons (30 ml) warmed cognac over birds and ignite.
When flames die down, cover casserole and simmer pheasants
over a low heat or in a slow oven until done, adding a little more
liquid if necessary.

Sauté mushrooms with garlic cloves in remaining butter and
oil. Season well and pour over birds. Finish cooking on an
absestos mat or in a slow oven, and just before serving sprinkle
with lemon juice. Serves 6 to 8.

PHEASANT IN RED WINE

2 young pheasants
4 shallots, finely chopped
2 tablespoons (30 ml) olive oil
3 tablespoons (45 ml) butter
1 pint (600 ml) red Burgundy
Mushroom stalks
1 tablespoon (15 ml) flour
Salt and freshly ground black pepper

GLAZED ONIONS
12 small onions
Salt
1 tablespoon (15 ml) butter
1 tablespoon (15 ml) granulated sugar

SAUTÉED MUSHROOM CAPS
12 button mushrooms
1 tablespoon (15 ml) butter
Salt and freshly ground black pepper

Clean birds. Put 2 shallots, finely chopped, and the pheasant liver into the cavity of each bird. Heat olive oil and 2 tablespoons (30 ml) butter in a large thick pan and sauté pheasants gently until they are a golden brown colour on all sides and almost tender.

Transfer pheasants to a large ovenproof casserole and keep warm. Pour red wine into pan in which you have cooked birds and cook over a high heat, amalgamating wine with the pan juices. Add mushrooms stalks and continue to cook until the liquid is reduced by half. Thicken the sauce with the remaining butter and flour. Simmer for a few minutes; strain through a fine sieve into a bowl and allow to cool slightly so that grease can be skimmed off the surface.

Pour wine sauce over the pheasants, correct seasoning and add Glazed Onions and Sautéed Mushroom Caps. Cover casserole and cook in a moderate oven (375°F/190°C/GM5) until pheasants and tender. Serves 4 to 6.

GLAZED ONIONS
Cook small white onions in boiling salted water until they are tender; drain well. Melt butter in a saucepan; add sugar and stir

until well blended. Add onions and cook slowly until they are glazed. Keep warm.

SAUTÉED MUSHROOM CAPS
Sauté button mushrooms in butter. Season to taste with salt and freshly ground black pepper. Keep warm.

PHEASANT À LA CRÈME

1 tender pheasant
Pheasant liver
4 tablespoons (60 ml) butter
2 tablespoons (30 ml) olive oil
2 tablespoons (30 ml) finely chopped carrot
2 tablespoons (30 ml) finely chopped onion
Generous pinch of thyme
1 bay leaf, crumbled
2–4 tablespoons (30–60 ml) cognac, heated
½ pint (300 ml) double cream
Butter
Cognac
White bread
Salt and freshly ground black pepper

Clean and truss pheasant, reserving liver; brown pheasant and liver on all sides in butter and olive oil in a flameproof casserole. Add finely chopped carrot and onion, thyme and bay leaf. Cover casserole and simmer for 20 minutes. Pour off excess fat and flame with heated cognac. Moisten with cream; cover casserole and simmer until pheasant is tender and sauce has reduced a little.

Mash the pheasant liver with a little butter and cognac, and spread a *canapé* of white bread with this mixture. Remove bird; pass the sauce through a fine sieve and correct seasoning.

Place pheasant on the *canapé* and cover with sauce, which should be quite thick. Serves 4.

NORMANDY PHEASANT

2 plump pheasants
4 tablespoons (60 ml) butter
2 large tart apples
1 wine glass Calvados
½ pint (300 ml) fresh cream
Juice of ½ lemon
Salt and freshly ground black pepper

Clean and truss 2 plump pheasants and sauté them in half the butter in a heavy-bottomed frying pan until they are nicely browned on all sides. Remove and keep warm.

Peel, core and slice apples, and sauté them in remaining butter until they are golden. Place apples in the bottom of an earthenware casserole; arrange pheasants on top and baste with the pan juices thinned down with Calvados; cook the birds in a moderate oven (375°F/190°C/GM5) for about 30 minutes.

Add cream and the juice of ½ lemon, and season to taste with salt and freshly ground black pepper. Return the casserole, covered, to the oven and cook until the birds are tender and the sauce is creamy and thick. Serves 4 to 6.

PHEASANT WITH GREEN APPLES

1 pheasant
4 oz (100 g) unsmoked bacon, diced
½ Spanish onion, finely chopped
1 clove garlic, finely chopped
2 tablespoons (30 ml) butter
2 tablespoons (30 ml) corn oil
4 small cooking apples
4 tablespoons (60 ml) Cointreau
½ pint (300 ml) cream
Salt and freshly ground black pepper

Sauté diced unsmoked bacon and finely chopped onion and garlic in butter and corn oil in a fireproof casserole until golden. Remove bacon and vegetables; reserve. Then brown pheasant on all sides in resulting fats. Remove pheasant and keep warm.

Peel, core and slice apples thickly, and sauté in remaining fat until they start to turn golden. Pour over Cointreau. Remove apples from casserole. Skim fat from pan juices. Return pheasant to casserole; surround with apple slices, bacon bits, onion and garlic, and allow to simmer, covered, for 10 minutes. Stir in the cream; add salt and freshly ground black pepper, to taste; cover and cook in a very slow oven (275°F/140°C/GM1) until tender.

When ready to serve: remove the pheasant and bacon bits to a clean casserole and keep warm; purée sauce and apples. Correct seasoning; reheat sauce; pour over pheasant and serve immediately. Serves 2 to 4.

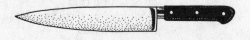

FAISAN AUX FRUITS

2 fat pheasants
2–4 tablespoons (30–60 ml) butter
Salt and freshly ground black pepper
4 tablespoons (60 ml) cognac
2 tablespoons (30 ml) game *fumet*
2 tablespoons (30 ml) lemon juice
2 tablespoons (30 ml) pineapple juice
4 slices fresh pineapple, halved
1 orange, peeled and cut in segments

To prepare birds: cut each bird into 8 serving pieces and sauté the wings, breasts and thighs in butter until golden. (Keep the drumsticks for another use; they are excellent devilled.) Season well with salt and freshly ground black pepper, and continue to cook until pheasant is tender. Remove pieces and keep warm.

To make fruit sauce: remove half the fat in the pan; add cognac and set alight; and then bring to a boil, stirring briskly to dissolve crusty bits on side of pan. Add a little *fumet* of game (made by boiling neck, carcass and giblets of birds for a minute or two in a very little water with finely chopped onion, salt and pepper); then add lemon and pineapple juices.

Arrange pieces of pheasant on a warm serving dish; garnish with pineapple and orange segments; pour over sauce. Serves 4 to 6.

PHEASANT MOUSSE

6 oz (175 g) pheasant breast
2 oz (50 g) ham
¼ pint (150 ml) very thick White Sauce (page 106),
using much less liquid
2 eggs
2 tablespoons (30 ml) softened butter
1 tablespoon (15 ml) dry sherry
Salt and freshly ground black pepper
Pinch of nutmeg
Grated lemon rind
¼ pint (150 ml) double cream, stiffly whipped
Clarified butter
A few cooked green peas, or finely chopped parsley
and truffles
Tomato Sauce (page 124)

Mince pheasant with ham, and pound until smooth in a mortar with thick White Sauce, 2 eggs and the softened butter. Rub mixture through a fine sieve into a bowl. Add sherry, salt, freshly ground black pepper, nutmeg and grated lemon rind. Mix well, then fold in stiffly whipped cream. Grease a plain mould with clarified butter; decorate with cooked green peas, or finely chopped parsley and truffles cut in fancy shapes; pour in the pheasant mixture and cover with greased paper. Place mould in a pan of boiling water and cook in a slow oven (350°F/180°C/GM4) until mousse is firm to the touch. Allow it to stand for a few minutes after removing it from the oven. Turn out mousse carefully on to a serving dish and pour Tomato Sauce around it. Serves 4 to 6.

Wild Duck

Wild duck is best when hung for at least 24 hours before cooking to enhance the flavour. Wipe ducks with a damp cloth, but do not wash before cooking. Eliminate any fishy flavour the duck might have by placing apples, onions or lemon in its cavity before cooking. I like to make a loose stuffing of equal parts of coarsely chopped oranges complete with skins, and onions, and flavour this with coarse salt, freshly ground black pepper and dried thyme and marjoram. This is a 'duck flavouring' stuffing, not one to serve with the duck, and it should be removed before the ducks are served. Wild duck should not be overcooked, for if so, it becomes dry and tough. Try serving it with an apricot or orange sauce.

ROAST WILD DUCK

2 wild ducks
Salt and freshly ground black pepper
Dried thyme
2 oranges
2 tart apples
2 Spanish onions
8 thin slices bacon
½ pint (300 ml) port

GARNISH
Orange slices
Watercress

SAUCE
2 tablespoons (30 ml) flour
Juice of 1 orange
Juice of 1 lemon
Port
Salt and freshly ground black pepper

Clean, pluck and singe wild ducks. Rub cavities with salt, freshly ground black pepper and dried thyme. Chop oranges (with peel), apples and onions coarsely, and stuff ducks loosely with this flavouring mixture, keeping remainder for roasting pans. Place ducks, breast sides up, on rack in roasting pans; cover breasts with bacon and pour port into pans. Roast ducks in a hot oven (450°F/230°C/GM8) for 20 minutes, basting several times with port. Remove bacon; baste well with pan juices and continue roasting until ducks are cooked rare. Crisp skins under grill; then transfer ducks to a heated serving dish and keep warm.

To serve: garnish with orange slices and fresh watercress. Serve with sauce. Serves 4.

SAUCE
Skim most of fat from pan juices, and stir in flour which you have dissolved in orange and lemon juice. Stir over a high heat until all crusty bits from bottom and sides of pan are incorporated into sauce, and sauce thickens. Then add port, and salt and freshly ground black pepper, to taste.

SALMIS OF WILD DUCK

2 wild ducks (roasted as above)
1 Spanish onion, finely chopped
4 shallots, finely chopped
2 cloves
Bouquet garni (4 sprigs parsley, 2 sprigs thyme,
1 bay leaf)
½ pint (300 ml) red Bordeaux
¾ pint (450 ml) Brown Sauce (page 114)
Salt and freshly ground black pepper
8 triangular *croûtons*, sautéed in butter

Cut breasts, wings and legs from ducks; remove skin and place pieces in a heatproof shallow casserole or chafing dish.

Combine finely chopped onion and shallots, cloves, *bouquet garni*, bones, skins and trimmings from ducks, and red wine in another saucepan; cook over a high heat until wine is reduced to half the original quantity. Add Brown Sauce, and salt and freshly ground black pepper, to taste; simmer gently for 20 minutes. Strain sauce over duck pieces and simmer on cooker or in a chafing dish at the table until duck is heated through. Garnish with *croûtons* and serve immediately. Serves 4.

Quail

So fat, so succulent, so tender, so full of wonderful flavour – quail need little or no hanging. In fact, they may be eaten the very day they are shot. I like quail *à l'estragon*, braised with stock, white wine and tarragon; *à la souvarov*, simmered in a sauce made rich with Madeira, truffles and *foie gras*; or as in the hills of France, surrounded with a vine leaf and then a 'bard' of fatty salt pork, and roasted on a spit. (Wonderful, too, for partridges.)

QUAIL WITH WHITE GRAPES

4 quail
Salt and white pepper
2 tablespoons (30 ml) flour
4 tablespoons (60 ml) butter
¼ pint (150 ml) dry white wine
2 tablespoons (30 ml) lemon juice
3 oz (75 g) seedless grapes
2 tablespoons (30 ml) blanched almonds, sliced

Clean quail; rub with a mixture of salt, pepper and flour. Melt the butter in a thick-bottomed casserole and sauté the birds in it until they are golden on all sides. Add wine and lemon juice; cover and cook over low heat for 15 to 20 minutes. Add seedless grapes and sliced blanched almonds, and cook for 5 to 10 minutes more, or until the birds are tender. Serves 4.

GRILLED QUAIL

4 quail
Salt and freshly ground black pepper
4 tablespoons (60 ml) butter
4 *croûtons* fried bread
Watercress
Bread Sauce (page 127)

Pluck, singe and draw the birds. Split them through the backbone and lay them flat without separating the halves.

Wipe them carefully and season with salt and freshly ground black pepper. Wrap in thickly buttered white paper and grill for 5 to 6 minutes on each side.

When the quail are ready to be served, remove paper and place each bird on a *croûton* of fried bread; garnish with springs of watercress. Serve Bread Sauce separately. Serves 4.

CAILLES EN CAISSES

4 quail
1 small can *mousse de foie gras*
Truffles
Well-flavoured stock (optional)
Brown Chaudfroid Sauce (page 117)
Chopped aspic jelly (page 76)

Bone quail and stuff them with *mousse de foie gras*, putting a truffle or part of a truffle in the centre of each. Sew them up, making them as neat a shape as possible.

Braise birds or poach them in well-flavoured stock until tender. Remove from pan and cool. Remove trussing threads and coat each quail with Brown Chaudfroid Sauce. When set, place each bird in an individual ramekin or soufflé dish just large enough to hold it. Garnish with chopped aspic jelly. Serves 4.

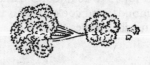

Woodcock and Snipe

Woodcock and snipe, the shore birds, are two of the most honoured species of game. Small and rather on the gamy side, their dark flesh has a strong, wild flavour. Quick-cooking birds – 10 to 20 minutes at the most – they should be hung 3 to 4 days before cooking. They are never drawn and every bit of them is eaten.

ROAST SNIPE

Snipe is usually kept until it is high, although some cooks prefer it fresh. Allow 1 snipe for each person. Pluck them very carefully as the skin is particularly tender. Do not empty them; just remove the gizzard. The head, too, is kept on. Skin it, remove the eyes and use the long beak for trussing the bird instead of a skewer. Press the legs and wings together, then draw the head round and run the beak through where the legs and wings cross.

Brush the snipe with melted butter and tie in a thin slice of fat bacon over the breast of each. Roast birds over charcoal or in the oven, basting them well with butter. Cooking time will depend upon how you like your birds – well done or with the flesh red – from 15 to 20 minutes. When ready, serve them on oblong *croûtons* of fried bread spread with a mixture of finely chopped cooked chicken livers and bacon rubbed through a sieve or, for special occasions, *foie gras*. Garnish with watercress and small pieces of fresh lemon. Serve gravy separately.

SALMIS OF WOODCOCK

4 woodcock
4 tablespoons (60 ml) dry white wine
4 tablespoons (60 ml) rich beef stock
2 lemons
Salt, freshly ground black pepper and nutmeg
1–2 tablespoons (15–30 ml) dry mustard
2½ oz (65 g) sliced mushrooms
1 tablespoon (15 ml) butter
1 tablespoon (15 ml) flour
2 tablespoons (30 ml) finely chopped parsley

Roast woodcock slightly (until about half cooked) and cut them into serving pieces. Be sure to cut woodcock on a serving dish to catch blood and juices. Arrange pieces in the blazer pan of a chafing dish.

Crush livers and giblets into serving dish with juices; add dry white wine, beef stock and juice of 2 lemons; stir in the finely grated peel of 1 lemon, and season to taste with salt, freshly ground black pepper, nutmeg and mustard.

Add sliced mushrooms, and pour this mixture over woodcock in blazer pan; place over heater and cook, stirring so that each piece of meat is thoroughly moistened and does not stick to the dish.

Do not let the *salmis* come to a boil. Just before serving, stir in a *beurre manié* made of butter and flour. Sprinkle with finely chopped parsley. Serves 4.

WOODCOCK AU FUMET

2 woodcock
2 slices bacon
Salt and freshly ground black pepper
Olive oil
2 shallots, finely chopped
½ pint (300 ml) champagne
½ pint (300 ml) port
2 tablespoons (30 ml) tomato concentrate
2 slices white bread
Butter
2 tablespoons (30 ml) sieved *pâté de foie gras*
2 tablespoons (30 ml) cognac

Hang woodcock for 4 to 6 days.

Clean and draw birds, reserving the livers. Truss legs close to the body; tie a piece of bacon around each bird; season generously

with salt and freshly ground black pepper, and roast in a fairly hot oven (425°F/220°C/GM7) for 10 to 15 minutes. Cut threads and discard bacon; cut 2 *suprêmes* (breast and wings) and legs from birds, and reserve.

Chop carcasses finely; put them in a saucepan with a little olive oil and finely chopped shallots, and simmer until shallots are soft. Add champagne, port and tomato concentrate, and continue cooking for a few minutes. Chop the raw livers; add them, together with the juices in the roasting pan in which the birds were cooked, to the chopped carcasses, and simmer sauce for ½ hour.

Cut bread slices in half; trim crusts and sauté slices in butter until golden. Spread with sieved *foie gras*. Place them on a heated serving dish. Warm woodcock *suprêmes* and legs through in a little butter; sprinkle with cognac, and flame.

To serve: arrange woodcock pieces on *canapés* and rub sauce over birds through a fine sieve. Serve immediately. Serves 2.

Rabbit and Hare

Some of the most famous dishes of Continental cookery are based on rabbit and hare: *civet de lièvre* (known in Britain as jugged hare), Flemish rabbit cooked with red wine and prunes, a *blanquette* of rabbit in a creamy saffron and lemon flavoured sauce, and French rabbit stew simmered with button onions and shallots in dry white wine.

But perhaps the most famous of all is *lièvre à la royale*, a noble preparation which varies in recipe region to region, but which generally combines a boned hare, stuffed with *foie gras* and finely ground meat, and perfumed with finely chopped mushrooms, truffles, cognac and herbs. It is then rolled in thin strips of fatty salt pork and simmered in stock and wine for 4 to 8 hours; its sauce is thickened just before serving with egg yolks, cream and the blood of the hare.

Rabbits and hares have fine-textured, lightly gamy meat, which resembles chicken somewhat in texture, but is apt to be less fatty. The female rabbit is generally more tender than the male. In many dishes the blood of the rabbit or hare is used to bind rich sauces, and it should be saved for this purpose. Most wild rabbits are improved by a marinade: red wine with a dash of vinegar, or white wine with a little lemon juice. A rabbit will serve 3 or 4 people; a hare, 6 to 8.

Wild rabbits are generally preferred to tame ones as they have a better flavour. The flesh of tame rabbits, however, is whiter and more delicate. When a hare is required for roasting, choose a leveret, a young hare under 1 year of age, as it will be more tender. An older animal is better for making jugged hare or hare soup.

To Joint a Rabbit or Hare

Cut off the four legs by the joints, leaving forelegs whole, but cut the hindlegs in two pieces, cutting through the bone with a chopper. Then cut the body across in five or six pieces, dividing the breast piece in two in order to make it flatter. Trim the pieces neatly, removing all the loose skin, which may be used with the neck for making stock or gravy. The liver, heart and kidney may also be served.

To Bone a Rabbit or Hare for a Terrine or Galantine

Clean and prepare the rabbit as usual, cut off the head and the forelegs, and lay the rabbit on its back on the chopping board. Begin boning at the neck by cutting through the thin layer of flesh which covers the breastbone. Press the knife close to the bone and raise the flesh from it on both sides. Then cut away the flesh from the long backbone, being careful not to cut through the flesh on the back of the rabbit, if possible. Disjoint the hindlegs carefully from the body and draw out the backbone. Now cut through the flesh of the legs and remove the bones as cleanly as possible. Also remove all the flesh from the forelegs which were cut off. When all bones have been removed, spread the rabbit on the board and cut away all sinews and trimmings. It will have rather a ragged appearance, but so long as there is a good straight piece of flesh from the back, this is all that is required. Lay the fleshy part from the legs on the back of the rabbit, and form all into an oblong shape. Season with salt and freshly ground black pepper, and stuff as desired.

RAGOÛT DE LAPIN

1 tender rabbit
18 button onions
12 shallots
3 tablespoons (45 ml) butter
3 tablespoons (45 ml) olive oil
Salt and freshly ground black pepper
2 tablespoons (30 ml) flour
Dry white wine
Bouquet garni (parsley, thyme, celery, bay leaf)
Chopped fresh tarragon or parsley

Sauté button onions and shallots in butter and olive oil until golden. Add rabbit, cut into serving pieces; season with salt and freshly ground black pepper, and sauté until well coloured. Transfer rabbit and vegetables to a heatproof casserole. Add 2 tablespoons (30 ml) flour to pan juices and stir until well blended. Add dry white wine and simmer, stirring continuously, until sauce has thickened. Add a generous *bouquet garni*. Pour sauce over rabbit pieces and vegetables, and simmer gently until rabbit is tender.

Sprinkle with chopped fresh tarragon or parsley. Serves 4.

LAPIN AUX PRUNEAUX

1 tender rabbit
½ pint (300 ml) red wine
4 carrots, sliced
1 Spanish onion, sliced
2 bay leaves
Salt and freshly ground black pepper
2 tablespoons (30 ml) butter
2 tablespoons (30 ml) olive oil
12 oz (350 g) dried prunes
1–2 tablespoons (15–30 ml) red currant jelly

Cut rabbit into serving pieces. Marinate in red wine for 24 hours with sliced carrots and onion, bay leaves, and salt and freshly ground black pepper, to taste. Drain and pat dry with paper towels or a clean cloth. Sauté pieces in butter and olive oil until they are well coloured. Add marinade juices and enough water to cover; add prunes which you have soaked in water overnight. Bring to a boil and skim carefully; lower heat and simmer gently for 1 hour, or until rabbit is tender.

Arrange rabbit pieces and prunes on serving dish; reduce the sauce over a high heat; correct seasoning; blend red currant jelly into sauce and pour over rabbit pieces. Serves 4.

BLANQUETTE DE LAPIN

1 tender rabbit
½ lemon
2 pints (1.1 lit) chicken or veal stock
1 Spanish onion, stuck with 2 cloves
4 carrots
Bouquet garni
Rice
Powdered saffron
2 tablespoons (30 ml) butter
2 tablespoons (30 ml) flour
2 egg yolks
¼ pint (150 ml) double cream
Juice of ½ lemon

Cut rabbit into serving pieces. Leave it overnight in cold water with ½ lemon. Rinse well. Blanch meat by putting it in cold water and bringing it slowly to a boil. Skim carefully and drain. Place blanched rabbit pieces in a deep heatproof casserole with enough chicken or veal stock (or stock and water) to cover; add a Spanish onion stuck with 2 cloves, 4 carrots cut into quarters lengthwise, and the *bouquet garni*, and bring to a boil. Skim; lower heat and simmer gently for 30 minutes. Add a handful of rice and a pinch of powdered saffron, and simmer until rabbit is tender.

Make a white *roux* by combining 2 tablespoons (30 ml) butter and 2 tablespoons (30 ml) flour in a saucepan. Add 1 pint (600 ml) of stock from the rabbit and stir well over a high heat until the sauce is smooth and creamy. Lower heat and simmer for 15 minutes, stirring from time to time. Remove saucepan from heat and 'finish' sauce by stirring in egg yolks, cream and the juice of ½ lemon.

Drain the rabbit pieces from the remaining stock. Clean the casserole; return rabbit pieces to it and strain sauce over meat through a fine sieve. Keep warm in oven with casserole covered until ready to serve. A little more fresh cream and a squeeze of lemon may be added just before serving. Serves 4.

TERRINE OF HARE

1½ lb (675 g) hare meat
A little butter
Salt and freshly ground black pepper
Pinch of nutmeg
1 teaspoon (5 ml) finely chopped thyme
1 tablespoon (15 ml) finely chopped parsely
¼ pint (150 ml) dry white wine
2 tablespoons (30 ml) brandy
1 lb (450 g) smoothly ground sausage meat
Slices of fat bacon
Flour and water paste

Any remains of uncooked hare may be used to make a *terrine*. Remove all bones, trim the flesh and cut it in small pieces, and then weigh it. Melt butter in a saucepan and sauté hare for a minute or two to stiffen the outside; do not let it brown. Place meat in a shallow bowl with salt, freshly ground black pepper and nutmeg, to taste, finely chopped thyme and parsley, and dry white wine and brandy. Marinate hare in this mixture for at least 2 hours. The sausage meat used should be very fine and smooth; if not sufficiently smooth when bought, put it through the mincer; pound it well and then sieve it. Combine sausage meat with the marinade liquids and the blood from the hare, if there is any, or the liver, pounded and sieved, to give the foremeat the taste and darkish colour of the game. Mix well; add marinated hare and mix again.

Line the bottom and sides of a *terrine* with thin slices of fatty bacon, then put in the mixture, which should fill it, forming a mound on the top. Cover the top with more fatty bacon and put on the lid. Seal round the join of lid and pot with a thick paste made of flour and water to keep in all the flavour of the meat while it is cooking. Make sure, however, that the little hole in the top of the lid is left open, or the *terrine* will burst in the cooking. If there is no hole in the lid, leave a small piece of the join unsealed.

To cook *terrine*; place it in a deepish pan with a little cold water round it and bring this to a boil over the heat. Then place it in the oven and cook until the meat is ready – 2 to 2½ hours. The water round the *terrine* should be kept boiling all the time; if it boils away, add more boiling water. Test the meat by running a needle in through the hole in the top, or if, on removing the cover, the fat on top looks quite clear and the meat moves about easily without adhering to the bottom and sides, it is sufficiently cooked. Remove cover and place a weighted plate on the *terrine* to compress it gently as it cools. Chill in refrigerator for at least 3 days before serving to allow flavours to ripen.

To keep *terrine*: a *terrine* like this will keep for 2 to 3 months in the refrigerator if sealed with a layer of melted lard. Other kinds of game may be used instead of hare.

JUGGED HARE

1 hare
18 small white onions
4 oz (100 g) fatty bacon, in 1 piece
2 tablespoons (30 ml) butter or dripping
2 tablespoons (30 ml) olive oil
2 tablespoons (30 ml) flour
Bouquet garni
½ pint (300 ml) red Burgundy
Salt and freshly ground black pepper
1–2 tablespoons (15–30 ml) tomato concentrate
4 oz (100 g) mushrooms, quartered
Vinegar

Ask your butcher to prepare hare, reserving the blood, which is a very necessary ingredient of this dish. Keep the saddle to serve roasted and cut remaining parts in serving pieces, chopping through the bones.

Peel onions and cut bacon into small thick strips. (If the bacon is very salty, the pieces should be blanched beforehand.) Melt butter or dripping with oil in a thick-bottomed heatproof casserole; sauté onions and bacon until lightly browned. Remove onions and bacon, and reserve; put in the pieces of hare and brown them in the same fat. When coloured on all sides, sprinkle with flour and brown that also. Now add *bouquet garni* and wine, and enough water to cover; season to taste with salt, freshly ground black pepper and tomato concentrate. Cover casserole and simmer gently for 2½ to 3 hours, or until the hare is almost tender. When ready, remove pieces of hare to a bowl and strain the sauce over them. Return to a clean casserole; add onions, bacon and quartered mushrooms, and continue to simmer for 20 minutes, or until both the hare and vegetables are cooked through. Then add the blood. Mix it first with a little vinegar and some of the sauce; strain it in beside the hare, mix well and bring to a boil. Be careful not to overboil it, or it will curdle. Serves 4 to 6.

LIÈVRE À LA BROCHE 'PAUL BOCUSE'

> 1 young hare (about 4½ lb/2.1 kg)
> Salt and freshly ground black pepper
> Powdered thyme and rosemary
> Dijon mustard
> Olive oil
> Rice pilaff
>
> SAUCE
> 2 shallots, finely chopped
> Pan juices
> 2 tablespoons (30 ml) wine vinegar
> ¾ pint (450 ml) sour cream
> 2 juniper berries, crushed

Do not marinate hare. Rub it with a damp cloth and put it on a spit. Season the hare inside and out with salt, freshly ground black pepper, powdered thyme and rosemary, to taste; then coat it generously with Dijon mustard. Sprinkle with a little olive oil and roast it on the spit from 35 to 45 minutes, or until the hare is tender but the flesh is still rose-coloured. Make sure there is a pan under hare to catch juices as it cooks.

Serve the hare with sauce and a rice pilaff. Serves 4 to 6.

SAUCE
Simmer finely chopped shallot in pan juices until soft; add wine vinegar, and scrape all crusty bits from the sides of the pan. Then add sour cream and crushed juniper berries, and reduce the sauce to a third of the original quantity. Strain.

Venison

Venison is a term for any antlered animal, whether it be moose, elk or deer. The flesh of venison should be dark and finely grained, and the fat firm, clear and white. It should be well hung before using, in order to acquire a gamy flavour. The flesh of the fallow deer is considered by many to be the best venison, and the buck is superior in quality to the doe. Buck venison is in season from June to the end of September, while the season for the doe is from October to the end of December.

The best joint for roasting is the haunch. The loin and neck are also highly esteemed. The shoulder and breast are better braised or made into a *ragoût*. Chops are usually cut from the loin or neck, and steaks from the legs.

Venison should be hung at least 2 weeks before being eaten. Many of the choicest cuts of venison – the steaks, chops, roasts and saddle – have virtually no fat at all, and so it is necessary to lard them with fatty salt pork or bacon. You can order a professional larding needle from any kitchen supply house. You will find it most useful for larding beef, veal, rabbit, hare and venison. I prefer to lard venison with fatty salt pork, as I think that smoked or salt bacon can give too strong a bacon taste to the meat. Long strips of fatty salt pork, when moistened with a little cognac and then rolled in powdered herbs, can do much to tenderize and moisturize meat and game, as well as give them additional flavour.

Another excellent tenderizer-moisturizer-flavourer is the marinade. All roasts of venison – legs, shoulders, fillets – except those of very young animals, should be marinated to ensure tenderness. The length of time for the marinade depends, of course, on a great number of things: your own tastes, the humidity and temperature of the atmosphere, and the nature and age of the game itself.

Meat for the marinade may be larded before immersion or after. It always seems to me that meat larded before marinating makes the marinade work faster. You can use either a raw marinade or a cooked marinade. And to hurry the process, you can even follow the lead of a famous game cook I know, who uses a hypodermic syringe to inject the marinade into the tissues of the animal.

The tender parts of a young animal – steaks, chops and the saddle – may be cooked without preliminary marinating. But the tougher cuts – leg, shoulder, etc. – and the meat from more mature animals, should be marinated for from 12 hours to several days in a cooked or raw marinade.

I prefer venison steaks cut quite thick, marinated overnight in equal quantities of olive oil and dry red wine, and then grilled over charcoal until they are rare but not bloody. Serve with an appetite and a purée of chestnuts or celery.

GRILLED VENISON STEAKS

4 venison steaks
Salt and freshly ground black pepper
2 bay leaves, crumbled
4 tablespoons (60 ml) olive oil
2 tablespoons (30 ml) lemon juice
4 tablespoons (60 ml) softened butter
Red or black currant jelly

Choose the steaks from the leg if possible, and have them cut from ¾ inch to 1 inch (18–25 mm) in thickness. Trim them neatly; season with salt, freshly ground black pepper and crumbled bay leaves, and marinate them in olive oil and lemon juice for 2 hours before cooking. Drain, and grill as you would beef, turning them often and allowing rather longer than for a beef steak. Venison must be served immediately, or it will become tough.

To serve: transfer steaks on to a heated serving dish and garnish with softened butter to which you have added red or black currant jelly, to taste. Serves 4.

VENISON STEAKS IN THE PAN

4 venison steaks, about 1 inch (25 mm) thick
2–4 tablespoons (30–60 ml) butter
4–6 tablespoons (60–90 ml) dry sherry
Salt and freshly ground black pepper
2 tablespoons (30 ml) finely chopped parsley
Red currant jelly

Sauté venison steaks in butter in a sauté or frying pan, turning them once or twice during cooking time, until they are sufficiently cooked. Moisten with dry sherry and season to taste with salt and freshly ground black pepper; turn the meat once more and then serve on a heated serving dish, garnished with pan juices and finely chopped parsley. Serve with red currant jelly. Serves 4.

HUNTER'S VENISON STEW

3 lb (1.4 kg) venison
Flour
3 Spanish onions, finely chopped
Butter
8 oz (225 g) unsmoked bacon, cut in 1 piece
6 cloves garlic
3 bay leaves
3 cloves
1 teaspoon (5 ml) mixed dried herbs
(marjoram, rosemary, thyme)
½ bottle red wine
3 large carrots, quartered
3 medium potatoes, quartered

Trim sinews and bones from venison, and cut the meat into 2-inch (5 cm) cubes. Roll them in flour. Sauté onions in butter in a large heatproof casserole until soft. Remove from pan and reserve. Dice unsmoked bacon, and sauté in remaining fat until golden. Remove and reserve.

Sauté venison in resulting fat until golden; then return sautéed onions and bacon to casserole; add garlic, bay leaves, cloves and dried herbs, and simmer, covered, in a very slow oven (300°F/150°C/GM2) for 2 hours.

Reduce wine over a high heat to half the original quantity; add to stew with quartered carrots and potatoes, and simmer for another hour. Serves 6.

VENISON EN CASSEROLE

2½ lb (1.1 kg) venison
4 oz (100 g) bacon, in 1 piece
2 tablespoons (30 ml) flour
¾ pint (450 ml) stock or water
1 Spanish onion, finely chopped
2 tablespoons (30 ml) red currant jelly
Bouquet garni (parsley, thyme, bay leaf)
2 tablespoons (30 ml) lemon juice
Salt and freshly ground black pepper
Forcemeat balls

Choose a nice fleshy piece of venison; wipe it and trim it carefully; cut it into 1-inch (25 mm) square pieces. Trim rind from bacon and cut it into rectangles. Sauté bacon pieces gently for a few minutes in a frying pan without allowing them to become too brown and crisp. Transfer bacon to a heatproof casserole, leaving the liquid fat in the pan.

Coat the pieces of venison with flour and sauté in bacon fat until well browned. Transfer venison to casserole with bacon. Add stock or water to frying pan and cook over a high heat, stirring all the brown crusty bits from the sides and bottom of the pan into the stock. Skim if necessary and strain over the venison. Add chopped onion, red currant jelly, *bouquet garni* and lemon juice, and season to taste with salt and freshly ground black pepper. Cover casserole and simmer venison gently until tender – 2 to 2½ hours. About 20 minutes before serving, add some small forcemeat balls made of sausage meat mixed with 1 egg and seasoned with dried herbs. Serves 4 to 6.

MARINATED VENISON STEAKS

4 thick steaks of venison, cut from the loin
Salt and freshly ground black pepper
½ Spanish onion, sliced
2 carrots, sliced
4 sprigs parsley
2 bay leaves
Thyme and rosemary
¼ pint (150 ml) dry white wine
Olive oil
2 tablespoons (30 ml) butter

SAUCE
2 tablespoons (30 ml) butter
2 shallots, finely chopped
1 tablespoon (15 ml) flour
6 tablespoons (90 ml) marinade juices, strained
½ pint (300 ml) sour cream
Lemon juice
Freshly ground black pepper

Season venison steaks generously with salt and freshly ground black pepper, and combine in a bowl with sliced onion and carrots, parsley, bay leaves, thyme and rosemary. Moisten with dry white wine and 6 tablespoons (90 ml) olive oil. Place bowl in the refrigerator and marinate steaks for 24 to 48 hours, turning them occasionally.

To cook steaks: remove venison from marinade, reserving marinade juices for further use, and pat dry. Heat 2 tablespoons (30 ml) each olive oil and butter in a large thick-bottomed frying pan, and sauté venison over a high heat for about 3 minutes on each side. Remove and keep warm.

Serve steaks on a heated serving dish with sauce. Serves 4.

SAUCE
Drain excess fat from frying pan and add 2 tablespoons (30 ml) butter. Sauté finely chopped shallots until soft; sprinkle with flour and cook, stirring, until the *roux* is lightly browned. Add 6 tablespoons (90 ml) strained marinade juices, the sour cream, and lemon juice and freshly ground black pepper, to taste.

CHAPTER FIFTEEN

Summer Food

Aglass of smoke-filled *pastis*, a dish of those perfect, hard, little green olives that are the natural fruit of Provence, and a parcel of bright blue sea stretching as far as the human eye can reach – and then some – is my idea of a summer meal of perfection. At least, the humble beginning of a summer meal that might continue, if I were marooned in one of the little fishing ports along the coast of sunny Provence, with a Provençal anchovy salad, made with salted anchovies, wine and olive oil, and spiked with fresh herbs and thin lemon slices. The whole is marinated until the anchovies are tender and soft, and the essence of the lemon and herbs has permeated the flesh of these delicious fish.

Another cool, summery-tasting appetizer that I enjoy preparing is *taramasalata*. I have no way of knowing, I am afraid, if my version (see recipe on page 563) approaches the authentic, for it, too, came to me via Provence, and is perhaps really only a more sophisticated version of Provençal *poutargue* – salted and smoked roe of tuna or grey mullet, sliced thinly and served as an *hors-d'œuvre* with freshly ground black pepper, olive oil and lemon juice. My *taramasalata* is a creamy fish pâté made with smoked cod's roe rather than tuna, and is quite delicious.

Freshly caught fish from the Gulf of Pampelonne, just thirty feet (10 m) across the sands from the open-air barbecues where they are cooked, is one of the great delights of St Tropez in the summer. Some of the little restaurants along the beach are beginning to do barbecued fish and lobster at lunch, and can be tempted to carry this on to late-night suppers under the stars. Everything here is of optimum freshness. The vegetables – and even the wines served at one or two of these restaurants – come from the farms and vineyards located in the flatlands just behind the beach. A meal I enjoyed there began with *salade niçoise* – tiny whole artichokes sliced with celery, onions, radishes, small green peppers, tomatoes, cucumber and lettuce, and garnished with black olives, quarters of hard-boiled egg, tuna fish and anchovies, dressed with a wine vinegar and olive oil dressing. This was followed by fresh sardines from the Gulf, brushed with a sauce of olive oil, lemon juice and fresh herbs, grilled over charcoal, and served with a dressing of melted butter and finely chopped tarragon. Melon and black coffee provided the finale to a perfect open-air meal.

Let barbecued fish with tarragon provide the focal point of an outdoor luncheon planned around your grill. Accompany the fish, if you like, with small new potatoes boiled in their jackets, served with nothing but coarsely ground salt and pepper, and lots of fresh butter. Precede the fish with a cold *ratatouille*, a fresh tomato salad dressed only with salt, pepper, finely chopped parsley and olive oil; or more exotically, with the *salade de tomates à la crème* which used to be the speciality of the Hôtel Fourrat in the Hautes Alpes: cut tomato slices thickly, sprinkle with freshly ground black pepper, salt, a little lemon juice and finely chopped onion, and mask with mayonnaise mixed with equal quantities of whipped cream.

Lobster makes delectable eating, too, when split, enfolded in fresh sprigs of tarragon, basil and chervil, and grilled to succulent, pink-shelled perfection over the coals. I like to dribble olive oil and lemon juice on them during cooking and serve them simply with melted butter to which finely chopped herbs and a little lemon juice impart their own special flavours.

Barbecue Breakfast

One of the most memorable outdoor meals of my life was a lazy Sunday morning barbecue breakfast several years ago on a noble terrace just outside New Orleans. Frosty mint juleps started the festivities; followed by steaming bowls of shrimp gumbo, and creamy scrambled eggs cooked over an open fire before our eyes; barbecued pompano, served with a most delectable Creole sauce composed of wine, olives, onions and herbs, was the highlight of the meal; fresh peaches in champagne, served in gossamer-thin glasses, provided the finale . . . a breakfast I shall never forget. And how easy – pompano notwithstanding – to recreate it at home for a Sunday outdoor breakfast-cum-lunch. Begin with a warming soup: New Orleans seafood gumbo – gumbo filé powder made of powdered sassafras leaves is now available in Britain – or Moroccan *harira*, the traditional 'break fast' soup of the Ramadan, based on stock vegetables and beans. Or start more simply with a Spanish omelette cooked over the coals and served right from the pan.

Follow with *rougets* or rainbow trout, rubbed with lemon, grilled over charcoal and basted during the cooking with a lemon or Creole barbecue sauce. End this outdoor meal on an upswing with fresh fruit cup – melon, peaches, raspberries and straw-berries – served in melon 'bowls', or peaches in champagne, and clear the way for the early noon festivities of life in the open air.

Barbecue Luncheon

A barbecue luncheon is fun for the guests and easy on the cook too. Start with an icy cool *gazpacho* in the Spanish manner – followed by barbecued beef and lamb kebabs, and a salad. Or why not begin your outdoor meal with the refreshingly different version of *salade niçoise* created by French theatrical producer, Sophie Babet, in her summer home on Cap d'Ail: 'Sophie's Salad' is a *savant* combination of layers of thickly sliced raw tomatoes, strips of baked green and red pepper, and sliced hard-boiled eggs, garnished with anchovies and ripe olives, and bathed in a fragrant green dressing (Vinaigrette Sauce with finely chopped fresh herbs and garlic). Follow with a summer *paella* . . . an all-in, one-dish, open casserole that contrasts the flavours and textures of chicken, lobster, prawns, and *chorizo*, the highly spiced Spanish sausage, the whole served with savoury saffron rice.

After-dark Barbecue Buffet

My favourite formula for entertaining in the hot months is a barbecue buffet party . . . smoke-flavoured barbecued meat and fish, combined with the finer elegances of a *fête champétre* served under the stars.

A choice of barbecued fish, grilled whole on the open coals, or individual skewers of lamb, beef and pork, marinated before cooking in wine, oil and spices, sets the meal off with a flourish. Two casseroles – an American seafood casserole of prawns, sole, scallops and lobster in a wine-flavoured cream sauce, and *bœuf à la bourguignonne*, tender chunks of beef simmered in red Burgundy with white onions and button mushrooms – provide a prepared-in-advance set of alternatives for the main course. Follow with a make-it-yourself salad – decorative bowls of prepared salad greens and raw vegetables, and a trio of salad dressings. Guests help themselves. Huge platters of assorted cheeses and fruits, and a tub filled with iced wines complete this easy entertaining pattern.

But whatever formula you choose, *al fresco* entertaining should be exciting and different, with a menu that owes everything to the imagination. To eat outdoors is no longer a choice between uncomfortable picnics by the roadside or rushing hot plates out into the garden. Today, thanks to the barbecue, it is one of life's finest pleasures. If you embrace the full scope of the barbecue instead of limiting your repertoire to steaks and chops, you will find that you have opened up a whole new range of tastes to your palate, for every dish cooked over charcoal seems to improve in flavour and alters subtly as it cooks to crusty goodness in the wood-scented smoke.

Barbecue Know-how

Watching the beach boys at work at their barbecues shows that keeping a fire under control once it is under way is easy when you know how. If you want a fire that sears quickly – perfect for grilling small fish, minute steaks or skewered meats – the charcoal should be piled about two or three inches (5–8 cm) high. If you need a lazy and more controlled heat for a whole leg of lamb or a large duck, the charcoal should be spread out in a single layer, with coals separated a little from each other.

Keep a circle of fresh charcoal at the outer edge of your fire and push it into the centre as needed. Do not put fresh coals on top of the lighted charcoal, or you will find that you have set up a dense smoke screen. A bulb syringe filled with water should be kept handy to tame flames when necessary.

It is important not to start cooking too soon with charcoal. For perfect grilling, charcoal should look ash-grey by day and have a warm, red glow after dark. If your charcoal is still flaming, it is too early to start cooking.

Barbecued meats are best if they are at room temperature when cooked. One to two hours out of the refrigerator is a good rule for steaks and chops; big roasts, several hours; chicken, about 30 minutes. This prevents meat being overdone outside and under-cooked inside.

Always give meat on the spit or grill a chance to warm up and relax over the coals before you start basting. The meat will absorb the flavours of your basting sauce better this way. A word to the wise: if your sauce has a tomato base, do not begin to use it until the last 15 minutes of cooking time. This gives a rosy brown glaze to barbecued meats and avoids unnecessary scorching.

One of the hazards of outdoor cooking is that fat dripping from the meat causes the fire to flare up and smoke. So keep coals under the meat for a short time until the meat becomes brown, then spread the coals in a circle with none directly under the meat. If flames still flare up, put a dripping pan under the meat. You will find that the meat will cook sufficiently even though there is no fire under it. If after the meat is done you still want a little more charring, push coals back under the meat and cook until it is as brown as you wish.

To keep grill or spit clean, use a wire brush, not steel wool. And always brush the grill with oil before grilling food on it, to prevent meats from sticking to it during cooking.

When grilling steak or lamb, cut a garlic clove in half and toss it on the coals for a wonderful flavour. For pork or ham on the spit, wait until meat is almost done and then drop a spiral of orange or lemon peel in the fire. I like to use herbs in this way too: a sprig of rosemary, a bay leaf or two, or a sprig of sage or thyme, make all the difference.

Provençal Hors-d'œuvre

Pepper: Choose sweet peppers – both yellow and green – and brush with olive oil. Drain and put them under the grill until they begin to turn colour. Slice peppers and dress with a well-flavoured Vinaigrette Sauce (page 691) to which you have added a little finely chopped garlic and parsley.

Tomatoes: Choose large ripe tomatoes; slice them in half and arrange in an *hors-d'œuvre* dish. Top with thinly sliced shallots or raw leeks and finely chopped parsley. Dress with a well-flavoured Vinaigrette Sauce.

Tuna fish: Slice canned tuna fish and arrange in an *hors-d'œuvre* dish. Top with slices of hard-boiled egg, thinly sliced spring onions and finely chopped parsley. Dress with a well-flavoured Vinaigrette Sauce.

Anchovy salad: See page 703.

Cold ratatouille: See page 561.

Green and black olives

SARDINE-STUFFED LEMONS

6 large fresh lemons
1 can sardines or tuna fish
5 oz (150 g) butter
Prepared mustard
Paprika and freshly ground black pepper
1 egg white, stiffly beaten
1 sprig fresh thyme, bay leaf or small green leaf per lemon

Cut off tops of lemons; dig out pulp with small spoon. Remove pips and reserve pulp and juice.

Mash sardines or tuna fish to a smooth paste with butter and mustard, and season to taste with paprika and freshly ground black pepper. Stir in juice and pulp of lemons together with stiffly beaten egg white. Correct seasoning and stuff lemons with this mixture. Chill. Top with a sprig of fresh thyme, a bay leaf or a small green leaf, and serve in egg cups. Serves 6.

COLD ŒUFS SAUMONÉES EN CROÛTE

6 round rolls
Butter
12 eggs
2 thin slices smoked salmon
4 tablespoons (60 ml) double cream
Salt and freshly ground black pepper
2 tablespoons (30 ml) finely chopped parsley

Slice tops off rolls and pull out interiors of rolls with your fingers. Brush rolls inside and out with melted butter and bake them in a slow oven (350°F/180°C/GM4) until they are golden brown. Cool.

Mix eggs slightly until whites and yolks are well mixed, but do not beat them.

Cut thin slices of smoked salmon into thin strips and heat for a moment in 2 tablespoons (30 ml) butter. Add eggs and cook, stirring constantly, over low heat. As eggs begin to set, add another 2 tablespoons (30 ml) butter, and the cream. Season to taste with salt and freshly ground black pepper. Cool.

Stuff rolls with scrambled egg mixture and sprinkle with finely chopped parsley. Serves 6.

AÏOLI SAUCE

4 fat cloves garlic per person
1 egg yolk for each 2 persons
Salt
Olive oil
Freshly ground black pepper
Lemon juice

Take 4 fat cloves of garlic per person and 1 egg yolk for each 2 persons. Crush garlic to a smooth paste in a mortar with a little salt; blend in egg yolks until mixture is a smooth, homogeneous mass. Now add olive oil, drop by drop at first, a thin, fine trickle later, whisking the mixture as you would for a mayonnaise. The *aïoli* will thicken gradually until it reaches a stiff, firm consistency. The exact quantity of oil is, of course, determined by the number of egg yolks used. Season to taste with additional salt, a little pepper and lemon juice. This sauce is served chilled, in a bowl. Guests help themselves.

AÏOLI SAUCE WITHOUT EGGS

4–6 cloves garlic
1 boiled potato, chilled
Lemon juice
Salt and freshly ground black pepper
Olive oil

Peel garlic and boiled potato. Pound garlic in a mortar until smooth; add potato and pound until it is well mixed with garlic. Add a little lemon juice, salt and freshly ground black pepper, to taste. Then, drop by drop, whisk in olive oil as you would for a mayonnaise, until *aïoli* is thick and smooth. Correct seasoning and serve.

VEGETABLES WITH AÏOLI SAUCE

6 potatoes
6 baby marrows
1 lb (450 g) new carrots
1 lb (450 g) green beans
6 ripe tomatoes
Salt and freshly ground black pepper
Aïoli Sauce (page 559)

Peel potatoes and cut into ½-inch (12 mm) cubes; wash and cut baby marrows, new carrots and green beans into ½-inch (12 mm) lengths. Boil each vegetable until tender but still quite firm. Do not overcook.

Seed and cut large fresh tomatoes into ½-inch (12 mm) cubes. Arrange vegetables in colourful groups on a large shallow serving dish; sprinkle with salt and freshly ground black pepper, to taste. Serve with Aïoli Sauce. Serves 6.

HARICOTS VERTS 'EN AÏOLI'

1 lb (450 g) green beans
Salt
4–6 tablespoons (60–90 ml) Aïoli Sauce (page 559)
Freshly ground black pepper
2–3 tablespoons (30–45 ml) finely chopped parsley

Cook beans in boiling salted water until tender – about 20 minutes. Drain well.

Mix while still warm with Aïoli Sauce. Toss well; season with salt and freshly ground black pepper; chill. Just before serving, toss well and sprinkle with finely chopped parsley. Serves 4.

RICE AND VEGETABLE SALAD

12 oz (350 g) rice
½ teaspoon (2.5 ml) powdered saffron
6 tablespoons (90 ml) dry white wine
1½ pints (900 ml) chicken stock
Salt and freshly ground black pepper
4 tablespoons (60 ml) cooked peas
4 oz (100 g) button mushrooms, quartered
½ cucumber, peeled, seeded and diced
4 stuffed olives, sliced
4 tomatoes, sliced
Ripe olives

DRESSING
6–8 tablespoons (90–120 ml) olive oil
2 tablespoons (30 ml) wine vinegar
4 tablespoons (60 ml) finely chopped parsley
1–2 cloves garlic, finely chopped
Dry mustard

Dissolve saffron in white wine; add it to hot chicken stock and combine in a large saucepan with rice, and salt and freshly ground black pepper, to taste. Cover pan and simmer until all the liquid is absorbed and the rice is tender – about 30 minutes.

Make a highly flavoured dressing with olive oil, wine vinegar, parsley, garlic and dry mustard, to taste.

Toss cooked saffron rice with peas, mushrooms, cucumber and stuffed olives in a bowl with dressing, and season generously with salt and freshly ground black pepper, adding more oil and vinegar if necessary. Garnish salad with sliced tomatoes and ripe olives. Serves 4.

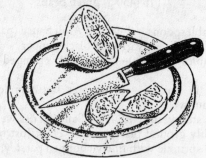

MUSHROOMS IN MUSTARD

1 lb (450 g) button mushrooms
Juice of 1 lemon
8 tablespoons (120 ml) olive oil
6 black peppercorns
2 bay leaves
1 tablespoon (15 ml) Dijon mustard
Salt
2 tablespoons (30 ml) finely chopped parsley

Wash and drain mushrooms. Trim ends of stems with a sharp knife and cut mushrooms in halves or quarters. Marinate in lemon juice and olive oil with peppercorns and bay leaves for at least 8 hours. Drain mushrooms (reserving marinade juices) and arrange them in an *hors-d'œuvre* dish.

To make a mustard sauce: combine 4 to 6 tablespoons (60–90 ml) marinade juices with Dijon mustard in a small jar, and shake until well blended. Add salt and a little more lemon juice or olive oil if necessary, and pour over mushrooms. Sprinkle with finely chopped parsley. Serves 4 to 6.

RATATOUILLE

8 tablespoons (120 ml) olive oil
2 Spanish onions sliced
2 green peppers, cubed
2 aubergines (eggplants), cubed or sliced
2 baby marrows, cut in ½-inch (12 mm) slices
4–6 ripe tomatoes, peeled, seeded and chopped
Salt and freshly ground black pepper
1 tablespoon (15 ml) chopped parsley
Pinch of marjoram or oregano
Pinch of basil
1 large clove garlic, crushed

Heat the olive oil in a large frying pan, add onion slices, and sauté until they are transparent. Then add the green peppers and aubergines (eggplants) and, 5 minutes later, the baby marrows and tomatoes. The vegetables should not be fried but stewed in the oil, so simmer gently in a covered pan for 30 minutes. Season to taste with salt and freshly ground black pepper, and add chopped parsley, marjoram, basil and crushed garlic; then cook uncovered for about 10 to 15 minutes, or until *Ratatouille* is well mixed and has the appearance of a *ragoût* of vegetables – which it is. Serve hot from the casserole, or cold as a delicious beginning to a summer meal. Serves 4.

RATATOUILLE IN TOMATO CASES

½ recipe Ratatouille (page 561)
6–8 tablespoons (90–120 ml) olive oil
2–3 tablespoons (30–45 ml) wine vinegar
Salt and freshly ground black pepper
Dry mustard
6 large ripe tomatoes
Finely chopped parsley

Prepare *Ratatouille*. Chill.

Combine olive oil and wine vinegar, and season to taste with salt, freshly ground black pepper and dry mustard. Toss *Ratatouille* in this dressing.

To prepare tomato cases: plunge tomatoes into boiling water, one by one, and remove their skins. Slice cap off each tomato and carefully scoop out all pulp and seeds. Cover loosely with foil and chill in refrigerator until ready to use.

Just before serving: fill tomato cases with *Ratatouille* mixture and sprinkle with finely chopped parsley. Serves 6.

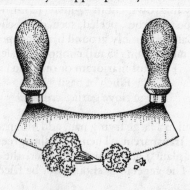

TARAMASALATA

1 jar smoked cod's roe (6 oz (175 g))
6 slices white bread
¼ Spanish onion, grated
1–2 cloves garlic, mashed
8 tablespoons (120 ml) olive oil
Juice of 1 lemon
1 tablespoon (15 ml) finely chopped parsley
Green olives
Hot toast

Place cod's roe in a mortar. Trim crusts from bread; soak bread in water; squeeze and add to cod's roe. Pound mixture to a smooth paste, and stir in onion and garlic. Then add olive oil and lemon juice alternately a little at a time, stirring well, until mixture acquires a smooth, uniform consistency. Strain through a fine sieve. (The above can be done in an electric blender, in which case the mixture does not need to be sieved.)

Serve in a salad bowl, sprinkled with finely chopped parsley and garnished with green olives. Serve with hot toast. Serves 4 to 6.

BARBECUED FISH

3 lb (1.4 kg) fresh fish fillets or steaks
(halibut, turbot, salmon or sea bass)
¼ pint (150 ml) olive oil
4 tablespoons (60 ml) wine vinegar
4 tablespoons (60 ml) dry sherry
2 tablespoons (30 ml) soy sauce
1–2 cloves garlic, finely chopped
1–2 bay leaves, crumbled
½ level teaspoon (2.5 ml) powdered ginger
1 level tablespoon (15 ml) sugar

Arrange fish fillets or steaks in a shallow glass or earthenware bowl. Combine remaining ingredients and pour over fish. Marinate in this mixture for at least 2 hours.

When ready to cook: place fish on a well-oiled grill over glowing charcoal (or in a flat ovenproof dish under grill of your cooker). Cook for 10 to 15 minutes, brushing from time to time with marinade juices. Turn and continue to cook until fish is done. Remove carefully to heated serving dish. Brush with remaining marinade and serve immediately. Serves 4 to 6.

GRILLED SEA BASS AUX HERBES

2 sea bass
2–3 tablespoons (30–45 ml) flour
2–3 tablespoons (30–45 ml) olive oil
Salt and freshly ground black pepper
2–3 sprigs each fennel, parsley and thyme

Flour cleaned fish lightly; brush with olive oil, and season to taste with salt and freshly ground black pepper. Stuff cavities of fish with herbs and grill for 3 to 5 minutes on each side, or until fish flakes easily with a fork. Baste fish with olive oil from time to time. Serves 4 to 6.

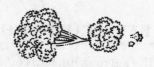

FLAMED SEA BASS AUX HERBES

2 sea bass, grilled as above
4–6 sprigs each rosemary, fennel and thyme
2–3 tablespoons (30–45 ml) hot cognac

Grill sea bass as above and remove them to a heated serving dish which has been covered with sprigs of rosemary, fennel and thyme. Top the fish with additional herbs; pour hot cognac over them and ignite. The burning herbs give the fish a delightful flavour. Serves 4 to 6.

Charcoal-grilled Steaks and Chops

Sirloin or rump steak: Should be at least 1½ inches (38 mm) thick. Brush whole steak with melted butter or olive oil; season generously with freshly ground black pepper and sear on both sides to hold in the juices. Then set grill about 4 inches (11 cm) from the coals and continue cooking, turning steak from time to time, until steak is done as you like it. I like it rare inside and crusty and brown (not black) on the outside. Slice steak into serving portions just before serving (about 12 oz/350 g for each portion). Timing: a 1-inch (25 mm) steak should cook rare in 3 to 5 minutes on each side; at 1½-inch (38 mm) steak, 4 to 7 minutes on each side; and a 2-inch (50 mm) one, 8 to 15 minutes on each side. Steaks thicker than 2 inches are just exaggerations and should be treated as roasts.

London broil: This cut of flavoursome flank steak, very popular in America, is grilled in one piece as above and then carved in very thin diagonal slices across the grain. This steak should be served very rare, as otherwise it will be tough. Timing: 3 to 6 minutes per side, according to thickness of steak.

Lamb steaks: One-inch (25 mm) thick steaks of lamb cut from the leg, brushed with a marinade sauce of olive oil, lemon juice and finely chopped garlic, are excellent when grilled over a charcoal or wood fire. The lamb steaks should be served rare for maximum flavour. Timing: 4 to 8 minutes per side.

Ham steaks: One-inch (25 mm) thick centre cuts of ham make delicious outdoor grills. Slit fat around edge of ham; brush steak with melted butter, and season generously with freshly ground black pepper before grilling over a low fire. Timing: 4 to 8 minutes per side.

Chops: One of the best outdoor grills I have ever tasted was also the simplest: thick veal chops cooked with halved tomatoes and large mushroom caps in a hinged grill. The chops and vegetables were brushed with melted butter, seasoned with rosemary, salt and freshly ground black pepper, and cooked over an open wood fire. Delicious. The fat from the chops and the flames gave a wonderful flavour to meat, and the tomatoes and mushrooms.

Lamb chops, veal chops and pork chops can all be grilled to perfection over wood or charcoal. But for the best results, the chops must be more than ¾ inch (18 mm) thick. Otherwise they tend to dry out in cooking.

Lamb chops and veal chops I prefer a little rare: pork chops, of course, should be better cooked, but still juicy. Always slit fat around chops in several places before cooking to prevent curling. Timing: for a ¾-inch (18 mm) lamb or veal chop, allow 2 to 5 minutes per side for rare; 5 to 8 minutes on each side for medium. For pork, allow 7 to 11 minutes. For a 1-inch (25 mm) lamb or veal chop, allow 3 to 6 minutes per side for rare; 6 to 10 minutes for medium. For a 1-inch (25 mm) pork chop, allow 9 to 14 minutes per side.

DAUBE IN THE ASHES

3 lb (1.4 kg) shin of beef, cut into 2-inch (5 cm) cubes
1 lb (450 g) unsmoked bacon, in 1 piece
3 Spanish onions, sliced
3 tablespoons (45 ml) olive oil
3 tablespoons (45 ml) butter
Flour
Coarse salt
Freshly ground black pepper
1–2 cloves garlic
1 strip dried orange peel
2 cloves
Bouquet garni (2 sprigs thyme, 4 sprigs parsley, 2 bay leaves)

Dice unsmoked bacon into large cubes; combine with sliced onions, olive oil and butter, and sauté in a heatproof casserole until onions are transparent. Sprinkle beef, cut into 2-inch (5 cm) cubes, with flour; add to casserole and continue to cook, stirring constantly, until beef browns. Then add coarse salt and freshly ground black pepper, garlic, dried orange peel, cloves and *bouquet garni*. Place a thick soup plate filled with cold water on top of the casserole to close it hermetically and place casserole in centre of hot ashes (bringing ashes up around casserole) for 2½ to 3 hours, replacing water in the soup plate as necessary.

For home cooking: place casserole in a preheated, very slow oven (275°–300°F/140°–150°C/GM1–2) for 2½ to 3 hours. Serves 4 to 6.

BARBECUED BEEF IN FOIL

2 lb (900 g) round of beef
Olive oil
4 medium-sized onions, quartered
4 medium-sized carrots

TOMATO BARBECUE SAUCE
½ small onion
1 clove garlic
1 sprig parsley
¼ pint (150 ml) tomato ketchup
2 tablespoons (30 ml) wine vinegar
2 tablespoons (30 ml) olive oil
1 teaspoon (5 ml) Worcestershire sauce
Freshly ground black pepper

Brush round of beef on both sides with oil, and grill until well browned on both sides. Place it on a double sheet of foil large enough to fold over roast; add quartered onions and carrots, and coat with Tomato Barbecue Sauce.

Fold foil over roast and cook for 45 to 60 minutes, or until meat is tender. Serves 4.

TOMATO BARBECUE SAUCE
Finely chop onion, garlic and parsley, and put in a large screw-top jar with all the other ingredients. Cover and shake vigorously until all ingredients are well blended. Allow to stand for 24 hours before using.

BOURBON BARBECUED LAMB

1 small leg of lamb, boned but not tied
Rice

MARINADE
¼ pint (150 ml) bourbon whisky
¼ pint (150 ml) olive oil
2 cloves garlic, finely chopped
2 bay leaves
¼ teaspoon (1.25 ml) each dried thyme,
tarragon and rosemary
Salt and freshly ground black pepper

Marinate lamb for 12 hours in marinade ingredients, turning meat several times during this period.

When ready to grill: build charcoal fire and burn until flames have subsided and coals are covered with ash. Drain lamb, reserving marinade; place it on grill about 7 inches (18 cms) from coals, and barbecue for 45 to 50 minutes, turning meat and brushing it with marinade every 10 minutes.

To serve: slice in thin strips and serve with rice. Serves 6.

LEMON GRILLED CHICKEN

3 young frying chickens, quartered
Salt and freshly ground black pepper

LEMON BARBECUE SAUCE
¼ pint (150 ml) olive oil
8 tablespoons (120 ml) lemon juice
2 tablespoons (30 ml) finely chopped onion
1–2 teaspoons (5–10 ml) dried tarragon
1–2 teaspoons (5–10 ml) finely chopped parsley
Salt, freshly ground black pepper and Tabasco

Sprinkle chicken with salt and freshly ground black pepper, and marinate in Lemon Barbecue Sauce for at least 4 hours.

When ready to grill: drain chicken pieces, reserving marinade juices, and place on grill about 6 inches (15 cm) from coals. Brush with marinade juices and cook slowly until tender – about 1¾ hours cooking time – turning chicken pieces and basting from time to time. Serves 6.

HERBED GUINEA FOWL

2 guinea fowl
2 cloves garlic, finely chopped
½ level teaspoon (2.5 ml) dried thyme
6 tablespoons (90 ml) softened butter
Grated peel of ¼ lemon
Lemon juice
Salt and freshly ground black pepper

Cut guinea fowl into quarters. Pound garlic, thyme, butter and lemon peel to a smooth paste with lemon juice, salt and freshly ground black pepper, to taste. Rub birds with this mixture; place in a well-buttered *gratin* dish and cook in a moderate oven (375°F/190°C/GM5) for 40 to 50 minutes, or until tender. Cool and wrap loosely in foil until ready to use. Serves 4.

CHILI CON CARNE WITH RED WINE

2 lb (900 g) lean beef
1 lb (450 g) fresh pork
1 Spanish onion, finely chopped
4 cloves garlic, chopped
2 tablespoons (30 ml) bacon fat
1 pint (600 ml) red wine
4 tablespoons (60 ml) chili powder
1 tablespoon (15 ml) flour
2 bay leaves
½ teaspoon (2.5 ml) powdered cumin
½ teaspoon (2.5 ml) oregano
Salt and freshly ground black pepper
Boiled red beans
Rice

Cut beef and pork into bite-sized cubes, trimming fat as you go. Brown meat, chopped onion and chopped garlic in bacon fat in a thick-bottomed heatproof casserole. Cover meat with red wine; bring gently to a boil. Cover casserole, lower heat, and simmer gently for about 1 hour.

Blend chili powder with flour in a little of the hot pan juices and add to the casserole at the same time as bay leaves, cumin and oregano. Season to taste with salt and freshly ground black pepper.

Simmer gently over low heat until meat is tender. The liquid should barely bubble if you want meat to be tender. Check seasoning, and serve with boiled red beans and rice. Serves 4 to 6.

Skewer Cookery

Skewer cookery can be great fun and delicious, and skewers can be made out of practically any food imaginable. I will always remember the Moroccan *brochettes* I enjoyed in the market-place at Marrakesh . . . liver, kidneys and, I think, heart, grilled on thin metal skewers over charcoal and brushed with the hottest pepper sauce imaginable. Mouth-searing outdoor eating at its best. If your palate takes to more delicate flavours, try beef, lamb or pork kebabs: cubes of tender meat, marinated in olive oil, lemon juice and soy sauce, flavoured with finely chopped shallots, garlic or onions, and a bay leaf or two. That is the host's job: then let guests prepare their own kebabs, alternating cubes of marinated meat with fresh vegetables, a bay leaf or two, and even cubes of bread, brushed with melted butter and finely chopped garlic. This is a perfectly easy formula for a summer party with a difference. And the choice of combinations is legion: serve bowls of small onions, either raw or poached, strips of green or red pepper, cubes of poached potato, mushroom caps, thin wedges of apple or tomato wrapped in bacon, whole small tomatoes, rum-soaked apricots and port-soaked prunes wrapped in bacon, cubes of fatty salt pork, small beef or pork burgers, and cubes of cooked ham.

French style: Marinate cubes of lamb in dry white wine, olive oil, fresh herbs and finely chopped garlic. Alternate on skewers with bay leaves and cubes of pork fat, and grill, basting with butter, until pink.

Italian style: Marinate beef cubes in red wine, oregano, garlic, olive oil, salt and pepper. Alternate with bay leaves and mushrooms, and grill, brushing with olive oil. Serve with Tomato Sauce (page 124).

Turkish style: Marinate cubed veal with dried thyme, crumbled bay leaf, crumbled rosemary, salt and a little lemon juice. Grill, and serve on rice.

Chinese style: Marinate pork cubes in soy sauce, honey, and *sake* or dry sherry, with finely chopped garlic and spring onions. Grill, and serve with soy sauce and mustard sauce.

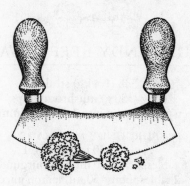

FISH SOUVLAKIA

2 lb (900 g) fresh halibut
4 tomatoes, thinly sliced
2 onions, thinly sliced
Rice pilaff

MARINADE SAUCE
6 tablespoons (90 ml) olive oil
6 tablespoons (90 ml) dry white wine
1–2 cloves garlic, finely chopped
½ onion, finely chopped
2 tablespoons (30 ml) finely chopped parsley
1 level teaspoon (5 ml) oregano
Salt and freshly ground black pepper

Combine Marinade Sauce ingredients in a mixing bowl. Cut fish into 1½-inch (38 mm) squares and toss in marinade mixture to make sure each piece of fish is properly covered with marinade. Place sliced tomatoes and onion on top; cover bowl with a plate and refrigerate for at least 6 hours. Turn fish several times during marinating period.

When ready to cook: place fish on skewers alternately with tomato and onion slices. Brush fish and vegetables with Marinade Sauce, and cook over charcoal or under grill of your cooker until done, turning skewers frequently and basting several times during cooking. Serve *souvlakia* with rice pilaff. Serves 4 to 6.

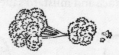

BURGUNDY BEEF KEBABS

3 lb (1.4 kg) steak
12 oz (350 g) mushroom caps
2–3 green peppers, cut into 1-inch (25 mm) squares

BURGUNDY MARINADE
¼ pint (150 ml) olive oil
6 tablespoons (90 ml) red Burgundy
2 tablespoons (30 ml) lemon juice
2 tablespoons (30 ml) soy sauce
1–2 cloves garlic, finely chopped
¼ teaspoon (1.25 ml) dry mustard
¼ teaspoon (1.25 ml) dried thyme
2 tablespoons (30 ml) finely chopped celery
½ Spanish onion, coarsely chopped
Salt and freshly ground black pepper

Cut meat into 1-inch (25 mm) cubes. Combine Burgundy Marinade ingredients in a large bowl; add meat; stir well and refrigerate overnight. When ready to use, drain meat and reserve marinade.

To grill: arrange beef cubes on long skewers, alternating with mushroom caps and green pepper squares. Grill over hot coals, turning meat and basting from time to time, until cooked as you like it. Serves 6.

CALIFORNIA BEEF KEBABS

2 lb (900 g) tender beef
4 tablespoons (60 ml) soy sauce
8 tablespoons (120 ml) olive oil
4 tablespoons (60 ml) finely chopped onion
1 clove garlic, crushed
Freshly ground black pepper
Pinch of powdered cumin
Green and red pepper squares
Button onions, parboiled
Tomatoes, quartered

Cut beef into 1-inch (25 mm) cubes and marinate in soy sauce, olive oil, chopped onion, garlic, freshly ground black pepper and powdered cumin for at least 2 hours. When ready to cook: arrange beef on skewers alternately with squares of green and red pepper, small white onions and quartered tomatoes. Grill as above. Serves 4.

BROCHETTES DE MOUTON

2 lb (900 g) tender lamb
½ pint (300 ml) olive oil
6 tablespoons (90 ml) lemon juice
1 tablespoon (15 ml) honey
1 clove garlic, crushed
2 bay leaves, crushed
Salt and freshly ground black pepper
Green and red pepper squares
Button onions, parboiled
Tomatoes, quartered

Cut lamb into 1-inch (25 mm) cubes. Combine olive oil with lemon juice, honey, crushed garlic and bay leaves. Season to taste with salt and freshly ground black pepper, and marinate lamb in this mixture for 2 to 4 hours.

Thread cubes of meat on skewers alternately with squares of green and red peppers, button onions and quartered tomatoes, and grill for 15 to 20 minutes, brushing frequently with the marinade. Serves 4.

MIXED GRILL 'SKUETS'

8 oz (225 g) boned sirloin
8 oz (225 g) boned shoulder of lamb
8 oz (225 g) lamb's kidney
4 tablespoons (60 ml) olive oil
4 tablespoons (60 ml) lemon juice
1 clove garlic, finely chopped
½ teaspoon (2.5 ml) each dried thyme and sage
Mushroom caps
Small white onions, parboiled

Cut beef and lamb into 2-inch (5 cm) cubes; cut kidney into thinner pieces. Marinate meats in olive oil and lemon juice with finely chopped garlic and herbs for at least 1 hour. Thread meats on skewers with mushroom caps and small parboiled onions. Grill. Serves 4.

PORK AND BEEF KEBABS

1 lb (450 g) pork, cut from leg
1 lb (450 g) round beef steak
8 oz (225 g) Spanish onions, finely chopped
Salt and freshly ground black pepper
Olive oil
4–6 tomatoes
4–6 small onions, poached
2 baby marrows, sliced
4–6 mushrooms caps

Have pork and beef cut into steaks about 1 inch (25 mm) thick; cut steaks into 2-inch (5 cm) squares. Combine meats and finely chopped Spanish onions in a bowl with salt, freshly ground black pepper and 6 to 8 tablespoons (90–120 ml) olive oil. Toss well, cover bowl with a plate and refrigerate overnight.

When ready to cook: remove meat from onion mixture (reserving onions for later use), and arrange pork and beef on 4 to 6 skewers alternately with tomato, poached onion, slices of baby marrow and a mushroom cap.

Brush meat and vegetables lightly with olive oil and cook over charcoal or under cooker grill until done, turning skewers frequently and basting several times during cooking. Roll skewers in reserved onion mixture and serve immediately. Serves 4 to 6.

INDONESIAN SKEWERED PORK

3 lb (1.4 kg) loin of pork, boned
Salt and freshly ground black pepper
2 tablespoons (30 ml) coriander
2 teaspoons (10 ml) cumin seed
1 Spanish onion, finely chopped
2 teaspoons (10 ml) brown sugar
4 tablespoons (60 ml) soy sauce
4 tablespoons (60 ml) lemon juice
8 tablespoons (120 ml) dry white wine
¼ teaspoon (1.25 ml) powdered ginger

Cut pork into 1-inch (25 mm) cubes and combine in a porcelain bowl with remaining ingredients. Mix well and allow pork cubes to marinate in this mixture for at least 4 hours, turning pork from time to time so that it becomes impregnated with all the flavours.

When ready to grill: drain and reserve marinade. Arrange 4 to 6 cubes of meat on each skewer; brush with marinade and grill for 5 minutes about 3 inches (8 cms) from the coals. Turn pork and baste with marinade every 5 minutes until pork is done – 20 to 25 minutes in all. Serves 6.

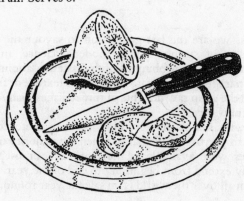

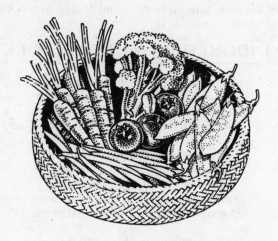

CHAPTER SIXTEEN
Vegetables

Alas, we are the last generation to savour the new, fresh tastes of spring. But is modern science, in giving us year-round bounty, robbing us of the taste sensations of the first tender asparagus, the delicate flavour and texture of fresh garden peas, and the crisp raw delights of tiny radishes, baby cucumbers and little new carrots?

Today, the season of everything has been stretched, so that if we were to prepare a calendar of when the majority of fruits and vegetables were available in the markets, our list would undoubtedly extend from beginning to end of the year. Gas-stored fruit from all over the world is on sale the year round, vegetables are frozen as soon as they are picked, even game is popped into deep-freeze by amateurs, so that what were the delights of a few weeks of the year now rumble on, half unnoticed, from January to December.

Of course, the convenience of this year-round bounty is enormous. Today, we could not do without our perennially present tomatoes, lettuce, celery and green peppers. Apples, pears and grapes from the Southern Hemisphere, citrus, melons and avocados from the Mediterranean, frozen and canned foods from the Americas, all help in the daily planning of our menus. But must we – in the first flush of excitement over the immense potential of accelerated freeze-drying – forget the subtle, wistful pleasures of seasonal foods?

I am afraid that when it comes to eating, I am a traditionalist; I want my tastes seasonally inspired. I like to feel the months rolling by; I want to make the most of the tender new spring vegetables: tiny new potatoes of the season's first digging, each one a fragile melting mouthful, served with mint or dill, and lemon butter; fresh garden peas, twice as sweet as the later, full-blown ones, simmered in butter with bacon, tiny white onions and shredded lettuce; carrots and mushrooms so young that a few minutes of gentle cooking in butter, or butter and cream, brings them to the peak of their perfection.

Asparagus, that most delicate of spring vegetables, I like thoroughly washed or scraped (they can be gritty), then simply steamed with the smallest amount of water and served hot with melted butter or Hollandaise Sauce, or à la polonaise. I think asparagus is important in its own right and should be served separately as a hot or cold hors-d'œuvre, or as a separate vegetable course.

And who can deny that a fresh, green salad is the very essence of spring? I like mine made of baby lettuces with the added peppery piquancy of watercress, bathed in an olive oil and wine vinegar dressing, with a hint of shallot and the merest breath of garlic to accent its delicate flavour. Later in the year, a little basil or eau-de-Cologne mint will add its touch to the harmony of the dish.

Young spinach leaves served raw with a French dressing, or steamed with a tablespoon or two of water and a drop of olive oil, are a sure sign to me that spring is here. I like them, too, cooked in this way, then chilled, and served with olive oil and lemon as a salad.

To Prepare Vegetables

Remove coarse or damaged leaves and decayed or discoloured parts from all vegetables before cooking. When freshly gathered, they should be washed just before cooking, but when bought commercially, it is often necessary to soak them in water for a short time in order to restore some of their original freshness.

Always soak close-leaved green vegetables such as cabbage, cauliflower and Brussels sprouts in water with a little lemon juice or vinegar for about ½ hour before cooking to remove insects.

Select vegetables that are crisp, fresh-looking and colourful. No amount of cooking and attention will revive a limp, tired one. It has lost its texture, a great deal of its flavour, and most of its goodness.

Do not peel vegetables unless absolutely necessary; most of the goodness is right under the skin or in the skin itself. Wash vegetables with a stiff vegetable brush or, in the case of mushrooms, tomatoes and very new potatoes, just wipe clean with a damp cloth.

Store cleaned vegetables in plastic bags or boxes in the re-frigerator to keep them crisp and fresh until ready to be used. Parsley and other herbs will keep green and fresh in this way for weeks.

To Cook Vegetables

Both French and Chinese cuisines treat vegetables with the reverence they deserve, cooking them in a little butter or oil, with just enough water, stock, wine or even steam to bring out their delicate flavours and textures.

The Chinese, particularly, are masters of the art of vegetable cookery. Serve your vegetables slightly crisp as they do, and not reduced to a pulpy, colourless mass. And follow their method of cutting vegetables across the grain into small uniform pieces, so that they will cook evenly and quickly when simmered in liquid or 'stir-fried' in vegetable oil.

STEAMING
The old-fashioned method of boiling vegetables in a pot full of water and then throwing the water away has much to condemn it;

so many of the valuable vitamins and trace elements are lost in the water. I far prefer to steam vegetables to obtain the utmost in flavour. The younger and more delicately flavoured vegetables can be cooked in this way in 15 minutes; older vegetables and more heartily flavoured vegetables can also be steamed if they are first blanched.

'WATERLESS' COOKING

I like to use heavy, shallow pans with tight-fitting lids for almost waterless cooking, with just a little chicken stock or water, and little butter or olive oil to add lustre and savour. When served hot with fresh butter, freshly ground black pepper and salt, or with a lemon- or mustard-flavoured sauce, you have a dish fit for the gods.

BRAISING

Another very good way of cooking vegetables to preserve maximum flavour is to braise them in a shallow heatproof casserole.

To Serve Vegetables

I have never been interested in the vegetable primarily as an accompaniment to meat or fish. Except in rare instances, potatoes or rice or noodles can do that with great ease. So take a page from the notebooks of the best French chefs, and serve vegetables as a separate course after the main course. This will allow guests to savour the flavour of meat, game or fish more fully, and permit you to add another texture and flavour surprise in your separate vegetable course.

One of the best vegetable salads in the world is chilled string beans *à la vinaigrette*: string beans cooked in very little water with a little butter or olive oil until just tender, not mushy and over-cooked, drained, and dressed with a Vinaigrette Dressing to which you have added finely chopped garlic and parsley. Try this, too, with broccoli or small Brussels sprouts. Delicious.

For interesting vegetable accompaniments to meat, try leeks or endive braised in oil and butter with a clove or two of garlic and a sprig of thyme; tomatoes or mushroom caps stuffed with a Provençal mixture of fresh breadcrumbs, finely chopped garlic and parsley; sliced mushrooms simmered for a moment only in butter and lemon juice with a hint of rosemary or thyme; or a noble *gratin dauphinois*, thinly sliced new potatoes cooked in cream with freshly grated Parmesan and Gruyère cheese.

Always serve vegetables as soon as possible after cooking; many lose flavour and texture if kept warm over any period of time.

Keep a vegetable juice jar for any liquid left over after cooking your vegetables. Strain the liquid into a special jar kept covered in the refrigerator for this purpose. Vegetable juices preserved in this way make wonderful flavour additives for soups, sauces and stews.

Artichokes

You have only to visit a Roman street market in mid-morning – the bustling Campo de' Fiori under the great, grey Palazzo Farnese, or the steeply inclined street just past the Trevi fountain – to see some of the most beautiful food in existence. Great platters of fish in all the colours of the rainbow; fruit and vegetables spilling from the stalls almost to the pavement; golden-yellow cheeses; milk-fed lambs and young kid no bigger than hares; tender young leaves of spinach; green cabbage and red cabbage, picked when still hardly more than sprouts – just right to be included raw, along with crisp pink radishes, in the salads so appreciated by the Romans; and minute purple artichokes, perfect for making one of Rome's most famous dishes, *carciofi alla romana* – young artichokes cooked Roman style – high on the list of specialities not to be missed in Rome.

Baked, fried, stuffed, puréed with rich cream as an accompanying vegetable, even in soup, the artichoke is a very versatile vegetable. Cook it in boiling water with a little salt, olive oil and lemon juice, and serve it cold *à la vinaigrette* as a first course, or hot as a separate vegetable course. Simmer artichoke hearts in olive oil and lemon juice, flavoured with a little finely chopped garlic and oregano, for a hot or cold *hors-d'œuvre*. Or serve halved or quartered hot artichokes with Hollandaise Sauce, or melted butter and lemon. I like, too, to stuff artichoke hearts with various ingredients – finely chopped mushrooms, minced chicken and herbs, or a mousse of green beans – or use them as decorative edible containers for Béarnaise or Hollandaise Sauce.

ARTICHOKES VINAIGRETTE

4 artichokes
Salt
Juice of ½ lemon
Vinaigrette Sauce (page 691).

Remove tough outer leaves of artichokes and trim tops of inner leaves. Trim the base and stem of each artichoke with a sharp knife. Cook until tender (30 to 40 minutes) in a large quantity of salted boiling water to which you have added the juice of ½ lemon. Artichokes are ready when a leaf pulls out easily.

When cooked, turn artichokes upside down to drain. Serve them cold with a well-flavoured Vinaigrette Sauce. Pull off a leaf at a time and eat the tender base of each leaf. Then remove 'choke' (fuzzy centre) and eat artichoke heart. Serves 4.

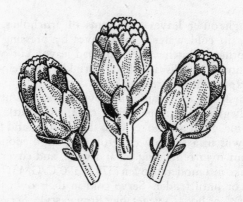

ARTICHOKES WITH GREEN MAYONNAISE

4 artichokes
Salt
Juice of ½ lemon
Green Mayonnaise (page 120)

Prepare and cook artichokes as in preceding recipe. Serve cold with well-flavoured Green Mayonnaise. Serves 4.

CARCIOFI ALLA ROMANA

6 small artichokes
Lemon juice
2 tablespoons (30 ml) finely chopped parsley
2–4 cloves garlic, mashed
2 tablespoons (30 ml) finely chopped fresh mint
2–4 anchovy fillets, mashed
4 tablespoons (60 ml) fresh breadcrumbs
Salt and freshly ground black pepper
¼ pint (150 ml) olive oil
½ pint (300 ml) dry white wine

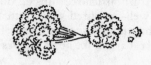

Trim tough outer leaves and stems of artichokes. Wash the artichokes in cold water. Open leaves by pressing artichokes against corner of kitchen table. Spread leaves; cut out 'chokes' (fuzzy centres) and discard them; sprinkle with lemon juice to prevent exposed hearts turning black.

Mix parsley, garlic, mint, anchovies, breadcrumbs, and salt and freshly ground black pepper, to taste, with a little of the olive oil and wine. Stuff artichokes with this mixture and place them, heads down, in a shallow casserole just large enough to hold them. Pour over remaining oil and wine, and cover with oiled paper. Bake in a moderate oven (375°F/190°C/GM5) for about 45 minutes, or until tender. Serve cold in their own juices as an *hors-d'œuvre*, or hot as a vegetable, Roman style. Serves 6.

Asparagus

Before asparagus was widely used as a food, it enjoyed a great reputation as a medicine for almost everything from toothache to heart trouble. The early Greeks and Romans enjoyed this delicious vegetable both fresh, as we do – and dried. The dried stalks were prepared by boiling them, making them perhaps the first dehydrated vegetable.

I like to serve asparagus hot with melted butter and lemon juice or Hollandaise Sauce, or cold with a *sauce ravigote* or *vinaigrette*. Asparagus tips make a delicious garnish for chicken, veal and ham in the Italian manner, and puréed asparagus makes a delicious soup.

To Prepare Asparagus

Wash the stalks thoroughly and, if sandy, scrub them gently with a vegetable brush. If there are some isolated leaf points below the head, remove them. To remove woody base, break stalks instead of cutting them. You will find that the stalk snaps off easily at the point where the tender part begins. Put the stalks in cold water as you clean and trim them.

To Cook Asparagus

I find it is best to sort home-grown asparagus into bundles of corresponding thickness, so that you can remove the thinner ones, as they will be ready before the thicker ends. Commercial bundles are usually graded to size already. Tie bundles securely in two places.

BOILING
Select a deep, narrow pan in which the asparagus stalks can stand upright, and pour in boiling water to just under the tips; in this way, the stalks can cook in water and the tender heads can cook in steam. Simmer gently – about 10 to 15 minutes from the time the water comes to a boil again after immersion is just about right. Slender stalks will take less time.

STEAMING
Lay asparagus stalks flat in a *gratin* dish; add 4 tablespoons (60 ml) chicken stock or water, 4 tablespoons (60 ml) butter, and salt and freshly ground black pepper, to taste. Place *gratin* dish in the top of a double steamer over boiling water (or on a trivet or brick to hold *gratin* dish over water in a large saucepan); cover pan and steam for 15 to 20 minutes, or until tender.

CHINESE QUICK STIR-FRYING

The Chinese cook asparagus in a most delicious manner. Cut stalks diagonally, making thin, slant-edged slices about 1½ inches (38 mm) long. Heat salad oil in a large frying pan or Chinese *wok*; add asparagus; sprinkle lightly with salt, freshly ground black pepper and monosodium glutamate, and cook over high heat, stirring, for 2 or 3 minutes. Add 4 tablespoons (60 ml) chicken stock or water; cover pan and cook over medium heat for 3 to 5 minutes, shaking pan frequently. Season to taste with soy sauce or lemon juice. Serve immediately. Asparagus segments should be cooked through but still crisp.

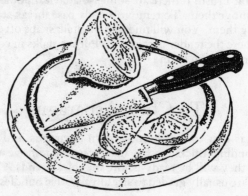

Asparagus Variations

Cook asparagus in any one of the ways above and serve with the following dressings:

1. Sprinkle blanched toasted almonds and melted butter over hot cooked asparagus.
2. Add diced hard-boiled egg to a well-flavoured Cream Sauce (page 107) and pour over hot cooked asparagus.
3. Add 2 tablespoons (30 ml) lemon juice and 2 tablespoons (30 ml) finely chopped parsley to 4 oz (100 g) melted butter, and pour over hot cooked asparagus.
4. Make a well-flavoured Vinaigrette Sauce (page 691); add finely chopped hard-boiled egg, parsley and gherkins, and pour over cold cooked asparagus. Serve cold as appetizer or separate salad course.

FRESH ASPARAGUS HOLLANDAISE

1 bunch fresh asparagus
Hollandaise Sauce (page 123)

Boil or steam asparagus as directed on page 583. Drain asparagus and serve with Hollandaise Sauce.

FROZEN ASPARAGUS TIPS WITH PROSCIUTTO

1 packet frozen asparagus tips, poached
Thin slices of prosciutto
Butter
2–4 tablespoons (30–60 ml) double cream
2–4 tablespoons (30–60 ml) freshly grated Parmesan

Wrap 2 poached asparagus tips in each slice of *prosciutto*. Fasten with wooden cocktail sticks. Arrange bundles in a well-buttered ovenproof dish, and sprinkle with double cream, freshly grated Parmesan and 2 oz (50 g) butter, diced. Bake in a preheated moderately hot oven (400°F/200C/GM6) for 5 minutes. Melt 2 oz (50 g) butter; pour over asparagus bundles and serve immediately. Serves 4.

ASPARAGUS POLONAISE

2 lb (900 g) asparagus
Pinch of sugar
Salt and freshly ground black pepper
1 tablespoon (15 ml) butter

POLONAISE SAUCE
4 oz (100 g) butter
3 oz (75 g) light breadcrumbs
2 hard-boiled eggs, finely chopped
1 tablespoon (15 ml) finely chopped chives

Wash and trim asparagus. Lay flat in a shallow saucepan and cook, covered, in a small amount of boiling water to which you have added sugar, salt, freshly ground black pepper and butter, until just tender – 10 to 15 minutes.

Drain asparagus and place on serving dish. Spoon Polonaise Sauce over it and serve immediately. Serves 4.

POLONAISE SAUCE
Melt butter in a saucepan; add breadcrumbs and sauté gently until light brown; then add finely chopped hard-boiled eggs and chives.

ITALIAN BAKED ASPARAGUS

1 lb (450 g) uncooked asparagus spears
2–4 tablespoons (30–60 ml) butter
2 tablespoons (30 ml) finely chopped onion
2 tablespoons (30 ml) finely chopped celery
1 tablespoon (15 ml) freshly grated Parmesan
1 tablespoon (15 ml) freshly grated breadcrumbs
4 canned Italian peeled tomatoes, diced
Salt and freshly ground black pepper
Pinch of oregano
Pinch of thyme

Melt butter in the bottom of a rectangular baking dish. Line bottom with asparagus spears; sprinkle with finely chopped onion, celery, cheese, breadcrumbs and diced canned tomatoes, and season to taste with salt, pepper, oregano and thyme. Cover dish and bake in a preheated moderate oven (375°F/190°C/GM5) for 45 minutes, or until tender. Serves 4.

Aubergines (Eggplants)

Carried into the Mediterranean area by the Arabs in the Early Middle Ages, the aubergine was a favourite with Greek, Turkish, Italian, French and Spanish cooks as far back as the twelfth century.

The Arabs used to scorch aubergines over charcoal, purée the creamy white flesh of the vegetable, season it with spices, and garnish it with sesame and pomegranate seeds. The Turks, Greeks and Armenians combine the aubergine in many recipes with lamb, onion and herbs, the most prized being the dish known as *moussaka*.

The aubergine has had a colourful career. At one time, it was thought that eating this exotic vegetable would cause insanity. Others damned it for its supposed aphrodisiac qualities. Today, we know the aubergine in Britain in two forms, egg-shaped and long-fruited, but in other parts of the world it is white, ash-coloured or brown, as well as the more familiar purple.

Do not peel aubergines. The skin contains a good deal of flavour and helps to hold the delicate flesh together in cooking. I always like to salt them, whether diced, sliced or cut in half, and allow them to drain for 1 hour, before using them in any one of the recipes below.

Use aubergines, diced and sautéed in butter or olive oil, as an exotic garnish for any of the following dishes: scrambled eggs, poached eggs, omelettes, fish, lamb or mutton chops or cutlets, and fried or casseroled chicken.

AUBERGINE AND GROUND BEEF CASSEROLE

4 medium aubergines, sliced
1 large onion, coarsely chopped
Butter
1½ lb (675 g) ground lean beef
¼ pint (150 ml) tomato concentrate
¾ pint (450 ml) water
1 level teaspoon (5 ml) salt
¼ level teaspoon (1.25 ml) freshly ground black pepper

Sauté chopped onion in 4 tablespoons (60 ml) butter until golden. Add the meat and cook, stirring continuously, until it is browned. Combine the tomato concentrate with the water; add salt and freshly ground black pepper, and pour sauce over meat. Bring to a boil and simmer for 5 minutes. Remove mixture.

Sauté aubergine slices in 8 tablespoons (120 ml) butter and place a layer of aubergine in the bottom of a well-buttered casserole. Using a slotted spoon, add a layer of drained beef, another layer of aubergine, then beef, and so on, until all the beef and aubergines have been used up.

Pour over the remaining sauce, and bake, uncovered, in a slow oven (350°F/180°C/GM4) until aubergines are tender. Serves 4.

AUBERGINES IMAM BAYELDI 'WHITE TOWER'

4 medium-sized aubergines
Salt
Olive oil
2 Spanish onions, sliced
2 cloves garlic, finely chopped
2 tablespoons (30 ml) finely chopped parsley
6 ripe tomatoes, seeded and chopped
4 whole tomatoes
Sugar
Freshly ground black pepper

Trim aubergines; cut in half lengthwise and scoop out some of the flesh, leaving shell about ¼ inch (6 mm) thick. Make 4 incisions lengthwise in each half, being careful not to cut through skin. Salt aubergine halves, making sure salt goes into incisions, and leave for 20 minutes. Wash aubergines, squeeze dry, and sauté in olive oil until they are soft and pliable. Reserve oil.

In another frying pan, sauté sliced onions in fresh olive oil until transparent. Add finely chopped garlic and parsley, and seeded and chopped tomatoes, and sauté for a few minutes more, stirring from time to time. Allow to cool.

Place sautéed aubergines cut side up in a fairly deep baking dish or shallow casserole. Stuff with onion and tomato mixture, spooning any left over around aubergines.

Slice 4 whole tomatoes and place slices on top of stuffing; sprinkle with a little sugar, salt and freshly ground black pepper, to taste.

Pour over the reserved oil; add a little water and cook in a slow oven (325°F/170°C/GM3) for 1 hour. Serves 4 to 6.

AUBERGINES AU GRATIN

4 aubergines, peeled and diced
Salt
4 tablespoons (60 ml) olive oil
Butter
1 Spanish onion, finely chopped
2 tablespoons (30 ml) tomato concentrate
6 tomatoes, peeled, seeded and coarsely chopped
1–2 cloves garlic, finely chopped
2 tablespoons (30 ml) finely chopped parsley
Freshly ground black pepper
Generous pinch each of allspice, cinnamon and sugar
Breadcrumbs

Peel and dice aubergines; salt them liberally and leave to drain in a colander for 1 hour. Rinse off salt with cold water and shake diced aubergines dry in a cloth. Combine olive oil and 2 tablespoons (30 ml) butter in a frying pan, and sauté aubergines until golden. Remove from pan, and in the same oil fry onion until soft and just turning golden, adding more oil if necessary. Add tomato concentrate, peeled, seeded and coarsely chopped tomatoes, and finely chopped garlic and parsley, and season to taste with salt, pepper, allspice, cinnamon and sugar. Simmer mixture, stirring occasionally, for 5 minutes. Add diced aubergines; pour into a buttered *gratin* dish (or individual soufflé dishes); sprinkle with breadcrumbs; dot with butter and bake in a moderate oven (375°F/170°C/GM5) for 30 minutes.

This Turkish dish makes an excellent *hors-d'œuvre*, served hot or cold. Serves 4 to 6.

TIAN À LA PROVENÇALE

4 small aubergines
4 small courgettes (baby marrows)
Olive oil
2 green peppers
2 red peppers
2 yellow peppers
4 cloves garlic, finely chopped
4 tablespoons (60 ml) finely chopped parsley
Thyme and marjoram
8 tomatoes
Butter
4 tablespoons (60 ml) fresh breadcrumbs

Cut aubergines and courgettes in thin strips, and sauté separately in olive oil. Cut peppers (green, red and yellow) in rings, and sauté as above. A few minutes before the end of cooking, sprinkle the aubergines and courgettes with 2 cloves garlic, finely chopped, 2 tablespoons (30 ml) parsley, and thyme and marjoram, to taste.

Cut tomatoes into thick rounds; place them in a buttered *gratin* dish, and cook *à la provençale* with remaining garlic and parsley, and the breadcrumbs.

Arrange cooked vegetables in a large ovenproof *gratin* dish, with the tomatoes in the centre, the aubergines on one side, and the courgettes on the other. Then place red, yellow and green pepper rings in a lattice over vegetables. Brown under the grill and serve immediately. Also good served cold. Serves 4 to 6.

Green Beans

French beans, *haricots verts*, string beans, just plain green beans –
whatever you choose to call them, they are fabulous fare. They
are at their very best, and unfortunately most expensive in the
markets, when they are at their smallest, and still stringless. All
that must be done before cooking is to 'top and tail' them, wash
them, and place them in a bowl with a little butter, salt and freshly
ground black pepper. Then steam them over water, or cook them
in boiling salted water, until they are tender. When they are a little
older, it is necessary to remove the filament or 'string' that binds
the two shells together. When they are older still (runner bean
size), it is best to cut them diagonally in thin slices before cooking
them as above.

Green beans should never be overcooked. For the ultimate in
flavour, they should remain a little firm to the bite – *al dente* like
Italian spaghetti or rice.

BASIC BOILED GREEN BEANS

1 lb (450 g) green beans
Salt and freshly ground black pepper
2 tablespoons (30 ml) butter
1 tablespoon (15 ml) finely chopped parsley

Cook beans in boiling salted water until tender – about 20
minutes. Drain; place in a heated serving dish. Season to taste
with salt and freshly ground black pepper. Top with butter and
finely chopped parsley. Serves 4.

BASIC STEAMED GREEN BEANS

1 lb (450 g) green beans
2 tablespoons (30 ml) finely chopped shallots or spring onions
2 tablespoons (30 ml) butter
Lemon juice
Salt and freshly ground black pepper

Place whole beans in a shallow *gratin* dish or bowl with finely chopped shallots or spring onions and butter, and steam over boiling water in a tightly closed saucepan or double steamer until tender – 15 to 20 minutes. Season to taste with lemon juice, salt and freshly ground black pepper. Serves 4.

GREEN BEANS À LA GRECQUE

1 lb (450 g) green beans
1 can tomato concentrate
1 pint (600 ml) water
4–6 tablespoons (60–90 ml) olive oil
½ Spanish onion, finely chopped
½ clove garlic, finely chopped
Salt and freshly ground black pepper

Top and tail green beans, and slice them in half lengthwise. Mix tomato concentrate with water, olive oil, and finely chopped onion and garlic. Put beans in a saucepan; pour over tomato-onion mixture, and season to taste with salt and freshly ground black pepper; bring to a boil. Lower heat and simmer gently, stirring from time to time, for ¾ hour, or until sauce has reduced and beans are tender. Serves 4.

CHINESE GREEN BEANS

1 lb (450 g) green beans
2 tablespoons (30 ml) peanut oil or lard
1 level teaspoon (5 ml) salt
¼ pint (150 ml) water
1 tablespoon (15 ml) soy sauce, *sake* or dry sherry

Wash and trim beans; break them into sections about 1 inch (25 mm) long. Heat oil or lard in a *wok* or frying pan; add beans and cook over medium heat for 1 minute, stirring constantly.

Add salt and water; cover pan and cook beans for 3 minutes. Remove cover and simmer, stirring from time to time, until all the water has evaporated – about 5 minutes. Add soy sauce, *sake* or dry sherry, to taste, and serve. Serves 4.

ITALIAN GREEN BEANS

1 lb (450 g) fresh green beans
6 tablespoons (90 ml) chicken stock
2 tablespoons (30 ml) olive oil
4 canned Italian peeled tomatoes, diced
Salt and freshly ground black pepper
Pinch of dried oregano (optional)
2 tablespoons (30 ml) finely chopped parsley

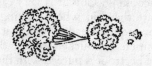

Combine chicken stock, olive oil and diced tomatoes in a sauce-pan, and bring to a boil. Add prepared green beans; season to taste with salt and freshly ground black pepper, and a pinch of oregano if desired. Cover saucepan and simmer gently for 1 hour. Remove cover and continue to simmer until excess moisture has evaporated and beans are tender. Sprinkle with finely chopped parsley and serve. Serves 4.

HARICOTS VERTS AU GRATIN

1½ lb (675 g) thin string beans
Salt
Butter
¾ pint (450 ml) double cream
Freshly ground black pepper
4–6 tablespoons (60–90 ml) freshly grated Gruyère
2 tablespoons (30 ml) freshly grated Parmesan

Poach string beans in salted water for 20 minutes, or until almost tender. Drain. Place in a well-buttered *gratin* dish and cover with cream. Season to taste with salt and freshly ground black pepper, and place in a preheated hot oven (450°F/230°C/GM8) for 20 minutes. Sprinkle with freshly grated cheeses; dot with butter and return to the oven until the cheese is golden brown and bubbling. Serves 6.

Beetroot

Beetroot, as we know it today, was introduced to Northern Europe in the sixteenth century. Colours vary from extremely dark red (almost purple) to bright red, and down the scale to off-white.

When you buy beetroots ready cooked, select those with a deep red colour; if they are to be cooked at home, choose beetroots with a sound skin, and be sure that this is not pierced or damaged in any way before cooking. Colour is very easily lost if water is allowed to penetrate the skin when cooking. For this reason, many cooks bake beetroot instead of boiling it.

Use beetroot simmered in chicken stock as the foundation for a delicious soup. The beetroot is puréed with the stock and double cream after cooking.

Serve sliced cooked beetroot with a lemon sauce slightly thickened with cornflour; use sliced beetroot as a garnish for green salads, potato salads and cold meats. Dice cooked beetroot and combine with diced cooked potatoes, cooked veal and pickled herrings, for an interesting supper or luncheon salad.

HARVARD BEETS

1 can or jar baby beetroots
1 level tablespoon (15 ml) cornflour
3 tablespoons (45 ml) vinegar or lemon juice
2 tablespoons (30 ml) sugar
Salt and freshly ground black pepper
1–2 tablespoons (15–30 ml) softened butter

Drain beetroots, reserving juice, and cut into even slices. Mix cornflour with ¼ pint (150 ml) reserved beet juice. Add vinegar (or lemon juice), sugar, and salt and freshly ground black pepper, to taste. Cook until thickened, stirring constantly. Add sliced beetroots; warm through. Just before serving, add softened butter and simmer until it has melted. Correct seasoning, adding more vinegar (or lemon juice), sugar or salt, as needed. Serves 4 to 6.

1 large cooked beetroot
1 teaspoon (5 ml) grated orange rind
¼ pint (150 ml) orange juice
2 tablespoons (30 ml) lemon juice
2 tablespoons (30 ml) sugar
1 level tablespoon (15 ml) cornflour
1–2 tablespoons (15–30 ml) butter
Salt

Peel and dice beetroot. Heat orange rind with orange and lemon juice. Mix sugar and cornflour, and stir into hot liquid. Cook, stirring constantly, until thickened. Add diced beetroot and butter; season to taste with salt, and heat through. Serves 4.

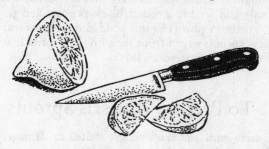

The Cabbage Family

Among the most maligned of our winter vegetables, the cabbage family – the common or garden 'sprout', green, white and red cabbage, and the more sophisticated cauliflower – are usually served boiled, with a pat of butter or margarine, gently swimming in their own water, almost invariably overcooked, and often – because of their advanced age – a trifle bitter to the taste. On festive occasions, a few boiled chestnuts or a cream sauce are added to these sorry dishes.

Yet how different these vegetables can be when treated with a little care and discrimination. Granted they must first be boiled or steamed, but they should be cooked only until the very moment of tenderness if their delicate fresh flavour is to be preserved.

Brussels Sprouts

I like to cook Brussels sprouts as in the directions below until just tender; then (1) toss them in butter in a frying pan, and just before serving, sprinkle with 4 tablespoons (60 ml) crisp crumbled bacon; (2) simmer them in butter with 4 tablespoons (60 ml) slivered almonds, and just before serving, sprinkle with lemon juice and finely chopped parsley; (3) simmer them in butter with a little garlic and fresh breadcrumbs, and just before serving, sprinkle with 4 tablespoons (60 ml) finely chopped cooked ham; (4) simmer them in butter, then moisten with sour cream; and (5) serve them as a delicious creamed soup – puréed, and simmered with a light cream sauce, made by combining 2 tablespoons (30 ml) each butter and flour with 1 pint (600 ml) each chicken stock and the liquid in which sprouts were cooked. Season to taste with butter, salt and freshly ground black pepper, and just before serving, stir in ¼ pint (150 ml) scalded double cream. Garnish with a few sprouts saved from the purée, or sprinkle with crisp crumbled bacon or watercress leaves.

To Prepare Brussels Sprouts

Cut off stem ends and remove any wilted or damaged outside leaves from small Brussels sprouts. (If Brussels sprouts are older, remove tough outside leaves entirely.) Soak sprouts in cold water with a little salt or lemon juice for 15 minutes.

To Cook Brussels Sprouts

Add sprouts to boiling salted water and simmer uncovered for 5 minutes. Cover pan and continue to cook for 7 (if very young) to 15 minutes longer, or until just tender. Drain well and season generously with salt and freshly ground black pepper. Use in any of the following ways.

BRUSSELS SPROUTS AU GRATIN

1 lb (450 g) small Brussels sprouts
Salt and freshly ground black pepper
Butter
1 pint (600 ml) well–flavoured cheese sauce
4 walnuts, finely chopped
2 tablespoons (30 ml) freshly grated breadcrumbs

Prepare and cook Brussels sprouts as above.

Place hot seasoned sprouts in a well-buttered ovenproof dish. Pour over well-flavoured cheese sauce.

Melt 4 tablespoons (60 ml) butter in a small saucepan; add finely chopped nuts and freshly grated breadcrumbs; simmer for a minute or two, then spoon over cheese sauce. Bake in a moderately hot oven (400°F/200°C/GM6) for 10 minutes. Serves 4.

BRUSSELS SPROUTS WITH BUTTERED BREADCRUMBS

1 lb (450 g) small Brussels sprouts
Salt and freshly ground black pepper
4–6 tablespoons (60–90 ml) toasted breadcrumbs
½ clove garlic, finely chopped
4 tablespoons (60 ml) butter
Lemon juice

Prepare and cook Brussels sprouts as above.

Combine hot seasoned sprouts in a frying pan with toasted breadcrumbs and finely chopped garlic, and sauté in butter until breadcrumbs are golden. Sprinkle with lemon juice, to taste. Serves 4.

BRUSSELS SPROUTS À LA POLONAISE

1 lb (450 g) small Brussels sprouts
Salt and freshly ground black pepper
4–6 tablespoons (60–90 ml) browned butter
Grated rind and juice of 1 lemon
4 tablespoons (60 ml) finely chopped parsley
Whites of 2 hard-boiled eggs, finely chopped

Prepare and cook Brussels sprouts as above.

Place hot seasoned sprouts in a heated serving dish; pour browned butter over them, sprinkle to taste with grated lemon rind, finely chopped parsley and egg white, and lemon juice. Serves 4.

Cabbage

There are three main types of cabbage:

Green: The common or green cabbage, sold everywhere, is bright green in the summer months, whiter, firmer and large in winter. The Savoy cabbage – a bright, deep green in colour, with a curly leaf – is much more delicate in flavour. I like to use its tender leaves for stuffed cabbage recipes.

White: White cabbage is used commercially for the preparation of sauerkraut, and is also used extensively for salads and cole slaw.

Red: Red cabbage is delicious, both raw and cooked. Always add lemon juice or vinegar to water when cooking this attractive vegetable, or it will turn purple in cooking. Red cabbage must be firm, and the outer leaves bright in colour. Cut the head in quarters and remove the heavy veins; then shred the rest of the cabbage on a coarse shredder. Often served raw as an *hors-d'œuvre* salad in France, red cabbage is equally delicious when shredded in this way, drained to the last drop of water in which it was cooked, and then simmered gently in butter or lard with diced apples and spices – a wonderful accompaniment to all pork dishes, goose and game.

CABBAGE CASSEROLE

1 head green cabbage (about 2 lb/900 g)
Salt
2 tablespoons (30 ml) cornflour
¾ pint (450 ml) milk
Coarsely grated Gruyère
Butter
Freshly ground black pepper and grated nutmeg

Remove and discard discoloured outer leaves from 1 head of green cabbage. Wash, core and shred cabbage, and soak in cold salted water for ½ hour. Drain; cook, covered, in a small amount of boiling salted water until just tender. Drain. Mix cornflour with a little hot milk; bring remaining milk to a boil in the top of a double saucepan; stir in cornflour mixture and cook over boiling water until mixture thickens. Add 6 tablespoons (90 ml) grated Gruyère, 4 tablespoons (60 ml) butter, and salt, freshly ground black pepper and nutmeg, to taste. Stir into cabbage and mix well. Turn the mixture into a well-buttered loaf tin; sprinkle with 4 tablespoons (60 ml) grated Gruyère; dot with butter and brown lightly in the oven. Serves 4.

RED CABBAGE

1 head red cabbage (about 2 lb/900 g)
2 tablespoons (30 ml) bacon fat
3 tart red apples, cored and sliced
½ Spanish onion, finely chopped
1 clove garlic, finely chopped
2–4 tablespoons (30–60 ml) wine vinegar
1 tablespoon (15 ml) flour
1–2 tablespoons (15–30 ml) brown sugar
1 teaspoon (5 ml) grated orange rind
Salt, freshly ground black pepper and grated nutmeg

Wash and shred cabbage, removing central core, ribs and outer leaves. Cook in bacon fat, in a covered saucepan, for 5 minutes. Add sliced apples and finely chopped onion and garlic, and bring to a boil with just enough water to cover. Cover, reduce heat, and simmer until tender but still crisp – about 15 minutes. Drain, reserving liquid.

Combine wine vinegar with flour and brown sugar, and stir in the reserved liquid. Cook, stirring, until thickened. Stir into cabbage; add grated orange rind, and season to taste with salt, freshly ground black pepper and nutmeg.

STEAMED STUFFED CABBAGE

1 Savoy cabbage
Butter
Tomato Sauce (page 124)

STUFFING
1 Spanish onion, chopped
Butter
8 oz (225 g) button mushrooms, chopped
1 lb (450 g) cooked ham, pork or veal, finely chopped
6 tablespoons (90 ml) cooked rice
Salt, freshly ground pepper and grated nutmeg
Chicken stock

STUFFING
Sauté chopped onion in 4 tablespoons (60 ml) butter until transparent; add mushrooms, and simmer, stirring constantly, until soft. In another pan, sauté ham in 2 tablespoons (30 ml) butter until golden; combine ham with vegetables and rice, and season generously with salt, freshly ground black pepper and nutmeg. Moisten with chicken stock.

Wash, trim and core cabbage; place it in a large saucepan. Cover with water and bring to a boil. Drain well. Cut out centre of cabbage in a circle with a diameter of about 2½ inches (7 cms), and scoop out to form a cup. Beginning with the outer leaves, separate leaves one by one, and fill each leaf with 1 to 2 tablespoons (15–30 ml) stuffing. Spoon remaining stuffing into cavity. Place cabbage in a well-buttered heatproof dish; cover loosely with foil and steam over boiling water in a covered pan until tender. Serve with Tomato Sauce. Serves 4.

Cauliflower

There are two basic methods of preparing cauliflower for the table – whole, and in florets. In either case never let the cauliflower become mushy. Undercook cauliflower so that each separate segment keeps its identity; mask it with a delicious sauce, and you will discover that it is one of your most delicious vegetables.

To Prepare Cauliflower

Trim stem and remove outer green leaves from cauliflower; wash and leave for ½ hour in cold salted water to which you have added a little lemon juice.

To Cook Cauliflower

WHOLE CAULIFLOWER
Measure enough water to cover cauliflower into a deep saucepan; add salt, to taste, and bring to a boil. Put cauliflower in the boiling water; bring to a boil again; then lower heat, cover saucepan and simmer gently for about 20 minutes, or until the cauliflower is just tender when pierced at the stem end with a fork. Do not over-cook. Drain well; arrange on a heated serving dish and top with melted butter, or a sauce or garnish.

CAULIFLORETS
If you do not intend to cook the head whole, break or cut cauliflower into florets. Prepare as above, but cook for 10 to 15 minutes only, so that florets are tender but not mushy. Drain florets and serve them with melted butter, or a sauce or garnish.

CAULIFLOWER SAUTÉ

1 cauliflower, cut into florets
Salt
4 tablespoons (60 ml) butter
Lemon juice
2 tablespoons (30 ml) finely chopped fresh herbs
(chives, chervil, parsley)

Clean cauliflorets and cook as above, but for 10 minutes only.
Drain well; sauté in butter and lemon juice until tender. Sprinkle
with finely chopped fresh herbs and serve immediately. Serves 4.

CAULIFLOWER AMANDINE

1 whole cauliflower
Salt
2 tablespoons (30 ml) blanched slivered almonds
4 tablespoons (60 ml) butter
Freshly ground black pepper

Clean cauliflower and cook as above. Drain. Sauté blanched
slivered almonds in butter; pour sauce over hot cauliflower,
and season to taste with salt and freshly ground black pepper.
Serves 4.

PAIN DE CHOU-FLEUR

1 whole cauliflower
Salt
3 egg yolks, well beaten
Softened butter
Freshly ground black pepper
Freshly grated nutmeg
½ pint (300 ml) Hollandaise Sauce (page 123)

Clean and cook cauliflower as above. Drain well and force
through a fine sieve. Beat in well-beaten egg yolks and 4 tablespoons (60 ml) softened butter, and season to taste with salt,

freshly ground black pepper and freshly grated nutmeg. Pour into a well-buttered soufflé dish or charlotte mould, and cook in a pan of hot water in a moderate oven (375°F/190°C/GM5) for 25 minutes. Turn out on to a heated serving dish and mask with Hollandaise Sauce. Serves 4.

Carrots

Particularly valuable for flavouring purposes in soups and stews, the carrot is a favourite standby – because of its bright colour, pleasing shape and delicate flavour – as a vegetable on its own. Ask anyone to name the most popular vegetables, and you will find the versatile carrot high on the list. Rich in both starch and sugar, carrots (generally those with a deep orange colour) are rich in carotene (pro-vitamin A) and contain many valuable mineral salts.

New carrots – so delicate that there is no suspicion of a woody core, so tender that a few minutes of gentle simmering in butter is all that is necessary to make them delicious – are best for serving as a vegetable. But the older ones, if carefully cooked to soften their somewhat woody fibre, can be used as the base for many delicious dishes, or as a prime flavourer for stocks, soups and stews.

To Prepare Carrots

Clean carrots with a stiff vegetable brush or with a stainless steel sponge. Do not peel carrots unless it is absolutely necessary – there is so much goodness in and just under the skin. If you do have to peel them, scrape them with the blade of your knife to remove only the smallest possible amount of skin.

Carrots may be diced, cubed, thinly sliced, diagonally sliced, cut into balls with a vegetable cutter, cut *en julienne* (matchstick-sized strips) or *en olives* (olive shapes).

Flavour carrots with butter, cream, sour cream, lemon juice, sherry, finely chopped parsley, dill and almonds.

To Cook Carrots

There is no reason on earth to boil carrots in a pot full of water. I far prefer to blanch them (place prepared carrots in a saucepan of cold water; bring to a boil and drain) and then simmer them for 15 to 20 minutes in 4 tablespoons (60 ml) butter add 4 tablespoons (60 ml) chicken stock (yes, even made with a cube), with sugar, salt and pepper, to taste. Delicious. Even more so if you add 4 tablespoons (60 ml) double cream and a sprinkling of finely chopped parsley or fresh mint just before serving. Sour cream is good, too.

CARROTS À LA BÉCHAMEL

Cook carrots as above; then, just before serving, add 4 to 6 tablespoons (60–90 ml) Béchamel Sauce (page 104).

CARROTS AUX FINES HERBES

Cook carrots as above; then, just before serving, sprinkle with 2 tablespoons (30 ml) each chopped parsley and chervil.

CARROTS À L'ORIENTALE

Cook carrots as directed, adding 2 tablespoons (30 ml) pre-soaked raisins at the same time as butter and chicken stock.

MOROCCAN CARROTS

2 lb (900 g) carrots, peeled and cut in quarters lengthwise
6 tablespoons (90 ml) water
6 tablespoons (90 ml) olive oil
2 cloves garlic
Salt and freshly ground black pepper
1–2 tablespoons (15–30 ml) vinegar
¼ level teaspoon (1.25 ml) cayenne pepper
¼ level teaspoon (1.25 ml) paprika
½ level teaspoon (2.5 ml) cumin powder
1–2 tablespoons (15–30 ml) finely chopped parsley

Blanch peeled quartered carrots in water to cover until water
boils. Drain; add 6 tablespoons (90 ml) each water and olive oil, 2
cloves garlic, and salt and freshly ground black pepper, and
simmer until carrots are tender. Drain; add vinegar, and generous
amounts of salt and pepper, and flavour to taste with cayenne,
paprika and cumin powder. Garnish with finely chopped parsley.
Serve cold as an appetizer. Serves 4 to 6.

HERBED CARROTS

1 lb (450 g) new carrots
2 tablespoons (30 ml) butter
2 tablespoons (30 ml) chicken stock or water
1 clove garlic, finely chopped
1 medium onion, finely chopped
1 tablespoon (15 ml) finely chopped parsley
Salt and freshly ground black pepper
½ level teaspoon (2.5 ml) rosemary
4 tablespoons (60 ml) cream

Wash carrots and cut diagonally into thin slices. Melt butter in
saucepan, and add chicken stock or water, sliced carrots, and
finely chopped garlic, onion and parsley. Season to taste with salt,
pepper and rosemary. Cover and cook over a low heat for 10 to 15
minutes, or until carrots are just tender.

Just before serving, stir in cream and season to taste. Serves 4.

CARROT RING MOULD WITH PEAS
AND ONIONS

2–3 lb (900 g–1.4 kg) new carrots
4 tablespoons (60 ml) butter
¼ pint (150 ml) chicken stock
1 tablespoon (15 ml) sugar
Salt
2 eggs
Butter
6–8 tablespoons (90–120 ml) grated cheese
Freshly ground black pepper
Cooked peas and button onions

Wash carrots; slice thickly and place in a saucepan; cover with cold water and cook over a high heat until water boils. Drain.

Simmer blanched carrots in butter, chicken stock and sugar, with salt, to taste, until carrots have absorbed the liquid without burning and are tender.

Mash carrot mixture and mix well with 2 eggs, 4 tablespoons (60 ml) softened butter, cheese, and salt and freshly ground black pepper, to taste. Press into a well-buttered ring mould and heat through in a slow oven (350°F180°C/GM4) for 15 minutes. Turn carrot ring out on a heated serving dish and fill centre with cooked peas and button onions. Surround with remaining peas and onions. Serves 6.

Chicory

I first met chicory as it should be cooked in France (where, incidentally, it is called *endive*), when I attended a small dinner party given by the great French *coiffeur*, Antoine, at a little *quai*-side restaurant in Villefranche. For a first course, on Antoine's recommendation, we all had *moules à la marinière* – gallons of tiny Mediterranean mussels steamed open in local white wine with a few finely chopped shallots, a hint of garlic and masses of finely chopped parsley – served with great simplicity in huge aluminium kitchen bowls.

Each one of the party chose a different course to follow, but we all had chicory. Simmered gently in a small iron *cocotte*, in a mixture of butter and olive oil with a splash of dry white wine, the chicory was lightly seasoned with salt and freshly ground black pepper, and not less than 5 sprigs of dried thyme and 5 fat cloves of garlic perfumed the whole. At first glance, too much of a good thing; but on tasting, perfection. A little rustic, perhaps, for urban tastes, but perfection none the less.

The lesson to be learned: chicory and water do not mix as well as chicory and butter or oil. If, perchance, you must boil the heads (see recipe for boiled chicory), do so in the minimum of water, and be sure to drain them well (I even press excess liquids out gently with a clean cloth) before serving them. Chicory has a delicate, bitter-sweet flavour that seems to demand intensification. I like to add one or more of the following: herbs, finely chopped onion, garlic, lemon juice, orange juice, dry white wine, Béchamel, Mornay or Vinaigrette Sauce. Chicory can be puréed – to serve as a vegetable, soup or soufflé. If slightly bitter, add a little sugar to pan juices.

BOILED CHICORY

8 heads chicory
½ pint (300 ml) salted water
4 tablespoons (60 ml) butter
Juice of ½ lemon
2 tablespoons (30 ml) finely chopped parsley

Trim root ends of chicory and wash well in cold water. Drain. Place chicory in a saucepan with boiling salted water, 2 tablespoons (30 ml) butter, and lemon juice, and cook for 20 to 30 minutes, or until tender. Drain thoroughly, reserving juices.

To serve chicory: boil reserved pan juices until reduced a little; pour over cooked chicory; sprinkle with finely chopped parsley and top with remaining butter. Serves 4.

CHICORY À LA BÉCHAMEL

8 heads chicory, cooked as above
½–¾ pint (300–450 ml) well-flavoured
Béchamel Sauce (page 104)

Cook chicory as in preceding recipe. Then place in a shallow ovenproof baking dish.

Add drained pan juices to hot Béchamel Sauce; pour over chicory and serve immediately. Serves 4.

BRAISED CHICORY

8 heads chicory
Butter
Salt and freshly ground black pepper
Juice of ½ lemon or orange

Trim root ends of chicory and wash well in cold water. Drain. Heat 4 tablespoons (60 ml) butter in a shallow fireproof casserole; add raw chicory, and season to taste with salt and freshly ground black pepper. Cover chicory with buttered paper. Cover casserole and simmer over a very low heat or in a slow oven (350°F/ 180°C/GM4) for 40 minutes, or until tender.

Turn chicory over from time to time, and 20 minutes after putting chicory in the oven, sprinkle with the juice of ½ lemon or orange. Serves 4.

CHICORY AU GRATIN

8 heads chicory
Salt
Juice of 1 lemon
4 thin slices cooked ham
Butter
6 tablespoons (90 ml) freshly grated Parmesan
½–¾ pint (300–450 ml) well-flavoured
Béchamel Sauce (page 104)
2 tablespoons (30 ml) freshly grated breadcrumbs

Trim root ends of chicory and wash well in cold water. Drain. Place chicory in a saucepan of boiling salted water with lemon juice, and simmer for 30 minutes. Drain well; then press in a clean cloth to remove excess moisture.

Roll each head in half-slice of ham and arrange in a well-buttered shallow heatproof casserole. Mix freshly grated Parmesan into Béchamel Sauce; pour over chicory; sprinkle with freshly grated breadcrumbs and 2 tablespoons (30 ml) melted butter, and cook in a moderately hot oven (400°F/200°C/GM6) for 10 to 15 minutes, or until sauce is bubbling and golden. Serves 4.

Courgettes (Zucchini)

Try this delicate, smooth-textured vegetable in any one of the following ways as an interesting first course, or as a separate vegetable course on its own.

FRIED COURGETTES

Peel courgettes; slice thickly or cut into thin strips about 2 inches (5 cm) in length, and soak in milk. Drain; dry well; roll in flour and deep-fry in hot oil until golden. Serve immediately.

GLAZED COURGETTES

Cut unpeeled courgettes into quarters lengthwise; slice each quarter into 2-inch (5 cm) segments and blanch in boiling water for about 3 minutes. Drain, and combine in a shallow saucepan with a little butter, and salt, freshly ground black pepper and sugar, to taste. Add a little light stock and simmer gently, covered, until liquid has almost disappeared and courgettes are glazed and tender.

COURGETTE SALAD

Cut unpeeled courgettes into thick slices or quarters and blanch in boiling salted water for 6 to 8 minutes. Drain well and chill. Just before serving, place courgettes in a salad bowl; add a well-flavoured French dressing and sprinkle lightly with finely chopped parsley, chervil or tarragon.

COURGETTE CASSEROLE

2 lb (900 g) courgettes, sliced
Salt
1 Spanish onion, finely chopped
Butter
2 eggs
6 tablespoons (90 ml) sour cream
8 tablespoons (120 ml) freshly grated Gruyère
Freshly ground black pepper
1 tablespoon (15 ml) breadcrumbs

Simmer courgettes in a little salted water in a covered saucepan until tender but still crisp – about 5 minutes. Drain; whisk in electric blender. Sauté onion in butter until transparent; add to courgette mixture with eggs, sour cream and 3 tablespoons (45 ml) grated cheese, and blend again. Season generously with salt and pepper.

Butter a shallow heatproof casserole; line it with 3 tablespoons

(45 ml) grated cheese and pour in the courgette mixture. Mix breadcrumbs with remaining cheese and sprinkle over the top. Bake in a slow oven (325°F/170°C/GM3) for 30 to 40 minutes, or until set. Serves 6.

STUFFED COURGETTES À LA PROVENÇALE

12 courgettes
Salt
Olive oil
Butter

PROVENÇALE STUFFING
6 oz (175 g) minced veal
2 tablespoons (30 ml) diced fat salt pork
1 onion, finely chopped
Olive oil
1 clove garlic, crushed
Fresh tarragon, minced
Fresh parsley, minced
1 egg, beaten
1 tablespoon (15 ml) grated Parmesan
4 tablespoons (60 ml) boiled rice
Courgette pulp
Salt and freshly ground black pepper

Simmer courgettes whole for about 5 minutes in salted water. Cut off tops; scoop out interiors, reserving pulp for stuffing.

PROVENÇALE STUFFING
Sauté meats and onion in olive oil. Mix garlic, herbs, beaten egg, grated cheese, rice and courgette pulp in a bowl, and then add them to the meat and onion mixture. Add salt and pepper, to taste. Sauté for a few minutes, stirring constantly.

Stuff scooped-out courgettes with Provençale Stuffing and place them in an ovenproof baking dish to which you have added a little olive oil; place a knob of butter on each courgette and bake in a moderate oven (375°F/190°C/GM5) for ½ hour. Serves 4.

COURGETTES IN RED WINE

12 courgettes
4 oz (100 g) finely chopped Spanish onion
4 tablespoons (60 ml) olive oil
2 tablespoons (30 ml) butter
¼ pint (150 ml) red wine
Salt and freshly ground black pepper
Lemon juice and olive oil
Finely chopped parsley

Cut courgettes into slices ½ inch (12 mm) thick and sauté with finely chopped onion in olive oil and butter for 5 minutes, stirring frequently. Add wine, and season to taste with salt and freshly ground black pepper. Simmer for 5 minutes.

Just before serving, sprinkle with a little lemon juice, olive oil and finely chopped parsley. Serves 4.

Leeks

The leek – first cousin of garlic and a well-known member of the onion tribe – is one of the simplest and homeliest of all winter vegetables. Known lovingly to the French as 'poor man's asparagus', the leek, none the less, lends its fine savour and earthy authority to many great French delicacies whose fame has travelled the world.

I like to combine leeks with onions and garlic as an aromatic threesome for the great French soups *pot-au-feu* and *poule-au-pot*; simmer leeks gently with a rolled roast of veal for a delectable *rôti de veau aux poireaux*; and purée leeks with cream, chicken stock and potatoes to make one of the finest cold soups in the world – *vichyssoise*. Try leeks on their own, puréed with chicken stock and cream, for a delicious cream of leek soup. Serve this versatile vegetable in a variety of ways: leeks *à la grecque* (leeks simmered in dry white wine and olive oil with finely chopped onions and carrots); leeks *à la vinaigrette* (leeks poached in water and served with Vinaigrette Sauce); leeks *au gratin* (leeks baked in a cream sauce); and leeks Mornay (poached leeks served with a well-flavoured cheese sauce).

To Prepare Leeks

While leeks may be one of the mildest flavoured members of the onion family, they are also apt to be one of the earthiest when freshly picked. To ensure that leeks are not gritty with sand or soil, trim off the roots and cut off the tops, leaving 1 to 3 inches (25–75 mm) of the green portion. Halve the leeks, leaving the halves attached at the root end. Wash thoroughly.

BOILED LEEKS

12 small leeks or 8 large ones
Salted water
2–3 tablespoons (30–45 ml) finely chopped parsley
Melted butter

Clean and trim leeks as above. Simmer in boiling salted water for 20 minutes, or until tender. Drain thoroughly.

Sprinkle with finely chopped parsley and serve with melted butter. Serves 4.

LEEKS À LA VINAIGRETTE

12 small leeks or 8 large ones
Salted water
6–8 tablespoons (90–120 ml) olive oil
2 tablespoons (30 ml) wine vinegar
Salt, freshly ground black pepper and mustard
Finely chopped parsley

Clean and trim leeks, and cook as in preceding recipe.

Arrange leeks in an *hors-d'œuvre* dish. Combine olive oil and vinegar with salt, pepper and mustard, to taste; pour over leeks and garnish with finely chopped parsley. Serves 4.

LEEKS IN BUTTER

12 small leeks or 8 large ones
4 oz (100 g) butter
Salt and freshly ground black pepper

Clean and trim leeks as above. Simmer in boiling water for 5 minutes. Drain thoroughly.

Place leeks in a shallow ovenproof baking dish; add butter, and salt and freshly ground black pepper, to taste, and cook in a moderate oven (375°F/190°C/GM5) for 35 to 40 minutes, or until tender. Serves 4.

LEEKS BÉCHAMEL

12 small leeks or 8 large ones
4 oz (100 g) butter
Salt and freshly ground black pepper
½–¾ pint (300–450 ml) well-flavoured Béchamel Sauce
(page 104)

Clean and trim leeks, and cook in butter as above. Drain pan juices; add to well-flavoured Béchamel Sauce; pour over leeks and serve immediately. Serves 4.

Mushrooms

The Greeks claimed mushrooms were the food of the gods. The Egyptians thought the common man so unworthy of these fragile fungi that only the Pharaohs were permitted to eat them. Now, cooks all over the world savour their earthy perfection.

The mushroom is one of the most delicious vegetables. Rich in phosphoric acid and albuminoids – on a nutritional level with lean beef – it is a healthy, digestible and nourishing food on its own.

There is, of course, small comparison between a wild mushroom and a cultivated one. To the true mushroom enthusiast, one *morel*, *chanterelle* or *girolle* is worth fifty of the commercial variety. But for the average city-dweller, denied the pleasures and skills of roaming fields and meadows in search of the wild varieties, the cultivated mushroom is a flavoursome, year-round food that adds much to the savour of good cooking.

Mushrooms last longer and keep better when refrigerated, but they should be used within two or three days of purchase.

Do not bother to peel fresh mushrooms. Just cut off sandy stem tips and wipe with a damp cloth, or wash quickly in cold water and dry thoroughly. If the mushrooms are not to be used immediately, keep them in cold water to which you have added a little lemon juice to preserve colour.

Do not overcook fresh mushrooms. They are naturally tender. I prefer to sauté them in butter, or butter and lemon juice, for 5 to 6 minutes only.

MUSHROOMS 'EN BROCHETTE'

36 button mushrooms (about 2 lb/900 g)
6 tablespoons (90 ml) melted butter
2 tablespoons (30 ml) olive oil
Lemon juice
Salt and freshly ground black pepper
Finely chopped garlic
Crushed rosemary

Clean mushrooms; remove stems (saving them for another use) and place 6 mushroom caps on each of 6 metal skewers. Combine melted butter and olive oil, and flavour to taste with lemon juice, salt, freshly ground black pepper, garlic and rosemary. Brush mushrooms with this mixture. Grill over charcoal or under the grill, turning mushrooms so as to brown them on all sides, and basting from time to time with sauce. Serve with grilled beef steak or lamb chops. Serves 6.

CHINESE MUSHROOMS

8 oz (225 g) mushrooms
2 tablespoons (30 ml) peanut oil or lard
½ tablespoon (7.5 ml) salt
¼ pint (150 ml) water
1 teaspoon (5 ml) cornflour

Heat oil or lard in a *wok* or frying pan; add mushrooms and salt, and stir over medium heat for 1 minute. Add water; cover pan and simmer for 3 minutes. Remove cover; add cornflour and simmer until thickened. Serve immediately.

MUSHROOMS À LA GRECQUE

1 lb (450 g) thickly sliced mushrooms
1 small can tomato concentrate (about 5 oz (150 g))
Water
2–3 tablespoons (30–45 ml) olive oil or butter
½ Spanish onion, finely chopped
½ clove garlic, finely chopped
Salt and freshly ground black pepper

Combine 1 can tomato concentrate and 2 cans water in a saucepan with olive oil or butter, finely chopped onion and garlic, and salt and freshly ground black pepper, to taste. Mix well; cover pan and bring to a boil; simmer gently over the lowest of heats, stirring from time to time, for 30 minutes, adding a little more water if necessary.

Add sliced mushrooms to sauce and simmer for 10 minutes. Serve hot as a vegetable; cold as an appetizer. Serves 4 to 6.

HERB-STUFFED MUSHROOMS

2 lb (900 g) open mushrooms
4 shallots, finely chopped
1 clove garlic, finely chopped
8 oz (225 g) sausage meat
1 tablespoon (15 ml) finely chopped chervil
1 tablespoon (15 ml) finely chopped tarragon
¼ teaspoon (1.25 ml) dried thyme
2 dried bay leaves, crumbled
Salt and freshly ground black pepper
Olive oil
Breadcrumbs
2 tablespoons (30 ml) finely chopped parsley

Wipe mushrooms clean with a damp cloth and trim stem ends.
Remove stems carefully from caps and chop them finely with
shallots and garlic. Mix thoroughly with sausage meat and herbs,
and season to taste with salt and freshly ground black pepper.
Sauté mixture in 2 tablespoons (30 ml) olive oil until golden.
Brush insides of mushroom caps with olive oil; fill them with
sausage mixture, and sprinkle lightly with breadcrumbs and
finely chopped parsley.

Pour 6 tablespoons (90 ml) olive oil into an ovenproof *gratin*
dish and heat through in the oven. Place stuffed mushroom caps
in the hot oil and cook in a moderate oven (375°F/190°C/GM5)
for 15 to 20 minutes.

Onions

The onion – the oldest known vegetable in the world – was
among the foodstuffs which fed the Egyptian workmen building
the Pyramids. Today, this versatile vegetable is served fried,
sautéed, boiled, baked, creamed and stuffed.

I used to love the great sandwiches of fried onions, red peppers
and sliced hot sausages we enjoyed in America when I was young.
Made of slices of bread with this hot, savoury mixture inside, they
were almost a meal in themselves. And in the summer, there were

fresh-tasting salads – red, green and white – containing sliced onion rings, tomatoes and green peppers.

Onions and carrots – glazed in a little chicken stock, butter and sugar – combine to make a perfect accompaniment to baked ham, or chicken in a cream sauce. And make onion and potato *gratinée* – a dish from Northern France. You will find it a wonderful change from the usual puréed potatoes with the Sunday joint. Creamy and rich, with its crusty top, it is a welcome addition to the winter vegetable theme.

A little finely chopped onion – a tablespoon or two (15–30 ml), no more – browned in butter, with a little finely chopped parsley and a hint of garlic, adds greatly to the savour of grilled beef steak or lamb chops. Add a whole onion, stuck with a pungent clove or two, to chicken or beef stock; serve a dish of creamed onions as an accompaniment to roast lamb. If onions are small enough, present them in a baked pastry case for added effect.

The larger onions imported from Spain and Portugal are much milder in flavour than our own, and are more suitable for serving as a vegetable. If onions tend to be strong in flavour, scald them in boiling water before cooking them.

CREAMED ONIONS WITH CLOVES

48 small white onions
Salt
4 tablespoons (60 ml) butter
8 whole cloves
1 teaspoon (5 ml) sugar
Freshly ground black pepper
1 level tablespoon (15 ml) flour
½ pint (300 ml) cream
Freshly grated Parmesan

Peel onions and cook in boiling salted water, uncovered, until almost tender. Drain, and rinse in cold water.

Melt 3 tablespoons (45 ml) butter in a large frying pan or casserole. Stick 8 onions with cloves. Add all the onions to the melted butter; sprinkle with sugar and cook over a low heat, shaking pan frequently, until onions are golden brown on all sides.

Transfer onions and pan juices to a shallow baking dish; season to taste with salt and freshly ground black pepper. Melt remaining butter in a small saucepan; add flour and stir until smooth. Add cream and cook, stirring constantly, until sauce is thick. Pour sauce over onions; sprinkle with freshly grated Parmesan and bake in a moderate oven (375°F/190°C/GM5) for 15 to 20 minutes. Serves 8.

ONION AND POTATO GRATINÉE

1 lb (450 g) Spanish onions, peeled
1 lb (450 g) large potatoes
¼ pint (150 ml) milk
2–3 tablespoons (30–45 ml) freshly grated Parmesan
2 eggs, well beaten
Freshly grated nutmeg
Salt and freshly ground black pepper
2 tablespoons (30 ml) freshly grated breadcrumbs
1–2 tablespoons (15–30 ml) melted butter

Put peeled whole onions in a large saucepan; cover with cold water and bring slowly to a boil. Drain. Cover with hot water and cook until tender. Drain. Peel potatoes and boil them. Put onions and potatoes through a *mouli-légume*, or 'rice' them. Add milk, grated cheese and well-beaten eggs. Beat mixture until soft and creamy; season to taste with freshly grated nutmeg, salt and freshly ground black pepper; sprinkle with breadcrumbs and melted butter, and bake in a slow oven (325°F/170°C/GM3) for 40 to 45 minutes. Serves 6 to 8.

ONIONS AND CARROTS

12 oz (350 g) small white onions
12 oz (350 g) small carrots
4 tablespoons (60 ml) butter
4 tablespoons (60 ml) chicken stock
Salt
1 level tablespoon (15 ml) sugar

Peel onions. Scrape carrots and slice them thickly. Place vegetables in a saucepan, cover with cold water and cook over a high heat until water boils. Remove from heat and drain. Replace vegetables in the saucepan; add butter and chicken stock, season to taste with salt and sugar, and simmer over a low heat until vegetables have absorbed all the liquid without burning, and have taken on a little colour. Serves 4.

Green Peas

Green peas – peas in the pod, that is – were first to disappear completely under the wheels of our modern Juggernaut, 'convenience living'. They have almost totally disappeared from the shops. While masses of exotic rarities are becoming commonplace at our greengrocers, fresh peas – once on sale everywhere – have moved against the current up into the rare luxury class.

It is really our fault. Frozen and canned peas are much easier to deal with. Their ready availability in freezer and larder is a constant boon to the hasty gourmet. But they are not the same thing. Nothing can match the flavour of peas freshly picked from the garden and popped, together with a few of the tenderest pods and a lettuce heart or a sprig of fresh mint, into the pan just before Sunday lunch. So try and wheedle your greengrocer into ordering fresh peas from the market; or beg them from your friends with kitchen gardens. As a last – or best – resort, grow them yourself.

Use peas – both fresh and frozen – in a variety of ways to lend colour and interest to meals. Fresh pea soup, made of puréed peas, chicken stock and cream, makes a flavoursome first course, served hot with *croûtons*, or chilled with finely chopped fresh mint or chives. A purée of fresh peas makes a refreshing change from that old standby, potatoes, as a brightly coloured accompaniment to grilled lamb chops. Or try a combination of peas, glazed carrots and button onions, piled in individual baked pastry cases, as a vegetable conversation-piece to accompany poached chicken with a Velouté Sauce.

To Cook Peas

The old-fashioned method of boiling peas in a pan of water and then throwing the water away has much to condemn it; so many of the valuable vitamins and trace elements are lost in the water, and the peas themselves lose so much of their flavour and identity. I far prefer to steam fresh peas to obtain the utmost in flavour; or cook them in heavy, shallow pans with tight-fitting lids for almost waterless cooking, with just a little chicken stock or water and a little butter to add lustre and savour. When served hot with fresh butter, salt and freshly ground black pepper, or with a few tablespoons of Chicken Velouté Sauce, they become food fit for the gods.

Always serve peas as soon as possible after cooking; they tend to lose flavour and texture if kept warm over any period of time.

BUTTERED PEAS

1 lb (450 g) frozen peas
4 level tablespoons (60 ml) butter
4 tablespoons (60 ml) chicken stock
Salt
1 tablespoon (15 ml) sugar

Place peas in a small saucepan; cover with cold water and cook over a high heat until the water boils. Remove from the heat and drain. Replace peas in the saucepan; add butter and chicken stock; season to taste with salt and sugar, and simmer over a low heat until the peas have absorbed the liquid and are tender. Serves 4.

Note: Frozen peas cooked in this manner may also be puréed to serve as a vegetable or folded into a soufflé; or, thinned with cream and well-flavoured chicken stock, to serve as a delicious soup.

PEAS AU GRATIN

1lb (450 g) cooked peas, fresh or frozen
4 oz (100 g) diced cooked ham
½ Spanish onion, finely chopped
Butter
½ pint (300 ml) cream, warmed
Salt and freshly ground black pepper
2 tablespoons (30 ml) freshly grated Parmesan
2 tablespoons (30 ml) freshly grated Gruyère

Sauté diced ham and finely chopped onion in 2 tablespoons (30 ml) butter until onion begins to take on colour. Combine with cooked peas and warm cream, and season to taste with salt and freshly ground black pepper. Pour mixture into a well-buttered casserole; sprinkle with freshly grated cheeses; dot with butter and cook under grill until top is golden. Serves 4.

PURÉE SAINT-GERMAIN

2 lb (900 g) frozen peas
1 lettuce heart, shredded
12 tiny spring onions, or ½ Spanish onion, sliced
3 sprigs parsley
4 oz (100 g) butter
4 tablespoons (60 ml) chicken stock or water
Sugar
Salt
2 boiled potatoes, puréed (optional)

Put peas in a saucepan with the shredded heart of a lettuce, spring onions, parsley, half the butter, chicken stock or water, and sugar and salt, to taste. Bring to a boil and cook slowly until peas are tender. When cooked, remove parsley and drain, reserving juices. Blend to a fine purée in an electric blender (or press through a fine sieve) and reheat in the top of a double saucepan, adding a little of the strained juices and the remaining butter. If purée is too thin, add puréed potatoes to lend body. Serves 4.

ROMAN PEAS

1 lb (450 g) shelled peas, fresh or frozen
2 tablespoons (30 ml) finely chopped Parma ham
½ Spanish onion, finely chopped
Butter
¼ pint (150 ml) well-flavoured beef stock
Sugar
Salt and freshly ground black pepper
1 tablespoon (15 ml) finely chopped parsley

Sauté finely chopped ham and onion in 4 tablespoons (60 ml) butter until onion begins to take on colour. Add peas and beef stock, and season to taste with sugar, salt and freshly ground black pepper. Simmer peas, covered, for 10 to 15 minutes. Just before serving, top with finely chopped parsley and a knob of butter. Serves 4.

Peppers

The pepper family, as we know it today, is vast and varied. Peppers come in hundreds of types, from the sweetest tasting to the hottest, from green to yellow to fiery red, or a mixture of all three. Many cooks are wary of buying red peppers. They think that all red types are hot. This is not so; a red pepper may be hot or mild, depending on the variety. It is useful to know that the 'sweet' green pepper ripens through yellow to brilliant red, but these more colourful versions are actually mellower and sweeter than the green, and a little less tough in texture.

Red or yellow peppers may be substituted for green peppers in any of the following recipes. Served cold, side by side on a bed of lettuce, or hot in a rich tomato sauce, they make a festive dish.

Serve peppers as a main course, as an accompaniment to roast and grilled meats, and as a vegetable garnish. The possible variations depend only on your own ingenuity and imagination.

Roasted or Grilled Peppers for Salads

Perfectionists prefer to peel the sweet pepper. The easiest way, I find, to prepare peppers in this way for use in appetizer salads and other dishes, is to grill or roast the peppers as close to the heat as possible, turning them until the skin is charred on all sides. The skins will rub off easily under running cold water. The peppers are then cored, seeded and sliced into thick strips, and marinated in a well-flavoured French dressing. Peppers prepared in this way will keep well under refrigeration, if packed in oil in tight sterilized jars.

ITALIAN PEPPER APPETIZER

4–6 green and red peppers
6 tomatoes, peeled and diced
2 cloves garlic, finely chopped
1 can anchovy fillets, drained and finely chopped
4 tablespoons (60 ml) dry breadcrumbs
Olive oil
Salt and freshly ground black pepper
2 tablespoons (30 ml) butter

Cut peppers in half lengthwise, and scoop out seeds and fibres. Combine diced tomatoes, finely chopped garlic and anchovies, breadcrumbs and 4 to 6 tablespoons (60–90 ml) olive oil. Season with salt and freshly ground black pepper. Stuff pepper halves with this mixture and arrange them in a well-oiled heatproof baking dish. Dot with butter and bake in a slow oven (350°F/

180°C/GM4) for 45 to 50 minutes, or until tender. Serve cold.
Serves 4 to 6.

TUNISIAN PEPPER AND TOMATO CASSEROLE

2 Spanish onions
Olive oil
6 ripe tomatoes, sliced
3 red or green peppers, diced
1 small can tomato concentrate
1–2 cloves garlic
Salt and freshly ground black pepper
⅛–¼ level teaspoon (0.6–1.25 ml) each
cayenne pepper and paprika
4 eggs
Powdered cumin

Slice onions thickly and sauté in 6 tablespoons (90 ml) olive oil until golden. Add sliced tomatoes, diced peppers, tomato concentrate and garlic, and simmer vegetables until soft and cooked through. Add 4 tablespoons (60 ml) olive oil; season to taste with salt, freshly ground black pepper, cayenne and paprika, and simmer for 5 minutes more.

To serve: spoon softened vegetables into individual casseroles or ovenproof serving dishes; break 1 egg into each dish and bake in a moderately hot oven (400/200°C/GM6) until eggs are just set – about 10 minutes. Sprinkle with a little powdered cumin. Serves 4.

TUNA-STUFFED PEPPERS

4–6 green peppers
2 slices white bread
Milk
1 egg, well beaten
4–6 tomatoes, peeled, seeded and chopped
16 ripe olives, pitted and chopped
1 can tuna fish (about 7 oz (200 g))
Salt and freshly ground black pepper
4 tablespoons (60 ml) olive oil

Trim stem ends of peppers, and scoop out seeds and fibres.

Trim crusts from bread; soak bread in milk until thoroughly moistened; drain. Mix together with beaten egg and chopped tomatoes and olives. Drain tuna fish; flake it, and add to stuffing mixture. Mix well, and season to taste with salt and freshly ground black pepper.

Stuff peppers with mixture and place in a heatproof baking dish which you have brushed with olive oil. Sprinkle peppers with remaining oil; cover dish and bake in a slow oven (350/180°C/GM4) for 45 to 50 minutes, or until peppers are tender. Serve immediately. Serves 4 to 6.

Potatoes

The potato is undoubtedly the world's number one vegetable. Yet its almost universal acceptance today dates from only the seventeenth and eighteenth centuries. Sir John Hawkins gets the credit for introducing the potato into Ireland in 1565; Sir Walter Raleigh planted it there in 1585. But it was not until the mid-nineteenth century that the potato became the important staple crop that it is today in Northern Europe, the British Isles and North America.

There are hundreds of ways of preparing potatoes. Some of the simplest ones are the best. Baked in the oven and rushed to the table, where they are slashed open with a quick cross-cut, to receive a pat of fresh butter and a sprinkling of coarse salt and freshly ground black pepper; or puréed with double cream and fresh butter; or crisp-fried in hot lard and oil – they are hard to beat. I like, too, to serve new potatoes no bigger than walnuts, hot and dry, in their jackets, with lashings of fresh butter, and pepper and salt. Or try the more sophisticated *gratin dauphinois* (new potatoes, peeled and thinly sliced, and cooked in the oven with double cream, and freshly grated Gruyère and Parmesan); *pommes de terre Anna* (new potatoes, peeled and thinly sliced, arranged in concentric layers in a well-buttered thick casserole, each layer brushed with butter, and baked in the oven until a crisp golden crust has formed); and potatoes O'Brien (sliced raw potatoes sautéed in butter and olive oil with finely chopped green pepper and pimento).

I liked, too, the hash-browned potatoes of my youth: the potatoes, first boiled in their jackets, were then peeled and coarsely chopped, before being browned in a heavy iron frying pan in equal quantities of butter and pork dripping. The potatoes were pressed down into the fat and cooked slowly until brown; it was always necessary to turn them once or twice at the beginning, to make sure that some of the crusty brown bits got into the interior of the potato cake. The entire bottom of the cake was then allowed to brown before the potatoes were turned over with a spatula, like an omelette, to brown on the other side. I recently enjoyed a different version of this delicious dish in France – *pommes de terre Lorette* grates raw potatoes coarsely; flavours them with a little chopped onion, salt and pepper, and fries them in butter and olive oil until brown on one side. The potatoes are then turned out on to a plate; more fat is added to the pan, and the potato cake is gently eased back into the pan to brown on the other side.

Choose potatoes best suited to your purpose: baking potatoes are large, with a fine, mealy texture when cooked. Use them for baking, and for soups and purées. New potatoes range in size from tiny ones no bigger than a walnut, to those of the size of a regular potato. Serve small new potatoes cooked in their jackets as above, or peeled and simmered gently in butter and lemon juice until tender; use larger ones for potato salads, and for cooked dishes such as *gratin dauphinois*, for which you want potato slices to keep their shape. Never bake a new potato.

Whenever possible, cook potatoes in their jackets. Most of the food value of the potato lies just under the skin and is lost if it is peeled away. If you prefer serving them without their jackets, the skins will slip off easily enough after cooking. If you peel raw potatoes, put them into a bowl of cold water immediately to prevent them changing colour.

Do not overcook potatoes. Test them with a fork – they are done when you can pierce them easily. Never allow them to become watery and mushy.

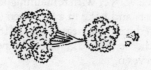

MRS BEETON'S GERMAN POTATOES

8–10 medium potatoes
3 oz (75 g) butter
2 tablespoons (30 ml) flour
½ pint (300 ml) broth
2 tablespoons (30 ml) vinegar
1 bay leaf (optional)

'Put the butter and flour into a stew pan; stir over the fire until the butter is of a nice brown colour, and add the broth and vinegar; peel and cut the potatoes into long thin slices, lay them in the gravy, and let them simmer gently until tender, which will be from 10 to 15 minutes, and serve very hot. A laurel-leaf [bay leaf] simmered with the potatoes is an improvement.'

SCALLOPED POTATOES WITH CHEESE

4 large baking potatoes
Butter
8 oz (225 g) Cheddar, grated
1 Spanish onion, finely chopped
4 tablespoons (60 ml) finely chopped parsley
Salt and freshly ground black pepper
½ level teaspoon (2.5 ml) paprika
¾ pint (450 ml) milk
¼ pint (150 ml) double cream

Peel potatoes and slice them thinly. Soak sliced potatoes in cold water for 10 minutes; drain and dry carefully. Butter a shallow baking dish generously and cover bottom of dish with a layer of potatoes. Season to taste with grated cheese (reserving 4 table-spoons/60 ml for later use), onion, parsley, salt, freshly ground black pepper and paprika. Cover with another layer of potatoes and season as above. Cover with remaining potatoes; pour in milk and cream to cover, and bake in a hot oven (450°F/230°C/GM8) for 10 minutes. Reduce oven heat to 350°F/180°C/GM4; sprinkle with remaining cheese and bake until the potatoes are tender – about 2 hours. Serves 6.

POMMES DE TERRE DUCHESSE

2 lb (900 g) potatoes
Salt
Butter
2 eggs
2 egg yolks
Freshly ground black pepper
Freshly grated nutmeg

Peel potatoes and slice them thickly; cook them, covered, in simmering salted water until soft but not mushy. Drain well; return potatoes to pan and remove all moisture by shaking pan over heat until they are dry.

Rub potatoes through a fine sieve; add 2 to 4 tablespoons (30–60 ml) butter, beating with a wooden spoon until mixture is very smooth. Combine eggs and egg yolks, and beat gradually into potato mixture. Season to taste with salt, freshly ground black pepper and freshly grated nutmeg, and beat until mixture is very fluffy.

If potatoes are to be used to garnish a meat, fish or vegetable dish, pipe mixture through a pastry tube to make a border; brush with butter and brown under the grill. Or pipe individual shapes with a pastry tube; brush with butter and brown under the grill.

GRATIN DAUPHINOIS À LA CRÈME

1 lb (450 g) new potatoes
½ pint (300 ml) milk
Salt and freshly ground black pepper
Butter
¼ pint (150 ml) cream
6 tablespoons (90 ml) freshly grated Gruyère
2 tablespoons (30 ml) freshly
grated Parmesan

Peel and slice potatoes thinly, and soak in cold water for a few minutes. Drain. Place sliced potatoes in a heatproof *gratin* dish; add milk; season to taste with salt and freshly ground black pepper, and cook for 20 minutes, or until half done. Drain.

Place drained potato slices in a buttered *gratin* dish; add cream; sprinkle with freshly grated cheeses; dot with butter and cook in a slow oven (350°F/180°C/GM4) for about 30 minutes, or until potatoes are cooked through. If top becomes too brown, cover dish with foil. Serve very hot. Serves 4.

SAUTÉED NEW POTATOES WITH HERBS

2 lb (900 g) small new potatoes
4 tablespoons (60 ml) olive oil
1 tablespoon (15 ml) each finely chopped parsley,
chervil and chives
4 shallots, finely chopped
1 clove garlic, finely chopped
Salt and freshly ground black pepper
Lemon juice

Peel small potatoes and cook whole in a frying pan with olive oil, and finely chopped herbs, shallots and garlic. Season potatoes to taste with salt, freshly ground black pepper and lemon juice, and sauté until cooked through and golden. Serve immediately. Serves 4 to 6.

POMMES DE TERRE SOUFFLÉES

1½ lb (675 g) new potatoes, peeled, dried and thinly sliced
1½ pints (900 ml) peanut oil
Salt

Bring oil to a boil. Place sliced potatoes in a frying basket and plunge them into the hot oil. They should begin to swell and colour in a few minutes. Remove basket from oil and allow potatoes to cool.

Bring oil to a boil again, this time a little hotter than before, and plunge the basket of sliced potatoes into it again. Continue to cook until potatoes are puffed and golden. Drain, season with salt, and serve immediately. Serves 4.

2 lb (900 g) potatoes
4 tablespoons (60 ml) butter
Juice of ½ lemon
½ beef stock cube
Salt and freshly ground black pepper

Peel potatoes and cut them in quarters lengthwise. Place in a *gratin* dish or shallow casserole with butter, the juice of ¼ lemon and ½ crumbled beef stock cube, and season to taste with salt and freshly ground black pepper. Cook in a moderately hot oven (400°F/ 200°C/GM6) for 15 minutes. Turn potatoes over and return to oven for 15 minutes more. Remove excess fat from dish; add remaining lemon juice and return to oven for 5 minutes more, or until tender. Serves 4 to 6.

Spinach

'Vegetables in England are served in all the simplicity of nature, like hay to horses, only a little boiled instead of dried.' This was the comment of some unknown disenchanted visitor to these isles.

For vegetables are our weak spot – all the world acknowledges that. And it is not the elaborate dishes that trip us up. It is in the simplest forms that we fail.

Take spinach, for example. An exotic from Persia, it was brought by the Moors to Spain, by the Spaniards to the Low Countries, by Flemish refugees to England. And after that great pilgrimage, we plunge it into cold water, boil it, and then force it on our children.

To Prepare Fresh Spinach

Because of its high water content, spinach should be cooked only in the water that clings to its leaves after washing. Do not boil in water. For a really superb flavour, add several tablespoons fresh butter, season to taste with salt and freshly ground black pepper, and cook as in the basic recipe below.

It is necessary to wash spinach well in several changes of cold water, at the same time removing any possible sand or grit, and all yellowed or damaged leaves and tough stalks.

To Cook Fresh Spinach

Wash 2 to 3 lb (900 g–1.4 kg) fresh spinach leaves in several changes of water, removing yellowed or damaged leaves. Drain thoroughly. Put leaves in a thick-bottomed saucepan with 4 tablespoons (60 ml) butter, and salt and freshly ground black pepper, to taste. Simmer gently, stirring constantly, until spinach is soft and tender. The mass of crisp leaves will begin to 'dissolve' almost at the first contact with the heat, and there will be just enough to serve 4 to 6 new spinach fanciers.

Spinach Variations

1. Purée fresh spinach, cooked as above; add double cream and butter, to taste; spread purée in a baked pastry shell and heat through for a delicious spinach flan.
2. Spread puréed spinach in a baked pastry shell as above; make 4 to 6 deep indentations in spinach with the back of a tablespoon; place 1 raw egg yolk in each indentation, and bake in a moderate oven until eggs are cooked through.
3. Spread puréed spinach in individual ramekins or shallow *gratin* dishes; place 1 or 2 poached eggs on each spinach bed; cover with hot Mornay Sauce (page 107); sprinkle with a little freshly grated Parmesan cheese – and you have poached eggs *à la florentine*.
4. Thin puréed spinach with double cream and chicken stock for a fresh-tasting, brightly coloured vegetable soup (see page 77).

BUTTERED SPINACH WITH HAM

2 lb (900 g) fresh spinach leaves
Butter
Salt and freshly ground black pepper
4 tablespoons (60 ml) diced cooked ham
4 tablespoons (60 ml) diced white bread

Wash spinach leaves in changes of water; drain. Put spinach in a thick-bottomed saucepan with 8 oz (225 g) butter, season to taste with salt and freshly ground black pepper, and cook, stirring constantly, over a fairly high heat until spinach is soft and melted. Transfer to a serving dish and keep warm.

Melt 2 tablespoons (30 ml) butter in a frying pan, and toss diced ham and diced bread in butter until golden. Fold ham and *croûtons* into spinach, and serve at once as a separate vegetable course. Serves 4.

CHINESE SPINACH

2 lb (900 g) fresh spinach leaves
3 tablespoons (45 ml) peanut oil or lard
1 teaspoon (5 ml) salt
1 tablespoon (15 ml) soy sauce, *sake* or dry sherry

Wash spinach leaves in several changes of water; drain and dry thoroughly. Heat oil or lard in a *wok* or frying pan; add spinach and salt, and cook over a medium heat for 3 minutes, stirring continually. Add soy sauce, *sake* or dry sherry, to taste. Serve immediately. Serves 4.

BEAN AND RAW SPINACH SALAD

1 lb (450 g) cooked kidney or broad beans
6–8 tablespoons (90–120 ml) olive oil
3 tablespoons (45 ml) wine vinegar or lemon juice
1 teaspoon (5 ml) each finely chopped fresh marjoram and basil
2 teaspoons (10 ml) finely chopped fresh parsley
1–2 cloves garlic, finely chopped
Salt and freshly ground black pepper
1 lb (450 g) young spinach leaves, raw
1 small onion, sliced

Mix cooked beans with a dressing made of olive oil and wine vinegar or lemon juice and finely chopped herbs and garlic. Add salt and freshly ground black pepper, to taste. Serve on tender young spinach leaves and garnish with onion rings. Serves 4.

Tomatoes

In 1518, Cortez discovered a small, tart, red, Mexican fruit – cousin of the deadly nightshade – that was to change the culinary history of the world. At first, the '*tomatl*', as it was called by the Aztecs, met with little favour in Spain. It was considered too tart as a fruit to be anything more than a herbal curiosity. Then an adventurous chef at the Spanish court tried combining it with onions, oil, vinegar and pepper, and created the world's most popular sauce.

Today, the tomato is one of the world's most popular fruits. In Britain alone, more than 600 million pounds (300 million kg) of fresh tomatoes are consumed every year. This means over 13 pounds (6 kg) per head every year for every man, woman and child in the country.

I like to serve stuffed raw tomatoes as a cold first course for summer luncheons, filled with (1) mashed flesh of avocado pear flavoured with salt, pepper, lemon and onion juice; (2) saffron rice, garnished with finely chopped olives, cooked ham, pimento and onions, and dressed with Vinaigrette Sauce (page 691); or (3) prawns in a Rémoulade Sauce (page 122).

Italian Tomato Sauce (page 125) is always a standby in my kitchen. It will keep for a week in the refrigerator. Use its sharp authority for pasta, for grilled fish, for grilled steak *pizzaiola*, and as a base for Italian devilled eggs. This light luncheon dish of poached eggs is usually served in individual heatproof ramekins.

Tomatoes may be grilled, stewed, baked, sautéed, jellied in aspic, stuffed with anything from clams to rice, made into sauces, soups, jellies, compotes, preserves and ketchups – and, of course, they may be eaten raw.

Tomatoes go with fish, meat, poultry, vegetables, rice, pasta and eggs. Try parsley, chervil, basil, tarragon and chives with raw tomatoes; thyme, fennel, bay leaf and marjoram with cooked tomatoes.

GRILLED ITALIAN TOMATOES

6 large ripe tomatoes
Butter
Salt and freshly ground black pepper
Dried oregano
1–2 tablespoons (15–30 ml) breadcrumbs
1 teaspoon (5 ml) finely chopped chives or onion
1–2 tablespoons (15–30 ml) freshly grated Parmesan

Cut tomatoes in half. Place tomato halves in a buttered baking dish. Season to taste with salt, freshly ground black pepper and dried oregano; sprinkle with breadcrumbs, finely chopped chives or onion, and freshly grated Parmesan. Dot tomatoes with butter and grill them 3 inches (8 cms) from the heat until tender. Serves 4.

SPINACH-STUFFED TOMATOES

8 large tomatoes
8 tablespoons (120 ml) hot cooked spinach
Butter
Salt and freshly ground black pepper
2 tablespoons (30 ml) freshly grated Parmesan

Slice tops off tomatoes; scoop out interiors carefully and discard.

Rub hot cooked spinach twice through a fine sieve; add butter, and season to taste with salt and freshly ground black pepper. Fill tomatoes with the hot purée; sprinkle with freshly grated Parmesan and dot with butter. Arrange filled tomatoes in a buttered baking dish and bake in a slow oven (350°F/180°C/GM4) for 5 minutes. Serves 4.

STUFFED TOMATOES

8 large tomatoes
Butter
4 tablespoons (60 ml) chopped spring onion
2 cloves garlic, finely chopped
2 tablespoons (30 ml) finely chopped parsley
8 oz (225 g) cooked ham, finely chopped
8 tablespoons (120 ml) shredded white bread
Salt and freshly ground black pepper
Breadcrumbs

Slice tops off tomatoes and scoop out interiors, being careful not to break cases. Chop pulp coarsely.

Melt 4 oz (100 g) butter in a large thick-bottomed frying pan, and sauté onions, garlic, parsley, ham and tomato pulp until onions are soft. Add shredded white bread which you have soaked in water and squeezed relatively dry. Season with salt and freshly ground black pepper, and stuff tomato cases with this mixture. Top with breadcrumbs; dot with butter and bake in a slow oven (350°F/180°C/GM4) for 20 minutes. Serves 4.

Other Fresh Vegetables

MRS GLASSE'S STEW'D CUCUMBERS

'Pare twelve Cucumbers, and slice them as thick as a Crown piece, and put them to drain, and then lay them in a coarse Cloth till they are dry, flour them and fry them Brown in Butter; pour out the Fat, then put to them some Gravy, a little Claret, some Pepper, Cloves, and Mace, and let them stew a little; then roll a Bit of Butter in Flour, and toss them up seasoned with Salt.'

BRAISED LETTUCE

4–6 small Cos lettuces
Butter
1 slice bacon, diced
½ Spanish onion, thinly sliced
2 small carrots, thinly sliced
¼ pint (150 ml) chicken stock
Salt and freshly ground black pepper
2 level teaspoons (10 ml) flour
Finely chopped parsley

Clean lettuces, leaving them whole. Pare the base of each lettuce to a point. Drop lettuces into a large saucepan filled with boiling water, and boil for 5 minutes.

Pour off water; plunge lettuces into a bowl of cold water for a few minutes. Drain lettuces and press out excess moisture.

Butter an ovenproof dish; place lettuces, diced bacon, and thinly sliced onion and carrots in dish, and add chicken stock.

Season to taste with salt and freshly ground black pepper, then cover and cook slowly until tender – about 45 minutes. About 5 minutes before you remove vegetables from heat, stir in 2 teaspoons (10 ml) butter which you have mixed to a smooth paste with 2 level teaspoons (10 ml) flour. Just before serving, sprinkle with parsley. Serves 4 to 6.

BRAISED FENNEL

4 fennel roots
Juice of ½ lemon
2 tablespoons (30 ml) olive oil or butter
¼ pint (150 ml) chicken stock
Salt and freshly ground black pepper
2 teaspoons (10 ml) butter
2 level teaspoons (10 ml) flour
Finely chopped parsley

Wash and trim fennel roots, and cut in half lengthwise. Put in a
heatproof dish with lemon juice, olive oil or butter, and stock.

Season to taste with salt and freshly ground black pepper, then
cover pan and cook slowly until tender – 30 to 40 minutes. Five
minutes before you remove vegetables from heat, stir in butter
and flour, mixed to a smooth paste. Just before serving, sprinkle
with finely chopped parsley.

STUFFED LETTUCE LEAVES

1–2 heads lettuce
1–2 tablespoons (15–30 ml) butter
4 oz (100 g) uncooked rice
1 pint (600 ml) hot beef stock
½ Spanish onion, finely chopped
2 oz (50 g) chopped mushrooms
2 tablespoons (30 ml) olive oil
4 oz (100 g) ham, finely chopped
2 tablespoons (30 ml) tomato concentrate
1–2 tablespoons (15–30 ml) finely chopped parsley

Separate lettuce leaves and wash well. Drain.

Melt butter in a thick-bottomed frying pan. Add rice, and sauté
until golden. Cover with ½ pint (300 ml) hot beef stock, adding a
little water if necessary, and cook, stirring constantly, until the
mixture comes to a boil. Reduce heat, cover pan, and cook slowly
for about 15 minutes, adding a little more beef stock if necessary.

Sauté chopped onion and mushrooms in oil, and add to rice
mixture. Mix in the finely chopped ham; season well. Place equal

quantities of the mixture on each lettuce leaf, and roll up, tucking ends in, to form neat 'packages'. Arrange them in a flat ovenproof dish. Blend tomato concentrate with remaining ½ pint (300 ml) hot beef stock; pour over stuffed lettuce leaves and bake in a moderate oven (375°F/190°C/GM5) for 30 minutes, or until done, basting frequently. Sprinkle with finely chopped parsley. Serves 4 to 6.

Dried Vegetables

Among the foods known longest to man – dried grains have been found in Peruvian and Aztec tombs, as well as among the remains of the lake dwellers in what is now Switzerland – they are also among the most versatile. Use beans – white haricot, red kidney, lentils, peas and flageolets – to give variety, richness and excitement to your winter meals. Feature them in warming country soups, or smooth purées to accompany meat, poultry or game. Make them, with pork, lamb, duck, goose or game, the highlight of an informal luncheon or supper. Serve a refreshing salad of cooked beans flavoured with onion, parsley, olive oil and wine vinegar.

To Soak Dried Beans, Peas and Lentils

Dried beans, peas and lentils are often soaked too long. Most recipes say overnight. I prefer to put them in cold water; bring them gently to a boil and then, with saucepan off the heat, allow them to steep in the water for 1 or 2 hours only. If soaked too long, they may ferment, which affects their flavour and makes them difficult to digest.

Haricot Beans

The dried seeds of the kidney or French bean – the pods are allowed to ripen fully and then the seeds are dried – are really natives of South and Central America. The very word *haricot* is a

French version of the Aztec, *ayacotl*. Dried haricot beans form a very valuable food, as they are cheap, nourishing and easily cooked. They will keep for months in a cool dry place, and are useful to fall back on when fresh vegetables are unobtainable.

Haricot beans should always be soaked first, and then cooked very thoroughly. Otherwise they may be difficult to digest.

Dried Peas

Dried peas are available in two forms: the whole green pea, and the split pea with outer skin removed. Use them as a vegetable instead of fresh green peas; add a few peas to a lamb or pork broth, or a stew that requires long cooking; purée them for a delicious accompaniment to pork, poultry or game; thin the purée down with milk, cream, dry white wine or water (or a combination of two or more of these) for an excellent pea soup. Make old-fashioned pease pudding, a favourite accompaniment to boiled pork.

Lentils

One of the most nourishing foods, more easily digested than either beans or peas, lentils figure prominently in vegetarian diets as a substitute for meat, fish or poultry.

Two kinds of lentils are usually sold in this country: the purple-green French or German lentils, which has a yellow-tinted interior, and the Egyptian lentil, usually sold without a coat, like a small, reddish-yellow split pea. The seed coat, when present, is dark brown.

Cook lentils with game, duck, goose, pork or sausages. Serve puréed lentils as a full-flavoured vegetable accompaniment to any meat. Make a rich country soup of lentils flavoured with onion, garlic and red or white wine. Serve cooked lentils spiked with an oil and vinegar dressing as an unusual appetizer salad.

Flageolets

These little green beans are used both fresh and dried as a garnish for meat dishes. Excellent with mutton and lamb. Usually sold in a dried state in this country and more expensive than white haricot beans, they make an excellent vegetable dish, especially puréed.

Lima or Butter Beans

Prepare and cook in the same way as haricot beans. They do not require such long soaking or cooking.

FRIJOLES – MEXICAN FRIED BEANS

1 lb (450 g) red beans
Salt
6 tablespoons (90 ml) lard

Soak beans overnight. Drain. Add water to cover; season to taste with salt, and cook slowly until very tender. Drain the beans and mash them. Add very hot lard, and continue cooking, stirring from time to time, until fat is absorbed by the beans. Do not let fried beans scorch. Serves 6 to 8.

The famous *frijoles refritos*, Mexican refried beans, are made by heating fat in frying pan, adding mashed fried beans, and cooking, stirring continuously, until beans are completely dry.

MEXICAN BEANS

1 lb (450 g) red kidney beans
1 Spanish onion, finely chopped
2 cloves garlic, finely chopped
Salt
2 tablespoons (30 ml) butter
1 tablespoon (15 ml) flour
½ teaspoon (2.5 ml) cumin powder
2 tablespoons (30 ml) Mexican chili powder
Bouquet garni (2 sprigs parsley, 2 sprigs thyme,
1 stalk celery, 1 bay leaf)
½ pint (300 ml) beef stock
Freshly ground black pepper

Place kidney beans in a large saucepan. Fill pan with water and bring gently to a boil. Remove saucepan from heat and let beans soak in hot water for 1 hour.

Drain, and simmer with finely chopped onion and garlic in salted water in a large casserole. After about an hour of cooking, taste them. If they are cooked, drain; if not, continue to simmer until they are tender, but do not let them burst. Drain.

Mix butter, flour, cumin powder and Mexican chili powder (a combination of powdered chilies, cumin seed, dried garlic and oregano) to a smooth paste. Combine cooked beans and chili paste in a saucepan. Add *bouquet garni*, beef stock, and salt and freshly ground black pepper, to taste, and simmer, stirring gently from time to time, for about ¾ hours, until sauce is smooth and rich. Remove *bouquet garni*. Serve immediately. Serves 4 to 6.

KIDNEY BEANS IN RED WINE

1 lb (450 g) red kidney beans
1 Spanish onion
Salt
1 tablespoon (15 ml) butter
1 tablespoon (15 ml) flour
Bouquet garni (2 sprigs parsley, 2 sprigs thyme,
1 stalk celery, 1 bay leaf)
Freshly ground black pepper
8 oz (225 g) fat bacon, diced
¼–½ pint (150–300 ml) red wine

Place kidney beans in a large saucepan. Fill pan with water and bring gently to a boil. Then let beans soak off heat for 1 hour.

Drain; simmer with onion in salted water in a large casserole until beans are almost cooked through – 45 to 60 minutes. Beans should remain fairly firm, otherwise they will break in subsequent cooking. Drain beans, reserving liquid, and remove onion.

Mix butter and flour to a smooth paste. Combine drained beans with butter and flour in a saucepan. Add ¼ pint (150 ml) bean liquor, *bouquet garni*, and salt and freshly ground black pepper, to taste, and simmer, stirring gently from time to time, for about 10 minutes, or until beans have absorbed flavour, adding more liquor if necessary. Sauté diced bacon until golden. Add to beans with red wine, and simmer gently until sauce is smooth and rich – about ½ hour. Remove *bouquet garni*. Serve immediately. Serves 4 to 6.

BOSTON BAKED BEANS

1½ lb (675 g) haricot beans
1 lb (450 g) salt pork or fatty bacon
2 onions, finely chopped
2 teaspoons (10 ml) dry mustard
Salt and freshly ground black pepper
4 tablespoons (60 ml) each dark treacle and
Demerara sugar
1 pint (600 ml) boiling water from beans
2–4 tablespoons (30–60 ml) tomato ketchup
2 tablespoons (30 ml) bacon fat
Sautéed onion rings, cooked sausages and frankfurters (optional)

Soak the beans overnight in cold water. Drain, cover again with fresh water, and allow to simmer on a low heat for about 1 hour, or until the skins of the beans burst when blown upon. Drain again, saving about 1 pint (600 ml) of the liquid. Scald the salt pork quickly; drain pork and cut slashes in the rind with a sharp knife. Cut pork in 2 pieces; place 1 piece in bottom of a large casserole; add beans and bury remainder of pork in the beans so that the rind just shows. Mix finely chopped onions, mustard, salt, pepper, treacle and sugar with reserved bean water, and bring to a boil. Pour this mixture over the beans, to cover. If necessary, add more boiling water. Place lid on casserole and bake in a slow oven (300°–325°F/150°–170°C/GM2–3) for 6 hours. From time to time add more boiling water, so that beans are kept covered and moist.

One hour before serving: stir 2 to 4 tablespoons (30–60 ml) tomato ketchup into the beans; drip the hot melted bacon fat over them and cook for 1 hour in a slow oven, uncovered, to colour beans and brown pork. If desired, add sautéed onion rings, cooked sausages and frankfurters just before serving. Serves 8.

PURÉE OF PEAS WITH SAUSAGES

1 lb (450 g) split peas
Salt
2 Spanish onions
2 cloves
Bouquet garni (2 sprigs parsley, 2 sprigs thyme,
1 stalk celery, 1 bay leaf)
4 oz (100 g) bacon, in one piece
¼ pint (150 ml) hot milk
Butter
Freshly ground black pepper
1 lb (450 g) sausages
2 tablespoons (30 ml) olive oil
6 tablespoons (90 ml) dry white wine

Place split peas in a large saucepan. Fill pan with water and bring gently to a boil. Remove saucepan from heat and let peas soak in hot water for 1 hour.

Drain peas, and cook in salted water with onions, cloves, *bouquet garni* and bacon until tender.

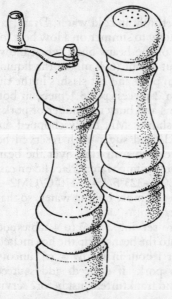

When cooked, drain. Remove onions, cloves, *bouquet garni* and bacon. (Bacon may be served at another meal.)

Force peas through a fine sieve. Combine in the top of a double saucepan with hot milk and 4 tablespoons (60 ml) butter, and simmer over water until smooth and thick. Season to taste with salt and freshly ground black pepper. Keep warm.

Simmer sausages in 2 tablespoons (30 ml) each butter and olive oil until cooked through. Remove sausages and keep warm. Pour off fat; add dry white wine to pan and cook over a high heat, stirring continuously until all crusty bits from sides of pan are blended into sauce.

To serve: arrange puréed peas in a heated serving dish. Arrange cooked sausages on top and pour over wine sauce. Serves 4 to 6.

LENTILS PROVENÇALE

1 lb (450 g) lentils
1 Spanish onion
Salt
4–6 tablespoons (60–90 ml) olive oil
1 clove garlic, finely chopped
1 small can anchovy fillets
4 oz (100 g) butter
Freshly ground black pepper

Place lentils in a large saucepan. Fill pan with water and bring gently to a boil. Remove saucepan from heat and let lentils soak in hot water for 1 hour.

Drain lentils and cook with onion in salted water until tender. The length of time for cooking lentils depends on their type and their age. In any case, after ½ hour look at them from time to time to see if they are cooked.

When ready, drain. Heat olive oil in a saucepan; add finely chopped garlic and lentils, and continue to cook, shaking pan from time to time, until lentils are heated through.

Pound anchovy fillets and butter to a smooth paste, and add to lentils, stirring in well. Season to taste with salt and freshly ground black pepper. Place in serving dish and serve very hot. Serves 4 to 6.

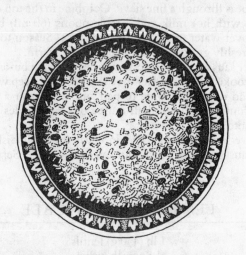

CHAPTER SEVENTEEN

Rice

It was in Signora Francesca's high-ceilinged kitchen that I first learned to cook 'in Italian'. I had come to Rome, after a year of touring Germany, to play a part in the Audrey Hepburn film *Roman Holiday*. All that long, somnolent summer, while waiting for the film to progress to where I was expected to take part, I spent the hot afternoons on the beaches of Rome's Lido . . . and my evenings in the little *trattorie* and *bottiglieri* around the Pantheon, the quarter of Rome I liked to call my own. Little by little my savings from the German Tour were exhausted, so I decided to move into an inexpensive *pensione* frequented by actor and dancer friends on the Via del Pantheon.

Signora Francesca's *pensione* was the complete third floor of an old *palazzo*, with a wonderful view of the square and its temple – the greatest complete building left to us by Imperial Rome. The Signora's cooking – *per le amici* – was famous in the quarter, and I soon fell into the habit of letting her cook for me. And then, as funds fell lower and autumn came on and still the film was not ready to bring in the *lire*, I used to remain with her while she prepared her simple dishes and help her cut up the vegetables for a *stufatino* . . . or prepare the tripe for a *trippa alla romana*. I learned the patience necessary to make the golden dough for tagliatelle, and the deft skill worn old hands can muster to chop the meats finely for the stuffings for cannelloni, ravioli and *agnolotti*.

Francesca was a soft-bodied old woman who loved to eat; often untidy, sometimes downright ill-tempered, she had a sincere goodness in her which nothing seemed to tarnish. I always think of her and that summer in Rome with a good deal of nostalgia . . . for those were happy days. And happy, too, was their sequel, my tour through Italy with Mario Carotenuto in his musical review, *Calvacata a Piedi* . . . a trip that was to take me through every major city of Italy and Sicily, and allow me to try at first hand the myriad regional specialities of the Italian cuisine that I have learned to love so well.

What teachers Mario and his company of actors, singers, dancers and musicians were! They knew every restaurant to visit and every famous regional dish to taste. I shall always be grateful to them for their warmth and enthusiasm as they guided me through the wonderful soups and *brodi* of the Italian provinces – delicate broths of beef or chicken – here mixed with beans, vegetables and pasta, there studded with subtly flavoured 'little monk's caps' of meat and herbs; the wonderful fish soups of the coastal towns; and *busecca*, an intriguing soup made of tripe. The varieties of pasta consumed on the way were, of course, legion . . . and how I loved it . . . *fettucine all' uovo*, thin egg noodles, freshly made, served with butter and finely grated Parmesan cheese; *spaghetti alla carbonara*, spaghetti, or sometimes macaroni, served with fried bacon or ham, and a sauce of finely grated Parmesan, fresh butter and the yolks of eggs; or just plain spaghetti, cooked to *al dente* tenderness and served *al aglio e olio* – with an oil and garlic sauce.

The great platters of *antipasti* were a delight to me; even the smallest country *trattorie* could boast of a plentiful and colourful assortment of *salame, prosciutto* and piles of sliced vegetables – both raw and cooked – dressed in olive oil and lemon juice with a hint of fresh basil or oregano. The delicious sweetness of fresh figs served with the salty pink raw ham of Parma was my discovery here . . . as was *cappon magro*, a huge mounted salad – practically a meal in itself – of vegetables, fish, mussels and lobster, bathed in a pungent garlic- and herb-flavoured sauce.

I loved, too, the simple salads of the Italians: tender green lettuce leaves dressed simply with lemon juice and olive oil; flavourful green peppers, baked soft and served cold with an oil and lemon dressing; and the cool taste of anise-scented fennel, thinly sliced and marinated in lemon and oil.

But I think the greatest surprise for me was the rice. Italians love rice and are wonderfully creative in their methods of cooking it. Not for them the pallid, slushy, plain-boiled variety so often served as a sop for the undistinguished gravies of curry and casserole. Instead they combine rice with butter, finely chopped onion and rich chicken stock, and simmer it gently until it is magically tender – neither mushy soft nor unpleasantly hard – but *al dente* just like their spaghetti. And then they flavour it with the heady taste of saffron, the earthiness of wild mushrooms or, for some special occasions, the excitement of thinly sliced white truffles. Nothing short of ambrosia . . . but then, they have had a head start on us. For if rice has been grown – and cooked to perfection – by the Chinese since 2800 BC, it was the Italians who introduced the mighty grain to the rest of Europe in the sixteenth century. Today rice from the Po Valley is exported to all of Europe and is a staple in the northern regions of Italy, as national in character as pasta and *polenta*.

Italian cooks respect rice; rarely, for example, do they wash it under the tap. Instead they clean it by placing it in cold water for a few minutes, carefully picking out the bits of grit, and then they rub it dry, after draining it, between the folds of a clean tea towel. Nor do they pour all of the cleaned rice into the liquid all at once. Francesca used to dribble it through her fingers, grain by grain, stirring it gently with a wooden spoon as she did so. Her stock for risottos was either chicken or beef, or a combination of chicken stock and dry white wine. For her *risotto alla milanese*, she liked to add diced fresh beef marrow to the butter in which the rice was cooked.

How to Cook Rice

The most common fault in the preparation of rice is overcooking. A good general rule, I think, is to cook rice for sweets and puddings thoroughly so that it is quite soft, but for main dishes to stop the cooking at the point where the rice just starts to get soft. Special care is required in handling rice once it is cooked. The grains mash very easily and, once cooked, they should never be stirred with a spoon, but tossed lightly with a fork. Serve your rice as soon as possible after cooking.

BOILED RICE
There are countless ways of cooking plain-boiled rice. Some cooks prefer to steam it in the Chinese manner; others insist that unless a knob of butter or a little oil is added to the cooking liquid, the grains will not separate. I like to boil it in a large, heavy saucepan capable of holding a good quantity of water. The secret for separate grains of white, fluffy rice is very simple indeed: just salt the water, add a little lemon juice to keep the rice white, and when the water is boiling well, dribble the grain into the liquid through your fingers, stirring all the while. Do not cover the pan; and allow rice to cook for 15 to 18 minutes. During the last 2 or 3 minutes of cooking time, watch the rice carefully, for the only real test is the 'taste test'. I always pick out one or two grains with a fork and taste them. When the rice is just right – with the granular core tender but not mushy – drain it through a large colander and keep warm over boiling water until ready to serve.

Serve the rice simply with butter and freshly grated Parmesan, or as they do it Italy during the truffle season, *coi tartufi bianchi*, the delicate sea-scented, garlic-flavoured white truffles of Alba.

RISOTTO
One of the easiest and most delicious methods of cooking rice is the risotto. Wash long-grain or Italian rice in cold water. Drain and dry thoroughly. Add 3 to 4 tablespoons (45–60 ml) butter, salt and pepper to taste, and enough chicken stock and dry white wine or beef stock, or a combination of the three, to cover the rice. Bring to a boil, stirring; reduce heat, cover tightly and simmer gently for 15 to 18 minutes. Uncover, toss lightly with a fork, add a little extra butter and some grated Parmesan, and

serve. The rice should have absorbed all the liquid and all the grains will be separate and moist.

If a rich chicken stock is used in cooking the rice, and you have sautéed the rice with a little finely chopped onion before adding the liquid, it will take on extra strength and flavour. Try adding to it 8 oz (225 g) of diced cooked chicken or lamb that has been heated in a little stock with ½ Spanish onion, finely chopped, and cooked until golden in 2 tablespoons (30 ml) butter or oil; the addition of a teaspoon or two (5–10 ml) of curry powder, ½ teaspoon (2.5 ml) powdered saffron, chopped nuts, diced raw apple or plumped up raisins will also do much to change the taste and quality of your risotto. This with a salad, followed by a sweet, or cheese and fruit, will make a delicious and satisfying meal.

FRIED RICE

Cooked rice, gently fried – whether the recipe is Chinese, Provençal or just plain home-inspired – can turn left-overs (cooked chicken, pork, shrimp or prawns, even vegetables) into a gourmet-style dish. Fried rice is not just one dish, it is a whole series of mouth-watering additions to your culinary repertoire, consisting first, of course, of rice, but with such delightful additions that the possibilities of variation are infinite. You must have perfectly boiled rice to start with; each grain dry, fluffy and distinct before you start. Then it is necessary only to pour a thin layer of corn or olive oil into your frying pan, add the rice, and stir over a high heat until it is golden. The possible additives are limitless; I know of one Chinese recipe which combines diced duck, chicken, Chinese sausage, fried egg, soy sauce, ham, shrimp and lobster. The recipes on page 663 are not quite so complicated.

BASIC ITALIAN RISOTTO

12 oz (350 g) rice
½ Spanish onion, finely chopped
Butter
1½–2 pints (900 ml–1.1 lit) hot beef stock
½ teaspoon (2.5 ml) powdered saffron
Salt and freshly ground black pepper
Freshly grated Parmesan

Place chopped onion in a deep saucepan with 4 tablespoons (60 ml) butter. Cook slowly for 2 to 4 minutes, taking care that the onion does not become brown. Add the rice and cook over medium heat, stirring constantly with a wooden spoon. After a minute or so, stir in a cup of hot beef stock in which you have dissolved the powdered saffron.

Continue cooking, adding stock as needed and stirring from time to time, until rice is cooked – 15 to 18 minutes. Correct seasoning. By this time all the stock in the pan should have been absorbed by the rice, leaving rice tender but still moist. Serve immediately with extra butter and freshly grated Parmesan. Serves 4 to 6.

RISOTTO CON FUNGHI

1 recipe Basic Italian Risotto (page 650)
6–8 dried mushrooms
8 oz (225 g) cooked ham, diced
6–8 tablespoons (90–120 ml) freshly grated Parmesan
Butter

Soak dried mushrooms for several hours in hot water. Drain; cut into small pieces and combine with diced cooked ham. Fold ham and mushroom mixture carefully into risotto cooked as above. Then stir in freshly grated Parmesan cheese; place rice in a well-buttered casserole; cover and cook in a preheated slow oven (350°F/180°C/GM4) for about 20 minutes. Serve immediately. Serves 4 to 6.

RICE WITH ITALIAN SAUSAGES

12 oz (350 g) rice
1 lb (450 g) Italian garlic sausages
Olive oil
Butter
1 Spanish onion, finely chopped
2 stalks celery, sliced
1 large can Italian peeled tomatoes
2–3 tablespoons (30–45 ml) tomato concentrate
1 clove garlic
1 tablespoon (15 ml) finely chopped parsley
Pinch of dried oregano
2 bay leaves
Salt and freshly ground black pepper

To prepare sausages for sauce: prick holes in sausages with a fine skewer or the point of a sharp knife; place in a frying pan just large enough to hold them and barely cover with water. Cook over medium heat until water evaporates. Remove sausages and brown in a little oil with butter, turning them from time to time, for 20 minutes. Allow to cool and slice into thin rounds.

To make sauce: combine chopped onion, sliced celery, Italian peeled tomatoes, tomato concentrate and garlic in a large saucepan. Add finely chopped parsley, oregano and bay leaves, and season to taste with salt and freshly ground black pepper. Simmer for 30 minutes, and then add sausage slices and simmer for 30 minutes longer.

To serve: cook rice as in Basic Italian Risotto recipe (page 650). Drain and serve immediately with Italian sausages and sauce. Serves 4 to 6.

RIZ AU FROMAGE

12 oz (350 g) rice
Butter
6 tablespoons (90 ml) freshly grated Gruyère
3 tablespoons (45 ml) freshly grated Parmesan
Double cream
Salt and freshly ground black pepper

Boil or steam rice in the usual way until tender but not mushy. Drain.

Butter a shallow heatproof casserole or deep *gratin* dish. Place a layer of rice on bottom of dish (using about a third of the rice); sprinkle with 3 tablespoons (45 ml) grated cheese (mixed Gruyère and Parmesan); sprinkle lightly with double cream; dot with butter, and season to taste with salt and freshly ground black pepper; continue this process until dish is full, using equal portions of rice each time, and finishing with a layer of grated cheese. Dot with butter and cook in a slow oven (350°F/180°C/GM4) for 15 to 20 minutes, or until top is golden. Serves 4.

BASIC PILAFF

12 oz (350 g) long-grain rice
½ Spanish onion, finely chopped
Butter
¾ pint (450 ml) well-flavoured stock
Thyme
Salt and freshly ground black pepper

Wash rice; drain and dry with a cloth. Sauté finely chopped onion in 4 tablespoons (60 ml) butter until a light golden colour. Add rice and continue to cook, stirring constantly, until it begins to take on colour. Then pour in hot stock, and season to taste with thyme, salt and freshly ground black pepper. Cover saucepan and place in a slow oven (350°F/180°C/GM4) for 15 to 20 minutes, or until the liquid has been absorbed and the rice is tender but not mushy. Serve with additional butter. Serves 4 to 6.

Curried Pilaff: Add 1 to 2 tablespoons (15–30 ml) curry powder to rice after you have browned it in butter. Continue to cook as above.

PARTY PILAFF

2 lb (900 g) uncooked rice
Butter
6 tablespoons (90 ml) olive oil
8 oz (225 g) fatty bacon, diced
2 Spanish onions, finely chopped
8 oz (225 g) celery, diced
4 oz (100 g) green pepper, chopped
4 lb (1.8 kg) diced cooked ham or turkey and ham
2 pints (1.1 lit) chicken stock
1 wine glass dry sherry
2 teaspoons (10 ml) Worcestershire sauce
Salt and freshly ground black pepper
12 oz (350 g) mushrooms, thinly sliced
4 tablespoons (60 ml) chopped parsley
Pitted ripe olives

Combine 6 tablespoons (90 ml) each butter and oil in a large heatproof casserole, and sauté diced bacon in it until golden. Remove bacon and reserve. Sauté chopped onion, celery and green pepper in resulting fats for 5 minutes. Then add diced ham (or diced ham and turkey) and sauté for 5 minutes more. Add bacon and uncooked rice, and cook for about 4 minutes more, stirring well, until rice begins to take on a little colour.

Pour chicken stock (made with chicken cubes), sherry and Worcestershire sauce into ham and rice mixture; season to taste with salt and freshly ground black pepper and bring to a boil. Cover casserole and bake in a moderate oven (375°F/190°C/GM5) for 30 minutes, or until rice is tender.

Sauté thinly sliced mushrooms in a little butter; add parsley and a handful of pitted olives, and heat through. Stir into casserole and serve. Serves 20.

CHICKEN LIVER PILAFF

6 oz (175 g) rice
Butter
1 tablespoon (15 ml) finely chopped onion
1 pint (600 ml) chicken stock
Pinch of saffron
2 tablespoons (30 ml) sultanas
Salt and freshly ground black pepper
8 oz (225 g) chicken livers
1 level tablespoon (15 ml) flour
½ pint (300 ml) well-flavoured Brown Sauce
(page 114)
4 tablespoons (60 ml) Madeira wine

To prepare pilaff: melt 1 tablespoon (15 ml) butter in a thick-bottomed saucepan and simmer finely chopped onion for a minute or two. Add the rice and stir until rice is well coated with butter. Do not let it colour. Add the stock, saffron and sultanas, and season to taste with salt and freshly ground black pepper. Cover saucepan and simmer rice gently for 15 minutes, or until tender. Correct seasoning; lightly stir in 1 tablespoon (15 ml) butter and press into a well-buttered ring mould. Bake in a slow oven (350°F/180°C/GM4) for 5 minutes.

To prepare chicken livers: cut green parts from livers; wash livers carefully and pat dry in a clean cloth. Dice livers; toss them lightly in seasoned flour and sauté in 2 tablespoons (30 ml) butter until lightly browned. Pour in Brown Sauce and wine; season to taste with salt and freshly ground black pepper. Simmer for a few more minutes, or until tender.

Turn rice ring out on a hot serving platter and fill with chicken livers. Serves 4.

HAM AND RICE CONTADINI

1½ lb (675 g) cooked ham, cut in cubes
Butter
4 tablespoons (60 ml) olive oil
Pinch of dried sage
Pinch of oregano
Freshly ground black pepper
1 Spanish onion, finely chopped
2 cloves garlic, crushed
4 oz (100 g) mushrooms, thinly sliced
12 stuffed olives, thinly sliced
1¼ lb (550 g) peeled tomatoes
2 tablespoons (30 ml) tomato concentrate
1 chicken stock cube
6 tablespoons (90 ml) dry white wine
1 lb (450 g) rice
Salt
Finely chopped parsley
Freshly grated Parmesan

Combine 2 tablespoons (30 ml) each of butter and olive oil in a thick-bottomed frying pan and sauté ham cubes until golden. Season to taste with sage, oregano and freshly ground black pepper.

Remove ham from pan; add 2 tablespoons (30 ml) butter and remaining oil, and sauté finely chopped onion and crushed garlic until golden. Add thinly sliced mushrooms and olives, and continue cooking for a minute or two. Stir in peeled tomatoes, tomato concentrate and chicken stock cube dissolved in dry white wine, and simmer gently, covered, for about 2 hours, adding a little water from time to time if necessary.

Just before serving, cook rice in rapidly boiling salted water until just tender. Drain rice and place on a hot serving dish. Add ham cubes to the sauce, correct seasoning and pour over rice. Sprinkle with finely chopped parsley, and serve with a knob of butter and grated Parmesan. Serves 6 to 8.

RIZ À LA BASQUAISE

12 oz (350 g) rice
1 Spanish onion, finely chopped
6–8 tablespoons (90–120 ml) olive oil
2–4 tablespoons (30–60 ml) tomato concentrate
¼ pint (150 ml) dry white wine
Salt and freshly ground black pepper
1 *Chorizo* sausage, sliced
12 pitted black olives
Butter
1 small can pimentos

Sauté finely chopped onion in olive oil until it just begins to turn golden in colour; add washed rice and stir until the oil has been absorbed by the rice. Stir in tomato concentrate which you have diluted in dry white wine, and add enough hot water to cover rice. Season to taste with salt and freshly ground black pepper. Arrange sliced sausage and pitted black olives on top of rice and fit a piece of well-buttered foil over casserole; cover casserole and cook over a low heat until water has evaporated and rice is tender but not mushy. Add canned pimentos cut into strips, and correct seasoning. Toss rice well just before serving. Serves 4 to 6.

RIZ PAYSANNE

12 oz (350 g) rice
6 oz (175 g) unsmoked bacon, cut in 1 piece
1 Spanish onion, coarsely chopped
4 tablespoons (60 ml) olive oil
Well-flavoured beef stock
Salt and freshly ground black pepper
2 tablespoons (30 ml) finely chopped parsley
1 tablespoon (15 ml) finely chopped chives or tarragon
2–4 tablespoons (30–60 ml) freshly grated Gruyère

Dice bacon and sauté chopped onion and bacon in olive oil until onion is soft and lightly golden. Stir in rice and continue to cook, stirring constantly, until all fat is absorbed by rice. Add well-flavoured beef stock to cover, and cook for 15 to 18 minutes, stirring occasionally and adding stock from time to time as needed. Season to taste with salt and freshly ground black pepper. When rice is done, all the stock in the pan should have been absorbed by the rice, which should be quite moist. Serve sprinkled with finely chopped herbs and cheese. Serves 4.

RICE WITH KIDNEYS AND BABY MARROWS

12 oz (350 g) rice
Salt
2 kidneys
4 baby marrows (about 4 inches (10 cms) each)
Butter
2 tablespoons (30 ml) olive oil
4 tablespoons (60 ml) fat bacon, diced
½ Spanish onion, finely chopped
1 tablespoon (15 ml) flour
Freshly ground black pepper
6 tablespoons (90 ml) dry white wine or Marsala
¾ pint (450 ml) hot beef stock
Finely chopped parsley
Freshly grated Parmesan

Cook rice in usual manner in boiling salted water, but for 10 minutes only; drain; cut kidneys into thin slices; cut baby marrows into long strips.

Combine 2 tablespoons (30 ml) butter, olive oil and diced

bacon in a deep saucepan, and sauté chopped onion in this mixture until transparent. Flour kidneys lightly and sauté them lightly in this mixture; add sliced marrows; season to taste with salt and freshly ground black pepper, and sauté until golden. Then stir in drained rice and cook until rice is golden. Pour dry white wine or Marsala and hot beef stock over it, and cook in a moderate oven (375°F/190°C/GM5) until rice is tender. Garnish with finely chopped parsley and serve with extra butter and grated Parmesan. Serves 4 to 6.

ITALIAN RICE CROQUETTES

12 oz (350 g) rice
1 chicken stock cube
1 pint (600 ml) milk
8 oz (225 g) chicken livers
2 tablespoons (30 ml) butter
2 tablespoons (30 ml) finely chopped onion
Salt and freshly ground black pepper
2 eggs, well beaten
4 tablespoons (60 ml) grated Parmesan
2 tablespoons (30 ml) finely chopped parsley
Breadcrumbs
Fat, for deep-frying
½ pint (300 ml) well-flavoured Italian Tomato Sauce
(page 125)

Crumble chicken stock cube into milk and bring to a boil. Add rice and cook, stirring from time to time, until rice is tender but not soft. Add hot water from time to time to keep rice from sticking. Drain and cool.

Sauté chopped chicken livers in butter with finely chopped onion until livers are cooked. Season livers to taste with salt and freshly ground black pepper, and fold into rice with 1 egg, well beaten, grated Parmesan and finely chopped parsley. Mix well and roll into balls or cork shapes. Roll in breadcrumbs, and then in remaining well-beaten egg, and then in breadcrumbs again. Chill.

When ready to serve, fry in deep hot fat. Serve with Italian Tomato Sauce. Serves 4 to 6.

ARANCINI

12 oz (350 g) rice
4 oz (100 g) chicken livers, chopped
1 Spanish onion, finely chopped
1 clove garlic, finely chopped
4 tablespoons (60 ml) olive oil
Salt and freshly ground black pepper
4–6 tablespoons (60–90 ml) tomato concentrate
¼ pint (150 ml) dry white wine
Butter
4–6 tablespoons (60–90 ml) freshly grated Parmesan
2 egg yolks, well beaten
2 eggs, well beaten
Breadcrumbs
Fat, for deep-frying

Sauté chopped chicken livers, onion and garlic in olive oil until vegetables are transparent. Season to taste with salt and freshly ground black pepper. Add tomato concentrate which you have diluted with dry white wine. Add enough water to make a creamy sauce; cover saucepan and simmer gently for 30 minutes.

Boil or steam rice in usual way until tender but not mushy. Drain well; butter lightly and season to taste with freshly grated Parmesan. Add well-beaten egg yolks and mix well. Then strain sauce from chicken livers into rice and mix well.

Form small balls the size of golf balls with seasoned rice mixture; then with your forefinger, dig a hole in the centre of each ball and put 1 teaspoon (5 ml) of liver mixture into each; pinch shut and reroll ball. Chill.

When ready to fry: dip *arancini* in beaten eggs and then in breadcrumbs, and fry in deep fat until golden. Serves 4 to 6.

BREAKFAST KEDGEREE WITH HAM

4 oz (100 g) rice
4 oz (100 g) cooked finnan haddock
4 oz (100 g) cold boiled ham
2 hard-boiled eggs
4 tablespoons (60 ml) butter
1–2 tablespoons (15–30 ml) tomato ketchup
2 tablespoons (30 ml) chopped watercress
Salt and freshly ground black pepper

Boil or steam rice in the usual way until tender but not mushy. Remove skin and bones from fish, and flake. Dice ham. Chop whites of hard-boiled eggs.

Melt butter in saucepan; toss rice in it. Add fish, ham and egg whites. Stir in ketchup and toss lightly over heat until hot. Stir in chopped watercress and correct seasoning. Grate egg yolks and scatter over kedgeree. Serve immediately. Serves 4.

WILD RICE WITH MUSHROOMS

12 oz (350 g) wild rice
Salt
Butter
4 tablespoons (60 ml) finely chopped spring onions
6 tablespoons (90 ml) diced ham
8 button mushrooms, thinly sliced
Freshly ground black pepper
2 tablespoons (30 ml) finely chopped parsley

Wash wild rice in cold water; drain; steam over salted boiling water for 30 minutes, or until tender. Melt 4 tablespoons (60 ml) butter in a frying pan; add chopped spring onions, diced ham and sliced button mushrooms, and sauté until lightly browned. Add steamed rice and continue to cook, tossing with a fork, for 5 minutes, adding more butter if necessary. Season to taste with salt and freshly ground black pepper, and sprinkle with finely chopped parsley. Serves 4 to 6.

Chinese Rice

Rice is very precious to the Chinese, and except at great banquets, is served throughout Chinese meals. It is so precious, indeed, that little Chinese boys are purportedly warned that for each grain left in their rice bowl a pock mark will appear on the face of their future bride.

A long-established manner of cooking rice in China is to steam it gently in a bamboo basket steamer which is placed over a pan of boiling water. Rice prepared in this way has an unusually loose and pleasant texture.

CHINESE STEAMED RICE

1 Chinese bowl long-grain rice
3 Chinese bowls cold water

Wash rice under cold running water, rubbing grains between fingers. Rinse with cold water until water is clear. Drain. Put rice in a large saucepan. Add water and boil for 3 minutes. Drain off water: put rice in a steamer and steam over water for 30 minutes. Serves 4.

CHINESE STEAMED RICE – CANTONESE STYLE

1 Chinese bowl long-grain rice
3 Chinese bowls cold water

Wash rice and drain as above. Add water and boil for 3 minutes. Drain off water; fill individual serving bowls three-quarters full to allow rice to expand, place bowls in a shallow pan of boiling water, and steam, covered, for 1 hour. Be sure to have enough boiling water to steam rice, but not enough to pour over into bowls. Add more boiling water from time to time as necessary. Serves 4.

CHINESE FRIED RICE WITH MUSHROOMS

2 bowls cooked rice
2 tablespoons (30 ml) oil
1 onion, chopped
4 oz (100 g) button mushrooms, coarsely chopped
1 tablespoon (15 ml) soy sauce
Salt and freshly ground black pepper

Heat frying pan, add oil and chopped onion, and fry until brown. Then add coarsely chopped mushrooms and fry until semi-cooked. Add cold cooked rice and sauté gently until the whole begins to brown, stirring occasionally. When mixture is hot, add soy sauce, and season to taste with salt and freshly ground black pepper. Serves 4, if served with 2 or more other dishes.

CHINESE FRIED RICE WITH MARINATED BEEF STRIPS

4 bowls boiled rice (1 day old)
4 spring onions
1 green pepper
2 thin slices fresh ginger
2 oz (50 g) fillet of beef
2–3 tablespoons (30–45 ml) lard
Salt and freshly ground black pepper
4 thin slices ham, diced
2 slices bacon, diced
4 eggs, lightly beaten
1 tablespoon (15 ml) corn oil

MARINADE SAUCE
½ clove garlic, finely chopped
½ teaspoon (2.5 ml) cornflour
½ teaspoon (2.5 ml) sugar
1 tablespoon (15 ml) soy sauce
2–3 tablespoons (30–45 ml) lard

Slice spring onions, green pepper and ginger into thin strips. Slice fillet of beef thinly and combine with Marinade Sauce ingredients.

Heat 2 to 3 tablespoons (30–45 ml) lard in a large frying pan and sauté thin strips of ginger and green pepper with salt and freshly ground black pepper, to taste, for 1 minute. Break in boiled rice and cook, stirring with a fork. When grains are hot and separated, stir in diced ham and bacon, and sauté with rice. Add beef and Marinade Sauce, and sauté until beef is tender. Fry lightly beaten eggs in corn oil and cook for 1 minute, stirring constantly. Fold into rice. Serves 4 to 6.

CHINESE FRIED RICE WITH SHRIMPS AND PEPPERS

2 bowls cooked rice
2 tablespoons (30 ml) oil
1 onion, coarsely chopped
4 oz (100 g) shrimps or prawns
½ green pepper, sliced
2 tablespoons (30 ml) chopped red pepper
1 tablespoon (15 ml) soy sauce
2 eggs, beaten
Salt

Heat pan, add oil and fry onion until brown. Add shrimps (or prawns) and peppers, and fry until semi-cooked. Then add cold rice and sauté gently, stirring continuously, until the whole begins to brown. When mixture is hot, add soy sauce, then the eggs, beaten with salt to taste, and sauté until done. Serves 4, if served with 2 or more other dishes.

CHAPTER EIGHTEEN

Pasta

O ne of my favourite places in the world to visit is Rome. I go there often at Christmas, I love it in the spring, and I once lived the year round in this ever-changing, always delightful city. The Romans differ from the other citizens of Italy – and from other Mediterraneans – in that they are quicker-tempered, more colourful, and more interested in the passing pleasures and problems of the moment. To mingle with them in their noisy, crowded streets, eat with them in the tiny *trattorie* and *bottiglieri* they call their own, live with them for any period of time, know them and love them, is one of life's purest pleasures. And much like the *Romani* themselves is the food they eat. Each market place and each restaurant presents a masterpiece of brilliantly coloured raw materials worthy of an Old Master . . . platters of rosy-fleshed *prosciutto*, the specially cured raw ham of Parma, served in the sun with purple figs or the golden warmth of ripe melon; fat, pink *scampi* and deeper-toned *salame* from Milan, Genoa and Bologna, in marbled rose and white; butter-yellow cheeses; baskets of scarlet plum tomatoes and glossy aubergines; and the creamy white pasta – the very symbol of the versatility of Italian food – displayed in every length and thickness, in ribbons and coils and shapes and shells of all sizes. And every shape and size – even though it is made of the same basic dough – seems to have a different flavour. To my mind there are few experiences more rewarding in the world than sitting down to a plate high with steaming pasta, bathed in a richly red tomato sauce, the whole topped by a freshly grated mound of flavourful Parmesan.

In most restaurants in Rome, chicken or beef consommé served with pasta, or pasta by itself – in all its myriad variations, spaghetti, spaghettini, minicotti, tagliatelle, macaroni and lasagne – alternates with gnocchi and risotto as a first course. Next comes meat or fish, followed by a green vegetable or a green salad. Last comes the cheese and fruit course, or a sweet: *zabaglione*, *zuppa inglese*, or a mound of *crème chantilly* encased in the lightest of pastries.

In Britain, we sometimes like to make a huge platter of Italian spaghetti the centre-piece of a buffet dinner or an informal luncheon. In this case, an *antipasto* platter of fresh vegetables, *salame* and olives should precede it. Follow with a green salad tossed with olive oil, wine vinegar and seasoning. French or Italian bread and, for a sweet, something light.

There seems to be no end to the ingenuity of Italian cooks when it comes to producing different variations on the pasta theme. I like to begin my Roman meals with a famous Roman speciality – *fettuccine all'uovo*, thin, fresh egg noodles served with butter and finely grated Parmesan cheese, or the green fettuccine of Florence, where the basic wheat-flour dough of the noodles is kneaded with finely chopped spinach. Sometimes I prefer *lasagne al forno*, wide ribbons of dough arranged in alternate layers with Ricotta and Mozzarella cheese, minced pork and veal, and slices of hard-boiled egg, the whole bathed in two unctuous sauces – a rich Béchamel and a special '*ragu*' *all romana*.

Then there are the spaghettis: *alla carrettiera*, spaghetti served with an aromatic sauce of tuna fish, mushrooms and *fines herbes*; *alla matriciana*, spaghetti with a sauce flavoured with chopped fat salt pork and onions; *alla carbonara*, spaghetti or macaroni served with fried bacon or ham and a sauce of finely grated Parmesan, butter and the yolk of eggs.

One of my favourites, perhaps, is fettuccine with cream sauce and mushrooms, a delicious combination of egg noodles, butter-simmered diced ham, mushrooms and onion, and a sauce made rich with egg yolks, cream and freshly grated Parmesan. This is a wonderful first course for a small after-theatre supper, as once the noodles are cooked, it can be prepared in a chafing dish at the table.

Basic Recipe for Home-Made Egg Pasta

The basic recipe for egg pasta – from which you make tagliatelle, lasagne, ravioli, cannelloni, agnolotti and tortellini – is relatively, simple. To make home-made pasta as it is made the length and breadth of Italy, you will need: 1 lb (450 g) flour, 1 level teaspoon (5 ml) salt, 3 well-beaten eggs, 4 to 5 tablespoons (60–75 ml) water, a large mixing bowl, a pastry board and a rolling pin.

Sift flour and salt into a large mixing bowl. Make a well in the centre and pour in beaten eggs. Add 2 tablespoons (30 ml) water, and mix flour and liquids together with your fingertips until the pasta dough is just soft enough to form into a ball, adding a tablespoon or two (15–30 ml) of water if the mixture seems too dry.

Sprinkle a large pastry board with flour and knead the dough on this board with the flat of your hand until dough is smooth and elastic (about 15 minutes), sifting a little flour on your hand and the board from time to time. Divide dough into 4 equal parts and, using a rolling pin, roll out one piece at a time into paper-thin sheets. To do this, roll out in one direction, stretching the pasta dough as you go, and then roll out in the opposite direction. Sprinkle with flour; fold over and repeat. The dough should be just dry enough not to stick to the rolling pin. Repeat this process of rolling, stretching and folding the dough another 2 or 3 times. Repeat with other pieces of pasta dough.

TO MAKE TAGLIATELLE (FETTUCCINE)
Prepare egg pasta as above. Roll out and dust liberally with flour. Fold loosely and cut into ¼-inch (6 mm) strips. Spread pieces out on a clean cloth to dry for at least 1 hour before cooking in the usual way.

TO MAKE LASAGNE
Prepare egg pasta as above. Dust with flour. Fold loosely and cut into 2-inch (5 cm) strips. Spread on a clean cloth to dry for at least 1 hour before cooking in the usual way.

TO MAKE CANNELLONI
Prepare egg pasta as above. Cut into 3 by 4 inch (8–10 cm) rectangles. Dry for 1 hour. Drop into boiling water for 5 minutes. Remove and drop immediately into cold water. Drain and spread on a clean cloth to dry. Fill as desired and bake until stuffing is cooked through. Serve with tomato sauce and freshly grated Parmesan cheese.

To Cook Pasta

One lb (450 g) of pasta serves 4 people for a main course, 6 people for a first course. Cook pasta in boiling salted water at least 6 pints (3.4 lit) of water per lb (450 g) of pasta.

Let water boil briskly for a minute before adding pasta. Instead of breaking long spaghetti or macaroni, hold a handful at one end and dip the other into the boiling water. As the pasta softens, curl it round in the pan until the whole length goes in. Do not cover. Stir at the start of the cooking to prevent spaghetti from sticking to the pan.

Cook pasta until tender but still firm – ‘*al dente*’, as the Italians say, which means just firm enough to bite comfortably, but not so soft that it is mushy. To test: lift out one strand with a fork and bite it. Do not overcook. When done, drain at once in a big colander, shaking it to remove as much water as possible. Serve pasta immediately.

TO KEEP PASTA HOT
If it is impractical to serve pasta immediately, set the colander of drained pasta over a saucepan containing a small amount of boiling water. Cover with a damp towel until ready to serve.

SPAGHETTI WITH MEAT BALLS

1 lb (450 g) spaghetti
Salt
Freshly grated Parmesan
Butter

MEAT BALLS
12 oz (350 g) finely chopped beef
8 oz (225 g) finely chopped pork
2 slices bread, soaked in milk and shredded
1 clove garlic, finely chopped
2 tablespoons (30 ml) finely chopped parsley
Salt and freshly ground black pepper
1 egg, lightly beaten
Flour
4 tablespoons (60 ml) olive oil

SAUCE
1 Spanish onion, finely chopped
1 clove garlic, finely chopped
2–4 tablespoons (30–60 ml) olive oil
1 small can mushrooms, sliced
1 large can Italian peeled tomatoes
6 tablespoons (90 ml) Italian tomato concentrate
1 bay leaf
1 small strip lemon peel
1 beef stock cube
Salt and freshly ground black pepper
1 tablespoon (15 ml) Worcestershire sauce

MEAT BALLS
Combine meat, bread soaked in milk and shredded, finely chopped garlic and parsley, salt and freshly ground black pepper and beaten egg. Mix well and shape into small meat balls. Dredge meat balls with flour and brown on all sides in hot olive oil. Remove from pan.

SAUCE
Sauté finely chopped onion and garlic in olive oil in a large, thick-bottomed frying pan until transparent. Add sliced mushrooms and sauté for a minute or two more. Then add peeled

tomatoes, tomato concentrate, bay leaf, lemon peel and beef stock cube, and season to taste with salt and freshly ground black pepper. Simmer gently, covered, for 1 hour, stirring from time to time. Just before serving, stir in Worcestershire sauce.

Return meat balls to sauce and simmer gently for 20 minutes.

Cook spaghetti in boiling salted water until just tender. Drain. Serve spaghetti with sauce and freshly grated Parmesan and butter. Serves 4.

SPAGHETTI ALLA BOLOGNESE

1 lb (450 g) spaghetti
Salt
Freshly grated Parmesan
Butter

BOLOGNESE SAUCE
2 tablespoons (30 ml) butter
4 tablespoons (60 ml) olive oil
4 oz (100 g) fatty salt pork or unsmoked bacon,
finely chopped
1 onion, finely chopped
2 carrots, finely chopped
1 stalk celery, finely chopped
8 oz (225 g) sirloin of beef, minced
1 strip of lemon peel
1 bay leaf
4 tablespoons (60 ml) tomato concentrate
½ pint (300 ml) rich beef stock
¼ pint (150 ml) dry white wine
Salt, freshly ground black pepper and grated
nutmeg
4 tablespoons (60 ml) double cream

Heat butter and olive oil in a large, thick-bottomed frying pan; add finely chopped fatty salt pork (or unsmoked bacon), onion, carrots and celery, and sauté over medium heat, stirring occasionally, until meat browns. Stir in raw minced beef and brown evenly, stirring continuously. Add lemon peel, bay leaf, tomato concentrate, beef stock and dry white wine, and season to taste with salt, freshly ground black pepper and nutmeg. Cover pan and simmer the sauce very gently for ½ hour, stirring occasionally.

Remove lemon peel and bay leaf, and simmer, uncovered, for ½ hour, or until sauce has thickened slightly. Add cream and simmer for 2 to 3 minutes more.

Cook spaghetti in boiling salted water until *al dente*. Drain. Serve with Bolognese Sauce and freshly grated Parmesan cheese. Dot with butter. Serves 4.

SPAGHETTI WITH SICILIAN ANCHOVY SAUCE

1 lb (450 g) spaghetti
Salt
2 tablespoons (30 ml) finely chopped parsley
Butter
Freshly grated Parmesan (optional)

SICILIAN ANCHOVY SAUCE
1–2 cloves garlic, finely chopped
6 tablespoons (90 ml) olive oil
10–12 anchovy fillets, diced
2 tablespoons (30 ml) dry breadcrumbs
Salt and freshly ground black pepper

Cook spaghetti in boiling salted water until *al dente* – tender but still firm. Drain and pour Sicilian Anchovy Sauce over it. Toss well and sprinkle with finely chopped parsley. Serve with butter, and freshly grated Parmesan if desired. Serves 4.

SICILIAN ANCHOVY SAUCE
Simmer garlic in olive oil until transparent; add diced anchovies and continue to cook, stirring, for 2 minutes. Stir in breadcrumbs, and season to taste with salt and freshly ground black pepper.

QUICK SPAGHETTI NAPOLETANA

1 lb (450 g) spaghetti
8 oz (225 g) bacon in 1 piece, diced
2 Spanish onions, finely chopped
Olive oil
Tomato concentrate
2 tablespoons (30 ml) melted butter
1 teaspoon (5 ml) sugar
Salt

Sauté diced bacon and finely chopped onions in olive oil until onions are transparent. Stir in desired amount of tomato concentrate diluted in boiling water. Add melted butter and sugar, and simmer for 15 minutes.

Cook spaghetti in salted boiling water until *al dente* – tender but still firm. Drain; add the sauce and serve. Serves 4.

FETTUCCINE WITH CREAM SAUCE AND MUSHROOMS

1 lb (450 g) fettuccine (egg noodles)
½ Spanish onion, finely chopped
Butter
4 oz (100 g) mushrooms, sliced
4 oz (100 g) ham, diced
¼ pint (150 ml) double cream
2 egg yolks
Freshly grated Parmesan
Salt and freshly ground black pepper

Sauté finely chopped onion in 2 tablespoons (30 ml) butter until transparent; add sliced mushrooms and diced ham, and continue to cook until mushrooms are tender, stirring from time to time. Combine double cream, egg yolks, 4 oz (100 g) butter, and freshly grated Parmesan, to taste, in the top of a double saucepan, and cook over water, stirring constantly with a wooden spoon, until sauce is thick and creamy. Do not let water under sauce come to a boil. Add salt and freshly ground black pepper.

Cook fettuccine in boiling salted water until *al dente* – tender but still firm; drain, mix with cream sauce, and toss. Garnish with ham, onion, mushrooms and freshly grated Parmesan. Serves 4.

FETTUCCINE ALLA BOLOGNESE

1 lb (450 g) fettuccine (egg noodles)
Salt
4 oz (100 g) freshly grated Parmesan

BOLOGNESE SAUCE
2 tablespoons (30 ml) butter
2 tablespoons (30 ml) olive oil
1 Spanish onion, finely chopped
8 oz (225 g) minced beef
Salt and freshly ground black pepper
¼ level teaspoon (1.25 ml) dried thyme or oregano
¼ pint (150 ml) dry white wine
2–4 tablespoons (30–60 ml) tomato concentrate

BOLOGNESE SAUCE
Heat butter and olive oil in a large frying pan, and sauté finely chopped onion until transparent. Add meat and cook, stirring constantly, until well browned. Season with salt, freshly ground black pepper, thyme or oregano, and wine in which you have dissolved tomato concentrate. Simmer over a low heat for 45 minutes, adding a little water from time to time when necessary.

Bring 6 to 8 pints (3.4 to 4.5 lit) well-salted water to a boil in a large saucepan. Add noodles and cook until tender but still firm. Drain the noodles and, while they are still very hot, pour Bolognese Sauce over them. Serve noodles with Parmesan cheese. Serves 4.

SPAGHETTI CON SALSA FREDDA

1 lb (450 g) spaghetti
Salt
8 tomatoes, peeled, seeded and diced
2 cloves garlic, finely chopped
16 fresh basil leaves, chopped
2 tablespoons (30 ml) chopped parsley
4–6 tablespoons (60–90 ml) warmed olive oil
Freshly ground black pepper
Freshly grated Parmesan

Cook spaghetti in boiling salted water until *al dente* – tender but still firm.

Mix together diced tomatoes, chopped garlic, basil and parsley. Moisten with olive oil; season generously with salt and freshly ground black pepper, and serve on drained hot spaghetti with freshly grated Parmesan cheese. Serves 4.

SPAGHETTI CON SALSICCE

1 lb (450 g) spaghetti
1 lb (450 g) Italian sausage, cut into small pieces
4 tablespoons (60 ml) olive oil
1 Spanish onion, finely chopped
2 cloves garlic, finely chopped
1 lb (450 g) ripe tomatoes
Salt and freshly ground black pepper
1–2 teaspoons (5–10 ml) brown sugar
½ teaspoon (2.5 ml) oregano, basil or marjoram
¼ pint (150 ml) dry white wine
4 tablespoons (60 ml) finely chopped parsley
Butter

Fry sausage in olive oil; add finely chopped onion and garlic, and continue cooking until vegetables begin to take on colour. Skin, seed and coarsely chop tomatoes. Add chopped tomatoes, salt, freshly ground black pepper and brown sugar, oregano, basil or marjoram, dry white wine and finely chopped parsley to onion mixture, and simmer gently for 15 to 20 minutes. Correct seasoning.

While sauce is simmering, cook spaghetti in rapidly boiling salted water until *al dente* – tender but still firm. Drain and place on a hot serving dish. Pour sauce over the spaghetti and serve with a generous knob of butter. Serves 4.

TRENETTE CON PESTO

1 lb (450 g) *trenette* (thin spaghetti)
Salt
Butter
Freshly grated cheese (Romano, Pecorino or
Parmesan)

PESTO SAUCE
2–3 cloves garlic, finely chopped
4–6 tablespoons (60–90 ml) finely chopped fresh basil
4–6 tablespoons (60–90 ml) finely chopped parsley
1 tablespoon (15 ml) pine nuts
6–8 tablespoons (90–120 ml) grated cheese (Romano,
Pecorino or Parmesan)
Olive oil
Freshly ground black pepper

Cook *trenette* in rapidly boiling salted water until just tender. Drain and place on a hot serving dish. Spoon Pesto Sauce over, and serve with a generous knob of butter and grated cheese. Serves 4.

PESTO SAUCE
Pound finely chopped garlic, basil, parsley, pine nuts and grated cheese in a mortar until smooth. Gradually add olive oil and whisk until sauce is smooth and thick. Season to taste with freshly ground black pepper.

FETTUCCINE ALLA CAPRICCIOSA

1 lb (450 g) fettuccine (egg noodles)
4 oz (100 g) veal, finely chopped
4 oz (100 g) butter
Salt and freshly ground black pepper
¼ pint (150 ml) red wine
½ pint (300 ml) well-flavoured Italian Tomato Sauce (page 125)
8 oz (225 g) peas
4 oz (100 g) fresh or dried mushrooms, sliced
1–2 slices Parma ham, cut in thin strips

Sauté finely chopped veal in half the butter until golden. Add salt, freshly ground black pepper and red wine, and simmer gently for 5 to 10 minutes. Add Tomato Sauce and continue cooking over a low heat for 30 minutes.

Cook peas in boiling salted water until tender; drain, and sauté with sliced mushrooms and ham in remaining butter until mushrooms are cooked through. Add to sauce.

Cook fettuccine in boiling salted water to *al dente* tenderness – tender but still firm. Pour sauce over them and serve immediately. Serves 4.

GREEN NOODLES ALLA CREMA

1 lb (450 g) green noodles
Salt
4 oz (100 g) butter
4 oz (100 g) freshly grated Parmesan
½ pint (300 ml) double cream

Bring 6 to 8 pints (3.4 to 4.5 lit) well-salted water to a boil in a large saucepan. Add green noodles and cook until *al dente* – tender but still firm.

While pasta is cooking, melt butter in a saucepan and stir in grated cheese and cream. Cook over a low heat, stirring constantly, until cheese melts and sauce is smooth.

Drain the noodles and, while they are still very hot, toss with the sauce. Serve noodles with additional Parmesan cheese. Serves 4.

TAGLIATELLE CON MORTADELLA

1 lb (450 g) tagliatelle (egg noodles)
Salt
4 tablespoons (60 ml) butter
4 oz (100 g) Mortadella, cut in thin strips
Freshly grated Parmesan

Boil noodles in salted water until they are cooked to *al dente* tenderness. Drain.

Melt butter in a thick-bottomed frying pan; sauté the Mortadella in it for 3 minutes. Toss the hot noodles with freshly grated Parmesan cheese, then with the Mortadella and butter sauce. Sprinkle with additional cheese and serve immediately. Serves 4.

BAKED TAGLIATELLE WITH MOZZARELLA AND TOMATO SAUCE

1 lb (450 g) tagliatelle (egg noodles)
4 tablespoons (60 ml) olive oil
1 Spanish onion, finely chopped
1 large can Italian peeled tomatoes
Salt
Freshly ground black pepper
Oregano
4 tablespoons (60 ml) butter
4 tablespoons (60 ml) freshly grated Parmesan
8 oz (225 g) Mozzarella cheese, diced

Heat olive oil in a saucepan and sauté finely chopped onion until transparent. Add Italian peeled tomatoes and season to taste with salt, freshly ground black pepper and oregano. Bring to a boil and cook over a medium heat for 15 minutes.

Cook tagliatelle in boiling salted water until *al dente* – tender but still firm. Drain.

Melt butter in a heatproof casserole. Add drained tagliatelle and toss well. Add half the Parmesan and Mozzarella, and toss again. Pour on the sauce; sprinkle with remaining cheeses and bake in a slow oven (350°F/180°C/GM4) until the Mozzarella begins to melt. Serves 4 to 6.

TAGLIATELLE CALEBRESE

1 lb (450 g) tagliatelle (egg noodles)
Salt
1 lb (450 g) Ricotta or cottage cheese
Freshly grated Parmesan
¼ pint (150 ml) hot water
2 tablespoons (30 ml) olive oil
4 tablespoons (60 ml) melted butter
Freshly ground black pepper

Cook tagliatelle in boiling salted water until *al dente* – tender but still firm.

Combine Ricotta or cottage cheese, 2 tablespoons (30 ml) grated Parmesan, hot water, olive oil and melted butter, and beat until smooth. Season to taste with salt and freshly ground black pepper. Heat in the top of double saucepan until warmed through.

Mix with tagliatelle; sprinkle with freshly grated Parmesan cheese and serve immediately. Serves 4.

ROMEO SALTA'S MACARONI WITH THREE CHEESES

1 lb (450 g) macaroni
Salt
2–4 tablespoons (30–60 ml) butter
6–8 tablespoons (90–120 ml) freshly grated Parmesan
4 tablespoons (60 ml) freshly grated Gruyère
4 tablespoons (60 ml) freshly grated Mozzarella cheese
Freshly ground black pepper
½ pint (300 ml) double cream

Cook macaroni in boiling salted water until just tender. Drain.

Toss drained macaroni in a casserole with butter, then toss with the three cheeses. Season to taste with salt and freshly ground black pepper; add the cream and toss again. Bake in a moderately hot oven (400°F/200°C/GM6) for 20 minutes, or until browned. Serves 4.

PASTA E FAGIOLI

8 oz (225 g) dried kidney or haricot beans
1 beef marrow bone, about 4 inches (10 cm) long
4 tablespoons (60 ml) tomato concentrate
4 pints (2.25 lit) cold water
1 Spanish onion
1 clove garlic
3 tablespoons (45 ml) olive oil
2 tablespoons (30 ml) freshly chopped parsley
1 teaspoon (5 ml) salt
Freshly ground black pepper and cayenne pepper
1 tablespoon (15 ml) dried oregano
8 oz (225 g) macaroni, broken in pieces
Freshly grated Parmesan

Soak dried beans overnight in cold water. Drain. Combine beans, marrow bone, tomato concentrate and water in a large saucepan. Bring to a boil; lower heat, cover, and simmer for 2 hours.

Chop onion and garlic finely, and sauté in olive oil until transparent. Add finely chopped parsley, salt, freshly ground black pepper and cayenne, to taste, and oregano, and simmer, covered, for about 20 minutes. Add macaroni and continue cooking until tender. Serve sprinkled with Parmesan cheese. Serves 4.

CANNELLONI RIPIENI

1 basic recipe Cannelloni (page 668)
Butter
Freshly grated Parmesan

FILLING
1 lb (450 g) button mushrooms, chopped
8 oz (225 g) cooked ham or veal, diced
½ Spanish onion, chopped
Butter
2 tablespoons (30 ml) olive oil
Freshly grated Parmesan
Salt and freshly ground black pepper

CHEESE SAUCE
2 tablespoons (30 ml) butter
2 tablespoons (30 ml) flour
1 pint (600 ml) hot milk
4 tablespoons (60 ml) grated Parmesan
Salt and freshly ground black pepper

Prepare one recipe of Cannelloni.

FILLING
Sauté chopped mushrooms, diced ham or veal, and onion in 2 tablespoons (30 ml) each butter and olive oil until vegetables are cooked through. Cool; add 2 tablespoons (30 ml) freshly grated Parmesan and season to taste with salt and freshly ground black pepper.

Place 2 tablespoons (30 ml) mushroom filling on each pasta square and roll it carefully around filling. Arranged filled cannelloni in a buttered shallow baking dish; cover with Cheese Sauce; sprinkle generously with grated Parmesan and bake in a slow oven (350°F/180°C./GM4) for about 30 minutes, or until golden brown. Serves 4.

CHEESE SAUCE
Melt butter in the top of a double saucepan; stir in flour to make a smooth *roux*; add hot milk gradually, stirring continuously; season to taste with grated Parmesan, salt and freshly ground black pepper. Cook, stirring from time to time, until sauce is smooth and thick.

LASAGNE VERDI AL FORNO

1 lb (450 g) green lasagne noodles
Salt
Butter
8 oz (225 g) Mozzarella cheese, diced
2 oz (50 g) freshly grated Parmesan
8 oz (225 g) Ricotta cheese, crumbled

MEAT BALLS
1 lb (450 g) lean beef, minced
4 eggs
½ loaf stale white bread
1 clove garlic, finely chopped
2 tablespoons (30 ml) finely chopped parsley
Salt and freshly ground black pepper

TOMATO SAUCE
1 Spanish onion, chopped
3 stalks celery, chopped
6 tablespoons (90 ml) olive oil
3 tablespoons (45 ml) tomato concentrate
3 lb (1.4 kg) tomatoes, peeled, seeded and chopped
1 teaspoon (5 ml) sugar
2 cloves garlic, chopped
Finely chopped parsley
Salt and freshly ground black pepper
2 tablespoons (30 ml) butter

MEAT BALLS
Combine beef and eggs in a large bowl, and mix well. Soak bread
in water until soft; squeeze dry and shred. Combine with meat
mixture, add garlic and parsley, and season to taste with salt and
freshly ground black pepper. Form into marble-sized balls.

TOMATO SAUCE
Sauté onion and celery in oil in a large frying pan until soft.
Transfer to a large pan and sauté meat balls in remaining fat until
golden.

Add tomato concentrate to remaining oil in pan and stir until
smooth. Then stir in chopped tomatoes and sugar, and cook for 5
minutes, stirring constantly. Press mixture through a fine sieve

into a large saucepan; add chopped garlic and parsley, and simmer mixture for 1 hour. Season with salt and freshly ground black pepper, and add butter; add meat balls and continue to simmer ½ hour longer, adding a little water if sauce becomes too thick.

Cook the green lasagne, 6 to 8 at a time, in boiling salted water until they are half done; drain carefully. Line a well-buttered baking dish with a layer of lasagne; remove half the meat balls from the Tomato Sauce with a perforated spoon, and spoon over lasagne; add a layer of diced Mozzarella cheese; sprinkle generously with grated Parmesan and crumbled Ricotta cheese, and moisten with well-seasoned Tomato Sauce. Repeat, using the same quantities, finishing with Tomato Sauce. Dot with butter and bake in a moderate oven (375°F/190°C/GM5) for about 30 minutes. Serves 4.

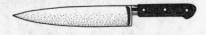

HOME-MADE RAVIOLI

Make ravioli dough as in basic recipe for pasta (page 667); divide dough in half; roll out ⅛ inch (4 mm) thick. Cut dough into strips 2 inches (5 cm) wide, and place a teaspoon (5 ml) of filling (see below and overleaf) at 2-inch (5 cm) intervals. Cover with another strip of dough. Then, with your finger press dough down around the filling. Cut dough into 2-inch (5 cm) squares and seal edges carefully with water. Set aside for 2 hours, and then cook as for any pasta.

MEAT FILLING FOR RAVIOLI

8 oz (225 g) cooked beef, minced
4 oz (100 g) cooked veal, minced
2 tablespoons (30 ml) butter
1 tablespoon (15 ml) olive oil
2 tablespoons (30 ml) grated Parmesan
2 tablespoons (30 ml) dry breadcrumbs
1 tablespoon (15 ml) finely chopped parsley
Nutmeg or cinnamon
Salt and freshly ground black pepper

Sauté minced beef and veal in butter and olive oil for 5 minutes. Cool; stir in grated Parmesan, breadcrumbs and parsley. Flavour to taste with nutmeg or cinnamon, salt and freshly ground black pepper.

SPINACH AND CHICKEN FILLING FOR RAVIOLI

6 tablespoons (90 ml) cooked chopped spinach,
pressed dry
8 oz (225 g) chicken, minced
2 tablespoons (30 ml) each butter, freshly grated
Parmesan and dry breadcrumbs
Nutmeg or cinnamon
Salt and freshly ground black pepper

Sauté chopped spinach and minced chicken in butter for 5 minutes. Cool; stir in grated Parmesan and breadcrumbs. Flavour to taste with nutmeg or cinnamon, salt and freshly ground black pepper.

GNOCCHI VERDI

2 lb (900 g) spinach
Butter
Salt and freshly ground black pepper
8 oz (225 g) Ricotta or cottage cheese
3 egg yolks
8 tablespoons (120 ml) freshly grated Parmesan
Sifted flour
Nutmeg

Wash spinach leaves in several changes of water, removing yellowed or damaged leaves. Drain thoroughly. Put leaves in a thick-bottomed saucepan with 4 tablespoons (60 ml) butter and season to taste with salt and freshly ground black pepper. Simmer gently, stirring constantly, until spinach is soft and tender. Purée cooked spinach and press dry.

Press liquid from Ricotta or cottage cheese in a sieve until it is very dry. Beat egg yolks in a large mixing bowl. Add drained cheese, spinach purée, 4 tablespoons (60 ml) grated Parmesan, 4 tablespoons (60 ml) melted butter, 2 tablespoons (30 ml) flour, and salt, freshly ground black pepper and nutmeg, to taste. Knead on a floured board until smooth. Let stand for 30 minutes, then roll into long sausages. Cut into ½-inch (12 mm) slices (gnocchi) and roll in flour.

Fill a large heatproof casserole with salted water. Bring to a boil; reduce heat to low and then add gnocchi carefully, one by one. Cook over a low heat until gnocchi rise to the surface. Drain well. Pour 4 tablespoons (60 ml) melted butter over them and sprinkle with remaining grated Parmesan. Serves 4.

GNOCCHI ALLA ROMANA

8 oz (225 g) Ricotta or cottage cheese
Butter
8 tablespoons (120 ml) grated Parmesan
3 egg yolks
4 tablespoons (60 ml) sifted flour
Salt and freshly ground black pepper and nutmeg

Sieve Ricotta or cottage cheese into a mixing bowl. Beat together 4 tablespoons (60 ml) each melted butter and grated Parmesan, and 3 egg yolks, and stir into cheese alternately with flour. Season to taste with salt, and freshly ground black pepper and nutmeg.

Spoon the mixture into a pastry bag fitted with a large plain nozzle. Holding pastry bag over a large saucepan full of boiling salted water, force mixture through nozzle, cutting it in 1-inch (25 mm) pieces (gnocchi) with scissors. Cook gnocchi for 6 or 7 minutes; remove with perforated spoon and drain on a clean cloth.

When ready to serve, arrange gnocchi in overlapping rows in a well-buttered shallow casserole or *gratin* dish. Pour 6 to 8 table-spoons (90–120 ml) melted butter over them and sprinkle with remaining Parmesan cheese. Bake in a slow oven (350°F/180°C/ GM4) for 10 minutes, and then brown under grill until golden. Serves 4.

POLENTA

1 lb (450 g) yellow cornmeal
2–2½ pints (1.1–1.4 lit) salted water
4 tablespoons (60 ml) butter
6–8 tablespoons (90–120 ml) freshly grated Parmesan

Bring water to a boil. Pour the cornmeal in slowly, stirring constantly with a wooden spoon. Continue cooking for 20 to 30 minutes, stirring frequently, until the *polenta* is thick and soft and leaves sides of pan easily; add a little more water if necessary. Stir in butter and freshly grated Parmesan cheese. Serves 4 to 6.

POLENTA GNOCCHI

1 recipe Polenta (above)
Butter
Italian Tomato Sauce (page 125)
Freshly grated Parmesan

Make *polenta* as above. Pour mixture on to a well-buttered baking sheet and spread out to ½-inch (12 mm) thickness. Allow it to cool and cut into small rounds with a biscuit cutter. Arrange gnocchi (*polenta* rounds) in overlapping rows in a well-buttered shallow baking dish and cover with Tomato Sauce. Dot with butter and sprinkle with freshly grated Parmesan. Brown in a hot oven (450°F/230°C/GM8) for 15 minutes. Serves 4 to 6.

POLENTA WITH CHICKEN LIVERS

1 recipe Polenta (above)
3 tablespoons (45 ml) butter
3 tablespoons (45 ml) olive oil
8 chicken livers, diced
1 slice bacon, about ¼ inch (6 mm) thick, diced
½ Spanish onion, finely chopped
½ pint (300 ml) chicken stock
¼ teaspoon (1.25 ml) dried sage
Salt and freshly ground black pepper

Heat butter and olive oil in a saucepan; add chicken livers, diced bacon and finely chopped onion; sauté, stirring constantly, until brown. Add chicken stock and dried sage, and season to taste with salt and freshly ground black pepper; simmer gently until tender – about 15 minutes. Keep warm.

Make *polenta* as above. Then pour *polenta* into a large heated serving dish and pour chicken livers over it. Serve immediately. Serves 4 to 6.

POLENTA PASTICCIATA

1 recipe Polenta (above)
Butter
4 tablespoons (60 ml) breadcrumbs
2 tablespoons (30 ml) freshly grated Parmesan
5 oz (150 g) freshly grated Mozzarella cheese
Italian Tomato Sauce (page 125)

Cook *polenta* as above. Butter a shallow baking dish, and sprinkle generously with breadcrumbs and freshly grated Parmesan. Spread a quarter of the *polenta* over it; cover with a quarter of the grated Mozzarella, and dot with 1 tablespoon (15 ml) butter. Repeat the layers until all the ingredients are used up. Bake in a moderate oven (375°F/190°C/GM5) for 15 to 20 minutes, or until well browned. Serve with well-seasoned Tomato Sauce. Serves 4 to 6.

CHAPTER NINETEEN

Salads

Many is the friend who comes to me with an 'absolutely delicious' new dressing for salad . . . 'Just take some brown sugar, some Worcestershire sauce, a little ketchup, olive oil, a dash of lemon . . . throw in a chopped clove of garlic or two, and let it sit for three days in a screw-top jar before you use it . . . and then you just add anything as you go along.' Like Grandma's stockpot, I suppose. The recipe is usually labelled Jamaican, Barbadian, or, heaven forbid, Italian.

This keeping of salad dressing ready for use in a jar is something I never could understand. So much better to mix your olive oil freshly with wine vinegar or with a hint of lemon juice. Mill your pepper into it to the exact proportion; add a pinch or two of coarse salt, and then improvise as you will: fresh herbs – chives, parsley, tarragon, basil – garlic, capers, olives, chopped hard-boiled egg. The choice is limitless and the results are always refreshingly different and delicious.

To me, salad is one of the highlights of the meal – whether I serve it Mediterranean and Californian fashion as the first course for a summer meal, or as a separate course, a crisp, green freshener on its own, perfect after a casserole or entrée, to be followed by cheese and fruit or a sweet.

To the purist, the very word salad evokes a vision of green lettuce leaves, carefully washed, dried leaf by leaf, liberally bathed with fruity olive oil, and flavoured with a touch of wine vinegar, a hint of garlic and a dusting of salt and freshly ground black pepper. Not for him the colourful concoctions of fruits, nuts and cream cheese so popular on the American side of the Atlantic. Nor does it mean lettuce, tomatoes, cucumbers and cress, doused with bottled salad cream, as it seems to far too often in England. A salad dressing worthy of the name does not come out of a jar or bottle but is mixed by the host or hostess just before serving.

Oscar Wilde once compared the making of a salad with brilliant diplomacy. 'The problem', he said, 'is entirely the same in both cases – to know exactly how much oil one must put in with one's vinegar.' And the quality of one's oil and vinegar are of the utmost importance as well. I like a fruity olive taste in my olive oil and prefer the oils from Provence or Tunisia for salads. If, for some reason, I use oil which is not fruity enough, I soak fat ripe olives in it for a day or two to give it body. Try this and you will be amazed at the results.

I usually prefer to mix salad dressing directly in the salad bowl – a wooden one, of course, and washed as seldom as possible – blending the olive oil and vinegar with pepper, salt, garlic and herbs, before I add the lettuce and salad greens. Then all I have to do at table is to give a final toss to the ingredients to ensure that every leaf is glistening with the dressing. A final check for flavour and the salad is ready to serve.

Cos lettuce, endive, chicory, young and tender spinach leaves, watercress and French *mâche* (corn salad) all make wonderful additives to a green salad. For a little variation in texture, add sliced or chopped celery, green pepper or fennel; or flavour with finely chopped shallots and chives, especially good with diced or finely sliced avocado pear. Epicures like to eat the avocado pear *au naturel* with just a touch of simple French dressing to fill the cavity. Try scoring the meat of the avocado into cubes with a knife before adding the dressing; this allows all the flavour of your dressing to permeate the avocado rather than remaining just on top. The cut squares look attractive too. In Britain, where we often get our avocados unripe, I like to dice the delicate buttery meat of the fruit; remove it entirely from the shell, and marinate it in French dressing with a hint of finely chopped chives. Then just before serving, refill the crisp green shells with the diced cubes which have been 'tenderized' and flavoured by the French dressing marinade.

Fennel on its own makes a delicious salad when dressed with olive oil and lemon juice and flavoured with a little coarse salt. The Italians use it in this way as an *hors-d'œuvre* and, combined with cucumber and radishes, as a salad.

To salad lovers with more catholic tastes, a salad can be made from almost any vegetable, meat, eggs, fruit or fish. Such salads make wonderful cold beginnings to summer meals . . . from the glorious plate of mixed salads and *charcuterie* which makes up the Italian *antipasto*, to the selection of *hors-d'œuvre* salad recipes you will find in Chapter 3. Try tomatoes *guacamole*, a Mexican variation on the familiar stuffed tomato theme (a highly spiced *guacamole* filling of creamy avocado pear is spiked with onion, lemon juice and Mexican chili powder); or, again in the Mexican line, Mexican crab salad (crabmeat, celery and pimento, dressed with well-flavoured mayonnaise and served in lettuce cups garnished with quartered tomatoes, hard-boiled eggs and ripe olives).

I like salads, too, as a complete meal in themselves . . . the perfect answer for summer luncheons in the country when served with hot garlic bread and followed by a mammoth tray of cheeses and a cooling sweet. Spanish seafood salad is a delicious example (coral chunks of lobster, pink prawns, and sole simmered in a *court-bouillon*, set in a bed of lettuce with cubes of cooked potato and jewel-bright peas); or Italian vegetable salad (garnished with tomatoes, sliced cucumber, green peppers and mushrooms, with a tangy anchovy dressing). Such salads are a boon to the hostess, for much of the preliminary preparation of fish, vegetables or meat can be done the day before. Of course, tired lettuce or an indiscriminate sprinkling of left-over meat and vegetables is guaranteed to take the heart out of any salad. So make your salads with the best and freshest ingredients only . . . *and* with a watchful eye for colour, taste and texture contrast.

Green Salads

TOSSED GREEN SALAD

1–2 heads lettuce
French Dressing (below)

Wash lettuce leaves well in a large quantity of water. They should be left whole, never cut. Drain well and dry thoroughly in a cloth or a salad basket so that there is no water on them to dilute the dressing.

To serve: pour French Dressing into salad bowl; arrange prepared lettuce leaves on top. Then at the table, give a final toss to the ingredients to ensure that every leaf is glistening with dressing. Check seasoning and serve. Serves 4 to 6.

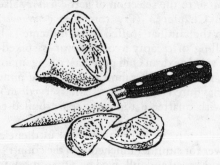

GREEN SALAD VARIATIONS
1. Add other salad greens in season – Cos lettuce, endive, chicory, batavia, young spinach leaves, watercress and French *mâche* (corn salad).
2. Add finely chopped garlic or shallots, or a combination of the two, to salad dressing.
3. Add fresh green herbs – finely chopped chervil, basil, tarragon, chives or *eau-de-Cologne* mint – to the dressing.
4. For crunch appeal, add diced celery, green pepper or fennel.

FRENCH DRESSING – VINAIGRETTE SAUCE

1 tablespoon (15 ml) lemon juice
1–2 tablespoons (15–30 ml) wine vinegar
¼ teaspoon (1.25 ml) dry mustard
Coarse salt and freshly ground black pepper
6–8 tablespoons (90–120 ml) olive oil

Mix together lemon juice, wine vinegar and dry mustard, and season to taste with coarse salt and freshly ground black pepper. Add olive oil, and beat with a fork until the mixture emulsifies.

SPECIAL VINAIGRETTE SAUCE

French Dressing
Finely chopped parsley
Finely chopped onion or chives
1 or more of the following: finely chopped green
olives, capers and gherkins
1 hard-boiled egg yolk, sieved

Make French Dressing as directed. Add a little finely chopped parsley and onion or chives, finely chopped green olives, capers or gherkins, and the sieved yolk of a hard-boiled egg.

CHILLED WATERCRESS SALAD

4 bunches watercress
2 oranges

CURRY DRESSING
6–8 tablespoons (90–120 ml) olive oil
2 tablespoons (30 ml) wine vinegar
1 tablespoon (15 ml) lemon juice
1 level tablespoon (15 ml) curry powder
Salt and freshly ground black pepper
1 teaspoon (5 ml) finely chopped shallots

Prepare watercress and chill in a damp towel. Peel oranges, cut into thin segments, and chill.

CURRY DRESSING

Combine olive oil, wine vinegar, lemon juice and curry powder. Season to taste with salt and freshly ground black pepper; and chill.

Just before serving, place watercress in a salad bowl; arrange orange segments on top; add finely chopped shallots to Curry Dressing and pour over salad.

Toss at table so that each leaf is glistening. Serves 4 to 6.

WATERCRESS AND SOY SALAD

2 bunches watercress
1 bunch radishes
4–6 stalks celery

SOY DRESSING
6–8 tablespoons (90–120 ml) olive oil
1 teaspoon (5 ml) sugar
1 tablespoon (15 ml) lemon juice
1 teaspoon (5 ml) soy sauce
Freshly ground black pepper and
monosodium glutamate

Prepare watercress and chill in a damp towel. Trim and slice radishes; slice celery.

SOY DRESSING

Combine olive oil, sugar, lemon juice and soy sauce, and season to taste with freshly ground black pepper and monosodium glutamate.

Just before serving, place watercress in a salad bowl; arrange sliced radishes and celery in centre. Add dressing and toss until every ingredient glistens. Serves 4 to 6.

WATERCRESS AND TOMATO SALAD

2 bunches watercress
4–6 ripe tomatoes, peeled, seeded and diced
½ cucumber, peeled, seeded and diced
4 stalks celery, sliced
Salt and freshly ground black pepper
French Dressing
1 clove garlic, finely chopped (optional)

Wash and pick over the watercress, drain well and wrap in a towel. Chill. When ready to serve, turn out into a large salad bowl. Arrange prepared tomatoes, cucumber and celery in centre; season to taste with salt and freshly ground black pepper, and toss with French Dressing, flavoured with a finely chopped clove of garlic if desired. Serves 4 to 6.

LETTUCE HEARTS 'LA NAPOULE'

2 small heads lettuce

'LA NAPOULE' DRESSING
6–8 tablespoons (90–120 ml) olive oil
2–3 tablespoons (30–45 ml) wine vinegar
½ level teaspoon (2.5 ml) paprika
¼ pint (150 ml) double cream
Salt and freshly ground black pepper

GARNISH
2 hard-boiled eggs
2 tablespoons (30 ml) finely chopped parsley

Wash and trim lettuce and cut hearts into quarters. Drain well; wrap in a clean towel and pat dry. Gather up the edges and corners of the towel, and shake out any remaining moisture; chill in the refrigerator until crisp.

'LA NAPOULE' DRESSING
Combine olive oil, wine vinegar, paprika and double cream; season to taste with salt and freshly ground black pepper; and whisk until creamy and thick.

GARNISH

Separate yolks from whites of hard-boiled eggs and rub yolks and whites separately through a wire sieve; chop parsley.

To serve: place 2 quarters of lettuce on each salad plate. Mask each quarter of lettuce with dressing and garnish a third of each portion with sieved egg white, a third with sieved egg yolk, and the remaining third with finely chopped parsley. Serves 4.

Luncheon or Appetizer Salads

SALADE DE TOMATES À LA CRÈME

12 ripe tomatoes
1 Spanish onion, finely chopped
6 tablespoons (90 ml) olive oil
2 tablespoons (30 ml) wine vinegar
Salt and freshly ground black pepper
6 tablespoons (90 ml) mayonnaise
4 tablespoons (60 ml) double cream
2 tablespoons (30 ml) chopped parsley

Cut the tomatoes in slices and place on a dish; sprinkle with finely chopped onion and moisten with a simple dressing, made with olive oil and wine vinegar seasoned with salt and freshly ground black pepper. Mix mayonnaise and cream, and cover tomatoes and onions. Sprinkle with parsley. Serves 4 to 6.

RUSSIAN TOMATO SALAD

4–8 ripe tomatoes
¼ pint (150 ml) double cream, whipped
4 tablespoons (60 ml) well-flavoured mayonnaise
1 tablespoon (15 ml) freshly grated horseradish
¼ teaspoon (1.25 ml) paprika
Salt and freshly ground black pepper
Lettuce leaves
2 tablespoons (30 ml) finely chopped parsley or chives

Peel tomatoes and chill until ready to serve. Combine whipped cream with mayonnaise, grated horseradish and paprika, and season to taste with salt and freshly ground black pepper. Chill.

When ready to serve, place tomatoes on lettuce leaves on individual salad plates and top with dressing. Garnish with finely chopped parsley or chives. Serves 4.

CHOUCROUTE FROIDE

1 Spanish onion, finely chopped
8 tablespoons (120 ml) olive oil
1 lb (450 g) sauerkraut
½ pint (300 ml) chicken stock
Salt and coarsely ground black pepper
1 clove garlic, finely chopped
2 tablespoons (30 ml) wine vinegar
2 hard-boiled eggs, quartered
1 beetroot, cooked and sliced

Sauté finely chopped onion in 2 tablespoons (30 ml) olive oil until golden but not brown. Place sauerkraut and onion in a heavy saucepan, and pour chicken stock over them. Simmer for ¾ hour.

Cool sauerkraut; season to taste with salt and coarsely ground black pepper, and mix with finely chopped garlic, remaining olive oil and the vinegar. Serve garnished with quartered hard-boiled eggs and thin slices of cooked beetroot. Serves 4 to 6.

DANISH CUCUMBER SALAD

2 cucumbers
1 tablespoon (15 ml) salt
Water and wine vinegar
2 tablespoons (30 ml) sugar
White pepper
2 tablespoons (30 ml) finely chopped parsley

Peel and slice cucumbers very finely. Sprinkle with salt and place under a weight in a glass bowl for at least 1 hour. Wash well; drain and dry thoroughly with a clean tea towel.

Combine water and wine vinegar, to taste; add sugar and white pepper and pour over cucumber slices. Leave salad in the refrigerator for 1 hour.

Just before serving, sprinkle with finely chopped parsley. Serve with grilled or fried meat, fish or chicken. Serves 6.

APPETIZER SALAD MARLY

8 oz (225 g) green asparagus tips, cooked
4 oz (100 g) button mushrooms
4–6 tomatoes

SAUCE MARLY
1 level tablespoon (15 ml) Dijon mustard
6 fluid oz (175 ml) thick cream
Juice of ½ lemon
Salt and freshly ground black pepper
A few drops of vinegar

Arrange cooked and drained asparagus tips on a long dish. Slice raw mushrooms thinly on top. Cut tomatoes into wedges and arrange around dish. Pour Sauce Marly over centre of dish. Serves 4.

SAUCE MARLY
Combine mustard, cream and lemon juice, and season to taste with salt, freshly ground black pepper and vinegar.

FRENCH VEGETABLE SALAD

6 large carrots
3 young turnips
3 large new potatoes
Salt
8 oz (225 g) string beans
½ cauliflower
6 tablespoons (90 ml) cooked peas
Well-flavoured French Dressing (page 691)
2 tablespoons (30 ml) finely chopped parsley

Scoop balls from raw carrots, turnips and potatoes with a potato scoop (or cut into cubes), and cook them in boiling salted water until tender but still firm – about 5 or 6 minutes. Drain and cool.

Cut string beans into 1-inch (25 mm) lengths and cook as above until tender but still firm. Drain and cool.

Break cauliflower into florets and cook as above until tender but still firm. Drain and cool.

Combine cooked vegetables and toss with a well-flavoured French Dressing. Sprinkle with finely chopped parsley. Serves 4 to 6.

CHEESE SALAD

8 oz (225 g) Gruyère, diced
1 small green pepper, finely chopped
12 black olives, sliced
4 tablespoons (60 ml) double cream
Salt and freshly ground black pepper
2 bunches watercress
Olive oil
Lemon juice or wine vinegar

Combine diced Gruyère, finely chopped pepper, sliced olives and cream. Season to taste with salt and freshly ground black pepper. Toss well and allow to marinate for at least 1 hour.

To serve: toss prepared watercress in a dressing of 3 parts olive oil to 1 part lemon juice or wine vinegar. Place cheese salad mixture in centre. Serve immediately. Serves 4.

COLD LAMB SALAD

Cold roast lamb
¼ Spanish onion, finely chopped
2 stalks celery, sliced
Olive oil
Tarragon vinegar
Salt and freshly ground black pepper
1 teaspoon (5 ml) finely chopped fresh tarragon
Finely chopped parsley

Slice lamb thinly and then cut into thin strips. Combine in a salad bowl with finely chopped onion and sliced celery. Pour over it a well-flavoured dressing made with olive oil and tarragon vinegar, and seasoned to taste with salt and freshly ground black pepper.

Just before serving, sprinkle with finely chopped tarragon and parsley. Serves 4.

CELERIAC SALAD WITH MUSTARD DRESSING

2 celery roots (celeriac)
Salt

MUSTARD DRESSING
6–8 tablespoons (90–120 ml) double cream
2 tablespoons (30 ml) olive oil
2–3 tablespoons (30–45 ml) lemon juice
1 tablespoon (15 ml) finely chopped onion
Dry mustard
Salt and freshly ground black pepper

Cook celeriac in boiling salted water until tender. Cook; peel and cut into thin strips.

MUSTARD DRESSING
Combine cream, olive oil, lemon juice and finely chopped onion, and dry mustard, salt and freshly ground black pepper, to taste. Blend well.

Marinate celeriac in this mixture overnight in the refrigerator. Serves 4 to 6.

HAM AND CHICKEN SALAD

8 oz (225 g) ham, sliced or diced
8 oz (225 g) chicken, diced
2 bananas, sliced
1 orange, separated into segments
1 avocado pear, peeled and sliced
¼ pint (150 ml) double cream
¼ pint (150 ml) mayonnaise (page 120)
1 tablespoon (15 ml) ketchup
1 teaspoon (5 ml) Worcestershire sauce
2 tablespoons (30 ml) lemon juice
2 tablespoons (30 ml) brandy
Salt and freshly ground black pepper
Lettuce leaves

Combine prepared ham and chicken with sliced bananas and orange and avocado segments in a mixing bowl. Whip the cream; blend in mayonnaise; add ketchup, Worcestershire sauce, lemon juice and brandy, and pour over meat and fruit mixture. Season to taste with salt and freshly ground black pepper, and mix carefully. Serve on lettuce leaves. Serves 4.

MAYONNAISE OF CHICKEN

4 tablespoons (60 ml) stiff mayonnaise
Lemon juice
Salt, celery salt and freshly ground black pepper
1 head lettuce, finely shredded
3 hard-boiled eggs, finely chopped
12 oz (350 g) cooked chicken, diced
4 stalks celery, diced
4 oz (100 g) tuna fish, diced

Thin mayonnaise with lemon juice and season to taste with salt, celery salt and freshly ground black pepper. Combine mayonnaise with shredded lettuce, finely chopped hard-boiled eggs and diced chicken, celery and tuna fish. Mix well. Add more mayonnaise and seasoning if desired. Serves 4.

RAW SPINACH SALAD

1 lb (450 g) raw spinach leaves
6–8 tablespoons (90–120 ml) olive oil
2–3 tablespoons (30–45 ml) wine vinegar
1 clove garlic, finely chopped
1 tablespoon (15 ml) finely chopped parsley
Salt and freshly ground black pepper
Dry mustard
2 hard-boiled eggs, cut in quarters
1 ripe avocado, peeled and sliced
1 small onion, thinly sliced

Wash spinach several times in cold water (spinach should be young and tender). Cut off stems; drain and chill until ready to use.

Make a dressing with olive oil, wine vinegar and finely chopped garlic and parsley, and salt, freshly ground black pepper and dry mustard, to taste.

Arrange spinach leaves in a salad bowl. Pour dressing over them; toss salad well and garnish with quartered hard-boiled eggs, sliced avocado and onion rings. Serves 4 to 6.

ITALIAN CAULIFLOWER SALAD

1 cauliflower
Salt

ITALIAN DRESSING
4 anchovy fillets, finely chopped
¼ pint (150 ml) olive oil
Juice of 1 lemon
Salt and freshly ground black pepper

Remove green leaves from cauliflower; trim stem and cut out any bruised spots. Break or cut into florets and poach in lightly salted water for about 5 minutes. Drain and place in a bowl of cold salted water until ready to use. Drain well.

When ready to serve, mix florets thoroughly with Italian Dressing. Serves 4 to 6.

ITALIAN DRESSING

Mix finely chopped anchovies with olive oil and lemon juice, and season to taste with salt and freshly ground black pepper.

ITALIAN PEPPER SALAD

2 lb (900 g) large, firm peppers (green, red and yellow)
¼ pint (150 ml) olive oil
2 cloves garlic, finely chopped
Lemon juice
Salt and freshly ground black pepper

Place peppers under the grill as close to the heat as possible, turning them from time to time until the skin is charred on all sides. Then rub the charred skins off under running water. Remove stems and seeds. Cut lengthwise into 1-inch (25 mm) strips. Rinse well and drain.

Place peppers in a salad bowl with olive oil and finely chopped garlic; add lemon juice, salt and freshly ground black pepper, to taste. Chill for at least 1 hour before serving. Serves 6.

POTATO SALAD WITH BACON

2–3 lb (900 g–1.4 kg) new potatoes
Salt
1 tablespoon (15 ml) sugar
2 tablespoons (30 ml) wine vinegar
4–6 thin slices bacon
Olive oil
Lemon juice
2 tablespoons (30 ml) finely chopped onion
2 tablespoons (30 ml) finely chopped parsley
Salt and cayenne pepper

Scrub new potatoes; cook in boiling salted water until just tender – 15 to 20 minutes; drain, peel and slice. Place potatoes in a bowl and sprinkle with sugar and wine vinegar. Toss gently.

Sauté bacon in a little oil until crisp. Drain well, pouring bacon fat over potatoes. Crumble or chop bacon finely and add to potatoes. Toss gently.

Combine 4 to 6 tablespoons (60–90 ml) olive oil with lemon juice and finely chopped onion and parsley, and season to taste with salt and cayenne pepper. Pour over salad. Serves 4 to 6.

Seafood Salads

BOUILLABAISSE SALAD 'FOUR SEASONS'

2 lobsters (about 2 lb (900 g) each)
2 dozen mussels
16 prawns
1 lb (450 g) crabmeat
3 oz (75 g) chopped celery
1 head lettuce
Very thinly sliced tomatoes
1 hard-boiled egg, finely chopped

DRESSING
8 fluid oz (225 ml) olive oil
8 tablespoons (120 ml) wine vinegar
4 tablespoons (60 ml) fish stock (reduced liquid in which
shellfish were cooked, or canned clam juice)
½ Spanish onion, finely chopped
2 tablespoons (30 ml) dry white wine
1 tablespoon (15 ml) finely chopped chives
Salt and freshly ground white pepper

All shellfish must be cooked and cooled. Using shallow salad bowl, arrange celery, lobster and crabmeat in centre of bed of lettuce. Place mussels, prawns and sliced tomatoes alternately around edge of bowl. Mix oil, vinegar, fish stock, onion, dry white wine and finely chopped chives; season to taste with salt and freshly ground white pepper, and pour over salad. Garnish with chopped hard-boiled egg and serve. Serves 4 to 6.

ANCHOVY SALAD

8–12 oz (225–350 g) salted anchovies
1 medium-sized onion, finely chopped
2 tablespoons (30 ml) finely chopped parsley
4 thin slices lemon
4 tablespoons (60 ml) olive oil
4 tablespoons (60 ml) red wine
Freshly ground black pepper

Wash anchovies in water until liquid is clear; dry them with a clean cloth and remove heads, tails and fins.

Strip anchovy fillets from bones and place in a bowl. Add finely chopped onion, parsley and lemon slices. Combine olive oil and red wine, and pour over the fillets. Season to taste with freshly ground black pepper and marinate anchovies for at least 2 hours before serving. Serves 4 to 6.

SWEDISH BUFFET SALAD

2 lb (900 g) cold poached halibut
4 tart eating apples
2 tablespoons (30 ml) butter
2 tablespoons (30 ml) cider
¼ pint (150 ml) sour cream
2 tablespoons (30 ml) grated horseradish
1 tablespoon (15 ml) prepared mustard
2 tablespoons (30 ml) lemon juice
Salt and freshly ground black pepper
2 hard-boiled eggs, finely chopped
Sprigs of fresh watercress

Carefully flake poached halibut. Peel, core and slice apples thinly. Combine butter and cider in a frying pan and sauté apple slices until soft, stirring constantly. Force apples and pan juices through a fine sieve and add sour cream, grated horseradish, prepared mustard and lemon juice.

Beat mixture until light and foamy, adding a little more cider if necessary, and toss flaked fish gently in this dressing. Season to taste with salt and freshly ground black pepper, and arrange salad in a glass serving bowl.

Decorate with finely chopped hard-boiled egg and sprigs of fresh watercress. Serves 6.

PROVENÇAL FISH SALAD

½ pint (300 ml) well-flavoured mayonnaise
(page 120)
1 clove garlic, finely chopped
1–2 anchovy fillets, finely chopped
1 tablespoon (15 ml) finely chopped basil or tarragon
2 tablespoons (30 ml) finely chopped parsley
1 tablespoon (15 ml) finely chopped capers
Lemon juice, to taste
1½ lb (675 g) cold poached fish, diced
6 large ripe tomatoes
Finely chopped parsley (for garnish)

Combine first 7 ingredients; toss diced cold poached fish lightly in sauce until well coated; pile fish mixture into tomato cases and garnish with finely chopped parsley. Serves 6.

To prepare tomato cases: plunge tomatoes into boiling water one by one, and remove their skins. Slice cap off each and carefully scoop out all pulp and seeds. Cover loosely with oil and chill in refrigerator until ready to use.

SEAFOOD SALAD

1 head lettuce, washed and chilled
1 head Cos lettuce, washed and chilled
8 oz (225 g) cooked prawns
8 oz (225 g) cooked lobster meat
8 oz (225 g) cooked white fish
8 oz (225 g) cooked crabmeat
4 ripe tomatoes
8 large ripe olives
Well-flavoured French Dressing (page 691)

Line salad bowl with lettuce and Cos leaves. Arrange prawns, lobster, white fish and crabmeat, cut in cubes, on bed of salad greens. Garnish with wedges of ripe tomato, and ripe olives. Serve with a well-flavoured French Dressing. Serves 4.

Fruit Salads

Strawberries, raspberries, white, red or black currants, grapes, oranges, bananas, apples, pears, apricots and peaches can all be used to make fruit salads of distinction. In winter, when fresh fruit is scarce, canned and dried fruits provide a very welcome addition.

Fresh fruit must be dry and perfectly ripe – hard, unripe pieces will spoil any salad. Peel oranges, taking every particle of white pith from them, and cut them into thin slices, or divide into sections, with pips removed. Peel plums, remove stones, and cut in halves or quarters. Use small grapes whole, but peel and halve the larger ones. Top and tail currants and berries carefully and wash if necessary. Always cut fruit with a silver knife.

I like to dress a fruit salad with a simple syrup made of sugar and water, spiked with fruit juice, wine or liqueur; or more simply, sprinkle the fruit with a little sugar and add fruit juice or wine.

Serve fruit salads in a salad bowl or in individual glass cups. Always allow salad to stand for some time after the dressing is poured over it; and the colder it is kept the better. It can be served either as a first course at luncheon or as a fresh fruit dessert at luncheon or dinner. Fruit salads may be garnished with grated coconut, shredded almonds, or chopped pistachio nuts or walnuts.

FRUIT SALAD WITH MINT DRESSING

1 grapefruit
2 oranges
2 apples
2 pears
1 small bunch grapes

MINT DRESSING
1–2 tablespoons (15–30 ml) finely chopped mint leaves
1 teaspoon (5 ml) finely chopped chives
¼ pint (150 ml) well-flavoured French Dressing (page 691)
Sugar

Peel and dice grapefruit and oranges. Core and dice apples and pears, but do not peel. Halve and seed grapes. Combine fruits and toss with Mint Dressing. Serves 4.

MINT DRESSING
Add finely chopped mint and chives to well-flavoured French Dressing. Sweeten to taste with a little sugar. Chill in refrigerator for at least 1 hour before using.

ORANGE SLICES IN RED WINE

8 oz (225 g) sugar
¼ pint (150 ml) water
Red Burgundy
1 clove
Cinnamon
Orange peel
2 strips lemon peel
4 large navel oranges

Make a syrup of sugar and water. Combine with ¼ pint (150 ml) red Burgundy, clove, cinnamon and 2 strips each orange and lemon peel. Boil until syrupy and reduced. Add another 2 tablespoons (30 ml) red Burgundy.

Peel oranges; divide into segments and remove all membrane and pith. Place orange segments in warm syrup and chill in refrigerator. Serve with slivers of fresh orange peel. Serves 4 to 6.

PEAR WALDORF SALAD

6 ripe pears
Juice of 1 lemon
6 stalks of celery, sliced
2 oz (50 g) halved walnuts
Mayonnaise or French Dressing (page 120 or 691)
1 head lettuce

Halve and core pears; cut into cubes and sprinkle with lemon juice. Add sliced celery and walnut halves. Toss together in mayonnaise or French Dressing according to taste, and pile into a salad bowl lined with lettuce leaves. Serves 4 to 6.

CARIBBEAN SALAD

1 can pineapple pieces (about 1 lb (450 g))
4 stalks celery, chopped
½ green pepper, sliced
½ red pepper, sliced
4 tablespoons (60 ml) coarsely chopped walnuts
4–6 tablespoons (60–90 ml) well-flavoured mayonnaise
Lemon juice
Lettuce

Drain pineapple pieces, reserving juices, and combine with celery, peppers, walnuts and mayonnaise. Add lemon juice and reserved pineapple juice, to taste. Arrange some lettuce leaves on individual salad plates and mound Caribbean Salad in the centre. Serves 4 to 6.

RED FRUIT BOWL

1 lb (450 g) red cherries, pitted
1–2 punnets ripe strawberries
1–2 punnets ripe raspberries
1 punnet red currants
Cognac
Lemon juice
Sugar

Clean the cherries, strawberries, raspberries and red currants, and combine in a bowl; marinate for at least 30 minutes in cognac, lemon juice and sugar, to taste. Chill. Serves 4 to 6.

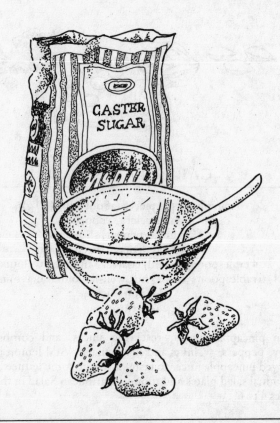

GREEK ORANGE AND OLIVE SALAD

3–4 ripe oranges
10–12 large black olives
1 tablespoon (15 ml) finely chopped onion
¼ pint (150 ml) well-flavoured French Dressing (page 691)
Salt and freshly ground black pepper

Peel and thinly slice oranges crosswise. Cut slices into quarters.
Pit and slice olives. Combine in a salad bowl with finely chopped
onion and French Dressing. Season with salt and freshly ground
black pepper, and toss before serving. Serves 4.

ROQUEFORT PEAR SALAD

4 ripe pears
Juice of 1 lemon
4 oz (100 g) Roquefort cheese
¼ pint (150 ml) double cream
1 tablespoon (15 ml) cognac
Paprika
Cos lettuce leaves
French Dressing (page 691)
Halved walnuts

Peel and core pears; cut into ¼-inch (6 mm) slices. Marinate in
lemon juice to keep from browning.

Combine Roquefort, cream and cognac, and mash to a smooth
paste. Add lemon juice (from pears) and paprika, to taste.

Sandwich cheese mixture between pear slices; place on a bed of
Cos lettuce leaves and dress with French Dressing; sprinkle with
halved walnuts. Serves 4 to 6.

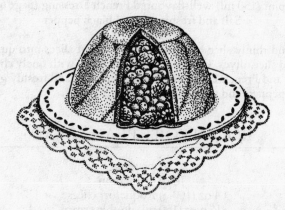

CHAPTER TWENTY
Puddings and Sweets

My first arrival in England was not auspicious. On my twenty-first birthday I disembarked at Plymouth – an involuntary pilgrim – en route to the front. The invasion of Normandy had just taken place; the first casualties were beginning to be listed; flying bombs were roaring over London; and the English were tired. To me, fresh from America, the exhaustion of the British people was extraordinary to see. They seem to have ceased to feel; the food was appalling – and the war was welcomed as a God-given excuse for all the pent-up puritanism of the people to come to the fore. To serve unimaginative food was looked on almost as a virtue; to enjoy a meal, a sin.

How different it was when I reached France. Here the nightmare was over, and feasting – with that skilful logic the French apply to their own comfort – was considered a patriotic gesture. So it was in France I stayed. For six years I lived in St Germain des Près, the most exciting quarter of what was the most exciting city in the world: creative, young, experimental – ready for every new experience, whether philosophical or physical.

But when I returned to England in 1953 for the Coronation, I might never have been here before, so different was it. Here was the Mrs Miniver-land I had imagined in my childhood. London was *en fête*, buildings garlanded, crowds jubilant, pageantry to the fore.

One meal summed up the change for me – and led me to stretch my three weeks' visit to twelve years. I was asked to tea by Sir Stephen Tallents, well known for his evocations of the country life. The very name of his house was almost parody – St John's Jerusalem. On my arrival, my host greeted me from the moat – knee-deep in water, rubber waders to the thighs, raking for the monastic relics that he discovered every now and then in the waters round his house.

Then tea itself. No bread and jam and cakes, but mounds of fresh strawberries and cream – strawberries such as I had never tasted before – and when we had eaten our way through an absolute mountain of them, Sir Stephen rose from the table to return a few minutes later with another great bowl of the fruit – still hot from the sun – brushed clean, not washed. Perfection!

As a boy, I loved the strawberry shortcake my father used to make. Thick, light, buttery scones (a baking powder American biscuit dough with extra butter and sugar added) were the secret here, sliced in half and buttered while still hot. Juicy, halved berries, sugared to taste, were ladled over the first layer; then came the top layer, and the whole was surmounted with more berries and lashings of cream piled high on top. Strawberries shortcakes like these were the star turn at the strawberry suppers that the church used to give every June. I think back to those summer suppers and wonder if children now still enjoy them as much as I did. The following sweets and puddings based on fresh fruits are among my favourites.

AMERICAN STRAWBERRY SHORTCAKE

SHORTCAKE
8 oz (225 g) plain flour
2 teaspoons (10 ml) baking powder
½ level teaspoon (2.5 ml) salt
2–4 tablespoons (30–60 ml) castor sugar
Softened butter
¼ pint (150 ml) milk
2 egg yolks, lightly beaten

BERRY MIXTURE
2 lb (900 g) fresh strawberries, sliced
Castor sugar
Lemon juice
½ pint (300 ml) double cream, whipped

SHORTCAKE (a sort of soft scone mixture)
Sift flour with baking powder, salt and sugar. Work in 4 table-spoons (60 ml) butter with a fork. Add milk and eggs little by little, stirring continuously, until mixture holds together but is still soft.

Turn out on a floured board. Roll out or pat into 4 rounds: place on a greased baking sheet and bake in a fairly hot oven (425°F/220°C/GM7) for 10 to 15 minutes, or until a pale golden colour.

To serve: split warm shortcakes in half, crosswise. Place bottom halves, cut sides up, on a serving platter, and spread with softened butter. Spoon half the sliced berries (to which you have added sugar and lemon juice, to taste) over buttered shortcakes, and top with other halves, cut sides down. Spoon on rest of sliced berries and whipped cream. Serves 4 to 6.

STRAWBERRIES ROMANOFF

2 lb (900 g) fresh strawberries
6 tablespoons (90 ml) icing sugar
3 tablespoons (45 ml) rum
3 tablespoons (45 ml) Cointreau
½ pint (300 ml) double cream
3 tablespoons (45 ml) Kirsch

Wash, drain and hull berries, and place in a bowl. Toss with 4 tablespoons (60 ml) icing sugar. Pour rum and Cointreau over them, and chill in refrigerator for at least 1 hour.

One hour before serving, whip cream until stiff; and remaining sugar, flavour with Kirsch and mix with the strawberries, tossing until every piece is coated. Keep cold until time to serve. Serves 8.

STRAWBERRY ORANGE

1 lb (450 g) strawberries
Orange juice, strained
Icing sugar
Whipped cream

Choose small strawberries – wild ones are best; combine them with strained orange juice and icing sugar, to taste, and allow to marinate in the refrigerator for at least 1 hour.

Serve in individual cups or bowls with a little whipped cream on top. Serves 4.

RASPBERRY BAVARIAN CREAM

1 packet frozen raspberries (10 oz (275 g))
Juice of 1 lemon
2 level tablespoons (30 ml) gelatine
4 tablespoons (60 ml) milk
2–4 tablespoons (30–60 ml) sugar
2 egg yolks
½ pint (300 ml) double cream
1 cup crushed ice

Defrost raspberries in a bowl with lemon juice.

Drain ¼ pint (150 ml) of the raspberry juices into a saucepan and heat just to simmering point. Pour the hot juice into the container of an electric blender. Add gelatine and milk; cover and blend at high speed for 1 minute.

Remove cover; add the sugar, raspberries and egg yolks. Then cover and blend at high speed for 5 seconds. Remove the cover, add cream and crushed ice, and keep blending until smooth. Pour into a mould and chill until set. Serves 4 to 6.

SUMMER FRUIT CUP

1–2 punnets strawberries
1–2 punnets raspberries
2 bananas, sliced
1 punnet red or white currants
4 oz (100 g) loaf sugar
¼ pint (150 ml) water
1 glass Claret or Burgundy
1 tablespoon (15 ml) brandy
1 tablespoon (15 ml) shredded pistachio nuts or coconut
Whipped cream and cookies or biscuits (optional)

Prepare the fruit and mix it lightly in a glass serving bowl. Boil the sugar and water together until they form a syrup; skim if necessary.

Allow the syrup to cool; then add wine and brandy, and pour over fruit. Stand in a cool place for several hours. Just before serving, sprinkle nuts or coconut over the top.

Whipped cream and cookies or biscuits may be served separately.

PINEAPPLE ROMANOFF

1 large pineapple
6 tablespoons (90 ml) icing sugar
3 tablespoons (45 ml) Cointreau
3 tablespoons (45 ml) rum
½ pint (300 ml) double cream
3 tablespoons (45 ml) Kirsch
Grated rind of 1 orange

Slice the pineapple, cut off the outer shell and the hard central core, and cut into segments. Toss segments with 4 tablespoons (60 ml) icing sugar. Arrange segments in a bowl suitable for serving at the table, and pour over them a mixture of Cointreau and rum; chill in the refrigerator.

One hour before serving: whip cream; add remaining icing sugar and flavour with Kirsch. Spoon whipped cream into marinated pineapple pieces, tossing until every piece is coated with creamy liqueur mixture. Top with finely grated orange rind, and keep cold until time to serve. Serves 6 to 8.

CHERRIES JUBILEE

1 large can pitted dark cherries
2 level tablespoons (30 ml) sugar
1 stick cinnamon
Juice and grated rind of ½ orange
1 teaspoon (5 ml) cornflour
4 tablespoons (60 ml) cognac
4 tablespoons (60 ml) cherry brandy
Vanilla Ice Cream (page 740)

Drain cherries and measure out ½ pint (300 ml) of the juice. Combine sugar, cinnamon, orange, juice, grated orange rind, cornflour and cherry juice, and bring slowly to a boil in blazer of chafing dish. Allow to bubble for 5 minutes, stirring from time to time, until sauce is reduced to desired consistency.

Add cherries and heat through. Heat cognac and cherry brandy, and pour over cherries. Ignite, and when flames die down, pour hot mixture over individual portions of Vanilla Ice Cream. Serves 4.

SUMMER PUDDING

8 oz (225 g) red or black currants
12 oz (350 g) cherries
8 oz (225 g) raspberries
¼ pint (150 ml) water
4–6 oz (100–175 g) sugar
Thin slices white bread
Custard Sauce (page 131) or whipped cream

Strip all stalks from currants; pit cherries; combine with raspberries, and wash if necessary. Place fruits with water and sugar in a saucepan, and simmer until sugar melts. Trim crusts from bread; cut each slice in half lengthwise and line sides of bowl or soufflé dish with bread. Cover bottom of dish with triangles of bread, and trim off bread slices at top edge of dish.

Fill dish with fruit mixture. Cut additional bread triangles to cover pudding. Place a flat plate on pudding: weight it and chill in refrigerator overnight.

When ready to serve, invert a serving dish and serve with Custard Sauce or whipped cream. Serves 6 to 8.

RHUBARB FOOL

1½ lb (675 g) young rhubarb
8 oz (225 g) sugar
2 tablespoons (30 ml) lemon juice
2 tablespoons (30 ml) butter
¾ pint (450 ml) cream, whipped
Sugar or lemon juice

Wash and trim young rhubarb stalks and cut into 1-inch (25 mm) segments. Combine rhubarb, sugar, lemon juice and butter in a thick-bottomed saucepan; bring gently to a boil, stirring continuously; lower heat and simmer, stirring all the time, for 5 to 8 minutes, or until rhubarb is soft but still keeps its identity.

Whisk in an electric blender until smooth, or press through a fine sieve. Allow to cool; then chill in refrigerator until ready to use. Just before serving, combine purée with whipped cream, and flavour to taste with sugar or lemon juice. Serves 4 to 6.

GOOSEBERRY FOOL

1½ lb (675 g) gooseberries
¼ pint (150 ml) water
4–8 oz (100–225 g) sugar
¼ pint (150 ml) custard
¼ pint (150 ml) double cream, whipped

Clean gooseberries and remove stems; wash gooseberries and put them in an enamelled saucepan with water and sugar. Cook until they are quite soft and then rub them through a fine sieve. Mix custard and whipped cream (reserving a little cream for garnish) with the gooseberry purée, and serve in a glass bowl or in individual glasses. Garnish with whipped cream. Serves 4 to 6.

ORANGES WITH CREAM

3 large oranges
¼ pint (150 ml) fresh orange juice
Sugar
½ pint (300 ml) double cream, whipped

Grate the rind of 1 orange and add to orange juice. Peel all the oranges and with a sharp knife cut off all the pith. Slice.

Place orange slices in overlapping rows in a shallow rectangular dish. Sprinkle with orange juice, and sugar, to taste.

Whip cream and add sugar, to taste; spoon over orange slices. Chill until ready to serve. Serves 4.

ORANGE DESSERT

3 tablespoons (45 ml) sugar
1 level tablespoon (15 ml) cornflour
6 tablespoons (90 ml) water
¼ pint (150 ml) orange juice
½ teaspoon (2.5 ml) finely sliced orange rind
2 tablespoons (30 ml) Cointreau
2 tablespoons (30 ml) cognac
Pinch of salt
Knob of butter
6 navel oranges
Sprigs of mint

Combine sugar, cornflour, water and orange juice in the top of a double saucepan. Cook over low heat, stirring constantly, until thickened. Remove from heat, and stir in orange rind, Cointreau, cognac, salt and butter.

To prepare oranges: cut through the rind of the oranges in a line from the stem almost to the bud end, forming 8 segments, and curl each segment inwards under the fruit at the base of each orange.

Loosen orange segments just enough so that they can be eaten easily with a knife and fork. Trim away any excess membrane and glaze lightly with sauce. Just before serving, pour remainder of the sauce over the orange sections and decorate with sprigs of mint. Serves 4 to 6.

ORANGES FLAMBÉES

4 large oranges
12 oz (350 g) sugar
4 tablespoons (60 ml) Grand Marnier

Remove bright outer peel carefully from oranges with a fruit parer; cut this zest into matchstick-sized pieces and reserve. Remove remaining pith from oranges and separate each orange into 8 sections.

Melt sugar in a small thick-bottomed saucepan, stirring constantly until it is a good caramel colour. Spear each orange segment with a fork and dip into caramel mixture. Place caramel-glazed orange segments thin sides up in a metal serving dish.

Stir *julienne* of orange matchsticks into caramel sauce and cook over a very low heat, stirring constantly. Drain and garnish each glazed orange section with caramelized zest.

When ready to serve: heat metal serving dish and flame with Grand Marnier. Serve immediately. Serves 4.

POIRES BELLE DIJONNAISE

4 ripe pears
Vanilla syrup (¾ pint (450 ml) water, 8 oz (225 g) sugar, vanilla extract)
1 pint (600 ml) Vanilla Ice Cream (page 740)
2 tablespoons (30 ml) cognac
Blackcurrant preserve
Crystallized violets

Peel, core and halve pears. Poach lightly in vanilla syrup. Cool in syrup and then put in refrigerator until ready to use.

Just before serving, spoon slightly softened Vanilla Ice Cream into individual chilled bowls; arrange 2 poached pear halves in each bowl and cover with a sauce made by combining 2 tablespoons (30 ml) each syrup and cognac with 1 small jar of blackcurrant preserve. Decorate with one or two crystallized violets. Serves 4.

POIRE VEFOUR

4–6 ripe fresh pears
Vanilla syrup (¾ pint (450 ml) water,
8 oz (225 g) sugar, vanilla extract)

PASTRY CREAM
6 oz (175 g) sugar
3 tablespoons (45 ml) flour
2½ tablespoons (38 ml) cornflour
¾ pint (450 ml) milk
6 egg yolks
4 tablespoons (60 ml) butter
Vanilla extract
Grand Marnier

GARNISH
Macaroon halves
Grand Marnier
Whipped cream
Sugar
Crystallized violets

To prepare pears: peel and core pears; slice in half and poach in a light syrup to which you have added plenty of vanilla. Allow to cool.

PASTRY CREAM
Combine sugar, flour and cornflour in the top of a double saucepan. Stir in milk and cook over direct heat, stirring all the time, until mixture comes to a boil. Boil for 1 minute. Beat egg yolks slightly and add a little hot milk mixture; then pour into saucepan with milk and sugar mixture, stirring constantly. Cook,

stirring, over hot but not boiling water, for 5 minutes. Strain and allow to cool slightly. Mix with butter and flavour to taste with vanilla and Grand Marnier.

To assemble dish: spread the bottom of a dish with half of the pastry cream. Allow to cool. Garnish with macaroon halves which you have sprinkled lightly with Grand Marnier. Cover lightly with remaining pastry cream and arrange poached pear halves on top.

Combine whipped cream with sugar and Grand Marnier, to taste. Decorate dish with whipped cream and crystallized violets. Serves 4 to 6.

CHOCOLATE MOULD

2 oz (50 g) chocolate
¾ pint (450 ml) milk
¼ oz (8 g) gelatine
1–2 oz (25–50 g) sugar
2 egg yolks
¼ teaspoon (1.25 ml) vanilla extract
Whipped cream

Break the chocolate into small pieces and put it in an enamelled saucepan with ¼ pint (150 ml) milk. Dissolve chocolate slowly, and cook until smooth. Then remove saucepan from heat, and add the remaining milk and the gelatine, sugar and egg yolks. Stir again over heat until the mixture is almost boiling, and the gelatine dissolved. Strain into a bowl; add vanilla extract. Allow to cool slightly; then pour mixture into a wet mould and set aside until firm.

When ready to serve, invert on a serving dish. Serve with whipped cream. Serves 4.

CHOCOLATE RUM MOUSSE

6 oz (175 g) sweet chocolate
5 eggs, separated
1 teaspoon (5 ml) vanilla extract
1 teaspoon (5 ml) instant coffee
1 tablespoon (15 ml) hot water
½ pint (300 ml) double cream
2 tablespoons (30 ml) rum

Melt chocolate in the top of a double saucepan over hot but not boiling water. Remove from heat and allow to cool. Beat egg yolks lightly and then beat them gradually into the melted chocolate. Flavour to taste with vanilla extract and instant coffee diluted in hot water.

Beat cream until thick; stir in rum and fold into the chocolate mixture. Beat egg whites until stiff and fold into the mixture a little at a time. Pour into a serving dish. Chill for at least 2 hours. Serves 4 to 6.

ZUPPA INGLESE

1 recipe Sponge Cake (page 810)
1½ pints (900 ml) milk
½ teaspoon (2.5 ml) vanilla extract
¼ level teaspoon (1.25 ml) powdered cinnamon
1 strip lemon peel
Pinch of salt
4 tablespoons (60 ml) sugar
1 tablespoon (15 ml) cornflour
8 egg yolks
6–8 tablespoons (90–120 ml) rum
Juice and grated rind of ½ orange
4 tablespoons (60 ml) Kirsch
Finely grated chocolate

Make sponge cake in 2 layers. Cool.

Combine milk, vanilla extract, cinnamon, lemon peel and salt in a saucepan, and bring just to boiling point. Remove from heat. Mix sugar and cornflour together in the top of a double saucepan. Add egg yolks and blend well. Gradually stir in the scalded milk, and cook over hot water, stirring constantly, until mixture is smooth and thick. Remove from heat. Cool. Remove lemon peel.

At least 2 hours before serving: place 1 cake layer in a serving dish; sprinkle with rum and orange juice, and cover with about two-thirds of the cooled custard mixture. Top with second layer; sprinkle with Kirsch and pour over remaining sauce. Chill.

Just before serving, remove from refrigerator and sprinkle with finely grated chocolate and orange peel. Serves 8.

RICE À LA ROYALE

3 oz (75 g) rice
½ pint (300 ml) milk
4 tablespoons (60 ml) sugar
Pears poached in syrup
Chopped pistachio nuts or shredded almonds

CUSTARD
4 egg yolks
½ pint (300 ml) milk
½ teaspoon (2.5 ml) cornflour
4 tablespoons (60 ml) sugar
Vanilla extract
2 sheets gelatine, dissolved in a little water
¼ pint (150 ml) double cream
2–3 tablespoons (30–45 ml) Kirsch

Simmer rice in milk and sugar until tender. Cool. Make the custard with egg yolks, milk, cornflour and sugar. Flavour to taste with vanilla extract; strain and divide into 2 equal parts. Add the gelatine, dissolved in a little water, to one part, and reserve the remainder to use as a sauce.

When the rice is cool, add custard containing gelatine along with 2 or 3 tablespoons (30–45 ml) double cream, and additional sugar if desired. Mix lightly and spoon into a china or glass serving dish.

Drain poached pears; pat them dry of syrup and arrange on top of rice. Add remaining cream to remaining custard; flavour with Kirsch and pour it around pears and over pudding. Sprinkle pears with chopped pistachio nuts or shredded almonds. Serve very cold. Serves 4 to 6.

CARAMEL CREAM

4 egg yolks
Light brown sugar
1 pint (600 ml) double cream

Beat egg yolks with 2 to 4 tablespoons (30–60 ml) light brown sugar until light and frothy. Bring cream to a boil in the top of a double saucepan; boil for 1 minute and pour over the egg yolks. Mix well; then return mixture to top of double saucepan and cook over hot but not boiling water, stirring constantly, for 2 or 3 minutes. Pour this custard into the heatproof dish in which it is to be served. Allow it to cool; then chill in the refrigerator.

Half an hour before serving, sprinkle a layer of sugar ⅛ inch (3 mm) thick on top and brown it quickly under a preheated grill. Grill must be very hot to caramelize surface. Chill again. Serve cold. Serves 4.

Baked Puddings

Simple Baked Puddings

The simplest puddings of all – milk puddings – can be made with or without eggs. Do not add eggs until the grain itself – barley, rice, tapioca or sago – is well cooked; the heat needed to cook the grain will curdle the eggs. One or two eggs to a pint of milk is the usual proportion. You will find that the pudding is lighter when the eggs are separated – and the whites, with a pinch of salt added, are beaten to introduce air into the pudding and make it rise.

Always wash all grains before cooking. The large kinds will cook better if they are pre-soaked in a little cold water before being cooked in milk.

A double saucepan is invaluable. If you use an ordinary saucepan, place an asbestos mat underneath it, or raise it slightly above the heat on a small trivet. Always rinse the saucepan out with cold water, or butter the bottom of it lightly, before adding milk. This helps to prevent the milk mixture from sticking or burning.

The simplest flavourings are always the best: grated lemon or orange rind, grated nutmeg, ground cinnamon or other spices.

When lemon or orange rind is used, grate it very thinly, then rub it into the sugar used in the pudding to help draw out the full citrus flavour. Cinnamon sticks, vanilla pods and bay leaves may also be used if they are first boiled in milk and then removed before grains are added.

Baked Milk Puddings

Milk puddings baked in the oven without pre-cooking in a saucepan should be baked in a very slow oven, otherwise the milk will boil over and burn before the grain has had time to swell and thicken the pudding. I find that several hours in a slow oven are much better than a shorter time in a hot one. However, if you have already cooked the rice or tapioca in a saucepan and the pudding is merely put into the oven to cook the eggs and brown the top, a fairly hot oven is satisfactory.

When baking a custard or other delicate pudding, place the dish containing it in a baking tin or shallow casserole, with a little hot water round it to avoid the danger of its boiling and curdling.

Some Basic Rules

Custard puddings are always baked in a very slow to slow oven (300°–325°F/150°–170°C/GM2–3).

Puddings containing suet, or other ingredients requiring thorough cooking, should be put in a slow to moderate oven (350°–375°F/180°–190°C/GM4–5).

Light batter puddings and those with beaten egg whites require a hotter oven to make them rise. I suggest 375°–400°F/190°–200°C/GM5–6.

Puddings with pastry require a hot oven to begin with (400°F/200°C/GM6) until the crust is set and begins to brown. Then the oven temperature may be lowered in most cases to 350°F/180°C/GM4.

A pudding that has to be baked should always be made a little moister than one for boiling or steaming, as the heat of the oven tends to dry it out. Always preheat your oven before baking.

SIMPLE RICE PUDDING

4 tablespoons (60 ml) rice
Butter
2 tablespoons (30 ml) sugar
Salt
Nutmeg or other flavouring
1¼ pints (750 ml) milk
¼ pint (150 ml) double cream
1 tablespoon (15 ml) finely shredded or chopped
suet or butter
Sultanas (optional)

Wash the rice, and put it in a well–buttered pie dish with the sugar, salt, and a little grated nutmeg or other flavouring. Pour in milk and double cream, and sprinkle the suet, very finely shredded or chopped, over the top. Bake the pudding in a slow oven (350°F/180°C/GM4) for 2 to 3 hours, or until the rice is quite soft. The slower it is cooked, the softer and creamier it will be. Sultanas may also be added if desired. Serves 4.

OLD ENGLISH RICE PUDDING

4 tablespoons (60 ml) rice
¼ pint (150 ml) water
1½ pints (900 ml) milk
Salt
Grated lemon rind
¼ pint (150 ml) double cream
Sugar
2 eggs, separated
Butter

Wash the rice, put it in an enamelled saucepan with the water, and boil until water is absorbed. Then add the milk, salt and a little grated lemon rind. Simmer slowly until the rice is thoroughly cooked, stirring occasionally with a wooden spoon. When ready, remove the saucepan from the heat, and when slightly cooled, stir in cream, 2 tablespoons (30 ml) sugar and egg yolks. Whisk egg whites until stiff and fold them lightly into mixture. Pour the mixture into a well-buttered pie dish, and bake in a slow (325°F/170°C/GM3) oven until nicely browned. Sprinkle with sugar. Serves 4.

BAKED APRICOT ROLL

8 oz (225 g) plain flour
1 level teaspoon (5 ml) baking powder
1 level teaspoon (5 ml) salt
1 tablespoon (15 ml) castor sugar
4 oz (100 g) chopped suet
6–8 tablespoons (90–120 ml) water
12 oz (350 g) apricot jam
Butter
Custard Sauce (page 131) or whipped cream

Combine flour, baking powder, salt, sugar and suet in a large mixing bowl. Work suet into dry ingredients with fingertips. Mix in enough water (6 to 8 tablespoons (90–120 ml)) with a fork to make dough leave sides of the bowl.

Roll dough into an oblong about 12 by 18 inches (30 by 45 cms). Spread with apricot jam and roll lengthwise into a large sausage shape. Seal edge with water and fold ends like an envelope.

Place on a large buttered baking tin and bake in a fairly hot oven (425°F/220°C/GM7) for 20 to 30 minutes, or until golden. Serve warm with Custard Sauce or whipped cream. Serves 8.

BAKED SULTANA PUDDING

8 oz (225 g) plain flour
Salt
1 teaspoon (5 ml) baking powder
Butter or lard
3 oz (75 g) sultanas
2–3 tablespoons (30–45 ml) sugar
A little candied peel, finely shredded
1 teaspoon (5 ml) vanilla extract
2 eggs, well beaten
6 fluid oz (175 g) milk
Cream

Sieve the flour, salt and baking powder into a bowl, and rub in 6 tablespoons (90 ml) butter or lard until free from lumps. Pick and clean the sultanas, and add them with the sugar, candied peel and vanilla extract. Make a well in the centre, add the well-beaten eggs, and then gradually mix in the milk. Mix together thoroughly. Put the mixture in a well-buttered cake tin, and bake in a moderate oven (375°F/190°C/GM5) for about 30 minutes, or until well risen and firm to the touch.

To serve: cut into squares, sprinkle with additional sugar and serve hot with cream. Serves 4 to 6.

RHUBARB CHARLOTTE

2 lb (900 g) rhubarb
1¾ lb (775 g) sugar
3 tablespoons (45 ml) lemon juice
Butter
Thin slices white bread
Brown sugar
Whipped cream

Wash and trim young rhubarb stalks and cut into 1-inch (25 mm) segments. Combine rhubarb, sugar, lemon juice and 3 tablespoons (45 ml) butter in a thick-bottomed saucepan; bring gently to a boil, stirring continuously; lower heat and simmer, stirring all the time, for about 5 minutes, or until rhubarb is soft but still keeps its identity.

Lightly butter a small charlotte mould or soufflé dish and dust with sugar. Trim crusts from bread; cut enough triangles to cover bottom of mould. Clarify butter; dip triangles of bread in butter one by one, and line bottom of mould, overlapping the triangles slightly. Line sides of mould with strips of bread dipped in clarified butter, also overlapping.

Fill the mould with rhubarb mixture; cover with overlapping triangles of bread dipped in butter. Sprinkle with a little brown sugar and bake in a moderate oven (375°F/190°C/GM5) for 30 to 35 minutes, or until the bread is golden. Let the mould stand for 5 to 10 minutes after being removed from the oven.

To serve: invert the charlotte on a heated serving dish. Serve with whipped cream. Serves 4 to 6.

BLACKBERRY AND APPLE SPONGE

2 lb (900 g) apples
8 oz (225 g) blackberries, hulled and washed
4 tablespoons (60 ml) castor sugar
Cream or Custard Sauce (page 131)

SPONGE
3 oz (75 g) butter
3 oz (75 g) castor sugar
2 eggs, beaten
4 oz (100 g) self-raising flour
1 oz (25 g) cornflour

Peel, core and slice the apples into a pie dish, and add hulled and washed blackberries and sugar. Make sponge by creaming butter and sugar, and adding eggs, flour and cornflour. Spread mixture over the fruit. Bake in a moderate oven (375°F/190°C/GM5) for 30 to 40 minutes. Sprinkle with a little castor sugar, and serve hot with cream or Custard Sauce. Serves 4 to 6.

BAKED CUSTARD PUDDING

4 egg yolks
2 egg whites
Castor sugar
Pinch of salt
½ teaspoon (2.5 ml) vanilla extract
1 pint (600 ml) milk
Butter

Beat the egg yolks and whites in a bowl with 2 tablespoons (30 ml) castor sugar, and salt and vanilla extract. Heat the milk without allowing it to boil, and pour it slowly on to the beaten eggs, stirring constantly. Strain the mixture into a well-buttered soufflé dish. Place the dish in a baking tin with a little cold water round it, and cook in a slow oven (350°F/180°C/GM4) for 50 to 60 minutes, or until the custard sets and the top is golden brown. The water in the tin will prevent the custard from becoming too hot and curdling. Sprinkle custard with a little castor sugar before serving. Serves 4.

BAKED BREAD AND BUTTER PUDDING

2–4 slices bread
Softened butter
2 eggs
1 pint (600 ml) milk
Castor sugar
Vanilla extract
2 tablespoons (30 ml) currants or sultanas

Remove crusts from bread; butter slices, and cut into thin strips.
Lay bread strips in a well-buttered Pyrex loaf dish. Dish should be
about half full. Whisk eggs in a mixing bowl; add the milk, and
sugar and vanilla extract, to taste. Mix well together and strain
over bread strips. Allow pudding to stand until bread is well
soaked. Sprinkle with currants or sultanas. Bake for 45 to 60
minutes in a slow oven (350°F/180°C/GM4) until golden brown
and firm to the touch. Sprinkle with sugar and serve hot. Serves 4.

COTTAGE PUDDING

10 oz (275 g) sifted plain flour
2 level teaspoons (10 ml) baking powder
½ level teaspoon (2.5 ml) salt
5 tablespoons (75 ml) softened butter
½ teaspoon (2.5 ml) vanilla extract
5 oz (150 g) sugar
2 eggs
8 fluid oz (225 g) milk
Lemon or Strawberry Hard Sauce (page 133)

Sift flour, baking powder and salt into a mixing bowl. Work softened butter and vanilla extract together until soft; add sugar gradually and continue beating until mixture is creamy. Separate eggs and beat yolks thoroughly into creamed mixture. Stir in a third of the flour mixture; and add a third of the milk. Repeat these ingredients alternately, ending with flour, until all ingredients are used. Beat egg whites until stiff and fold gently into batter. Pour into greased mould and bake for 30 to 40 minutes in a preheated slow oven (350°F/180°C/GM4). Cool slightly and serve topped with Lemon or Strawberry Hard Sauce. Serves 4 to 6.

QUEEN OF PUDDINGS

2 oz (50 g) fresh breadcrumbs
Butter
3 tablespoons (45 ml) sugar
Grated lemon rind
Vanilla extract
1 pint (600 ml) milk
3 egg yolks
3 tablespoons (45 ml) apricot or
strawberry jam
Lemon juice

MERINGUE
4 egg whites
Castor sugar

Combine breadcrumbs with 3 tablespoons (45 ml) each butter and sugar. Flavour to taste with grated lemon rind and vanilla extract. Bring the milk almost to a boil in a small saucepan; pour it over the crumb mixture and let it soak for 10 minutes. Then stir in egg yolks; pour the mixture into a well-buttered deep pie dish and bake in a moderate oven (375°F/190°C/GM5) for 20 to 25 minutes, or until set. Remove from oven and allow to cool.

When cool, spread with apricot or strawberry jam flavoured to taste with lemon juice.

Beat egg whites until stiff but not dry; fold in castor sugar to taste. Pile meringue on pudding in high peaks and bake in a slow oven (350°F/180°C/GM4) until meringue is lightly browned. Serves 4 to 6.

APPLE AMBER PUDDING

1½ lb (675 g) apples, peeled, cored and sliced
2–4 tablespoons (30–60 ml) granulated sugar
2 tablespoons (30 ml) butter
Grated rind of 1 lemon
2 egg yolks, beaten
1 recipe Shortcrust Pastry (page 755)
2 egg whites
1 tablespoon (15 ml) castor sugar
Vanilla extract
Glacé cherries
Angelica

Combine apples, sugar, butter and grated lemon rind in a saucepan, and simmer gently, stirring from time to time, until mixture is reduced to pulp. Beat mixture with a wooden spoon until perfectly smooth, or rub it through a sieve; then add beaten egg yolks.

Line a pie dish with shortcrust pastry and pour apple mixture into it. Bake in a moderate oven (375°F/190°C/GM5) for 30 to 40 minutes, or until the pastry is cooked and the apple mixture set. Whisk egg whites until stiff; flavour with 1 tablespoon (15 ml) castor sugar and a few drops of vanilla extract. Pile meringue on top of the pudding; decorate with a few pieces of glacé cherry and angelica. Return to a cool oven until lightly browned. Serves 4.

BROWN BETTY

1½ lb (675 g) apples, peeled, cored and sliced
Butter
6 oz (175 g) browned breadcrumbs
2 tablespoons (60 ml) golden syrup
¼ pint (150 ml) water
½ teaspoon (2.5 ml) cinnamon
Sugar
Cream

Place a layer of sliced apples in a buttered pie dish. Sprinkle some of the breadcrumbs over them, and dot with butter. Put in some more apples and repeat these alternate layers until all the apples and breadcrumbs are used up. The top layer should be breadcrumbs.

Mix syrup with water and cinnamon, and pour this over the top. Sprinkle with sugar and dot with butter. Place the pie dish in a tin containing hot water, and bake in a moderate oven (375°F/190°C/GM5) for 1 hour, or until the apples are soft. Serve with cream. Serves 4.

Boiled and Steamed Puddings

When fresh suet is used in a pudding, it should be hard and dry. Any fresh suet may be used, although beef suet is generally preferred. Remove all skin and fibre before shredding the suet finely with a knife on a chopping board. Dust it over generously with flour (taken from the quantity required for the pudding), and then chop it finely with a knife. A long, pointed knife is best. Hold down the point of the knife on the board with one hand and work the handle end up and down with the other. The more finely the suet is chopped, the lighter the pudding will be.

To Prepare the Mould

A pudding which is to be steamed or boiled must be put into a well-buttered mould or bowl. To butter the pudding mould: make sure that it is perfectly dry; then brush it with fresh clarified butter. Put a little of the butter into the mould or bowl, melt it in a warm place, and then run fat around the sides, or paint it on with a brush. Butter a piece of white paper to cover the pudding at the same time. I sometimes coat the buttered mould with fine browned breadcrumbs, biscuit crumbs or brown sugar, or I decorate it with raisins, almonds, or sticks of candied peel or preserved fruits. Or I coat the mould with melted caramel instead of butter. Always prepare the mould before you make the pudding. A plain mould is best for light puddings as it is easier to turn out, but a more decorative mould may be used for the more solid kinds based on flour and suet.

To Steam a Pudding

Fill mould or bowl three-quarters full (or even less if pudding mixture is very light and spongy) to allow the mixture to rise.

Cover the top of the mould or bowl with a piece of buttered paper, twisting it on so that it does not fall down the sides; place it in a saucepan with just enough hot water to reach half-way up the mould; put a tight-fitting lid on the pan, and keep the water at simmering point until the pudding is cooked. If water boils down, add more hot water. Custard puddings must be steamed very slowly and carefully, as extreme heat will curdle the eggs and make the pudding watery. With the lighter puddings, I always put a saucer or old plate at the bottom of the saucepan to raise the pudding mould a little away from the direct heat of the stove.

A steamer may be used instead of a saucepan to steam puddings; in this case, the water must be kept boiling underneath the pudding during cooking time.

Alternatively, the mould containing the pudding may be placed in a deep tin or saucepan with boiling water around it, and then cooked in the oven instead of on top of the stove. I find this a more convenient method, as it saves space on the top of the stove, and you can easily regulate oven temperature.

To Boil a Pudding

A pudding mixture may either be boiled in a bowl covered with a cloth, or in a cloth only. If you use a bowl, fill it completely with your pudding mixture; then top pudding with a round of bread, which is afterwards removed. This prevents water from soaking into the pudding and making it soft. To enclose pudding: wring out a clean cloth that has been soaked in boiling water: sprinkle it lightly with flour and fix it firmly over the bowl by tying a string under the rim of the bowl in a loop knot so that it can easily be untied. Bring up the four corners of the cloth and tie them over the top of the pudding, or fasten them together with a safety-pin.

If no bowl is used, prepare a pudding cloth in the same way: put the pudding mixture in the centre and draw all the sides of the cloth together, leaving enough room for the mixture to swell. Tie firmly with string.

Plunge the pudding into a large saucepan of boiling water – there must be sufficient water to cover it completely – and keep it boiling steadily for the required time, keeping a kettle of boiling water on hand to fill up the saucepan when necessary.

To Turn Out a Pudding

Lift pudding out of the saucepan and allow it to stand for a minute or two, because the first steam escaping from the pudding is apt to crack it if unprotected by the bowl or cloth in which it has been cooked. Remove the cloth or paper from the top; take hold of the bowl or mould with a cloth and shake it gently to ensure that the pudding is coming away quite freely from the sides. Turn it out on a hot serving dish and remove the mould carefully.

When pudding is boiled in a cloth, lift it on to a colander or sieve and let it drain for a minute or two. Then untie the string, remove cloth gently from the sides of the pudding, turn it out on a hot serving dish and pull the cloth carefully away.

STEAMED APRICOT PUDDING

Butter
3 oz (75 g) castor sugar
3 oz (75 g) plain flour
2 eggs
8–10 canned apricot halves
Pinch of cinnamon
Rind and juice of 1 lemon
2 level teaspoons (10 ml) baking powder
½ pint (300 ml) Apricot Sauce (page 132)

Cream 3 oz (75 g) butter in a bowl; add the sugar, and then gradually add the flour and eggs. Beat well until light and frothy. Drain the pieces of apricot and cut them in small pieces; add them to the mixture with the cinnamon, lemon rind and lemon juice, and last of all the baking powder. Mix well and pour into a well-buttered pudding mould. Cover with buttered paper and steam for 1½ to 2 hours, or until the pudding is well risen and firm to the touch. When ready, turn out and strain the Apricot Sauce over pudding. Serves 4.

CHOCOLATE BREAD PUDDING

3 oz (75 g) semi-sweet chocolate
Butter
¼ pint (150 ml) milk
2 oz (50 g) castor sugar
2 eggs separated
5 oz (150 g) breadcrumbs
1 level teaspoon (5 ml) baking powder
Cinnamon
Vanilla extract
Chocolate or Custard Sauce (page 133 or 131)

Dissolve chocolate with 2 oz (50 g) butter in the top of a double saucepan; add milk and simmer gently. Sieve sugar over the top; add egg yolks and half the breadcrumbs, and mix well. Stir in remaining breadcrumbs, baking powder, cinnamon, and vanilla extract, to taste.

Whip egg whites to a stiff froth. Fold them into mixture at the last moment, and then pour mixture into a well-buttered pudding mould; cover with buttered paper and steam for 1 to 1½ hours, or until the pudding is well risen and feels firm to the touch. Serve with Chocolate or Custard Sauce. Serves 4.

CHELSEA PUDDING

4 oz (100 g) suet
4 oz (100 g) breadcrumb
4 oz (100 g) plain flour
Salt
1 teaspoon (5 ml) baking powder
4 oz (100 g) currants
4 oz (100 g) raisins
8 fluid oz (225 ml) treacle or molasses, slightly warmed
8 fluid oz (225 ml) milk
Butter
Custard Sauce (page 131) or a jam sauce

Chop suet finely and mix with breadcrumbs, flour, salt and baking powder. Mix well together with the tips of the fingers, then add the currants and raisins, carefully washed. Make a well in the centre; add slightly warmed treacle, then gradually add milk, beating all together. Pour mixture into a well-buttered mould; cover with buttered paper and steam steadily for 3 hours. When ready, turn out and serve with Custard Sauce or a jam sauce. Serves 4 to 6.

BARONESS PUDDING

8 oz (225 g) plain flour
½ teaspoon (2.5 ml) salt
1 teaspoon (5 ml) baking powder
1 oz (25 g) castor sugar
4 oz (100 g) suet, chopped
4 oz (100 g) sultanas
¼ pint (150 ml) milk
Butter
Apricot or Custard Sauce (page 132 or 131)

Sieve flour, salt and baking powder into a mixing bowl; add sugar, finely chopped suet, and sultanas.

Mix dry ingredients together thoroughly; make a well in the centre and gradually pour in enough milk to make a softish dough (about ¼ pint/150 ml).

Pour the mixture into a well-buttered bowl which you have decorated with a few sultanas; cover with buttered paper and steam steadily for 3 hours. Serve with Apricot or Custard Sauce. Serves 4 to 6.

NÈGRE EN CHEMISE

6 oz (175 g) butter
8 slices white bread
1¼ pints (750 ml) double cream
4 oz (100 g) blanched almonds, ground
6 oz (175 g) castor sugar
4 oz (100 g) bitter-sweet chocolate
8 eggs
Icing sugar

Cream butter. Soak bread, trimmed of crusts, in ½ pint (300 ml) double cream. Add to butter with ground blanched almonds, sugar, and chocolate which you have melted over hot water and cooled. Beat the mixture with electric mixer until smooth; then beat in eggs one by one.

Pour the mixture into a tall mould. Cover or seal the mould and place in a large saucepan of boiling water (the water should come half-way up the mould). Cover the saucepan and steam the pudding for 1½ hours, adding more boiling water from time to time if necessary. Whip remaining cream; sweeten to taste with icing sugar. Serve immediately. Serves 6.

SPONGE PUDDING

Butter
2 tablespoons (30 ml) jam
4 tablespoons (60 ml) castor sugar
1 egg, well beaten
4 oz (100 g) plain flour
4 fluid oz (100 g) milk
1 level teaspoon (5 ml) baking powder
1½ teaspoons (7.5 ml) vanilla extract
Grated rind of ½ lemon
Pinch of salt

Butter a pudding basin and coat bottom with jam. Cream 4 tablespoons (60 ml) butter with sugar in another bowl; add beaten egg and half the flour. Beat well, and then add the milk and remaining flour. The mixture should have the consistency of a thick batter that will just drop from the spoon. Beat again, and finally add baking powder, vanilla extract, lemon rind, and salt, to taste. Pour the mixture into the prepared basin; cover with buttered paper and steam for 1 to 1½ hours, or until well risen and firm to the touch. When ready, turn out and serve quickly. Serves 4.

STEAMED CHERRY PUDDING

8 oz (225 g) fresh cherries
3 oz (75 g) brown breadcrumbs
2½ oz (65 g) castor sugar
Grated rind of ½ lemon
¼ pint (150 ml) double cream
2 egg yolks, beaten
2 egg whites
Butter
Juice of ½ lemon
4 fluid oz (100 ml) water
Red food colouring (optional)

Combine breadcrumbs, 1½ oz (40 g) castor sugar and grated lemon rind in a mixing bowl. Wash, pick and stone the cherries, and add three-quarters of them to breadcrumb mixture. Scald cream and pour it over the crumbs and fruit. Stir in beaten egg yolks. Beat whites until stiff and fold into mixture.

Pour the mixture into a well-buttered mould or bowl; cover with a piece of buttered paper, and steam slowly and steadily for about 1½ hours, or until pudding is well risen and firm to the touch.

Combine remaining cherries, lemon juice, water and 1 oz (25 g) sugar in a saucepan; bring to a boil; reduce heat and simmer gently for 15 minutes. Tint sauce with red food colouring if necessary. Invert the pudding carefully on a hot dish; pour the sauce around it and serve immediately. Serves 4.

STEAMED GINGERBREAD PUDDING

4 oz (100 g) suet
4 oz (100 g) sifted plain flour
1 teaspoon (5 ml) ground ginger
1 cup dry breadcrumbs
½ teaspoon (2.5 ml) ground cinnamon
3 oz (75 g) brown sugar
1½ teaspoons (7.5 ml) baking powder
Pinch of salt
8 fluid oz (225 ml) treacle or molasses
1 egg, well beaten
8 fluid oz (225 ml) milk
Butter
Custard Sauce (page 131)

Chop suet finely and mix it in a bowl with sifted flour, ground ginger, breadcrumbs, cinnamon, brown sugar, and baking powder, adding salt to taste. Make a well in the centre; pour in the treacle and well-beaten egg, and gradually mix in the dry ingredients, adding the milk slowly as you mix. Beat for a minute and pour the mixture into a well-buttered mould. Cover with buttered paper and steam steadily for 2 to 3 hours, or until well risen and firm to the touch. When ready, turn out and serve with Custard Sauce. Serves 4 to 6.

Ice Creams

The best ice creams are those made with double cream and fresh fruits or other flavourings. Very good ones can also be made with equal parts of custard and cream, with flavouring added.

Plainer creams are made with custard only.

Always be careful when adding sugar to the basic ice cream mixture. If the mixture is too sweet, it will not freeze properly, and if not sweet enough, it will be hard and rough.

Refrigerator Method

Set dial of your refrigerator at maximum about 1 hour before you make ice cream. Make ice cream; pour mixture into ice trays and put in freezing compartment. Stir mixture every 30 minutes until it is half frozen; then leave for 2 or 3 hours, or until it is frozen hard.

Freezer Method

Set dial of freezer at 'quick freeze' about 1 hour before you make ice cream. Make ice cream; pour into a mixing bowl and place bowl in freezer until mixture is half frozen. Then whisk mixture thoroughly with a rotary whisk and pour it into the containers of your choice. Return to freezer for 2 to 3 hours, or until it is frozen hard.

VANILLA ICE CREAM

4 egg yolks
4 oz (100 g) sugar
Pinch of salt
¾ pint (450 ml) single cream
1–2 teaspoons (5–10 ml) vanilla extract

Beat egg yolks, sugar and salt until light and lemon-coloured. Scald single cream, and add to egg and sugar mixture, whisking until mixture is well blended.

Pour mixture into top of a double saucepan and cook over water, stirring continuously, until custard coats spoon.

Strain through a fine sieve; stir in vanilla and freeze as above.

APRICOT ICE CREAM

½ pint (300 ml) apricot purée
½ pint (300 ml) double cream, lightly whipped
Lemon juice
2–3 tablespoons (30–45 ml) apricot liqueur
2–3 drops red food colouring
Castor sugar

Make the apricot purée by rubbing canned apricots through a hair sieve, using some of the syrup. The purée must not be too thick. Mix the cream, lightly whipped, into the purée; then add lemon juice, apricot liqueur and enough red food colouring to give the mixture a good apricot colour. Sweeten to taste and freeze in the usual way. Serves 4.

Note: Fresh apricots may be used, but they must be stewed until soft in a syrup of sugar and water.

PRALINE ICE CREAM

4 oz (100 g) almonds
4 oz (100 g) sugar
Lemon juice
Oil
1 pint (600 ml) warm custard (see Vanilla
Ice Cream opposite)
½ pint (300 ml) double cream
Liqueur or cognac

Blanch almonds; chop them roughly and dry well. Combine sugar in a small saucepan with lemon juice; melt it carefully over a medium heat until it takes on a good caramel colour. Add chopped almonds and stir constantly until they are brown also. Pour the mixture on to a flat tin that has been greased with salad oil, and let it cool.

When praline mixture is cold and hard, reduce it to a powder by pounding it in a mortar. Add this powder to the warm custard; then cool and half freeze. Whip cream, fold into custard with a little liqueur or cognac, and freeze again until sufficiently stiff. Serves 4.

CHOCOLATE ICE CREAM

2–3 oz (50–75 g) chocolate
2–3 tablespoons (30–45 ml) milk
½ pint (300 ml) custard (see Vanilla Ice Cream page 740)
½ pint (300 ml) double cream
Sugar and vanilla extract

Grate chocolate and dissolve it over low heat in 2 to 3 tablespoons (30–45 ml) milk. Add melted chocolate to custard and strain into a bowl. Whip the cream lightly; mix with chocolate custard; sweeten to taste and add a few drops of vanilla. Freeze in the usual way. Serves 4.

LIQUEUR ICE CREAM

1 pint (600 ml) double cream
4 oz (100 g) castor sugar
Maraschino or other liqueur

Whip cream; add sugar. Flavour it to taste with Maraschino or liqueur of your choice. Mix well and freeze. Serves 4.

TANGERINE ICE CREAM

6 tangerines
4 oz (100 g) castor sugar
1 pint (600 ml) double cream

Grate the rind of 3 tangerines very lightly and rub rind into the sugar. Put this flavoured sugar in the top of a double saucepan with half the cream, and scald until sugar is quite dissolved.

Remove from the heat and cool. Strain the juice of the 6 tangerines into this mixture. Whip remaining cream and fold into mixture. Freeze in the usual way. Serves 4.

BISCUIT TORTONI

½ pint (300 ml) double cream
2 egg whites
Castor sugar
Salt
4 oz (100 g) chopped toasted almonds
Sherry, Marsala or cognac

Whip cream. Beat egg whites; add sugar and salt, to taste, and continue beating until mixture is stiff and glossy. Fold chopped almonds (reserving 2 tablespoons (30 ml) for garnish) into egg mixture with whipped cream. Stir in sherry, Marsala or cognac, to taste, and spoon mixture into 6 to 8 individual soufflé dishes or custard cups. Sprinkle with reserved almonds and freeze in the usual way. Serves 6 to 8.

BANANA ICE CREAM

5 bananas, peeled and sliced
½ pint (300 ml) chilled custard (see Vanilla Ice Cream
page 740)
Grated rind and juice of 1 orange
¼ pint (150 ml) double cream, whipped
Castor sugar
1–2 tablespoons (15–30 ml) Maraschino or other liqueur
Yellow food colouring (optional)

Flavour custard with grated orange rind. Rub ripe bananas through a sieve to make ¼ pint (150 ml) banana purée. Add strained orange juice, chilled custard and whipped cream to banana purée, and flavour to taste with sugar and 1 to 2 tablespoons (15–30 ml) Maraschino or other liqueur. Colour slightly if desired with yellow food colouring. Freeze in the usual way. Serves 4.

Water Ices

When making delicate water ices – with a fruit juice or fruit purée base – it is best to prepare a sugar syrup first. If you intend to mould your water ice, always add a little dissolved gelatine to the hot syrup.

SYRUP FOR WATER ICES

8 oz (225 g) sugar
1 pint (600 ml) water
Juice of ½ lemon

Combine sugar and water in an enamelled saucepan; bring to a boil and boil for 10 minutes, removing any scum that rises. Add lemon juice and strain through a muslin-lined sieve. This recipe makes 1¼ pints (750 ml).

PEACH WATER ICE

½ pint (300 ml) peach purée (see method)
½ pint (300 ml) syrup for ices (see above)
Juice of 1 lemon
2–3 drops almond extract
2–3 drops red food colouring

Rub peaches through a hair sieve until a sufficient quantity of purée is obtained. Add syrup to the fruit purée, and flavour to taste with strained lemon juice and almond extract. Tint mixture slightly with red food colouring. Cool and freeze in the usual way. Serves 4.

GRAPE WATER ICE

1 lb (450 g) muscat grapes
½ pint (300 ml) syrup for ices (see above)
Juice of 2 lemons
1 tablespoon (15 ml) orange-flower water
½ glass Marsala
Finely chopped pistachio nuts

Wash grapes; crush them and rub them through a hair sieve. Strain syrup and lemon juice over the grape purée; add orange-flower water and Marsala, and allow to cool. Freeze in the usual way. Serve water ice piled up in small cups and sprinkled with finely chopped pistachio nuts. Serves 4.

ORANGE WATER ICE

12 oz (350 g) sugar
1½ pints (900 ml) water
¾ pint (450 ml) orange juice
¼ pint (150 ml) lemon juice
Finely grated rinds of 1 orange and 1 lemon

Bring sugar and water to a boil; boil for 5 minutes. Cool slightly, and add orange juice, lemon juice, and grated orange and lemon rind. Cool; strain through a fine sieve and freeze in the usual way. Serves 6 to 8.

PINEAPPLE WATER ICE

1 can pineapple slices
½ pint (300 ml) syrup for ices (see above)
Juice of 1 lemon, strained
Vanilla extract or Kirsch
Yellow food colouring

Chop the pineapple and pound it in a mortar with a little pineapple syrup. Rub it through a fine sieve. To ½ pint (300 ml) of this purée add ½ pint (300 ml) syrup, the strained lemon juice, and vanilla

extract or a little Kirsch. Tint with a little yellow food colouring.
When cold, put in the freezer and freeze until stiff enough to pile
up in ice cups. Serves 4.

STRAWBERRY WATER ICE

½ pint (300 ml) strawberry purée (see method)
½ pint (300 ml) syrup for ices (see page 744)
Juice of 1 lemon, strained
Red food colouring
2 egg whites

Rub ripe strawberries through a hair sieve. Combine fruit purée,
syrup, strained lemon juice, and enough red food colouring to
make a pink ice. When quite cold, freeze in the usual way. Whisk
egg whites until stiff and stir into the mixture when it is half
frozen. Then continue the freezing until the ice is sufficiently stiff
for serving. Serves 4.

BLACKCURRANT ICE

1 pint (600 ml) blackcurrants, topped and tailed
Juice of 2 lemons, strained
3–4 oz (75–100 g) granulated sugar

Place half of the blackcurrants in an electric blender and blend for a
few seconds until puréed. Repeat the process with the remaining
currants, and add them to the first purée. Add the strained lemon
juice to the sugar and stir well. Add to the fruit purée. Place in
freezing tray of refrigerator and freeze until almost stiff – about 1
hour. Put half the blackcurrant in the blender and blend until
softened to sherbet consistency. Repeat with second half. Spoon
into chilled glasses and serve at once. Serves 4 to 6.

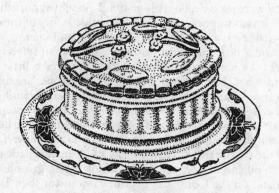

CHAPTER TWENTY-ONE

Pies and Pastries

'How lucky you are to be able to cook,' people often say, rather as if I had discovered the secret of the Philosopher's Stone. But after all, people have been trying to make food palatable for tens of thousands of years, and it is only one step further to try and make it delicious. There is no real secret, just a series of basic rules that are easy to master and, once learned, they are found to apply to the whole range of cuisine, from the highest to the most simple.

The trouble is that people are put off by the mystique of the great chefs. It is true that real masters work for years to perfect some exotic sauce, but concert pianists and prima ballerinas also have to practise every day to keep up their technique, and you do not ignore music or dancing simply because you cannot reach their level.

But with cooking it is different. Some people tell me almost with pride that they do not attempt, or really enjoy, elaborate dishes; but you would never catch those same people boasting that they were tone-deaf or colour-blind. So why ignore the sense of taste? It is as important and as pleasurable as any of the others. Pastry-making is a case in point. The basic combination of flour, fat, air and a little cold water or egg yolk is as simple as child's play. Yet the variations, once you have acquired a little know-how and what the French cooks call a *tour de main*, are limitless. From a simple farmhouse shortcrust to the ethereal ramifications of featherlight *pâte feuilletée* is only a series of easy steps. The Orientals, in their wisdom, started it first by combining flour and water; and the fame of their *won ton*, *shao m'ai* and *pastes* has gone around the world; the Ancient Greeks and Romans made pastries rich with oil and honey; and in the Middle Ages, great houses in Britain and on the Continent became famous for their fabulous mounted set pieces containing everything from game to pickled eggs, mushrooms, spices and vinegar.

The pies of early Tudor days bore little resemblance to the confections we now call by that name. The very word 'pie' came into use when a pastry full of live birds was opened up, and the birds – magpies – began to chatter the moment the crust was lifted. Animated pies soon became a court fad. At the coronation of Henry VII, a 'custard pye' served at the banquet was carried in by four strong men 'richle clad in red and gold', who placed it on the royal table. When His Majesty cut the first slice, out flew a flock of birds followed by the court hunchback, 'whereupon the lords and ladies laughed mightily'. My version of custard pie is, I am afraid, much simpler. And pastry-making and pie-making today are simpler, too.

It is in the realm of pies, flans and tarts that the French have so much to teach us. In England, a pie is usually a solid affair of beefsteak and kidney or oysters and chicken, covered in short-crust pastry, or an equally deep dish of apples flavoured with cloves. Welcome as these riches are, I far prefer the lighter talents of the French cook, who fills featherlight pastry shells with savoury as well as sweet fillings to delight the adventuresome palate.

French savoury tarts make wonderful appetizers, served warm or cold. They are perfect for spring luncheons or as a recipe to carry over into outdoor meals with a difference. For the tart – like the omelette or the soufflé – is the perfect carry-all for a host of vegetables and fruits, forming the perfect beginning, or ending, to a meal.

You will find my favourite recipes for savoury and sweet tarts, pies, raised pies and basic types of pastry on the following pages, as well as a recipe for a new kind of pastry which you do not roll out, but press into shape in pie, tart or flan tins with your fingers. This 'fingertip' pastry approaches the famous *pâte sablée* of French pastry cooks. It is rich in flavour, crumbly in texture, and very easy to make. At times I add a drop or two of water to the basic dough, or a sprinkling of lemon juice and a little cinnamon. This pastry is good for all kinds of rich dessert tarts or, with a little less icing sugar in the basic mix, it can be used to lend distinction to savoury tarts of all kinds.

Anyone who has visited the Mediterranean coast of France or the western coast of Italy is familiar with the savoury tomato and onion tart spiked with the salty tang of anchovy and black olives. These pastries come in every shape and size, and the cases range from bread dough to *brioche* dough.

I once gave lunch to two famous writers to celebrate the first stage of work on my new house at St Tropez – one, the most gifted and prolific journalist of our time, and the other, the author of one of this generation's great classics. Provençal tomato and onion tart seemed to me to be the perfect beginning for such a meal.

'Too salty for me,' said the journalist, with his usual forthright honesty. 'Best thing I've ever eaten,' replied the author. So how can one tell? I myself love it, and include the recipe here for you to judge for yourself. Of course, it *is* salty. How could any dish garnished with anchovy fillets and ripe olives be anything else? But it is the saltiness of the Mediterranean that I love; the appetizing saltiness of an *anchoïade*, the high sharp flavour of a *salade niçoise*, the earthy simplicity of an Italian pizza. It is a dish reminiscent of sun-washed lunches on the fisherman's port at St Tropez; of moonlight picnics on the beach at Pampelonne. A dish to be washed down with the cooling *vin rosé* of Provence; the centre-piece, if made large enough, for an informal cocktail party on a Mediterranean terrace. Try it and see.

Individual mushroom and bacon tarts provide a new variation on the familiar quiche theme. To make these savoury tarts, combine crisp mushrooms slices with crisply fried bacon and a little finely chopped parsley in a custard mixture of cream and beaten eggs, and serve these delicious hot appetizers in bite-sized tart shells to accompany drinks; or in individual pastry shells or an elegant flan ring for a distinctive first course for luncheon or dinner.

Canned crab, lobster, prawns or shrimps, or poached diced fish can also be used to advantage in this basic recipe. And to get away from the fish and shellfish theme, diced poached sweetbreads and mushrooms, or a combination of minced veal and fresh pork, moistened with dry white wine, are well worth trying.

The first revelation of just how delicious a French fruit flan could be – and how different from the Anglo-Saxon concept of fruit pie – was the fresh strawberry tart served to me in a small Left Bank restaurant when I first lived in Paris. The pastry was a cinnamon-flavoured *pâte sablée* rich with butter and as sandy in texture as its name leads one to suppose. Chilled ripe strawberries were packed cheek to cheek in this delicate pastry shell. And that was all – no glaze, no cream, no other flavouring was added to mar its perfection. A sauce made of chilled puréed fresh raspberries was served with it. A fruit tart at its very possible best.

Another favourite way with fruit tarts is the French manner of serving sliced apples, pears, plums, strawberries, blueberries, peaches or raspberries in a pastry case, on a fragile Kirsch-flavoured *crème pâtissiére*, the fruits themselves topped with a golden apricot glaze. I give you the recipe for this cream topped with glazed slices of fresh peaches on page 786. Use this same recipe as summer fruits come into season with the fruit of your choice as star performer.

Making Perfect Pastry

Pastry-making requires a certain amount of practice before you can acquire a *tour de main*. So do not be discouraged if you are not successful with your first tart or pie. If you are a new hand at pastry-making, I suggest you begin with one of the simpler kinds of pastry, especially those in which the fat is well mixed with flour before the rolling begins – shortcrust and suet crust. Then you can try the more difficult kinds later.

Basic Ingredients

Butter or fat: Several different kinds of fat may be used for pastry-making: butter, lard, dripping, clarified fat, margarine and various kinds of vegetables fat now on the market. I like to use butter for all the finer kinds of pastry, and fresh unsalted butter for puff pastry. When the butter is too soft, it should be put in the refrigerator for a short time before using.

Lard or margarine may be used (or a mixture of butter and lard) for more inexpensive pastry. If dripping is used, it must be carefully clarified and all trace of gravy or meat juices removed.

Suet is used principally for making boiled or steamed pastry. The fat taken from the kidney is the best, and beef suet is generally preferable to mutton.

Flour: I use plain flour for most pastries, but for the finer kinds such as puff pastry, choux pastry, etc., I find it best to use cake flour or a combination of three parts flour to one part cornflour. All flour should be very dry and for pastry-making it should be sieved. This not only ensures that it is free from lumps but also makes the pastry lighter.

Baking powder: When the supply of butter or fat is limited, baking powder helps to give lightness to the plainer kinds of pastry. When it is used, the pastry should be baked as soon as possible after liquids are added.

Liquids: Water (and sometimes lemon juice) is usually the only liquid required for mixing pastry. It must be as cold as possible, and in hot weather a piece of ice should be added to it. The exact amount of water to use is not always given in pastry recipes as so much depends on the consistency of the fat used and also on the consistency of the flour. The finer the flour, the more liquid it will require. For richer pastries, add a beaten egg or the yolk of an egg to the amount of water used.

To Prepare Pastry

See that all utensils used – pastry board, basin, rolling pin, etc. – are clean and cool. The board or marble should be smooth and perfectly flat. Use it for pastry-making only.

Clean, dry hands are a must for pastry-making. In the summer, when hands are apt to be warm, mix the pastry as much as possible with a knife or a pastry cutter to keep it cool.

Make pastry in as cool a place as possible; the colder it is kept during the making, the lighter it will be. In hot weather, pastry should be wrapped in foil or a damp cloth and allow to 'repose' in the refrigerator for at least ½ hour before it is used.

Liquids should be added to flour as quickly and lightly as possible. Some cooks do this on the board or slab by making a well in the centre of the flour and pouring the water into the centre as they mix. I find that mixing it in a large mixing bowl is much easier.

When handling pastry, never rub little pieces off the fingers on to the pastry or the pastry board as these tend to form hard lumps when cooked.

To Roll Out Dough

Sprinkle the pastry board with flour; lay the dough on it and work lightly with the hands until free from cracks. Flour a rolling pin; press down the pastry and then with sharp quick strokes roll pastry on one side only to the thickness required.

Roll pastry lightly and try to press equally with both hands. When rolling flaky or puff pastry, always roll away from you, using short quick strokes and lifting the rolling pin between each stroke.

Never allow pastry to stick to the board, but lift occasionally on the rolling pin and dust some flour underneath. If anything has stuck to the board, scrape it off carefully with a knife before beginning to roll again.

Always sprinkle flour over board and pastry through a flour sifter to make it finer and lighter, using as little flour as possible for this, as too much tends to make the pastry hard.

If the rolling pin sticks to the pastry, dust with a little flour and brush it off again lightly with a small brush kept for this purpose.

To Bake Pastry

A fairly hot oven is required for pastry, for if it is not hot enough the butter will melt and run out before the starch grains in the flour have had time to burst and absorb it. If the oven is too hot, however, the pastry will burn before it has risen properly. For puff pastry, the thermometer should register about 350°F/180°C/GM4 to begin with, and when the pastry is well risen the heat may be reduced to about 325°F/170°C/GM3. For meat pies, about 300°F/150°C/GM2 will be hot enough, and for the plainer kinds of pastry the temperature may be a little lower still.

Pastry should never be baked in an oven in which meat is being roasted, or with any other dish that generates steam, as moist heat is apt to destroy its crispness. When baking pastry, open and close the door as gently as possible and never more often than is absolutely necessary.

If pastry becomes too brown before it has cooked sufficiently, cover it over with a piece of aluminium foil or a double sheet of paper that has been lightly sprinkled with water. If the pastry is not to be used at once when taken from the oven, allow it to cool slowly in the warm kitchen. Light pastry tends to become heavy when cooled too quickly.

TO BAKE 'BLIND'
Line a pie tin with pastry, fluting the edges; chill. Prick bottom with a fork; cover bottom of pastry with a piece of waxed paper or aluminium foil; cover with dried beans; and bake in a hot oven (450°F/230°C/GM8) for about 15 minutes, just long enough to set the crust without browning it. Remove beans and paper or foil and allow to cool. Fill with desired filling and bake in a moderate

oven (375°F/190°C/GM5) until done. The beans can be reserved in a storage jar and used again.

TO BAKE PASTRY SHELL ONLY
Bake 'blind' as above for 15 minutes; remove beans and foil; lower heat to 375°F/190°C/GM5 and bake for 10 to 15 minutes. If crust becomes too brown at edges, cover rim with a little crumpled foil.

To Glaze Pastry

Pastry is generally glazed before being put in the oven, except when it has to be baked for a long time.

When a rich deep colour is wanted on a meat pie, brush over the pastry with egg yolk mixed with a very little water. For a lighter colour, use the egg (yolks and whites together), or egg and milk, or, for the plainer kinds of pastry, milk alone.

Sweet pastry is generally glazed with lightly beaten white of egg and sugar, with milk, or with water and sugar.

SHORTCRUST PASTRY
FOR SAVOURY TARTS AND PIES

8 oz (225 g) plain flour
1 teaspoon (5 ml) castor sugar
Squeeze of lemon juice
Pinch of salt
4 oz (100 g) butter, diced
Iced water

Sift flour and sugar into a mixing bowl. Add lemon juice, salt and butter; cover well with the flour and rub together lightly with the tips of the fingers until the mixture resembles fine breadcrumbs. While rubbing, keep lifting the flour well up in the bowl, so that air may mix with it and the butter is not made too soft.

When pastry is thoroughly mixed, make a well in the centre and add cold water very gradually, mixing with one hand or a knife. Add very little water – 1 to 3 tablespoons (15 to 45 ml) – or pastry will be tough instead of short.

Roll out and bake as directed on page 753.

RICH BISCUIT CRUST

A richer pastry can be made in the same way, using 5 or 6 oz (150–175 g) of butter and adding the yolk of 1 egg beaten with a little water for mixing.

Roll out and bake as directed on page 753.

SHORTCRUST PASTRY FOR DESSERT TARTS AND PIES

8 oz (225 g) plain flour
1 tablespoon (15 ml) icing sugar
Squeeze of lemon juice
Pinch of salt
4 oz (100 g) butter, diced
½ teaspoon (2.5 ml) vanilla extract
Iced water

Sift flour and sugar into a mixing bowl. Add lemon juice, salt, butter and vanilla extract; cover well with the flour, and rub together lightly with the tips of the fingers until the mixture resembles fine breadcrumbs. While rubbing, keep lifting the flour well up in the bowl, so that air may mix with it and the butter is not made too soft.

When pastry is mixed, make a well in the centre and add cold water very gradually, mixing with one hand or a knife. Add very little water – 1 to 3 tablespoons (15 to 45 ml) – or pastry will be tough instead of short.

Roll out and bake as directed on page 753.

RICH BISCUIT CRUST

A richer pastry for dessert tarts and pies can be made in the same way, using 5 to 6 oz (150 to 175 g) of butter and adding the yolk of 1 egg beaten with a little water for mixing.

Roll out and bake as directed on page 753.

CREAM SHORTCRUST PASTRY

8 oz (225 g) plain flour
1 tablespoon (15 ml) castor sugar
Pinch of salt
4 tablespoons (60 ml) butter
About ¼ pint (150 ml) double cream

Sift flour, sugar and salt into a mixing bowl. Add butter; cover well with the flour and rub together lightly with the tips of the fingers. While rubbing, keep lifting the flour well up in the bowl, so that air may mix with it.

Add cream gradually, mixing with one hand or a knife.

Roll out and bake as directed on page 753.

RICH SHORTCRUST PASTRY

8 oz (225 g) plain flour
½ level teaspoon (2.5 ml) salt
1 level tablespoon (15 ml) icing sugar
5 oz (150 g) butter
1 teaspoon (5 ml) lemon juice
1 egg yolk, beaten with 1 tablespoon (15 ml) water
1–2 tablespoons (15–30 ml) water

Sift flour, salt and icing sugar into a mixing bowl. Dice slightly softened butter and add to flour mixture. Using pastry blender or two knives scissor fashion, cut in butter until blend begins to crumble. Then rub in butter with the tips of fingers until mixture resembles fine breadcrumbs. Do this very gently and lightly or the mixture will become greasy and heavy. Add lemon juice and beaten egg yolk and water mixture gradually, all the time tossing gently from bottom of bowl with a fork; add water until crumbs adhere when pressed.

Shape dough lightly into 2 flattened rounds, wrap in plastic and put in refrigerator for at least an hour, or overnight, to ripen and become firm.

If chilled dough is too firm to handle, leave it at room temperature until it softens slightly.

Pat one ball of dough on a floured pastry board with a lightly floured rolling pin to flatten and shape it. Then roll from the centre to edges until pastry is ⅛ inch (3 mm) thick and 2 inches (5 cm) larger in diameter than pie tin. Fold in half and lift into position over tin. To prevent shrinkage, press pastry into pan without stretching. Use in the following ways:

Two-crust pie: Fill with fruit, moisten edge, cover with top crust and press to seal. Trim off excess pastry; press edge with fork or crimp with fingers. Cut gashes in top for the steam to escape. Bake in a moderately hot oven (400°F/200°C/GM6) until crust is brown and fruit is tender – about 30 minutes.

One-crust pie: Using scissors, trim pastry ½ inch (12 mm) beyond edge of pan. Fold edge under and crimp with fingers. Fill with uncooked mixture; bake as directed on page 753.

Pastry shell: Line pan with pastry and prick bottom and sides well with fork. Bake 'blind' in a hot oven (450°F/230°C/GM8) for 15 minutes. Remove beans and foil; lower heat to 375°F/190°C/GM5, and bake for 10 to 15 minutes longer.

ROUGH PUFF PASTRY

8 oz (225 g) plain flour
Pinch of salt
Squeeze of lemon juice
4 oz (100 g) chilled butter
Iced water

Sieve flour and salt into a clean, dry bowl, and add lemon juice. Put the butter in the bowl, cover it over well with the flour, and then break it into pieces the size of a hazelnut. Have some iced water in a jug ready for mixing, and make a well in the centre of the flour and butter. Mix very lightly with the right hand or with a knife, pouring the water in gradually with the left hand until you have added enough to bind the mixture together.

Flour the board or marble slab and turn the dough out on it. Flour the rolling pin and roll the dough out carefully into a strip about 10 inches (25 cms) in length and 6 to 7 inches (15 to 18 cms) wide. Lift occasionally while rolling, and dust some flour underneath the pastry to prevent it from sticking.

Roll the pastry on the one side only, and roll it away from you in short quick strokes. When rolled to the required length, fold it in three, and press down lightly with the rolling pin.

Turn the pastry half round, bringing the joins to the right-hand side, and roll again in the same way as before.

Fold again in three; half turn and roll again, repeating this until the pastry has had three rolls and three folds. The fourth time you roll the pastry out, roll to the size and shape you require.

If pastry becomes too soft while rolling, return it to the refrigerator before completing the process. It is improved by being wrapped in waxed paper and kept for a few hours before using. It will keep for several days if kept like this in the refrigerator.

A richer pastry can be made by using 6 oz (175 g) butter (instead of 4 oz/100 g) to 8 oz (225 g) flour. A well-beaten egg may be used for mixing, along with a little water.

CORNFLOUR SHORTCRUST PASTRY

3 oz (75 g) cornflour
4 oz (100 g) plain flour
1–2 oz (25–50 g) castor sugar
½ teaspoon (2.5 ml) baking powder
Squeeze of lemon juice
4 oz (100 g) butter
1 egg yolk, mixed with a little milk or water

Sift cornflour, flour, sugar and baking powder into a mixing bowl. Add lemon juice and butter; cover well with the flour and rub ingredients together lightly with the tips of the fingers until the mixture resembles fine breadcrumbs. While rubbing, keep lifting the flour well up in the bowl, so that air may mix with it and the butter is not made too soft.

When pastry is mixed, make a well in the centre and gradually add egg yolk mixed with a little milk or water, mixing all the time with one hand or a knife.

Roll out and bake as directed on page 753.

FLAKY PASTRY

10 oz (275 g) plain flour
Generous pinch of salt
Squeeze of lemon juice
7 oz (200 g) butter
Iced water

Sieve flour and salt into a clean, dry bowl and add lemon juice. Divide butter into 4 equal parts. Take one of these pieces and rub it into the flour with the tips of the fingers until mixture is quite free from lumps. Then add just enough iced water to form dough into one lump. Mix with hands as lightly as possible and turn out on to a floured board. Knead lightly until free from cracks, and then roll out into a long narrow strip, rather less than ¼ inch (6 mm) in thickness. Take one of the remaining portions of butter, and with the point of a knife put it in even rows of small pieces all over the pastry, leaving an inch (25 mm) margin without butter round the edges. (If butter is too hard, work it on a plate with a knife before commencing.)

Now flour the surface lightly, and fold the pastry exactly in three. Turn the pastry half round, bringing the joins to the right-hand side, and press the folds down sharply with the rolling pin so as to enclose some air.

Roll the pastry out again into a long narrow strip, and proceed as before until the two remaining portions of butter have been used. If the butter becomes too soft during the rolling, refrigerate the pastry for a short time before completing the process.

The last time, roll the pastry out to the desired thickness, and if it requires widening, turn it across the board and roll across. Never roll in a slanting direction, or the lightness of the pastry will suffer. This pastry is not quite as rich as puff pastry. It may be kept for several days in the refrigerator if wrapped in waxed paper or in a damp cloth.

FINGERTIP PASTRY

SWEET
8 oz (225 g) plain flour
Pinch of salt
2 tablespoons (30 ml) icing sugar
5 oz (150 g) softened butter
1 egg yolk
4 tablespoons (60 ml) cold water

SAVOURY
8 oz (225 g) plain flour
Generous pinch of salt
1 level tablespoon (15 ml) icing sugar
5 oz (150 g) softened butter
1 egg yolk
4 tablespoons (60 ml) cold water

Sieve flour, salt and sugar into a mixing bowl. Rub in the butter with the tips of fingers until mixture resembles fine breadcrumbs. Do this very gently and lightly, or mixture will become greasy and heavy. Beat egg yolk; add cold water; sprinkle over dough and work in lightly with your fingers. Shape moist dough lightly into a flattened round; wrap in plastic and leave in refrigerator for at least 1 hour to ripen.

If chilled dough is too firm for handling, allow to stand at room temperature until it softens slightly. Then turn it on to a floured board and roll out as required. Press into pie tin (or individual tins) with your fingers and prick with a fork.

Bake 'blind' in a preheated oven (450°F/230°C/GM8) for 15 minutes; lower heat to 350°F/180°C/GM4 and bake for 30 minutes. If crust becomes too brown at edges, cover with a little crumpled foil.

PUFF PASTRY (PÂTE FEUILLETÉE)

8 oz (225 g) plain flour
Generous pinch of salt
Squeeze of lemon juice
8 oz (225 g) butter, diced
Iced water

Sieve flour and salt into a clean, dry mixing bowl, and add lemon juice and a quarter of the diced butter. Rub together lightly with the tips of your fingers until the mixture resembles fine bread-crumbs. Then mix with just enough iced water to make a rather stiff dough. Turn this out on to a floured board and work it well with the hands until it no longer sticks to the fingers and is perfectly smooth. Then roll it rather thinly into a square or round shape. The remaining butter to be used should be as nearly as possible of the same consistency as the dough, so work it with your hands into a neat thin cake and place it in the centre of the dough. Fold dough up rather loosely, and flatten the folds with a rolling pin. Then roll the pastry out into a long narrow strip, being careful not to allow the butter to break through.

Fold dough exactly in three; press down the folds and lay the pastry aside in a cool place for at least 15 minutes. This is called giving the pastry one 'turn'; seven of these operations are usually required for puff pastry.

The next time the pastry is rolled, place it with the joins at your right-hand side and the open ends towards you. Give it two turns this time, and again put it in the refrigerator for at least 15 minutes.

Repeat this until the pastry has had seven rolls in all, one roll or turn the first time, and after that two each time with an interval between.

The object of cooling the pastry between rolls is to keep the butter and flour in the distinct and separate layers (in which the rolling and folding has arranged them), and on which the lightness of your pastry depends.

When rolling, keep the pressure of your hands on the rolling pin as even as possible.

After you have given the pastry its last roll, put it in the refrigerator for ½ hour before using it, then roll to the required thickness. This pastry will keep for several days in the refrigerator if wrapped in a piece of waxed paper or in a damp cloth.

VOL-AU-VENT CASE

1 recipe Puff Pastry (page 760)
Butter
Water
Beaten egg

Cut a circle 8 inches (20 cms) in diameter out of a sheet of cardboard to use as a pattern for making a *vol-au-vent* case of puff pastry.

Place the pattern on puff pastry which you have rolled out ¼ inch (6 mm) thick. Cut round the pattern with a sharp, pointed knife. Place the circle of dough on a buttered baking tin. Brush the surface with cold water; lay a second circle of puff pastry (made in the same way) on it and, with the point of your knife slanting inwards, incise a circular cut in the top circle of pastry about 1 inch (25 mm) from the outside edge. Then, again with the point of the knife, press the inner top disc away from the incision to prevent pastry edges from closing up again during cooking.

Brush the surface with beaten egg, without touching the sides, and bake in a hot oven (450°F/230°C/GM8) for 5 to 10 minutes. Reduce heat to 375°F/190°C/GM5 and bake for 25 to 30 minutes more. Remove from oven; remove cover and dig out greasy centre without damaging the case. Use baked *vol-au-vent* case immediately or within 6 hours for best results.

INDIVIDUAL VOL-AU-VENT CASES

1 recipe Puff Pastry (page 760)
Butter
Water
Beaten egg

Cut a circle 2½ inches (7 cms) in diameter out of cardboard to use as a pattern, and proceed as above, making 1 *vol-au-vent* shell for each serving.

Baked *vol-au-vents* will keep for several days in a tightly closed container.

CHOUX PASTRY (PÂTE À CHOUX)

¼ pint (150 ml) water
2 tablespoons (30 ml) butter
1 tablespoon (15 ml) sugar
Pinch of salt
4 oz (100 g) plain or cake flour, sifted
3–4 eggs
A few drops of vanilla extract

Combine water, butter, sugar and salt in a small saucepan, and bring to a boil. Remove saucepan from heat and add sifted flour. Return pan to the heat and stir mixture with a wooden spoon until the dough is compact and dry, and leaves the sides of the pan. This mixture (called a *panada* in culinary terms) should not be over-cooked or it will become oily.

Remove the saucepan from the heat and add the eggs one at a time, beating each one in very thoroughly until the dough is of a good consistency – not too stiff or it will not rise properly, not too soft or it will spread and lose its shape. Add vanilla extract, to taste. Allow to cool before using.

SUET CRUST OR PASTRY

8 oz (225 g) plain flour
Pinch of salt
¼ level teaspoon (1.25 ml) baking powder
4 oz (100 g) suet
Cold water or milk

Sift flour, salt and baking powder into a clean, dry mixing bowl. Shred the suet very finely with a sharp knife. Place on a chopping board and sprinkle with some of the flour; then chop it very finely, using enough flour to prevent it sticking to the board and knife. The more finely the suet is chopped, the better the pastry will be. When ready, mix it thoroughly with remaining flour in the bowl, rubbing all the ingredients together lightly with the tips of your fingers.

When thoroughly mixed, make a well in the centre of the dry ingredients and add cold water or milk very gradually, mixing the dough with your hand or with a knife. Form into a smooth soft dough, and turn out on to a floured board, leaving the bowl quite clean. Work lightly with the hands until free from cracks, then flour a rolling pin and roll out to the thickness required. Roll on one side only, taking care that the pastry does not stick to the board or rolling pin. Lift it gently at the sides from time to time, dusting a little flour under and over as required. Use no more flour than is necessary for this purpose, as too much tends to make the pastry hard.

Use suet pastry for fruit and meat puddings, roly-poly pudding, dumplings, etc.

ARTICHOKE TARTS VINAIGRETTE

4 cooked or canned artichoke hearts
4 hard-boiled eggs
1 thick slice cooked ham, diced
½ cucumber, peeled, seeded and diced
4 stalks celery, sliced
Well-flavoured Vinaigrette dressing
6 individual baked pastry shells
Finely chopped fresh herbs
Mayonnaise (page 120)

Dice artichoke hearts and hard-boiled eggs into large pieces and combine in a bowl with diced cooked ham, cucumber and celery. Moisten liberally with a well-flavoured Vinaigrette dressing (3 parts olive oil, 1 part wine vinegar, dry mustard, finely chopped garlic, salt and freshly ground black pepper).

When ready to serve; fill baked pastry shells with artichoke and egg. Sprinkle each tart with finely chopped fresh herbs and top with a dab of stiff mayonnaise. Serves 6.

CHINESE PASTRY FOR SHAO M'AI, WON TON AND SPRING ROLLS

7 oz (200 g) sifted plain flour
½ level teaspoon (2.5 ml) salt
8 tablespoons (120 ml) warm water
Cornflour

Sift flour and salt into a mixing bowl, make a well in the centre, and pour warm water into it. Mix with a fork or spoon until well blended. Knead well until dough is soft and pliable. Then cover dough with a damp cloth and allow to stand for 30 minutes.

Sprinkle cornflour on a pastry board and roll out pastry very thinly. Cut into 3-inch (8 cm) squares with a knife or rotary pastry wheel, using a square or rectangle as a guide. For Chinese egg rolls: cut into 6-inch (15 cm) squares.

SAVOYARD LEEK AND SAUSAGE FLAN

Pastry for 8- or 9-inch (20 or 23 cm) pie shell
1 medium-sized onion
1 oz (25 g) cooked ham
4 button mushrooms
Salt and freshly ground black pepper
Butter
1 tablespoon (15 ml) flour
8 fluid oz (225 ml) milk
Freshly grated nutmeg
1 egg yolk
2 tablespoons (30 ml) double cream
4 small pork sausages
Olive oil
4 small poached leeks
2 oz (50 g) grated Parmesan

Chop onion, ham and mushrooms finely. Place this mixture in a saucepan with salt, freshly ground black pepper and 2 tablespoons (30 ml) butter. Sauté gently until the onion is transparent. Set aside. Combine flour and 2 tablespoons (30 ml) butter in the top of a double saucepan. Cook for 10 minutes, stirring from time to time, without letting flour take on colour. Pour in cold milk and cook, stirring from time to time, until sauce becomes smooth and thick. Season to taste with salt, freshly ground black pepper and a little grated nutmeg. Remove from the heat and stir in the egg yolk with a wire whisk. Add cream. Sauté the sausages in a little butter and olive oil until golden, but not cooked through.

Place onion, ham and mushroom mixture in the bottom of a pie shell which you have baked 'blind' for 10 minutes in a hot oven (450°F/230°C/GM8). Place sausages and leeks alternately in spoke fashion on this mixture; pour over the sauce and sprinkle with grated cheese. Return to a slow oven (325°F/170°C/GM3) and bake for 30 to 40 minutes, or until custard is firm and golden brown. Serve very hot. Serves 4 to 6.

INDIVIDUAL MUSHROOM AND BACON TARTS

6 individual pastry cases
3 slices bacon
Butter
3 tablespoons (45 ml) finely chopped onion
8 oz (225 g) mushrooms, thinly sliced
3 tablespoons (45 ml) finely chopped parsley
3 eggs, lightly beaten
6 fluid oz (175 ml) cream
Salt and freshly ground black pepper

Line individual tart tins with pastry, fluting the edges; chill. Prick bottoms with a fork and bake 'blind' in a hot oven (450°F/230°C/GM8) for about 15 minutes, just long enough to set the crusts without browning. Allow to cool.

Sauté bacon in butter until crisp. Sauté chopped onion in resulting fat until transparent, and drain. Crumble bacon and combine with thinly sliced mushrooms, sautéed onion and chopped parsley. Spoon mixture into tart cases.

Beat eggs lightly; add cream, and season to taste with salt and freshly ground black pepper. Pour custard mixture into tart shells and bake the tarts in a slow oven (325°F/170°C/GM3) for 30 to 40 minutes, or until the crusts are brown and the custard has set.

FRENCH ONION TART

PÂTÉ BRISÉE PASTRY
8 oz (225 g) plain flour
Generous pinch of salt
1 level tablespoon (15 ml) icing sugar
5 oz (150 g) softened butter

ONION FILLING
2 Spanish onions
5 oz (150 g) butter
1 tablespoon (15 ml) flour
3 eggs
¼ pint (150 ml) cream
¼ pint (150 ml) milk
Salt and freshly ground black pepper
Freshly grated nutmeg

PÂTÉ BRISÉE
Sieve flour, salt and sugar into a mixing bowl. Rub in the softened butter with the tips of the fingers until the mixture resembles fine breadcrumbs. Do this very gently and lightly or the mixture will become greasy and heavy. Roll into a ball and chill for ½ hour or more.

When ready to use, turn on to a floured board and knead or pat pastry lightly into a round. Place in a 10-inch (26 cm) pie tin and press out with fingertips to line pie tin (no rolling is necessary). Finish edge of pastry as usual and prick bottom with a fork to avoid air bubbles while cooking. Bake in a hot oven (450°F/230°C/GM8) for 10 minutes. Cool slightly and fill with Onion Filling.

ONION FILLING
Chop onions finely; sauté in butter until transparent. Cool; add flour, eggs, cream and milk, and mix well. Season to taste with salt, freshly ground black pepper and freshly grated nutmeg.

Pour mixture into pie shell and cook in a slow oven (325°F/170°C/GM3) for 30 to 40 minutes. Serve very hot. Serves 4 to 6.

PRAWN AND LOBSTER QUICHE

PASTRY
8 oz (225 g) plain flour
1 level tablespoon (15 ml) icing sugar
Generous pinch of salt
5 oz (175 g) softened butter, diced
1–2 tablespoons (15–30 ml) iced water

QUICHE FILLING
¼ pint (150 ml) double cream
¼ pint (150 ml) milk
¼ pint (150 ml) canned clam juice
4 eggs
1 can lobster (7 oz/200 g)
4 oz (100 g) prawns

PASTRY

Sieve flour, sugar and salt into a mixing bowl. Rub in softened butter a little bit at a time with the tips of the fingers until mixture resembles fine breadcrumbs. Do this very gently and lightly or mixture will become greasy and heavy. Add just enough iced water to make a good dough. Shape dough lightly into a flattened round, wrap in foil or plastic and put in refrigerator for at least 1 hour to ripen and become firm. If chilled dough is too firm for handling, leave at room temperature until it softens slightly. Then turn out on to a flavoured board and roll out in usual manner; place in a 9-inch (23 cm) pie tin and press out with fingertips.

Prick with a fork; cover with a piece of foil; fill with dried beans and bake 'blind' in a preheated oven (450°F/230°C/GM8) for 15 minutes. Remove beans and foil. Allow pastry shell to cool.

QUICHE FILLING

Beat cream, milk, clam juice and eggs with a whisk. Place chunks of lobster and prawns on the baked pastry shell. Pour the beaten egg mixture over the lobster and prawns. Bake in a slow oven (325°F/170°C/GM3) for 30 to 40 minutes, or until the custard is set and golden brown. Serves 6 to 8.

PROVENÇAL TOMATO AND ONION TART

1 recipe Savoury Fingertip Pastry (page 760)
1 egg yolk, beaten
4 tablespoons (60 ml) olive oil
6 large ripe tomatoes
2 tablespoons (30 ml) tomato concentrate
Freshly ground black pepper
3 Spanish onions
2 tablespoons (30 ml) butter
Freshly chopped rosemary
2 tablespoons (30 ml) finely grated Parmesan
1 can anchovy fillets
Black olives
Olive oil

Line a pie tin with pastry, fluting the edges; chill. Brush with a little lightly beaten egg yolk and bake in a hot oven (450°F/230°C/GM8) just long enough to set the crust without browning it. Allow to cool.

Heat olive oil in a pan; add ripe tomatoes, peeled, seeded and chopped, tomato concentrate, and freshly ground black pepper, to taste. Cook over a low heat until excess moisture is cooked away, mashing occasionally with a wooden spoon to form a purée. Slice Spanish onions and simmer in butter with a little freshly chopped rosemary until soft and golden, but not brown.

Sprinkle bottom of pastry case with freshly grated Parmesan; add onions and then cover with the tomato purée. Arrange anchovies in a lattice-work on top and place a black olive in the centre of each square. Brush olives and anchovies lightly with oil, and bake in a slow oven (350°F/180°C/GM4) for about 30 minutes.

SMOKED SALMON QUICHE

4 eggs
¼ pint (150 ml) double cream
¼ pint (150 ml) milk
¼ pint (150 ml) canned clam juice
Salt, freshly ground black pepper and
grated nutmeg
8 individual pastry cases (about 4 inches/10 cms
in diameter)
Thinly sliced smoked salmon
Butter

Whisk eggs together with cream, milk and canned clam juice. When well mixed, season to taste with salt, freshly ground black pepper and grated nutmeg.

Prick bottoms of pastry cases with a fork and bake 'blind' in a hot oven (450°F/230°C/GM8) for about 15 minutes, just long enough to set the crusts without browning them. Allow to cool.

Fill pastry cases with egg mixture; cover with thin slices of smoked salmon; and dot with butter. Bake in a slow oven (325°F/170°C/GM3) for 30 to 40 minutes, and serve immediately. Serves 8.

KOULIBIAK AU POISSON 'L'AUBERGE D'ARMAILLE'

1¾ lb (775 g) salmon
Butter
4 oz (100 g) button mushrooms, finely chopped
½ Spanish onion, finely chopped
4 tablespoons (60 ml) butter
1 recipe Flaky Pastry (page 759)
8 oz (225 g) cooked rice
2 tablespoons (30 ml) finely chopped parsley
4 hard-boiled eggs, sliced
Salt and freshly ground black pepper

Cut salmon into thin slices and sauté in butter until tender. Cool. Sauté finely chopped mushrooms and onion in 4 tablespoons (60 ml) butter until onion is transparent. Cool.

Roll pastry into 2 rectangles about 6 by 8 inches (15 by 20 cms).

Combine rice with mushroom and onion mixture; sprinkle with finely chopped parsley and gently fold in salmon and sliced hard-boiled egg. Place this mixture on one layer of pastry; season to taste with salt and freshly ground black pepper; and top with remaining pastry, pinching pastry well together. Decorate with pastry leaves and bake in a moderate oven (375°F/190°C/GM5) for 30 minutes. Serve hot. Serves 6 to 8.

CHINESE SPRING ROLLS

8 oz (225 g) raw pork, finely chopped
4 oz (100 g) shrimp, finely chopped
4 tablespoons (60 ml) finely chopped water chestnuts
8 tablespoons (120 ml) bean sprouts
4–6 Chinese mushrooms, soaked and
finely chopped
1 slice fresh ginger root finely chopped
2 spring onions, finely chopped
Lard or peanut oil
1–2 tablespoons (15–30 ml) *sake* or dry sherry
1–2 tablespoons (15–30 ml) soy sauce
Freshly ground black pepper
1 recipe Chinese Pastry (page 765)

Combine first 7 ingredients and sauté in lard or peanut oil until golden. Then stir in *sake* (or dry sherry), soy sauce and freshly ground black pepper, to taste.

Roll out Chinese pastry dough thinly and cut into 6-inch (15 cm) squares. Place about 2 tablespoons (30 ml) of filling in the centre of square, cover filling with one corner of dough and roll up to the middle. Turn the two opposite ends (which you have moistened with water) on to the roll to seal the ends. Then continue rolling up to the farthest tip. Moisten tip to seal. Continue until all filling is used up.

Heat cooking oil to frying temperature and lower (ends first to keep them from unrolling) as many rolls as possible without crowding. Fry until golden brown. Drain and serve immediately. If rolls are not to be served immediately, they can be reheated in a hot oven.

Meat, Poultry and Game Pies

Almost any kind of meat can be used to make a rich, full-flavoured pie – beef, mutton, veal, pork, rabbit, poultry or game – used separately or with two or three different kinds combined to make one pie. Hard-boiled eggs, mushrooms, oysters, diced bacon, chopped onions, sliced potatoes and forcemeat balls or sausage meat are often added to give flavour and extra contrast to the pie fillings.

Always cut solid meat into bite-sized cubes or in thin slices which you then roll up before putting in the pie. Game and poultry should be jointed, with the larger bones removed. If you plan to serve your pie cold, season it more generously than if you are going to serve it hot. Grated lemon rind and finely chopped herbs and onions are good flavour additives.

Pack meat rather loosely in the pie dish and pile it high in the centre like a dome. I sometimes put an egg cup or pie funnel in the centre of the dish to help hold up the crust. A little liquid – water, wine, stock or gravy – should then be poured in. If any bones and trimmings have been taken from the meat, make them into a simple stock while the pie is cooking, and then use this stock for filling up the pie just before serving. A really good gravy is very important to a pie. When it is to be served cold, this gravy should be a jelly. So add a little gelatine to the hot stock.

Tender meats are best for making pies; but if a cheaper and less tender cut is being used, be sure to cook it partially before you put on the crust by covering the meat-filled pie dish with another dish or close-fitting lid, and placing it in a slow oven (325°F/170°C/GM3) for 1 hour or longer. Or, if you prefer, meat and aromatics may be put into a large closed container and steamed for an hour or so.

In every case, the contents of the pie must be quite cold before the pastry cover is put on.

To Cover a Meat Pie

Rough puff or flaky pastry will be required to cover the average pie.

Roll the pastry out into an oblong shape about ¼ inch (6 mm) thick. From this cut a strip about 1 to 1½ inches (25–38 mm) in width, or a little wider than the rim of the pie dish. Wet the rim of the dish with cold water and place the strip around the rim, wetting one of the edges to make them stick at the join. Do not overlap the pieces, or one part of the edge will be thicker than the rest. Brush the strip of pastry with cold water. Cut out a piece of pastry large enough to cover the top of the pie dish and place it over the pie, making sure that the pastry does not stretch or drag over the dish. With a sharp knife cut off any pieces of pastry hanging round the dish; then hold the dish up with one hand, and with the other hand trim neatly round the edges of the pie, inclining the knife so that the edges of the crust will slope outwards.

Flour the first finger of the left hand and keep pressing the back of it down on the rim of the pastry, while with the blunt edge of a floured knife you press the edges evenly all round to make them look like the leaves of a book.

To scallop edges: Draw the blunt edge of a knife across the rim of the pie at ½-inch (12 mm) intervals, bringing the knife up and in, while with the thumb of your left hand you press the pastry down just in front of the knife. Make a hole in the centre of the pie with a knife, and brush over with beaten egg, omitting the outer edge. Roll out the pastry trimmings and use them to decorate the pie.

To make leaves: Cut the pastry into strips about 1½ inches (38 mm) wide; trim them into leaf-shaped pieces, marking each one with the blunt edge of a knife to imitate the veins of a leaf. Make 7 to 9 of these leaves for a centre ornament. Arrange them so that they radiate from the hole in the centre of the pie towards the edge of the dish. One or two roses or tassels may also be added.

To make a rose: Take a small piece of pastry about the size of a hazelnut and work into it as much dry flour as it will take up. Roll it out as thin as a sheet of paper and cut it into a square. Fold in four to make a smaller square. Lay this square, cut sides up, over the point of the first finger, drawing the edges down around the finger. Cut a cross in the centre of the pastry; remove it from the finger and squeeze the edges together. Open out the petals in the centre to form a rose.

To make a tassel: Roll out a small piece of pastry in a strip about 1 inch (25 mm) wide. Cut this strip across like a fringe to about two-thirds of its width and then roll up lengthwise, pinching the base together to open the fringe of the tassel.

When the pie is decorated, brush it over with a little beaten egg or with egg and milk before baking.

To Bake and Serve the Pie

Place the pie on a baking tin and put it in a hot oven (450°F/230°C/GM8) for 30 minutes, or until the crust has risen and set and is beginning to brown. Then reduce heat to 325°F/170°C/GM3 so that the meat may cook more slowly. As soon as the crust is dark enough, it should be covered with a double piece of paper or foil until the pie is cooked. Test the meat by running a skewer in through the hole in the top. As soon as the pie is done, remove it from the oven. Heat some good stock or gravy and pour it in the hole through a funnel or out of a small cream jug. Wipe the dish with a wet cloth before serving.

BEEFSTEAK AND KIDNEY PIE

2 lb (900 g) thick beef steak, cut into large bite-sized pieces
12 oz (350 g) calf's kidney
Salted water
2 tablespoons (30 ml) plain flour
1 level teaspoon (5 ml) salt
¾ level teaspoon (3.75 ml) freshly ground black pepper
4 tablespoons (60 ml) butter or suet
4 shallots, finely chopped
½ pint (300 ml) rich beef stock
1 bay leaf
1 teaspoon (5 ml) chopped parsley
A pinch each powdered cloves and marjoram
Flaky pastry (page 759)

Clean kidney, split, remove fat and large tubes, and soak in salted water for 1 hour. Dry kidney and cut into ¼-inch (6 mm) slices.

Mix flour, salt and ½ level teaspoon (2.5 ml) freshly ground black pepper, and roll beef and kidney in this mixture.

Melt butter or suet in a thick-bottomed saucepan or iron casserole and sauté finely chopped shallots until golden. When shallots have taken on a little colour, add the beef and kidneys, and brown them thoroughly, stirring almost constantly. Moisten with beef stock and add remaining freshly ground black pepper, bay leaf, chopped parsley, powdered cloves and marjoram; stir; cover and simmer over a low flame for 1 to 1¼ hours, or until meat is tender. If liquid is too thin, thicken with a little flour mixed to a smooth paste with water.

Grease a deep baking dish, place a pie funnel in centre of dish, add meats and liquid, and allow to cool. In the meantime, make flaky pastry crust and place over meat, moistening and pinching edges to dish. Make vents in the pastry to allow steam to escape and bake in a hot oven (450°F/230°C/GM8) for 10 minutes. Lower heat to moderate (375°F/190°C/GM5) and continue baking for 15 minutes, or until pastry crust is golden brown. Serves 4 to 6.

GAME PIE

2 partridges or pheasants
12 oz (350 g) veal cutlet
8 oz (225 g) cooked ham
6 tablespoons (90 ml) cognac
6 tablespoons (90 ml) red wine
1 tablespoon (15 ml) finely chopped parsley
2 tablespoons (30 ml) finely chopped onion
Salt and freshly ground black pepper
Butter
3 tablespoons (45 ml) olive oil
4 oz (100 g) button mushrooms, quartered
¼ teaspoon (1.25 ml) dried thyme
1 bay leaf
½ pint (300 ml) well-flavoured game stock
Puff pastry (page 760)
1 egg yolk

Cut partridges (or pheasants) into serving pieces, removing bones where possible. Cut veal and ham into ½-inch (12 mm) strips.

Marinate meats in cognac and red wine for at least 4 hours, with finely chopped parsley and onion, and salt and freshly ground black pepper, to taste.

Line a deep pie dish with strips of ham and veal; sauté partridge or pheasant pieces in 3 tablespoons (45 ml) each butter and olive oil until golden, then place them on this bed; top with quartered mushrooms, and season generously with salt, freshly ground black pepper, dried thyme and a bay leaf. Pour over marinade juices and game stock, and dot with 2 tablespoons (30 ml) diced butter.

Line the edges of the pie dish with puff pastry, and then cover pie with puff pastry. Make a hole in the centre and decorate with pastry leaves. Brush with egg yolk and bake in a hot oven (450°F/230°C/GM8) for 20 minutes, or until pastry begins to brown; then reduce heat to moderate (375°F/190°C/GM5) and continue baking for 1½ to 2 hours, or until the meat is tender and the pastry brown and crisp.

CHICKEN AND GROUSE PIE

1 small roasting chicken
1 fat grouse
1 pint (600 ml) red wine
Flour
8 oz (225 g) bacon, in 1 piece
4 oz (100 g) butter
Salt and freshly ground black pepper
¼ teaspoon (1.25 ml) crumbled rosemary
¼ teaspoon (1.25 ml) crumbled thyme
12 button onions
12 little chipolata sausages
2 tablespoons (30 ml) olive oil
3 hard-boiled eggs
Flaky pastry (page 759)
Beaten egg yolk

Cut chicken and grouse into serving pieces, and marinate for 2 days in red wine. Drain and dry pieces well. Sprinkle pieces generously with flour.

Dice bacon and blanch it by placing it in cold water and

bringing it slowly to a boil. Drain. Sauté bacon in butter until golden; remove bacon and sauté chicken and grouse pieces in remaining fat until golden. Pour over the juices of the marinade; add bacon bits, salt, freshly ground black pepper, and crumbled rosemary and thyme.

Blanch onions in boiling water for 10 minutes; drain and add to casserole. Bring to a boil; reduce heat and simmer for 1½ hours, uncovered. If the sauce reduces too much, add more wine or a little boiling water. Cool.

Sauté sausages in olive oil. Shell eggs and slice in quarters. Arrange pieces of chicken and grouse in a large deep pie dish around a pie chimney; top with sausages and quartered hard-boiled eggs, and pour in sauce, together with onions and bacon bits. Cover with flaky pastry; brush with beaten egg yolk and bake in a hot oven (450°F/230°C/GM8) for 10 minutes. Lower heat to moderate (375°F/190°C/GM5) and continue baking for 15 to 20 minutes, or until pastry is golden brown. Serves 6.

Raised Pies

Raised pies can be made in two different ways: (1) raised by hand, or (2) shaped and baked in a special mould for the purpose.

When the pie is to be raised by hand, I like to use a hot-water crust. In this way the pastry can easily be formed into the desired shape while the dough is still warm. Then, as the pastry cools, it hardens and retains the desired form.

When the pie is to be formed in a mould, I prefer a richer crust made with equal quantities of butter and lard, and mixed with an egg. Butter alone is apt to make too soft a crust. A raised pie mould usually opens at the side for easier removal.

Small pies are either raised by hand or shaped in tin rings or rims.

Almost any of the fillings given for an ordinary meat pie may be used for a raised pie.

Raised pies are generally served cold; to look right and cut well, they should be rather solid in texture. This is why they should be filled up with jellied stock which, when set, fills up all the spaces. For the same reason, a good *farce* or sausage meat is frequently used in the packing of a raised pie.

RAISED PIE CRUST

3 tablespoons (45 ml) lard
About ¼ pint (150 ml) milk or water
4 oz (100 g) plain flour
¼ teaspoon (1.25 ml) salt

Put the lard and milk or water in a small saucepan and bring to a boil without allowing them to reduce in quantity. Sieve the flour and salt into a clean dry bowl and make a well in the centre. Pour in the hot liquid, mixing at first with a spoon or knife as it is rather hot, then turning quickly by hand until all is formed into one mass. Turn dough out on a floured board and knead lightly until free from cracks. Use while still warm for raised pies.

RICH RAISED PIE CRUST

8 oz (225 g) plain flour
½ teaspoon (2.5 ml) salt
2 tablespoons (30 ml) butter
2 tablespoons (30 ml) lard
1 egg yolk
Water (up to ¼ pint/150 ml)

Sieve the flour and salt, and rub in the butter and lard in the same way as for Shortcrust Pastry (page 754). Bind together with the yolk of an egg and a little water, keeping the pastry as dry as possible. Knead well, wrap it in a wet cloth or muslin, and let it rest for ½ hour. Then use as required.

POULTRY OR GAME RAISED PIE

1 lb (450 g) rich raised pie crust (above)
Butter
1 tender chicken or pheasant
Freshly ground nutmeg and allspice
Salt and freshly ground black pepper
1 lb (450 g) sausage meat
8 oz (225 g) veal cutlet, diced
8 oz (225 g) cooked ham, diced
Beaten egg
½ pint (300 ml) strong gravy or stock

Make a stiff rich raised pie crust as directed above; butter a raised pie mould and line it with pastry.

Bone chicken or pheasant; lay it, skin side down, on a clean cloth, and season generously with nutmeg, allspice, salt and freshly ground black pepper. Spread a layer of sausage meat over boned bird; cover with a layer of diced veal and season generously again. (Raised pies, always served cold, need a lot of seasoning.) Cover with a layer of diced ham, and then another layer of sausage meat. Form bird into a roll to fit pie mould, bringing edges of skin together at the back.

Line pastry case with sausage meat; place stuffed bird in the pie, and fill any cavities with remaining veal, ham and sausage meat; top with sausage meat. Wet edges of pie; put on pastry lid, pinching edges together well. Cut a hole in centre of pastry top, and decorate top with leaves made of scraps of remaining pastry, reserving one for later use. Brush pastry with beaten egg and bake pie and reserved leaf in a hot oven (450°F/230°C/GM8) until pastry begins to brown; cover pie loosely with foil; reduce heat to 375°F/190°C/GM5 and cook for about 2 hours, or until meat feels tender when a sharp knife or skewer is run through hole at the top.

In the meantime, make a good strong gravy or stock with the chicken or pheasant bones and any trimmings left from bird, veal or ham. When pie is ready, pour in stock through hole at the top. Cover hole with reserved pastry leaf and allow pie to cool.

Note: Make sure gravy is considerably reduced before being poured into pie, as it must form a jelly when cold.

VEAL AND HAM RAISED PIE

1 lb (450 g) raised or rich raised pie crust (page 778)
2 egg yolks, well beaten
Forcemeat stuffing
1 lb (450 g) shoulder of veal, diced
Freshly ground nutmeg and allspice
Salt and freshly ground black pepper
8 oz (225 g) ham, diced
Beaten egg white
½ pint (300 ml) strong gravy or stock

FORCEMEAT STUFFING
1 lb (450 g) shoulder of veal, minced
1 lb (450 g) fat bacon, minced
2 eggs, well beaten
Salt and cayenne pepper
Freshly ground mace and nutmeg
Freshly grated lemon peel
1 tablespoon (15 ml) freshly chopped parsley
¼ level teaspoon (1.25 ml) dried thyme

To raise a pie crust in the traditional manner with your hands is a difficult task that can only be achieved with practice. A simpler method is to roll out the pastry and cut 2 rounds or oval pieces for the top and bottom crusts, and a piece long enough for the sides. Place the bottom piece on a buttered baking sheet and fasten sides to it with beaten egg yolk, pinching edges well together.

Line pastry shell with forcemeat stuffing; cover with a layer of diced veal, and season generously with freshly ground nutmeg, allspice, salt and freshly ground black pepper. Cover this with a layer of diced ham; then a layer of forcemeat and a layer of diced veal, and season generously as above. (Raised pies, always served cold, need a lot of seasoning.) Continue until the meat rises about an inch (25 mm) above the pastry, finishing with a layer of forcemeat, and filling all cavities of the pie. Brush top edges of pie crust with beaten egg; carefully put on the cover, pinching the edges well together. Make a hole in the middle of the lid, and decorate the pie with pastry leaves made from scraps of pastry, sticking leaves on with beaten egg white. Reserve 1 pastry leaf for later use. Brush pastry with beaten egg yolk, and bake the pie and reserved pastry leaf in a hot oven (450°F/230°C/GM8) until pastry begins to brown; then cover pie with foil; reduce heat to 375°F/190°C/GM5 and cook about 2 hours, or until meat feels tender when a sharp knife or a metal skewer is run through hole at the top of the pie.

Remove pie from the oven; place a funnel in hole at top and pour in strong gravy or stock. Seal hole with baked pastry leaf and allow pie to cool. Serve cold.

Note: Make sure gravy is considerably reduced before being poured into pie, as it must form a jelly when cold.

FORCEMEAT STUFFING
Combine minced veal, fat bacon and beaten eggs together, and flavour to taste with remaining ingredients.

Sweet Pies

APPLE STREUSEL

6 tart eating apples
Juice of 1 lemon
1 unbaked pastry shell
2 oz (50 g) sugar
½ level teaspoon (2.5 ml) cinnamon
¼ level teaspoon (1.25 ml) nutmeg or allspice

STREUSEL TOPPING
3 oz (75 g) brown sugar
3 oz (75 g) plain flour, sifted
Grated rind of 1 lemon
6 tablespoons (90 ml) softened butter

Peel and core apples, cut into eighths and toss in lemon juice. Arrange prepared apples in unbaked pastry shell. Combine sugar and spices, and sprinkle over apples.

STREUSEL TOPPING

Combine brown sugar, flour and grated lemon rind, and cut softened butter into mixture until crumbly, with a pastry blender or 2 knives. Sprinkle mixture over apples and bake in a hot oven (450°F/230°C/GM8) for 15 minutes. Reduce oven temperature to 350°F/180°C/GM4 and bake for 30 minutes. Serves 6.

BANANA CREAM PIE

1 baked pastry shell, shortcrust or rich biscuit crust (page 755)
3 bananas, sliced
Juice of 1 lemon
¼ pint (150 ml) double cream, whipped

VANILLA CREAM
4 oz (100 g) sugar
3 tablespoons (45 ml) cornflour
¾ pint (450 ml) milk
5 egg yolks
½–1 teaspoon (2.5–5 ml) vanilla extract
2 teaspoons (10 ml) Kirsch

VANILLA CREAM
Combine sugar and cornflour in the top of a double saucepan. Stir in milk and cook over direct heat, stirring constantly, until mixture comes to a boil. Boil for 1 minute. Beat egg yolks slightly; add a little hot milk mixture and stir into milk and sugar mixture. Cook, stirring, over hot but not boiling water until thickened – 5 to 10 minutes. Strain and cool; then add vanilla extract and Kirsch.

Combine sliced bananas and lemon juice in a shallow bowl and toss.

Place a layer of drained banana slices in the bottom of baked pastry shell; cover with half the Vanilla Cream; arrange layer of banana slices on this and cover with remaining Vanilla Cream. Top pie decoratively with remaining banana slices and garnish with a ring of whipped cream. Serve cold but not chilled. Serves 6.

COFFEE CHIFFON FLAN

1 9-inch (23 cm) prebaked flan case
1 level tablespoon (15 ml) powdered gelatine
4 tablespoons (60 ml) cold water
¾ pint (450 ml) milk
4 eggs, separated
4 oz (100 g) castor sugar
2 level tablespoons (30 ml) powdered coffee
¼ pint (150 ml) double cream, whipped
¼ teaspoon (1.25 ml) salt
Coarsely grated chocolate

Soak gelatine in cold water. Warm the milk.

Cream together egg yolks, half the sugar, and coffee. Pour on warm milk, stirring constantly; return to heat and cook gently until custard just coats the spoon. Cool. Dissolve gelatine over gentle heat; stir into cooled coffee custard. Fold in whipped cream.

Whisk egg whites with salt until stiff but not dry; then whisk in remaining sugar a little at a time. Whisk coffee custard and fold gradually into beaten egg whites; turn into prebaked flan case and decorate with coarsely grated chocolate.

CHOCOLATE CREAM PIE

2 oz (50 g) bitter chocolate
8 oz (225 g) sugar
2 tablespoons (30 ml) cornflour
¼ level teaspoon (1.25 ml) salt
¾ pint (450 ml) milk
2 eggs, well beaten
2 tablespoons (30 ml) butter
½ teaspoon (2.5 ml) vanilla extract
1 baked pastry shell

GARNISH
½ pint (300 ml) double cream
2 oz (50 g) sugar
½ teaspoon (2.5 ml) vanilla extract
½ oz (15 g) bitter chocolate, coarsely grated

Melt chocolate over hot water in the top of a double saucepan. Combine 8 oz (225 g) sugar, cornflour and salt in a bowl. Gradually stir in milk; then stir mixture into melted chocolate. Cook over boiling water, stirring constantly, for 10 minutes, or until thick. Pour hot mixture into well-beaten eggs a little at a time, stirring after each addition. Return to top of double saucepan and cook, stirring occasionally, for 5 minutes. Remove from heat; add butter and ½ teaspoon (2.5 ml) vanilla extract. Cool. Pour mixture into baked pastry shell.

GARNISH
Whip cream and blend in the sugar and vanilla extract. Garnish pie with a ring of whipped cream and sprinkle grated chocolate on top of the whipped cream. Chill and serve. Serves 6.

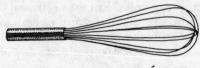

LEMON SOUFFLÉ PIE

4 egg yolks, well beaten
6 oz (175 g) sugar
4 tablespoons (60 ml) lemon juice
¼–½ level teaspoon (1.25–2.5 ml) ground nutmeg
1 teaspoon (5 ml) grated lemon rind
1 teaspoon (5 ml) vanilla extract
Salt
4 egg whites
1 baked pastry shell

Combine egg yolks, a third of the sugar, and lemon juice. Flavour to taste with nutmeg and cook over water, stirring constantly, until mixture thickens. Remove from heat. Mix in grated lemon rind and vanilla extract. Cool.

Add salt to egg whites and beat until soft peaks form; gradually add remaining sugar and beat until stiff. Fold into warm lemon mixture.

Spoon mixture into baked pastry shell and bake in a slow oven (325°F/170°C/GM3) for about 30 minutes, or until golden brown. Serves 8.

LEMON SPONGE TART

2 tablespoons (30 ml) butter
6 oz (175 g) sugar
3 eggs, separated
2 tablespoons (30 ml) plain flour
¾ pint (450 ml) milk
Juice of 3 lemons
Grated rind of 1 lemon
I unbaked pastry shell

Cream butter and blend with sugar and egg yolks until light and creamy. Sprinkle with flour; then mix in milk, lemon juice and rind. Whisk egg whites until stiff; fold into lemon mixture. Pour lemon mixture into unbaked pastry shell and bake in a slow oven (350°F/180°C/GM4) for approximately 45 minutes.

TARTES AUX PÊCHES

6 small peaches
8 oz (225 g) sugar
¼ pint (150 ml) water
Cinnamon
¼ pint (150 ml) red Burgundy
6 individual pastry cases

Pour boiling water over peaches in a bowl and peel. Slice in half and remove stones. Poach peaches, uncovered, in syrup made of sugar, water, and cinnamon, to taste, for about 15 minutes. Add Burgundy and continue to cook, uncovered, over a low heat until fruit is tender – about 15 minutes.

Put peaches in a deep bowl. Reduce liquid over high heat to the consistency of a light syrup. Pour syrup over the peaches and put in the refrigerator to chill.

Put 2 halves together and set a re-formed peach inside each pastry case; glaze with reduced syrup. Serves 6.

FRENCH PEACH FLAN

1 baked fingertip shell (page 760)
Fresh peaches, sliced

FRENCH PASTRY CREAM
4 oz (100 g) sugar
3 tablespoons (45 ml) cornflour
¾ pint (450 ml) milk
5 egg yolks
½–1 teaspoon (1.25–2.5 ml) vanilla extract
2 teaspoons (10 ml) Kirsch

APRICOT GLAZE
6 tablespoons (90 ml) apricot jam
3 tablespoons (45 ml) water
1 tablespoon (15 ml) rum, brandy or Kirsch (optional)

FRENCH PASTRY CREAM
Combine sugar and cornflour in the top of a double saucepan. Stir in milk and cook over direct heat, stirring all the time, until mixture comes to a boil. Boil for 1 minute. Beat yolks slightly, add a little hot milk mixture and pour back into milk and sugar mixture, stirring. Cook, stirring, over hot but not boiling water until thickened – 5 to 10 minutes. Strain and cool. Add vanilla extract and Kirsch; cover with waxed paper and refrigerate until well chilled.

Half-fill baked pastry shell with French Pastry Cream and arrange slices of fresh peaches in rows on this bed. Coat with golden-coloured Apricot Glaze.

APRICOT GLAZE
Heat apricot jam and water in a small saucepan, stirring constantly, until mixture melts. Strain and, if desired, stir in rum, brandy or Kirsch. Keep warm.

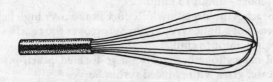

SOUR CREAM–SULTANA PIE

8 oz (225 g) sugar
½ level teaspoon (2.5 ml) powdered cinnamon
½ level teaspoon (2.5 ml) nutmeg or allspice
Salt
2 eggs, beaten
½ pint (300 ml) sour cream
2 tablespoons (30 ml) lemon juice
4 oz (100 g) sultanas
1 unbaked pastry shell

Combine sugar, spices, salt, beaten eggs, sour cream, lemon juice
and sultanas. Mix until all is thoroughly blended. Pour into pastry
shell and bake in a slow oven (350°F/180°C/GM4) for 1 hour, or
until filling has set. Cool. Serves 8.

CUSTARD PIE

1 level tablespoon (15 ml) cornflour
¾ pint (450 ml) milk
Grated rind of ½ lemon
4 tablespoons (60 ml) sugar
½ teaspoon (2.5 ml) vanilla extract
Salt
3 eggs
1 unbaked pastry shell

Mix cornflour smoothly with a little milk; combine remaining
milk with lemon rind in the top of a double saucepan and simmer
gently over water for 15 minutes. Strain hot milk into cornflour
and return to double saucepan; cook over water, stirring constantly, until thickened. Add sugar, vanilla extract and salt, to
taste; cool.

Beat eggs and add them to custard mixture. Mix well.

Prick bottom of unbaked pastry shell with a fork; cover with a
piece of foil or waxed paper; weight this with dried beans and
bake 'blind' in a preheated hot oven (450°F/230°C/GM8) for 15
minutes. Remove foil and beans. Allow pastry shell to cool.

Pour custard mixture into pastry shell and bake in a moderate oven (375°F/190°C/GM5) for 25 to 30 minutes, or until the pastry is cooked and the custard has set. Serve cooled but not chilled. Serves 8.

VARIATIONS: ·

Cherry custard pie: Add 1 cup pitted sour cherries soaked in 4 tablespoons (60 ml) cherry brandy (add the brandy, too) to mixture and bake as above.

Pear custard pie: Add 2 ripe pears (peeled, cored and thinly sliced) which you have soaked in 4 to 6 tablespoons (60–90 ml) Kirsch to mixture (add Kirsch, too) and bake as above.

EGGNOG PIE

¼ pint (150 ml) single cream
3 egg yolks
3 oz (75 g) granulated sugar
Salt and freshly grated nutmeg
1 teaspoon (5 ml) gelatine
2 tablespoons (30 ml) cold water
2 tablespoons (30 ml) rum
1 tablespoon (15 ml) brandy
½ teaspoon (2.5 ml) vanilla extract
3 egg whites
¼ pint (150 ml) double cream
1 baked pastry shell

Scald cream in the top of a double saucepan. Combine egg yolks, sugar, salt and freshly grated nutmeg, and stir into the scalded cream. Cook, stirring constantly, over water until the mixture coats a spoon.

Soften gelatine in water; add to custard mixture and stir until dissolved. Add rum, brandy and vanilla extract; strain custard into a glass bowl and chill until mixture begins to set. Whisk egg whites until stiff; whip cream. Fold egg white and cream into custard mixture and pour into a baked pastry shell. Chill.

Just before serving, sprinkle with a little freshly grated nutmeg.

AUTUMN PEAR FLAN

1 9-inch (23 cm) rich shortcrust flan case
(page 755)
6–8 pears

PASTRY CREAM
4 oz (100 g) sugar
4 level tablespoons (60 ml) cornflour
¾ pint (450 ml) milk
5 egg yolks
½–1 teaspoon (2.5–5 ml) vanilla extract
2 teaspoons (10 ml) Kirsch

WINE SYRUP
6 oz (175 g) sugar
½ pint (300 ml) red wine
Pared rind of 1 lemon
4 cloves
1-inch (25 mm) piece of root ginger
1–1½ teaspoons (5–7.5 ml) red food colouring
1 level teaspoon (5 ml) gelatine
4 tablespoons (60 ml) cold water
Juice of 1 lemon
¼ pint (150 ml) thick unsweetened apple purée

PASTRY CREAM

Combine sugar and cornflour in the top of a double saucepan. Stir in milk and cook over direct heat, stirring all the time, until mixture comes to a boil. Boil for 1 minute. Beat yolks slightly, add a little hot milk mixture and pour back into milk and sugar mixture, stirring. Cook, stirring, over hot but not boiling water, until thickened (5 to 10 minutes). Strain and cool. Add vanilla extract and Kirsch; cover with waxed paper and refrigerate until well chilled.

Peel and core pears. Dissolve sugar in wine with lemon rind, cloves and ginger. Bring to a boil and cook for 3 minutes. Reduce heat to simmering point, stir in red food colouring and poach pears very gently, turning occasionally, until tender but not mushy. Remove from syrup and cool.

Soak gelatine in cold water and add with lemon juice and apple purée to the hot syrup. Mix thoroughly until smooth; cool.

Half-fill flan case with Pastry Cream; re-form pears and arrange on pastry base. Cover pears with red apple-wine sauce. Serves 6 to 8.

PEARS IN PASTRY SABAYON

6 pears
¼ pint (150 ml) syrup (4 oz (100 g) sugar 8 tablespoons
(120 ml) water)
¼ pint (150 ml) apricot jam
Cream (optional)

PASTRY
9 oz (250 g) plain flour
1 level teaspoon (5 ml) salt
4 tablespoons (60 ml) lard
4 oz (100 g) softened butter
Water, to mix

SABAYON SAUCE
4 egg yolks
4 oz (100 g) sugar
6 fluid oz (175 ml) Marsala
1 tablespoon (15 ml) cognac

PASTRY

Sift flour and salt together; rub in lard and half the butter until mixture resembles fine breadcrumbs. Add sufficient water to form into a ball which will just hold together, and knead firmly but quickly until smooth. Allow to rest in a cool place for 15 minutes. Roll out into an oblong and spread remaining butter over surface. Fold in half, seal edges, rest for 5 minutes and roll out to ⅛-inch (3 mm) thickness. Cut 6 pastry rounds large enough for pears to sit upon and cut remainder of pastry into thin strips.

Poach pears in syrup and apricot jam; cool, and place 1 pear on each pastry round. To make cage of pastry strips for each pear: cross 2 strips at right angles; seal well with water and place cross at top of each pear. Snip strips at base and seal well with water. Place pears in pastry on baking sheet and bake in a moderately hot to hot oven (400°–450°F/200°–220°C/GM6–7) for 20 minutes, or until pastry is set. Remove and brush with reduced glaze. Serve with cream or Sabayon Sauce. Serves 6.

SABAYON SAUCE

Beat egg yolks and sugar in the top of a double saucepan until yellow and frothy. Add Marsala; place over hot water and cook, stirring constantly, until thick and foamy. Stir in cognac and chill.

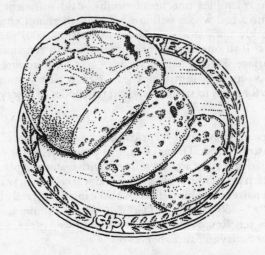

CHAPTER TWENTY-TWO
Cakes and Breads

During the long summer vacations spent on the New England shore when I was a boy, I used to like to stay in bed late in the mornings. Late, that is, except when I knew my father was up early making his favourite breakfast: home-made baking powder biscuits and his own particular brand of rich breakfast coffee. My father was an early riser, and joining him for breakfast meant getting up before seven. But it was worth it. I still remember those summer mornings, sitting by the kitchen stove so that we could take biscuit by biscuit out of the pan as they became ready.

Dad was a breakfast buff. He didn't like cream in his coffee – 'too rich' – and he didn't like just milk – 'too measly'. His favourite brew – and thus mine – was a combination of equal parts of milk, cream and, believe it or not, evaporated milk. This we thought was ambrosia. And then would come the biscuits – light, fluffy, butter-scented affairs that would literally melt in your mouth. The flour was carefully sifted, I remember, and baking powder helped, but it was the light touch and the lack of fuss and bother that made those biscuits what they were. And they were masterpieces . . . I have rarely met their equal since.

Dad's light touch with biscuits was carried over into the magic realm of home-made breads. He never bothered about any other kind of cooking; that was my mother's job, and sometimes my brother Bud's. But if some cooks took pride in their cakes, some in their jams and jellies, and others in their pastry, my father always said that an honest loaf of bread, baked at home, was an accomplishment that any man could be proud of. So together, in the early summer mornings, we would make home-made bread at least once a week, with enough crusty loaves to last the family four days or more. I remember the actual manipulation of the warm elastic dough as if it were yesterday. And I just have to close my eyes to smell again the warm, sweaty odour of the yeast and the wonderful aroma of the bread baking in the oven. I look back on it today as one of the most nostalgically satisfying memories I know. For there is no taste and fragrance in the world quite like that of freshly baked bread, served warm from the oven, with a pot of unsalted butter.

Breads and Hot Breads

Novice cooks are often afraid to attempt yeast-raised mixtures. But baking with yeast is not really difficult if you realize that yeast, unlike other raising agents, is a living plant requiring gentle warmth in order to perform. Not enough heat and your bread will be heavy and soggy. Too much heat and the yeast will be killed. And like any other plant, yeast requires food to thrive, and this it obtains from carbohydrates in the flour and sugar, and from the moisture used in making the dough.

Home-baking is as easy as it is pleasant. The miracle of bread is accomplished when the heat of the oven transforms the self-risen dough into an airy, flavoursome loaf covered with a crisp, golden crust. Let modern ovens, perfect flours and dried yeasts take all the guesswork out of baking.

TO PREPARE YEAST SPONGE
Heat water to lukewarm; pour into a small bowl and sprinkle with dried yeast and sugar. Heat milk enough to melt butter, and then cool to lukewarm. Allow yeast to soak in water for a few moments before stirring; then allow it to set for 10 minutes before combining yeast and water mixture with lukewarm milk and butter mixture.

TO SET YEAST SPONGE (CLASSIC METHOD)
Warm a large mixing bowl and sift flour and salt into it. Make a well in the centre and strain in yeast and milk mixture. Then rock the bowl gently so that some of the flour falls down into the liquid, and shake an equal thickness of flour over the top so that the yeast is embedded warmly in the midst of the bowl of flour.

Cover the mixing bowl with waxed paper or foil and then with a clean wool blanket; stand it in a warm place for about 20 minutes to start the yeast working.

For a quick method, see Step 2 in the recipe for Home-made White Bread overleaf.

TO MIX THE DOUGH
Your dough should be soft and elastic – almost sticky – to allow the yeast to perform perfectly. So gently mix in the flour surrounding the yeasty part, and go on doing this to the dough until it forms one even mass. It will be sticky at first and the moist parts will stick to your fingers, so keep dipping your hands in the dry part of the flour and sprinkling dry flour on the damp places. The proper action is a gently rocking action which should leave the sides of the bowl relatively dry.

TO KNEAD THE DOUGH
Place dough on a lightly floured board and press down on dough with the heel of your hand, punching the dough away from you. (If you dust your hands lightly with flour from time to time, it will prevent sticking.) Then fold dough over towards you; press

down lightly and away from you. Give dough a quarter-turn to the left and repeat. Continue this procedure, folding and turning, for about 7 minutes, or until the dough feels elastic and the surface is satiny in texture. At this point it will no longer stick to the board or to your hands.

RISING
Wash and warm mixing bowl again; dry thoroughly and brush with melted butter. Place ball of dough in the bowl and brush lightly with melted butter.

Cut a deep cross in the top of the dough with a knife; cover bowl with paper or foil and with a blanket, and set it to rise again for 1 hour.

BAKING
Have ready some warm loaf tins, lightly buttered and floured. Punch down dough with your fists. Turn it out on to a lightly floured board and knead it for 2 or 3 minutes. Then cut it into equal portions – large enough to half-fill the loaf tins. Knead each piece until smooth and place in the tin, pressing it into the corners.

Cover dough lightly and allow to rise again until it has almost reached the top of the tin.

Place the loaves in a hot oven (450°F/230°C/GM8) for the first 15 minutes. Then reduce oven heat to moderate (375°F/190°C/GM5) and continue cooking until loaves are golden brown. Or, more simply, bake at a steady temperature of 400°F/200°C/GM6.

FINISHES FOR BREAD OR ROLLS
Brush bread or rolls with milk or egg white and scatter one of the following over the surface: poppy seeds, crushed cardamom, coriander, anise or caraway. Crushed coarse salt is used for onion breads.

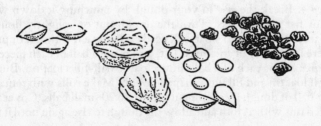

HOME-MADE WHITE BREAD

¾ pint (450 ml) milk
4 oz (100 g) butter
1–1½ teaspoons (5–7.5 ml) salt
¾ pint (450 ml) lukewarm water
1 tablespoon (15 ml) sugar
1 level tablespoon (15 ml) dry yeast
2¾ lb (1.25 kg) sifted plain flour
Melted butter

Step 1: Bring milk to a boil. Remove from heat and add butter and salt. Cool to lukewarm. Fill small bowl with lukewarm water; sprinkle sugar and yeast over the surface; after a few minutes, stir well. Then mix dissolved yeast into *lukewarm* milk. (If milk is too hot, it will kill yeast.)

Step 2: Warm a large mixing bowl with hot water. Dry well and sift half the flour into it. Make a well in the centre; pour in yeast-milk mixture and mix well. Gradually stir in remaining flour. When the dough leaves the sides of the bowl, you have used enough. Turn dough out on to a lightly floured pastry board and knead thoroughly with the heel of your hand until dough is satin-smooth and elastic.

Step 3: Brush a large mixing bowl with melted butter. Place ball of dough in the bowl and brush with melted butter. I always cover the bowl completely with a piece of waxed paper or foil, and then with a wool blanket to keep it warm. Your dough will rise best in a warm room, free from draughts. If too warm, your dough will rise too quickly and be coarse-textured. If it rises too little, it will be heavy and soggy. After about 1 hour, test if dough has risen the correct amount by pressing your finger into it. If, when you remove your finger, a dent remains, the dough is ready.

Step 4: Break the rise in your dough by punching it down with your fist a few times. Turn the dough out on a lightly floured board. Divide it into 4 parts. Knead each part a few times, or until there is no trace of stickiness left, and make a ball of each piece.

Step 5: Shape each of 3 balls into a loaf to half-fill a loaf tin. Butter each loaf tin and fill with shaped dough. Make rolls with remaining ball of dough by shaping it into 16 to 20 small balls. Cover the filled tins with a cloth and allow the dough to rise again until it has nearly doubled in bulk. Use finger dent test again: if finger leaves a dent in the dough, your bread is ready for the oven.

Step 6: Bake in a preheated moderate oven (375°F/190°C/GM5) for 45 to 60 minutes. Bake rolls for 15 to 20 minutes. Remove bread and rolls from pans, and if you like a crisp crust, allow them to cool uncovered on a rack. If you prefer a softer crust, cover with a towel while cooling.

HOME–MADE WHOLEMEAL BREAD

¾ pint (450 ml) milk
4 oz (100 g) butter
1 teaspoon (5 ml) salt
¾ pint (450 ml) lukewarm water
1 tablespoon (15 ml) Barbados or moist brown sugar
2 level tablespoons (30 ml) dry yeast
1¾ lb (800 g) wholemeal flour
1 lb (450 g) sifted plain flour
Melted butter

Steps 1, 2 and *3*, as above, using ingredients listed on the left.
Step 4: Divide dough into 3 parts and knead each piece until there is no trace of stickiness left. Then shape each into a round loaf and place on a floured baking sheet. Cover with a cloth and allow to rise again for 30 to 40 minutes. Bake in a preheated moderately hot oven (400°F/200°C/GM6) for about 1 hour.

Remove bread from pans, and if you like a crisp crust, allow loaves to cool uncovered on a cake rack. Cover with a towel for a softer crust.

FRENCH BREAD

1 tablespoon (15 ml) butter
1 tablespoon (15 ml) salt
1 teaspoon (5 ml) sugar
1 level tablespoon (15 ml) dry yeast
¼ pint (150 ml) lukewarm water
1½ lb (675 g) sifted plain flour
Yellow cornmeal

Combine butter, salt and sugar in a large mixing bowl. Add ¾ pint (450 ml) boiling water and stir until all is dissolved. Cool to lukewarm. In a separate bowl, sprinkle yeast over ¼ pint (150 ml) lukewarm water to soften. Stir; then strain into butter mixture and mix thoroughly. Now stir in flour, a quarter at a time. Beat until smooth, then add remaining flour little by little, working it in well with your hands.

Place dough on a lightly floured board and knead well until dough is smooth and elastic. Transfer dough to a large, warm, buttered bowl, cover with waxed paper or foil, and with a piece of clean blanket, and leave to rise in a warm place, away from draughts and direct heat, for about 1½ hours, or until dough has doubled in bulk.

Punch dough down with your fist and let it rise again until double in bulk – this time for about 1 hour.

Butter a large baking sheet and sprinkle it lightly with cornmeal (for a crunchy bottom crust). Divide the dough into 3 equal parts and roll each part into a rectangle 8 by 14 inches (20 by 35 cms) on a lightly floured board. Your dough should be so elastic at this point that it will resist rolling, but with a little effort this can be done. Roll the long side of the rectangle towards you in a tight neat roll – it should be about 1½ inches (38 mm) in diameter. Pull it into shape if necessary. Place the 3 long rolls, seam sides down, on prepared baking sheet, and let them rise until double in size.

Brush tops with cold water and make 3 or 4 diagonal slashes across each loaf. Bake loaves in a preheated moderately hot oven (400°F/200°C/GM6) for 50 minutes to 1 hour, brushing the tops with cold water every 15 or 20 minutes.

Keep a shallow pan of hot water in the oven while loaves are baking. This, together with the frequent brushing with water, will give the good crisp crust of real French bread.

ITALIAN BREAD

1 pint (600 ml) warm water
2 level tablespoons (30 ml) dry yeast
2 lb (900 g) sifted plain flour
1 level tablespoon (15 ml) salt
Butter
Yellow cornmeal
1 tablespoon (15 ml) water
1 egg white

Pour warm water into a large warmed mixing bowl; sprinkle with yeast; stir after 5 minutes and then stir in a quarter of the flour. Beat well; add salt and gradually beat in all but a quarter of the flour. Turn out dough on to a lightly floured board. Cover; leave to rest for 10 minutes. Knead by hand for about 20 minutes, or until dough is very elastic; knead in remaining flour.

Place dough in a lightly buttered bowl, turning once to grease surface. Cover with waxed paper or foil, and a piece of clean blanket, and leave to rise in a warm place, away from draughts and direct heat, for about 1½ hours, or until dough has doubled in bulk.

Punch the dough down with your fist and let rise again until double in bulk – this time for about 1 hour. Turn out on a lightly floured surface. Divide in half and form each part into a ball. Cover; allow dough to rest for 10 minutes.

Roll each half of the dough into a rectangle 15 by 8 inches (39 by 20 cms), about ½ inch (15 mm) thick. Roll up tightly, beginning at short side and sealing well as you roll. Taper ends by rolling out with hands until loaf measures 10 to 11 inches (25 to 28 cms) in length. Place loaves, seam side down, on buttered baking sheets sprinkled with cornmeal (for a crunchy bottom crust). Add 1 tablespoon (15 ml) water to egg white and beat lightly; brush over tops and sides of loaves. Cover with a damp cloth, but do not let it touch dough. Leave to rise in a warm place until double in bulk (1 to 1½ hours).

For a crisper crust, place shallow pan filled with boiling water on lower rack of oven during baking.

Bake in a moderate oven (375°F/190°C/GM5) for 20 minutes; brush with egg white again and continue baking 20 minutes more, or until well browned and done. Cool.

VIENNA BREAD

¾ pint (450 ml) milk
1 oz (25 g) sugar
2 teaspoons (10 ml) salt
1½ oz (75 g) butter
2 level tablespoons (30 ml) dry yeast
¾ pint (450 ml) lukewarm water
3 lb (1.4 kg) sifted plain flour
1 egg white, lightly beaten
2 tablespoons (30 ml) sesame seeds

Heat milk until almost boiling. Remove from heat and stir in sugar, salt and butter until all are dissolved. Cool to lukewarm.

Sprinkle yeast over ¾ pint (450 ml) lukewarm water to soften. Stir; then strain into milk mixture with half the flour. Beat until smooth, then add remaining flour, working it in well with your hands.

Place dough on a lightly floured board and knead well until dough is smooth and elastic.

Transfer dough to a large buttered bowl, cover with waxed paper or foil, and a piece of clean blanket, and leave it to rise in a warm place, away from draughts and direct heat, for about 1½ hours, or until double in bulk.

Punch the dough down with your fist and divide into 3 equal parts. Knead each part on a floured board and shape into long loaves, 12 inches (30 cms) in length. Make several diagonal cuts across the top of each loaf and place loaves several inches apart on a buttered baking sheet.

Let dough rise again until double in bulk; brush with lightly beaten egg white and bake in a preheated fairly hot oven (425°F/220°C/GM7) for 50 minutes. Remove from oven; brush again with egg white and sprinkle with sesame seeds. Bake 10 minutes longer.

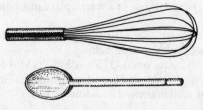

SULTANA BREAD

1 lb (450 g) plain flour
1 teaspoon (5 ml) salt
1 oz (25 g) butter
½ oz (15 g) dry yeast
1 teaspoon (5 ml) castor sugar
½ pint (300 ml) lukewarm milk
1 teaspoon (5 ml) vanilla extract
4 oz (100 g) sultanas, washed and drained

Sieve flour and salt into a mixing bowl and rub in butter with your fingertips until mixture is smooth and free from lumps. Make a well in the centre.

Sprinkle yeast and sugar over lukewarm milk in a small mixing bowl; after a few minutes, stir well. Add vanilla extract, and strain into the centre of the dry ingredients. Gradually mix the dry ingredients from the sides of the bowl into the yeast mixture with your hands until a thick batter is formed. Cover the bowl and stand it in a warm place for about ¾ hour. Sprinkle with carefully washed and drained sultanas; mix all into a soft dough; turn out on a floured board and knead for a few minutes. Put the dough in a well-buttered and floured loaf tin and leave in a warm place to rise. When well risen, bake in a hot oven (450°F/230°C/GM8) until bread is done.

OLD ENGLISH SPICE BREAD

1 lb (450 g) plain flour
2 oz (50 g) castor sugar
1 level teaspoon (5 ml) powdered ginger
¼ level teaspoon (1.25 ml) powdered cinnamon
1 oz (25 g) softened butter
¼ pint (150 ml) milk
¼ pint (150 ml) cream
½ oz (15 g) dry yeast
Salt
1 tablespoon (15 ml) orange-flower water
1 egg white, lightly beaten
1–2 oz (25–50 g) shredded almonds

Sieve flour, sugar, ginger and cinnamon into a warmed mixing bowl and rub in butter until the mixture is smooth and free from lumps. Make a well in the centre.

Combine milk and cream in a saucepan and heat until lukewarm. Pour into a small bowl and sprinkle with dry yeast and a little salt; after a few minutes, stir well. Add orange-flower water, and strain into the centre of the dry ingredients. Make into a light dough.

Sprinkle dough with flour; cover the bowl and stand it in a warm place for 1½ to 2 hours, or until the dough is well risen and feels light and elastic to the touch.

Turn out on a floured board and knead lightly. Form into small balls, and place them in a buttered and floured bread pan. Brush over with lightly beaten egg white; sprinkle with shredded almonds which have been dried in the oven; and bake in a moderate oven (375°F/190°C/GM5) until crisp and golden.

BRIOCHES

1 lb (450 g) plain flour
½ oz (15 g) dry yeast
Salt
Lukewarm water
4 eggs
2 tablespoons (30 ml) sugar
4–6 oz (100–175 g) butter, slightly softened
1 egg yolk, beaten with a little water

Make a yeast sponge: sieve 4 oz (100 g) flour into a small mixing bowl and make a well in the centre. Sprinkle yeast and a pinch of salt into 4 tablespoons (60 ml) lukewarm water; after a few minutes, stir well. Strain yeast mixture into the centre of the flour. Make into a soft dough. Roll this in a little flour to make a ball and cut it across the top with a sharp knife. Place 'sponge' in just enough warm water to cover it while you are preparing the dough – about 15 minutes. Keep the water warm but not hot over a saucepan, and the 'sponge' will swell to 2 to 3 times its original volume.

To make the dough: sieve 12 oz (350 g) flour into a mixing bowl and make a well in the centre. Add eggs to well, and mix in the flour gradually to make a soft dough. When well mixed, turn dough out on a lightly floured board and knead it until the dough becomes smooth and elastic and no longer sticks to your fingers. Then mix in the sugar, a pinch of salt and the slightly softened butter. When these are well incorporated, drain the 'sponge'; place it in the centre of the other dough, and mix the two doughs lightly. Place the dough in a floured bowl, cover it and let it stand in the natural heat of the kitchen for about 3 hours, by which time it should have swelled to twice its original volume. Beat the dough down to make it fall again, and set it in a cool place until the next day, beating it down again if it rises too much. It may be kept for 24 hours in this way so long as it is not allowed to rise too much.

Butter small *brioche* moulds or medium-sized custard cups. Roll dough into a sausage shape. Cut off pieces of dough to make balls about 2 inches (5 cms) in diameter and place one in each mould. Snip top of each ball with scissors to form a cross and set a second small ball in the centre of the cross. Place the *brioches* in a warm place to rise until double in size. Brush tops over with egg yolk beaten with a little water, and bake in a fairly hot oven (425°F/220°C/GM7) for 15 to 20 minutes, or until brown.

To make a large *brioche*: butter a soufflé mould and tie a strong band of buttered white paper round the outside to give it more height. Half-fill the mould with *brioche* dough and set it in a warm place to rise. When the dough fills the mould, put it in a moderate oven (375°F/190°C/GM5) to bake for 30 to 40 minutes, or until brown.

ROLLS

8 fluid oz (175 ml) milk
1 oz (25 g) butter
1 teaspoon (5 ml) salt
4 tablespoons (60 ml) lukewarm water
1 tablespoon (15 ml) sugar
1 level tablespoon (15 ml) dry yeast
12 oz (350 g) plain flour
Melted butter

Step 1: As in recipe for Home-made White Bread (page 796).
Step 2: Add half quantity of flour and beat thoroughly for 2

minutes in electric mixer. Add enough of remaining flour to make a dough just barely firm enough to handle.

Step 3: Turn dough out on a lightly floured pastry board and knead thoroughly with the heel of your hand until dough is satin-smooth and elastic. Leave to rise for 1 hour.

Step 4: Form dough into small balls and arrange on butter baking sheets. Brush with melted butter. Cover with a cloth and allow to rise until double in bulk – about 1 hour.

Step 5: Bake in a fairly hot oven (425°F/220°C/GM7) until well browned – 15 to 20 minutes. Makes about 18.

BREAKFAST ROLLS

1 lb (450 g) plain flour
2 oz (50 g) butter
½ oz (15 g) dry yeast
1 teaspoon (5 ml) salt
½ pint (300 ml) lukewarm water

Sieve flour; rub in butter and make a well in the centre. Mix yeast with salt and lukewarm water. Strain into centre of flour and mix up quickly into dough. Turn out on a well-floured board and knead until smooth. Form dough into a long roll and cut across in pieces about 3 inches (8 cms) in length. Place them on a buttered and floured baking sheet and set to rise in a warm place for about 1 hour. When well risen, bake rolls in a moderate oven (375°F/190°C/GM5) for 15 to 20 minutes, or until brown and crisp.

MILK ROLLS

1 lb (450 g) plain flour
½ teaspoon (2.5 ml) salt
2 teaspoons (10 ml) baking powder
2 oz (50 g) butter
About ½ pint (300 ml) milk
Melted butter (optional)

Sieve flour, salt and baking powder into a mixing bowl and rub in butter with your fingertips as lightly as possible. Make a well in the centre and add enough milk to make a softish dough. Mix quickly and lightly, then turn out on a floured board and form the dough into small rolls. Place them on a greased and floured baking sheet, and bake at once in a moderate oven (375°F/190°C/GM5) for 15 to 20 minutes, according to size of rolls. When brown and crisp, brush the rolls over with a little milk or melted butter to glaze them.

BAKING POWDER BISCUITS

8 oz (225 g) plain flour
3 level teaspoons (15 ml) baking powder
½ level teaspoon (2.5 ml) salt
2–3 oz (50–75 g) softened butter
¼ pint (150 ml) milk

Sieve flour, baking powder and salt into a mixing bowl. Rub softened butter into mixture with pastry blender or your fingers; then add milk, stirring mixture quickly, until you have soft but not sticky dough.

Knead dough with floured fingertips on a lightly floured board just enough to shape it into a smooth ball; roll or pat out lightly to ½-inch (12 mm) thickness and cut in rounds with a floured glass or biscuit cutter. Bake on a greased baking sheet in a hot oven (450°F/230°C/GM8) for about 15 minutes, or until biscuits are golden brown. Makes 12.

POPOVERS

¾ pint (450 ml) milk
½ level teaspoon (2.5 ml) salt
1 oz (25 g) melted butter
5 eggs, lightly beaten
8 oz (225 g) sifted plain flour

Combine milk, salt, butter and eggs. Add flour and beat until smooth. The batter should have the consistency of thick cream. Half-fill well-buttered baking cups and bake in a fairly hot oven (425°F/220°C/GM7) for 15 minutes. Reduce temperature to 375°F/190°C/GM5 and bake for 15 to 20 minutes longer. Makes 12 to 16 popovers.

Cakes

If bread is the staff of life, then cakes must surely be counted as one of life's great blessings . . . proper symbols for festivities, feasting and friendship. 'That takes the cake' is an expression from my early childhood, a hangover, no doubt, from almost a century before, when a giant cake was given as the prize to the winners of the Cake Walk – a popular dance and a competition held in the American Deep South.

At different periods of history, cakes have been credited with everything from deciding political fates to starting a revolution. Today they can be criticized only for adding an extra inch or two to our long-suffering waistlines. And if it becomes necessary one day to choose between a delicious chocolate or coconut cake or taking in a notch in my belt, I am afraid that I will 'take the cake' every time.

My mother was a great cake-maker. I still cherish today a hidden nostalgia for the *Blitz Torte* – a Viennese cake of egg whites and ground nuts, dusted with cinnamon and served with chilled whipped cream – that my mother used to make for my early birthdays. And those superb Viennese *torten*, with their rich fillings and icings, are still among my favourites today, as are the rich wet chocolate cakes: the world-famous *Sacher Torte*, the secret recipe of Sacher's in Vienna; American Devil's Food Cake with chocolate or tart lemon icing; mocha layer cake, a subtle blend of chocolate and coffee spiked with rum; and light-textured Angel Cake; liqueur-soaked *baba-au-rhum*; and the delicate *madeleines* so beloved by Proust that he began *À la recherche du temps perdu* with a loving evocation of their delicate splendour.

My mother knew that no matter how carefully the cake mixture was prepared, the success or failure of her cakes would depend almost entirely upon the proper oven heat. She used to watch her oven carefully. Some, she said, were inclined to burn at the bottom, while in others the top was the hottest part. Every time we went away for a holiday to a rented house on one of the New York lakes or on the New England shore, she would make a test sponge cake to see how the new oven behaved, for she said it was only by experience and careful watching that the capabilities and faults of individual ovens could be learned. Today, of course, with our well-regulated modern ovens and temperature controls, cake-making is no longer fraught with problems.

There is no branch of cooking, however, where greater care and accuracy are required than in cake-making. I recommend strongly that if you are new to baking, you should follow cake recipes carefully, without altering quantities or cooking times, until you have made the recipe at least twice. Then experiment as you like.

The handling of the cake has much to do with its lightness. Some cooks seem to have a knack of turning out light cakes and pastry, while others have to practise before their creations are a success.

Always preheat your oven before making your cake, especially for those cakes which include baking powder. They will spoil if they have to stand waiting for the oven to heat, and even more so if they are put into an oven that is not hot enough. You will find a moderate oven is best for most cakes; rather hotter for small and light cakes than for thicker fruit cakes.

Assemble all ingredients and cake tins before you start to make the cake. If fruit is included in the recipe, prepare it in advance.

In some cake mixtures – especially the plainer ones – the butter or fat is rubbed into the flour; in others, it is beaten to a cream before the other ingredients are mixed with it; and in still other mixtures, the eggs or egg yolks are creamed with the sugar, and the butter is added in a melted form according to the nature of the cake.

1. When a cake rises in a cone in the centre, this indicates that your oven was too hot when you started baking. As a result, the sides of the cake hardened with a crust before the mixture had time to rise.
2. If the cake rises at one side, your oven is hotter on one side than the other. Correct this by turning the cake from time to time during baking.
3. If the bottom of the oven is too hot, place an asbestos mat underneath the cake to prevent the bottom burning.
4. Do not open the oven door for at least 5 minutes after the cake has been put in, and then only with the greatest care. Do not slam the oven door; it can be fatal to the successful rising of the cake. Handle a cake carefully during baking. Moving or shaking it during baking is almost certain to cause it to fall.
5. Be sure the cake is sufficiently cooked before removing it from

the oven. Small cakes are ready if they feel firm when gently touched with the finger. Larger cakes should be tested by running a warm skewer into the centre. If the skewer comes out sticky, the cake is not cooked enough; but if it is dry, the baking is finished.

6. Allow cakes to stand for a minute or two before removing them from the cake tins; you will find that they turn out more easily.

7. Always cool cakes on a wire cake rack so that the air gets around the bottom and sides.

8. The time given for baking in the following recipes is to be used as a guide only. Your oven and your personal taste will tell you when the cake is done.

PREPARATIONS OF CAKE TINS

Always prepare your cake tins before you mix ingredients for your cake, as most cakes will spoil if the mixture has to wait while you prepare the tins.

To line a round cake tin with paper: Cut a double band of paper 2 or 3 inches (5–8 cms) deeper than the cake tin and rather longer than the circumference. Fold up an inch (25 mm) of this band on the double fold and make a mark. Open out and make cuts along the marked–off inch (25 mm) of the paper an inch (25 mm) or so apart. Arrange this band inside the cake tin, making the notched section of paper lie flat on the bottom of the tin. Then cut a double round of paper to fit inside the tin and lay it smoothly on the bottom. The paper must lie perfectly flat; there must be no wrinkles. If the cake tin is very large, three or four folds of paper may be used. If the cake mixture contains a fair amount of butter, no grease is required, but if there is little or no fat in the cake ingredients, the paper and tin should be brushed lightly with clarified butter.

To line a flat tin with paper: If the tin is very shallow, the paper will not need to be shaped, but just pressed in smoothly and folded or snipped at the corners. Brush with clarified butter if necessary. Sometimes I dust the buttered paper with a mixture of flour and sugar as well.

For scones or small cakes: Butter a flat baking sheet and sprinkle it lightly with flour. Knock the edge of the sheet against the table after flouring so that surplus flour is shaken off.

For sponge cakes: Tie a double band of paper round the outside of the tin to project 2 or 3 inches (5–8 cms) above the top edge. Coat the inside of the tin and the paper with melted clarified butter. Do not use butter that is too liquid, or your coating will be too thin. Dust lightly with equal quantities of flour and castor sugar to give sponge cake a light dry coating, turning the mould round and round until every part is coated. Knock tin against side of table to shake off surplus flour and sugar.

Small cake tins: Brush tins with clarified butter and dust with flour and sugar.

I always like to have 2 oz (50 g) each of sieved flour and sugar, ready mixed in a lightly covered storage jar, for the preparation of cake tins.

TO KEEP CAKES

Do not store cakes until quite cold. Large cakes will keep best if wrapped in paper and put in a tin box with a tight-fitting lid. Fruit cakes which have to be kept for any length of time should be wrapped in greaseproof paper and then in a sheet of ordinary paper or a clean cloth. For small cakes the box should be lined with paper.

STALE CAKES AND BISCUITS

Many puddings and sweets can be made with the remains of stale cakes and broken biscuits. Small pieces of white cake such as sponge and Madeira cake, if too small for other purposes, can be made into crumbs by rubbing them through a wire sieve, and these can be used instead of breadcrumbs for many sweets. The crumbs will keep for some time if they are dried in a slow oven and then stored in a jar with a tight-fitting lid.

Use larger pieces of cake to make trifles and other puddings after soaking them with a little liqueur, wine or fruit juice.

SPONGE CAKE

6 egg yolks
8 oz (225 g) sugar
2 tablespoons (30 ml) lemon juice or water
Grated rind of ½ lemon
Generous pinch of salt
3 oz (75 g) plain flour, sifted 4 times
1 oz (25 g) cornflour
6 egg whites

Beat egg yolks, sugar, lemon juice or water, lemon rind and salt until light and fluffy (5 minutes at high mixer speed). Sift flour and cornflour, and mix into egg yolk mixture a little at a time. Whisk egg whites until soft peaks form, and fold gently into yolk mixture.

Divide mixture into 2 unbuttered cake tins. Cut through mixture gently several times to break up any large air bubbles. Bake in a slow oven (350°F/180°C/GM4) for 25 to 30 minutes. Test by denting lightly with finger; if the cake is done, the dent will spring back.

Invert layers on wire racks. When cool, loosen edges and remove from tins.

ANGEL CAKE

2 oz (50 g) cake flour
1 oz (25 g) cornflour
1 teaspoon (5 ml) cream of tartar
Salt
8 egg whites
4 oz (100 g) castor sugar
1 teaspoon (5 ml) orange-flower water or
vanilla extract
½ teaspoon (2.5 ml) almond extract
Glacé Icing (page 825)

Sieve flour and cornflour two or three times with the cream of tartar. Add a pinch of salt to egg whites and beat as stiffly as possible. Sieve sugar and mix it into beaten egg whites. Mix in the flour and cream of tartar mixture gradually, and then the orange-flower water or vanilla, and almond extract. Do not stop beating after the mixing is begun, and keep the mixture as light as possible. Pour into a floured but ungreased tin; cut through mixture twice with a spatula, and bake on the lowest rack of a preheated moderate oven (375°F/190°C/GM5) for 35 to 40 minutes. Test the cake with a fine skewer before removing it from the oven and do not allow it to become too brown. When ready, turn the cake upside down on a sheet of paper, and leave it until the tin can be slipped off easily. Serve cake plain, or ice with Glacé Icing.

LEMON LAYER CAKE

4 oz (100 g) butter
4 oz (100 g) sugar
3 egg whites
8 oz (225 g) plain flour
1 teaspoon (5 ml) baking powder
About ¼ pint (150 ml) milk

LEMON FILLING
Grated rind and juice of ½ lemon
1–2 tablespoons (15–30 ml) sugar
3 egg yolks, well beaten
1 tablespoon (15 ml) water
1 small piece butter

Beat butter and sugar together until light and creamy. Whip egg whites to a stiff froth. Sieve flour with baking powder. Add milk and flour alternately to the butter and sugar mixture. Fold in egg whites and mix very lightly. Pour the mixture into 2 sandwich cake tins which have been greased and lined with paper. Bake in a moderate oven(375°F/190°C/GM5) for about 20 minutes, or until a light brown colour and well cooked. Turn out to cool, and serve with the following filling between the two layers.

LEMON FILLING

Combine grated rind and strained juice of ½ lemon in the top of a double saucepan, and add sugar, egg yolks and water. Cook over water, stirring continuously, until thick and smooth. Stir in butter. Remove from heat and allow the mixture to cool before using it.

BISCUITS À LA CUILLER

6 oz (175 g) sugar
6 egg yolks
¼ teaspoon (1.25 ml) vanilla extract
6 oz (175 g) plain flour, sifted 4 times
6 egg whites, stiffly beaten
Powdered sugar

Cream sugar with egg yolks and vanilla extract in a warm bowl until fluffy and almost white. Then fold in flour carefully, a third at a time; fold in stiffly beaten egg whites. Place a piece of waxed paper on a baking sheet. Force mixture through a piping bag on to paper; each finger should be 3 inches (8 cms) long by 1¼ inches (3 cms) wide; sprinkle lightly with powdered sugar and bake in a slow oven (325°F/170°C/GM3), with door open, until light brown. Remove from the paper with a thin metal spatula while they are still warm. When cool, put them together in pairs to keep moist.

MADELEINES

2 oz (50 g) butter
4 oz (100 g) castor sugar
4 eggs, separated
3 oz (75 g) flour, sifted
1 oz (25 g) cornflour, sifted
Vanilla extract
1 tablespoon (15 ml) cognac
Beaten egg white
Icing sugar or Glacé Icing (page 825)

Whisk butter and sugar in electric mixer until light and creamy. Then beat in egg yolks one by one with a little of the flour. Whisk egg whites until stiff and add them alternately with remaining flour and cornflour. Add vanilla extract and cognac, and mix very lightly. Half-fill *madeleine* moulds or other tiny individual moulds, buttered and dusted with flour, with this mixture, and bake in a moderate oven (375°F/190°C/GM5) for 25 to 35 minutes, or until well risen and nicely browned. Brush with beaten egg white and dust with icing sugar, or ice with Glacé Icing.

CHOCOLATE CAKE

4 oz (100 g) butter
8 oz (225 g) sugar
2 oz (50 g) unsweetened chocolate melted
over hot water
1 teaspoon (5 ml) vanilla extract
2 eggs, well beaten
6 oz (175 g) plain flour
2 oz (50 g) cornflour
½ teaspoon (2.5 ml) salt
2 level teaspoons (10 ml) baking powder
¼ pint (150 ml) milk

Cream butter and beat in sugar, chocolate, vanilla extract and eggs. Sift flour and cornflour with salt and baking powder. Add to first mixture alternately with milk. Spread in shallow pan or two 9-inch (23 cm) layer cake tins. Bake for about 30 minutes in a slow oven (350°F/180°C/GM4).

ENGLISH COCONUT CAKE

8 oz (225 g) softened butter
6 oz (175 g) castor sugar
8 oz (225 g) dried coconut
3 eggs, well beaten
12 oz (350 g) plain flour
4 oz (100 g) cornflour
1 teaspoon (5 ml) baking powder
Grated lemon or orange rind
About 8 fluid oz (225 ml) milk

Beat softened butter and sugar in electric mixer until light and creamy. Add the coconut and well-beaten eggs. Sieve flour, cornflour and baking powder, and add grated orange or lemon rind, to taste. Fold into the sugar and butter mixture gradually, adding enough milk to make the mixture just soft enough to drop from the spoon. (A cake made with milk should never be too moist.) Pour the mixture into a lined cake tin and bake in a moderate oven (375°F/190°C/GM5) for 1½ to 2 hours, or until nicely risen and firm.

CHOCOLATE ROLL

2 oz (50 g) chocolate
1 tablespoon (15 ml) water
4 oz (100 g) butter
2 oz (50 g) sugar
2 eggs
4 oz (100 g) sifted plain flour
Vanilla extract
½ teaspoon (2.5 ml) baking powder
Vanilla Butter Icing (page 824)
Chocolate Butter Icing (optional, page 824)
Powdered sugar

Grate or shred the chocolate and melt it slowly with water without allowing it to boil. Cream butter and sugar. Add 1 egg and a quarter of the flour, and beat until well mixed. Add remaining egg and then the rest of the flour, beating until all is well mixed. The lightness of the roll depends upon the mixture being well beaten. Flavour with cooled melted chocolate and vanilla extract, to taste. Stir in baking powder and mix well.

Line a rectangular baking tin with waxed paper. Butter the paper well and spread the batter evenly over it. (The mixture should not be more than ¼ inch (6 mm) thick, or it will not roll well when baked.) Bake the cake in a moderately hot oven (400°F/200°C/GM6) for 10 to 15 minutes, or until well browned and firm to the touch.

Turn the cake out on to a board dusted with sugar; remove the paper from the cake; sprinkle more sugar over the top of the cake; trim the edges and roll up quickly. When cold, unroll; spread with Vanilla Butter Icing and then re-roll the cake. Ice with Chocolate or Vanilla Butter Icing if desired, or dust with powdered sugar.

CHOCOLATE LAYER CAKE

4 oz (100 g) butter, softened
Grated rind of 1 orange
Grated rind of 1 lemon
8 oz (225 g) castor sugar
4 egg yolks
6 oz (175 g) plain flour
1 teaspoon (5 ml) cream of tartar
1 teaspoon (5 ml) carbonate of soda
2 oz (50 g) cornflour
¼ pint (150 ml) milk
4 egg whites
Chocolate Butter Icing (page 824)
Chocolate Glacé Icing (page 826)
Preserved fruits or finely chopped pistachio nuts

Whisk softened butter in electric mixer until light and creamy. Combine grated orange and lemon rind with sugar and add to butter, beating them well together. Beat in egg yolks with a spoonful of flour. Combine cream of tartar and carbonate of soda with remaining flour and cornflour, and add them gradually to the other ingredients along with the milk. Whip egg whites to a stiff froth, and fold them quickly and lightly into the cake mixture. Bake in a lined cake tin in a slow oven (350°F/180°C/GM4) for 1 to

1½ hours, or until cake is well risen and firm to the touch. Turn out of the tin and allow to cool. Then cut the cake in 3 to 4 layers; spread each layer with Chocolate Butter Icing and assemble cake again. Ice with Chocolate Glacé Icing and decorate with preserved fruits or finely chopped pistachio nuts.

CHOCOLATE ICE BOX CAKE

8 egg yolks
6 oz (175 g) sugar
¾ pint (450 ml) milk
½–1 teaspoon (2.5–5 ml) vanilla extract
2 level tablespoons (30 ml) gelatine
4 tablespoons (60 ml) cold water
1½ oz (40 g) bitter chocolate, melted
2 tablespoons (30 ml) melted butter
4 tablespoons (60 ml) rum or Kirsch
¾ pint (450 ml) double cream
Sponge fingers
Kirsch and water
Whipped cream
Walnuts

Combine egg yolks and sugar in the top of a double saucepan and work the mixture with a wooden spoon until smooth. Bring the milk to a boil and add vanilla extract; then add milk gradually to the yolk mixture, stirring rapidly with a wire whisk. Cook over boiling water until the mixture becomes smooth and thick. Do not allow mixture to boil, or it will curdle.

Soften the gelatine in cold water and add it to the hot custard, stirring until it dissolves. Cool the custard but do not let it set. Divide the custard into two portions and add melted chocolate, melted butter and rum or Kirsch to one portion. Whip cream until stiff and fold half of it into each of the two mixtures.

Line the sides of a medium spring-form cake tin with sponge

fingers dipped in equal quantities of Kirsch and water. Fill the mould with alternating layers of chocolate and vanilla cream, allowing each layer to set in refrigerator for about 30 minutes before adding the next.

Set the cake (still in its pan) in the refrigerator to chill for at least 12 hours, or overnight.

When ready to serve, remove the sides of pan from the cake, leaving the cake in the bottom of the pan. Top with whipped cream and walnuts.

SACHER TORTE

6 oz (175 g) butter, softened
6 oz (175 g) sugar
6 oz (175 g) bitter-sweet chocolate
6 egg yolks
1 teaspoon (5 ml) vanilla extract
8 egg whites
8 oz (225 g) sifted plain flour
Apricot glaze
Chocolate Glacé Icing (page 826)
Whipped cream, chilled

I have no idea if this recipe is the original one from Sacher's famous coffee-house in Vienna; all I know is that it is one of the most deliciously rich cakes I know. Mother used to make it for winter coffee parties and serve it with whipped cream.

Whisk softened butter and sugar in the electric mixer until smooth and light-coloured. Melt chocolate; cool to lukewarm and beat into butter and sugar mixture. Then beat in egg yolks one by one. Flavour with vanilla extract.

Whisk egg whites until stiff and fold into cake mixture alternately with sifted flour.

Butter and flour a spring-form cake tin; spoon cake mixture into tin and bake in a slow oven (350°F/180°C/GM4) for 45 minutes to 1 hour (testing for doneness after 45 minutes).

Let cake cool in the tin overnight. Remove the rim and spread top and sides of cake with a thin layer of apricot glaze. Then ice the entire cake with Chocolate Glacé Icing. Serve with chilled whipped cream.

APPLE TORTE

2 tart eating apples
1 egg
6 oz (175 g) sugar
2 oz (50 g) plain flour
1 level teaspoon (5 ml) baking powder
Pinch of salt
¼ teaspoon (1.25 ml) almond extract
2 oz (50 g) walnut, chopped
Butter
Whipped cream

Peel, core and slice apples. Beat egg lightly; add sugar and apple
slices. Then combine flour, baking powder, salt, almond extract
and chopped walnuts, and stir into apple mixture. Mix well. Pour
into a well-buttered baking dish or soufflé dish and bake in a slow
oven (325°F/170°C/GM3) for 25 minutes. Serve topped with
whipped cream.

BLITZ TORTE

TORTE
4 oz (100 g) butter
4 oz (100 g) castor sugar
3 egg yolks
3 oz (75 g) plain flour
1 oz (25 g) cornflour
2 level teaspoons (10 ml) baking powder
½ level teaspoon (2.5 ml) cinnamon
6 tablespoons (90 ml) single cream
½ teaspoon (2.5 ml) vanilla extract

TOPPING
3 egg whites
6 oz (175 g) castor sugar
½ teaspoon (2.5 ml) vanilla extract

GARNISH
Whipped cream
Powdered sugar
Cinnamon

TORTE

Cream butter and sugar until light and fluffy. Add egg yolks one at a time, beating until well mixed. Combine flour, cornflour, baking powder and cinnamon, and stir into butter mixture alternately with cream to which you have added vanilla extract. Spread mixture evenly in 2 spring–form sandwich tins.

TOPPING

Beat egg whites until stiff; then beat in sugar and vanilla extract, beating until mixture is thick and glossy. Spread topping evenly over *Torte* and bake in a slow oven (325°F/170°C/GM3) for 25 minutes, then at 350°F/180°C/GM4 for 30 minutes. Cool; then carefully remove cakes from tins.

Just before serving, place 1 *Torte* on serving dish, meringue side down, and cover with whipped cream. Add top layer of *Torte* and dust lightly with powdered sugar and cinnamon. Serves 12.

STRAWBERRY TORTE

TORTE
2 oz (50 g) butter
4 oz (100 g) castor sugar
4 egg yolks
½ teaspoon (2.5 ml) vanilla extract
3 oz (75 g) plain flour
1 oz (25 g) cornflour
2 level teaspoons (10 ml) baking powder
4–6 tablespoons (60–90 ml) cream

TOPPING
4 egg whites
8 oz (225 g) sugar
½ teaspoon (2.5 ml) vanilla extract

FILLING
1 punnet fresh strawberries, crushed
and sweetened
½ pint (300 ml) cream, whipped

GARNISH
Powdered sugar and cinnamon

TORTE

Combine butter, sugar, yolks, vanilla extract, flour, cornflour, baking powder and cream, and beat until smooth. Spread mixture in two 8- or 9-inch (20 or 23 cms) sandwich tins.

TOPPING

Beat 4 egg whites until stiff. Gradually blend in sugar, beating continuously. Add vanilla extract, to taste.

Spread topping over *Torte*. Bake in a very slow oven (300°F/150°C/GM2) for 30 minutes. Allow to cool in tins.

FILLING

Blend strawberries, crushed and sweetened, with whipped cream.

Just before serving, place 1 *Torte* on serving dish, topping side down, and cover with filling. Add top layer of *Torte* and dust lightly with powdered sugar and cinnamon. Serves 12.

FRENCH MERINGUE CAKE

CAKE
6 eggs, separated
6 oz (175 g) sugar
2 tablespoons (30 ml) water
Grated rind of 1 lemon
Generous pinch of salt
3 oz (75 g) plain flour
1 oz (25 g) cornflour
Butter
Apricot jam

MERINGUE
3 egg whites
Sugar and salt

GARNISH
Canned apricots

CAKE
Beat egg yolks, sugar, water, lemon rind and salt until light and fluffy (5 minutes in mixer at high speed). Sift flour and cornflour, and gradually blend into egg yolk mixture. Whisk egg whites until stiff but not dry and fold gently into yolk mixture. Line inside and bottom of 2 cake tins with buttered paper. Pour in mixture and bake in a slow oven (350°F/180°C/GM4) for 45 minutes, or until golden brown. Invert cakes on wire rack and cool. The next day cut the cakes into thin layers; spread with apricot jam and re-form cake.

MERINGUE
Beat egg whites until stiff; add sugar and salt, to taste. Spread cake with meringue mixture and bake in a fairly hot oven (425°F/220°C/GM8) as you would a meringue.

Just before serving, decorate with drained apricot halves.

SABAYON CAKE

CAKE
6 eggs, separated
6 oz (175 g) sugar
2 tablespoons (30 ml) water
Grated rind of 1 lemon
Generous pinch of salt
6 oz (175 g) plain flour
2 oz (50 g) cornflour
Butter

SABAYON SAUCE
6 oz (175 g) sugar
Grated rind and juice of 1 orange, made up to
¼ pint (150 ml) with water
3–4 tablespoons (45–60 ml) Marsala or sherry
1½ tablespoons (22 ml) brandy

ORANGE TOPPING
1 egg
5 oz (150 g) sugar
1 oz (25 g) plain flour
Grated rind and juice of 1 orange
½ pint (300 ml) double cream, whipped

GARNISH
4 oz (100 g) chopped toasted almonds

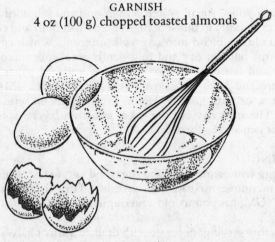

CAKE

Beat yolks, sugar, water, lemon rind and salt until light and fluffy (5 minutes at high mixer speed). Sift flour and cornflour, and mix into egg yolk mixture a little at a time. Whisk egg whites until soft peaks form and fold gently into yolk mixture. Place equal quantities of batter in 3 lb (1.4 kg) 8-inch (20 cm) cake tins which have been buttered and lightly dusted with flour. Cut through mixture gently several times to break up any large air bubbles. Bake in a slow oven (325°F/170°C/GM3) for 45 minutes, or until golden brown. Invert layers on wire racks. When cool, loosen edges and remove from tins.

SABAYON SAUCE

Place sugar, orange rind, juice and water in a saucepan, and simmer gently for 20 minutes. Remove from heat and add Marsala or sherry, and brandy.

ORANGE TOPPING

Place all topping ingredients except cream in the top of a double saucepan and heat, stirring, until thick and smooth. Cool; fold in whipped cream.

Brush 2 cake layers liberally with Sabayon Sauce; spread with Orange Topping, and put all layers together. Brush top and sides of cake with sauce, spread with topping and pat chopped almonds firmly around sides of cake. Serves 8 to 12.

Cake Icings
Butter Icing

Butter icing must be quite cold and hard before it is used. In hot weather, put icing in refrigerator before using it. If a large plain cake is to be iced, it is usual to split cake once or twice and spread icing between layer. I sometimes blend a little double cream into the icing just before using. Spread a thin coating of the icing on the top and sides of the cake, and put most of the icing into a forcing bag, with a rather large pipe on the end of it. Force out the icing on the cake in stars or scrolls, and do it as quickly as possible, before the heat of your hand has time to soften the icing.

BASIC BUTTER ICING

6 oz (175 g) butter
8 oz (225 g) icing sugar
Vanilla, rum, Maraschino, Curaçao, etc.

Place butter in a mixing bowl and beat with a wooden spoon or spatula until it is like whipped cream. Sieve sugar, and blend it gradually into the cream butter. Add flavouring of your choice – vanilla, rum, Maraschino, Curaçao, or any of the others below, and the icing is ready for use.

CHOCOLATE BUTTER ICING

Make icing as above. Dissolve 2 oz (50 g) unsweetened chocolate in a little water or milk; cool and mix with icing.

STRAWBERRY OR RASPBERRY BUTTER ICING

Add a few drops of essence of strawberry or raspberry to Basic Butter Icing. Colour pink.

ORANGE OR LEMON BUTTER ICING

Grate the rind of an orange or lemon; rub into 2 oz (50 g) of the sugar to be used for the icing. Make icing as above and colour with a little yellow colouring.

Glacé Icing

Glacé Icing may be poured over the cakes, or individual cakes may be dipped into it. If a large cake is to be iced, put it on a wire stand placed on a sheet of white paper, and pour over enough icing to cover the top only, or the top and sides, as desired. Any icing that runs over may be gathered up and used again. Small cakes may be iced in the same way. They may be held on the point of a palette knife over the pan of icing, and the icing poured over them, or they may be dipped right into the icing. Always decorate cakes while icing is still soft.

BASIC GLACÉ ICING

8 oz (225 g) icing sugar
1–2 tablespoons (15–30 ml) water or other liquid

This simple soft icing is quickly and easily made. Sieve sugar into an enamelled saucepan. Add 1 to 2 tablespoons (15–30 ml) water or other liquid and stir over a medium heat with a wooden spoon until warm. Do not let the icing become too hot, or it will be lumpy. As sugar melts, icing becomes softer, so keep liquid to a minimum. Icing should be thick enough to coat back of wooden spoon. It will then be of the right consistency for coating a cake. If icing becomes too soft, stiffen it by adding a little more sieved icing sugar. But end result is better if this does not have to be done.

LIQUEUR GLACÉ ICING

Make Glacé Icing as above, using any liqueur to moisten the sugar along with a little water. Add colouring if desired.

RASPBERRY OR STRAWBERRY GLACÉ ICING

Make Glacé Icing as above, flavouring with raspberry or strawberry essence and colouring it pink. Strawberry or raspberry syrup may be used instead of water.

CHOCOLATE GLACÉ ICING

Melt unsweetened chocolate with a very little water until smooth. Flavour Glacé Icing with a little vanilla. Combine with chocolate, beating well. Use immediately. I sometimes add a small piece of butter to give the icing a glossy appearance. Do not let icing boil, or it will lose its shine.

COFFEE GLACÉ ICING

Make icing as above, using clear black coffee or instant coffee (dissolved in a little hot water) to moisten the sugar. Flavour with a few drops of vanilla extract.

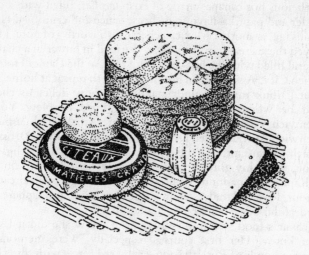

CHAPTER TWENTY-THREE

A Guide to Cheese

O n a trip to Mexico some years ago, I discovered – along with the delights of its ancient cities, its sunswept beaches, its regional cuisine – the deft use Mexican cooks make of local cheeses. I particularly liked the cheese soups I tasted there: *sopa mexicana*, a well-flavoured chicken stock enriched with cream, garnished with fine strips of cooked chicken breast and raw avocado pear, and topped with crumbled cream cheese; and *sopa con queso*, chicken stock simmered with cinnamon, paprika, onions, tomatoes and Mexican cheese.

Mexican cooks use crumbled cream cheese, too, as a garnish for some of their heartier soups of corn or black beans, to top bean casseroles and *tortillas*, or as a tangy filling for baked green chile peppers.

Delicious hot canapés made of crisp *tortillas*, filled with a chili powder and paprika-flavoured cheese sauce and crumbled *Chorizo* sausage, is another Mexican cheese dish worthy of note. I first enjoyed these crisp corn pancakes, warmed in butter in a chafing dish and filled with the hot cheese mixture, at the Bamer Hotel in Mexico City. A wonderful hot fingerfood to repeat at home.

But I think my first understanding of how delicious cheese could be when cooked was when I lived in New York's Greenwich Village and used to frequent a small, dark *bistro* on Greenwich Avenue called Drossie's, or more correctly, Drossie's Russian Restaurant. For the *cognoscenti*, Drossie was a delightful person, with tiny glittering eyes, raven locks and parrot nose, a pre-Raphaelite madonna of pre-Gingold vintage, who breathed humour, love and understanding into the simple atmosphere and wonderful food so beloved by her familiars.

Drossie's food was impossibly cheap. How she did it I shall never know. Her first courses, especially, were memorable: steaming bowls of Russian soup – ruby red *borsch* with thin slices of onion, duck and beetroot shining faintly through its translucent depths, and golden-toned *stchi*, breathing hints of cabbage, onion and tomato – both served with generous dollops of sour cream.

Red caviar dressed with sour cream and a wedge of lemon was another appetite whetter that found favour at Drossie's, as was her special chicken liver *pâté* served with black bread. But the greatest of all these for me were her cheese *blini à la Drossie* – paper-thin pancakes wrapped around cinnamon-flavoured cottage cheese, the whole fried until crisp in butter and oil, and served hot, topped with chilled sour cream.

On my last trip to Greenwich Village, I looked hopefully for Drossie and her Russian Restaurant on Greenwich Avenue, but alas, it exists no more, and Drossie is either serving her excellent specialities to a favoured few in the back streets of some other great city, or to the angels themselves.

One of the most versatile, as well as one of the most ancient, foods known to man, cheese can be served at every course throughout the meal, from appetizer to dessert. In France alone, over 400 different varieties of cheese are still produced – 400 different flavours, each with its own character, its own history, its own special pleasure. Of these, about 100 are produced commercially, and at least thirty are available regularly in Britain. Add to this the famous cheeses of Switzerland, Denmark, Germany and Italy, not to mention the sizeable cheese-producing industry in Great Britain, and you get some idea of the complexity and excitement of this vast subject.

Many people are sticklers about cheese. French friends swear that it must come in one place only in the meal, after the main course or salad, and definitely before the sweet. Italians are apt to be content with a slice of Grana or Provolone with a crisp apple or succulent pear in place of dessert. Americans team it haphazardly with salad, the worst of all worlds, for cheese's perfect partner is wine, and everyone knows that wine is an enemy of salads. The English prefer their cheese after the sweet, a hangover from the days when it served as a savoury prelude to port.

If cheese is to serve as a preparation for port, I am all for it. But if this is just habit, with no port forthcoming, I range myself on the side of the French, and prefer it in what I consider its natural place, after the main course or salad, so that the wines served with it can be in the same *gamme* as those served with the meat.

But wherever it comes in the meal, one cannot but agree with Hilaire Belloc that it is a profound matter. Perhaps it is just this profundity that is its worst enemy. For the choice of a perfect cheese in prime condition, and of the correct accompaniments – wine, bread, butter, biscuits, etc. – often prove to be pitfalls for the unwary.

I give you here a list of some of my favourites.

BEL PAESE

A soft but firm Italian cheese – its yellow-cream richness is mild and delicately flavoured – Bel Paese is a non-aggressive cheese, delicious with fruit. Served almost exclusively as a dessert cheese, it can be used, if necessary, as a substitute for Mozzarella in certain cooked recipes. Bel Paese keeps well, its flavour tending to sharpen as it ages. Serve at room temperature.

Companion wines: Beaujolais, red and dry white Italian wines

BRIE

Talleyrand called this soft, creamy French cheese 'the King of Cheeses'. Brie comes in thin, yellow-crusted cartwheels – the

---

trade calls it 'red' – dusted with a powdery white mould. Delicious when soft and a little runny, apt to be chalky when under-ripe, Brie smells of ammonia when past its prime. It is available in Britain by the slice, in individual, wedge-shaped, wooden boxes, or cut to order from the whole.

Brie used to be produced by individual farmers, and in consequence had a subtle variety of flavours. Today the production is industrialized, and the cheese has, alas, lost much of its subtlety and flavour, with a tendency to be oversalted to keep it from becoming too runny when cut.

Brie de Meaux is the best known, and the largest in diameter. *Brie de Provins* is not as wide and a little thicker. *Brie de Coulommiers* has cream added to the original mixture, and is eaten fresh.

Brie is at its mellow best as a dessert cheese; try it, too, as the flavour accent for cheese pastry. The optimum season is from November to June.

Companion wines: Corton, Pommard, Nuits St Georges

BURRINI
These pear-sized Italian cheeses with a soft but firm texture resemble twin gourds more than anything. Pale yellow in colour,

with an earthy tang, Burrini enclose a small egg of fresh butter in the outer layer of golden cheese. Cut it across in slices so that butter and cheese come with each slice. Burrini are strung together with raffia.

Companion wines: Chianti, Beaujolais, Nuits St Georges, *vini dei castelli*

CAERPHILLY
Caerphilly is a semi–soft cheese with a close, flaky texture, much like Cheddar, but white in colour. Caerphilly used to be made of partially skimmed milk, but today it is manufactured from full–cream milk. It is produced in Somerset, where it is packed while still warm into small hoops, to give a cheese weighing about 8 lb (3.8 kg). Caerphilly is an unripened cheese, sold in a matter of days after being formed and soaked in brine.

Excellent toasted, Caerphilly cuts well for sandwiches; but it is at its best when eaten with fresh bread and ale. It is a great favourite with children because of its mild flavour, and it is easily digestible.

Companion wines: *Rosés*, dry white Burgundies, dry sherry, ale

CAMEMBERT
One of the world's favourite cheeses, smooth-textured Camembert originated in the town of Camembert, Normandy, created by a French farmwife, Madame Harel, almost two centuries ago. Today, there is a statue in the main square of the town to celebrate this fairly recent addition to France's cheeses. Camembert, available here in creamy rounds, fairly thick, with a yellowish-orange, mould-covered crust, or in individual foil-wrapped portions, is at its best when it is pale yellow, slightly runny and soft. The faintly bitter taste of Camembert – attributed to the straw on which it is matured – fairly cries out for a piece of crusty French bread, a Claret or a Burgundy, and a slice of ripe pear. Camembert is available all year round, but the best quality cheeses are found in the months of January, February, March and April.

Camembert cooks well: Camembert toasts and Camembert fritters; try it, too, soused in dry white wine.

Companion wines: Clos Vougeot, Côtes Rôties, Hermitage, dry cider

CHEDDAR

By far the most popular English cheese, Cheddar is slightly darker than milk, cream to soft gold in colour, and close and buttery in texture. It tends to go flaky when mature, crumbly when aged, and has a full, clean, slightly nutty flavour. Cheddar is delicious with a crust of fresh farmhouse bread. Cheddar cooks well, if a trifle too greasily, for soufflés and fine sauces.

Companion wines: Clarets, Burgundies, ale, beer, cider

CHESHIRE

The oldest English cheese, probably being made when Britain was first visited by Caesar's legions. Crumbly in texture and not as flaky as Cheddar, Cheshire cheese is very slightly salty in flavour and reddish gold in colour.

Companion wines: Beaujolais, ale, beer, cider

BLUE CHESHIRE

A rarer cheese than Cheshire, and a great favourite with epicures, this aged cheese has a rich flavour which is deliciously different. Blue Cheshire is veined with blue and green, hence its name.

Companion wines: Clarets, Burgundies, ale, beer, cider

CHÈVRE

The Chèvre family numbers a variety of cheeses made of goat's milk. Creamy, yet chalky in texture, with a distinctive flavour all its own, this cheese is usually eaten fresh, though some are eaten very ripe. Chèvre comes in a variety of shapes, the most common of which is a cylindrical loaf. Salty when not quite ripe, it is at its best when there is a little green mould on the outside skin. Serve Chèvre with French bread and butter, and a robust red wine or dry *rosé*.

Companion wines: Beaujolais, Beaujolais Fleurie, Brouilly, *vins rosés*

DANISH BLUE

Danish Blue is a quick ripener, whiter and sharper in flavour than other Danish cheeses. Its green and blue veining is a characteristic of this popular cheese. As it ripens, it becomes creamier in texture and flavour. Use Danish Blue to give added zest to cocktail dips;

cream it with butter and brandy, and use it as a spread, or to fill crisp celery stalks; crumble a little into a French dressing for a green salad with a difference.

Companion wines: Châteauneuf-du-Pape, Hermitage, Côtes Rôties

DERBY
A very mild cheese, pleasantly firm, and not unlike Cheddar in appearance, but milder in flavour. Known as the working man's cheese in Victorian times, Derby goes supremely well on a hot summer day in the country. Serve with dark bread and an apple.

Companion wines: Beaujolais, ale, beer, cider

DERBY SAGE
Derby Sage used to be made especially for harvest time and Christmas from milk in which bruised sage and parsley had been steeped overnight. Today, this mild-flavoured cheese is available throughout the year. The green and white milks are kept separate until the curds are ready to be vatted, then mixed together. A most attractive addition to the cheese-board.

Companion wines: Beaujolais, ale, beer, cider

EDAM
A decorative red cannonball, Edam can be mild in flavour or a little sharp, according to its age. The proper way to serve it is to cut a small round lid from the top from which the rest of the cheese is extracted with a sharp spoon or scoop. Replace lid after using to keep cheese soft. Try a thick wedge of Edam teamed with black bread and butter and a slice of apple for a morning snack.

Companion wines: Beaujolais, dry white and light red wines, cider

EMMENTHAL
Commonly called Swiss cheese, Emmenthal comes in tremendous straw-coloured wheels, which are aged for varying lengths of time to achieve a faintly waxy texture and huge glistening 'eyes'. This is a perfect cheese for the table, besides being one of the greatest cooking cheeses in the world. Emmenthal is produced with both whole milk and skimmed milk, and resembles its cousin, Gruyère, except that it is softer in texture

and flavour. Use Emmenthal (and/or Gruyère) for cooked dishes of all kinds. Available all year.

Companion wines: Corton and all the red Burgundies, Riesling, beer

GORGONZOLA
Gorgonzola originated in the town of the same name near Milan more than 1,000 years ago. It is a creamy, richly flavoured cheese with blue-green veins, riper in flavour than other blue cheeses, and softer and creamier in texture. Gorgonzola is remarkably good with fruit, or with crusty bread and butter and a hardy red wine. Like most blue cheeses, Gorgonzola combines well with butter and oil for dips, spreads and sauces. Try it in the German manner, '*passiert*', pounded with butter and then forced in coiled ribbons through a large holed colander.

Companion wines: Barolo, Chianti, *vini dei castelli*

GOUDA
A junior version of Edam, this fresh Dutch cheese can often be a trifle young and rubbery when found in the markets. Give it a little time to age before using it. Gouda melts well and is useful for toasted cheese sandwiches.

Companion wines: Beaujolais, dry white and light red wines, cider

GRUYÈRE
Produced in the valley of Gruyère and the Swiss cantons of Fribourg, Neufchâtel and Vaud, Gruyère cheese is creamier, richer in flavour, and smoother in texture than Emmenthal and, more important to the novice shopper, it has tiny or almost non-existent eyes. Its melting quality is unbeatable, hence its use in *fondue*.

The most delicious of Gruyères – and hence the most difficult to come by – is the supreme aged Gruyère, which is delightfully rich, nutlike, and practically holeless.

Add a little freshly grated Parmesan for extra flavour. I find that Gruyère and/or Emmenthal marries wonderfully with Parmesan for soufflés, sauces and casseroles. The high flavour of one complementing the subtle smoothness of the other, when blended with cream and chicken stock, makes a most delicious cheese combination. Gruyère is available all year round.

Companion wines: Chambertin and all the red Burgundies, Riesling, beer

LEICESTER
Crumbly and flaky, much like Cheshire cheese in texture, Leicester has a deep orange-red colour. It keeps well, but is best when young and mild. Good with salads and watercress. Excellent as one of the components of Welsh rarebit.

Companion wines: Beaujolais, ale, beer, cider

LIVAROT
Produced in the cantons of Livarot and Vimoutiers in Normandy, Livarot is made of cow's milk. Round and flat, with a rather strong odour, it matures for four to six months, covered with hay, in special caves, where the cheese is placed after being encircled with a sort of covering called '*laiche*'.

Livarot is at its best from November to June. A little too strong for some tastes, it is nevertheless a great favourite with many.

Companion wines: Pomerol, Corton, dry cider

MARIBO
A whipped milk cheese, golden yellow in colour, with innumerable irregular holes, Maribo is a mild, creamy Danish cheese, with a faintly acid flavour when young, and strong and more definite when mature. Good with grapes. An excellent sandwich cheese.

Companion wines: Beaujolais and the red wines of Bordeaux, Bourgogne and the Côtes du Rhône

MAROILLES
Originating in a little French town, Thierache, in a region of woods and prairies, Maroilles is a soft-textured cheese with a reddish crust, square in shape, with a rich, redolent odour. It takes three to four months to mature in very humid caves. The cheese is washed with a wet brush and turned every sixteen days during the maturing process. At its best from October to June.

Companion wines: Nuits St Georges, Pommard, beer

MOZZARELLA

Once made exclusively of buffalo milk, now more ordinarily made of cow's milk, Mozzarella is an excellent culinary cheese, perfect for deep-frying, for topping pizzas, or to add its creamy flavour to baked lasagne or macaroni. In Italy, Mozzarella is eaten fresh with its buttermilk dripping from it.

Companion wines: Chianti, Soave, *vini dei castelli*

PARMESAN

Named after the ancient duchy of Parma, where this cheese was first produced 2,000 years ago, Parmesan is in reality the generic name for a family of hard cheeses known in the Italian peninsula as '*grana*'. Parmesan, made of skimmed milk mixed with rennet and saffron, is matured for one year in a cool store before being covered with a black-coloured mixture of oil, wine and *fumo nero*; it is then matured for at least one year longer at a higher, more moist temperature. Parmesan's dry texture keeps for years and gains in aromatic flavour.

Primarily known as a cheese for use in cooked dishes and for sprinkling over cooked dishes, *grana* is eaten as a dessert cheese in its home country. Use freshly grated Parmesan in sauces for spaghetti and rice dishes, and try sliced Parmesan cooked in alternate layers with sliced potatoes. Parmesan is available throughout the year.

Companion wines: Lambrusco, Barolo, Chianti, *vini dei castelli*

PONT L'EVÊQUE

Pont l'Evêque, made in familiar square moulds, is cured for four months to develop its rich, creamy texture, heavy crust and typical odour. Its flavour is ripe rather than mild, stronger in taste than either Brie or Camembert. Best avoided in its early stages and after it has passed the mark, Pont l'Evêque is one of the noblest of French cheeses. It is available all year round, but is at its best from October to June.

Companion wines: Moulin à Vent, white Burgundy, dry cider

PORT DU SALUT (PORT SALUT)

Early in the nineteenth century, a community of Trappist monks returning from exile installed themselves in the ancient monastery of Notre Dame du Port Salut, at Entrammes on the banks of the Mayenne in France, and began to produce for their own consumption a lightly cooked, moulded cheese with a firm crust, that has since become famous. Port Salut keeps well and has an agreeable flavour. Available all year round.

Companion wines: Anjou, Chinon, Musigny, Corton

ROQUEFORT
A hardy traveller since early Roman times, Roquefort is made with ewe's milk and mouldy bread, hand mixed, packed into glazed earthenware moulds, and matured in the natural caves of the Rouerge district of France, where moist winds called '*fleurines*' impart their own flavour and quality to this world-famous cheese. Pliny described the delights of Roquefort in the first century; Charlemagne claimed it as one of his special favourites; and nearer our own time, Curnonsky, France's prince of gastronomes, chose it as the finest cheese to bring out the best in France's great wines.

Roquefort is often used in salad dressings: either crumbled into a French dressing, or blended to a creamy sauce with sour cream and lemon juice. I like it combined with poached cauliflorets as an appetizer salad, or as a superb spread for grilled steak. Try Roquefort, too, creamed with butter and spiked with a drop of

brandy, as a stuffing for two-inch (5 cm) lengths of raw celery. Available all year round.

Companion wines: Chambertin, Châteuneuf-du-Pape, Hermitage; in fact, all the red wines of Bordeaux, Bourgogne and the Côtes du Rhône

STILTON
One of England's most famous cheeses, Stilton is sometimes called the world's most regal blue cheese. When properly ripened, its blue mould should be evenly distributed all over the surface in wide-branching veins; the background colour of the cheese is a rich cream, not anaemic white. Best season for this richly flavoured cheese is between November and April.

Companion wines: Clarets, Burgundies

TOMME
Tomme is in reality a whole family of cheeses, the most famous of which is *Tomme de Savoie*, a mild-flavoured, cream-coloured, smooth-textured, moulded cheese of the Savoy region of France. Other varieties: *Tomme au fenouil*, flavoured with fennel, and *Tomme au marc de raisin*, covered with a protective and flavourful layer of crushed grape pips. There is also a lesser known *Tomme de Brach*, made from ewe's milk and with a quite different flavour. They are available all year round.

Companion wines: Moulin à Vent, Hermitage, St Julien

CHAPTER TWENTY-FOUR

I Remember Christmas

Christmas has always been a great event in my family. The early years of my childhood have left me with a string of half-remembered moments, glittering in my memory like the silver ornaments on a Christmas tree. I remember the first happy time when I was allowed to take part in the preparations for Christmas instead of being kept in the wings, waiting to see 'what Santa brought me'. And ever since, it has been the preparations for Christmas that have excited me more than the presents – welcome as they are – or the actual event.

I remember my mother baking cookies weeks before the holidays, each type cut or formed into traditional shapes; the spice-flavoured *Lebkuchen*, the sugar-coated butter cookies, the

I REMEMBER CHRISTMAS

chocolate *tuiles*, the little Christmas stars, the decorated angels, the icebox cookies and gingerbread spears, gay little wreaths covered with crushed pistachio nuts, tiny, perfect marzipan apples, and rich, rum-scented chocolate truffles.

I remember getting out the boxes of Christmas ornaments and Christmas lights, kept carefully from year to year, with every year some new treasure added. For trimming the tree was a hilarious family pastime on Christmas Eve, a time to stay up late and help with the festivities. And when the tree was finished and everyone had laid his gifts underneath it, to be opened in the morning, there was champagne, and the first taste of Mother's cookies.

I remember the warm, steamy odours of the Christmas pudding, the pleasures of helping with the brandy butter, the chilled excitements of my father's special Christmas Morning egg-nog with apple brandy, made with apples from his own trees – the secret element that gives an indescribable hidden warmth to this Christmas drink.

I remember the 'Yankee Christmases' of my boyhood at my grandmother's farm, with their traditional roast turkey and cran-berry sauce, served with candied sweet potatoes and chestnut purée, and followed by mincemeat and pumpkin pies.

But best of all, perhaps, now that I am older and memories are beginning to sort themselves out into a clearer pattern, were the Christmases spent at *Tante* Gustel's.

Tante Gustel, my mother's German aunt and my great-aunt, was an out-and-out eccentric. She lived in what seemed to my childish eyes to be a veritable fairyland of exciting objects, but what to my mother's more adult reasoning was a vast array of Victorian furniture, silver epergnes, whatnot stands, and statuary of doubtful origin, all tucked into a tall, narrow house far too small to hold them. *Tante* Gustel for her sins – and I suspect for her pleasures – ran a pig farm just outside New York, and there this full-bosomed, crimson-faced martinet held full sway over a blond husband half her years – my Uncle Teddy – and a retinue of German servants and farm labourers to whom her word was law. If *Tante* Gustel had one love other than pigs and food, it was diamonds. I still remember those first visits to her, fighting valiantly as I was swept up into those militant but loving arms, pressed against that hot, moist face – kicking, squirming, every-thing but biting to be let down – for *Tante* Gustel hurt. All the children in the family knew that. First of all, her moustache bristled as she kissed you, and then there were her diamonds, for thrice-married *Tante* Gustel collected diamonds as other people collect postage stamps or recipes. And at sixty-three, her large, broad, *gemütlich* bosom was studded with clips, brooches, stars, pendants, baubles and scimitars of every size, all encrusted with tiny glittering points of absolute agony for any bare arms or legs that were caught up against them.

But once this moist-eyed initiation to the service of love was over, *Tante* Gustel became a boy's best friend. First of all, there was *Schnaps*, for no young man, no matter what his age, should be allowed to make such a journey in such cold without the help of a little *Schnaps*. Christmas ceremony number one was the opening of the cut-glass *Schnaps* decanter in front of the glistening Christmas tree with its waxen Christmas angel on top. The tree itself was lit with hundreds of tiny candles (no electric bulbs here), the lower branches weighted down with little fluted glass baskets, as glistening as the Christmas ornaments of blown glass that they imitated so well, filled with tiny candies, home-made cookies, glazed nuts and sugared fruits. The whole house was rich with scents and warmth and love, from the sharp spiciness of the *Schnaps* by the tree, to the hot, steamy odour of roast goose *mit Apfelpurée und Sauerkraut*, which wafted in from *Tante* Gustel's kitchen.

I loved it, and I loved Teddy's great barrels of German beer in the cellar. For this was ceremony number two: 'Ted's hour', my mother called it, when all the men of the family went solemnly downstairs to clink glasses by the barrels with the blond young giant who, I always suspected, was the only person who really knew how much it hurt to be pressed up against *Tante* Gustel's diamonds.

And there was sliced stuffed goose neck, sent down in thick slices from the kitchen to help stay Christmas appetites, its crisp golden casing made from the neck of the Christmas goose, stuffed with sausage meat, duck and goose liver, and chopped truffles, subtly flavoured with dry white wine, garlic, cinnamon, cloves and mace. It was a triumph.

As for our Christmas dinner, it, too, had a pattern as fixed as the recipes for the holiday cookies, the sliced stuffed goose neck, and the frosted and glazed fruits which always formed wonderfully eatable decorations on the sideboard in the dining-room.

On Christmas Day, the table had its best white damask cloth, ironed to a smooth satin finish; silver sparkled on every available surface in the room, and my great-aunt's best Meissen china provided the perfect foil for the Teutonic richness of the food. *Tante* Gustel was not one for half-measures when it came to feeding her loved ones, and the feast was always of gargantuan proportions. A huge roast goose, served with tart apple sauce and stuffed with savoury sauerkraut, was flanked on one side by a tender ham, cut down from the smoke-house ceiling, where it had hung since last year's killing, and on the other side by great bowls of puréed potatoes thickened with butter and fresh cream, puréed yellow turnips flavoured with cinnamon and mace, and tiny Brussels sprouts covered in golden buttered breadcrumbs. Fresh-baked soft white rolls, melting hot, were there in plenty, and around these portentous head-liners was scattered a series of minor dishes of mustard pickles, spiced peaches and salted almonds, for those who had the room or the disposition to add to the bounty already on their plates.

At a signal from *Tante* Gustel, we would pile into the small crowded dining-room, with its flock wallpaper and crystal chandelier. Teddy carved, *Tante* Gustel fussed and beamed, the two maids served, and the rest of us set to with gusto and devotion, secure in the knowledge that hot mince pies with lemon-iced pastry, and *Kugelhupf* waited for us in the kitchen.

Tante Gustel, Teddy, my mother, all are dead now; the pig farm is gone, victim of urbanization and the steady growth of New York. There are only the diamonds left, glittering somewhere, less brightly now, like my Christmas memories.

GOOSE WITH SAUERKRAUT STUFFING

1 goose
1¼ lb (550 g) fat salt pork
2–3 Spanish onions, coarsely chopped
3–4 cooking apples, peeled, cored and diced
4–6 tablespoons (60–90 ml) brown sugar
Salt and freshly ground black pepper
Dried thyme
3 teaspoons (15 ml) caraway seed
3–4 lb (1.4–1.8 kg) sauerkraut

Dice salt pork and sauté in a frying pan until transparent. Add coarsely chopped onions and fry until onions are transparent. Add diced apples and toss with onions and salt pork. When onions and apples are golden, add brown sugar, salt, freshly ground black pepper, thyme and caraway seed. Remove from heat. Drain sauerkraut, and toss with apple and onion mixture.

Wash goose inside and out. Rub cavity with a little salt and freshly ground black pepper. Stuff with apple-sauerkraut; truss goose and sew up the vent. Prick goose all over with a fork, and place it on a rack over a roasting pan. Rub exterior of goose with salt, freshly ground black pepper and a little dried thyme. Roast in a moderately hot oven (400°F/200°C/GM6) for 20 minutes; then reduce heat to 350°F/180°C/GM4 and continue to roast until tender, allowing 20 minutes per pound (450 g). Baste goose from time to time with a little hot water, and prick it occasionally to allow fat to escape, pouring the fat off as it accumulates in the pan.

POULARDE ST HONORÉ

1 roasting chicken

FILLING
8 oz (225 g) cooked ham
2 tablespoons (30 ml) tomato concentrate
3–4 tablespoons (45–60 ml) double cream
Salt
Paprika and freshly ground black pepper
2–3 drops red food colouring (optional)

GARNISH
Cooked carrot, truffle, and white of hard-boiled egg,
cut in fancy shapes
Aspic jelly (page 76)

Roast or cook chicken *en casserole* until golden and very tender. When cold, ease the legs away from the body without quite separating them, and carefully remove the flesh from the breast in one long piece on each side. Cut away the upper part of the breast bone with kitchen shears, leaving the chicken quite hollow in the centre, ready for the filling. Lay breast fillets on a board, skin side up, and cut them into slices lengthwise without quite separating the pieces.

FILLING

Trim ham, removing all gristle and skin, and chop or mince it finely. Pound it well in a mortar with tomato concentrate. Add cream gradually, until mixture has a creamy consistency, without being too soft. Season to taste with salt, paprika and freshly ground black pepper. Tint lightly with red food colouring if desired.

To decorate: fill hollow of the chicken with ham mixture, re-forming the whole bird. Lay the breast pieces on each side, separating the slices a little to show some of the white. Decorate the top, where the filling shows, with pieces of cooked carrot, truffle, and white of hard-boiled egg, or any other garnish preferred, covering the filling entirely. Brush over with slightly liquid aspic jelly and allow to set. Serve chicken surrounded with chopped aspic.

HAM À LA JURASIENNE

1 Spanish onion, coarsely chopped
2 carrots, coarsely chopped
6 tablespoons (90 ml) butter
2 tablespoons (30 ml) flour
½ pint (300 ml) well-flavoured beef stock
1 level tablespoon (15 ml) tomato concentrate
Bouquet garni (parsley, thyme, bay leaf)
Salt and freshly ground black pepper
8 tablespoons (120 ml) port
4 oz (100 g) freshly grated Gruyère
1 egg
¼ pint (150 ml) double cream
4 thick slices cooked ham

Sauté coarsely chopped onion and carrot in a heatproof casserole with 4 tablespoons (60 ml) butter until golden. Sprinkle lightly with flour; moisten with beef stock to which you have added tomato concentrate, a *bouquet garni*, and a little salt and freshly ground black pepper; simmer gently for 20 minutes. Strain sauce and add port.

Mix freshly grated Gruyère, egg and double cream to a smooth paste in a bowl.

Sauté ham slices in 2 tablespoons (30 ml) butter; place slices in a heatproof *gratin* dish; spread Gruyère mixture on each slice and pour over the sauce. Place dish in a slow oven (325°F/170°C/GM3) for 15 minutes, or until sauce is golden and bubbly. Serves 4.

COLD GAMMON OF BACON WITH CUMBERLAND JELLY

1 gammon of bacon (10–12 lb/5–6 kg)
Vegetables for soup
2 bay leaves
6 peppercorns
Toasted breadcrumbs
Cloves, brown sugar, dry mustard, and cider or
fruit juice (optional)

CUMBERLAND JELLY
½ jar red currant jelly
Rinds of 1 orange and 1 lemon
Juice of 2 oranges and 1 lemon
1 level tablespoon (15 ml) dry mustard
½ oz (15 g) gelatine
¼ pint (150 ml) port
2 tablespoons (30 ml) Cointreau

Wash gammon well; do not take off rind; soak for 24 to 48 hours to remove salt, changing water several times.

Cover gammon completely with cold water and bring very slowly to boiling point to open pores gradually, extract salt, and at the same time help to increase the temperature of any cold core within the joint.

Change water; add vegetables for soup, bay leaves and peppercorns, and bring slowly to boiling point again; reduce heat immediately when boiling point is reached and allow temperature to drop to simmering point; cover. Simmer until cooking is complete – about 20 minutes per pound (450 g) for an average-sized gammon.

Allow gammon to cool in the water in which it was cooked. If you are going to serve it cold, do not remove rind until well set. I leave it on overnight. Then remove skin, sprinkle fat with toasted breadcrumbs, or, if you prefer, score fat criss-cross. Stud with cloves; sprinkle with brown sugar and a little dry mustard, and brown in the oven for 20 to 30 minutes, basting from time to time with cider or fruit juice. Serve with Cumberland Jelly.

CUMBERLAND JELLY

Pare rind of 1 orange and 1 lemon as thinly as possible, and cut into fine short strips; blanch for 5 minutes in boiling water. Reserve.

Combine red currant jelly with strained orange and lemon juice in a saucepan, and simmer until jelly has melted. Add a small quantity of this to the mustard, mix well, and return to pan.

Soak gelatine in port and Cointreau for 5 minutes; then dissolve gently over heat and add to red currant jelly mixture. Allow to cool a little before spooning jelly into a glass serving dish or crock. Just before it sets, stir in blanched orange and lemon rind.

Christmas Left-overs

TRUFFLED TURKEY SALAD

8 tablespoons (120 ml) stiff mayonnaise
1 small can black truffles
Salt, celery salt and freshly ground black pepper
1 head lettuce, finely shredded
4 hard-boiled eggs, finely chopped
1½ lb (675 g) cooked turkey, diced
4 stalks celery, thinly sliced

Thin mayonnaise with juice from a small can of black truffles, and season to taste with salt, celery salt and freshly ground black pepper. Add 2 tablespoons (30 ml) finely sliced black truffles to sauce; then combine sauce with shredded lettuce, finely chopped eggs, diced turkey and sliced celery. Mix well. Add more mayonnaise and seasoning if desired. Serves 4.

TURKEY HASH

1 lb (450 g) diced turkey meat
Salt and freshly ground black pepper
1 egg, beaten
2 tablespoons (30 ml) whipped cream
Breadcrumbs
Butter

SAUCE
2 level tablespoons (30 ml) butter
2 level tablespoons (30 ml) flour
¼ pint (150 ml) milk
¼ pint (150 ml) double cream

SAUCE
Melt butter in a saucepan; add flour and cook until *roux* just starts
to turn golden. Add milk and cook, stirring constantly, until
sauce is reduced to about half the original quantity. Stir in double
cream.

Add ½ pint (300 ml) sauce (above) to turkey mixture; season to
taste with a little salt and freshly ground black pepper, and pour
into a heatproof *gratin* dish. Combine remaining sauce with
beaten egg; fold in whipped cream. Spread over creamed turkey
mixture. Sprinkle with fresh breadcrumbs, dot with butter, and
brown in a hot oven (450°F/230°C/GM8) or under the grill.
Serves 4.

HAM AND APPLE SALAD

1 slice ham, ½ inch (12 mm) thick
6 oz (175 g) Danish Blue cheese
3 red eating apples
Juice of 1 lemon
French Dressing (page 691)
Lettuce
Chopped green pepper and parsley

Cut ham into ½-inch (12 mm) squares. Roll cheese into small
balls. Dice apples, leaving peel on, and dip in lemon juice to

preserve their colour. Toss apples and ham in well-flavoured French Dressing. Line a dish with lettuce leaves, and fill with cheese balls, ham and apple. Sprinkle with chopped green pepper and garnish with parsley. Serve with additional French Dressing. Serves 4.

DUCK AND ORANGE SALAD

Diced meat of 1 roasted duck
4 shallots, finely chopped
2 stalks celery, sliced
Olive oil and wine vinegar
Salt and freshly ground black pepper
Rosemary
4 small oranges, peeled and separated into sections
Lettuce
8–10 black olives

Combine diced duck, finely chopped shallots and sliced celery with a dressing made of 3 parts olive oil to 1 part wine vinegar. Season to taste with salt, freshly ground black pepper and rosemary. Toss well. Allow duck to marinate in this mixture for at least 2 hours.

Just before serving, add orange sections; toss again, adding more dressing if required. Line a glass salad bowl with lettuce leaves; fill with salad and garnish with black olives. Serves 4.

Christmas Pâtés and Terrines

French cooks have brought the making of *terrines* and *pâtés* to a fine art. From truffle-studded *pâté de foie gras* in all its richness, to the more homely versions of chunky-cut *pâté de campagne*, this dish is a choice morsel on restaurant menus the world over.

Chicken liver *terrine* is surprisingly easy to make, yet you will find that is adds another dimension to an ever-popular theme. A simple combination of fresh chicken livers, marinated for 2 hours in port, and then minced with sausage meat and ham, the whole is flavoured with dry white wine, garlic and bay leaves, wrapped in thin slices of bacon, and baked in the oven until cooked through.

I like to make it 3 days before it is to be served – long enough for its flavours to blend and ripen – and I always serve it with thin strips of freshly made toast and butter, as a delicious first course for a dinner party.

CHICKEN LIVER TERRINE

1¼ lb (550 g) fresh chicken livers
6 tablespoons (90 ml) port
Generous pinch of thyme
4 bay leaves
4 slices ham
12 oz (350 g) sausage meat
3 slices bread
A little milk
¼ pint (150 ml) dry white wine
½ clove garlic, finely chopped
Freshly ground black pepper
Thin slices streaky bacon, or bacon and pork fat
Melted lard

Place fresh chicken livers in a bowl; add port, a generous pinch of thyme, and 2 bay leaves, crumbled. Allow the livers to marinate in this mixture for at least 2 hours.

Put three-quarters of the chicken livers through a mincer with ham, sausage meat, and bread which you have soaked in a little milk. Stir in ¼ pint (150 ml) dry white wine to make a rather wet mixture. Then add ½ clove garlic, finely chopped, and freshly ground black pepper, to taste. Mix well.

Line a *pâté* mould (I use a Pyrex one) with thin slices of streaky bacon. For a more subtle flavour, ask your butcher to give you paper-thin strips of larding pork fat; place the strips between 2 sheets of waxed paper, and pound them as thinly as possible. Then use thin strips of pork fat alternately with strips of streaky bacon to line your *pâté* mould.

Spread half of the liver and sausage mixture in the bottom of the mould; add whole chicken livers, and cover with remaining liver and sausage mixture.

Top with thin strips of bacon and 2 bay leaves; cover mould; place in a pan of boiling water and cook in a moderate oven (375°F/190°C/GM5) for 1¼ to 1½ hours. Place a weight on *pâté* – all excess juices will pour over edges of mould – and allow to cool. When cold, coat with a little melted lard. Chill in refrigerator for 2 to 3 days before serving.

TERRINE AUX FOIES DE VOLAILLE

8 oz (225 g) lean pork
8 oz (225 g) fat bacon
6 oz (175 g) poultry livers
2 cloves garlic
4 small shallots
4 eggs, beaten
2 tablespoons (30 ml) cornflour
3 tablespoons (45 ml) dry white wine
4 tablespoons (60 ml) Cointreau
Salt, freshly ground black pepper and
grated nutmeg
1 sprig thyme and 1 bay leaf
Madeira Aspic (page 76)

Put lean pork, fat bacon, poultry livers (chicken or duck, or a combination of the two) through the finest blade of your mincer, together with garlic and shallots. Combine mixture in a large bowl with beaten eggs, cornflour, dry white wine, Cointreau, and salt, pepper and grated nutmeg, to taste. Mix well.

Place a sprig of thyme, a bay leaf and the *pâté* mixture in an earthenware *terrine*: cover the *terrine*, place in a pan of water and cook in a slow oven (325°–350°F/170°–180°C/GM3–4) for about 1½ hours. At the end of the cooking, add Madeira Aspic.

The addition of Cointreau in this recipe removes any bitterness from the poultry livers.

FRENCH LIVER TERRINE

8 oz (225 g) liver sausage, diced
2 tablespoons (30 ml) mayonnaise
2 tablespoons (30 ml) cream
Salt and freshly ground black pepper
Lemon juice or brandy
Toast, crackers, or thin slices of rye or
pumpernickel bread
Sieved hard-boiled egg yolks or
finely chopped parsley

Combine liver sausage, mayonnaise and cream in a blender, and flavour to taste with salt, freshly ground black pepper, and lemon juice or brandy; whirl until smooth. Serve on toast, crackers or thin slices of rye or pumpernickel bread, or pack into small individual crocks or a *terrine*, and decorate with sieved hard-boiled egg yolks or finely chopped parsley.

TERRINE OF THE FARM 'FOUR SEASONS'

1 large capon or small turkey
1 lb (450 g) veal shoulder
1 lb (450 g) pork shoulder
1 lb (450 g) ham
6 fluid oz (175 ml) cognac
2 bay leaves
1 teaspoon (5 ml) thyme
1 teaspoon (5 ml) salt
Freshly ground black pepper
8 oz (225 g) veal, minced
8 oz (225 g) pork, minced
8 oz (225 g) pork fat, minced
8 oz (225 g) ham, minced
4 eggs
Strips of pork fat
Flour and water paste

Bone a large capon (or small turkey); remove the breast fillets and the meat of the breast without disturbing the skin.

Cut veal shoulder, pork shoulder and ham into 1-inch (25 mm) squares; place in a large bowl with capon skin and meat; marinate with cognac, bay leaves, thyme and salt, and freshly ground black pepper, to taste.

Combine minced veal, pork, pork fat and ham with eggs; mix well.

Remove skin from marinade and dry it. Line a deep casserole or *terrine* with a few thin slices of pork fat, and then with turkey or capon skin, outside down, so that some of the skin hangs over the sides. Mix minced meats by hand with cubed meats and seasonings. Place a layer of this mixture in bottom of casserole; roll strips of fillet in chopped parsley and herbs, and arrange on top. Cover with remaining meat mixture. Fold overlapping skin over this, and top with thin slices of pork fat. Cover casserole, and seal it with a flour and water paste. Bake in a pan of hot water in a 350°F/180°C/GM4 oven for about 2 hours, or until fat is clear. (Remove seal after 1¾ hours to check on this.) If all the broth is not cooked out, return to oven for another 15 to 20 minutes. Place weights on *terrine* (about 6 to 8 lb/3–3.8 kg) and allow to cool. Chill in refrigerator.

HOME-MADE PÂTÉ

8 oz (225 g) cooked beef, lamb or veal
6 oz (175 g) sausage meat
2 slices white bread, trimmed
Milk
2 shallots, finely chopped
1 small onion, finely chopped
3 tablespoons (45 ml) finely chopped parsley
1 tablespoon (15 ml) finely chopped chervil (optional)
2 egg yolks
Salt and freshly ground black pepper
Butter
Gherkins or well-flavoured French Tomato Sauce
(page 124)

Put cooked beef, lamb or veal through mincer with sausage meat. Soak bread in a little milk and squeeze almost dry. Add soaked bread to meat with finely chopped shallots, onion, parsley and chervil. Add egg yolks, and salt and freshly ground black pepper, to taste, and spoon mixture into a well-buttered *pâté* mould. Cook in a slow oven (350°F/180°C/GM4) for 1 hour.

Serve cold with gherkins, or hot with well-flavoured Tomato Sauce.

TERRINE OF PHEASANT

1 medium-sized pheasant
1 small onion, sliced
2 small carrots, sliced
2 sprigs parsley
1 bay leaf
Salt
Pinch of thyme
3 fluid oz (75 ml) Madeira
3 fluid oz (75 ml) cognac
8 oz (225 g) fresh lean pork
1 lb (450 g) fresh fat pork
1 egg, beaten
½ clove garlic, crushed
Freshly ground black pepper
Madeira Aspic (page 76)

Split pheasant down the back; open it out flat and cut the meat from each breast into strips. Place strips in a bowl with sliced onion, carrots, parsley, 1 bay leaf, ½ teaspoon (2.5 ml) salt, a pinch of thyme, Madeira and cognac. Let meat marinate in this mixture for 2 hours, then drain. Strain marinade, reserving juices.

Cut remaining meat from the pheasant, and combine with lean pork and half the fat pork. Chop finely; add beaten egg, crushed garlic, ½ teaspoon (2.5 ml) salt, freshly ground black pepper, to taste, and the reserved marinade. Blend until very smooth.

Line a *terrine* or earthenware casserole with thin strips of remaining fat pork, thinly sliced. Spread a third of the meat mixture over the bottom, and arrange marinated strips on it. Add alternate layers of meat mixture and marinated strips. Then add alternate layers of meat mixture and breast meat, finishing with the meat mixture.

Cover casserole; place it in a pan of hot water and bake in a moderately hot oven (400°F/200°C/GM6) for about 1½ hours. Remove cover and place a weighted plate on the *terrine* to compress it gently as it cools. When cold, unmould *terrine* and turn out on a board. Scrape fat from surface; wash and dry casserole, and return *terrine* to it, bottom side up. Pour Madeira Aspic around it, cooled but still liquid, and chill until set.

FONDANT DE VOLAILLE 'AUBERGE DU PÈRE BISE'

1 large capon (about 3½ lb (1.6 kg))
½ pint (300 ml) dry sherry
2 tablespoons (30 ml) cognac
6–8 tablespoons (90–120 ml) Noilly Prat
4 sprigs thyme
1 bay leaf
4 sprigs parsley
2 tablespoons (30 ml) port
4 shallots
2 carrots
½ Spanish onion
2 cloves garlic
6–8 peppercorns
8 oz (225 g) pork fat
1 lb (450 g) lean pork
2 tablespoons (30 ml) coarse salt
Freshly ground black pepper
8 oz (225 g) *foie gras*
1 oz (25 g) pistachio nuts
Thin strips pork fat (about 1 lb (450 g)
Diced *foie gras* (optional)
Salted flour and water paste

Skin chicken and remove meat from bones, leaving breasts whole. In a large porcelain bowl, combine sherry, cognac and Noilly Prat with herbs, port, shallots, carrots and onion, all finely chopped, and garlic and peppercorns. Add chicken pieces and marinate in this mixture for at least 12 hours.

Dice pork fat and 8 oz (225 g) lean pork, and combine with

coarse salt, and freshly ground black pepper, to taste. Leave in the refrigerator for 6 hours to prevent meat changing colour during cooking. Pass through the finest blade of your mincer.

Place chicken pieces in a roasting pan with remaining pork, diced, and roast in a hot oven (450°F/230°C/GM8) for 5 minutes, or until meat has coloured slightly. Then strain marinade juices over meat and continue to cook for 5 minutes more.

Remove chicken breasts, and pass the remaining chicken pieces and pork juices through the finest blade of your mincer, blending in *foie gras* at the same time. Combine minced pork and pork fat with chicken mixture; stir in pistachio nuts and remaining marinade juices, and place *pâté* mixture in refrigerator to 'relax' for 2 to 3 hours.

When ready to cook: line a large *terrine* or *pâté* mould with paper-thin strips of pork fat; fill a quarter full with *pâté* mixture; scatter diced *foie gras* over this for a really luxurious *terrine*, as served at Père Bise; cover with a layer of *pâté* mixture and place marinated chicken breasts on this. Repeat alternate layers of *pâté* mixture and diced *foie gras*, ending with *pâté* mixture. Top with thin strips of pork fat; cover *terrine* and seal edges with a dough made of flour, water and salt, so that no moisture escapes. Place *terrine* in a pan of boiling water and bake in a preheated slow oven (325°F/170°C/GM3) for 1 hour.

Keep *pâté* in refrigerator for 2 to 3 days before serving.

PÂTÉ OF DUCK

1 tender duckling
1 lb (450 g) veal
8 oz (225 g) diced bacon
2 tablespoons (30 ml) savoury biscuit or cracker crumbs
Salt and freshly ground black pepper
Nutmeg
1 egg, well beaten
1 glass dry sherry
4 oz (100 g) thinly sliced bacon
1 onion, thinly sliced
1 lemon, thinly sliced
1 bay leaf
Flour and water paste

Bone a tender duckling and cut the flesh in small pieces. Dice veal roughly, removing skin. Put veal, diced bacon and duck trimmings through the finest blade of your mincer twice to make a fine *farce*. Add biscuit or cracker crumbs; season to taste with salt, freshly ground black pepper and a little nutmeg, and moisten with well-beaten egg and sherry. Mix thoroughly. Line a *terrine* with sliced bacon. Put in a layer of the *farce*, then some pieces of duck, more *farce*, and so on, until the dish is full. Cover with sliced bacon, and top with thin slices of onion and lemon, and a bay leaf. Put on the lid and seal the join with a paste made of flour and water. Bake in a slow oven (350°F/180°C/GM4) for 1½ to 2 hours, or until the pieces of duck feel quite tender when they are pierced with a skewer. (Remove pastry seal after 1½ hours to check on this.)

Remove lid of *terrine* and place a weighted plate on the *pâté* to compress it gently as it cools. Chill in refrigerator for 2 to 3 days before serving.

Christmas Cookies

BRANDY SNAPS

4 oz (100 g) butter
4 oz (100 g) castor sugar
4 oz (100 g) golden syrup
4 oz (100 g) sifted plain flour
½ level teaspoon (2.5 ml) ground ginger
A few drops of vanilla extract

Combine butter, sugar and syrup in the top of a double saucepan, and cook over water until melted. Remove from heat and mix in flour gradually. Add ground ginger and flavour with a few drops of vanilla extract. Pour the mixture in small rounds on to well-buttered baking sheets and bake in a moderate oven (375°F/190°C/GM5) for about 10 minutes. When ready, remove the snaps with a palette knife and twist them round cornet moulds or round the handle of a wooden spoon. Remove them when quite cold.

SCOTCH SHORTBREAD

8 oz (225 g) plain flour
8 oz (225 g) rice flour
12 oz (350 g) butter, diced
4 oz (100 g) castor sugar
1 teaspoon (5 ml) vanilla extract or grated lemon rind
1 egg
2 tablespoons (30 ml) double cream

Sieve flour and rice flour into a mixing bowl, and rub in butter with your fingertips. Add sugar and vanilla extract or lemon rind. Whisk egg with cream in a small bowl and pour over dry ingredients. Mix to a smooth paste with your hand, using more cream if necessary.

Turn out on a floured board and knead lightly until free from cracks. Flour a rolling pin and roll the dough out to about ¾ inch (18 mm) thickness. Stamp it out in small rounds with a cutter, and place the biscuits on a buttered and floured baking sheet. Roll the scraps again and cut out more biscuits until all dough is used up. Bake biscuits in a slow oven (325°F/170°C/GM3) for 30 minutes, or until lightly coloured. Sprinkle with sugar while still hot and transfer to a cake rack to cool.

MACAROONS

4 oz (100 g) ground almonds
8 oz (225 g) castor sugar
Squeeze of lemon juice
3–4 egg whites
Rice paper
Icing sugar
Blanched and split almonds

Combine ground almonds and sugar in a mixing bowl; beat in lemon juice and enough of the egg whites, one by one, to make mixture just moist enough to drop from a spoon. Put mixture into a forcing bag with a plain pipe at the end, and force out small portions on rounds or squares of rice paper. Dust over with icing sugar (to make macaroons crack on top) and place half a blanched and split almond on the top of each one. Bake in a slow oven (350°F/180°C/GM4) for 30 to 40 minutes, or until well browned, dry and well risen. Cool macaroons on a cake rack, and break off any scraps of rice paper that extend beyond the edges. Makes 12.

PFEFFERNÜSSE

8 oz (225 g) sifted plain flour
1 oz (25 g) cornflour
1 level teaspoon (5 ml) baking powder
1 teaspoon (5 ml) cinnamon
½ level teaspoon (2.5 ml) powdered cloves
½ level teaspoon (2.5 ml) mace
¼ level teaspoon (1.25 ml) white pepper
2 eggs
8 oz (225 g) sugar
1 teaspoon (5 ml) grated lemon rind
4 tablespoons (60 ml) finely chopped candied citron
Butter
Icing sugar

Sift together flour, cornflour, baking powder and spices. Beat eggs and sugar until light and fluffy. Stir in dry ingredients, lemon rind and citron. Roll dough into a long thin roll 1 inch (25 mm) in diameter; cut off small pieces and roll into 1-inch (25 mm) balls. Place balls about 1 inch (25 mm) apart on a well-buttered baking sheet. Cover with foil and leave overnight. Bake in a slow oven (350°F/180°C/GM4) for 20 minutes. Remove from baking sheet and cool on wire racks. When cold, roll in icing sugar. Store in a tightly covered cake tin for about 1 week to 'ripen'. Makes about 4 dozen cookies.

GINGERBREAD COOKIES

12 oz (350 g) sifted plain flour
1 teaspoon (5 ml) allspice
1 teaspoon (5 ml) ginger
1 teaspoon (5 ml) cinnamon
1 level teaspoon (5 ml) salt
½ level teaspoon (2.5 ml) soda
6 oz (175 g) butter
4 tablespoons (60 ml) brown sugar
8 tablespoons (120 ml) golden syrup
6 tablespoons (90 ml) milk

Sift together flour, spices, salt and soda. Blend butter, sugar and golden syrup. Add sifted dry ingredients alternately with milk. Mix well. Chill overnight in the refrigerator.

Roll out dough and cut out shapes with cookie cutters. Place cookies on a well–buttered baking sheet, and bake in a moderately hot oven (400°F/200°C/GM6) for 10 to 12 minutes. Makes about 3 dozen cookies.

Christmas Sweets

CHRISTMAS SNOWBALL BOMBE

3 tablespoons (45 ml) diced candied cherries
3 tablespoons (45 ml) diced candied pineapple
3 tablespoons (45 ml) diced candied citron
2 tablespoons (30 ml) dried sultanas
1 tablespoon (15 ml) dried currants
Kirsch
1½ pints (900 ml) Vanilla Ice Cream (page 740)
1 pint (600 ml) double cream
½ teaspoon (2.5 ml) vanilla extract
Sugar
Crystallized violets
Small holly leaves

Moisten all fruits with Kirsch and let stand for 2 hours, stirring from time to time. Combine fruits and liqueur with softened Vanilla Ice Cream and mix well. Pack mixture into a round *bombe* mould (or fill 2 small pudding basins and press together to form sphere) and freeze until solid.

Just before serving: unmould 'snowball' on to a chilled serving dish. Whip cream; flavour with vanilla extract, and sugar and Kirsch, to taste; fill a pastry tube fitted with 'rosette' nozzle. Mask ice cream completely with whipped cream rosettes; garnish with crystallized violets and small holly leaves. Serves 4 to 6.

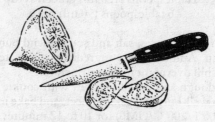

BRANDIED PEARS

2 lb (900 g) sugar
1 teaspoon (5 ml) vanilla extract
1 long strip lemon peel
2 cloves
2 pints (1.1 lit) water
6 lb (3 kg) ripe pears
Brandy

Combine sugar, vanilla extract, lemon peel, cloves and water in large saucepan, and bring to a boil, stirring constantly. Lower heat and simmer, uncovered, for 15 minutes.

Halve, core and peel pears. Add them to syrup and simmer gently, uncovered, for 30 to 40 minutes, or until pears are translucent and soft. Remove from syrup with a slotted spoon.

Sterilize 4 pint (600 ml) jars; leave in hot water until ready to fill. Place 4 tablespoons (60 ml) brandy in each hot jar. Half-fill jars with drained pears; add 2 tablespoons (30 ml) brandy to each jar. Fill jars with remaining pears, add 2 final tablespoons (30 ml) brandy, and fill with strained syrup to within ½ inch (12 mm) of top. Cap jars and store.

SHERRIED PRUNES

2–3 lb (900 g–1.4 kg) dried prunes
2 lb (900 g) sugar
1 teaspoon (5 ml) vanilla extract
4 slices lemon
2 cloves
2 pints (1.1 lit) water
1 bottle sherry

Soak prunes overnight in cold water. Drain.

Combine sugar, vanilla extract, lemon slices, cloves and water in a large saucepan, and bring to a boil, stirring constantly. Lower heat and simmer, uncovered, for 15 minutes. Add prunes to sugar syrup and simmer gently, uncovered, adding more water if necessary, for 30 to 40 minutes, or until prunes are almost cooked through. Remove prunes from syrup with a slotted spoon.

Sterilize 4 pint (600 ml) jars; leave in hot water until ready to fill. Fill jars almost to the top with drained prunes. Fill half full with sherry and add strained syrup, to cover. Cap jars and store.

PORT-'N'-PIPPINS

1½ lb (675 g) small Cox's Orange Pippins,
peeled and cored
8 oz (225 g) sugar
1 pint (600 ml) water
1 inch (25 mm) cinnamon stick
1 inch (25 mm) whole ginger
Rind of 1 lemon
1 glass port
Red food colouring (optional)
Whipped cream (optional)

Combine sugar, water, cinnamon and ginger in a saucepan with the thinly peeled rind of 1 lemon, and boil for 10 minutes. Strain and cool. Pour this syrup over the apples in a bowl; cover with a plate and marinate overnight.

The following day, transfer apples and syrup to an enamelled saucepan and simmer until tender.

Remove apples with a slotted spoon and arrange in a shallow serving bowl. Add port to syrup and strain it over apples. A few drops of red food colouring may be added to syrup if desired, and apples may be decorated with a little whipped cream.

ORANGE JELLY QUARTERS

5 thin-skinned oranges
¼ pint (150 ml) port
½ oz (15 g) gelatine
¼ pint (150 ml) water
1 lemon
4 oz (100 g) sugar
Sponge fingers and cream (optional)

Wash oranges well; pare 1 orange very thinly and steep peel in port for 1 hour. Soak gelatine in half the water; stir over heat until dissolved.

Slice remaining oranges in half, and scoop out pulp and juices, reserving orange shells. Remove pips from pulp. Combine juice and pulp of all oranges and the lemon with sugar and remaining water. Strain dissolved gelatine and port into orange mixture. Fill emptied orange shells with mixture; cool, and chill. When set, cut into halves again. Serve alone, or with sponge fingers and cream. Serves 4.

PORT WINE OR CLARET JELLIES

½ pint (300 ml) port or claret
½ pint (300 ml) water
4 oz (100 g) sugar
1 tablespoon (15 ml) red currant jelly
1 inch (25 mm) cinnamon stick
3 cloves
Rind and juice of 1 lemon
1 oz (25 g) gelatine
2–3 drops red food colouring (optional)
Whipped cream (optional)

Combine water, sugar, red currant jelly, cinnamon and cloves in an enamelled saucepan. Add very thinly peeled lemon rind, strained lemon juice, and gelatine which you have dissolved in a little water. Stir over heat until gelatine is dissolved. Simmer for a few minutes; then add port or claret. Do not boil again. Strain through a piece of muslin, and if necessary, add a few drops of red food colouring to improve colour. Cool.

When nearly cold, pour into 1 large, or several small, moulds that have been rinsed out with cold water. Chill until firm. Turn out when ready to serve, and decorate with whipped cream if desired.

BRANDIED CREAM FOR CHRISTMAS CAKE OR PUDDING

5 egg yolks
4 oz (100 g) icing sugar
2 tablespoons (30 ml) plain flour
½ pint (300 ml) milk
½ teaspoon (2.5 ml) vanilla extract
¼ pint (150 ml) double cream, whipped
Sugar
Brandy

Whisk egg yolks with icing sugar; then beat in flour. Bring milk to a boil and add vanilla extract; stir into egg and sugar mixture; cook over water, stirring continuously, until smooth and thick. Remove from heat, and cool. Then add whipped cream, sweetened to taste with sugar. Stir in brandy, to taste.

BRANDIED CREAM FOR CHRISTMAS CAKE OR PUDDING

Index